THE *Viandier* OF TAILLEVENT

THE Viandier OF TAILLEVENT

An Edition of
all Extant Manuscripts

Edited by
Terence
Scully

University of Ottawa Press

Printed and bound in Canada

ISBN 0-7766-0174-1

Canadian Cataloguing in Publication Data

Taillevent, 1326-1395.
The viandier of Taillevent

Text in Old French of Le viandier de Guillaume Tirel dit Taillevent, followed by the English translation. Introd. and commentaries in English.
Bibliography: p. ISBN 0-7766-0174-1

1. Cookery–Early works to 1800. 2. Cookery, French. I. Scully, Terence, 1935- . II. Title. III. Title: Le viandier de Guillaume Tirel dit Taillevent.

TX707.T3513 1988 641.5 C88-090325-2E

Données de catalogage avant publication (Canada)

Taillevent, 1326-1395.
The viandier of Taillevent

Texte en vieux français de Le viandier de Guillaume Tirel dit Taillevent, suivi de la traduction anglaise. Introd. et commentaires en anglais.
Bibliographie: p. ISBN 0-7766-0174-1

1. Cuisine—Ouvrages avant 1800. 2. Cuisine française. I. Scully, Terence, 1935- . II. Titre. III. Titre: Le viandier de Guillaume Tirel dit Taillevent.

TX707.T3513 1988 641.5 C88-090325-2F

This book is printed on acid-free paper

Cover design by Communications Graphiques Gagnon et Bélanger

Contents

Acknowledgements

I wish to express my gratitude to Carl Langford of the Computing Centre of Wilfrid Laurier University for his unfailing helpfulness in the preparation of the Texts section of this edition; to Lois Macdonald for having laboured cheerfully over the typing of a good part of its first rough draft; to André Donnet and Grégoire Ghika of the Archives du Valais, Switzerland, for their assistance in paleographic matters; to Janet Shorten of the University of Ottawa Press and Peter Smith for their proficiency; and most particularly to D. Eleanor Scully for her culinary counsel and gastronomic gusto.

INTRODUCTION

Introduction

The Manuscripts

The collection of culinary recipes that is known as the *Viandier* of Guillaume Tirel or "Taillevent" is extant today in four manuscripts. A fifth was recently destroyed.

VAL Sion (Switzerland), Archives cantonales du Valais, S. 108.

A parchment roll from the second half of the thirteenth century; 13 cm wide x 194.5 cm long; written on both sides, although the text occupies only two-thirds of the verso. This roll contains only the *Viandier*. A fragment which must have measured some 8 to 10 cm has been cut away from the top of the roll; on the recto this missing portion may have held the title of the work as well as several of the first recipes; on the verso it probably held the recipes that in other copies are called *Soupe en moustarde* (§83) and *Civé d'oeufs* (§84), as well as the beginning of the *Brouet d'Alemagne* (§85). Capitals, which vary between one and two lines in height, are in red, as are some whole recipe titles.

> *Incipit*: *Boully larde prenez vostre grain lardes bouilli larde / et metez cuire en yaue ....*
>
> *Explicit*: ... *en huille boullez tresbien metez du formage auec qui ueult / Explicit / Nomen scriptoris est petrus plenus amoris.* [Two lines below this and centred on the page are a group of letters—perhaps *gein*—which appears to be a signature.]

See André Donnet, "Inventaire de la Bibliothèque Supersaxo," *Vallesia*, 29 (1974), p. 84.

This manuscript was reproduced in photo-facsimile by Jérôme Pichon and Georges Vicaire in their edition of *Le Viandier de Guillaume Tirel dit Taillevent* (Paris, 1892), pp. 227–252. An edition of it was published by Paul Aebischer, "Un manuscrit valaisan du *Viandier* attribué à Taillevent," in *Vallesia*, 8 (1953), pp. 73–100. Aebischer points out that the early date[1] of the Valais manuscript indicates that the Guillaume Tirel who was studied by Pichon and Vicaire could not have been the author of the original version of the *Viandier*.

MAZ Paris, Bibliothèque Mazarine, 3636 (*olim* 1253), ff. 219r–228 r.

Fifteenth century. In-folio, paper. In the *Catalogue général des manuscrits des bibliothèques publiques de France. Paris. Bibliothèque Mazarine*, vol. 3, this volume is qualified as a "Recueil d'extraits, de notes de médecine, de tableaux de mathématiques et d'astrologie, etc." The *Viandier* does not occupy a full gathering of the manuscript.

---

[1] "L'écriture de notre manuscrit sédunois est très soignée, d'une belle gothique de la seconde moitié du XIIIe siècle, ou au plus tard des toutes premières années du siècle suivant": Paul Aebischer, "Un manuscrit valaisan du *Viandier* attribué à Taillevent," *Vallesia*, 8 (1953), p. 74.

Incipit: *Taillevent maistre queux du roy de France par cy enseigne a toutes gens / pour apparoillier a maingier en cusine de roy duc conte marquis barons / prelas & de tous aultres seigneurs, bourgois merchans et gens douneur / Pour dessales tous poutages ....*

Explicit: ... *et la graisse de vostre / rost puis vercel sur vostre rolz adressiez par escuelles.*

In their edition of the *Viandier*, Pichon and Vicaire present only fourteen recipes from the Mazarine manuscript, those recipes "qui se trouvent dans ce manuscrit et ne figurent pas dans celui de la Bibliothèque Nationale."[2] This version of the *Viandier* has not otherwise been published.

BN Paris, Bibliothèque Nationale, fonds français, 19,791.

Fourteenth century. In-4°, vellum, bound in parchment with several sheets of paper next to this binding. The text is written in a single gathering of nine sheets of vellum beginning on the recto of f. 1 and ending in the middle of f. 18v. The folios were not originally numbered. Cue letters are indicated for the rubricator, and space is left for capitals, though these were never inserted. At the foot of f. 1r the name (?) *A. Delpriey* can be read; and at the foot of f. 18v the following notation appears: *Cest viandier fu achete a Paris par moy Pierre Buffaut lan m.ccc.iiij*^{xx}*xij ou pris de vj s. par.*

Incipit: *Cy comence le Viandier Taillevent maistre queux du Roy nostre sire ....*

Explicit: ... *fleur de canelle saffran garingal noys mugaites / Explicit.*

This manuscript provided the basis for the edition of *Le Viandier de Guillaume Tirel dit Taillevent* by Pichon and Vicaire; their reading of the *BN* text is found at pp. 1–34 of that publication.

VAT Rome, Vatican City, Biblioteca Vaticana, Regina 776 (*olim* 233 and 2159), ff. 48r–85r.

First half of the fifteenth century. Paper, 85 folios, 21 cm x 15.2 cm, bound in parchment. Capitals are in red at the beginning of most paragraphs; capitals in the incipit alone are ornamented. The first work in this manuscript, a *Jugement des songes enigmatiques* (ff. 1r–46v), was originally paginated, but then these numbers were changed when this work was incorporated into the present manuscript. At that time the whole volume was given a folio numbering. Folio 47, separating the two works, remains blank recto and verso.[3]

Incipit: *Cy commence le Viandier Taillevent maistre queux du Roy de France ouquel sont contenues les choses qui s'ensuivent ....*

Explicit: ... *cuisses de vostre chappon et versez vostre sausse dessus.*

A transcription of the version of the *Viandier* contained in *VAT* was appended by Pichon and Vicaire to their edition of *BN* after Siméon Luce drew their attention to the

---

[2] These are Recipes 2, 7, 28, 86, 104, 111, 127 and 171–177 in the present edition. Pichon and Vicaire make a number of errors in transcribing these texts of *MAZ*.

[3] The catalogue of *Codices Reginenses* in the Vatican Library has not yet progressed to the point where our manuscript 776 has received an official description. See, however, Pichon and Vicaire's "Avant-Propos" concerning the *VAT* manuscript, pp. 45–70.

existence of the Vatican manuscript.[4] Sylvie Martinet was responsible for a "Nouvelle édition augmentée et refondue" of the Pichon and Vicaire work, an edition that expanded the Table Alphabétique to include page references to the Vatican version as well as to *BN*.[5]

Saint-Lô Saint-Lô, Archives de la Manche, Série E, Archives de la baronnie de la Haye-du-Puits, ff. 39v–46r.

Fifteenth century. Small in-folio, paper, 46 ff. The folios were numbered at some time after the manuscript was compiled, and a note indicated that ff. 24, 42, 43, 44 and 45 were missing. According to Pichon and Vicaire, there was some trace of two folios having been torn away, but there was no indication that any substantial amount of the text of the *Viandier* was missing: "Il paraît," Pichon and Vicaire write of the contents of this manuscript, "à quelques recettes près, assez conforme au ms. conservé rue de Richelieu."[6] In the Saint-Lô manuscript the *Viandier* followed *Le Journal de la Recepte / de la terre et baronnie de la haie-Dupuis pour ung an commenchant / au terme saint michiel lan mil iiij^c chinquante & quatre et finissant / lan revolu & acomply tant en argent grains fromens et / advoinne sail poyure commin poullailles oefz et autres choses* .... This manuscript was destroyed in a fire on June 6, 1944; as far as is known, no copy was ever made of it, in whole or in part. Pichon and Vicaire refer to only seven passages in "le ms. de la Haye-du-Puits" in order to confirm readings in the *BN* manuscript they are editing.

Apart from the above five manuscripts, Pichon and Vicaire mention the trace of a manuscript that seems to have contained a copy of the *Viandier* but which, like the Saint-Lô manuscript, has disappeared. This volume is described in the *Inventaire du duc de Berry de 1416. Art. 919*: "Un gros volume, escript en françoys, de lettre de court, ouquel sont contenuz les livres qui s'ensuivent: [ten items] ... et ou derrenier est le Viendier Taillevent." This large-format, leather-bound volume appears catalogued also in the *Inventaire de Sainte-Geneviève*; the Duke paid 200 gold écus for it in 1404.[7]

---

[4] *Romania*, 21 (1892), pp. 306–309. For Luce, comparisons between only a few passages in *BN* and *VAT* "suffisent pour mettre en évidence et hors de toute contestation la supériorité du texte du Vatican" (p. 309). Luce was reviewing the Pichon and Vicaire edition of the *Viandier*. This edition, based on the *BN* text, made only occasional reference to *MAZ* and the Saint-Lô manuscript, and initially took no account of either *VAL* or *VAT*.

[5] The first edition (1892) of the *Viandier* by Pichon and Vicaire was printed in only 354 copies by Techener for the Société des Bibliophiles (lxviii–178 pp., with index; Bossuat 5611). This was followed the same year by a *Supplément au Viandier de Taillevent. Le manuscrit de la Bibliothèque vaticane* (paged 183–297, with index). The revised edition by Sylvie Martinet amalgamated the two indexes, and was until recently available in reprint from Slatkine (Geneva) or Daniel Morcrette (Luzarches).

[6] Pichon and Vicaire, *Viandier*, p. lii.

[7] See Pichon and Vicaire, *Viandier*, p. iv, n1. Louis Stouff also reports that a copy of "le *Viandier* de Tirel de Taillevent" is recorded in the possession of a canon of Arles in the late fifteenth century: "Y avait-il a la fin du moyen-âge une alimentation et une cuisine provençales originales?" *Manger et Boire au Moyen Age*, 2 vols. (Paris, 1984); vol. 2, p. 98.

In their *Bibliographie* Pichon and Vicaire describe fifteen printed editions of the *Viandier* of Taillevent dating between 1490 and 1604.[8] In order to "faire voir à nos lecteurs sous quelle forme s'est produite, de 1490 à 1604, l'œuvre de Taillevent," they reproduce the text of what they consider to be the oldest printed edition.[9] Far from being useful in illuminating obscurities in the extant manuscripts, these printed editions frequently contain such errors and mutilations of the earlier texts that their use by contemporary purchasers must have led to remarkable culinary adventures.

General Editorial Considerations

When editing an early text that is extant in several varying versions, paleographers have normally attempted at the outset to determine which of the available versions appears to be the best. Standard editing procedure then requires that all of the remaining versions be placed in some sort of relationship with this base text so that scribal errors, omissions or additions—variants of any nature—can be identified and the wording and spelling of the text restored to an earliest or "original" form, at least in the critical apparatus. If the range of variations is sufficiently broad, the text chosen to be presented to the modern reader should ideally be as faithful as possible to what the author had probably intended.

In the case of the *Viandier* of Taillevent, if classic procedures were followed the base text would undoubtedly be that offered by the Vatican manuscript of this work. Pichon and Vicaire were clearly rueful to have learned of this manuscript only as their edition, based on the version found in the Bibliothèque Nationale, had gone through the press. "Le manuscrit du Vatican est très important," the scholars note, "car, outre qu'il est plus étendu que ceux de la Bibliothèque Nationale, de la Bibliothèque Mazarine et des Archives de la Manche (ms. de la Haye-du-Puits), il est infiniment plus correct."[10] Even had these

---

[8] *Ibid.*, pp. lii–lxviii. A useful guide to early printed cookbooks is provided by the article of Alain R. Girard, "Du manuscrit à l'imprimé: le livre de cuisine en Europe aux XVe et XVIe siècles," in J.-C. Margolin and R. Sauzet, eds., *Pratiques et discours alimentaires à la Renaissance* (Paris, 1982), pp. 107–118.

[9] Pichon and Vicaire, *Viandier*, pp. 143–199. This text of the oldest printed edition is followed in Pichon and Vicaire's work (pp. 203–209) by a copy of the additions made by Pierre Gaudoul to his printed edition of the *Viandier* between 1532–1537. In an article entitled "La source des additions de Pierre Gaudoul au *Viandier* de Taillevent" in *Bibliothèque d'Humanisme et Renaissance: Travaux et Documents*, 16 (1954), p. 208, Georgine Brereton shows that Pierre Gaudoul took as the first thirteen recipes of his chapter 2 ("S'ensuit la façon de composer les potaiges des choses dessusdictes," ff. 71–72) the whole of Book VII of the *Platine en françoys*.

[10] Pichon and Vicaire, *Viandier*, p. 49. It is important, though, not to be too quick to condemn the reading offered by any single manuscript for a particular passage. As a case in point, Aebischer seems to have an ill-founded *parti-pris* against the Valais version of the *Viandier*. About the reading in *VAL* of Recipe 66, for instance, he says, quite wrongly, "Cette recette est inexactement reproduite: le texte de V [Vatican Library] et N [Bibliothèque Nationale] est bien meilleur. *Au loing*, par exemple, est une erreur pour *au loin*": *Vallesia*, 8 (1951), p. 92, n78. A number of Aebischer's emendations of *VAL*, inspired by a comparison with *BN* or *VAT*, were in fact ill-advised.

editors known of the Valais manuscript, they would undoubtedly still have preferred to use the Vatican version as a base—again, had they learned of *it* in time.

But the fact that the Vatican manuscript presents the most detailed of the four presently extant texts—or at least the longest, the most extensive text—should not be taken to indicate that it is the best source. Contrarily, one may argue that the very distension of the Vatican text (199 "recipes" as against 140 in *BN*, 133 in *MAZ*, and 128 in *VAL*) means almost certainly that it does not represent, even remotely, the earliest version. In matters of cookbooks the earliest version, the one closest to the author's original draft or compilation, is very likely to be the shortest and most elementary of all eventual versions. This is true no matter what the dates at which subsequent manuscript copies happen to have been made.

Cookbooks by their nature invite modifications by their users. Succeeding generations of copies will naturally tend to incorporate all manner of editorial changes into the text. On the one hand these modifications will include a variety of "corrections" or explanations, clarifications of one sort or another; on the other hand, we can expect especially to find accretions in the form of favourite supplementary recipes. Material may even be dropped from a cookbook, though this rarely, one imagines; such deletions would probably occur if a user judges some material not at all apt to be practical, either because a resultant dish is deemed unpalatable or because a main ingredient is normally difficult to obtain. The nature of cookbooks is to grow, and generally to "improve," at least according to the changing tastes of the times. For this very reason a later copy, while perhaps an improvement gastronomically, does not represent a more desirable text for that scholar who is concerned above all with examining a best text, where "best" means closest to the original.

It is true that, as with literary works, there may well be several "original" texts for any cookbook. The professional life of Guillaume Tirel, the Taillevent studied by Pichon and Vicaire,[11] seems to have spanned some sixty-five years between 1330 and 1395. It is not at all beyond the realm of possibility that, as master cook to Charles V, he prepared a second version of the compendium of recipes that now bore his name, a sort of reedition of his masterwork, as he grew in experience and celebrity—and as too, perhaps, he noticed flaws or oversights in what he had already written or copied. Many of the variants found in *BN* and *VAT* undoubtedly originated as marginal or interlineal notations in some earlier version.[12] Surely Taillevent would have annotated his own working copy of the work in

---

[11] Archival and archaeological evidence about the life of Guillaume Tirel, "Taillevent," is examined extensively by Pichon and Vicaire in the Introduction (pp. vi–xxxix) to their edition. To some extent those pages take up conclusions published much earlier by Pichon in an article in the *Bulletin du Bibliophile* (Techener) of June 1846. A summary of his findings is offered later in this present Introduction. Given the solid biographical data assembled by Pichon, and the paleographic evidence presented by the Valais manuscript, Aebischer arrives at the necessary conclusion that Guillaume Tirel was not the original author of the *Viandier*, but merely adopted the text of this work—such, perhaps, as it existed in *VAL*—as his own by prefacing it for posterity with his name. See *Vallesia*, 8 (1953), p. 80.

[12] See, for example, the case of the word *coulez* in Recipe 10 *VAL*.

such a way, and surely this revised version could quite possibly have been any one of those missing source manuscripts which we shall identify as *X, Y* and *Z*.

In the case of an *author*'s revision of any work, the later version would doubtless be textually "better." But this is true as a principle over the whole tradition of the *Viandier*. To the extent that every user of used this book—every dilettante or practitioner, every gastronome, chef or humble pastry baker—made the slightest change in its text, he became a sort of author and provided his own successor with what he considered to be a better text. For this reason we may posit that every deliberate change in a cookbook is, in principle, a gastronomic "improvement."

Clearly, of course, many of the variants we find in the *Viandier*'s extant copies are scribal blunders, pure and simple, of the oldest, most ubiquitous sort; these we shall always have with us. But we are still faced with the problem, acute in the case of the *Viandier*'s four manuscripts, of whether earliest is indeed best.

The Valais manuscript is certainly the oldest and stylistically the most laconic of the four. Any obvious errors in its copy of the text are few in number and tend generally to be of a classic sort.[13] The fifteenth-century Mazarine copy, though the product of a scribe who seems close to being totally ignorant in culinary matters, shows frequent signs that its source (which we shall call *X* in this edition) attempted to make serious improvements in what was traditionally available. There are found in *MAZ*, alone among the extant copies, an interpolated recipe[14] as well as several remarkably detailed amplifications of particular procedures.[15] Such modifications indicate that the source that *MAZ* drew upon for his particular copy had been revised by a capable, practising cook. Yet alongside this evidence of professional competence, *MAZ* presents his reader with an equally remarkable array of mistakes, blunders which occasionally amount to sheer nonsense.[16] His omission of the titles above the majority of recipes after §63, his placing of a wrong title over another recipe,[17] and his copying of the recipes for eight different fish, undistinguished from one another, in a single paragraph, without break, punctuation or rubric[18]—all of this nonchalance about his subject matter is bewildering. *BN*, though this copy was probably written during Taillevent's lifetime,[19] occasionally attempts to abbreviate the directions given in his text by reducing a phrase to a single word; in a few cases this abbreviation results only in obscurity. The scribe is furthermore frequently quite careless in his copying.[20] And either an idiosyncratic gastronomic prejudice against sea-fish, or

---

13 See, for example, the end of Recipe 77 *VAL*.

14 Recipe 81.

15 See 36 *MAZ*, 37 *MAZ*, "Soient plumey en aigue," and the *Nota* of 42 *MAZ*.

16 See *-er* as a past participle, and *-ez* as an infinitive, 36 *MAZ* and 49 *MAZ*; and *la portemine*, 38 *MAZ*.

17 In Recipe 70, the title *Lamproye fresche* identifies the recipe for preserved lamprey.

18 Recipes 131 to 146.

19 The date 1392 is inscribed by a purchaser on a fly leaf: see above.

20 For example, in 39 *BN*, where *cameline* has become *a la canelle*; in 54 *BN*, regarding mallards; in 61 *BN*, in which *dessus* is written *deffaites*; the *nois noiguetes* in 68 *BN*; and the blunder—rather serious, as one can imagine—of writing *mout* rather than *moins* in 74 *BN*.

a regional dearth in the supply of sea-fish, prompts him to omit many of the recipes in that particular chapter. *VAT*, like *MAZ* a comparatively late version, is generally elegant in his script and careful in his copy. Though his basic source is closely related to that of *BN*, *VAT* appends two substantial series of recipes to the end of his copy of the *Viandier*. Furthermore, he, or his immediate source, demonstrates a certain independence of inspiration by continually inserting recipes for miscellaneous dishes throughout the body of the work he was copying.[21] He frequently enriches a recipe by specifying additional ingredients or an alternative manner of preparation.[22]

All four of the manuscripts present texts which, while different, and imperfect in different ways, are individually valuable. There is, in fact, no good reason why we might not suppose Taillevent himself to have been responsible for the originals of any or all of the last three versions, those contained in *MAZ*, *BN* or *VAT*. Or, to put the conclusion another way, there seems to be no good reason for paying less attention to any one of the four manuscripts than to the others.

The search for a base manuscript for an edition of the *Viandier* is a futile and pointless quest. While all four manuscripts have very similar formats and material, each has peculiar traits in its variants, variants which of course may in many cases be attributable either to the copyist of that particular manuscript or to the "author" of that version of the text. That these are indeed different persons—the various cooks who used their *Viandier* and altered its contents, and the scribes who merely reproduced those modified copies—seems clear in every case but that of *VAL*, the earliest copy.

Whether Guillaume Tirel is the author of the oldest version of the *Viandier* is another moot question. That Guillaume Tirel was known as Taillevent, and that he spent all of his working life in or near the kitchens of various members of the French royal family during much of the fourteenth century, has been adequately proven by Pichon and Vicaire.[23] But while the *MAZ*, *BN* and *VAT* manuscripts all begin with some acknowledgement that the *Viandier* to follow is the work of Taillevent,[24] the oldest and shortest text, that of *VAL*, seems to antedate the life—certainly the "productive" professional life—of Guillaume Tirel. What is intriguing is that this manuscript has been mutilated at its beginning; if it ever had a title or attribution—the sort of *incipit* we find in the later versions of the *Viandier*—it has been cut away. Why would anyone cut away the beginning of any manuscript? Since the Valais roll was clearly a functioning kitchen cookbook—despite its several manifest errors—much rubbed[25] and even splattered with grease, it is unlikely to have been decorated with an irresistible miniature or illuminated initial letter among its first lines.

---

[21] Recipes 58, 59, 96, 115, 131 and elsewhere.

[22] Among many possible examples of such amplifications in *VAT*, see the seasonal distinctions that may appropriately be observed in preparing §38, the new Recipe 41, the specific small birds mentioned in §45, the long addition in §47, and the directions for serving in Recipes 64 and 65.

[23] See Note 11, above.

[24] According to Pichon and Vicaire, the text copied in the Saint-Lô manuscript was anonymous.

[25] The ink is rubbed and the skin is smooth particularly along the right margin between Recipes 126 and 146, as if fingers had frequently held the roll open at that point. On the recto side of the roll this area corresponds to Recipes 23–27, which contain the more popular broths.

One is tempted to conjecture that the *incipit* itself might have explained the mystery, that it may have been cut away simply because of the text it contained. The *incipit* may well have borne an indication either of the title of the work, or of its author, or perhaps of both. In any case it is very much a pity that we are prevented from reading what, if anything, the Valais scribe had written in his very neat gothic minuscule at the head of this much-used codex. We may speculate that the first lines of *VAL* contained the names of neither Taillevent nor the *Viandier*, but rather some other identification.

This Edition

Because no single manuscript version of the *Viandier* is patently preferable to the others—either because of its fidelity to what Guillaume Tirel, *alias* Taillevent, may or may not have written, or may or may not have appropriated and altered, or because of the obvious superiority of the recipes or ingredients, or because of the clarity of the exposition found in that manuscript—a conscientious editor of the *Viandier* is lead inexorably to eschew the traditional procedure whereby one version is consecrated the base text and the three other manuscript versions relegated to what would have to be very extensive footnotes. Even more unsatisfactory is the method adopted by Pichon and Vicaire, a sequential and separate presentation of whole texts—in the case of Pichon and Vicaire, the texts of *BN* and *VAT*—accompanied by a tentative and wholly inadequate system of footnotes which relate a limited number of features or passages in one text to corresponding features or passages in the other. In their footnotes Pichon and Vicaire incorporate as well a very few references to variants in the Saint-Lô manuscript; despite the fact that they seem to have had free access to this latter copy, they made no attempt to reproduce it even partially, as they did with half a dozen recipes from *MAZ*.

Because each of the four extant manuscript versions of the *Viandier* is more or less related to the others, each can shed some amount of light upon obscurities encountered in the others. Such mutual illumination, no matter how slight, is afforded in most cases of multiple manuscript copies. In the case of the *Viandier*, though, where there is no preeminent version, it is vital that an editor allow each manuscript reading to be examined to the fullest extent in the light of all of the others at every stage in the tradition of the text. By the same token, it is vital that the demonstration of significant variants in the tradition not be left to an editor's determination of what is pertinent. All too often editorial emendations, even if they are acknowledged in footnotes, reveal more of the editor's perceptions, and ignorance, than they clarify the text.[26] Adjustments to spelling, the supplying of apparently missing words, the omission of apparently gratuitous words or letters must always be considered highly hazardous by the responsible editor, to be

[26] A case in point is two instances in the *Viandier* in which the verb *faire* may seem to a modern reader to require a dependent infinitive, §18 *VAL* and §91 *VAL*; *faire* is, however, quite adequate and correct alone here, without need of emendation. Aebischer in particular sins in this respect, inserting into the text of *VAL* no fewer than seven unnecessary words or phrases—some of which "emendations" seriously alter the intended sense of a passage. See, for example, *Vallesia*, p. 87, n33. At one point in this edition of *VAL* (p. 92, n85), a word which is "restored" by means of brackets is indeed written in the text.

resorted to only when there is available absolutely no other means of suggesting that a deficiency of some sort may possibly exist in the copy.

All of the manuscript versions must be presented in full. They must be allowed to show exactly the text that a contemporary reader had in his hand, probable errors, obscurities, alterations, everything—but only what the scribe wrote.[27] They should further be presented in such a way that comparisons between these versions are as easy and as fruitful as possible. With an effective layout of texts, a significant variant in an otherwise dependable copy becomes obvious. The reader is placed in the best position to decide whether, given two or more possible readings, one of them is preferable. It is by means of such a juxtaposition of texts, moreover, that the manuscript tradition of the *Viandier* may most clearly be demonstrated.

The format used for the presentation of the texts in this present edition should prove of the maximum usefulness in showing *all* variants clearly, and in helping to establish what were the probable relationships between the four manuscripts. Furthermore, and perhaps most usefully, a close juxtaposition of all four manuscript readings should help the historian trace a significant period, some 125 years, of the history of French culinary practice. Given the relatively small number of copies that were apt to have been made of the *Viandier* up to the fifteenth century, each of the extant manuscripts surely represents an important avatar of the work, reflecting changes in gastronomic taste, development in culinary techniques, and varying conditions of alimentation, the provision of foodstuffs.

Editorial Practice

In setting forth the texts of the *Viandier*'s recipes the editor's policy has been to reproduce the manuscript readings as faithfully as possible.

To the extent that this is feasible, phrases that correspond in the various readings are aligned vertically. If it is apparent that different expressions in two versions represent the same procedure, those expressions are aligned in order to facilitate a comparison of terminology. Where an ingredient or procedure is absent in one manuscript but mentioned in another, the space representing the absence is filled with a broken line to draw the reader's attention to the variant. In certain instances all of the ingredients or procedures are present in two recipes but the order of their presentation varies: in those cases the alignment of texts has made it occasionally necessary to leave a blank space at some point in the text. A typical layout of the *Viandier*'s texts is shown here:

VAL	*salmonde,*	– –	*gingenbre,*	*canelle,*	*girofle, noys muguetez,*
MAZ	sanemonde,	– –	gigimbre,	cannelle,	giroffle, noix muguetes,
MAZ2	salemonde,	– –	gigimbre,	cannelle,	
BN	salmonde,	*vin aigre,*	*gingembre,*	*fleur de canelle,*	

[27] I would continue to advocate this policy even where it may be considered "clear" and "obvious" that errors have been made in the manuscript copy. For instance, in 7 *VAL*, *tamper* should probably have been written *tramper*; in 19 *BN*, *boullés*, *broyés* (because this is what the other manuscripts have); in 4 *MAZ*, *souffrir*, *souffrit* (because this is what correct usage requires that the scribe ought to have written, even though he did not).

VAL *poivre long,* – – – – *saffren*
MAZ poivre long, – – – – saffrain
MAZ2 poivre long, giroffle, graine de paradis, ung pol de saffrain, noix nuguetes;
BN *poivre lonc, girofle, graine de paradis, poudre de saffren et noix mugaites;*

In this brief passage (from Recipe 162) the reader can see clearly that the version copied by the manuscript of the Bibliothèque Nationale has modified the list of ingredients by introducing into it vinegar and, in common with the second version of this recipe copied by the Mazarine manuscript, grains of paradise (melegueta pepper). All other ingredients here remain a part of all of the manuscripts that reproduce this recipe, although an alteration in the order of these ingredients can be observed.

A title is supplied for each recipe. Even though in many instances this title must be an editorial compromise between a variety of versions offered by the several manuscripts, a common name is for this very reason a practical expedient which will help identify individual versions of a recipe. These same titles identify the respective recipes in their English translation (below).

Footnotes to the text of a recipe and to the commentary on the text are numbered in a sequence which belongs to *that recipe alone*. In a few place where a text and its commentary are brief, the sequence of note numbers at the foot of the page overlap to the extent that two 1s or 2s appear. The editor hopes that no undue confusion will result from the duplication of these numbers.

The *Viandier* Tradition

In attempting to determine what the family of manuscripts that constituted the *Viandier* of Taillevent may have been, we have kept two probabilities in mind. First, despite the fact that *VAL* is the earliest manuscript of the work we know as the *Viandier*, it is neither an original nor did it have a *direct* influence upon any of the later copies we possess. This becomes clear as the texts are compared. Second, while we believe in principle that Guillaume Tirel could have produced the version contained in any one of the other three extant manuscripts, claiming, rightly or wrongly, authorship of the original *Viandier*, none of *those* manuscripts, *MAZ*, *BN* or *VAT*, is either an "original," a faithful copy of an original, or a copy that had a direct influence upon any other extant manuscript copy. This is a notable peculiarity of these manuscripts of the *Viandier*: while obviously related, none of the copies is directly, clearly and consistently dependent upon any other copy.

In this family of copies the relationship seems to be as between cousins and nephews, or perhaps, at the closest, as between brothers. One is forced always to suppose an intervening copy (and perhaps even, early in the tradition, a second "*O*" from the hand of Guillaume Tirel) that introduces variants into various branches of the tradition. The same error, however, is rarely found in two copies. *VAL*, from the late thirteenth century,[28]

[28] See Aebischer's discussion about the dating of the Valais manuscript, in *Vallesia*, pp. 72 and 77–84; see especially the conclusion on p. 84: "Le fait est là, en tout cas, indiscutable: que S [*VAL*] est un manuscrit de cent ans presque plus ancien que N [*BN*]."

is most closely related to the fifteenth-century *MAZ*. *MAZ*, though late and, because of its extensive variants, most obviously derived from the annotated copy of a competent practising cook, seems in many details to be most faithful to the primitive *O*. It is this copy *O* that one assumes to be at the primordial origin of *VAL* and of the whole subsequent tradition—onto which a later *O* of Guillaume Tirel may or may not have been grafted. The fifteenth-century edition of the *Viandier* that Pichon and Vicaire reproduce (pp. 141–199) seems, in that section containing the traditional *Viandier* recipes, more closely related to *MAZ* than to any other existing manuscript copy. The following diagram seems to provide a basis for understanding the peculiar relationships among our extant versions, provided that one has assumed an absolutely minimal number of manuscript copies.

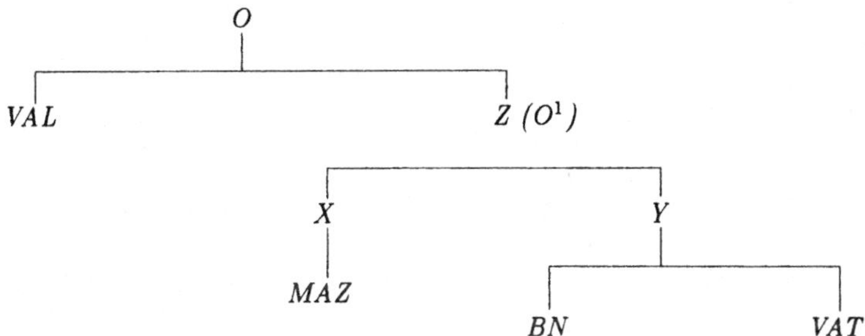

What is noticeable in this stemma is that we are still led to suppose the existence of a good number of copies intervening between the four subsisting manuscripts. In the attempt to reestablish a family tree of this sort, conjecture always plays an enormous role, of course. While the simplest scheme may be the safest one to propose, it is likely that the actual manuscript history of the *Viandier* was much more complex than what has been essayed in the diagram above. Useful cookbooks are used, by the household manager if not by the cook himself. They may even become dusted with powders, splattered with sauces, burnt or smudged with hot spoons used to hold them open. Probably more than any other type of book they are subject to the vagaries of an unprotected existence and the influences of an unfriendly environment.

There may not be many that actually disappeared into the broth vat, but it is true that actual working copies of mediæval recipe books do not seem to have survived very well.[29] All three of the later copies of the *Viandier* are clean and relatively neat, even if

[29] Just how many relatively distinct and independent cookbooks were compiled in the late Middle Ages, and how many copies of these ever were made, is of course an even more uncertain matter. In the prologue to his *Du fait de cuisine*, Maistre Chiquart, chief cook to the Duke of Savoy, working at one of the most enlightened courts of Europe in the early 1400s, states that he does not have and never has had a cookbook in his possession. "Me avés requis et commandé," he writes to his lord, "que ... je voulsisse par escript laissier aucune science de l'art de cuysinerie et de cuysine ... [mais] par pluseurs foys j'ay cecy reffusé ... car je n'ay nuls livres ouz escriptz

the transcriptions themselves are occasionally careless. The appearance of these copies, their actual production, ranges up to the rubricated elegance of the *BN* copy. All three are obviously library copies of the *Viandier*; it is the working copies which have disappeared. These latter copies, which we shall have to imagine—with their interlineal and marginal notations, their smudged, illegible words, their intercalated favorite recipes, their expunctuations or cancellations—these chefs' copies would be very precious to us, had they survived, to bridge the gaps between our fine copies that disagree so much among themselves. It would be safe to affirm that the significant changes, those at least that are deliberate and intended as improvements, are made only in the light of practice and of material results. It is the practitioner who corrects, clarifies or amplifies recipes in his own copy of a cookbook, and it is these "improved" versions that are used when library or scriptorium copies are made, or when the work is propagated to a neighbour's or a relative's household.

Because of the similarities and differences between the four *Viandier* manuscripts, it is useful, as I have suggested, to suppose the existence of four further manuscripts, more or less direct sources of the extant copies. "*O*" can still be the designation of the earliest, most rudimentary form of the *Viandier*. This is not *VAL*, because of the errors and peculiarities in *VAL*'s copy that are not transmitted to other copies.[30] On the other hand, *MAZ*, *BN* and *VAT* frequently share passages and terminology not found in *VAL*,[31] and this agreement suggests their dependence upon another manuscript that has not survived. I call this hypothetical manuscript "*Z*." So substantial are these common differences between the three later manuscripts and *VAL* that we may look upon *Z* as an important source version in the *Viandier* tradition. It is tempting to imagine, as I have suggested, that Guillaume Tirel may have been responsible for *Z*. From *Z* on, then, this work would indeed have become *Le Viandier de Taillevent*.

A contradiction between the culinary and the textual qualities of *MAZ*, already pointed out, leads to a hypothesis about a third influential but missing manuscript. Of all four manuscripts, *MAZ* appears to be the most inattentively copied.[32] Yet at the same

faysans de cecy mencion ne memoyre": *Du fait de cuisine*, ff. 11r–v; ed. Terence Scully, *Vallesia*, 40 (1985), p. 130.

It is clear that such books as the *Viandier* were not best-sellers at late-mediæval scriptoria. Perhaps what we should bear in mind is the exortation placed at the end of the *Enseignements*: "Quiconques veut servir en bon ostel, il doit avoir tout ceu qui est en cest roulle escrit en son cuer ou en escrit sus soi. Et qui ne l'a, il ne puet bien servir au grei de son mestre" (ed. Lozinski, p. 179). The cook's memory was undoubtedly one of his most valuable assets.

[30] The *VAL* scribe miscopied, for instance, *des [o]eufs* for *des foies* (Recipe 19) and *blanc* for *liant* (Recipes 20 and 21). *VAL* has peas and beans combined in a single recipe (§11) whereas in later manuscripts these are treated separately.

[31] For instance, Recipes 43, 101 and 135 seem to have been introduced into the *Viandier* in a copy which influenced only *MAZ*, *BN* and *VAT*.

[32] Concerning the absence of titles in *MAZ*, it should be noted that the scribe copying *MAZ* has left extraordinarily wide margins on his pages. It may be that there was a plan to add marginal rubrics—which would, however, have duplicated those titles that are already written ahead of

time, of all of the manuscripts copying the traditional body of recipes of the *Viandier*, *MAZ* shows the soundest individual modifications, alterations which, as I have suggested, point to contributions from a professional chef. This person must have been responsible for the source of *MAZ*, "*X*," a revised copy of the *Viandier* which may or may not have contained the supplementary material of Recipes 171–177. Despite the professional flair evinced in *X*, however, this copy seems to have had no influence in the extant corpus of manuscripts other than upon *MAZ*.

BN and *VAT* are textually close, related perhaps to the extent of sharing a common immediate source. This common source, whether immediate or not, is "*Y*," the product of a chef who, among his other characteristics, seems to have liked pasties, or worked for a patron who did. To the older, more traditional methods of food preparation that use boiling and roasting, he adds a number of recipes and variants of recipes that involve baking in an oven without the use of a shell of pastry.[33] *Y* seems to have been a working copy on which someone has inserted amplifications and clarifications above the line or in the margin in such a way that *BN* occasionally fails to understand their sense and miscopies them. *VAT*, however, does normally show these modifications incorporated properly into his text.[34] Unique among the extant manuscripts, *VAT* contains a Table of Contents. This Table anticipates several recipes not in fact actually copied by *VAT* but existing, one has to assume, in *VAT*'s source. It is reasonable to suppose, therefore, that this source must have been even more ample than the *Viandier* we find in either *BN* or *VAT*, and must consequently have been the most extensive version of whose existence we have any evidence. The *VAT* Table does not include the two series of supplementary material (Recipes 178–187 and 188–220) appended after the list of spices (Recipe 170) which concluded the *Viandier* in *Y*.

There are three series of recipes added to the traditional corpus of the *Viandier* which is copied by the four manuscripts. *MAZ* has a set of seven additional paragraphs, written in the same hand, describing the preparation of dishes apparently unrelated to any of the material already copied. These dishes include two sauces, two meat dishes, two egg dishes and one for deep-fried fritters. This brief assortment of recipes is what one might expect of a cook, perhaps *X*, who wanted to add several of his own favourite preparations to the *Viandier* he had been using or had copied. In any case, these recipes tend to be rather more detailed in the culinary steps they outline, and more precise in their style than what was copied before.[35] New words of a technical nature appear here,[36] and new ingredients are mentioned.[37] Most curiously, this supplementary material in *MAZ* is followed by nine

---

their recipes. It still remains unclear, though, how any system of marginal rubrics could have distinguished between the unbroken series of untitled recipes we find in *MAZ* between Recipes 135–146 and Recipes 158–161.

[33] For example, Recipes 121 and 151.

[34] See, for example, the qualification *tout cru* inserted by *Y* in Recipe 4. As well, *Y* introduces a number of new recipes into the *Viandier*, including §168.

[35] See particularly Recipes 173, 175 and 177.

[36] For example, the verb *gratusier* in Recipe 176.

[37] These new ingredients include herbs in particular: *espinoches*, *marjolienne*, *orvale*.

further recipes for sauces, seven of which had just been copied by *MAZ* from his original source, but two of which,[38] while likewise in the *Viandier* tradition and copied by other manuscripts, had not previously been taken up and reproduced by *MAZ* in the earlier series of sauces. All but one of the nine recipes in this repeated series of sauces now bear names, whereas previously not a single one was named, and the texts of these recipes are considerably altered.

Both of the other series of supplementary recipes are found only in the *VAT* manuscript. They are copied by a hand slightly different from the one that wrote to the end of Recipe 170. First is a sequence of ten prescriptions for curing, improving and preserving wines, which section of text is headed "Le fait des vins." Following these, and up to the end of the manuscript, a very substantial collection of thirty-three recipes for prepared dishes occupies eleven and one half folios. These dishes are quite varied in nature, representing several categories of preparation already found in the *Viandier*, and are in a very general way organized in a logical sequence of stews, broths, flans, tortes, crêpes, pies and finally *entremets*. In most cases these added recipes are considerably more complex than before; they are for dishes whose presentation is designed to be more impressive, dishes that may in the broadest sense quite properly be termed *entremets*. It is worth noting that several of those last preparations that are actually designated as *entremets* are not in fact dishes intended eventually to be eaten, nor are they even composed of any edible parts. These later *entremets* are, rather, simply ingenious show-pieces. The prose style of both sections of the supplementary material in *VAT*, from Recipe 178 to the end, is less laconic than that found in his copy of the traditional work, a little more prosy, more explicit and generally more helpful in the instructions the writer addresses to the cook.[39]

New words appear in these later, appended sections of *VAT*'s *Viandier*.[40] Significantly, too, we find new ingredients, foodstuffs never previously used in the traditional *Viandier*, and a few not found in either of the other fourteenth-century French works, the *Enseignements* and the *Menagier de Paris*.[41] The fifteenth-century cook outlines a few

---

[38] Recipes 166 and 167.

[39] The direction for slicing or drawing chicken meat into strips is both specific and figurative in Recipe 189: "Le charpir ainsi qu'on charpiroit lainne." The logical cohesion of the instructions is assured by such terms as *ledit*, as in "Deffaictes lesdictes espices et ypocras emsemble" (Recipe 188).

[40] These terms, almost technical neologisms, such as *compettement* and *raisonnablement*, *duisable*, *finer* and *fricture*, usually have to do with the proper, competent preparation of culinary dishes. A new syntactical practice found in these later texts may also be pointed out here: the author occasionally places a preposition, without expressing its object, after a verb and, following the preposition, the object of the verb: " Et y mecter cuire avec poivre ront": "Set round pepper to boil with it" (Recipe 173).

[41] Examples of these new ingredients in the *Viandier* are *annis blanc ou vermeil*, *grenade*, *gingembre de mesche*, *cynamome* (which is prescribed in combination with *canelle* in Recipes 188 and 206); and as colorants, alkanet and the orchil lichen known as *tournesoc*. Sugar is much more frequently employed in these last recipes. We find as well a new term *menues espices* (Recipes 191 and 206), apparently with the sense of the former *fines espices*.

novel procedures here.[42] And interestingly there is as well a tentative move to indicate a little more specifically the relative quantities of some ingredients that enter into these new dishes,[43] although these indications are still by no means as precise as they are made by Chiquart, who was writing at roughly the same time as *VAT* was copied. A fire made of coal is more frequently prescribed in these new recipes in an effort to obtain a more even, regulated, low fire.[44] And in general one senses in the fifteenth-century writer of *VAT* a certain professional consciousness that the terse style of the earlier *Viandier* did not allow to penetrate. The phrase "ainsi que compaignons sçaivent bien la maniere"[45] reminds the reader that the culinary techniques described in these pages belong to the masters of a craft.

The Order of the Recipes in the *Viandier*

By the more or less extensive use of chapter rubrics, all four manuscripts of the *Viandier* indicate that the work has a reasoned layout.[46] The sequence of recipes throughout the traditional part of the work—that is, exclusive of the additions made by *MAZ* and *VAT*—is determined primarily by the recognition of two general types of *viande*, on the one hand that of land animals and fowl, both domestic and wild, and, on the other, that of fish and other aquatic creatures. As well, the *Viandier* makes use of several further, subsidiary categories into which fourteenth-century dishes can be sorted, according to the circumstances of their use and according to the methods employed in their cooking and preparation.

The collection opens[47] with an assortment of dishes of simple boiled meats from four-

---

[42] In Recipes 188 and 192, for instance, *hippocras*, a spiced wine, is used as a medium in which to steep the ground spices, just as Chiquart at roughly the same time is specifying another variety of spiced wine called *claret* for the same purpose. And in Recipe 191 chicken and veal are cooked together and combined in a dish, a procedure that has become quite common, even normal, in the recipes of Chiquart.

[43] "De l'ypocras selong la quantité que on veult faire du potaige"; "De la chappleure de deux ou de trois pains blans"; "Et de girofle un peu moins que de graine."

[44] For his two-day banquet at the beginning of the fifteenth century Chiquart requires only two cart-loads (*charrestés*) of firewood but a whole "barn-full" (*une grant grange pleine*) of coal (*Du fait de cuisine*, f. 15v).

[45] Recipe 212 in *VAT*.

[46] The Valais roll shows the fewest internal divisions, bearing chapter names only twice: before Recipe 155, "Saulcez non boulluez," and before Recipe 163, "Saulcez boulluez." Of the other manuscripts, *BN* is most particular to insert chapter designations. The composition of the various versions of the *Viandier*, including the sequence in which the recipes are copied in each manuscript, can most easily be seen in the chart that accompanies this Introduction.

[47] The helpful hints on removing salt from a stew—probably because preserved meat had been inadequately desalinated previous to going into the pot—or on removing a burnt taste from a stew that was inattentively left over too hot a fire, do not in all likelihood form part of the original *Viandier*. It is not surprising, though, that these items were inserted later at the head of the work in order to help the cook deal immediately with the ever-present problems associated with salted

footed animals, both domestic and wild, fresh and salted. At Recipe 10 begins a new division for which only the *Y* manuscripts indicate a title: "Potages lians." The section should undoubtedly, and more accurately, be headed: "Potages lians *de char*." This latter qualification is implied in Recipe 96[48] and refers either to the main ingredient or perhaps, by extension, to the meat days upon which these dishes may properly be eaten. The second chapter in the *Viandier* contains various recipes for meat broths, stews and similar preparations. They continue to share with the dishes of the first chapter the common feature of the meat being boiled in a pot; however, in every case now the meat is prepared in conjunction with some sort of sauce which combines a liquid, other than just water, with a thickener, flavouring and colorant.

Beginning with Recipe 31 is a chapter of recipes for a variety of roast meats, particularly of domestic animals which, according to the Galenic humoral theory, are deemed to be more moist by nature—and generally a little more cool—than wild animals, and therefore more suitable for the roasting process.[49] A series of dishes for fowl (Recipes 44 to 59) may have been conceived as a subdivision in the chapter on roast meats; in every case these birds are cooked by roasting and are then dressed with an appropriate condiment or sauce.

Following these roasts are fourteen *entremets*, dishes suitable for presentation between the first and second servings (*assises, assiettes* or *mets*) of a dinner. The *entremets* in the *Viandier* is generally lighter than a normal preparation, yet at the same time somewhat fancier. The substance of an *entremets* can be meat, poultry or fish, treated in an unusual way, or it can be a dish of boiled cereal, a sort of porridge. Recipes 73 and 74 (*Froide sauge* and *Sourps de porcelet*) at the end of the chapter are really counterparts, and as such are illustrative of one other sort of logic that occasionally determines the arrangement of the recipes in the *Viandier*.[50]

According to *BN*, Recipe 75 (*Comminee de poisson*) opens a series of "Potaiges lians"; the series should properly be titled "Potaiges lians sans char," the name given to this chapter in the Vatican Table. In much the same way as the Recipes 73 and 74 just mentioned form a pair, several of the recipes in this section of meatless stews are counterparts to recipes that have already been presented in the second chapter of the *Viandier*[51] and are

---

meat and unregulated heat. Meat and fish that have been preserved in salt form an important basis for the *Viandier*'s recipes, and the regulation of the heat to which a pot is exposed is always a primary concern to the various writers throughout the book.

48 The Table at the beginning of *VAT* alone names the chapter which opens with Recipe 75, "Potaiges lyans sans chair." For a discussion of the sense of several generic terms applied to liquid culinary preparations, see Jean-Louis Flandrin, "Brouets, potages et bouillons," *Médiévales*, 5 (1983), pp. 5–14; and Liliane Plouvier, "Cuisine: et le potage fut … ," *L'Histoire*, 64 (Feb., 1984), pp. 79–81.

49 See the section on Culinary theory and practice, below.

50 So the two *Comminees* of Recipes 12 and 13 are juxtaposed; and the *Boussac* of Recipe 20 is related to the *Hondous* of Recipe 21, of which the *Hochepot* of Recipe 23 is in turn a derivative.

51 The *Comminee de poisson* (Recipe 75) is, for instance, a counterpart to the *Comminee de poullaille* (Recipe 12); the *Brouet vergay d'anguilles* (Recipe 76) is a counterpart to the *Brouet*

clearly designed to provide the cook with ready alternatives for menus during Lent or on the meatless days of the week.[52]

The chapter "Viandes pour malades" is a common feature in mediæval health handbooks and in many early cookery books.[53] The *Viandier*'s assortment of para-medicinal dishes for the sick includes a caudel and a gruel, two chicken dishes for meat days and a dish using perch for a fish day. This choice of dishes is entirely typical of such chapters.

Recipes for fish are expressly grouped into three categories: fresh-water fish, round sea-fish and flat sea-fish.[54] The order of fish in each chapter seems to follow the ideal order

---

vergay for meat days (Recipe 26); the *Gravé de loche* (Recipe 77) is a counterpart to the *Gravé de menus oiseaus* (Recipe 18); and so forth.

52 According to Recipe 195, one of the fifteenth-century additions, the meat-days or butcher-days (*jours maslés*) of the week are Sunday, Tuesday and Thursday. Concerning foods appropriate for the fast-days of Lent, see the *Libre del coch* of Mestre Robert, ed. Veronika Leimgruber (Barcelona, 1982), §169; and Hans Wiswe, *Kulturgeschichte der Kochkunst* (Munich, 1970), p. 87.

53 For doctors' prescriptions of foods and dishes appropriate for sick persons, see Arnaldus de Villanova, *De modo preparandi cibos et potus infirmorum*, in the *Opera omnia* (Lyon: Tardif, 1586), vol. 2, p. 177 f.; and, together with general hygiene for the sick, the convalescent and those living in times of plague, the *De regimine sanitatis* attributed to the same author, in Book 2, ch. 30–36; the *Regimen sanitatis* of Magninus Mediolanensis, Part 4; and Bernard de Gordon, *De cibis* (Bibliothèque Nationale, ms. lat. 16,189, ff. 195v–199v). See also Musandinus, *Summa de preparatione ciborum et potuum infirmorum*, ed. Salvatore de Renzi, *Collectio Salernitana*, vol. 5, pp. 254–268. Martin de Saint Gille, writing his *Commentaires sur les Amphorismes Ypocras* in Avignon between 1362 and 1365, amplifies upon the type of foods suitable for the sick, which foods he calls in French *diete estroite ou subtille*: "Diete subtille ou estroite est contenu ... en viandes de grant quantité et de petit nourrissement, si comme tisanne non coullee, puree de pois, ou en viandes de petite quantité, si comme poucins, oefz, poissons": ed. Germaine Lafeuille (Cambridge, Mass., 1954); see the Glossary. A chapter in Alonso de Chirino's *Menor daño de la medicina*, ed. M.T. Herrera (Salamanca, 1973), p. 127, deals with *viandas sótilas* intended for the sick, and is still, at the beginning of the fifteenth century, inspired by Hippocrates and Celsus. In Arnaldus de Villanova's *Souverain remede contre l'epedimie* (Lyon: Claude Nourry, 1501), ch. 4 is devoted to an outline of the foods to be consumed during the plague.

Among cookery manuals of this period that contain a section of sick-foods, see the *Tractatus* whose Book 4 has a rubric that reads, "De condimentis delicatis dominorum, ad naturam confortandam et appetitum provocandum": ed. Marianne Mulon, *Bulletin Philologique et Historique* (Paris, 1968 [pub. 1971]), p. 391. The *Menagier de Paris* has both seven "Buvrages pour malades" and eight "Potages pour malades" (in the Brereton and Ferrier edition, §§297–319; in the Pichon edition, pp. 237–243). Chiquart's *Du fait de cuisine* concludes with a "Titre des viandes pour malades" which groups sixteen dishes for "fellés ou acterves de personnes, ou detenuz d'aucunes infirmités et maladies" (f. 92v).

54 These three divisions of fish correspond to a distinction made by natural scientists since the time of Pliny the Elder in his *Natural History*, Book 9, ch. 36. It is a distinction that the *Menagier de Paris* continues to adopt with divisions titled "Poisson de mer ront" and "Poisson de mer plat" (ed. Brereton and Ferrier, respectively pp. 236—though without the word *ront*—

of preference as this was determined by physicians and scientists of the day, with the most favoured fishes dealt with first. At the end of the third of these chapters (Recipe 148 f.), there are recipes for several varieties of shellfish.

A brief section is constituted by Recipes 152, 153 and 154 which are for miscellaneous additional dishes. Intended originally perhaps to provide further possibilities for Lent, these recipes, and particularly the order of them in the various manuscripts, pose problems about the interrelationships of those manuscripts.

Two chapters on sauces close the most rudimentary form of the *Viandier*, as *VAL* reproduced it. A distinction is made between sauces according to whether they are prepared cold or hot. The cold sauces tend to make preponderant use of cinnamon or garlic, whereas in the hot sauces pepper or ginger is the principal ingredient.

A list of spices used in the *Viandier* follows the sauce recipes in *BN* and *VAT*. Apparently a compilation of *Y*, this list provides the user of the book with a sort of preliminary check-list with which he could examine the stocks in his condiment larder.[55]

Culinary Theory and Practice

We are fortunate to possess a work from the beginning of the fourteenth century that indicates that culinary practice at this time must have been determined in large measure by contemporary medical theory. When, in about 1332, the physician and doctor Magninus Mediolanensis (Maino de' Maineri) composed his *Regimen sanitatis*, he devoted a series of ten chapters in its Part 3 to a systematic examination of the qualities of all foodstuffs generally in use in the households of his contemporaries.[56] For this analysis Magninus is clearly indebted in particular to the Galenic tradition as this body of theory distinguishes the nutritive and humoral qualities of each species of grain, vegetable, fruit, animal, animal product and so forth. While his work, in this respect, resembles a number of similar

---

and 240; ed. Pichon, pp. 194—with *ront*—and 201). The *Enseignements* has a rubric that its most recent editor Lozinski reads as "Ici enseingne des pessons reaus e des autres viandes" (p. 186): the qualification after *pessons* should undoubtedly read *reans* or *reons*. Pichon and Vicaire (*Viandier*, p. 223) omit this word altogether, and in his edition of the work (p. 222) Douët-D'Arcq gives no indication that there is a chapter rubric at this point. (For the various editions of the *Enseignements*, see n71, below.)

[55] The Roman gastronome Apicius in his *Excerpta*, which is edited along with his *De re coquinaria* by G. Giarratano and F. Vollmer (Leipzig, 1922), p. 77 f., has a similar list of spices that ought to be in the home so that no seasoning may be wanting, whether seeds or dry ingredients. The *Menagier de Paris* (ed. Brereton and Ferrier, pp. 186 and 190; ed. Pichon, pp. 111 and 122) composes the same sort of inventory in the form of two shopping lists of items to be procured "*a l'espicier*" in order honourably to prepare food for a formal dinner either in May or in September.

[56] A native of Milan, Magninus taught for a while in the medical faculty at the University of Paris before serving as personal doctor to Andreas of Florence, Bishop of Arras between 1331 and 1334, to whom he dedicated his *Regimen sanitatis*. Magninus died about 1364. See Ernest Wickersheimer, *Dictionnaire biographique des médecins en France au moyen age*, 2 vols. (Paris, 1936), vol. 1, p. 533.

outlines compiled in the thirteenth and fourteenth centuries, it is remarkable for the detail and thoroughness of its examination of foodstuffs.

For anyone interested in late-mediæval cookery this Part 3 of Magninus' *Regimen sanitatis* is especially precious because it contains as well a chapter entitled "De saporibus et condimentis" in which the physician defines the medical function of culinary sauces and, in view of this function, enumerates at great length the sauces appropriate to a wide variety of those meats and fishes analysed by him in other chapters of Part 3.[57] Because every noble household in Europe at this time had attached to it at least one doctor who necessarily was familiar with current medical doctrine, there can be little doubt that the cooks of these households were required to be guided directly or indirectly by this doctrine.[58]

---

[57] The chapter "De saporibus et condimentis" is chapter 20, occupying ff. 112r–115v in the edition published by Johannes de Westfalia (Louvain, 1482): *Regimen sanitatis Magnini Mediolanensis Medici famosissimi Attrebatensi Episcopo directum*. What appears to be a slightly modified version of the material in this chapter 20 of the *Regimen* was copied also in a manuscript (Naples, Biblioteca Nazionale, VIII. D. 35, ff. 52–53v) under the title "Opusculum de saporibus." This latter version was published by Lynn Thorndike in *Speculum*, 9 (1934), pp. 183–190: "A Mediaeval Sauce-Book." This article contains biographical data on Magninus, as well as a transcription of that abbreviated part of the chapter "De saporibus et condimentis" (part II, chapter 24) that appears in the *Regimen sanitatis* attributed to Arnaldus de Villanova: *Hec sunt opera Arnaldi de Villanova*, ed. Thomas Murchius (Lyons: Fradin, 1504), ff. 54v–79v. See Terence Scully, "The *Opusculum de saporibus* of Magninus Mediolanensis," *Medium Ævum*, 54 (1985), pp. 178–207.

[58] Several pieces of evidence exist to demonstrate this direct, daily influence of medical personnel upon the food consumed by a fourteenth-century aristocrat. At the court of Burgundy at this time "six médecins veillent sur la santé de Monseigneur, en particulier sur son alimentation. Placés derrière lui pendant les repas, ils conseillent ou déconseillent les plats qui passent." See Charles Commeaux, *La vie quotidienne en Bourgogne au temps des ducs Valois (1364–1477)* (Paris, 1979). One of the most important early English cookery books, the *Forme of Cury* (*c.* 1390), states in its foreword that it was "compiled by assent and avyssement of maisters of phisik and of philosophie" dwelling at the court of Richard II (see the Warner edition, p. 1). At the conclusion of the *Diversa servicia* we read: "Explicit de coquina que est optima medicina" (ed. Hieatt and Butler, p. 79). "One of the duties of Edward IV's physician was to 'stond muche in the kynges presence at his meles, councellyng his grace whyche dyet is best'. Besides consulting with the steward and master cook as to the day's menu, the royal physician would also sit at the king's table to see that he ate nothing harmful to his health": Colin Clair, *Kitchen and Table* (London, 1964), p. 63.

The close rapport between food and medicine at this time is apparent in the incorporation in the *Kochbuch Meister Eberhards* of a dietetic in its second section: see the study by Wolfgang Hirth, "Die Diätetik im Kochbuch des Küchenmeisters Eberhart von Landshut und eine deutsche Regel der Gesundheit nach Arnald de Villanova," *Ostbairische Grenzmarken*, 8 (1966), pp. 273–281. The rapport is apparent also in the practice of copying cookbooks in the same manuscript volume as medical treatises: the *MAZ* copy of the *Viandier* was itself placed beside a treatise of the famous doctor Bernard de Gordon; the *Tractatus* and *Liber de coquina* appear in the same manuscript as an Arab medical dietetic, the *Liber de ferculis*.

Magninus states that condiments served originally to make foods more palatable and therefore more digestible. However, according to Magninus, sauces now play a much more important role in the regimen of any healthy man: they work to counteract any harmful superfluities in the foodstuffs that are to be consumed. They help render the digestion of various foods safe as well as easy. A fundamental premise for the use of condiments is expressed succinctly: "Sauces vary according to the foods for which they are made, because this or that food requires this or that sauce, as the cooks of the great well know."[59] Because the temperament of man is moderately warm and moderately moist, dishes in which the net nature of all ingredients approximates this, or dishes whose nature is at least temperate in relative temperature and humidity, are to be preferred. The cooks of the great lords had therefore to be aware of the humoral qualities of all of the foodstuffs that passed through their hands. They had to know what by its nature could safely be ingested, and to recognize what combinations of ingredients, of meats and sauces, were either requisite or permissible in view of the health of the lord and his court.

For this same reason the method employed to cook any meat or fish must be appropriate for that meat or fish. In the process of cooking, the exposure to moisture, whether water or oil, and to heat will tend to increase or decrease the natural relative moistness of the flesh, and either to moderate or intensify its relative warmth. In this regard the principle to which mediæval physicians subscribed is simply that dry meats should be boiled and moist meats should be roasted: "Boiling ... tempers dryness and roasting, moistness."[60] According to the proximity to temperateness of these natural qualities in the flesh, a modification in temperature and in humidity could be desirable, or alternatively could perilously disturb the healthy humoral balance within the person who is to consume the food.

The various authors of the *Viandier* do not illustrate in all their detail the recommendations that Magninus makes in his chapter "De saporibus et condimentis"—either with

[59] "Diversificantur sapores ratione cibariorum pro quibus fiunt. Nam alia et alia cibaria indigent alio et alio sapore, sicut sciunt dominorum coci": Magninus, *Regimen sanitatis*, part 3, ch. 20, *ed. cit.*, f. 113v. In the *Opusculum de saporibus* Magninus amplifies this rule somewhat: "Quanto cibi sunt temperatiores et temperamento propiores, tanto minus ex saporibus est comedendum cum eis. Et similiter sapores eis competentiores sunt et esse debent temperamento propiores, et econverso quanto cibi sunt magis lapsi a temperamento tanto indigent saporibus magis lapsis ad oppositum lapsus ciborum; unde si cibi declinant ad frigidum et humidum et viscosum, sapor debet esse calidus et siccus et subtiliativus, et econverso si cibi sunt calidi et sicci, sapor debet esse frigidus et humidus" (ed. Thorndike, *loc. cit.*, pp. 186–187). See also the *Regime tresutile et tresproufitable pour conserver et garder la santé du corps humain*, ed. Patricia W. Cummins (Chapel Hill, 1976), pp. 19ff.

[60] "Elixatio ... obtemperat siccitatem et assatio humiditatem": Magninus, *Regimen sanitatis*, part 3, ch. 17, *ed. cit.*, f. 100v. See also J. Albini, *De sanitatis custodia* (1341–1342), ed. G. Carbonelli (Pinerolo, 1906), p. 81; and the *Regime tresutile*, ed. Cummins, p. 25, where boiling is stipulated for rabbit and stag, and roasting for pork and lamb. Because for the most part fowl are considered to be of a warm and moist nature, partaking as they do of the temperament of air, they are normally roasted in the *Viandier*.

regard to how each meat should be cooked or with regard to the most suitable sauces to be used to dress each. Singular tastes and peculiar gastronomic traditions, to say nothing of economic considerations—the cost and relative availability of certain foodstuffs—doubtless influenced the cooks of individual households. What is usually reflected in the *Viandier*, however, is a culinary practice that recognizes in a general way the doctrines propagated by contemporary medical schools concerning the most wholesome means of cooking and preparing particular meats and the most salubrious condiments to be consumed in conjunction with them.[61]

Of the various cooking processes, roasting imparts the most heat to a meat, and dries it out the most: this process is most appropriate for a cold, moist meat, such as pork; beef, being relatively warm and dry, should not ideally be roasted but should be boiled instead.[62] While boiling imparts a high degree of moisture to a meat, it does not warm it nearly as much as does roasting. That boiling was probably the usual treatment accorded beef by cooks using the *Viandier* seems evident by the ubiquitous requirement of beef broth in the *Viandier*'s recipes.[63] Frying, a process intermediary between roasting and boiling in its effects, warms moderately and, because of the oil or grease used in the pan, lends a moderate amount of moisture to a meat: mature poultry has a meat whose relatively dry and cool properties make frying suitable at some point in its preparation.[64]

Sauces make use of a liquid base (water or broth, wine, vinegar or verjuice[65]) in which

---

[61] For particular choices made in the *Viandier* recipes, either in cooking method or in saucing, as these are determined specifically by the humoral qualities of the foodstuffs being prepared, see the commentary to the various recipes, below.

[62] Pork is the first item in the *Viandier*'s section on roast meats, whereas the meat of wild animals, venison, is boiled. "Or, devés savoir que totes chars c'on use, ou eles sont domesces ou eles sont sauvegines .... Et sachiés que totes sauvegines sont plus caudes et plus seches que les domesces ... ": *Le régime du corps de Maître Aldebrandin de Sienne. Texte français du XIIIe siècle*, ed. Louis Landouzy and Roger Pépin (Paris, 1911).

[63] As a result of the attention paid to the natural temperament of foodstuffs, a recipe for roast beef is simply not found in the *Viandier*: beef is considered to be the driest of all domestic meats, and roasting to be the most drying of all cooking processes. Such a preparation of such a meat would risk generating either cholera or melancholy in the person consuming it.

[64] "Inter carnes volatilium laudabilium in regimine sanitatis quedam sunt temperatiores et temperamento propinquiores. Alie sunt minus temperamento propinque. Temperatores quedem sunt galline juvenes, galinarum, pulli et juvenes pingues capones que tamen ad aliqualem caliditatem et humiditatem declinant": Magninus, *Regimen sanitatis*, ch. 17, "De carnibus," *ed. cit.*, f. 102r. Furthermore, according to Aldobrandino, chicks enjoy a moist nature common to most young creatures of any species—veal is more moist than beef, for example; with age hens have become both drier and cooler in temperament: see *Le régime du corps*, *ed. cit.*, p. 128. See also Albini, *De sanitatis custodia*, *ed. cit.*, pp. 77–79, and the *Regime tresutile*, *ed. cit.*, p. 24, where explicit distinctions are made between the proper treatments for meats according to whether the animals they come from are domestic or wild, young or old, male or female.

[65] The three grape products, wine, vinegar and verjuice, vary broadly in their temperatures. While all three are dry in the second, or moderately strong, degree, wine is warm in the second

are infused spices and herbs, with occasionally the admixture of other agents for binding, colour or taste.[66] In a noble household in the late Middle Ages spices were not merely the property of a culinary or gastronomic domain. They belonged under the management and control of the court apothecary, who dispensed spices in exactly the same way he dispensed drugs—and for the same reasons.[67] Spices were held to be varieties of drug, which functioned by acting upon and altering the humoral state, the temper, of the person or thing to which they are applied. For their sick patients, doctors prescribed medicines that were frequently composed in large measure of those same spices used in the kitchen.

Spices are generally of a dry nature (an exception being ginger) and warm, varying in these respects merely between high (cinnamon and cloves) and extreme (mustard and pepper). Plain Cameline Sauce is basically a cinnamon and vinegar sauce whose ingredients make it moderately warming and very drying in its effects: it is appropriate for use with such temperate meats as venison (when boiled, because venison is normally by nature a dry meat) or veal (when roasted, because it is a relatively moist meat). Similarly, almonds are ubiquitously used in dressings and sauces because their qualities approximate those of the human temperament, being moderately warm and moist.[68] Cold and moist fish such as tench and eel require the special warming and drying treatment provided by Green Sauce whose principal ingredient, parsley, is considered to be very warm and very dry.

---

degree, vinegar is on the other hand moderately cool in the second degree, and verjuice is even more cool, in the third degree. The *Viandier* will frequently specify that a relatively cool meat be cooked in water and wine in order to warm it: wild boar and capons (castration alters the warm nature of male animals) are so treated regularly. And, similarly, ground liver is normally steeped in a wine mixture because animal viscera are considered generally to be both cool and moist.

[66] The *Regime tresutile*, *ed. cit.*, p. 59, typically sets out principles to be followed in preparing sauces in the summer and in the winter, and advises the reader of the effects of such sauce ingredients as sage, pepper, garlic and parsley. On the seasonal availability of meats, domestic and game, month by month, see Louis Stouff, *Ravitaillement et alimentation en Provence aux XIVe et XVe siècles* (Paris, 1970); and J.-P. Sosson, "La part du gibier dans l'alimentation médiévale," *La chasse au moyen âge* (Paris, 1980), pp. 347–359.

[67] In 1416 an apothecary of Amadeus VIII of Savoy received payment for spices delivered to the Count's cook, Chiquart, specifically for the making of a lamprey sauce (the *Viandier*'s Recipe 69): "Libravit Iohanni Belleni appothecario pro specibus suprascriptis ab eodem emptis pro dicta salsa lampree facienda et tradictis dicto magistri Chiquardo. Et primo pro una libra zinziberis albi, . I. flor. . VI. gross. ; dimidia libra cinnamoni, . VI. den. gross. ; uno quarterono grane paradisi, . III. den. obl. gross. ; uno quarterono piperis, . II. den. , . I. quart. ; uno quarterono garioffilorum, . IIII. obl. gross. dimidio quarterono gallericorum, . IIII. den. obl. gross." Mara Castorina Battaglia, "Notizie sui farmaci usati alla corte di Savoia dal 1300 al 1440," *Minerva Medica*, 69 (1978), p. 511, n32.

[68] See Magninus, *Regimen sanitatis*, ch. 12, "De fructibus"; *ed. cit.*, f. 90v; and Aldobrandino, *ed. cit.*, p. 154. Almond milk, made from almond paste steeped in a liquid and then strained, served as a more durable alternative to cow's milk, whose use seems reserved in the *Viandier* for preparations that require a binding agent.

The *Viandier* Among Early Cookery Books[69]

Only three works of a similar nature in northwestern Europe may possibly antedate the *Viandier* that we read in *VAL*. The first of these is the brief collection of twenty-nine recipes in Anglo-Norman dialect that is introduced by the rubric "Coment l'en deit fere viande e claree."[70] This collection dates from the end of the thirteenth century. While a few of the preparations outlined here, dishes such as the *Gelye* of §9, bear some resemblance to preparations in the *Viandier*, by far the greater part of its contents belong to a distinctly different tradition.

The earliest continental French recipe collection is the slightly more extensive work, of some forty-six recipes, whose incipit reads: "Vez ci les enseingnemenz qui enseingnent a apareillier toutes manieres de viandes."[71] The composition of this "Little Treatise" has been very tentatively placed at about 1300.[72] Whether or not the *Enseignements* was known to the writer of the original *Viandier*, or, conversely, whether the author of the *Enseignements* may have read *O*, are possibilities that in all likelihood will remain only that. In any case, similarities between the two works do exist at an elementary level in the general layout of the various dishes within each collection: meats/fowl/*entremets*/fish. Both works share as well certain broadly-known dishes. However, where the recipes in the *Viandier* are organized according to the type of dish a meat will enter into, or according to the manner in which these dishes are prepared, the *Enseignements* begins with a sequence of dishes appropriate for each of the meats themselves: pork/beef/veal/mutton/kid and lamb. That similarities exist between dishes described in two French cookbooks dating from approximately the same period should, of course, be expected. There is, however, no firm textual evidence of any direct influence one way or the other between these two early collections.

---

69 Here and in the commentary that accompanies the texts of the *Viandier* it will be the editor's practice to refer to early recipe collections by means of an abbreviated title. The complete title and full bibliographic information are in all cases supplied in the Bibliography (below).

70 *Viande e claree* is edited by Constance B. Hieatt and Robin F. Jones as collection "A" in "Two Anglo-Norman Culinary Collections Edited from British Library Manuscripts Additional 32085 and Royal 12.C.xii," *Speculum*, 61 (1986), pp. 862–866.

71 This work has been edited on three occasions and with varying titles: *Enseignements*, ed. by Grégoire Lozinski as Appendix I in his *Bataille de Caresme et de Charnage* (Paris, 1933), pp. 181–187; *Traité de cuisine écrit vers 1300*, ed. Pichon and Vicaire in their edition of the *Viandier de Guillaume Tirel dit Taillevent* (Paris, 1892), pp. 213–226; and *Traité de cuisine écrit vers 1306*, ed. L. Douët-D'Arcq, in "Un petit traité de cuisine écrit en français au commencement du XIVe siècle," *Bibliothèque de l'École des Chartes*, 21 (1860), pp. 216–224. In the present study references to this recipe collection will normally be double: firstly to the *Enseignements* as edited by Lozinski, with page and line number; and secondly to the edition of this work published by Pichon and Vicaire, with the page numbers of the text as they read it.

72 See in the previous note the titles that two of its editors have given this work. According to Pichon and Vicaire the language of the *Petit traité* "nous donneroit peut-être le droit de faire remonter l'époque de sa composition aux dernières années du XIIIe siècle" (p. 213, n1).

Finally, of the three early recipe compilations the significance of the hoariest should be considered briefly. This is the work that Rudolf Grewe calls the *Northern-European Cookbook.*[73] Of German origin and extant now in four distinct versions, this cookbook was undoubtedly composed in the first half of the thirteenth century and is therefore the earliest known mediæval collection of culinary recipes. In it we find a few dishes that bear a resemblance to dishes in the *Viandier*, but once again it is quite evident that as a collection it has no close relationship with the French work.

Almost the same conclusion must be reached concerning two Latin recipe collections that appear to have been written likewise near the beginning of the fourteenth century.[74] These are the *Liber de coquina* and the *Tractatus de modo preparandi et condiendi omnia cibaria.*[75] Again, certain preparations in one or the other of these works have counterparts in the *Viandier* but there is, with one exception, no evidence of direct borrowing in either direction. The one exception is the series of wine recipes of which a number of passages are echoed in the *Viandier*—not in its original form but among the additions appended in the *VAT* copy toward the beginning of the fifteenth century.

The *Viandier* did have significant influence, however, upon two works that clearly postdate it, although in all likelihood it will never be possible to declare whether this influence was direct or indirect. Whole sections of the *Viandier* were incorporated more or less textually into the Fifth Article of the Second Distinction of the *Menagier de Paris* (*c.* 1393)[76] and many individual recipes from the *Viandier* appear in whole or in part in

---

[73] The different manuscript sources of this German work have been edited separately: see the Bibliography, below. The work as a whole has recently been studied and translated into English by Rudolf Grewe in "An Early XIII Century Northern-European Cookbook," in *Current Research in Culinary History: Sources, Topics and Methods* (Boston, 1986).

[74] See Marianne Mulon, "Recettes médiévales" in *Annales: Economies, Sociétés, Civilisations,* 19 (1964), pp. 933–937; and this same article reprinted under the title "Les premières recettes médiévales" in Jean-Jacques Hémardinquer, *Pour une histoire de l'alimentation* (Paris, 1972), pp. 236–240. Mulon's survey provides a good introduction to the whole area of early French cookbooks. Of somewhat less value is the Introduction ("Notes sur l'histoire de la cuisine française") to Bertrand Guégan, *Le cuisinier français* (Paris, 1934), pp. ix–xxi. For a general survey of French food, see Alfred Gottschalk, *Histoire de l'alimentation et de la gastronomie*, 2 vols. (Paris, 1948), vol. 1, pp. 257–352.

[75] These Latin works were edited and published together by Marianne Mulon, "Deux traités inédits d'art culinaire médiéval," *Bulletin Philologique et Historique (jusqu'à 1610)* (Paris: Comité des Travaux Historiques et Scientifiques, 1968 [publ. 1971]), pp. 369–435. The text of the *Tractatus* is at pp. 380–395; that of the *Liber de coquina*, pp. 396–420.

[76] This encyclopedic work has had two modern editions, of which the more recent is *Le Menagier de Paris. A Critical Edition*, ed. Georgine E. Brereton and Janet M. Ferrier (Oxford, 1921). Previously the *Menagier* was published by Jérôme Pichon, *Le ménagier de Paris, traité de morale et d'économie domestique composé vers 1393 par un bourgeois parisien*, 2 vols. (Paris, 1846); this edition was reprinted by Slatkine, Geneva, in 1970. Most references to the *Menagier* in the present study will include both editions, in the above order: for the first, reference is usually to Brereton and Ferrier's paragraph number (§) in the Fifth Article of the Second Distinction (pp. 191–283);

the later work. These borrowings prove useful to a reader of the *Viandier* because where the *Viandier* occasionally assumes that procedures need not be explained in detail, or even mentioned to the professional cook for whom the work is designed, the latter work usually makes no such assumption. The author of the *Menagier* includes cuisine merely as one item among a broad range of practical household arts of which he considers his young bride to be totally ignorant. When the bourgeois author instructs the inexpert new mistress of his house on culinary procedures, these instructions frequently illuminate the sense of certain otherwise obscure passages in the *Viandier*. Neither Brereton and Ferrier nor Pichon in their respective editions of the *Menagier*—nor, it should be added, Pichon and Vicaire in their edition of the *Viandier* itself—make any serious attempt to compare similar recipes in the two works, or to allow parallel passages to shed much light one way or the other. In the Notes below we have tried to indicate where similarities exist in the two works, and the extent to which the *Menagier* has been willing to accept totally what was in his source. With surprising regularity, though, the bourgeois author expresses reservations about the versions of the recipes he is copying.

The second work influenced significantly by the *Viandier* is the *Livre fort excellent de cuysine tres-utile et proffitable*, of which a number of editions were printed in Paris and Lyons from about 1540, and which went through several changes of name and several minor modifications of contents during the sixteenth century.[77] In their edition of *BN*, Pichon and Vicaire make occasional comparisons between the *Viandier*'s recipes and those of the *Grand cuisinier*, a derivative of the *Livre fort excellent*, printed in Paris by Jean Bonfons. While many of the recipes in the *Viandier* and in the *Grand cuisinier* are indeed similar, the relationship between the two texts appears much less close than that which exists between the texts of the *Viandier* and the *Menagier*.

A third French cookery book to appear after the *Viandier*, one which quite clearly drew no inspiration from it but which in places may clarify a reading of it, is the *Du fait de cuisine* of Maistre Chiquart Amiczo.[78] This extensive work, written in 1420 by the *maistre queux* of Amadeus VIII, first Duke of Savoy and eventual Pope Felix V, contains several of the *Viandier*'s more common dishes and affords the most detailed view we presently possesss of the techniques of food preparation in a late-mediæval princely household.

A final late-mediæval manuscript of recipes in French should be mentioned. While relatively short (48 recipes), the anonymous *Recueil de Riom* from the middle of the

---

for the second, Pichon's edition, the page number is always that of the second of the two volumes where the article concerning food preparation is located, pp. 124–272.

[77] *Livre fort excellent de cuysine tres-utille & proffitable contenant en soy la maniere dhabiller toutes viandes* ... (Lyon: Olivier Arnoullet, 1542). This work seems to be at the origin of *Le Grand Cuisinier de toute cuisine, tresutille et prouffitable contenant la maniere dhabiller toutes viandes tant chair que poisson* ... (Paris: Jehan Bonfons, n.d.; later editions 1560, 1566, 1575, etc.); *La Fleur de toute cuysine, contenant la maniere d'habiller toutes viandes tant chair que poisson* ... (Paris: Alain Lotrian, 1543; and Paris: N. Chrestien, 1548); and *Le livre de honneste volupté, contenant la maniere d'habiller toutes sortes de viandes, tant Chair que Poisson* ... (Lyon: Benoist Rigaud, 1588; not to be confused with Platine, *De l'honneste volupté*).

[78] Ed. Terence Scully, *Vallesia*, 40 (1985), pp. 101–231.

fifteenth century contains what appears to be most of the standard, relatively commonplace dishes of the day.[79]

Because, as Thomas Austin himself says, "Much of the scientific cookery in England was of course French,"[80] it is from time to time useful to compare the *Viandier*'s recipes with those that appear in collections copied in that country. Apart from the Anglo-Norman *Viande e claree*, already mentioned, the earliest English culinary work is found in the manuscript B.L. Royal 12.C.xii.[81] This compilation of thirty-two recipes is still written in French and is dated by its more recent editors at between 1320 and 1340. While clearly having absolutely no direct relationship with the *Viandier*, these recipes do shed occasional light upon our texts. The same observation can be made about the famous late-fourteenth-century *Forme of Cury*,[82] and several lesser collections similarly in English and similarly from the fourteenth century.[83] From the fifteenth century come the English *Liber cure cocorum*,[84] and the several culinary manuscripts edited by Thomas Austin.[85] While this English cookery, whether copied in Anglo-Norman or in English, may owe a general debt to France for much of its inspiration, no particular links with the *Viandier* or its long continental French tradition are evident.

Two fourteenth-century Italian recipe collections, the *Libro della cocina*, by an anonymous Tuscan, and the *Libro per cuoco*, by an anonymous Venetian,[86] may likewise usefully

---

[79] Ed. Carole Lambert, *Le recueil de Riom et la Manière de henter soutillement: Deux receptaires inédits du XVe siècle* (Montreal, 1988).

[80] Thomas Austin, *Two Fifteenth-Century Cookery-Books* (London, 1888; repr. 1964). "The words which denote methods of cooking, and the names of the finished dishes are almost exclusively French. So also are very nearly all the non-indigenous materials, *e.g.* spices, some of the fruit, the wine": M.J. Sergeantson, "The Vocabulary of Cookery in the Fifteenth Century," *Essays and Studies*, 23 (1938), p. 37. *Cf.*, however, Constance B. Hieatt's defence of the originality of early English cookery in "The Roast, or Boiled, Beef of Old England," *Book Forum*, 5 (1980), pp. 294–299; and again in the same author's "'Ore pur parler del array de une graunt mangerye': The Culture of the 'New Get', *circa* 1285," *Acts of Interpretation: The Text in its Contexts, 700–1600*, ed. E. Talbot Donaldson, Mary J. Carruthers and Elizabeth D. Kirk (Norman, Okla.: Pilgrim Books, 1982), pp. 219–220 and n3.

[81] This collection was edited by Paul Meyer in the *Bulletin de la Société des Anciens Textes Français*, 19 (1893), pp. 38–56; and again by Constance B. Hieatt and Robin F. Jones as Collection "B" in their article "Two Anglo-Norman Culinary Collections ...," *Speculum*, 61 (1986), pp. 859–882.

[82] Ed. Samuel Pegge (London, 1780); also ed. by Richard Warner in *Antiquitates Culinariae: Curious Tracts on Culinary Affairs of the Old English* (London, 1791), pp. 1–35; and most recently by Constance Hieatt and Sharon Butler in their collection of several early English cookery texts, *Curye on Inglysch* (London, 1985); part IV, pp. 93–154.

[83] These works, *Doctrina faciendi diversa cibaria, Diversa servicia, Utilis coquinario* and *Goud Kokery*, are edited by Hieatt and Butler in *Curye on Inglysch*, parts I, II, III and V, respectively.

[84] Ed. Richard Morris (London, 1862).

[85] *Two Fifteenth-Century Cookery-Books* (Oxford, 1888).

[86] Both of these works have most recently been published by Emilio Faccioli in his collection

be read in order to appreciate the broad international influence exerted at this time by French cuisine in general, though once again there is no apparent direct rapport between these Italian (or Catalan, Portuguese or German) recipe books and the *Viandier*.[87]

With the growth in the number of modern editions of early culinary recipe collections our understanding of the nature of late-mediæval European cookery is expanding.[88] Besides the works mentioned above, numbers of other recipe collections from England, Germany, Italy, Catalonia, Castile and Portugal—to say nothing of the Arab domains of Spain and North Africa—all invariably shed at least some glimmer of light upon what is copied in the *Viandier*. The Bibliography below was compiled with the intention of indicating to

---

of early Italian recipe books, *Arte della cucina*, 2 vols. (Milan, 1966), vol. 1, pp. 19 f. and 61 f. respectively.

[87] For a review of Italian cookery of this period, the following may usefully be consulted: Jean-Louis Flandrin and Odile Redon, "Les livres de cuisine italiens des XIVe et XVe siècles," *Archeologia Medievale*, 8 (Florence, 1981): "Problemi di storia dell'alimentazione nell'Italia medievale," pp. 393–408; Emilio Faccioli, "La cucina," *Storia d'Italia*, 5/1 (Turin, 1973), "I documenti"; Lorenzo Stecchetti (pseud. for Olindo Guerrini), *La tavola e la cucina nei secoli XIV e XV* (Florence, 1884); and Maria Luisa Incontri Lotteringhi della Stufa, *Desinari e cene dai tempi remoti alla cucina toscana del XV secolo* (Florence, 1965). The first essay in particular, that of Flandrin and Redon, presents a clear analysis of the contents of the three earliest Italian cookery books (the *Libro della cocina*, the *Libro per cuoco* and the *Libro de arte coquinaria*, c. 1450, of Maestro Martino), as well as of the *De honesta voluptate* of Platina (*alias* Bartolomeo Sacchi, 1421–1481); Flandrin and Redon draw some comparisons between these Italian works, and the *Viandier* and the *Menagier*, and compare early French and Italian cuisine briefly.

Concerning early Iberian cookery, see the Introduction to the *Libre de sent soví (Receptari de cuina)* by Rudolf Grewe (Barcelona, 1979), pp. 7–58. Similarly for early German cookery, see Gerhard Eis, *Die mittelalterlich Fachliteratur* (Stuttgart, 1968), pp. 27–29, and in particular the excellent general study of Hans Wiswe, *Kulturgeschichte der Kochkunst* (Munich, 1970). For an edition of the earliest German cookbook see *Das Kochbuch Meister Eberhards: Ein Beitrag zur altdeutschen Fachliteratur* by Anita Feyl, Diss., Albert-Ludwigs-Universität, Freiburg im Breisgau, 1963, pp. 13–32. While the influence of Arabic cookery upon mediæval European culinary practice must remain largely conjectural, see in this regard Claudia Roden, "Early Arab Cooking and Cookery Manuscripts," *Petits Propos Culinaires*, 6 (1980), pp. 16–27; Maxime Rodinson, "Les influences de la civilisation musulmane sur la civilisation europénne médiévale dans les domaines de la consommation et de la distraction: l'alimentation," *Atti del Convegno Internazionale della Accademia Nazionale dei Lincei* (Rome, 1971), pp. 479–499; C. Anne Wilson, "The Saracen Connection: Arab Cuisine and the Mediæval West," *Petits Propos Culinaires*, 7 (1981), 13–22 and 8 (1981), pp. 19–27; and particularly Toby Peterson, "Arab Influence on Western European Cooking," *Journal of Medieval History*, 6 (1980), pp. 317–341.

[88] For surveys of the genre of the mediæval cookbook, see Bruno Laurioux and Odile Redon, "Émergence d'une cuisine médiévale: le témoignage des livres," in *Matériaux pour l'histoire des cadres de vie dans l'Europe occidentale (1050–1250): Cours d'agrégation sous la direction de H. Bresc* (Nice, 1984), pp. 91–101; and the article by Marianne Mulon, "Recettes médiévales," referred to previously.

the interested reader some of the more prominent primary sources in this area. Secondary sources, studies and commentaries, also have a place in the Bibliography. Evidence about mediæval European food and cookery is gleaned not only from the multitude of changing recipes which must be analysed and compared, but from such broadly disparate sources as economic studies, household accounts, travel documents, medical treatises, archeology and legal testaments.[89] What a society eats is intimately related to what that society is and does. That food is one of man's absolute necessities means that it must be a principal object of study by anyone who seriously hopes to understand the history of humanity.

But more than merely an object of academic study, food exists to be consumed—and always with a certain degree of pleasure. For this reason the reader will find appended after the English translation of the *Viander*'s texts a tentative menu of recipes adapted from a few of those found in our collection. It will be obvious that the modern cook who is willing to experiment with these suggestions will not be preparing a fourteenth-century banquet. Nor should he or she expect to set out a *disner* or *souper* similar to one of the extensive meals of twenty or thirty dishes outlined by the *Menagier*'s menus. The intention of D. Eleanor Scully, who worked up the modern adaptations, and myself is more humble. Our hope is simply to afford the reader an opportunity to prove in the surest way possible that this cuisine that Taillevent has transmitted to us is sound, that his recipes remain for the most part practical and, above all, that the food they produce is good.

Taillevent

The life of Guillaume Tirel, professionally better known by his *nom-de-cuisine*, Taillevent—the name by which the *Viandier* will always be qualified—is best summed up by Siméon Luce:

> Né vers 1315, enfant de cuisine au service de la reine Jeanne d'Evreux, dès 1326, queux de Philippe de Valois, en 1347 et 1349, écuyer de l'hôtel et puis queux du dauphin de Viennois, en 1355, queux du duc de Normandie en 1359 et 1361, queux et sergent d'armes de ce même dauphin, duc de Normandie, devenu le roi Charles V en 1368, premier queux dudit roi en 1373 et 1377, successivement écuyer de cuisine, premier écuyer de cuisine et maître des garnisons de Charles VI en 1381, 1388, et 1392, l'auteur du *Viandier* mourut certainement en 1395, à l'âge d'environ quatre-vingts ans, comme M. Pichon l'a très bien vu en s'appuyant sur une date à demi effacée, mais restituée avec beaucoup de sagacité, de la dalle tumulaire du musée de Saint-Germain.[90]

[89] The interdisciplinary nature of any serious study of mediæval cookery is obvious throughout the excellent doctoral thesis of Barbara Santich, *Two Languages, Two Cultures, Two Cuisines: A Comparative Study of the Culinary Cultures of Northern and Southern France, Italy and Catalonia in the Fourteenth and Fifteenth Centuries*, The Flinders University of South Australia, 1987. For this scholar the cuisine that must be studied is that which transcends mere necessity and becomes a vital constituent of "culture" (p. 47).

[90] From the review by Siméon Luce of Pichon and Vicaire, *Le Viandier de Guillaume Tirel dit Taillevent*, in *Romania*, 21 (1892), p. 307. As appendices to their edition, pp. 257–284, Pichon

It is clear from this biography that, because of his professional competence, Taillevent earned and held the respect of the most powerful individuals of fourteenth-century Europe. The simple qualification found in the *incipit* of his *Viandier* attests to the man's preeminence among his peers: "Taillevent, maistre queux du roy de France."

and Vicaire publish passages from twenty-one fourteenth-century documents in which the name of Guillaume Tirel (frequently qualified with the phrase "dit Taillevent" or "alias Taillevent") appears. A brief review of Guillaume Tirel's life and work was compiled by Liliane Plouvier, "Taillevent, la première star de la gastronomie," *L'Histoire*, 61 (Nov. 1983), pp. 93–94.

Contents of the Manuscripts

	Valais	Mazarine
	[*Incipit* cut away.]	Taillevent maistre queux du roy de France par cy enseigne a toutes gens pour apparoillier a maingier en cusyne de roy, duc, conte, marquis, barons, prelas et de tous aultres seigneurs, bourgois, merchans et gens d'ouneur *(127)*
1.		1. Pour dessalés tous poutaiges
2.		2. Pour oster l'arsure de toutes viandes
2A.		3. Pour ce mesme
3.		4. Boulitures de grosses chairs
4.		5. Haricocus de mouton
5.	1. Boully lardé *(recto)*	6. Boullir larder
6.	2. Venoison de cherf fraiche	7. Venoisson de serfz fresche
7.	3. Sangler frais .... Sangler salé et cerf	8. Sangler et serfz salez *(128)*
8.	4. Chevreau sauvage	9. Chevrieulx saulvaige
9.		
10.	5. Chaudin de porc	10. Chauduin de porc
11.	6. Cretonnee de pois vers ou de fevez	11. Cretonnés de pois nouviaulx
11A.		12. Cretonnee de feves nouvelles
12.	7. Conminee de poullaille	13. Conminee de poullaille
13.	8. Comminee d'almandes	
14.	9. Brouet de canelle	14. Brouet de cannelle
15.	10. Brouet gorgié	15. Brouet georgé *(129)*
16.	11. Brouet roucet	16. Brouet rousset
17.	12. Une soringne de haste menue de porc	17. Menue haste de porc
18.	13. Gravé de menus oiseaux	18. Grainné de menus oysiaulx
19.	14. Blanc brouet de chapons	19. Blanc brouet de voulaille
20.	15. Bonsax de lievrez et de conins	20. Boussat de lievres
21.	16. Hondous de chapons	21. Hondel de chappons *(130)*
22.	17. Brouet d'Alemagne de char ...	22. Brouet d'Alemaigne
23.	18. Hochepot de poullaile	23. Hoichepoult de poulaille
24.	19. Soutil brouet d'Angleterre	24. Soubtilz brouet d'Angleterre
25.	20. Brouet de verjus	
26.	21. Brouet vergay	25. Brouet vergay
27.	22. Rappé	26. Rappé

Bibliothèque Nationale	Vatican Table	Vatican
Cy comence le Viandier Taillevent maistre queux du Roy nostre sire, pour ordenner les viandes qui cy aprés s'ensuivent. Premierement *(1r)*	Cy commence le viandier taillevent maistre queux du Roy de France ouquel sont contenues les choses qui s'ensuivent. Et premierement *(48r)*	Cy aprés s'ensuit comment on fait les chosses dessusdites. Premierement *(51r)*
1. Pour dessaller tous potages	1. Pour dessaler toutes manieres de potaiges	1. Pour dessaller toutes manieres de potaiges
2. Pour oster l'arsseure de tous potages	2. Pour oster l'arsure des potaiges que l'en dit aours	2. Pour oster l'arsure d'un pot que l'en dit aours
3. Bouture de grosse char	3. Bousture de grosse chair	3. Boulture de grosse chair
4. Hericoq de mouton	4. Hericoc de mouton boully lardé	4. Hericoc de mouton
5. Bouli lardé *(1v)*		5. Bouly lardé *(51v)*
	5. Venoison de cerf et de chevreau sauvaige	6. Venoison de cerf et de chevrel sauvaige fresche
6. Senglier fais .... La salee	6. Venoison de sanglier	7. Venoison de sanglier frez. Le salé
7. Chevriaulx sauvages		
8. Chappons aux herbes ou veel	7. Chappons aux herbes	8. Chappons aux herbes ou veel
Potaiges lians	Potaiges lyans	Potages lyans
9. Chaudun de porc	8. Chaudun de porc	9. Chaudun de porc
10. Cretonnee de pois novieux	9. Cretonnee de poys nouveaux et de feves nouveaux	10. Cretonnee de poys nouveaulx *(52r)*
11. Cretonnee de feuves nouvelles *(2r)*		11. Cretonnee de feves nouvelles
12. Conminee de poulaille		12. Comminee de poullaille
14. Cominé d'almendes *(2v)*	10. Comminee d'amendes	13. Comminee d'amendes *(52v)*
13. Brouet de canelle	11. Brouet de canelle	14. Brouet de canelle
15. Brouet gorgié	12. Brouet georgié	15. Brouet georgié
16. Brouet rousset	13. Brouet rousset	16. Brouet rousset *(53r)*
17. Une vin aigrete	14. Une vinaigrete	17. Une vinaigrette
18. Civé de menus oisiaux	15. Gravé de menuz oiseaulx	18. Gravé de menuz oyseaulx *(53v)*
19. Blanc brouet de chappons *(3v)*	16. Blanc brouet de chappons	19. Blanc brouet de chappons
20. Bousac de lievre ou de conis	17. Boussac de lyevres	20. Boussac de lievres ou de connins
21. Houdous de chappons	18. Houdons de chappons	21. Hondons de chappons *(54r)*
22. Brouet d'Ailmengne de char ...	19. Brouet d'Almaigne *(48v)*	22. Brouet d'Allemangne
23. Hochepot de poullaille *(4r)*	20. Hochepot de poulaille	23. Hochepot de poullaille
24. Sutil brouet d'Engleterre	21. Soutif brouet d'Angleterre	24. Soustil brouet d'Angleterre *(54v)*
25. Brouet de vergus	22. Brouet de verjus	25. Brouet de verjus de poullaille ...
26. Brouet vergay *(4v)*	23. Brouet de vergay	26. Brouet vertgay
27. Rappé	24. Rappé	27. Rappé *(55r)*

	Valais	Mazarine
28.	23. Civé de veel	27. Civel de veaul *(131)*
29.	24. Cyvé de lievres	28. Civel de livre
30.		
		Chappitre de roz
31.	25. Porc rosti	29. Porc rotis
32.		30. Viaul rotis
33.	26. Fraise de veel	31. Fraise de veaul
34.	27. Mouton rosti	32. Mouton rotis
35.	28. Chevreax, aigneaux	33. Chevrieulx et aigneaulx rotis
36.	29. Oyes	34. Oyes rotiees
37.	30. Poles rosties	35. Poulés rotis *(132)*
38.	31. Chapons, gelines, hetoudeaux	36. Chappons, gelines et estoudeaulx
39.	32. Connins	37. Conins rotis
40.		
41.	33. Lievrez en rost	38. Lievres en rolz
42.	34. Bourbier de sanglier	39. Bourbier de sangler
43.		39a. Et nota que toute venoison fresche
44.	35. Pigons rostis ...	
45.	36. Menus oiseaux	40. Menus oysaulx en rolz
46.		
47.	37. Perdris	41. Cigne
48.		
49.	38. Cygnez	42. [unnamed]
50.	39. Paon	46. Pavons saulvaiges *(133)*
51.	40. Faisans	44. Faisans
52.	42. Segoignez	43. Cigogne
53.	41. Herons	45. Haron
54.	43. Malars de riviere	48. Malart de reviere
55.	44. Oitardes, gentez, gruez	47. Ostardes, gentes et gruees
56.		
57.	45. Cormorans	
58.		
59.		
60.	46. Porcelet farcy	49. Pourcelet falcis

Bibliothèque Nationale	Vatican Table	Vatican
	25. Civé de veel	28. Civé de veel
28. Civé de lievres	26. Civé de lievres	29. Civé de lievre
29. Civé de conis	27. Civé de connins	30. Civé de connins *(55v)*
	28. Mouton et beuf a la poree	
	29. Le janbon de porc a la rappee	
	30. Le chappon au vertjus	
	31. Le chappon et le trumel de beuf au jaunet	
	32. Le janbon sallé avec l'eschinee et les andoylles	
	33. Le janbon bruslé fraiz aux poreaulx mengié au poivre chault	
Chapitres de ros *(5r)*	Rostz	Cy ensuivent les rostz de chair
30. Porc	36. Oes, porc	31. Rost de porc
31. Item veel	37. Veel	32. Veau
32. Pour faire fraise de veel	38. Frase de veel	33. Pour faire frase de veel ...
33. Mouton en rost	39. Mouton	34. Mouston en rost *(56r)*
34. Chevriaux, aingniaux	34. Chevreaux	35. Chevreaux, aigneaux
	35. Aigneaulx	
35. Oues en rost	36. Oes, porc	37. Oes et oysons en rost
36. Poulés	40. Poullés	38. Poullés et poucins *(56v)*
37. Chappons, hetoudiaux, gelines *(5v)*	41. Chappons *(49r)*	39. Chappons, gelines, hettoudeaulx en rost
	42. Gelines	
	43. Hettoudeaulx	
38. Conis en rost	44. Connins	40. Connins, lappereaulx
		41. Chappons de haulte gresse en pasté
39. Livres en rost	45. Lyevres	42. Lyevres en rost *(57r)*
40. Bourbier de sanglier	46. Bourblier	43. Bourbier de sanglier frez
	47. Sanglier	
41. Toute venoison freiche	48. Toute venoison	44. Toute venoison fresche
42. Pijons rostis ...	49. Pignons	45. Pijons roustiz ... *(57v)*
43. Menus oysiaux	50. Menuz oyseaulx	46. Menuz oyseaulx ...
44. Plouviers, videcoqs *(6r)*	51. Plouviers	47. Plouviers et videcoqs
	52. Videcocz	
45. Perdrix	53. Perdriz	48. Perdriz
46. Truterelles	56. Tourtourelles	49. Turturelles *(58r)*
47. Cinne	57. Cynes	
48. Paon	58. Paons	50. Paon, cine
49. Faisans	59. Faisans	51. Faisans
50. [S]ogoingnes	60. Cycongnes	52. Sigongnes *(58v)*
51. Heron *(6v)*	61. Herons	53. Heron
53. Malars de riviere	63. Malars	55. Malartz de riviere
52. Uistardes, grues, gantes	62. Oetardes	54. Outardes
54. Butor	64. Butors	56. Butor
	65. Buhoreaulx	
55. Cormorant	66. Cormorans	56. Cormorant
		58. Poches et telles manieres d'oiseaulx de riviere
		59. Sarcelle *(59r)*
56. Pourcel farci	67. Pourcellés farciet	36. Pourcelet ou cochon farsy

	Valais	Mazarine
		Chappitre d'entremés
61.	47. Faux grenon	50. Faulx grenons *(134)*
62.	48. Menus droies de piés, de foyez et de jusiers	
63.	49. Formentee	55. Fromentee *(135)*
64.	50. Garlins	51. [unnamed]
65.	50a. [unnamed]	52. [unnamed]
66.	51. Poulaille farcie	53. Poulaille farcie
67.		54. [unnamed]
68.	52. Gelee de poison qui porte limon ou de char	56. [unnamed]
69.	53. Lamproie frache a la saulce chaude	
70.	54. Lamproie a la galentine	57. Lamproye fresche
71.	55. Ris	
72.	56. Cisne revestu en ces plumes et atout sa pel	
73.	57. Froide sauge	58. Brouet vergay de poullaille
74.	58. Sourps de porcelet	59. [unnamed] *(136)*
75.	59. Conminee de poisson	60. [unnamed]
76.	60. Brouet vert gay d'anguilles	
77.	61. Gravé de loche	61. Graigne de louche
78.	62. Chaudumet a becquet	62. Civel de beschet
79.	63. Une soringne	
80.	64. Brouet saraginois	63. Brouet serrazinés
81.		64. Lemprions
82.	65. Cyvé d'oittrez	65. Civé d'ostres *(137)*
83.	*(verso)* [cut away?]	66. [unnamed]
84.	[cut away?]	67. [unnamed]
85.	66. [beginning cut away]	68. [unnamed]
86.	67. Lait de prouvance	69. [unnamed]
87.	68. Brouet vert d'eufs et de formage	70. [unnamed] *(138)*
88.	69. Brochet	71. [unnamed]
89.	70. Gavé de parche	72. Graine de louche
90.	71. Coulis de poullez	73. Colis d'ung poulet
91.	Eaue rousse de chappon ou de poulle pour malade	74. [unnamed]
92.	73. Chaudeau flamen	75. Chaudel flamant
93.	74. Gruyau	76. [unnamed]
94.	75. Coulis de perche	77. Colis d'unne perche
95.	76. Blanc mengier d'ung chappon pour ung malade	78. Blanc maingier d'ung chappon
96.		

Bibliothèque Nationale	**Vatican Table**	**Vatican**
Chapitres d'entremés *(7r)*	Entremetz	Ensuivent les entremez
57. Faus guernon	68. Faulx grenon	60. Faulxgrenon
58. Menus doies: piés, foies, guisiers	69. Menuz droiz	61. Menuz piez, foyes et juisiers
59. Formentee *(7v)*	70. Froumentee	62. Fromentee *(59v)*
60. Taillés	73. Tuilleiz	63. Tailliz
61. Millot *(8r)*	74. Millet	64. Milet
62. Poullaille farcie	75. Poulaille farcie	65. Poullaille farcie *(60r)*
63. Gelee de poisson qui porte limon ou de char *(9r)*		69. Gelee de poisson a lymon et de chair *(61r)*
64. Lemproie franche a la saulce chaude *(9v)*	76. Lamproye fresche	70. Lamproye fresche a la saulce chaude *(61v)*
65. Lemproie en galentine	77. Lamproye en galentine	71. Lamproye en galantine *(62r)*
66. Ris engoullé au jour de mengier char *(10r)*	78. Ris engoulé	66. Rix engoullé a jour de mengier chair *(60v)*
67. Entre més de cine revesté de sa piau atoutes les plumes	79. Entremetz d'un cine reves tu	67. Entremez d'un cigne revestu en sa peau atout sa plume
68. Une froide sauge *(10v)*	71. Froyde sauge	68. Une froide sauge
69. Soulz de pourcel	72. Soux	72. Soux de pourcel *(62v)*
Potaiges lians	Potaiges lyans sans chair	
70. comminee de poisson	80. Comminiee de poisson	73. Comminee de poisson
71. Brouet vergay d'anguilles	81. Brouet vertgay d'anguilles	74. Brouet vertgay d'anguilles
72. Gravé de loche *(11r)*	82. Grané de loche	75. Gravé de loche
73. Chaudumel au bescuit	83. Chaudumé au bescuit	76. Chaudumel au bescuit *(63r)*
74. [U]ne soringne		77. Une soringue
	84. Brouet sarrasinois	78. Brouet sarrasinois *(63v)*
75. Civé d'oistres *(11v)*	85. Civé d'oestres	79. Civé d'oistres
76. Soupe en moustarde	86. Souppe en moustarde	80. Souppe de moustarde
77. Civé d'oeufs *(12r)*	87. Civé d'oeufz	81. Civé d'oeufz *(64r)*
78. Civé d'Almengne	88. Brouet d'Alemaigne	82. Brouet d'Almaigne d'oeufz
78a. [unnamed]	89. Layt lié *(49v)*	83. Lait lyé de vache
79. Brouet d'oeufs et du fromage	90. Brouet vert d'oeufz	84. Brouet vert d'oeufz et de frommage
80. Une saulce jaunete sur poisson froit ou chaut *(12v)*	91. Sausse jaunete	85. Une saulce jaunette de poisson froit *(64v)*
81. Gravé de perche	92. Grané de perches	86. Gravé de perche
	93. Poivre civé [?] de poisson	
	94. Layt de provence	
	Brouetz et aultres choses	
82. Couleis d'un poulet	95. Coulleiz d'un poullet	87. Couleiz d'un poulet
83. Eaue rose d'un chappon ou poulle *(13r)*	96. Eaue rose	88. Eaue rose d'un chappon ou poulle *(65r)*
84. Chaudiau flamenc	97. Chaudeau flamment	89. Chaudeau flament
85. Gruiau d'orge *(13v)*	98. Ung gruyau d'orge	90. Ung gruyau d'orge mondé
86. Couleis de perche	99. Ung coulleiz de perche	91. Ung couleiz de perche *(65v)*
87. Blanc mengier d'un chappon	100. Blanc mengier de chappon	92. Blanc mengier d'un chappon pour ung malade
	101. Comminiee de poisson	93. Comminee de poisson

	Valais	Mazarine
		Chappitre de poisson d'aigue doulce *(139)*
97.	77. Lux	79. [unnamed]
98.	78. Brochet	80. [unnamed]
99.	79. Barbillons	82. Barbillons
100.	80. Bar	81. Le bar
101.		83. [unnamed]
102.	81. Carpe	84. Carpe
103.	82. Perche	85. Perche
104.	83. Tanchez	86. Tanche
105.	84. Bresme	87. Roussaille
106.	85. Poulaille	88. [unnamed]
107.	86. Anguillez	89. [unnamed]
108.	87. Cheneveaux	90. Chenernes *(140)*
109.	88. Truitez	91. Tructes
110.	89. Pinperneaulx	92. Pipenalx
111.	90. Loche	93. Louche
112.	91. Gaymeaux	
113.		
114.	92. Lamproions	94. Lamprions
115.		
116.	93. Ablez	95. Abletes
117.	94. Eccrevissez	
		Chappitre de poisson de mer
118.	95. Porc de mer	96. [unnamed]
119.	96. Maquereaulx frais	97. Gornaulx, rougés
120.	97. Gournalx, rougez	98. Rouget
121.	98. Congre	99. Congre
122.	99. Mellus	100. [unnamed] *(141)*
123.	100. Chien de mer	101. Chien de mer
124.	101. Saulmont frais	102. Salmon fres
125.	102. Mullet	103. [unnamed]
126.	103. Morue fraiche	103a. La fresche
127.	104. Grapois	104. Crappois
128.	105. Egreffin	104a. [unnamed]
129.		
130.	105a. [B]rete	105. Brete
131.		
132.	106. Truite saulmonoise	

Bibliothèque Nationale	Vatican Table	Vatican
Chapitres de poisson d'eaue doulce *(14r)*	Poissons d'eaue doulce	S'ensuit des poissons d'eaue doulce
88. Lus	102. Luz	94. Lux *(66r)*
89. Brochet	103. Brochet	95. Brochet
90. Barbillons	104. Barbillons	97. Barbillons
91. Le bar		96. Bar
92. Alouse	120. Alozes d'eaue doulce	98. Aloze
93. Carpes	105. Carpes alozees	99. Carpes
94. Perche	106. Perches	100. Perche
	107. Tenches	101. Tanche
95. Bresme *(14v)*	108. Bresmes	102. Bresme *(66v)*
96. Baissaille	109. Rossaille	103. Rossaille
97. Chevriaux	112. Anguilles	104. Anguilles
	111. Chevesneaulx	
98. Truites	113. Trutes	105. Truite
99. Pimperniaux	114. Pinperneaulx	106. Pinperneaulx
	110. Loche *(50r)*	107. Loche
100. Guemual	115. Gaymel	108. Gymiau *(67r)*
		109. Meinuise
102. Lamprions	116. Lamproyons	111. Lamproyons
	117. Setailles	112. Santoilles
101. Ables	118. Ables	110. Ables
103. Escrevices *(15r)*	119. Escrevisses	113. Escrevisses
	121. Vendoises	
	122. Gardons	
Chapitres de poisson de mer ront	Poisson de mer ront	Poisson de mer ront
104. Porc de mer	123. Porc de mer	114. Porc de mer
108. Maquerel frais	128. Maquereaulx	120. Maquerel frez
105. Gornault, rouget, grimodin	124. Gourneaulx	115. Gournault, rouget, grimondin *(67v)*
	146. Rouget	
	145. Grimondins	
	144. Lamproyes	
106. Congre *(15v)*	125. Congre	116. Congre
	126. Mellanz	117. Merluz
107. Chien de mer	127. Chiens de mer	118. Chien de mer
109. Saumont frais	129. Saumon	119. Saumon frez *(68r)*
110. Mulet	130. Mulet	121. Mulet
111. Morue franche	131. Morue	122. Morue fresche
	133. Grappois	124. Grappois
	132. Angrefin	123. Moruaulx et aigreffins *(68v)*
	134. Orfin	125. Orfin
	135. Brete	126. Braytte
		127. Colin
	136. Truite saumonneresse	128. Truitte saumonneresse

	Valais	Mazarine
133.		
134.		
135.		106g. [unnamed]
136.	107. Raye	106. Raye
137.	108. Turbot	106a. [unnamed]
138.		
139.	109. Bresme	106b. [unnamed]
140.	110. Limonde	106c. [unnamed]
141.	111. Doree	
142.		
143.	112. Alose	106d. [unnamed]
144.		
145.	113. Aspellens	106e. [unnamed]
146.	114. Esturgon	106f. [unnamed]
147.	115. Perche	107. [unnamed] *(142)*
148.		
149.	116. Hanons	108. [unnamed]
150.	117. Moullez	109. [unnamed]
151.		
152.	129. Flans, tartez en karesme qui ont saveur de formage	110. Pour faire flaons et tartres en karesme qui auront savour de fromaige
153.	130. Pour faire poree de cresson	111. [unnamed]
154.		

Bibliothèque Nationale	**Vatican Table**	**Vatican**
Chapitre de poisson de mer plat *(16r)*	Poisson de mer plat	Poisson platz de mer
112. Pleis	147. Pleiz	129. Pleys
	148. Balaine	
113. Flais	149. Flez	130. Flaiz
114. Solles	150. Solles	131. Solles *(69r)*
115. Raie	151. Raye	132. Roye
116. Turbot	152. Turbot	133. Turbot
117. Barbues	153. Barbue	134. Barbue
118. [B]resme	154. Bresme	136. Bresme *(69v)*
	155. Sancte	
	156. Tune	
	157. Lymande *(50v)*	137. Lymande
	158. Doree	135. Doree
	159. Carreletz	
		138. Truitte saumonneresse
119. Alouse cratoniere *(16v)*	137. Aloze de mer	139. Aloses
	138. Fuccus	
120. Ables	139. Ables	140. Alles de mer
		141. Esperlans
121. Esturjon	140. Esturjon	142. Esturjon
122. Seiche	141. Seiche	143. Seiche *(70r)*
		144. Oestres
125. Hanons	142. Honnons	146. Hannons *(70v)*
126. Moules *(17v)*	143. Moules	145. Moules
127. Escrevices de mer		147. Escrevices de mer
Viande de quaresme		
123. Pour faire flaons et tartes en quaresme *(17r)*	177. Pour faire flans et tartes en karesme	148. Pour faire flans ou tartres en karesme
124. Poree de cresson	176. Poree de cresson	148. Poree de cresson
		150. D'autres menuz potaiges
	178. Pour faire aultres flans et tartes	
	179. Pour faire pastés en pot	

	Valais	Mazarine	Mazarine 2
	Saulcez non boulluez		Chappitre de saulses
155.	118. Cameline	112. [unnamed]	125. Saulse cameline
156.	119. Aulx camelins	113. [unnamed]	126. Haulx camelins
157.			
158.	120. Aulx vers	113a. [unnamed]	
159.	121. Aulx a harens frais	113b. [unnamed]	
160.		113c. [unnamed]	
161.	122. Saulce vert	113d. [unnamed]	127. Saulse verde
162.	123. Saulce a garder poison	114. [unnamed]	128. Saulses pour garnir poissons de mer
	Saulcez boulluez		
163.			
164.	124. Poivre jaunet	115. [unnamed]	129. [unnamed]
165.	125. Poivre noir	116. [unnamed]	130. Poivre noir
166.	126. Saulce de lait de vache		131. Jasse de lait de vaiche
167.	127. Sauce de aulx		132. Jansse aux haulx *(145)*
168.			
169.	128. Une poitevinee	117. [unnamed]	133. Sause portemie
170.			
171.		118. [cameline mustard sauce] *(143)*	
172.		119. [marjoram sauce]	
173.		120. [stewed poultry]	
174.		121. [stewed mutton]	
175.		122. [tortes of herbs, cheese & eggs]	
176.		123. [an egg dish] *(144)*	
177.		124. [clary fritters]	

Bibliothèque Nationale	Vatican Table	Vatican
Saulces non boullues	Sausses non boullues	Saulces non boullues et comment on les fait *(71r)*
128. Cameline	160. Cameline	151. Pour faire cameline
129. Aulx camelins	161. Aux camelinez	152. Aulx camelins
130. Aulx blans	162. Aux blans	153. Aulx blans
131. Aulx vers	163. Aux vertz	154. Aulx vers
	164. Rappee	
	165. Aux atout la cotelle	
132. Aulx a herans frais	166. Aux aux harens fraiz	155. Aulx a harens frez
133. Saulce verte	167. Sausse vert	
134. Une saulce a garder poisson de mer	168. Une soussie	
	169. Une bonne sausse de jance pour morue aux aulx	
Saulces boullues *(18r)*	Sausses boullues	
		156. La barbe Robert ... Taillemaslee *(71v)*
135. Poivre jaunet	170. Poivre jaunet	
136. Poivre noir	171. Poivre noir	
137. Jance au lait de vache	172. Janse de lait	
138. Jance aux aulx	174. Janse aux aux	
139. Jance de gingembre	173. Jance de gingenbre sans aux	
140. Saulce poetevine	175. Une poitevine	
140a. Espices qui appartienent en ce present viandier *(18v)*		156a. Espices qu'il fault a ce present viandier

[The following recipes are found in the **Vatican** manuscript alone. They do not appear listed in the **Vatican Tab**

S'ensuivent aucuns remedes et experimentz touchans le fait des vins et autres choses *(72r)*

178. 157. Pour amender et faire vermeulx moust ou vin nouvel pour vendre tantost
179. 158. Pour garder vin d'engresser et d'estre trouble
180. 159. Pour tous vins degresser
181. 160. Pour garir vin boucté *(72v)*
182. 161. Pour garir vin bouté qui sente le fust, le mugue ou le pourry
183. 162. Pour garir vin qui trait a aigreur *(73r)*
184. 163. Pour garir vin enfusté
185. 164. Pour vin qui a la seive brisiee
186. 165. Pour esclarcir vin roux en yver
187. 166. Pour vin vermeil esclarcir *(73v)*
188. 167. Potaige appellé menjoire *(74r)*
189. 168. Lassis de blanc de chappon *(74v)*
190. 169. Gravé d'escrevisses *(75r)*
191. 170. Ung rozé a chair *(75v)*
192. 171. Une trimolette de perdrix *(76r)*
193. 172. Brouet de daintiers de cerf et cervoisons
194. 173. Flaons cochus *(76v)*
195. 174. Doreures *(77r)*
196. 175. Coqz heaumez *(77v)*
197. 176. Tourtes parmeriennes *(78r)*
198. 177. Tostees dorees
199. 178. Blanc mengier party *(78v)*
200. 179. Layt lardé *(79r)*
201. 180. Tourtes de layt *(79v)*
201A. Buignetz et roysolles de mouelle [only the name is copied]
202. 181. Crespes grandes et petites *(80r)*
203. 182. Pipesfarces
204. 183. Alouyaulx
205. 184. Dyapré *(80v)*
206. 185. Tuillé *(81r)*
207. 186. Tailliz de karesme *(81v)*
208. 187. Pastez nourroys
209. 188. Petis pastez lorez
210. 189. Herissons *(82r)*
211. 190. Petz d'Espaigne
212. 191. Espaules de mouton farcies. Motes et mangonneaulx *(82v)*
213. 192. Cignes revestuz *(83r)*
214. 193. Paons [revestuz] *(83v)*
215. 194. Entremetz de paintrerie: le chevalier au cigne
216. 195. Une tour *(84r)*
217. 196. Saint George et sa pucelle *(84v)*
218. 197. Saincte Marthe
219. 198. Entremetz plus legiers
220. 199. La poulse pour ung chappon gras *(85r)*

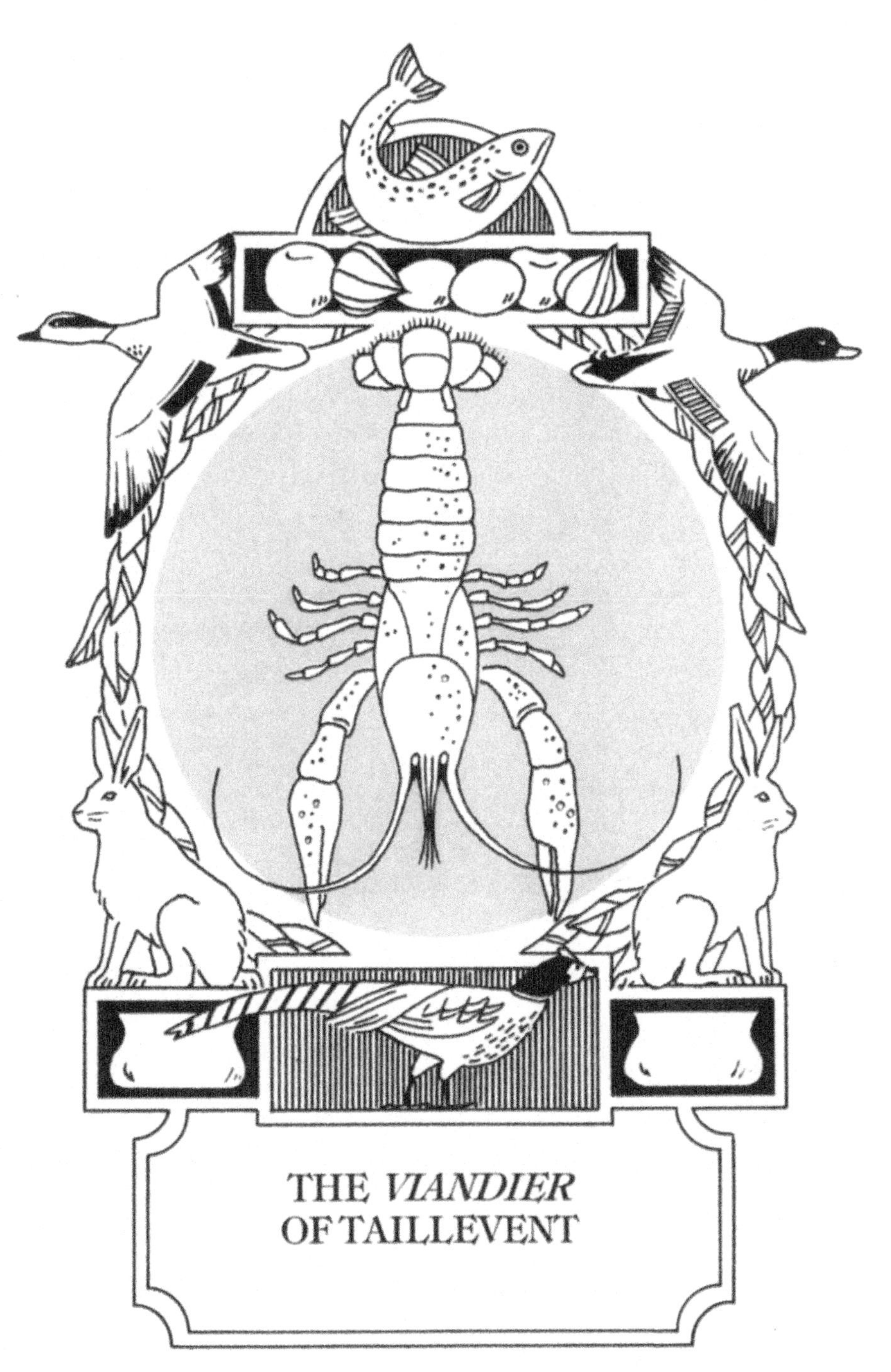
THE *VIANDIER*
OF TAILLEVENT

Texts and Commentary

Incipit

MAZ Taillevent maistre queux du roy de France par cy enseigne a toutes gens pour apparoillier a maingier en cusyne de roy, duc, conte, marquis, barons, prelas et de tous aultres seigneurs, bourgois, merchans et gens d'ouneur.

BN *Cy comence le Viandier Taillevent maistre queux du Roy nostre sire, pour ordenner les viandes qui cy aprés s'ensuivent. Premierement:*

VAT **Cy aprés s'ensuit comment on fait les chosses dessusdites. Premierement:**

1. Pour dessaler ...

MAZ	Pour dessalés tous poutaiges
BN	*Pour dessaller tous potages*
VAT	**Pour dessaller toutes manieres de potaiges qui seroient trop sallez**

MAZ	sans y mectre	aigue ne vin ne aultre liqueur.	Prener
BN	*sans y metre ne oster.*	– – – – – – –	*Prennés*
VAT	**sans y rien mettre ne oster.**	– – – – – – –	**Prenez**

MAZ	une touaille blainche	et la ployer en deux ou en trois doubles et
BN	*une nappe blanche*	– – – – – – – – – –
VAT	**une nappe bien blanche**	– – – – – – – – – –

MAZ	la moilliez un petit	puis la mectre sur vostre pout	bien loing du
BN	– – – –	*et mettés sur vostre pot,*	– – –
VAT	– – – –	**et la mettez sur vostre pot,**	– – –

MAZ	feu sur charbons en boillant	et le tourner souvent	d'ung coustel[1]
BN	– – – – – –	*et la tournés souvent,*	– – –
VAT	– – – – – –	**et la retournez souvent;**	– – –

MAZ	et d'aultre.	
BN	– –	*et tirés arriere le pot du feu.*
VAT	– –	**et convient traire le pot loing du feu.**

[1] *coustel*: understand *cousté*, modern *côté*.

The first four recipes of the *Viandier* appear in *MAZ*, *BN* and *VAT* but are not attested in the *VAL* manuscript. The part cut away at the top of the *VAL* roll may have contained all of these recipes; or, what is more likely to have been the case, if we may judge by the number of lines which appear to be missing from the top of the back of *VAL*, only Recipes 3 and 4. *O* is apt to have begun with the recipes for boiled meats (§§3 and 4, below).

Of the three versions of Recipe 1, *MAZ(X)*[2] inserts several amplifications. Of a technical nature, these additions are intended to render the directions for this operation fully explicit. Undoubtedly for the same purpose, *MAZ(X)* relocates the instructions about the intensity of the heat required under the boiling pot; by copying the phrase at the end of the recipe, *Y* (with *BN* and *VAT*) maintains what seems to have been an earlier addition.

The *Menagier*[3] makes literal use of the version found in *VAT*, except that in *VAT* the words "qui seroient trop sallez" have been added to the title, just in case the verb *dessaler* might prove insufficiently clear or explicit.

2. Pour oster l'arsure ...

MAZ	Pour oster l'arsure de toutes viandes.	Vuydiez premierement
BN	*Pour oster l'arsseure de tous potages.*	– – – – –
VAT	**Pour oster l'arsure d'un pot que l'en dit aours.**	– – – – –

MAZ	vostre poutaige du pout ou il sera en ung aultre poult neufz,	puis
BN	– – – – – – – – – – – – – – –	*Prenés*
VAT	– – – – – – – – – – – – – – –	**Prenez**

MAZ	prener du levain	de paste crue	liez deans ung blanc drappel et
BN	*un pou de levain*	– – –	*et le liés en un drapel et*
VAT	**ung pou de levain**	– – –	**et le liez en ung drappelet blanc et**

MAZ	le mectre dedans vostre poutaige	et ne l'y lessez.
BN	*metés ou pot,*	*et ne l'i lessiés gueires.*
VAT	**gectez dedans le pot,**	**et ne luy laissiez guaires demourer.**

2A. Pour ce mesme

MAZ Pour ce mesme. Prener des noix et les pertussiez tout oultre de chascunne part, puis les laver bien et les faictes boulir en vostre viande.

---

[2] Because clearly the extant copy of the *Viandier* which we call *MAZ* was not copied by someone who knew much about cookery, we must assume that the practical variants that we find in *MAZ* probably originated in some copy previous to *MAZ*, but after *Z*. *X* appears to have had access to an unknown source outside the *Viandier* tradition, or at the very least we may conjecture that *X* was written or directed by a professional cook of some initiative, experience and imagination. *MAZ(X)* adds an alternative for Recipe 2, as well as the *unica* of Recipes 67 and 170–176, and he provides variant versions for Recipes 156–167.

[3] §345 in the Brereton-Ferrier edition; p. 262 in the Pichon edition. See also Eberhard, §19.

MAZ(X) again has unique material here, a first step ("vuydiez premierement ... ") intended to help ensure the success of this remedy for a burnt taste in a stew or broth. This addition requires a change later of the word *pot* to *poutaige*.[1] A second alteration in the *MAZ* text is found in the qualification of *levain* by the phrase *de paste crue*. This *levain de paste*, known today as sourdough, provided by process of fermentation the carbon dioxide gas which would to some extent absorb a burnt taste. By specifying *crue*, *MAZ* assures that the fungus cell is still active.[2]

In the additional prescription offered by *MAZ* (Recipe 2A), walnuts, high in protein and higher in fat content than either almonds or pine nuts, are suggested as an alternative means to counteract the burnt taste.[3]

[Boulitures]

3. Bouliture de grosse chair

MAZ	Boulitures de grosses chairs comme beuf, porc, mouton. Cuysiez en
BN	*Bouture de grosse char, c'est porc, buef, mouton. Cuit en*
VAT	**Boulture de grosse chair, si est beuf, porc et mouton. Cuit en**

MAZ	aigue et sel et maingier aux hauls blans ou a verjus reverdi,
BN	*eaue et sel, et mengier aux aulx blans ou vers ou au verjus*
VAT	**eaue et en sel, se mengue, le beuf aux aulx vertz en esté,**

MAZ	– – – – – – – – – – – – – –
BN	– – – – – – – – – – – – – –
VAT	**blans en yver, et le porc et le mouton aussi a bonne sausse vert ou**

MAZ	– – – – – – – – – – – – et y mecter a cuyre
BN	– – – – – – *se elle est freiche;* – – – –
VAT	**il n'y ait point de vin se la chair est freische;** – – – –

MAZ	pierressy, saulge, ysouppe; et la salee maingier a la moustard.
BN	– – – – – – – *et sallee, a la moustarde.*
VAT	– – – – – – – **et se elle [est] sallee, a la moutarde.**

---

[1] This step appears in the *Menagier de Paris* (§346; p. 263) where the text that follows it is very close to that of *VAT*. The first step was probably omitted by a derivative of *Y*, upon which version both *BN* and *VAT* depended.

[2] A starter for sourdough was regularly sold in Paris streets. See "Eve pour pain!" in the *Crieries de Paris* of Guillaume de la Villeneuve, ed. Étienne Barbazan and Dominique Méon in *Fabliaux et contes des poètes françois*, 4 vols. (new ed.; Paris: B. Warée, Imprimerie de Crepelet, 1808), vol. 2, p. 278, l. 39.

[3] See Jasper Guy Woodroof, *Tree Nuts: Production, Processing, Products*, 2 vols. (Westport, Conn., 1967), vol. 1, p. 59.

The term *grosse* used to qualify the meat of this recipe refers to the properties which make it more or less digestible.[1] A foodstuff consisting of fine, easily digestible particles is called *subtile*. It is generally held that a *grosse* meat should be boiled in order to render it more susceptible to transformation into chyme and chyle, and hence into blood. The first of the meats mentioned here, beef, is always subjected to boiling in late-mediæval cookery because its dry nature makes it unsuitable for roasting.[2] Beef *bouillon* is a kitchen staple and enters into a relatively large percentage of made dishes in the *Viandier* and in other recipe collections of the period.

MAZ(X) seems to suggest *verjus reverdi* as an alternative serving sauce for these three boiled meats, whereas *verjus* is not qualifed in *BN*, and does not even appear in *VAT*. This type of verjuice sauce is not common in mediæval recipe books;[3] *MAZ(X)* realizes that it would be useful to list those ingredients—parsley, sage, hyssop—which will lend a distinct green colour to the verjuice.[4]

---

[1] Speaking of the difference in foods appropriate for peasants on the one hand and nobles on the other, the *Regime tresutile* states: "Les rustiques et aultres gens de grande labeur et excercité doibvent estre refectionés de viandes plus grosses, car [en] yceulx la vertu digestive est forte et ne doit pas user de viandes subtiles, come sont poussins, chapons et chair de viau, car icelles chairs ce brullent en l'estomac ou incontinent ceroient digerees et ainsi seroit chose necessaire de les souvent refectioner. Les nobles et ceulx qui vivent d'oiseaulx doivent user diete [de] subtile substance, car en eulx la vertu digestive est debile, et ne peult digerer grosses viandes, comme sont chers de porcz salees et chairs de beuf, et de poissons qui desceiche" (ed. Cummins, p. 107).

[2] In her article on early English cooking, "The Roast, or Boiled, Beef of Old England," *Book Forum*, 5 (1980), pp. 294–299, Constance B. Hieatt is surprised that that most typical of modern English dishes, roast beef, is not found in mediæval England. "Chars de buef est froide et seche de se nature et engenre gros sanc et melancolieus ... ": Aldobrandino da Siena, *Le régime du corps de maître Aldebrandin de Sienne* (Paris, 1911), p. 123. The *Regime tresutile* (*ed. cit.*, p. 21) refers to Isaac's *Dietæ universales* in its comment to l. 27 of the *Regimen sanitatis salernitanum*: "Chair de chievre et de beuf sont grandement mauvaises et dures et difficiles a digerer, et engendrent gros sanc melancolique."

[3] Chiquart (*Du fait de cuisine*, f. 26r.) does recommend that a sauce called *verjust verd* be used on roast goat kid, though he does not mention its ingredients.

According to Aldobrandino, verjuice is "fait de roisins qui ne sont mie meur, et de forcetes [tendrils of the vine] et de vicaus, et d'autres coses aigres, si a celle meisme nature, si com de refroidier le caut, et d'amortir l'arsure de l'estomac ki vient de cole" (p. 119). The *forcetes* that Aldobrandino mentions as providing verjuice are the *boujons* listed for the *Viandier* by *VAT* in §170 as a source for a tart flavour. More than a century later Platina writes: "De acore. Quod agrestam vulgo dicunt, et Omphacium Plinii, id acorem Macrobii autoritate dixerim. Omphax enim (ut dixi) uvam adhuc acerba significat. Quare igitur magis appellent oleum ex bacca immatura omphacium quam agrestam, quae ab omphace fit, non satis video. Acorem vero ita Macrobius exprimit. Acetum acerbius acore est ... " (*De honesta voluptate*, f. 22v).

[4] Parsley and sage are regularly combined to provide a green food-colouring (*e.g.* in Recipes 26 and 87). Hyssop, an aromatic mint-flavoured herb which is rare in fourteenth-century cookery, is used in the *Viandier* only in combination with these first two green herbs (see also Recipe 4).

It seems strange that this verjuice sauce should disappear from the *Viandier* as *VAT* copies it, and that *BN* should seem to include it only as an alternative to white and green garlic sauces, until we realize that *BN* has blundered in his reading of his source. The wording in *Y* (and perhaps already in *Z*) allowed *BN* to understand that there were three different sauces here, while in reality there are only two: these are the white and green garlic sauces.[5] For the second of these *MAZ* supplies the ingredients list, though somewhat inexplicitly: verjuice (used in both types of garlic sauce), and the three herbs. The colours white and green refer of course not to the colour of the garlic—which is never distinguished in any of the mediæval health handbooks, *tacuina*, or botany manuals—but rather to the colour of the finished sauce. *Y* adds the clarification that these first sauces apply only to fresh, boiled meats, a distinction seemingly assumed by *MAZ*; the treatment of the salted meats, when boiled, will follow and conclude the recipe.

VAT distinguishes specific applications for the white and green sauces according to the season in which the meat is eaten, but this distinction is required for beef alone; boiled pork and mutton call for something different, a green sauce made without wine. This sauce, whose ingredients will be given later in the chapter of the *Viandier* which is devoted to unboiled sauces,[6] combines parsley, ginger, white bread,[7] vinegar and verjuice. The vinegar (according to *MAZ*) is to predominate over the verjuice. Pork and mutton resemble one another in that both are considered moist meats, pork being cold,[8] however, and mutton somewhat warmer.[9] When a moist meat is boiled it requires a sauce that will counteract not only the natural humidity of the meat but the humidity added to it by the cooking process as well. Parsley, being warm and dry in the third degree,[10] functions to this end in a serving sauce, and is aided further by the liquid base of the sauce. Wine, verjuice and vinegar are all moderately dry liquids, differing from one another only in their temperatures: verjuice is the coldest of the three, vinegar is temperately cool and wine is moderately warm.[11] By explicitly excluding wine from the sauce for pork and mutton, *VAT* shows that what is desired is a sauce that is particularly drying and cooling. Beef, being by nature dry and cold, does not call for the same type of sauce, even when considerably warmed and humidified by boiling.

---

[5] The recipes for these two sauces appear later in the *Viandier*, Recipes 157 and 158.

[6] Recipe 161. This recipe does not appear in the *VAT* manuscript itself, although it is listed in the *VAT* Table.

[7] The variant recipe contained in *MAZ* adds sage to these dry ingredients, and offers the cook a choice between vinegar and verjuice for a base liquid.

[8] *Le Régime du corps de maître Aldebrandin de Sienne: Texte français du XIIIe siècle*, ed. Louis Landouzy and Roger Pépin (Paris, 1911), p. 122.

[9] Aldobrandino, p. 124.

[10] Constantinus, Platearius, Aldobrandino, and the *Hortus sanitatis*.

[11] "Est a noter que les raisins sont de trois manieres, car les aulcuns sont vers et aigres et en est fait le verjus, et iceulx restraindent le ventre et amortissent la fureur de la coleur du sanc et vault moult es fluys coleriques. Les aultres sont meurs, doulz et recens, desquelz procede le bon vin ... " (*Regime tresutile*, p. 34, f. 23v). For the respective qualities of wine, verjuice and vinegar, see Aldobrandino, pp. 117–118, 119 and 120.

4. Hericoc de mouton

MAZ	Haricocus de mouton. Prener vostre mouton et le tailliez par morceaulx,
BN	*Hericoq de mouton.* - - - - - - *Tout cru, et le metés frire*
VAT	**Hericoc[1] de mouton. Prenez vostre mouton et le mettez tout cru soubzfrire**
MAZ	puis le mecter souffrire en sain de lac et oignons aveques
BN	*ou sain de lart, depecié par menus pecies,[2] aveques oingnons*
VAT	**en sain de lart, et soit despecié par menuez pieces, des ongnons menuz**
MAZ	en ung pout couvert sur les charbons, et houchez souvent;
BN	*minciés,* - - - - - - - - - - - - - -
VAT	**meiciez avec,** - - - - - - - - - - - - - -
MAZ	puis quant il sera bien souffrir mecter dedans de vo boillon du beufz
BN	- - - - - - - *et deffaites du boullon de buef;*
VAT	- - - - - - - **et deffaictes de boullon de beuf;**
MAZ	et lessiez boulir; puis adjouster vin, verjus, parressy, saulge,
BN	- - - - - - - - - *du vergus, percil, ysope et*
VAT	- - - - **et y mettez du vin et du verjus et macis, ysope**
MAZ	ysouppe —et du saffrain qui le veult; et tout ce faicte boulir ensamble
BN	*sauge;* - - - - - - *et boullés tout ensemble;*
VAT	**et sauge;** - - - - - - **et faictes bien boullir emsemble.**
MAZ	jusque ad ce qu'il soit cuit. - - - - - - Et ad ce faire
BN	- - - - - - - - *et fine poudre d'espices.*
MAZ	est bon le colz et la poiterine du mouton.

The *hericoc* is a dish of mutton with chopped onions and herbs.[3] The present recipe is an instance in which *MAZ(X)* amplifies the text he has received from the *Viandier* tradition.

[1] *Hericoc*: the scribe wrote *Hericot*, but then crossed the *t* high as if to make it into a *c*.

[2] *pecies*: *sic*.

[3] The Haricot is a old French dish of long tradition. Its name derives from a Frankish verb that by the twelfth century had become *harigoter*, "to shred." See also the *Arricoch* in the *Libre de sent soví*, Appendix I, p. 59; and *Meritoch* and *Nerricoch*, with what appears to an agglutinated article, in the *Libre del coch*, §§63 and 80 (though note Barbara Santich's warning against "culinary *faux amis*": *Two Languages*, pp. 67–68). The *Haricot de mouton* in the *Recueil de Riom*, §20, calls for onion, parsley, beef broth, verjuice and *pouldre*. In the *Grand kalendrier et compost des bergiers* (orig. ed. 1499; repr. Paris, n.d., p. 88) *Hericoq* consists of grilled breast of mutton, onions, white ginger, cinnamon, cloves, grains of paradise, verjuice and salt. See Liliane Plouvier, "Les métamorphoses du Haricot de mouton," *Ambiance culinaire*, (Jan. 1988), pp. 80–81.

While it is only after the instruction to fry the mutton that *BN* and *VAT* mention that the meat is to be cut up,[4] *MAZ(X)* puts this operation in its proper place, ahead of the frying. He specifies the use of a covered pot in which to fry the mutton and, further, that the contents of the pot be stirred and that the pot be placed over the coals. *X* is enough of a cook to expect that the liquid added to the fried meat should be boiled, although he has to repeat this instruction when he comes to it later. As a postscript he advises which cuts of pork are most suitable for this treatment. *Y* adds that the onions with which the chopped pork is fried are themselves to be chopped.

The phrase *tout cru* found in *BN* and *VAT* indicates that the mutton is not to be boiled or parboiled. Boiling was a common first step in cooking, before subjecting a meat to the processes of frying or of roasting. These processes will more or less dry a meat while imparting to it the particular final taste and texture required by a particular dish. *Y* therefore makes it clear that this present recipe is quite different from the preceding one, §3, where mutton is simply boiled.

In the list of herbs that constitute the sauce, *VAT* replaces parsley with mace. Such a substitution may perhaps have originated in a rather mysterious mention that *BN* makes of spice powder: "et fine poudre d'espices." The source of this particular ingredient is unlikely to have been *Y* unless *VAT*, reading *Y*, could not understand the phrase and decided therefore to omit it. Mace is, though, one of the "fine" spices;[5] *VAT* may simply be specifying a particular fine spice from among those that *Y*, with a collective term, had left a little vague. However, the *Hericot de mouton* copied by the *Menagier de Paris*[6] is similar to the *VAT* version of the dish here, with three exceptions: the mutton is to be parboiled before frying; no mention is made of either wine or verjuice; and parsley is found listed together with mace, hyssop and sage. It may well be, then, that the *VAT* manuscript is *missing* an herb, parsley, which was indeed written in a common source for both *VAT* and the *Menagier*.

Another, and much simpler, explanation for the mention of "spice powder" in *BN* may also be that this is being suggested as a serving garnish.[7]

The name of the dish is given a peculiarly Latin appearance in the *haricocus* of *MAZ*.

5. Bouli lardé

VAL *Boully lardé.*[1] *Prenez vostre grain,* - - - - - - - -

---

[4] *Z* probably offered a text somewhat similar to what we read in *BN*, with the past participle *depecié*, following the direction *le metés frire*, but designating or intended to apply to the meat which was set to fry. *VAT* misinterprets this past participle, making it a separate, and apparently subsequent, step.

[5] "Minues espices comme giroffle et macit" (Chiquart, f. 21r). In the *Viandier*, *BN* alone uses the term *fines espices* (in Recipes 20, 23 and 77, as well as here), preferring it as a sort of handy abbreviation for a list of specific spices. In no subsequent use, however, does mace appear in the spice list of the other manuscripts.

[6] *Menagier*, §64; p. 148.

[7] See, for example, Recipes 101, 120, 147.

[1] In most cases throughout *VAL*, the name of the recipe is written a second time either at the

MAZ	Boullir larder. Prener vostre grain – – – – – – – –
BN	*Bouli lardé. Prennés vostre grain* – – – – – – – –
VAT	**Bouly lardé. Prenez vostre grain—entens que c'est ma chair ou**

VAL	– – – *lardés et metez cuire en yaue et vin,*
MAZ	– – – – – et le mecter boulir en aigue et en vin,
BN	– – – *et le lardés et cuisés en eaue, vin,*
VAT	**ma veneison—et le lardez et le mettez cuire en eaue ou en vin,**

VAL	– – – – – – *et y metez cuire du masit, sel; et saffren,*
MAZ	et qu'ilz soit bien larder; et y mecter a cuire de mascit et du saffrain
BN	– – – – – – – – *et percil metés seulement; et du saffren,*
VAT	– – – – – – – – **et mettez du macis seullement; et du saffran,**

VAL	*qui veult.*
MAZ	tant seullement.
BN	*qui y veult.*
VAT	**qui veult.**

This is the first extant recipe in *VAL*. The nature of the dish *Bouilly lardé* is suggested by its name.

Three variants among the manuscripts are worth noticing in particular. *VAL* includes salt among the ingredients, whereas *MAZ* explicitly excludes it by saying that these ingredients should include mace and saffron alone in addition to the liquids. This *sel* is undoubtedly an error in *VAT*: *O* probably read, "du masit seul saffren qui veult." *Z*, not understanding these qualifications, made *seul* into an adverb which *MAZ(X)* then proceded to apply to both ingredients, eliminating the choice that had been allowed for the second. Another variant is found in *BN*'s substitution of parsley for mace, as in the previous recipe. And, thirdly, the only manuscript to specify which meat or *grain* is appropriate for this recipe is *VAT*, whose scribe writes that one may use either *chair*—not, it should be noted, as distinct from *poisson*,[2] but rather denoting meat from domestic animals—or *veneison*—that is, game meat. This is hardly a specification since all that *VAT* indicates in effect is that one may use any meat whatsoever. The phrase does not seem to serve any purpose, but may well be in some way suggested by the following recipe which is intended exclusively for game meat.

The *Bouilly lardé* is still a relatively simple dish which appropriately adds fat and warmth to those meats—generally of game animals, large and small—that are considered to possess a dry nature.[3] In the *Menagier de Paris* this dish is derived from the *boussac*

---

right-hand end of the first line of its text or in the space remaining at the end of the preceding recipe. With this first extant recipe in the roll, the name is repeated after the command *lardés*.

[2] The only *bouilli lardé* described by Chiquart is for the fish tench (f. 62r).

[3] Domestic meats possess, on the contrary, a nature that is generally more cool and more moist. Magninus distinguishes clearly between these two general classes of meat and specifies sauces

made for rabbit,[4] and is appropriate specifically for stag-meat, that is, "venison" in the modern English sense.[5]

6. Venoison de cerf fraiche

VAL	*Venoison de cherf fraiche.*			*Parboullie, lardee*	
MAZ	Venoisson de serfz fresche.			Parbouler et lardés	
VAT	**Venoison de cerf et de chevrel sauvaige fresche.**			**Pourboullue et lardee**	

VAL	*au long par dedans;*	*puis metés cuire*	*en autre yaue,*	*et du*
MAZ	au loing dedans la chart	et puis mecter cuire	er une aigue	et du
VAT	**au long,** – – –	– – – – –	– – –	**et du**

VAL	*masit et du vin grant foison;*	– –	*a la cameline;*
MAZ	mascit et vin a grant foisson,	– –	et maingier a la cameline;
VAT	**macis, et du vin grant foisson;**	**bien cuire**	**et mengier a la cameline;**

VAL	*et en pasté, parboullie et puis lardee.*	
MAZ	et en pasté parboulir et lardez,	et mecter dedans de la fine
VAT	**et mise en pasté, pourboullie et lardee,**	– – – – – –

MAZ	poudre.	
VAT	– –	**et mengee a la cameline.**

After dealing with the meats of domestic animals in Recipe 5 the *Viandier* turns to the other category of meats from four-footed animals, game-meat or venison. The treatment of this meat, whose generally dry nature lends itself properly to boiling, will occupy this and the following two recipes; as well, Recipe 43, for *Toute venoison fresche*, will offer a couple of universal rules for its preparation.[1]

Fresh stag-meat, when it is boiled, is prepared as a variety of *bouilly lardé*, which requires the meat to be parboiled and in which the pork strips are applied to the inside

---

appropriate, in relative warmth and moisture, for each (*Regimen*, ch. 17). See also Aldobrandino, p. 121.

[4] *Menagier*, §82; p. 153.

[5] *Menagier*, §90; p. 156. See also §80; p. 153.

[1] On the relative importance of venison and of domestic meats in Flanders at the end of the fourteenth century, see J.-P. Sosson, "La part du gibier dans l'alimentation médiévale," *La chasse au moyen âge* (Paris, 1980), pp. 347–359: "La consommation de gros gibier (cerfs, biches, sangliers) est très loin d'être exceptionnelle et ne paraît pas sensible aux saisons. ... Ovins, puis porcins et bovins dominent très largement" (p. 351).

of the meat.[2] The dish calls for a serving sauce known as Cameline.[3] This manner of preparing and serving venison seems to have been well established in late-mediæval cookery. The procedure, including a recipe for the cameline sauce, is described at the beginning of the thirteenth century in the *Northern-European Cookbook* in §7 for *Herensalsin.*[4] Venison is regularly served together with bowls of yellowish *Fromentee* (see below, Recipe 63).

When this meat is to be baked in a pastry shell, it undergoes a similar treatment of parboiling and larding.

BN chooses to omit the recipe for fresh stag, putting in its place a recipe for roe deer (§8) that consists merely of a reference to the absent recipe for stag! We can usually suppose, in the case of such an omission by a particular manuscript, that the meat in question was perhaps not normally available to the persons for whom the manuscript was copied,[5] or perhaps for reasons of personal taste that it was not normally eaten by them. However, the fact that *VAT* combines these meats here in Recipe 6, rather than in Recipe 8, making use of a reference back to this recipe for fresh stag as the other three manuscripts do, suggests that *Y* may have indicated somehow that Recipe 8 ought to be moved back to the position occupied by Recipe 6, and that *BN* misunderstood this attempt to link the two recipes in this way. *BN* does in fact copy the part of Recipe 6 that deals with the meat in a pasty, but this procedure applies of course only to the deer-meat of Recipe 8.

The text of the *Menagier*[6] is close to that of the *VAT* version for *Venoison de cerf*, although roe deer is dealt with separately later.[7]

7. Sanglier

VAL	*Sangler frais.*	*Faites cuire en vin et en yaue et getez*
MAZ	- - - - - - -	- - - - - - - - -

[2] Stag-meat is recognized as being cold and dry in its qualities, that is, possessing a melancholic complexion: "Amplius consueverunt homines sani existentes uti carnibus leporinis et cuniculorum et cervorum. Et iste carnes sunt melancolice et talem humorem habent generare. Unde tales carnes cum perveniunt ad antiquitatem simpliciter sunt evitande. Meliores autem sunt cum sunt partui propinque ut siccitas earum obtemperetur ab etate. Et predicte carnes sunt simpliciter evitande nisi sint pinques. Nam ex earum pinguedine obtemperatur siccitas" (Magninus, *Regimen sanitatis*, ch. 17). The *Viandier* safely compensates for any lack of natural fat in the stag-meat by barding it with pork. *Cf.* the *Venoison de serf au soupper*, in which the stag-meat is larded, in the *Recueil de Riom*, §17. This recipe is copied next to one for *Venoison de sangler frez* (*Recueil de Riom*, §18), which is the *Viandier*'s Recipe 7.

[3] Cameline sauce is accorded the premier position in the order of recipes copied in the *Viandier*'s later chapter on sauces (Recipe 155).

[4] See *Ein mittelniederdeutsches Kochbuch*, ed. Wiswe, §71.

[5] Chiquart, writing at the court of Savoy, recognizes the very great importance of deer-meat (*chevrieu*) on the table of his master; an interesting preparation called *Chyvrolee* is designed for this meat and is unique to the *Du fait de cuisine* (§13, f. 34r).

[6] *Menagier de Paris*, §85; p. 154. Brereton and Ferrier erroneously read the *Menagier*'s recipe as for *venoison de beuf*—clearly a contradiction in itself.

[7] *Menagier*, §88; p. 155.

BN	*Senglier frais. Cuit en vin et en eaue;* –
VAT	**Venoison de sanglier frez. Cuit en vin et en eaue;** –

VAL	*le premier boullon; a la cameline ou au poivre aigret. Sangler sallé*
MAZ	– – – – – – – – – – – – – Sangler et
BN	– – – – *a la cameline ou au poivre egret; la salee,*
VAT	– – – – **a la cameline et au poivre aigret; le salé,**

VAL	*et cerf. Metez tamper,*[1] *puis lavés tresbien*
MAZ	serfz salez. Mecter vostre chart tramper, puis – – –
BN	– – – – – – – – – – – –
VAT	– – – – – – – – – – – –

VAL	– – *et getés le premier boullon et lavez d'eaue fraiche,*
MAZ	la bouler et gectez le premier boillon et la lavez d'aigue fresche,

VAL	*et lessiez reffroidier;* – – – *puis le metés par*
MAZ	puis la lessiez reffroidier sur une nappe; puis la trainchiez par

VAL	*lachez et metez boulir une petite onde en yaue et*
MAZ	lesches et mecter boulir une petite unde par moitié aigue et par

VAL	*moitié vin blanc; puis pelés chastaingnez cuitez en la brese et le*
MAZ	moitié vin blanc; puis pillez chastaignes cuites – – et

VAL	*metez en plast, et drecez vostre boullon avecques de la venoison;*
MAZ	mectez ou plaut, et dressiez vostre venoison et de son aigue avecques;

VAL	*mangier a la motarde.*
MAZ	et maingier a la moustarde.
BN	*a la moustarde.*
VAT	**a la moustarde.**

Still dealing with fresh wild meats—that is, with *venoison*, as *VAT* correctly inserts the term—the *Viandier* turns to a consideration of wild boar meat. For some reason *MAZ* omits the recipe for fresh boar yet still copies the detailed treatment prescribed for salted boar meat. Both *VAL* and *MAZ* equate salted boar and salted stag for this latter recipe; *Y*, however, has deleted any reference to salted stag meat, as well as the whole of the recipe for the preparation of these meats.

---

[1] *tamper*: *sic.*

One new sauce is mentioned in this recipe: *poivre aigret* is apparently the same as *poivre jaunet*,[2] a boiled sauce combining pepper, ginger and saffron.[3] It is to be regretted that *MAZ* did not copy the recipe for fresh boar because at Recipe 99, as dressing for the fish *barbillons*, the other manuscripts call again for the sauce *poivre aigret*, whereas *MAZ* specifies *rapee*. This *rapee* is one of the sauces listed among the non-boiled sauces in the Table to the *VAT* manuscript, but for some reason its recipe was not reproduced when the copyist came to it. In the Table it is located just after the recipe for green garlic sauce, used in Recipe 3, and may very well have been a type of non-boiled yellowish pepper sauce prescribed for fresh boar and for *barbillons* in earlier versions of the *Viandier* at a time when pepper was still much in vogue.

Another sauce, for salted boar and stag, is the mustard sauce already mentioned for salted mutton; in no other recipe is it mentioned as a garnish for meats,[4] although the first of the unique additions in the *MAZ* manuscript—following the sauce section, and itself undoubtedly a sauce as well—combines mustard, red wine, cinnamon and sugar.[5] There is no mention of boiling this mixture. As with all of the recipes in this part of *MAZ*, the sauce is unnamed. The practice of serving salt venison with its own bouillon is echoed in Recipe 122 where stockfish is served in the same way.

8. Chevreau sauvage

VAL	*Chevreau sauvage.*	*Doit estre aparrelliez a mangier*	*comme le cerf*
MAZ	Chevrieulx saulvaige.	Soit apparoillier et maingier	en la fourme
BN	*Chevriaux sauvages.*	- - - - - - - -	*comme serf.*

VAL *frais.*
MAZ et maniere comme le serfz frest cy dessus desclairiz et diviser.

BN *Item, en pasté, parboullie et lardee; mengier comme dit est.*

[2] The *Menagier* (§281; p. 232) copies the recipe of the *Viandier*'s sauce *poivre jaunet* but calls it *poivre jaunet ou aigret*. The *Sent soví* describes a sauce consisting of pepper and "molt vinagre" (ch. 90), this latter ingredient explaining the qualification *aigret*. In the Anglo-Norman collection *Viande e claree*, *pevre gresse* is made with grape juice, "probably sour," Hieatt and Jones speculate (p. 870, §19.1). Concerning the use of pepper in mediæval cookery, see in particular Bruno Laurioux, "Et le poivre conquit la France," *L'Histoire*, 67 (1984), pp. 79–81.

[3] These are the ingredients listed later in Recipe 164. At that point a choice is offered between verjuice and/or vinegar.

[4] Mustard—presumably a mustard sauce—is frequently prescribed as a dressing for fish. *Sinapis* being warm and dry in the fourth, or most extreme, degree according to all such authorities as Aldobrandino, Crescentius and Platearius, a sauce made from it is suitable for the cold, moist flesh of most fish. A recipe for a mustard sauce composed of mustard, honey and vinegar is found in Grewe, *Northern-European Cookbook*, §8.

[5] Recipe 171, below.

Wild goat (*chevreau*, a diminutive of the Latin *capra*) in *VAL* is called roe deer (*chevrieulx*, Latin *capreolus*) in *MAZ* and *BN*. The treatment of this meat is the same as that of fresh stag; *VAT* has already combined the two meats in Recipe 6 where the first is still called wild goat kid (*chevrel*). It is probable that at some very early stage in the tradition of the *Viandier* an author or scribe added the epithet "wild" in an attempt to obviate any confusion inherent in the words *chevreau/chevriaux*. There is no doubt that it is the deer which is meant here, and that this meat is still part of, and the concluding item in, the section on *venoison*.

Despite the name applied to Chiquart's dish, *Une chyvrolee de cerf*, this is indeed in his case a stew for deer-meat, with wine, spices (including mace) and herbs; it might indeed be a distant derivative of the *Viandier*'s preparation.[1]

9. Chappons, veel, aux herbes

BN *Chappons aux herbes ou veel. Cuisés en eaue, et du lart, percil,*
VAT **Chappons aux herbes ou veel. Mettés les cuire en eaue, lart, persil,**

BN *sauge, ysope, - vin, verjus, saffren et gingembre.*
VAT **sauge, ysope, coq, vin, vertjus; saffran et gingembre se vos voulez.**

The recipes for boar and deer appear to conclude the opening section of the original *Viandier*; this deals with large cuts of meat which are to be boiled or otherwise cooked without being greatly reduced in size or changed in appearance. Manuscript *Y* has taken the opportunity of this division in the book's composition to insert a recipe for capons. One assumes that *Y* chose this particular point in the collection, rather than some place later among the other domestic fowl—at about Recipe 36 or so—because this first part of the *Viandier* is devoted to meats that are to be boiled. Generally speaking, fowl are normally subjected to a roasting process (in Recipes 36 ff.), whether on a spit or a grill, perhaps because of what was considered to be their essentially moist nature.[1] Both capons and veal, however, being young meats, enjoy a temperate nature and, with the admixture of appropriately drying and warming herbs and spices, can safely undergo boiling and the increase in moisture consequent on this cooking procedure.[2]

VAT's addition of *coq* (costmary or dittany) to the list of potherbs in this recipe is remarkable because it is the only time in any of the manuscripts of the *Viandier* that this herb is used.

---

[1] *Du fait de cuisine,* §13, f. 35r.

[1] In his *Du fait de cusine*, Chiquart cites from memory what appears to have been accepted as a classic culinary rule concerning the advisability of roasting fowl: "Si volucris verrat, qui torret eam, procul errat; / Sed procul ab igne volucrem de flumine torre" (f. 15r).

[2] "Vous devés savoir que chars de buef se diversefie selonc sen eage dont on le trueve, si com chars de beuf qui alaite ki doune melleur norrissement, et plus legierement se cuist por ce qu'il est caus et moistes por l'alaitier qu'il fait ... " (Aldobrandino, *ed. cit.*, p. 123). See also *Sanitatis conservator*, p. 18, l. 584.

The punctuation near the end of this recipe in *VAT* is problematic: because saffron and ginger are listed after the liquids, they are likely intended to be considered separately as optional ingredients in the cooking sauce.[3] What is further possible is that they are intended as a garnish—optional in the case of *VAT*—with which the meat, capons or veal, is to be dressed when it is served.

Potages lians (BN, VAT) ❧

10. Chaudun de porc

VAL	*Chaudin de porc.*	*Cuisiez,*	*puis le despechiez*
MAZ	Chauduin de porc.	Cuilz vostre chauduin en aigue,	puis tailliez
BN	*Chaudun de porc.*	*Cuisés en eaue,*	*puis la metés*
VAT	**Chaudun de porc.**	**Cuisiez le en l'eaue et**	**puis le decoupez**

VAL	*par morceaux,*	*puis frisiez en saing de lart;*	*prenez gingembre,*
MAZ	par morceaulx	et frissez en sain de lart;	et prener gingimbre,
BN	*par pieces*	*et frisiés en sain de lart;*	*du gingembre,*
VAT	**par morceaulx**	**et frisiez en sain et en lart;**	**puis prenez gingenbre,**

VAL	*poivre long, saffran, et*	– –	*du pain hallé et metez*
MAZ	poivre long, saffrain, et	– –	pain bruler lequel soit
BN	*poivre lonc et du safren,*	– –	*pain hallé, et*
VAT	**poivre long et saffran, et**	**puis prenez**	**pain hallé, et mettez**

VAL	*tramper en boullon de buef*	– – – – – – – –	*ou*
MAZ	tremper en boillon de beuf	—car son boillon sent le sain—	ou en
BN	*trempés*[1] *en eaue de buef*	*—car son boullon sent le fians—*	*ou en*
VAT	**tremper en boullon de beuf**	**—car son boullion sent le fiens—**	**ou,**

VAL	*eaue boullie ou lait de vache;*	– – – – – – –
MAZ	lait de vaiche,	et le passez parmi l'estermine;
BN	*lait de vache qui veult,*	*et passés parmi l'estamine;*
VAT	**se vous voulez, en lait de vache,**	**et passez par my l'estamine;**

VAL	*prenez verjus esgrené*	*cuit en yaue et metez les grenez en*
MAZ	puis prener verjus esgrenez	cuit en aigue et mecter les grains en
BN	*puis prennés esgrené*	*cuit en eaue et metés les grains en*
VAT	**puis prenez vertjus de grain**	**cuit en eaue et mettez les grappes en**

---

[3] In the *Recueil de Riom* a recipe of *Chappons et* [read *es*?] *herbes et trumeaux de beuf* (§16) calls for "du saffran, de la canelle, et du gingibre de mesche entier."

[1] *trempes* followed by a *d* that is stroked out.

VAL	*vostre potaige*	– – – – –	*quant vous devés servir, et*
MAZ	vostre poutaige	ou dedans les escuelles	sur le point de servir;
BN	*vostre potage*	– – – – –	*sur le point de servir, et*
VAT	**vostre potaige**	– – – – –	**sur le point de servir, et**

VAL	*filés moiaux de eufs*	*et coulez.*
MAZ	fillez moyeux d'euf dedans	et boulés bien.
BN	*fillés moieux d'uefs dedans*	*et faites boulir.*
VAT	**fillez moyeulx d'oeufz dedans**	**et faictes boullir.**

The four versions of the *Chaudun de porc* offer interesting variants, even though the texts generally agree closely. Copy *Z* has made two substantial additions. The explanation why beef broth should be preferred for the infusion of the toast, rather than the broth of the boiled pork viscera itself, has been modified—or misread—by *MAZ(X)* or by *Y*: because it is difficult to think that either *X* or even *MAZ* could misunderstand the word *fians* ("dung, excrement"), or disagree with the relevance of the term to those parts of the pig that are being boiled, it might be safe to suppose that *Z* had in fact written *sain* (hog fat with a distinct taste). This amounts to speculating that the less likely reading was in fact the original reading, simply because it *is* the less likely. In a sense *Y* "corrects" his copy of the text by improving upon the explanation, or at least by finding what seems to be a better, more plausible one.[2]

A second addition by *Z* is the instruction that the spice mixture is to be sieved before it and a mash of unripe grapes are added to the pot.

A final variant is found in the last directive in the recipe—according to which, *MAZ*, *BN* and *VAT* agree, the sauce, with egg yolks just added in, is to be boiled; *VAL* alone has the verb "strain" rather than "boil." The order of the actions in *VAL* is strange because one would expect the egg yolks to be strained before being added to the main mixture; this is a common procedure, and is indeed the case in Recipe 12.[3]

---

[2] The *Menagier de Paris* offers no choice in the matter of the liquid in which the spices are to be steeped: "Soient alayez du chaudeau" (§97; p. 160). The author does, however, append an explanatory comment later: "*Nota* que le sel et vinaigre ostent la freschumee." In all probability this comment was suggested by the text of the *Viandier* which the Menagier had in front of him and which, as *Y* did, refers to the *freschumé*, or excremental odour, of the broth in which pork viscera have been boiled. It is equally clear, though, that he does not consider such a smell to constitute an insuperable restriction on the use of this liquid because other ingredients can be added to the pot that will effectively check the odour. If the Menagier feels his source to be unsound in objecting to the *freschumé* of this pork bouillon, this may perhaps provide a slight additional argument that the original word in our text was *sain* rather than *fian*.

[3] The *Menagier*'s version of the recipe does not make use of eggs. In the recipe for *Ung broet de chauldun de porc*, §19 in the *Recueil de Riom*, we read, "dez moyoux d'eufz, coler ou entregecter . . . ." In the *Liber de coquina* (part II, §59), a recipe for *Calcatum* or *Calcadum* outlines a broth for cow intestines, but uses fried onions and has no taste of verjuice. *Cf.* also the *Galdafra* in the *Liber de coquina* (part II, §57), and the *Gualdafra* in the *Libro della cocina* (pp. 35 and 36).

The position of the verb *coulez* in *VAL*, and the different verb appearing in the other manuscripts, seem to suggest that *coulez* may have been an interlinear or marginal insertion in an early manuscript, perhaps some cook's attempt to obviate the possibility of the eggs separating or hardening inappropriately in the mixture. If this was the case, though, the notation must have been misunderstood by *Z* and by all later manuscript copies, perhaps because the specific meaning of the word or the intent behind it was not clear. The *Chaudun de porc* is the first recipe in a section of what *Y* calls *Potaiges lians*, that is, stewed preparations of a more or less thick consistency. The *chaudin*, *chauduin* or *chaudun* is a collective term designating the entrails of any animal.[4] According to the *Enseignements*, *chaudin de porc* should be roasted and served with a garlic sauce or verjuice.[5] The author of the *Menagier* does not seem to be greatly dependent upon the text of the *Viandier* for his treatment of *Chaudun de pourceau*. In various fifteenth-century English recipe collections there are *chawdwyn* and *chaudoun* that use swans' and fish viscera, but all of these English recipes depend upon ginger, pepper and vinegar to compose the dish's characteristic taste.[6]

11. Cretonnee de pois nouveaulx

VAL	*Cretonnee de pois vers*	*ou de fevez.*	*Cuisiez,*	–
MAZ	Cretonnés de pois nouviaulx.	– – –	Cuissiez les pois,	–
BN	*Cretonnee de pois novieux.*	– – –	*Cuisés les*	*jusques*
VAT	**Cretonnee de poys nouveaulx.**	– – –	**Cuissiez les**	**jusques**

VAL	– –	*purés*	*et frisiez en saing de lart; prenez*
MAZ	– –	puis les purez bien	et les frissez en sain de lart; puis
BN		*au purer*	*et frisiés en sain de lart; puis prennés*
VAT	**au purer**	**et puis les purez,**	**et les frisiez en sain de lart; puis**

VAL	*lait de vache*	– – –	*et boulez une onde,*
MAZ	prener lait de vaiche	– – –	et le bouler une onde et
BN	*lait de vache*	*ou d'almendes*	*et le bouillés*[1] *une onde, et*
VAT	**prenez lait de vache**	– – –	**et le**[2] **boulliez une onde, et**

[4] "Le chaudun, ce sont les boyaulx que l'en dit l'*entrecerele* des boyaulz, et aussi sont ce les boyaulx menuz dont l'en fait boudins et saulcisses, et aussi en est la pance" (*Menagier de Paris*, §12; p. 128).

[5] *Enseignements*, p. 181, l. 23; *Petit traité de cuisine*, p. 214.

[6] Among those edited by Austin, pp. 76, 95, 108, 114; and the *Forme of Cury* (ed. Warner, §§143 and 115; ed. Hieatt and Butler, *Curye on Inglysch*, part IV, §§147 and 118). The *Utilis coquinario* (part III in Hieatt and Butler) contains a *Chauden for potage* (§6) which resembles the *Viandier*'s dish except that neither vinegar nor verjuice is specified.

[1] *bouilles* followed by *on* stroked out.

[2] *le* followed by *frisez* stroked out.

VAL	*metez tramper ung pou de pain dedens;*	*prenez gingembre,*
MAZ	mecter tremper ung pol de pain dedans;	puis broyer gigimbre
BN	*metés – – vostre pain dedans vostre lait;*	*prennés gingembre*
VAT	**mettés tremper vostre pain dedans le lait;**	**et faictes**[3] **gingenbre**

VAL	*saffren*	*desfait de vostre lait, faitez boulir;*
MAZ	et saffrain,	destramper de vostre lait et faicte boulir;
BN	*et saffren broié*	*et deffaites de vostre bouillon, et faites boulir;*
VAT	**et saffran brayer**	**et le deffaictes de vostre lait, et faictes boullir;**

VAL	*prenez poullez cuis en eaue,*	*frisiez par quartiers,*
MAZ	puis prener polés cuys en aigue	et les frissiez par quartiers
BN	*prenés poulles cuites en eaue*	*et les metez dedans par quartiers*
VAT	**et puis prenez poulles cuites et**[4] **eaue**	**et les despeciez par quartiers**

VAL		*metez boullir avec;*	*traiés*
MAZ		et mecter boulir avecques;	puis tirez arriere
BN	*et frisiés;*	*puis metés boullir aveques;*	*puis traiés arriere*
VAT	**et les frisiez,**	**puis mettez boullir avecques;**	**puis traiez arriere**

VAL	*du feu, fillés*	*des eufs grant foison*[5] *dedens.*
MAZ	du feu et fillez	grant foisson de moyeuf d'euf dedans, et puis dressiez.
BN	*du feu et fillés*	*moieux d'oeufs grantfoison.*[6]
VAT	**du feu et y fillez**	**grant foison de moyeulx d'oeufz.**

The variants in this recipe are found largely in *BN* and are not sound. The spices are steeped in the bread-and-milk mixture, but for this latter *BN* writes *bouillon*—a *lapsus* committed perhaps under the influence of the verb *boulir* that follows. It may perhaps also be a deliberate choice of word because *BN* has previously provided the alternative of almond milk for cow's milk, and *bouillon* may seem to him to offer a safe technical term to designate inclusively both of these liquids. *Y* changes the meat from *poulet* to *poule.* After this meat is boiled, *BN* probably reads in *Y* the direction "metez par quartiers" but, trying to clarify this, writes "metez dedans par quartiers"; after this the direction, "et frisiés" only adds to the nonsense.

Cretonnee de pois and the following *Cretonneee de feves* may, by their titles, seem out of order among these meat stews yet they are in reality varieties of chicken preparation, as are the next three recipes. Furthermore, because of their dependence upon spices and

[3] *faictes* followed by *boullir* stroked out.

[4] *et*: *sic.*

[5] *grant foison* inserted above the line.

[6] *grantfoison*: the *t* is added over the *n* of *granfoison*.

milk[7] and because of the final addition of egg yolks in each recipe, they are related to the *Chaudun* that precedes them. The term *cretonnee* appears to be a derivative of *cremium* and *cremare*, indicating that the deep frying of the peas or beans is historically the essential step in the preparation of this dish.[8]

The recipe using peas is echoed in Chiquart's treatise under the name *Une gratunee de pollas*, though as usual in much greater detail than here and with some additional ingredients.[9]

11A. Cretonnee de feves nouvelles

MAZ Cretonnee de feves nouvelles. Soit fait par la fourme et maniere
BN *Cretonnee de feuves nouvelles. Auxi comme dit est des poes[1] nouviaux.*
VAT **Cretonnee de feves nouvelles. Ainsi comme celles de poys cy devant.**

MAZ du cretonnee des pois noviaulx.

The *feves* used in mediæval cookery are the broad bean, *Vicia faba*, cultivated for food since the earliest times and the only vegetable known as bean in Europe until the sixteenth century. Beans of the *Phasiolus* family (coco, french, snap, string, wax, lima, navy, haricot and flageolet beans) are a new-world vegetable.

12. Comminee de poullaille

VAL *Conminee de poullaille. Cuisiez en vin et en eaue,*
MAZ Conminee de poullaille. Cuissiez vostre poullaille en aigue et en vin,
BN *Conminee de poulaille. Cuisés la en vin et en eaue,*
VAT **Comminee de poullaille. Cuissiez la en vin et en eaue,**

VAL	*despeciés par cartiers,*	*frisez en saing de lart;*	
MAZ	despeciez par quartiers	et frissiez en sain de lart;	puis
BN	*puis la despeciés par quartiers,*	*et la frisiés en sain de lart;*	
VAT	**et puis la despeciez par quartiers**	**et frisez en sain de lart;**	**puis**

[7] The *Menagier* provides for milk in his *Chaudun de pourceau* as an alternative to the meat bouillon: "Et aucuns font le potage de espices et lait, comme cy dessus est dit de cretonnee" (§97; p. 161). See also the *Gratonea lactis* of the *Liber de coquina*, III, §1. Concerning the thickeners that the *Menagier* uses in his *Cretonnee* (§95; p. 159), see Note 3 to Recipe 12 (below).

[8] "*Cremium*, a *Cremare*: Siccamentum lignorum vel frixorum in patella: et etiam quod remanet in patella aridum de carnibus post pinguedinem liquefactum, dicitur Cremium ... (Joan. de Janua)" (DuCange, 2, 614c). See also Tobler, 1, 1043, and *FEW*, 16, 314. For a slightly different version of this dish see Eberhard, §4, *Ein essenn von gebratenn arbeissenn.*

[9] *Du fait de cuisine*, §62, f. 86v.

[1] *poes*: the *e* appears to have been changed from an *i*.

VAL	*metez ung pou de pain trampé en vostre pot, coullez*
MAZ	prener ung pol de pain et mecter tramper en vostre boillon, couler
BN	*prennés un pou de pain trempé en vostre boullon, et le coullés*
VAT	**prenez ung pou de vin et en trempez vostre boullon, et le coulez**

VAL	*et metez boullir avec vostre grain; prenez ung pou de gingembre*
MAZ	et mecter boulir avecque vostre grain; broyer ung pol de gigimbre
BN	*et metés boullir aveques vostre grain; prennés un pou de gingembre*
VAT	**et le mettez boullir avec vostre grain; puis prenez bien pou de gingenbre**

VAL	*et de commin desfait de verjus;*[1] – – – –
MAZ	et de conmin et deffaicte de – – – – –
BN	*et un pou de comin, deffaites de verjus et de vin; puis prenez*
VAT	**et de commin deffait de verjus et de vin; puis prenez**

VAL	*moiaux de eufs grant foison, et lez batez, coullés, fillez*
MAZ	moyeux d'euf grant foisson et les bater, coler et fillés
BN	*moyeux d'oeufs grant foison, et batés lez bien – et fillés*
VAT	**moyeulx d'oeufz grant foison, et les batez bien – et les fillez**

VAL	*dedens;* – – – – – – – *gardez qu'il n'arde.*
MAZ	dedans, – – – – – – – et gardez bien qu'il ne arde.
BN	*avequez vostre potage arriere du feu.* – – – – – –
VAT	**en vostre potaige arriere du feu; et gardez qu'il ne tourne.**

This *comminee* is the second recipe in the series of poultry dishes. Variants appear in the later stages of the recipe as the two spices are infused in a liquid before being added to the pot. Wine has been added to the verjuice by the two *Y* manuscripts; *VAL* mentions only verjuice, but a curious variant is found at this point in *MAZ* where, because neither verjuice nor wine is listed among the ingredients, the spices seem to be mixed directly with the item that follows, the egg yolks. Such a procedure is unique in the *Viandier*; it is likely a matter of an omission on the part of *MAZ(X)*.

At the stage at which the egg yolks are to be added, *VAL* and *MAZ* say that these should be strained, whereas *Y* omits this particular instruction. We are reminded of Recipe 10 in which only *VAL* makes any mention of straining the egg yolks. While *Y* may not consider this step to be important enough to keep, *VAT* himself does recognize the danger that the yolks may set in the hot mixture, rather than blending evenly throughout it. There is, too, the possibility that it was *Y* who inserted this warning and that *BN*, perhaps not understanding the sense of the verb *tourner* in this context, chose to leave it out.

The *Menagier*, never timid about adding personal comments about his source material, takes exception to the use of egg yolks in this recipe. His source probably raised the

[1] *deuerius* followed by *dup* which is stroked out.

possibility that the yolks might coagulate (as we find in *VAT*), and the *Menagier* feels constrained twice to remark that the function of the eggs in this recipe is not as a binding agent: they are there solely to lend their colour to the mixture as an alternative to saffron.[2] Moreover, referring directly to his source—in all probability *Y* or a close derivative of *Y*—the *Menagier* notes, "Pain est lyoison, et il est dit apres 'oeufz', qui est aultre lyoison; et il doit souffire de l'une, sicomme il est dit ou chappitre de la cretonnee."[3]

The name *comminee* derives from the major spice in the dish, cumin. This ancient aromatic seed-like fruit of a herbaceous plant was much prized as a stimulant of the appetite in the Middle Ages.[4] Ginger and cumin are both present in all three *comminees* presented in the *Viandier*.[5]

13. Comminee d'almandes

VAL	*Comminee d'almandes.*	*Cuisez vostre poullale en yaue,*	*puis*
BN	*Cominé d'almendes.*	*Cuisiés vostre poulaille en eaue,*	*et la*
VAT	**Comminee d'amendes.**	**Cuisiez bien vostre poulaille en eaue,**	**et la**

VAL	*coppez par quartiers, frisez en saing de lart;*	*prenez almandrez,*
BN	*descoupés par quartiers et frisiés en sain de lart;*	*prennés almendes*
VAT	**despeciez par quartiers et friolez en sain de lart;**	**puis prenez amendes**

[2] *Menagier de Paris*, §98; p. 161.

[3] *Ibid.* The author has indeed inserted a brief dissertation on various thickeners, their uses and advantages, into his copy of the *Cretonnee de poiz nouveaulx ou feves nouvelles* (§95; p. 159). While the *Viandier* uses both bread (with saffron) and egg yolks in Recipe 11 for *Cretonnee*, the *Menagier* omits the bread, includes the saffron, and uses the egg yolks only grudgingly: "Ja soit ce que qui le veult faire lyant de moyeulx de oeufz, filez les dedens." He continues by examining the qualities of each of the thickeners that a cook might choose: "Car iceulx moyeulx d'eufz jaunissent assez, et si font lyoison. Maiz le lait se tourne plustot de moyeulx d'oeufz que de lioyson de pain et du saffren pour coulourer. Et pour ce, qui veult lyer de pain, il couvient que ce soit pain non levé et blanc; et sera mis trempé en une escuelle avec du lait ou avec du boullon de la char, puis broyé et coulé par l'estamine. ... Encores pouez vous faire autre lyoison: c'estassavoir des poiz mesmes ou des feves broyees, puiz coulez. Si prenez laquelle lyoison que mieulx vous plaira. Car quant est de lioyson de moyeulx d'oeufz, il les couvient batre, couler par l'estamine, et filer dedens le lait apres ce qu'il a bien boulu et qu'il est trait arriere du feu avec les poiz nouveaulx ou feves nouvelles et les espices. Le plus seur est que l'en preigne ung petit du lait et destremper les oeufz en l'escuelle, et puis encores autant, et encores, tant que les moyeulx soient bien destrempez a la culier avec foison de lait; puis mectre ou pot qui est hors du feu, et le potage ne se tournera point."

[4] See Matthaeus Platearius, *Circa instans: Le livre de simples medecines*, ed. Paul Dorveaux (Paris, 1913), *s.v. comin*. See also Aldobrandino, Crescentius, *Commodorum ruralium*, the *Hortu sanitatis*, and Amédée Salmon, "Remèdes populaires du moyen âge" in *Études romanes dédiées à Gaston Paris* (Paris, 1891), p. 258–259, §§4 and 46.

[5] Recipes 12, 13 and 75.

VAL	– *broiez,*		*desfaites du boullon, metez*
BN	*pellees,* – – –		*deffaites de vostre boullon et metés*
VAT	– **et les[1] brayés, et les deffaictes de vostre boullon et mettez**		

VAL	*boullir sur vostre grain;*	*prenez gingembre et commin desfait*
BN	boullir sur vostre grain,	*et gingembre et comin deffait*
VAT	**boullir sur vostre grain;**	**et prenez gingenbre et commin deffait**

VAL	*de vin et de verjus, metés ung pou de pain blanc.*
BN	*de verjus et de vin; et tousjours se lie[2] d'elle mesmes.*
VAT	**de vin et de verjus; et tousjours se lye elle mesme.**

The *Comminee d'almandes* is different from the "standard" *Comminee de poullaille* in the use it makes of ground almonds, and in the omission of the egg yolks that are called for in the previous recipe.

In a variant at the end of this recipe we can trace the culinary thinking of *Y*. Earlier versions added white bread in order to assure that the mixture should thicken; *Y*, however, not only omits any mention of this bread but asserts quite positively, as if to refute the previous versions, that any further binding agent on top of the ingredients already listed is not at all necessary: "Tousjours se lie d'elle mesmes."[3] Concerning *VAL*'s *pain blanc*, we may speculate whether the origin of this ingredient lay perhaps in a misreading, by some ancestor read eventually also by *Z* or *Y*, of the word *lyant*. This seems quite likely to have been the case a little later in both Recipes 20 and 21. All three dishes are meant to be thick. See also the same problem with the word *blanc* in Recipe 15.

BN appears to have misread the word *pellees*,[4] copying *brayés*—though such an error, as a mere scribal *lapsus*, does seem unlikely. It might be noted that in the next recipe, for *Brouet de canelle*, all four manuscripts agree that the almonds are expressly *not* to be skinned.

14. Brouet de canelle

VAL	*Brouet de canelle.*	*Cuisiez vostre poulaille en vin ou en eaue,[1]*
MAZ	Brouet de cannelle.	Cuisiez vostre poulaille en aigue et en vin,

---

[1] *les* followed by *fillez* stroked out.

[2] *lie*: the manuscript shows *lielle*.

[3] Almond oil is high in protein (and low in carbohydrates) and does in fact bind a mixture when heated. See Woodroof, *Tree Nuts*, vol. I, p. 59.

Almond milk was usual in mediæval cookery where, in more recent times, with ready refrigeration facilities, a cook might use animal milk. Ground almonds, drawn out with a liquid, provided a valuable milk that was not as subject to spoilage as animal milk, could not be watered by an unethical merchant, and was acceptable for consumption on lean or fast days (see Recipe 152, below).

[4] Applied to nuts, the verb *peler* refers to the removal of the inner skin which lies between the husk and the kernel.

[1] *eaue* followed by *a* expunctuated.

BN	*Brouet de canelle.*	*Cuisés vostre poulaille en eaue et vin,*
VAT	**Brouet de canelle.**	**Cuissiez vostre poulaille en vin ou en eaue,**

VAL	*ou telle char que vous vourez;*	*metez par quartiers,*
MAZ	- - - - - - - - -	puis despeciez par quartiers et
BN	*ou autre grain,*	*et despeciés par quartiers et*
VAT	**ou tel grain comme vous vouldrez,**	**et le despeciez par quartiers et**

VAL	*friollés;*	- - -	*prenez almandrez toutes saiches*	-
MAZ	frissez	en sain de lart;	et prener amandres seches	- -
BN	*friolés;*	- - -	*prennés almendez toutes seiches*	*et cuisés*
VAT	**friolez;**	- - -	**puis prenez amendes toutes seiches**	**et cuisez**

VAL	*sans peller et de la canelle grant foison,*	*broiez, coulez,*
MAZ	sans pillez et de la cannelle grant foisson,	broyez, couler et
BN	*sans peller et de canelle grant foison,*	*broiés, coullés, et*
VAT	**sans peler et de canelle grant foison,**	**et brayez et coullez, et le**

VAL	*desfaitez du boillon;*	-	*faitez boullir avec*
MAZ	deffaicte de vostre boillon	-	et faicte boulir avec
BN	*deffaites de vostre boullon*	*de buef et*	*bulliés bien aveques*
VAT	**deffaictes de vostre boullon**	**de beuf et**	**faictez bien boullir avecques**

VAL	*grain, du verjus,*	*avec gingembe,*	*girofle, graine*
MAZ	vostre grain, et du verjus,	avec gigimbre,	giroffle, grainne
BN	*vostre grain, et du verjus;*	*et prennés gingembre,*	*girofle, graine*
VAT	**vostre grain, et du verjus;**	**et prenez**	**girofle et graine**

VAL	*de paradis;*	- - - - - - -	*et soit liant.*	
MAZ	de paradis;	- - - - - - -	et soit tresbien lyant.	
BN	*de paradis;*	- - - - - - -	*et soit liant.*	
VAT	**de paradiz,**	**braiez et mettez emsemble;**	**et soit lyant**	**et fort.**

A fifth recipe for poultry allows the substitution of any other meat, but is similar to the previous recipe in its use of almonds—the only thickener made use of in both dishes—ground with the major spice here, cinnamon.[2] *MAZ(X)* eliminates the option of an alternative meat in this broth.

All manuscripts agree from the beginning that the almonds are dry—as opposed to fresh and green fruit—but *Y* seems to have inserted the rather strange direction that the

---

[2] In Chiquart's work the name of a similar dish is *Broet camelin*. Such a use of an adjective of colour in order to identify a particular broth or a dish of any sort is common; the next two recipes in the *Viandier* are for *Brouet georgé* (§15) and *Brouet rousset* (§16). Concerning the culinary genre *brouet*, see J.-L. Flandrin, "Brouets, potages et bouillons," *Médiévales*, 5 (1983), pp. 5–14.

almonds are to be "cooked" before being ground and stirred into the pot. The cooking of totally dry almonds is so strange that one wonders whether both *BN* and *VAT* may not in fact have misread the word which they copied as *cuisés*. One possibility is that *Y* may have shown a verb related to *croise*, the shell of a nut:[3] the almonds are to be shelled—an operation perhaps more readily performed on dry nuts than on fresh—but not skinned. The verb may have been *croissir* or *croissier*, in the sense of "break open [the shells of the nuts]."[4] A second possibility is that *cuisés* may represent the adjective *crues*: the nuts are to be dry and raw. Strangely enough, both of these possibilities are allowed by the reading which the *Menagier* has of this recipe: "Puiz prenez des amandes crues et sechez a toute l'escorche et sans peler . . . ."[5] In this case, *a toute l'escorche* is used to reinforce *crues et sechez*, but this may well be the result of an effort on the part of the *Menagier* to understand a word, *croises* or *croisés*, which he knows only as a noun.[6]

The final significant variant in the recipe for cinnamon broth is *VAT*'s omission of ginger from the list of spices.

The punctuation in *VAL* and *MAZ* after the word *avec* is determined by the sentence structure of *BN* and *VAT*: "et prennés gingembre . . . ." Because these last spices are not explicitly infused in any liquid, it may well be that *VAL* and *MAZ* should read, "du verjus avec gingembre . . . "; in that case *Y* is in error in dropping *avec* and introducing a new clause, "et prennés gingembre . . . ."

In *VAT* an epithet *fort* is added to describe the appearance of the finished dish, but in the *Menagier* we find the advice, "et soit liant et *sor*." Either adjective is reasonable here, but a similar dish in Chiquart's collection may provide some illumination. Chiquart describes both a *Broet camelin* (made of poultry and served with pork, kid, veal or lamb) and a fast-day variation of this, a *Broet camelin de poissons*, for which the recipe requires "cynamomy a grant foyson affin qu'il porte la couleur du cynamomy."[7] The colour of both of these cinnamon dishes would be the reddish-brown represented by the adjective *sor*.

15. Brouet georgié

VAL	*Brouet gorgié.*	*Prenez tel grain*	–	*comme vous voldrez,*
MAZ	Brouet georgé.	Prener telz grain	–	conme vous voudrois
BN	*Brouet gorgié.*	*Prennés vostre grain*	–	– – – – –
VAT	**Brouet georgié.**	**Prenez tel grain**	**vollaille**	**que vous vouldrez**

[3] The term *croyse*, is used a number of times in the *Viandier* for, specifically, the shell of an almond nut.

[4] See Tobler, 2, 1081, *croissier*, and 1082, *croissir* or *croistre*.

[5] *Menagier de Paris*, §102; p. 163.

[6] Chiquart wrote in his recipe for *Broet camelin*: "Hayés grant quantité d'amandres . . . et les nectoyés bien des croyses . . . et les pisés bien et adroit sans plumer . . . " (*Du fait de cuisine*, §7, f. 26v).

[7] *Du fait de cuisine*, §31, f. 57v. The feminine adjective *cameline* is commonly used, of course, to designate the reddish-brown cinnamon sauce of late mediæval cookery.

VAL	*despeciés par pieces;*	*prenés persin*	– –	*et oingnons menus*
MAZ	et despeciez par pieces;	et puis parsin	effuellé	et oignons menuz
BN	*et le despeciés;*	*et prennés percil*	*effueillis*	*et oingnons menus*
VAT	**et la despeciez;**	**et prenez persil**	**effeullié**	**et ongnons menuz**

VAL		*et metez frire en saing de lart;*	*prenez des foiez*
MAZ	menusiez	et souffrire en sain de lart;	puis prenez des foyes
BN	*minciés*	*et metés sus frire en sain de lart;*	*puis prennés deffoies,*
VAT	**missiez**	**et mettez souffrire en sain de lart;**	**puis prenez des foyes**

VAL	*et du pain halé*	*desfait*	– –	*du boillon du beuf, faitez*
MAZ	et pain bruler,	deffaicte	– –	de boillon de beuf et faicte
BN	*pain halé,*	– – –	*et vin et*	*boullon de buef, et faites*
VAT	**et pain hallé,**	**et deffaictes**	**de vin et**	**de boullon de beuf, et faictes**

VAL	*boulir ensemble;*	*puis affinez gingembre,*	*saffren, girofle*
MAZ	boulir ensemble;	puis affiné gigenbre,	giroffle et saffrain,
BN	*bien boullir en semble;*	*puis affinés gingembre,*	*girofle, saffran,*
VAT	**bien boullir tout ensemble;**	**puis affinez gingenbre,**	**saffren,**

VAL	*deffait de verjus;*	*et que le boillon soit blanc*
MAZ	deffaicte de verjus;	et que le brouet soit blanc,
BN	*et deffaites de vergus;*	*et que vostre bouillon soit* –
VAT	**deffaictes de verjus;**	**et que vostre boullon soit blanc brun,**

VAL	*et liant.*
MAZ	et lyant conme une seringne.
BN	*liant.*
VAT	**et lyant comme une soringue.**

The two broths at this point in the *Viandier*, the *Brouet gorgié* or *georgié*, and the *Brouet rousset* (§16), are related to one another in some of the ingredients they use and in the manner of preparing them. They differ in their requirements of several different spices, which spices determine the peculiar appearance of each dish and hence its name.

The first of the pair is a general-purpose broth using poultry, as is the case in the previous recipes, or any other meat. *VAT* makes it apply exclusively to poultry, but the insertion of this limitation at the beginning of his copy of the recipe is likely his own doing.

Two minor variants are found here in the copies: *Y* adds wine to the beef bouillon in which the toast and liver are steeped, and *VAT* omits one of the spices, cloves.

A serious problem is posed toward the end of the recipe, not because of a variant but because three of the manuscripts agree on the word *blanc*. There is, however, no similar agreement about just what is *blanc*. Whether this is the beef bouillon or the broth, or whether bouillon here means in effect the finished broth as a prepared dish or sauce, it is very difficult to imagine how a mixture of parsley, fried onions, liver, toast, ginger and saffron could possibly turn out "white." The reader feels that one of the *Menagier*'s sarcastic comments would be apropos here. Even *VAT* recognizes the difficulty and, alone, tries to qualify the colour that he copies.[1] *BN* solves the problem in typical fashion by simply omitting the word altogether from his copy. In all probability, either *O* read "que le brouet soit blant et liant," and we must understand *blant* in the sense of "mild,"[2] or else an early copy contained only the word *lyant* which at some point was misread as *blant*. If we suppose the first hypothesis, *blant* or *blanc* would be the opposite of *aigu*[3] and *fort d'espices*[4]: there is to be no predominant spice, as in the previous recipe, but a *bland* balance of relatively mild ingredients. Of these ingredients the blended colour of parsley and saffron alone stands out; they alone might be considered to give a characteristic quality to the dish. In any case, in the *Du fait de cuisine* the *Broet georgé* has apparently by definition an orange cast to it.[5]

Z attempted to define the degree of stiffness of the finished dish by comparing this broth to a *soringue*—a thick preparation we see only at Recipe 79. It is this comparison that is taken up by the *Menagier*.

16. Brouet rousset

VAL	*Brouet roucet.*	*Prenez tel grain*	*comme vous voldrez,*	*et*
MAZ	Brouet rousset.	Prener tel grain	conme vous voudrois	et
BN	*Brouet rousset.*	*Prennés vostre grain*	– – – – –	*et*
VAT	**Brouet rousset.**	**Prenez tel grain**	**comme vous vouldrez,**	**et**

VAL	*oingnons copez par rouellez et persin esfeulié,*	*et metez surfrire*
MAZ	oignons par rouelles et parsin effuellé,	frisiez
BN	*oingnons minciés par rouelles et percil effueillié,*	*et metés sus frire*
VAT	**ongnons missiez par rouelles et persil effueillié,**	**et mettez souffrire**

VAL	*en saing;*	*et prenez*	–	*foyez*	*et coullez*	*ou boillon*
MAZ	en sain de lart;	puis deffaictes	–	foyes	– –	de boillon
BN	*en sain de lart;*	*puis prennés*	*pain et*	*foies,*	*et coullés*	*ou bouillon*
VAT	**en sain de lart;**	**et puis**	**pain et**	**foyes,**	**et coulez**[1]	**en boullon**

---

[1] The *Menagier*, too, indicates that the colour is darker: "Et doit ce potage estre brun de sain et lyant comme soringue" (§103; p. 164). The *soringue* (Recipe 79, below) is one of the darkest and thickest of stews.

[2] *blanc*: "flatteur, caressant, pacifique" (Godefroy).

[3] *Cf.* Recipe 28 where *VAT* uses *agu* to describe the biting taste of vinegar in a dish.

[4] Cf. Recipes 28, 29 and 182.

[5] In elaborating the *Broet georgé* the cook should add only sufficient saffron "pour lui donner la couleur dudit broet" (Chiquart, *Du fait de cuisine*, §37, f. 63v). In the *Menagier*'s recipe for *Brouet georgé* (§103), the term *frangié* is used in contradistinction with *houssié* in describing variants of the dish: for the *Menagier* the version properly called *frangié* is coloured a reddish-yellow with saffron, much like the *Viandier*'s dish.

[1] *et coulez*: repeated and stroked out.

VAL	*de beuf et en vin,*	*et metez boulir avec*[2] *vostre grain;*	*puis affinez*
MAZ	de beuf – –	et mecter boulir avec vostre grain;	puis affiner
BN	*de buef et en vin*	*et metés boullir aveques vostre grain;*	*puis prennés*
VAT	**de beuf et en vin**	**et mettez boullir avec vostre grain;**	**et puis affinez**

VAL	*gingenbre, canelle,*	–	*grainne de paradis,*	*fleur*
MAZ	gigimbre, cannelle,	giroffle,	graine,	fleur
BN	*fines*[3] *espices: gingembre, canelle,*	*girofle,*	*graine de paradis,*	*fleur*
VAT	**gingenbre, canelle,**	**girofle,**	**graine,**	**fleur**

VAL	*de canelle,*[4]	*et defaitez de verjus.*	
MAZ	de cannelle,	deffaicte de verjus;	et qu'il soit bien roux.
BN	*de canelle,*	*destrempés de vergus;*	*et soit rous.*
VAT	**de canelle,**	**et deffaictes de vertjus;**	**et soit roux.**

The russet broth derives its characteristic colour largely from a combination of spices that includes grains of paradise but that excludes saffron.[5] *Z* adds cloves to this spice list; *Y* adds bread as a thickener together with the liver.

The *Menagier* points out that, apart from a change of spices, the essential difference between *Brouet georgé* and *Brouet rousset* is that the former begins with chopped onions whereas the latter uses sliced onions.[6]

17. Haste menue de porc / Une vinaigrete

VAL	*Une soringne de haste menue de porc.*	– – – – – –
MAZ	Menue haste de porc.	Prener une haste de porc
BN	*Une vin aigrete.*	*Prennés menue hate de porc,*
VAT	**Une vinaigrette.**	**Prenez la menue haste du porc**

VAL	*metez*	*par piescez*	*rostir en la broche*	*et ne le cuisiez pas de*
MAZ	et mecter	– –	rotir en broches	et ne soit pas cuite du
BN	– –	– –	– – – –	*et ne la rosticiés pas trop;*
VAT	**et mettez**	– –	**rostir,**	**et ne la laissiez mie trop**

2 *auec* is inserted above the line.

3 *BN* has misread the word *affines*.

4 *grainne de paradis fleur de canelle* inserted above the line.

5 *BN* is partial to the term *fines espices*: see also Recipes 20 and 77. In Chiquart's *Broet rosé* alkanet root is fried in oil, then added to the broth, after all of the other ingredients, "en si bon point et aviz que la coulleur dudit boullon soit plus sur la couleur rosee que de goules" (*Du fait de cuisine*, §8, f. 28v). In the manuscript B.L. Royal 12.C.xii the dish called *Rosee* (§12 in the edition by Meyer, p. 52, and by Hieatt and Jones, p. 867) is both coloured and flavoured by cinnamon and rose petals; it bears little resemblance to the *Viandier*'s preparation.

6 *Menagier de Paris*, §104; p. 164.

VAL *tous poins;* – – – – *metez frire en saing, et oignons avec,*
MAZ tout point; – – – – – – – – – – puis la
BN *puis la descoupés, et oingnons par rouelles, et*
VAT **cuire; puis la decouppez, et ongnons par rouelles, et mettez**

VAL – – – *en ung pot sur lez charbons,*
MAZ souffrisiez en sain de porc; – – – – – – – – – –
BN *frisiés en sain de lart* – – – *dedans un pot sur le charbon*
VAT **souffrire en son saing ou en aultre dedans ung pot sur le charbon,**

VAL *et hochiez souvent; et quand il sera surfrit, metez boulon*
MAZ – – – – – – – – puis prener foyes et couler en boillon
BN *et ostés souvent le pot; et quant il sera cuit si y metés bouillon*
VAT **et hochez le pot bien souvent; et quant il sera bien souffrit si y**

VAL *de beuf, vin plain, metez sur vostre grain;*
MAZ de beuf et du vin; – – – – –
BN *de buef plain,* – – *et metés boullir sur vostre grain;*
VAT **mettez boullon de beuf et du vin, et mettez boullir sur vostre viande;**

VAL *prenez gingembre, graine de paradis, ung pou de saffren*
MAZ puis affinez gigimbre, grainne et ung pol de saffrain,
BN *puis affinés gingembre, graine de paradis et un pou de saffren,*
VAT **puis affinez** – – **graine de paradiz et ung pou de saffren,**

VAL *defait de vin aigre, bouly tout ensemble.*
MAZ deffaicte de vin aigre et faicte boulir tout ensamble; et se
BN *deffaites de vin aigre et metés tout boullir ensemble; et se*
VAT **et deffaictes de vinaigre et mettez boullir tout emsemble; et se**

MAZ lye d'elle mesme.
BN *doit lier de soi mesmes, et est brune.*
VAT **doibt lyer de luy mesmes et estre brunet.**

The *soringue* is, as Recipe 15 has pointed out, a type of thick broth.[1] This generic name of the dish is not found for this preparation of the *haste menue* in any other manuscript

[1] A recipe for a dish similar to this is one found in the *Enseignements* (p. 181, l. 24; *Petit traité de cuisine*, p. 214), where its name is *Haste menue en brouet*. See also *Une vinesgrete de menuz hastez de porc* in the *Recueil de Riom* (§2), where the items of pork that could be mounted on small roasting-spits (*menuz hastez*) are listed: "c'est assavoir foyez, ratez et frasez." The *Vinegrete* in the *Forme of Cury* (§61; Hieatt and Butler, part IV, §62) does not specify the use of a roasting-spit for the first stage in the preparation of this dish.

The name *soringue* or *soringne* which *VAL* alone applies to this preparation seems to be inspired by the processes by which the meat is cooked. In Catalan and Provençal the verb

than *VAL*, even though the reference to it in Recipe 15 is contained in both *MAZ* and *VAT*. For the present dish *MAZ* prefers simply the collective name of the meat to be used, which appears to comprise pork spleen, liver and kidney,[2] while *Y* introduces a new name, *Vinaigrete*. The inclusion of an indefinite article by *Y* in this name, *Une vinaigrete*, suggests that the genre may have been more broadly recognized by cooks than his single example in the *Viandier* would seem to indicate. *Une vinaigrette*, again with the indefinite article, is the name for the dish copied in the *Menagier*.[3] Chiquart has only a *sorengue* of eels; his version of *Une vinaigrete* makes use of just pork liver rather than the combination of organs designated by *haste menue*, and of cinnamon rather than saffron; but the dish remains similar otherwise.[4]

The curious addition that *MAZ(X)* makes of livers is perhaps an echo of Recipes 15 and 16. This ingredient may perhaps also point to a culinary tradition to which the *Enseignements* belonged, because its sauce for pork "spleen" requires both ground liver and toast, with pepper and various other spices.[5]

Y inserts a concluding comment about the brown colour of the *Viandier*'s *Vinaigrete*. This the *Menagier* takes up with an exclamation: "Brune: Comment sera elle brune, s'il n'y a du pain hallé?" His recipe, therefore, calls for toast, as does that of Chiquart, although with the protein available in the chopped spleen and liver, any wheat-flour product would be quite superfluous as a binder: as *Z* had already stated, "se lye d'elle mesme."

The origin of the name *Vinaigrete* may lie in such a version of the dish as we find in the *Enseignements* where vinegar (together with ground toast, either as colorant or thickener) is poured into this preparation as a final ingredient. It was clearly intended in

---

sosenguar is a synonym for *sofrire*. "Si vols ffer sosengua a conils o a lebres ho qualque carn te vuylles, moltó, vadell, cabrit, sien ffetes peces menudes, e sien sosenguades, ho en altra manera apellades sofrites, ab grex de cansalda, ho en holi ho en sagí" (*Sent soví*, §81). This frying operation may be preceded by a preliminary roasting or parboiling, but is always done with onions and is always followed by a boiling in a spiced broth. See Grewe, *Sent soví*, p. 55, and the *Soringue d'anguilles* at Recipe 79, below.

[2] The *Menagier* provides a definition of the collective term *haste menue*, or *hastelet*, under the general rubric of "Yssues d'un porc": "La haste menue c'est la rate, et a icelle tient bien la moictié du foye et les rongnons; et l'autre moictié du foye tient a la froissure entre le mol et le cuer" (§12; p. 128; see also §266). This *froissure* is used in the *Viandier*, but is of a calf: see *Fraise de veel*, Recipe 33, below.

[3] *Menagier*, §105; p. 164. For the roasting of the *haste menue*, see later in the *Menagier*, §363; p. 268.

[4] *Du fait de cuisine*, §57, f. 81v.

[5] A hot, dry spice such as pepper is appropriate for a cold, moist meat such as pork, and particularly for its viscera; *cf.* the long pepper stipulated for the earlier *Chaudun de porc* (Recipe 10). For the *Menue haste de porc* prepared here in Recipe 17, rather than the pepper used by the *Enseignements*, the *Viandier* has substituted grains of paradise, melegueta pepper. "Plus connue aujourd'hui sous le nom de *maniguette*. On l'emploie pour donner du montant aux eaux-de-vie et aux vinaigres, et surtout pour falsifier le poivre" (Pichon and Vicaire, p. 6, n4). The nineteenth-century use of melegueta pepper with vinegar is noteworthy.

the *Enseignements* that the flavour of this vinegar should predominate. Any cook who followed the recipe copied in the *Viandier* would have to be generous in the amount of vinegar he used to steep the spices.

18. Gravé de menus oiseaulx

VAL	*Gravé de menus oiseaux*	*ou de tel grain comme on veult.*
MAZ	Grainné de menus oysiaulx.	Prener menus oysiaulx tel que vous voudrés,
BN	*Civé de menus oisiaux.*	*Prennés vostre grain*
VAT	**Gravé de menuz oyseaulx**	**ou telle viande comme vous vouldrez.**

VAL	*Metés surfrire en saing tres bien;*	*prenez pain halé*
MAZ	mecter souffrire tresbien;	puis prenez pain bruler,
BN	*et metés frire en sain de lart tresbien;*	*puis prennés pain hallé*
VAT	**Mettez souffrire en sain de lart tres bien;**	**puis prenez pain brulé**

VAL	*desfait de boullon de beuf,*	*coullez, metez avec vostre*
MAZ	deffaicte de boillon de beuf,	couler et mecter avec vostre
BN	*et deffaites de boullon de buef,*	*et coullés et metés aveques vostre*
VAT	**et deffaictes de boullon de beuf,**	**coullez et mettez avec vostre**

VAL	*grain;*	*affinez gingembre, canelle et ung pou de verjus;*	*faitez*
MAZ	grain;	puis affiner gigimbre, cannelle et ung pol de verjus,	et faicte
BN	*grain;*	*affinés gingembre, canelle, un pou de vergus.*	*et faut*
VAT	**viande;**	**puis affinez gingenbre, canelle et ung pou de vertjus,**	**et faictes**

VAL	*tout ensemble.*		
MAZ	boulir tout ensamble;	– – –	et ne doit pas estre trop lyant.
BN	*boulir en semble;*	*et doit estre tendre*	*et non pas trop liant.*
VAT	**boullir emsemble;**	**et doibt estre tendre**	**et non pas trop lyant.**

Examples of what may properly be included among the "menus oiseaux" to be prepared for this dish are specified later by *VAT* in Recipe 45: "menuz oyseaulx comme allouettes, cailles, mauvilz et autres."

There cannot be as much assurance about the sense of the word *gravé* found here in the *Viandier* for the first time. Although the manuscripts at various places occasionally show the word as *grané*, or perhaps *grane*, almost as often the *n* in this word could be either an *n* or a *v*. The present case illustrates our dilemma well: *VAL* writes *grave* (*gravé*) quite clearly; *MAZ* doubles the *n*, leaving no doubt about what he understands the word to be; and *BN* chooses—one is tempted to say, cautiously—another word altogether, *civé*;[1] and finally in *VAT* the word could be either *grané* (*grane*) or *gravé*. It is perhaps a passage in

[1] *Cf.* the *Cibarium ex sylvaticis* in Platina, f. 48r: "Cibarium, quod vulgo corrupto vocabulo *civerum* appellant, sic facto . . . ."

which we might benefit from the relative proven dependability of the various manuscripts. Ironically, though, the two which are more or less immediate products of working cooks, *VAL* and *MAZ(X)*, despite the obvious scribal sloppiness in *MAZ* itself, represent the two contrary possibilities. The sense of *grané* is relatively easy to deduce as a derivative of the word *grain*.[2] This sense can readily be seen in the way *MAZ* chose to spell his *grainné*. It is the word *gravé* that poses the problem. The word did exist; scribes here and in other works[3] attest repeatedly to the early existence in French of the form with a *v*, but its origin still remains somewhat of a mystery.[4]

The recipe is copied in all four manuscripts with few material changes. *Y* adds a note about texture ("doit estre tendre") which must be meant to apply to the meat.

The verb *faitez* in *VAL*, found there alone, whereas other manuscripts show *faictes boullir* or *faut boulir*, does not require an accompanying infinitive. The verb is not causative in *VAT* but merely supposes an implied object: "Do [it] all together."[5]

The *Menagier*,[6] the *Du fait de cuisine*[7] and the *Recueil de Riom*[8] all have similar recipes, the *Menagier* and the *Recueil de Riom* adding in poultry liver as a binder. The *Menagier* further appends a note that the sauce should be *claret*.

19. Blanc brouet de chappons

VAL *Blanc brouet de chapons.* *Cuis*
MAZ Blanc brouet de voulaille. Cuisiez poulés ou chappons

---

[2] Emilio Faccioli, in his *Arte della cucina*, 2 vols. (Milan, 1966), vol. 2, p. 397, defines the old Italian *brodo granato* as a "brodo pieno di piccoli grumi"; the term occurs three times as a variety of dish in the fourteenth-century *Libro della cocina* edited by Faccioli. See also the *Liber de coquina* whose editor, Mulon, glosses a word *granatum* as a "potage dit 'grané'" (p. 428), although at its only occurence, in the *Liber de coquina*, part II, §1, the *n* of this word appears as a *u* or *v*: "Postea insimul bulliantur quousque brodium sit grauatum" (p. 400). And see the *Brodecto granato* (for chicken, with fried onions, herbs and saffron) in the Libro "A" (§58) of the *Due libri di cucina*. Gunnar Tilander in *Glanures lexicographiques* (Lund, 1932), p. 135 wrote that "*Grané* se rattache à *grain*, expression fréquente dans Taillevent ... "; he rejected Pichon's transcription of *gravé* in the *Menagier*.

[3] Cf. the recipe for "La maniere coment l'en deit fere gravee" in the *Viande e claree* (§29), which dates from the end of the thirteenth century. The *Menagier de Paris* has *gravé* consistently in all of its manuscripts; see p. 151 of the Pichon edition, n1. The *Du fait de cuisine*, which was dictated in large part by Chiquart himself, shows clearly *gravé* in all half-dozen instances of the term.

[4] The *Oxford English Dictionary*, *s. v. gravey*, suggests that *gravé* in French derived through scribal error (repeated?, over considerable time?) from *grané* but, given the obvious etymological sense of the form *grané*, such an error seems difficult to imagine.

[5] *Cf.* Recipe 91 *VAL*: "Faitez jusques ace que le chapon soit cuit."

[6] *Menagier de Paris*, §74; p. 150.

[7] *Du fait de cuisine*, §19, f. 40r.

[8] *Recueil de Riom*, §7: *Ung grane d'alouestez*.

BN	*Blanc brouet de chappons. Cuisiés*
VAT	**Blanc brouet de chappons. Cuis**

VAL	*en vin et en eaue; despeciés par membrez et frisiez*
MAZ	en vin et en aigue, puis les despiciés par membres et les frissiez;
BN	*en vin et en eaue, puis despeciés par membres et frisiés*
VAT	**en vin et en eaue, puis despeciez par membres et frisiez**

VAL	*en saing;*	*broiez amandez et des broions de chapons,*
MAZ	– – –	puis broyer amandres et des broyons
BN	*en sain de lart;*	*puis boullés d'almendes et des brans de chappons*
VAT	**en sain de lart;**	**et puis brayez amendes et des brahons de voz chappons**

VAL	*et des eufs*	*desfais de boillon,*
MAZ	et des piez de ladicte poulaille,	deffaicte de vostre boillon
BN	*et foiez,*	*et deffaites de vostre bouillon*
VAT	**et des foyes,**	**et deffaictes de vostre boullon**

VAL	*metez boullir sur vostre grain;*	*prenez gingembre,*	*canelle,*
MAZ	et mecter sur vostre grain;	puis prener gigimbre,	cannelle,
BN	*et metés boulir sus vostre grain;*	*puis prennés gingembre,*	*canelle,*
VAT	**et mettez boullir sur vostre viande;**	**puis prenez gingenbre,**	–

VAL	*giroffle, grene de paradis, poivre long, garingal*
MAZ	giroffle, garingal, poivre long, graine,
BN	*girofle, poivre lonc, caringal, graine de paradis,*
VAT	**girofle, garingal, poivre long, grainne de paradiz,**

VAL	*desfait de vin aigre;*	*boullez tout ensemble,*
MAZ	deffaicte de vin aigre;	bouler tout ensemble,
BN	– – – – – – –	*et faites tout boullir en sembre;*
VAT	**et deffaictes de vin aigre**	**et faictes bien boullir ensemble;**

VAL	*et y fillez moiaux de eufs bien batus,*	*et coulez.*
MAZ	et y fillez moyeux d'eux batuz,	et coulez.
BN	*et y fillés moieux d'oeufs bien batus.*	
VAT	**et y fillez moyeulx d'oeufz bien batuz;**	**et soit bien lyant.**

This white broth is related to the standard *blanc mangier* (Recipe 95 in the *Viandier*) in that it is basically a mixture of chicken and almonds. The colour of the dish, with its six spices and its egg yolks, is not of course white;[1] the *blanc* of its name is probably

[1] The spice galingale, which appears again in §§24, 68 and 80, is mentioned in the *Menagier* (§290; p. 235) as an alternative to alkanet as a source of a red colorant.

a transformation of *blant*—as it may also have been at the end of Recipe 15, above. Both almonds and chicken were held to be particularly suitable for persons with digestive problems and were relied upon regularly to form the bases of a bland diet.[2] Ginger—reinforced here by grains of paradise, a relative of pepper—is the predominant spice and is likewise a favourite "digestive."

The major variant in this recipe is found at the beginning of the sauce: *VAL* shows eggs to be added to the almond and capon paste,[3] *MAZ* chicken feet, *BN* and *VAT* livers. Despite our conviction that *X*, the source for *MAZ*, was copied or edited by a competent cook, the scribe copying *MAZ* itself frequently misread, misunderstood or miscopied his original. This phrase, following "broions de chapons," is undoubtedly a case in point: in all likelihood the word *piez* in *MAZ* originally read *foiez*; the binding agent for this element of the sauce had been changed by *Z* from eggs—egg yolks are to be added in, later, anyway—to chicken livers.

Less significant variants occur in *BN*, which has *boullés d'almendes* rather than *broyés d'almendes*. *VAT* omits cinnamon from the list of spices.

The *Menagier de Paris* has a recipe for a *Brouet de chappons*—that is, without the qualification *blanc*—which is a close copy of *Y* or a derivative of *Y*, except that the *Menagier* omits the beaten egg yolks at the end.[4] This omission is merely one instance of the *Menagier*'s general distrust of eggs as a binder.

Chiquart's *Broet blanc sur chappon*[5] is a preparation similar to the *Viandier*'s, although ginger and grains of paradise are the sole spices specified by Chiquart. Despite its title in the *Du fait de cuisine*, this is essentially a sauce, made with chicken meat and other ingredients, to be poured over other meats (pork, kid and veal are suggested) when these are served.

20. Boussac de lievres, connins

VAL	*Bonsax de lievrez et de conins.*	*Halez en broche*
MAZ	Boussat de lievres.	Halez en broches voz lievres ou
BN	*Bousac de lievre ou de conis.*	*Hallés en broche*
VAT	**Boussac de lievres ou de connins.**	**Hallez les en broche**

VAL	– –	*ou sur le greil, decopés par membres*
MAZ	voz connins	ou sur le gril, puis[1] mecter per membres
BN	– –	– – – – – – – – – –
VAT	– –	**ou sur le grail, puis les decouppez par membres**

[2] The *Menagier de Paris* follows up this recipe immediately with the *Viandier*'s *Blanc mengier de chapons pour malades* (§107; p. 165). The two preparations are similar in nature.

[3] The capon meat to be ground with the almonds is specifically termed *broions* or *brahons*. This is dark, muscle meat. It is, as the *Sent soví* indicates, distinct "del blanch dell pits [breast] e de les ales, so és [that is] lo blanch" (ch. 49).

[4] *Menagier*, §72; p. 149.

[5] *Du fait de cuisine*, f. 19v; this is the first recipe in Chiquart's collection of eighty.

[1] *puis* ends a page and is repeated at the top of the following page.

VAL	*et metés surfrire en saing;*	*prenez blanc pain defait de boullon*
MAZ	souffrire en sain;	puis deffaicte de boullon de beuf pain
BN	*et suffrisiés en sain de lart;*	*prenés pain brullé et vin et bouillon*
VAT	**et frisiez en sain de lart;**	**puis prenez pain brullé, du boullon**

VAL	*de beuf et de vin cler,*	– –	*faitez boullir ensemble;*
MAZ	blanc et y mecter du vin,	couler	et faicte boulir tout ensamble;
BN	*de buef,*	*coulés,*	*boullés en semble;*
VAT	**du beuf et y[2] mettez du vin,**	**et coullez**	**et faictes boullir ensemble;**

VAL	*prenez gingembre, canelle, girofle, grene de paradis*
MAZ	puis prener cannelle, gigimbre, giroffle, graine de . . . ,
BN	*puis prennés finez espices sans saffren,*
VAT	**et puis prenez gingenbre, canelle, girofle, graine de paradiz,**

VAL	*desfait de verjus;*	*et soit brun, et non guerez blanc.*
MAZ	deffaicte de verjus;	et soit brunt, et non riens lyant.
BN	*destrempé de verjus;*	*et soit brun noir, et non pas trop liant.*
VAT	**et deffaittez de vertjus;**	**et soit brun noir, et non pas trop lyant.**

The four scribes show some hesitation, or at least lack of unanimity, over the proper name of the dish. The *n* that *VAL* shows in *Bonsax* is exceptional; it is likewise doubtful just what the final *x* represents, whether the word should perhaps be read as *bousaus* or *bousacs*. The *Menagier* reproduces the form of the name found in *VAT*—and apart from the omission of one spice, cinnamon, its recipe is identical with the *VAT* version. At the beginning of the fifteenth century in Savoy, Chiquart wrote *buchat*, his *u* being occasionally the equivalent of *ou* in standard Francian.[3]

The *boussac* or *boussat* may at its origin have been little more than a boiled sauce whose name derived from the verb "to boil." The Savoyard *buchat* seems related to the Italian verb *bullicare*.[4]

BN's habit of abbreviating his copy is seen as he writes "finez espices sans saffren" instead of ginger, cinnamon, cloves and grains of paradise; in Recipe 79, *BN* similarly substitutes "fines espices sans poivre" for the same four spices.[5] In the last phrase of *VAL*'s version, the word *blanc* may very well have been *lyant* in his source.

---

[2] *y* repeated, this *y* stroked out.

[3] The *Buchat de connins* of Chiquart (*Du fait de cuisine*, §20, f. 41v) is similar to the *Boussat/Boussac* of the *Viandier*. One peculiarity of Chiquart's recipe is the use of a bouquet of herbs that is placed in the pot with the cooking meat. See also the *De busach de conills* in the *Libre del coch* (§155) and the *Boussac de lievres* in the *Recueil de Riom* (§35), though this latter version is a very much simpler dish than the *Viandier*'s.

[4] See also DuCange 1, 713b, *Bossex*—"Dolium" (an earthenware jug for storing grain): this preparation, *Boussac de lievres*, may be simply "Jugged hare."

[5] Though the term *fines espices* was broadly recognized in mediæval culinary circles, there is little agreement upon exactly what it designated. For Chiquart the *minues espices* include ginger,

21. Hondous de chappons

VAL *Hondous de chapons. Cuisiez en vin et en eaue,*
MAZ Hondel de chappons. Cuisiez vos chappons en aigue et vin,
BN *Houdous*[1] *de chappons. Cuisiés les en vin et en eaue,*
VAT **Hondons de chappons. Cuisiez les en vin et en eaue,**

VAL *despeciez par menbres, friolez en saing;*
MAZ puis despeciez par menbres et les frissiez;
BN *puis les metés par quartiers et friolés en sain de lart;*
VAT **et despeciez par membres et les friolez en sain de lart;**

VAL *prenez ung pou de pain brullé, desfait de boullon,*
MAZ puis prener ung pol de pain brulez, deffaicte de vostre boillon,
BN *puis prenez un pou de pain brullé, deffait de vostre boullon,*
VAT **et prenez ung pou de pain qui soit brullé, deffait de vostre boullon,**

VAL *faitez boullir avec vostre grain;*
MAZ et faicte boulir avec vostre grain;
BN *et boulliés aveques vostre grain;*
VAT **et faictes boullir avec vostre viande;**

VAL *affinez gingembre, canele, giroffle, graine de paradis,*
MAZ puis affiner gigibre, cannelle, giroffle, graine de paradis,
BN *puis affinés fines espices sans saffren,*
VAT **puis affinez gingenbre, canelle, girofle et grainne de paradiz,**

VAL *deffait de verjus; ne soit pas trop blanc.*
MAZ deffaicte de verjus; et ne soit pas tropt lyant.
BN *deffaites de vergus; et ne soit pas trop liant.*
VAT **et deffaictes de verjus; et ne soit mie trop lyant.**

---

grains of paradise, pepper, cinnamon, nutmeg, mace and cloves (*Du fait de cuisine*, f. 43r). The *Sent soví* (§219) provides a recipe (with quantities) for the mixture of spices that it terms *salsa fina*: ginger, cinnamon, pepper, cloves, mace, nutmeg and saffron. In the *Libro per cuoco* the author included a paragraph (§73) for *Specie fine a tutte cosse*: "Toy una onza de pevere e una de cinamo e una de zenzevro e mezo quarto de garofali e uno quarto de zaferanno" (ed. Faccioli, p. 86). What is understood to be included in the collective term *fines espices* or *menues espices* is naturally apt to vary from period to period and from cook to cook. Pegolotti (*Pratica della mercatura*, pp. 293–297) identifies *spezie minute* by means of a preceding dot in his list of such merchandise. Lopez and Raymond gloss "minute spices" as "those wares which sold in small quantities at high prices": Robert Sabatino Lopez and Irving Woodworth Raymond, *Medieval Trade in the Mediterranean World* (New York: Columbia University Press, 1961), p. 108.

[1] *Houdous*: the scribe who was reponsible for the *BN* copy does not distinguish consistently between *n* and *u*. Following this *houdous*, for instance, he writes *de chappous cnisies* ....

The *Hondous* is related to the previous *Boussac* in that both are relatively simple, thin sauces of the same four spices, and both serve as dressing over a fried meat—in this second case, capons. The *Menagier* copies the *Viandier*'s Recipe 21 but gives it the name *Hardouil de chappons*.[2]

The two minor variants found in the previous recipe are duplicated here: *BN* abbreviates the four spices in the same way as he did in Recipe 20; and *VAL* writes *blanc* again, this again probably representing a misreading of the word *lyant*.

22. Brouet d'Alemagne de char

VAL	*Brouet d'alemagne de char de connins ou de poullale.*	
MAZ	Brouet d'alemaigne.	Prener
BN	*Brouet d'ailmengne de char—ou de conis ou de poulaille.*	*Prenés*
VAT	**Brouet d'allemangne de chair de connins et de poullaille.**	**Prenez**

VAL	- - - - - - - -	*Despeciez, metez surfrire en saing*
MAZ	chart de connins ou de poulaille	et les despeciez per morceaulx et des
BN	*vostre char*[1]	*et la despeciés et suffrisiés en sain*
VAT	**vostre chair**	**et la despeciez et la mettez souffrire**

VAL	*et oignons menus;*	*affinez amendez*
MAZ	oignons menuz menusiez, et frissiez en sain;	puis affinez amendres
BN	*de lart et oingnons menus minciés;*	*puis affinés almendes*
VAT	**en sain de lart, et de l'ongnon menu missié;**	**puis affinez amendes**

VAL	*grant foison, destrempez de vin et de boullon de beuef,*	
MAZ	grant foison, deffaicte de boillon de beuf et de vin	et
BN	*grant foisson, deffaites de vin ou de bouillon de buef,*	*puis*
VAT	**grant foyson et destrempez de vin et de boullon de beuf,**	**puis**

VAL	*faitez boullir avec vostre grain;*	*affinez gingenbre, canelle,*
MAZ	faicte boulir avec vostre grain;	puis affiner gigimbre, cannelle,
BN	*faictes boullir aveques vostre grain;*	*puis affinés gingembre, canelle,*
VAT	**faictes boullir avec vostre grain;**	**puis affinez gingenbre, canelle,**

VAL	*grene de paradis, girofle, nois muguetez;*	- - - -
MAZ	giroffle, graine de paradis, noix minguetes,[2]	et ung pol de saffrain
BN	*girofle, graine de paradis, nois mugaites,*	*bien pou de saffran;*
VAT	**girofle, grainne de paradiz, noiz muguetes,**	**bien peu de saffran;**

---

[2] *Menagier de Paris*, §100; p. 162. One of the *Menagier* manuscripts has *hourdouil* (see the variants in Brereton and Ferrier and in Pichon). The similarity between this form *hourdouil* and the *houdous* written by *BN* is interesting.

[1] *char*: the last two letters are missing in a hole in the manuscrit *BN*.

[2] The form *minguetes* that was written by *MAZ* ("noix minguetes": nutmegs) should undoubtedly read *miuguetes*.

VAL *soit sur jaune,* *liant,* *deffait de verjus.*
MAZ qu'il soit sur jane coulour et lyant, deffaicte de verjus.
BN *et soit sur le jaune,* – – *defait de verjus.*
VAT **et soit sur le jaune et lyant, deffait de verjus.**

The qualification in the name of this dish may appear to be overly specific: "de char de connins ou de poullale." The word *char* in the title, however, should properly be understood to qualify the category of preparation to which the broth belongs. This is a "brouet de char," a broth for meat-days, as distinct from a broth intended for consumption on lenten or fasting days.[3] There are a number of dishes in the section of *Potages lyans sans chair* (Recipes 75–89) that are counterparts to the current series of *Potages lyans de chair* (Recipes 10–30). The *Brouet d'Almaigne d'oeufz* (§85 in that meatless chapter) corresponds to the present *Brouet d'Alemagne de char*.

MAZ(X) demonstrates his professional competence by inserting the chopped onions *before* the instruction to fry, so that the onions and meat are clearly to be fried together.

VAL alone shows cloves among the spices to be added to the mixture.[4] If cloves were present in *O* they must have been omitted by *Z*. Contrarily, either saffron was accidentally dropped by *VAL*—which seems unlikely because he did copy the advice about the dish being yellowish in colour—or *Z* has again been responsible for a significant textual modification, having added a little saffron to the ingredients in order to assure that the dish has the colour specified by *O*. The *Brouet d'Alemaigne* in the *Menagier de Paris*[5] adds veal to the possible meats for this recipe. Liver is further added there as a binding agent, but the almonds are omitted. This omission of the almonds is remarkable because the peculiar character of the German Broth seems to be determined by its use of onions and almonds together.[6] While Chiquart alters the meats and the procedures a little, his basic ingredients for the broth—onions, almonds, and spices—remain the same as in the *Viandier*.

---

[3] The *Du fait de cuisine* offers both types of recipe: a *Broet d'Alemagny* made with capons and to be served over pork, lamb, kid or veal (§2, f. 20r); and a *Broet d'Alemagny de poyssons* (§25, f. 51r). Later in the *Viandier*, among those additions made to *VAT* in the fifteenth century, the meat-days of the week (the *trois jours maslés de la sepmaine*) will be declared to be Sunday, Tuesday and Thursday (in Recipe 195). The meat version of this dish is the first in the *Recueil de Riom*.

[4] The *Browet d'Alemaigne* found in Royal 12.C.xii (§15 in the edition both of Meyer, p. 52, and of Hieatt and Butler, p. 867) lists as ingredients only almonds, cloves, cubebs and onions. No meat is specified there for the sauce; this is, however, to be yellow, as is stated in the *Viandier*.

[5] *Menagier*, §108; p. 165.

[6] *Cf.* Austin, p. 19, *Bruet of Almaynne*. Note also in the *Forme of Cury*, §47 and the *Liber Cure Cocorum*, ed. R. Morris (London, 1862), p. 11, where the name of the dish has become *Brewet of almony* (according to Warner, p. 11; Hieatt and Butler choose the reading *Almayne*, p. 108 and *Breuet of almonde* respectively. "Germany," *Almayne*, has understandably been converted to "almonds," *almony, almonde*. Other English versions of this recipe are contained in the *Diversa cibaria*, §15, and the *Utilis coquinario*, §22 (at pp. 46 and 87 respectively in the Hieatt and Butler edition).

23. Hochepot de poullaille

VAL	*Hochepot de poullaile.*	
MAZ	Hoichepoult[1] de poulaille.	
BN	*Hochepot de poullaille.*	
VAT	**Hochepot de poullaille.**	**Prenez vostre poullaille et**

VAL	*Metez par membres surfrire*	*en saing de lart;*
MAZ	Mecter vostre poulaille souffrire par menbres;	– – –
BN	*Metés par membres suffrire*	*en sain de lart;*
VAT	**la despeciez par membres et la mettez souffrire**	**en sain de lart;**

VAL	*prenez ung pou de pain brullé*	*et dez foyes*
MAZ	et prener ung pol de pain bruler	et des foyes,
BN	*broiés pain brullé*	*et vos foies,*
VAT	**puis prenez ung pou de pain brullé**	**et des foyes de la poullaille,**

VAL	*deffais de vin et du boillon de beuf,*	*metez boullir*	
MAZ	et deffaictes de boillon de beuf et de vin,	et mecter boulir	avec
BN	*deffaites de bouillon[2] de buef,*	*et metés bouillir*	*aveques*
VAT	**et deffaictes de vin et de boullon de beuf,**	**et mettez boullir**	**avec**

VAL	*vostre grain;*	*affinez gingembre, canelle, grene de paradis*
MAZ	vostre grain;	puis affiner gigimbre, cannelle, graine de paradis,
BN	*vostre grain;*	*puis affinez fines espices,*
VAT	**vostre grain;**	**puis affinez gingembre, canelle et grainne de paradiz,**

VAL	*deffait de verjus;*	*et doit etre noiret et cler.*
MAZ	deffaicte de verjus;	et doit estre noir cleré et non pas tropt noir.
BN	*deffaites de verjus;*	*soit noir cler et non pas trop.*
VAT	**et deffaictes de vertjus;**	**et doibt estre claret noir et non pas trop.**

The *Hochepot de poullaille* is another relatively simple preparation reminiscent of the *Hondous de chapons* (§21). The basic differences between the two recipes are that in the *Hochepot* the parboiling step is omitted—the poultry being fried directly, or raw—and liver is added to the toast binder. The *Menagier*, while not giving any details specifically about his *Hochepot de volaille*, has placed it immediately after his *Hardouil de chapons*, the *Viandier*'s *Hondous*; the only directions for making the *Menagier*'s *Hochepot de volaille* are that it "soit fait ainsi, et soit non claret."[3] There is no mention in the *Menagier* of liver being added, which should account for much of the darker colour of the *Hochepot*, although he does explicitly contradict Taillevent with his advice that the dish ought not be *claret*.

1 Pichon and Vicaire read the word as *horchepoult*.

2 *bouillon*: the first *o* is inserted above the line with caret.

3 *Menagier*, §101; p. 163.

As it happens, it is just here, with this instruction about the appearance of this dish, that the manuscripts of the *Viandier* reveal the most hesitation. *VAL* is straightforward in his phraseology; *Z* appears to have made a modification in the adjectives and, in a attempt to explain the word *claret*, felt compelled to add what we might look upon as a regrettable qualification: "et non pas trop." This qualification appears not entirely to have satisfied *MAZ(X)*.

The contradiction found in the *Menagier* may be understandable in the light of the indecision, or plain confusion, shown in the various earlier versions.

As a name, a culinary genre, *hochepot* is not common in recipe collections of this period. Hieatt and Butler, and Austin, have published recipes for *Goos in hogepotte*[4] that are not similar enough to our *Hochepot* to warrant any comparison. We may surmise that the dish had too much in common with other dishes to ensure for itself much of a tradition, and that the French name—which means simply "stir-pot"—was not sufficiently distinctive or clearly appropriate for a preparation such as this.

24. Soutil brouet d'Angleterre

VAL	*Soutil brouet d'Angleterre.*	*Prené chastaingnez cuitez et pelés,*
MAZ	Soubtifz brouet d'Angleterre.	Prener chastaignes cuites et pilez,
BN	*Sutil brouet d'Engleterre.*	*Des chataingnes pellees cuites,*
VAT	**Soustil brouet d'Angleterre.**	**Prenez chastaignes cuites pellees,**

VAL	*et moiaux de eufs cuis et ung pou de foie de porc;*	*broier tout*
MAZ	et moyeuf d'euf cuis en ung pol de foye de port;	broyer tout
BN	*et moyeux d'oeufs cuis et un pou de foye de porc*	*tout broié*
VAT	**et moyeulx d'oeufs cuis en vin, un pou de faye de porc,**	**et broyez**

VAL	*ensemble, destrampés d'un pou de eaue tiede, coulez;*
MAZ	ensamble, destramper d'ung pol d'aigue tiede et coulez; puis
BN	*ensemble, destrempé d'un pou d'eaue tiede ensemble, coullés;*
VAT	**tout ensemble et destrempez d'un pou d'eaue tyede, puis coullez;**

VAL	*affinez gingembre, girofle, canelle, garingal, poivre long, graine,*
MAZ	affinez gigimbre, cannelle, graine, garingal, poivre long, espit et
BN	*affinés poivre lonc,*
VAT	**affinez gingenbre, gyrofle**

VAL	*de saffren;*	- - - - -	*fetez boullir emsemble.*
MAZ	saffrain	pour donner couleur,	et faicte boulir tout ensamble.
BN	*de saffren,*	- - - - -	*et faites boullir tout en semble.*
VAT	**et saffran**	**pour donner coulleur,**	**et faictez boullir ensemble.**

---

[4] *Curye on Inglysch*, part II, §22 and part IV, §33; and *Two Fifteenth-Century Cookery-Books*, p. 18. See *hotchpot* in the *Oxford English Dictionary*.

The *Soutil brouet* is a meatless boiled soup, which might be used as a sauce. The epithet "subtle" refers not to the ingenuity required to compose this dish or to its exquisiteness, but rather to its digestibility. *Subtilis* is a medical qualification applied to foodstuffs that are readily converted into various humours and chyle by the body.[1] This conversion is rendered more or less rapid and easy in part by the size of the particles composing any ingested substance: where the components are fine, the substance is said to be subtle.[2] In a sense, too, the *Brouet d'Angleterre* might be considered *soutil* because, lacking the chunks of meat present in most of the pottages we have seen in this section, and the finely chopped meat that a *gravé* typically would have, this dish is relatively homogenous in texture.

For this recipe, the major problem found among the manuscripts is in the lack of agreement about which spices should be included in it. *MAZ* is fairly faithful in copying the spice list that *VAL* has: only cloves are not found;[3] *MAZ* adds instead a spice called *espit*. This aspic is a rare spice in mediæval cookery; it appears elsewhere as one of several exotic ingredients in the *Menagier*'s *gelee*.[4] Most curiously *BN* and *VAT* abbreviate this spice list drastically, and not in the same way. All that these two versions agree upon is the saffron which, apparently, gives its characteristic colour to the *Soutil brouet*. It is likely that *VAT* had access to a more extensive spice list for the dish in its manuscript source because the text of this recipe in the *Menagier* is virtually identical with that of *VAT*. However, the bourgeois author's spice list includes "gingembre, canelle, giroffle, graine, poivre long, garingal, et saffren pour donner couleur"—in other words, exactly the same spices as are copied by *VAL*, though not found in *VAT*.[5]

Of all of the entrails of a boar, the *Menagier* notes that only the liver is worth keeping, "qui semble qu'il soit propre pour faire soutil brouet d'Angleterre."[6]

25. Brouet de verjus

VAL *Brouet de verjus. Prenez poulaille ou tel grain comme vous vouldrez,*
BN *Brouet de vergus. Prenez vostre poullaille ou autre grain,*
VAT **Brouet de verjus de poullaille ou de tel grain comme vous vouldrez.**

[1] The *Regimen sanitatis* of Magninus Mediolanensis distinguishes between foods that are generative of gross humours and those that produce subtle humours; pork and stag-meat are among the former, the meat of roe deer and lamb are among the latter (part 3, ch. 17). See also Bartholomaeus Glanvilla, *De proprietatibus rerum*, Book 6.

[2] Aldobrandino reports that philosophers hold clean rainwater to be "mieudre de totes autres por ce qu'ele est plus soutius, car par la subtilité veons nous qu'eles corrunpent [*i.e. digest*] trop [*very*] plus legierement que les autres" (*ed. cit.*, p. 18).

[3] Cloves are mentioned by *VAT*, so that it is not likely that *VAL* indulged in a private addition that was apart from the tradition it received.

[4] *Menagier de Paris*, §251; p. 218. The spice, *Lavandula spica* L, is called *spic* in the French version of Platearius's *Circa instans*. See also Aldobrandino, *ed. cit.*, p. 97.

[5] *Menagier de Paris*, §109; p. 166.

[6] *Menagier*, §91; p. 157.

VAL *cuisiez en vin et en eaue, et du verjus tant qui le sente;*
BN *cuisés en vin et en eaue et verjus, et que le goust de verjus passe*
VAT **Cuisiez en vin, en eaue et en verjuz tellement que le goust du verjus passe**

VAL – – – *prenez gingembre, ung pou de pain, desfaitez du boullon, et*
BN *tout; broiés gingembre, un pou de pain deffait de vostre bouillon, et*
VAT **tout l'autre; puis broyez gingenbre et** – – – – – – – – –

VAL *de moiaux d'eufs grant foison; passez parmy l'estamine tout*
BN *moyeux d'oeufs grant foison; coullés tout*
VAT **des moyeulx d'oeufz tous cruz grant foison et passez tout parmy l'estamine**

VAL *ensemble, metez boullir, puis metez sur vostre grain quant il sera*
BN *ensemble,* – – – *puis metés sur vostre grain quant il sera*
VAT **ensemble et mettez boullir, puis gectez sur vostre grain quant il sera**

VAL *bien friolé* – – – – – – *pour li doner goust.*
BN *friolé —du lart a cuire.*
VAT **friolé —et mettez du lart au cuire pour luy donner goust.**

MAZ omits this recipe, a simple combination of verjuice and ginger, the ginger being part of the thick yellow sauce, the verjuice instilling its taste into the meat as it is cooking.

Either *Z* or *Y* has attempted a couple of textual improvements. The expression "tant qu'il le sente" probably was felt not to be sufficiently clear, so it is rephrased: "Que le goust de verjus passe tout." The other modification is the result of an effort to improve an obvious oversight on the part of *O*. When drafting this recipe *O* forgot to mention the last stage in the preparation of the *grain*: after the meat is boiled, it is—and this is a normal procedure, as we have seen—to be fried[1] in pork fat. The omission is corrected by the insertion of the words "quant il sera bien friolé" at the end of the recipe when the *grain* is again mentioned, though the correction at this point is awkward.

Y inserts another phrase, "du lart au cuire," after "friolé" and before "pour li doner goust." If we are to believe *VAT*, it is the frying, presumably in pork fat, which will add taste to the meat; if, on the other hand, we understand *cuire* in its usual sense, the bacon is to be thrown into the pot just as the *grain* is undergoing its initial boiling and flavouring with verjuice.[2] If the second procedure is intended, then surely "pour luy donner goust" in *VAT* is superfluous: the wine and the strong verjuice would seem already to have imparted sufficient, or at least a quite distinct, taste. The *Menagier*'s recipe for *Brouet de verjus*[3] is not particularly helpful in resolving our difficulty because he both boils the meat with

[1] In part to seal the juices in, and also in part to brown the meat in order to give it an appetizing appearance.

[2] This use of bacon is by no means uncommon: Chiquart advises it frequently.

[3] *Menagier de Paris*, §111; p. 167. The *Recueil de Riom*'s *Brouet de verjust* (§4) has the same two-stage cooking procedure, without mentioning any use of pork.

bacon and then later fries it in *bon sain doulx*! The *Menagier* at least believes that the presence of bacon in the boiling pot is appropriate for this dish. A concluding, and perhaps telling, observation is that this procedure is to be followed in the next recipe, for *Brouet vergay*, in which the *MAZ* version makes it clear that the piece of pork is boiled in order to add flavour to the dish.

BN has, as usual, omitted some of the text—that rather important step in which the sauce is boiled.

26. Brouet vergay

VAL	*Brouet vergay.*	*Cuisiez tel grain que vous volez*
MAZ	Brouet vergay.	Cuisiez tel grain conme vous voudrois
BN	*Brouet vergay.*	*Prennés vostre grain*
VAT	**Brouet vertgay.**	**Cuisiez tel grain comme vous vouldrez**

VAL	*en vin ou en eau ou boullon de beuf,*	*du lait avec,*
MAZ	en aigue ou en vin ou en boullon de beuf,	et du lart pour donner saveur,
BN	*cuit en eaue et bouillon de buef,*	*et du lart,*
VAT	**en vin et en eaue et en boullon de beuf,**	**et de lart pour luy donner goust,**

VAL	*friolez vostre grain;*	*prenez gingembre,*	–
MAZ	et puis friolez vostre grain;	puis affinez gigimbre,	–
BN	*si le friolés;*	*puis prennés gingembre,*	*saffren,*
VAT	**puis convient bien frioler vostre grain;**	**puis affinez gingenbre,**	**saffren,**

VAL	*percin, ung pou de sauge,*	– –	*moiaux d'eufs,*
MAZ	parressi et ung pol de sauge,	– –	– – –
BN	*percil et un pou de sauge*	*qui veult,*	*et moyeux d'uefs tous crus,*
VAT	**persil, ung pou de sauge**	**qui veult,**	**et des moyeulx d'oeufz tous cruz,**

VAL	*du pain parmy,*	– – – – – –	*deffait de vostre boillon,*
MAZ	– – –	et coulez parmi l'estermine,	deffaicte de vostre boillon
BN	*du pain,*	*passés par l'estamine,*	– – – – –
VAT	**et du pain,**	**tout passé parmy l'estamine,**	**deffait de vostre boullon,**

VAL	*du verjus;*	*et du formage, qui veult.*
MAZ	et de verjus;	et de fromaige qui . l veult.
BN	*et du vergus;*	*et du fromage qui veult.*
VAT	**et i fault ung pou de verjuz;**	**et de bon froumage qui veult.**

A colour described as *vergay* in a food is normally the result of a mixture of ingredients which are green and yellow. In practice this usually means a combination of green herbs, especially parsley, with saffron.[1] The *Brouet vergay* of this recipe has parsley and sage—together with some ginger for flavouring—mixed first of all, in the *VAL* version, with egg yolks alone for the *gay* effect, and then later with saffron as well. At what period the saffron was added to the recipe, in order to reinforce the colour provided by the yolks, is difficult to judge because *MAZ* has omitted the passage that would have contained a mention of both of the thickeners, the yolks and the eggs, and perhaps of the saffron as well if this additional colorant was introduced by *Z*. The *Menagier*, whose text is closely related to that of *VAT*, inserts a comment that the function of the egg yolks is "pour lier"; they should, furthermore, says our knowledgeable bourgeois, be considered merely as alternatives to the ground bread in this respect.[2]

The procedure of adding a piece of pork as a flavorant to the pot in which the *grain* is being cooked, a procedure we see for the first time copied somewhat hesitantly in the previous recipe, is still not understood as such by *VAL* who writes *lait* for *lart*; the justification of the procedure—"pour donner goust"—is copied this time by *MAZ*, although *BN* persists in skipping it.

27. Rappé

VAL	*Rappé.*	- - - - - - - - - -	*Metez grain*
MAZ	Rappé.	Mecter vostre grain halez en broches,	puis
BN	*Rappé.*	- - - - - - - - - - -	*Metés vostre grain*
VAT	**Rappé.**	- - - - - - - - - - -	**Mettez vostre grain**

VAL	*surfrire en saing, halé;*	*premierement prenez du pain*
MAZ	souffrissiez en sain;	puis prener du pain
BN	*frire en sain de lart sur le charbon;*	*trempés du pain*
VAT	**souffrire en sain de lart;**	**puis prenez du pain**

VAL	*et le metez tramper*	*en boullon,*	*passé parmy l'estamine*
MAZ	et le mecter tremper	en boillon de beuf	et passis parmi l'estermine
BN		*en bouillon de buef*	*et le coullés*
VAT	**et mettez tremper**	**en boullon de beuf**	**et passez parmy l'estamine**

VAL	*et getez sus;*	- - - - - - - - - - -
MAZ	et gectiez sur vostre grain;	puis affiner gigimbre et deffaicte de verjus
BN	*et metés sur vostre grain;*	*puis affinés gingembre, deffait de verjus*
VAT	**et gectez sur vostre grain;**	**puis affinez gingenbre, deffaictes de verjus**

[1] "Pain, persil, saffren bien pou en la verdeur pour le faire vertgay": Recipe 76. *Cf.* also Recipes 73, 87 and 163. This is the colour that English recipes describe as *gawdy green*, literally "joyous green": see, for instance, the instruction "Colour it gawdy grene" in the *Forme of Cury* (Hieatt and Butler, p. 124, §115.)

[2] *Menagier de Paris*, §112; p. 167.

VAL - - - - - - - - - - *prenez groisellez ou*
MAZ et de vin, et mecter sur vostre grain; puis prenez grousselles ou
BN *et de vin, mis en vostre boullon; prennés des grosselles ou*
VAT **et de vin, et mettez sur vostre grain; puis prennez de groiselles ou**

VAL *verjus boulu bien pou, et metez en vos escuelle et drecés sus.*
MAZ verjus esgrenez en aigue et mecter dedans le[1] escuelles et dressiez.
BN *du verjus esgrené et metés dedans.*
VAT **du verjus en grain et mettez dedans.**

The *grain*, whichever one may be chosen by the cook,[2] undergoes two cooking stages in this recipe for *Rappé*, roasting and frying, although initially the *Viandier*'s indication of the first stage was so meager—only the adjective *halé* alludes to it—that either *Y* or *Z* seems to have missed it altogether. *BN* and *VAT* set the raw meat frying immediately; *MAZ* alone picked up the significance of the adjective *halé* and amplifies upon the laconic style so common in *VAL*.[3]

VAL contains a very serious oversight, an instance perhaps of lineal haplography: the preparation of the binding and the preparation of the spice both conclude with an instruction that these mixtures are to be cast over the frying meat. The similarity in the two sections of text may explain why *VAL* has omitted the spice preparation entirely.

BN has this spice preparation added directly to the sauce in the frying pan rather than poured over the meat. If *BN* is not merely in error, this sauce would have to be used as a basting in order to obtain the same effect as in the other versions.

The name of this dish, *rappé*, is fairly common in mediæval cookery books. It normally designates a dish in which fresh grapes are an ingredient or constitute a garnish.[4] The

---

[1] *le*: *sic*.

[2] *Rappé* is a type of sauced dish, made of mashed grapes, whose general-purpose sauce, *rappee*, is listed in the *VAT* Table (after Recipe 158) among a number of other unboiled sauces. No recipe for this *rappee* is copied by *VAT* at that point in his reproduction of the book, however, perhaps because this earlier recipe for the dish *Rappé* could already be read in the *Viandier*.

[3] The *Menagier* (in §113; p. 168) indicates that the meat is to be boiled and then fried in lard. Spices to be used include "grainne, gingembre, etc." When being served, the meat is dressed with the sauce, which in turn is covered with boiled *verjus de grain* or—the same alternative offered by the *Viandier*—boiled currants.

[4] In English recipe books of the period raisins are used rather than fresh grapes, and usually in combination with other fruits. See Austin, pp. 16 and 28; and Hieatt and Butler, part II, §§50, 61 and 87; part III, §18; and part IV, §85 (in Warner's ed. of the *Forme of Cury*, §83). The English names, *Rapey, Rapy, Rapee* and *Rapes* clearly have nothing to do with turnips, as Hieatt and Butler suggest (p. 210).

For Cotgrave (1611) *rappé* is an only slightly fermented grape juice: "A verie small wine comming of water cast upon the mother of grapes, which have beene pressed; also, the wine which comes from a vessell filled with whole and sound grapes (divided from the cluster) and some wine among; which being drawne out, is supplyed by the leavings of good wine, put into the vessell, and revived and kept in heart a whole yeare long by the said grapes" (*s. v. rapé*).

phrase found here in *VAL*, "prenez ... verjus boulu," is a shorter form of what *VAL* wrote in Recipe 10 (for *Chaudun de porc*): "Prenez verjus esgrené cuit en yaue et metez les grenez en vostre potaige." In this earlier recipe *VAT* "corrects" the word *grains* (copied by *MAZ* and *BN* from *Z* and *Y*) to *grappes* because the cook is to use boiled seedless grapes.[5] An alternative to grapes are *groisellez*—currants, red or white—likewise boiled. As *VAL* alone mentions, though, this fruit, whether grapes or currants, should be boiled only slightly (*boulu bien pou*) in order that the *rappé* have its characteristic consistency.

28. Civé de veel

VAL	*Civé de veel.*	*Rosti tout cru en la broche*	– –
MAZ	Civel de veaul.	Soit viaul rotis tout cruz en broche	ou sur le gril
BN	*Civé de lievres.*	*Rosticés tout cru en broche*	*ou sus le gril*
VAT	**Civé de veel.**	**Rosti en broche**	**ou sur le greil**

VAL	*sans trop laissier cuire, decopés et metés*
MAZ	sans tropt lessiez cuire, puis coppez par pieces et mecter
BN	*sans trop lessier cuire, descouppés par pieces et*
VAT	**sans trop laissier cuire, decouppez par pieces et mettez**

VAL	*surfrire en saing,*	*et oingnons menus;*
MAZ	souffrire,	et oignons menuz menusiez;
BN	*frisiés en sain de lart*	*et oignons menus minciés*[1];
VAT	**souffrire en sain,**	**et couppez ongnons bien menuz frire avec;**

VAL	*prenez pain roussi*	*destrampé de vin et de puree*
MAZ	puis prener pain rotis,	destramper de vin et de puree de pois
BN	*prennés pain hallé*	*deffait de vin et de bouillon de beuf*
VAT	**puis prenez pain brullé**	**deffait de vin et de boullon de beuf**

VAL	*ou de boullon,*	*faite boulir avec vostre grain;*
MAZ	en boillon de beuf	et faicte boulir avecques vostre grain; puis
BN	*ou de puree de pois*	*et boullés aveques grain;*
VAT	**ou de puree de poys**	**et faictes boullir avec vostre grain; puis**

VAL	*affinez gingembre, canelle,*	–	*graine de paradis,*	*saffren*
MAZ	affiner gigimbre, cannelle,	–	graine de paradis	et saffrain
BN	*affinés gingembre, canelle*	–	– – – –	*et saffran,*
VAT	**affinez gingenbre, canelle,**	**girofle,**	**grainne de paradiz**	**et saffran**

---

[5] The *Menagier* expatiates on the preparation of this fruit: "Puiz ayez vertjus de grain ou groseilles qui soient boulyes une onde en la paelle percee ou en autre eaue, ou drappel, estamine, ou autrement, c'estassavoir pour oster la premiere verdeur" (§113; p. 168). This *premiere verdeur* which is quickly to be boiled off is the excessive acidity of the unripe grapes.

[1] The scribe wrote only five vertical strokes for the *min* of *mincies*.

VAL	- - - - - - -	*deffait de verjus et de vin aigre;*
MAZ	pour lui donner couleur,	deffaicte de verjus et de vin aigre.
BN	- - - - - - -	*deffaites de verjus et de vin aigre;*
VAT	**pour luy donner couleur, et le**	**deffaictes de verjus et de vin aigre;**

VAT **et soyt liant, et assez d'ongnons, et que le pain soit brun,**

VAL	- - - -	*fort d'espices.*	
BN	- - - -	*et soit fort espicé.*	
VAT	**et agu de vin aigre et**	**fort d'espices,**	**et doibt estre jaunet.**

In *BN* the scribe copied the wrong name, *Civé de lievres*, for the dish following the *Rappé*, although the recipe that *BN* proceeds to reproduce after this name is indeed the one called veal stew in the other manuscripts. *BN* omits one of the spices, grains of paradise, whereas *VAT* adds one, cloves. Besides this addition, *VAT* makes others of an interpretive nature, toward the end.

The four manuscripts use four different terms to indicate the degree to which the bread is to be toasted: it is to be *roussi*, *rotis*, *hallé*, and *brullé*. An interesting spectrum of browns is thus covered here, from a light tan or russet through to a very dark shade. The exact depth of colour of the toast is important, here and in other dishes that make use of bread or toast as a thickener, because this particular ingredient will help determine the hue of the finished dish. It should be observed that colour is always a prime consideration in mediæval gastronomy. Since the *Civé de veel* is to possess a yellowish shade derived from the saffron in it—a colour defined by *VAT* as *jaunet*—the warning issued by the *Menagier* is quite apropos: the cook should select "pain roussi seulement, ou chappelleures de pain non brulé, pour ce qu'il seroit trop noir pour civé de veel."[2]

Three of the qualities that *VAT* emphasizes in his version of this recipe enter into a definition of the generic name of the dish. The *civé*, *civet* or *civel* is by nature thick, oniony and spicy. To ensure the proper thickness, the *Viandier* uses puree of peas here for the first time, to reinforce the action of the usual toast; finely chopped onions will lend all of their flavour to the meat and to the dish as a whole; and, in the third place, the three standard aromatic spices—ginger, cinnamon and grains of paradis, to which *VAT* adds cloves—are used in the sauce in sufficient quantities that even *VAL* says that it is "fort d'espices"! The colour of any *civé* will vary somewhat according to the meat it is made for, but the basic qualities will remain. Of these the essential one, for which the dish may have received its name, is the onions. More properly the original ingredient was chives,[3]

[2] *Menagier de Paris*, §115; p. 168.

[3] In Latin, the word is *cepae*. This term, however, denoted all types of onions including the Old French *cives*, "chives," and the Old French *ongnon*. The *Enseignements* has a recipe for a *chivel* of pork in which the ingredients include chopped pork, fried onions, pepper and spices (p. 181, l. 14; *Petit traité*, p. 214). A later dish in the same work is called "cuttle-fish *en chivé d'oignons*" (p. 187, l. 118; p. 225). By the fifteenth century the word *civet* is related to the Latin *cibarium*; see Recipe 18, n1.

but *oingnon* is always the name of the vegetable in early French recipe books.[4]

29. Civé de lievres

VAL *Cyvé de lievres. Doit estre noir et le pain bien brulé*
MAZ Civel de livre. Il doit estre noir et le pain bien bruller
BN *Civé de lievres.* [Printed with the *Civé de veel*, above.]
VAT **Civé de lievre. Doibt estre noir et le pain bien brullé**

VAL - - - - - - *et fait comme cely de veel,*
MAZ - - - - - - et soit fait conme de veaul,
VAT **pour luy donner couleur, et se fait de telles estoffes que celuy de veel,**

VAL *mez on ne doit laver la char.*
MAZ mais hon ne doit point laver la chart.
VAT **et ne fault point laver le lyevre.**

BN does not copy the couple of lines of this recipe for *Civé de lievres*, in all probability because he had already mistakenly copied the name of the dish over the previous recipe.[1]

The difference between veal stew (Recipe 28) and hare stew, apart from the major ingredient, is largely one of colour: the latter is to be dark, this colour being in part a function of the darkness of the toast used as a thickener.[2]

30. Civé de connins

BN *Civé de conis. Doit estre ainsi fait comme civé de lievres*
VAT **Civé de connins. Doibt estre fort et non mie si noir comme**

BN *ou bousac, comme dessus est dit.*
VAT **celuy de lyevre ne sy[1] jaune comme celuy de veel, mais entre deux;**

et se fait de teles estoffes comme cellui de veel.[2]

---

[4] The *Regimen sanitatis* of Magninus Mediolanensis (in Part 3, Ch. 14, "De radicibus") distinguishes only between *porri albi*, *allea* and *cepe*.

[1] A comparison can be made between the *Viandier*'s *Civé de lievre* and a dish called *Llepre a schiberi* in the Nice manuscript, §8, f. 3r. In this latter preparation pepper predominates.

[2] "Faire asler du pain tant qu'il soit assez noir" (*Recueil de Riom*, §10: *Ung civé de lievres*). See also the *Menagier*, §116; p. 169.

[1] *sy* followed by *no* stroked out.

[2] The last phrase, *mais entre deux ... de veel*, is added by a later hand into the space left between this recipe and the following chapter heading.

It is probably *Y* who added the new entry for rabbit stew, but the versions of this recipe that *BN* and *VAT* show have little in common. It is again the colour that, according to *VAT*, defines this particular variant of the *civé* genre. *BN*'s comparison between a *Civé de conis* and the *Bousac de lievre ou de conis* (Recipe 20) is interesting, for while the rabbit is roasted and then fried, as for the other dish, the earlier recipe uses no onions, has white bread rather than toast, and is a loose rather than a stiff mixture. Although the spice combination is similar, there is no saffron in a *boussac*; this colorant is, though, a usual ingredient in a *civé*. The significant similarity between the two dishes seems therefore for *BN* to be the two-fold cooking procedure the meat is to undergo.

Rostz de chair (MAZ, BN, VAT)

31. Porc rosti

VAL	*Porc rosti.*	– – – – –	– – – – –
MAZ	Porc rotis.	Au verjus;	et aulcuns y mectent
BN	*Porc.*	*Au verjus;*	*aucuns y metent*
VAT	**Rost de porc.**[1]	**Se mengue au verjus;**	**et aucuns y mettent**

VAL	*Dez oignons desoubz,*
MAZ	au dessoubz oignons,
BN	*des oingnons,*
VAT	**des aulx en la lechefricte avec le sain qui chiet du rost,**

VAL		*du vin et du verjus;*
MAZ		vin, verjus;
BN		*vin et verjus.*
VAT	**des ongnons,**	**du vin et du verjus, et en font saulse;**

VAL	*lardé rosti, a poudre d'espicez et de saffren, au verjus;*

VAL	*et en pasté,*	*au saffren, a poudre d'espices,*	*et au verjus.*
MAZ	et en pasté,		au verjus de grain.
VAT	**aussi porc mis en pasté,**		**se mengue au verjus.**

The first recipe in the new section, which *VAT* titles "Rostz de chair," is for pork. The dish *Porc rosti* is an appropriate choice to open this chapter since, according to contemporary medical doctrine, cold and moist meats should be roasted (rather than boiled, fried or

[1] *porc* is clearly written *port* by *VAT*.

baked),[2] and since pork is universally recognized by the same authorities as the coldest and moistest meat of all four-footed animals.[3]

Such a roast as this does not entail a very complex procedure for its cooking. At its simplest, this dish requires only a basting sauce and a serving sauce; both of these are provided in the above recipe. *VAL* does not even mention a serving sauce; it is only *VAT* who indicates at the beginning that verjuice is a serving sauce rather than merely part of the name of the dish: *Porc au verjus*. *Z* has made the onions optional in the basting sauce. *VAT* offers the option of strengthening this sauce by adding garlic to it.

Two further modes of preparing pork do not appear in all of the manuscripts. *VAL* alone suggests wrapping (or barding) a pork roast with bacon—a remarkably unusual procedure which runs quite contrary to classical teaching. In all likelihood *VAL* is in error here. His recipe for this *lardé rosti*, as he terms it, was probably accidentally copied from the following section on roast veal; *VAL* has not reproduced Recipe 32, and in fact the "third" method of preparing pork, in a pasty, is likewise in *VAL* similar to what is found in the following recipe for preparing veal in a pasty. In copying this present Recipe 31 his eye seems simply to have skipped on to Recipe 32.

In the *Viandier* tradition, therefore, we may safely surmise that there are in this chapter just two recipes for pork: roasted, or baked in a pasty.

With regard to the alternative dish, pork pie, *MAZ* and *VAT* agree at least in part. The *Menagier de Paris* specifies that the cook should put "du vertjus de grain dessus" when serving pork pie,[4] so it seems that *VAT* omitted the important qualification "de grain."[5] This garnish is reminiscent of what is used in the *Rappé* (Recipe 27).

32. Veel rosti

MAZ	Viaul rotis.	Soit pourboulir, et larder	et rotis;	a pouldre d'espices
BN	*Item, veel.*	*Soit parboulli et lardé;*	– –	*a la cameline;*
VAT	**Veau.**	**Fort pourboully et lardé;**	– –	**se mengue a la cameline;**

MAZ	ou saffrain;	et en pasté,	a poudre fine de gigimbre
BN	– –	*item, veel en pasté:*	*prennés poudre d'espices,*
VAT	– –	**et en pasté,**	**mettez y de la pouldre d'espices,**

MAZ	et de cannelle.		
BN		*saffran*	*et vergus.*
VAT	**du lart et du**	**saffren;**	**et se mengue au verjus.**

---

[2] "Et est diligenter notandum que carnes ... declinantes ad humiditatem debent assari ut earum humiditas temperetur" (Magninus, *Regimen sanitatis*, ch. 17 "De carnibus").

[3] "Chars de porch, sor totes chars de bestes, est plus froide et plus moiste, et devés entendre ce de le domesce, car li chars de porc sauvaige [*i.e.* boar], a comparison a le domesce, si est caude et seche ... " (Aldobrandino, p. 122).

[4] *Menagier*, §373; p. 271.

[5] It might be noted, however, that the sixteenth-century usage reported by Randle Cotgrave allowed *verjus*, unqualified, to denote the juice grapes themselves: "*Verius*: m. Veriuyce; especially that which is made of sowre, and unripe grapes; also, the grapes whereof it is made."

Veal is a relatively temperate meat.[1] In order that it not be excessively dried during the roasting process, the cook must take two preliminary, precautionary steps: parboiling will raise the degree of moisture in the veal; then wrapping it in bacon strips will provide a protective coating against the intensity of the flame under the spit or grill. The *Menagier* makes an interesting comment about this second procedure, saying, "Ainsi le souloit l'en faire,"[2] suggesting by this a certain respect for the *Viandier* as his prime source, even though in his opinion the work might in his own time represent a somewhat outdated procedure. He demonstrates again as well his complete independence of taste.

MAZ names spices here that *VAL* in the previous recipe indicated (erroneously?) were for a basting sauce. *Y* (that is, *BN* and *VAT*) does not mention any ingredients for a basting sauce, but states that the roast should be served with cameline sauce as a dressing. The *Menagier* shares *Y*'s version.

A second possibility for a veal dish—as above for pork—calls for fine spices[3] to be baked with the meat in a pasty, to which spices *Y* adds saffron, and *VAT* alone adds bacon. As with the pork, veal pie is to be eaten with verjuice, perhaps "verjus en grain," the mash of verjuice grapes seen in the recipe for *Rappé*. *Y* probably had merely the phrase "au verjus,"[4] amplified by *VAT*, but typically abbreviated by *BN* (*saffran et vergus*) so that verjuice seems to be one of the ingredients in the pie itself.

33. Fraise de veel

VAL *Fraise de veel.*
MAZ Fraisse de veaul. Prenez la

---

[1] Beef is dry, but young animals are by nature more moist than the mature member of the species. See, for example, J. Albini, *De sanitatis custodia*, ed. Carbonelli (Pinerolo, 1906), part 2, dist. 2, tract. 2, ch. 3, "De diversitate nutrimenti ex parte etatis animalum": "Carnes autem decrepitorum non bene nutriunt quia aquisiuerunt superfluam siccitatem ut in pluribus. animalia autem in quorum complesione dominatur siccitas. tempore lactationis postquam iam sunt formata aliqualiter et post illud. laudabilius nutriunt quam in sequenti tempore. nam propter propinquitatem ad tempus quo nata fuerunt et quia lacte nutrientur. temperatam et convenientem habent humiditatem et bonum generant nutrimentem. si bono modo coquinentur sicut patet de carnibus vitulorum lactantium et edorum" (p. 78).

[2] *Menagier de Paris*, §144; p. 179. The *Menagier*'s own recipe—his preferred alternative—for roast veal calls for the meat to be seared first, then larded and roasted.

[3] Concerning this blend of unspecified *poudre d'espices*, see the results of a study by Jean-Louis Flandrin in "Internationalisme, nationalisme et régionalisme dans la cuisine des XIVe et XVe siécles: le témoignage des livres de cuisine," *Manger et Boire au Moyen Age*, vol. 2, p. 85 which show that the percentage of recipes requiring such a mixture is 49% in the *Libro della cocina*, 44.8% in the *Forme of Cury*, but only 8.7% in the *Viandier*. The authors of the *Viandier* seem to be more concerned with specifying the particular spices to be employed than in resorting to a general-purpose mixture.

[4] This phrase (*au verjus*, or *a la cameline*, or *a la jansse*), which indicates the serving sauce with which a dish is to be garnished, appears baldly, without explanation, in Recipes 34 and 35, and becomes common later in the *Viandier*, particularly in the recipes for fish.

BN	*Pour faire fraise de veel.*	*Prennés vostre grain*
VAT	**Pour faire frase de veel que l'en appelle charpie.**	**Prenez vostre grain**

VAL	– – – –	*Decopez tres menu,*	*friolez en saing de lart;*
MAZ	et la cuisiez	et la coppez bien menue	et la friolez en sain;
BN	– – – –	*et descouppés bien menu,*	*puis le frisiés en sain;*
VAT	**s'il est tout cuit,**	**et decouppez bien menu,**	**puis le frisiez en sain de lart;**

VAL	*broiez gingenbre, saffren*	*et eufs crus*
MAZ	puis broyer gigimbre, saffrain	et euf crus deffait de verjus
BN	*et broiés gingembre, saffren;*	*prennés oeux tous crus,*
VAT	**et puis brayez gingenbre, saffren,**	**et batez des oeufz tous cruz**

VAL	*et les fillez par desus*	*en fruiant.*
MAZ	et fillez par dessus;	et fait l'on le veel qu'il soit bien froit.
BN	*fillés sur*	*vostre friture;*
VAT	**et les fillez sur**	**vostre grain ou sain;**

VAT	**brayez espices, mettés de la pouldre d'espices—combien que**

BN	– – – – – – – –	*mengiés au verjus vert.*
VAT	**aucuns n'y en veullent point, et le menguent**	**au verjus vert.**

Fraise de veel is not dealt with by the *Menagier*, although all four manuscripts of the *Viandier* have copied it, and recipes are given for it in the *Enseignements*[1] and in Chiquart's *Du fait de cuisine*.[2] The *fraise* of a calf is, however, at least defined by the *Menagier*: "La fraze c'est la caillette, la pance et les boyaulz, lesquelz les tripiers vendent tous nettoyez, lavez et appareilliez, trempans en belle eaue necte."[3] A satisfactory translation of *fraise* is "tripe."

None of the influential (and hypothetical) manuscripts in the *Viandier* tradition—those that I call *X*, *Y* and *Z*—appears to have noticed that an assumption was made by *O* that the meat in this recipe is to be boiled before the steps outlined in the text are begun. *MAZ* and *VAT* on their own insert explicit references to this preparatory step: "la cuisiez" (writes *MAZ*), and "s'il est tout cuit ... " (adds *VAT*).[4]

[1] In the *Enseignements* there is a dish called *Char de veal a la charpie* (p. 182, l. 33; *Petit traité*, p. 215).

[2] *Du fait de cuisine*, §61, f. 85v. The *Sent soví* contains as well several recipes for the preparation of *ffrexures* which bear certain resemblances to what is in the *Viandier*. See also the *Froyse* edited by Austin, pp. 45 and 86; and the *Liber cure cocorum*, p. 50.

[3] *Menagier de Paris*, §14; p. 128.

[4] According to Rudolf Grewe, the first stage in preparing the *ffrexures* of the *Sent soví* consists always of a boiling or parboiling of the calf's mesentery before it is fried (§121, n2). This remains the modern culinary procedure.

The process by which the spices and eggs are to be added gives rise to a number of variants among the manuscripts, perhaps because of the term that appears in *VAL*. *Fruiant* is the present participle of the verb *fruire*, a variant form of *frire*. *MAZ(X)*, or perhaps *Z*, realizes that the eggs will coagulate if fried with the meat, and so directs that the eggs-and-spice mixture is to be added *after* the meat is fried (*froit*, past participle of *frire* or *fruire*). *Y* tries to avoid the difficulties caused by the participles of this verb by altering the sentence in order to use the noun *friture*. *VAT* in turn tries to clarify the word *friture*[5] by writing that the mixture should be poured over the *grain* as it is lying *in* the grease ("ou sain").

Y adds advice about the proper serving sauce for veal tripe, *verjus vert*. This is the sauce which *MAZ* had called *verjus reverdi* in Recipe 3 and then later again in Recipe 34.[6] It is a broadly recognized sauce, but *VAT* apparently considers this to be a less desirable alternative to a simple sprinkling with spice powder.

The *VAT* title for this recipe includes an alternate and more descriptive name for the dish: *Charpie*. This name is used twice in the *Enseignements*[7] for this treatment of veal in which the meat is cut into very slender strips or shredded into its fibres.[8]

34. Mouton rosti

VAL	*Mouton rosti.*	- -	*Au sel menu ou a la cameline ou verjus.*
MAZ	Mouton rotis.	Il se mainge	a sel menuz, a la cameline ou au verjus vert.
BN	*Mouton en rost.*	- - -	*Au sel menu ou a la cameline ou au verjus.*
VAT	**Mouston en rost.**	- - -	**Au sel menu, a la cameline ou au verjus.**

Only *MAZ(X)* among all the copies of this brief recipe makes it explicit that the fine salt, cameline sauce, and (green) verjuice are to be to used as serving sauces.

---

[5] *VAT* uses the word *friture* only once, and that is in the supplementary material toward its end (Recipe 190).

[6] *MAZ* listed the ingredients for this *verjus reverdi* in §3: ground green herbs in verjuice.

[7] *Enseignements*, p. 182, l. 33; *Petit traité de cuisine*, p. 215.

[8] Tilander (*Glanures*, p. 43) had surmised that the noun *charpie* was a composite: "Probablement appelée ainsi parce qu'il était permis d'en manger les jours de jeûne"; he offered no further rationale for this explanation of the term.

The verb *charpir* is used in Recipe 189 (*q. v.*) where the sense, "to shred," is defined by the text, and in the *Enseignements* (p. 184, l. 121; *Petit traité*, p. 220) where the cook is told how to cut the meat, which in that case is chicken: "Charpez la char bien menu eschevelee [*i.e.* like a hair]." Recipe 189 (for *Lassis de blanc de chappon*) indicates that such treatment should reduce the meat to strings or strands of fibres much like carded wool: "Prendre tout le blanc du chappon et le charpir ainsi qu'on charpiroit lainne."

35. Chevreaux, aigneaux

VAL	*Chevreax, aigneaux.*	*Metez en eaue bollante,*
MAZ	Chevrieulx et aigneaulx rotis.	Mecter les en aigue boillant
BN	*Chevriaux, aingniaux.*	*Boutés en eaue boullant*
VAT	**Chevreaux, aigneaux.**	**Reffaictes les en eaue boullant**

VAL	*plumés,*	- - - - -	*halés en broche,*
MAZ	- -	et les tirés tantoust,	puis les halés en broches,
BN	- -	*et traiés tantost,*	- - - - -
VAT	- -	**et les tirez tantost hors**	**et les hallez ung pou en la broche**

VAL	*lard'es,*	*rosticiez;*	*a la camelline.*
MAZ	larder et	rotissez;	et maingier a la cameline.
BN	*lard'es et*	*metés en broche;*	*a la cameline.*
VAT	**et puis les lardez;**		**et mengiez a la cameline.**

Kid and lamb are parboiled, as veal was, before being roasted. *VAT* uses the verb ***reffaire*** here for the first time.[1] It is a proper technical term, attested only from the fourteenth century in this context and in the sense it has throughout the *Viandier*. ***Reffaire*** means to boil (normally a meat) briefly but sufficiently to engorge the object's cells with moisture; subsequent cooking, whether by roasting, frying or baking, will as a result of this plumping be more penetrating, less dessicating and toughening. Barding is frequently used in conjunction with this parboiling, particularly for a dry meat.[2]

Plumés, a direction found in *VAT* at the point where the other manuscripts have an instruction to take the meat from the water, seems to be an error, perhaps for *pluniés*.[3] In any case *plumer* is used elsewhere in the *Viandier* only with the sense of removing skins from almonds or of plucking feathers from a goose.[4]

---

[1] The word here is probably *VAT*'s own insertion. The *Menagier* (§145; p. 179), who is quite conversant with proper culinary jargon, and who normally seems eager to show it, uses only the word *boutez* that we find in *BN*. Compare this with the tenderizing treatment that the *Menagier* accords the roe deer: "Chevrel sauvage ... soit bouté en eaue boulant et retiré tantost pource qu'il est plus tendre que cerf" (§88; p. 155). He does, however, in §258 (pp. 223–224), outline the procedure denoted by the verb *reffaire*, which proper term he does use at that point.

[2] "Assum exquavis carne hoc modo facies, si annicula erit, ubi modicum ebullierit ex cacabo exemptam illaridabis, voluique ad ignem iubebis, quo ad bene coquatur" (Platina, f. 47r: "Toute chair vieille et dure rostiras a cette façon / et premierement la parbouliras dedans ung chaulderon / apres la larderas tresbien et mettras en broche et icelle feras tourner jusques a ce qu'elle soyt cuyte": *Platine en françois*, f. 57r).

[3] See the verb *plungier* in Recipes 104 *VAT*, and 120.

[4] Recipe 36. There is a possibility that *VAL* may have picked up this word accidentally from the next recipe—but then for some reason may have omitted it, of all words, when he came to copy §36.

BN reveals a certain hesitancy about the roasting of this parboiled meat. The *Viandier* directs that the meat is to be browned on a spit before being covered with strips of bacon, a procedure that will sear the whole of the surface of the meat and protect its juices as it is roasted; *BN*, however, omits this searing step, bards the meat directly and then sets it on the spit. Even *VAT* is cautious about searing: "Hallez ung pou," he writes. The *Menagier*, with *BN*, omits the step altogether.

36. Oyes

VAL	*Oyes.*	- - - - - - - - - - - - - -
MAZ	Oyes rotiees.	Plumey a sec, puis les reffaicte en aigue chaude
BN	*Oues*[1] *en rost.*	- - - - - - - - - - - - - -
VAT	**Oes et oysons en rost.**	- - - - - - - - - - - - - -

MAZ et copper les alles, le colz et les piez; et les rotissiez sans larder;

VAL		*aux aulx blancs ou vers,*	*ou poivre noir ou jaune.*
MAZ	et les maingier	aux haulx blans ou vers,	ou a poivre noir ou jane;
BN		*aux aulx blans ou vers,*	*ou au poivre jaunet*[2] *ou noir.*
VAT	**se menguent**	**aux aulx blans ou vers,**	**ou poivre noir ou a la jance;**

MAZ qui veult, aux haulx boulir.[3] Et les yssues se doivent bien laver
unesfois ou deux avec du sel et de l'aigue, et mectre sur l'oye envouleper,
ait du foye, de la teste, des alles, des piez et des aultres yssues;
l'on les doit mectre cuire en ung pout avec char salee, puis les lessiez
reffroidiez; et les maingier au vin aigre et a parressy avant que l'oye
soit rotier car c'est le premier que l'on doit maingier de l'oye,
et est appellez la petite oye.

VAT **et aucuns les menguent a la saulse saint Merry, c'est assavoir aulx
destrempez a la petite oue ou que on a d'aultre eaue grasse. Et
sont aucuns bons frians, quant l'oe ou l'oyson sont rostiz, qu'ilz
les portent aux oyers saint Merry ou au carrefour saint Sevrin ou
a la porte Baudés coupper et les despecier par lesdiz oyers qui les
mettent tellement que par morceaulx et par lez que, en chascun morcel,
a pel, chair et os, et le font tres gentement.**

---

[1] *Oues*: the first letter is missing in a hole in the manuscript.

[2] The sauce is written clearly *januet* by *BN* here and in Recipes 49, 60, 63, 72, 79, 124 and 162.

[3] Read this alternative sauce as *haulx boulis*; *cf.* *lessiez* and *rotier* below, which function as an infinitive and past participle respectively.

The goose enjoyed a preeminent position among roasting fowl in mediæval gastronomic esteem, owing in large measure to the high degree of moisture its meat contains and its consequent appropriateness for roasting.[4] The recipe for roast goose in the *Viandier* is not extensive or complex. Only the serving sauce receives attention in all four manuscripts. All four sauces listed as alternatives by *VAL*, *MAZ* and *BN* are among those described later in the sauce section of the *Viandier*; they are therefore more or less standard preparations. To be noted in passing is that both garlic and pepper are held by all of the major authorities to be extremely, even dangerously, warm and dry in the fourth degree.[5]

VAT has what appears to be a variant for the yellow pepper sauce: *la jance*. While this is quite a common sauce, described along with the others in Recipes 168, 157, 158, 165 and 164 respectively, the word *jance* may very well be a misreading of *janet* by the scribe.[6]

The *Enseignements* specifies a garlic sauce for roast goose in summer and a hot pepper sauce in winter.[7] The *Menagier de Paris* serves goose in winter either with a white garlic sauce or with *VAT*'s *jance*.[8] For *rost d'oyes* the *Recueil de Riom* offers a recipe for a *Saulse d'aux de Bresbant* which consists of garlic, egg yolks and verjuice.[9] Chiquart specifies *jance* for gosling.[10]

The two long commentaries appended quite independently by *MAZ* and by *VAT* attest to the popularity of roast goose as a dish. *MAZ(X)*'s note provides a definition of *la petite oye* that is useful in turn in the reading of *VAT*'s note.[11]

---

[4] Eberhard (§24) warns that goose should not, in fact, be boiled because with this cooking method its grease will not be separated from the meat of its carcass. He warns also that the consumption of goose drippings is dangerous for fat people.

[5] Platearius, Aldobrandino, Crescentius, the *Nef de santé*, etc.

[6] The opposite possibility, *jane* copied for *jance*, is seen in Recipe 121 *MAZ*.

[7] *Enseignements*, p. 183, l. 68; *Petit traité*, p. 217.

[8] *Menagier*, §148; p. 180.

[9] *Recueil de Riom*, §42.

[10] *Du fait de cuisine*, f. 26r.

[11] Regarding "la petite oye," see the *Menagier*'s recipe (§71; p. 149) titled *Potage d'une petite oe*. Neither Brereton and Ferrier nor Pichon offer an explanation of this "petite oe" in the *Menagier*. Though the preparation which is described in the *Tractatus*, part II, §9, has no name, it is undoubtedly a variation of a *petite oie*.

Pichon and Vicaire have their own note on the *oyers rôtisseurs* of Paris between the thirteenth and fifteenth centuries (p. 87, n3 in their edition). See Étienne Boileau, *Réglemens sur les arts et métiers de Paris, rédigés au XIIIe siècle et connus sous le nom du Livre des mestiers*, Collection de documents inédits sur l'histoire de la France, A 55, ed. G.-B. Depping (Paris: Crapelet, 1837), pp. 175–178 ("Des Cuiseniers. C'est l'ordenance du mestier des oyers de la ville de Paris") and 356–357. See also Lebault, pp. 331–332. Concerning the place names mentioned by *VAT*, *saint Merry*, the *carrefour saint Sevrin* and *la porte Baudés*, see *Les rues de Paris*, ed. Étienne Barbazan and Dominique Méon in *Fabliaux et contes de poètes françois*, 4 vols. (Paris, 1808), vol. 2, pp. 266, 241 and 271, respectively.

37. Poules rosties / Poulés rostis

VAL	*Poles rosties.*	- - - - - - - - - - - -
MAZ	Poulés rotis.	Soient plumey en aigue, rotis, larder; et maingier
BN	*Poulés.*[1]	- - - - - - - - - - - -
VAT	**Poullés et poucins.**	- - - - - - - - - - **Se menguent**

VAL	*A la cameline ou verjus ou froide[2] sauge;*	*en pasté,*
MAZ	a la cameline ou a verjus vers ou a la froide sauge;	ou en pasté
BN	*A la froide sauge ou verjus en rost;*	*ou en pasté,*
VAT	**a la froyde saulge ou en rost;**	**ou en pasté,**

VAL	*pourdré[3] d'espices, morceaux de lart;*	*au verjus vert.*
MAZ	soient mis morcellet de lart, poudre d'espices;	et verjus de grain.
BN	*aux espices et du lart a cuire;*	*et vergus de grain.*
VAT		**au verjus vert en esté**

VAT	**ou sangle en[4] yver.**

For this sort of roast poultry *VAL* states that hens (in the feminine) are to be the meat whereas the other manuscripts have either pullets or chicks. *MAZ(X)* alone writes the details of the roasting procedure with which none of the *Viandier*'s main manuscripts seems to have bothered. The three serving sauces of *VAL* are reproduced by *MAZ*—though with *verjus vers* rather than plain verjuice.[5] *Y* seems to have left out cameline sauce as a possible dressing, putting the cold sage sauce first. *VAT* carelessly skips the word *verjus* itself, making *en rost* the nonsensical alternative.

The name *Froide sauge*, used for one of the sauces here, is as commonly used to designate a cold dish of chicken, for which a recipe is detailed below at §73. The *Viande e claree* recipe for *Saugee* describes how to make this green sauce, and then tells the cook to drop cold meat into it just before serving.[6]

The recipe for chicken pie is uniform in three of the manuscripts, *VAT* alone not copying either of the details for the making of it.[7] The serving sauce for this pie shows a number of variants. *VAL* has the green verjuice which *MAZ* used on roast mutton and that *Y* used on veal tripe. *MAZ* and *BN* have *verjus de grain*, the grape mash seen in the recipe for *Rappé* (§27). *VAT* copies the green verjuice seen in *VAL*, though its use is

---

[1] *Poules*: the first letter is missing in a hole in the manuscript.

[2] *froide* is written *foride* by *VAL*.

[3] *pourdre*: *sic*.

[4] *en* followed by *este* stroked out.

[5] See the same penchant in *MAZ(X)* for green verjuice as a garnish in preference to plain verjuice in Recipe 34 as well.

[6] Ed. Hieatt and Jones, §3, p. 863.

[7] The *Menagier* (§159; p. 185) covers *poucins*, "chicks," in a pie with strips of bacon, these latter being the pieces of *lart* found in the *Viandier*.

limited to the summer months, and in winter no serving sauce at all is to be used. Such a pattern of choices offered by the four manuscripts in the matter of a sauce seems to indicate both that the text of *Z* at this point probably read "verjus de grain," and that *VAT* has been free in deciding not to suggest its use.[8]

38. Chappons, gelines, hetoudeaux

VAL	*Chapons, gelines, hetoudeaux.*	*En rost,*
MAZ	Chappons, gelines et estoudeaulx.	Soient mis en roz, et maingier
BN	*Chappons, hetoudiaux, gelines.*	-
VAT	**Chappons, gelines, hettoudeaulx.**	**En rost,**

VAL *a la saulce de most ou la poitevine ou la jance.*
MAZ et maingiera la saulse de mol ou a la portemine ou a la gence.
BN *Au moust ou a la poetivine ou a la jance.*
VAT **a la saulce de moulst en esté, ou a la[1] poitevine en yver, ou a la jance;**

et si fait l'en bien celle saulce comme de moulst en yver, c'est a savoir, de vin et de succre bolu[2] ensemble.

These fowl, capons, hens and cockerels, are suitable only for roasting, although the sauces used on them are as varied as those for the pullets and chicks of the previous recipe. Recipes for *sauce poitevine* and for the various *jances* are included later in the *Viandier*.[3] These sauces tend in their basic form to be rather bland,[4] as undoubtedly likewise is the

---

[8] It is only in Recipes 10 and 27 that *VAT* uses this "sauce"—and even in §27 it is called, perhaps somewhat hesitantly, *verjus en grain*. This is particularly a summer garnish because it requires the cook to have access to relatively fresh, unripe grapes. Regarding the seasonal availability of verjuice, see the *Menagier*, §§266, 279 and 294; pp. 228, 232 and 237. According to the work's bourgeois author, in July old verjuice has become weak, whereas the new is still too *vert*; at harvest time it is best to mix the old and the new. The physicians of the time held verjuice by its nature to exert a strong cooling influence upon anyone who consumes it; Aldobrandino advises that it be used only in the spring and summer (ed. Landouzy and Pépin, pp. 64 and 119). The *Recueil de Riom* has a *Rost de poullaille, de poussins, du verjust* (§36).

[1] *ou* followed by *en* stroked out; *la* followed by *poti* stroked out.

[2] *moulu* stroked out, with *bolu* inserted above.

[3] These are Recipes 169 and 166–168 respectively. The name *portemine* written by *MAZ* (above) curiously is repeated as *portemie* in *MAZ*'s second recipe for the sauce (Recipe 169).

[4] Since the qualification *aux aulx* is not found for *la jance* suggested here by all four manuscripts, this sauce is unlikely to be the particular one described in Recipe 167. Since the basic ingredient in any *jance* is ginger, it would be safe to assume that what is meant as a possible serving sauce in the present recipe is the plain *Jance de gingembre* (§168), copied later by only *BN*. This variety of *jance* is indeed a relatively mild mixture of ginger, almonds and verjuice. The *sauce poitevine* is likewise based on ginger, an exceptional spice in that it tends to be somewhat ("temperately") moist as well as warm. These qualities endow ginger with a particular affinity to human nature, and render it therefore both safe and beneficial for human consumption.

sauce de most, for which we have no recipe in the *Viandier*.

The *Menagier* does, however, fortunately provide a recipe titled *Moust pour hetoudeaulx*,[5] together with two additional variants for seasons in which the principal ingredient, must, is not available. Similarly, the bourgeois author supplies the ingredients for an ersatz *moust* for those same periods in the year when fresh grape juice is not available: "Se fait en tout temps de vin, vertjus et foison succre."[6] This is in effect the sense of the *VAT* addition by which the cook is told what to substitute for must in winter.

The *poitevin* sauce, making use as it does of chicken livers, would tend to be of a "warmer" nature than a sauce whose basis is must, which is temperate, that is, closer to neuter in temperature.[7] For this reason *VAT* sees *la poitevine* as more appropriate for winter use.[8] A suitable alternative, for the same reason, is a sweetened (*i. e.* "warmed") wine.

39. Connins rostis

VAL	*Connins.*	*Parboulis, lardés, rostis;*
MAZ	Conins rotis.	Soient pourboulir, larder et rotis;
BN	*Conis en rost.*	*Parboulis et lardés;*
VAT	**Connins, lappereaulx.**	**Soient poubouliz et lardez et mis en rost;**

VAL		*a la cameline.*		
MAZ	et maingier	a la cameline.		
BN		*a la canelle;*	*et en pasté,*	- - - - - - -
VAT	**et mengiez**	**a la cameline;**	**et en pasté**	**soient pourbouluz et lardez**

VAT	**et mis tous entiers ou par grans pieces en pasté, et y mettre de**

BN	*en poudre d'espices.*
VAT	**la pouldre d'espices; et soient mengiez a la cameline ou au verjus.**

[5] "Prenez roisins nouveaulx et noirs et les escachez [*grind*] ou mortier et boulez ung boullon. Puis coulez par une estamine et lors gectez dessus vostre pouldre de petit gingembre et plus de canelle, ou de canelle seulement *quia melior*, et meslez ung petit a une cuillier d'argent, et gectez croustes, ou pain broyé, ou oeufz, ou chastaignes pour lyer, dedens, du succre roux, et draciez" (*Menagier de Paris*, §290; p. 234). This particular sauce may of course have little to do with what Taillevent had in mind.

[6] *Menagier de Paris*, §150; p. 181. A must sauce is found in both the *Tractatus*, part I, §19 and the *Liber de coquina*, part V, §13: must is simply to be boiled until it is of the consistency of honey. In the *Due libre*, Libro A, §46, a must sauce—must boiled away until only a third of the original quantity remains—is used as a base for a mustard sauce. The syrupy product of this boiling is what DuCange calls "le raisiné": *s.v. sapa*.

[7] Aldobrandino, *ed. cit.*, pp. 136 and 145–146.

[8] The *Menagier* enunciates as a universal rule that sauces made in winter should be "stronger," that is reinforced with warm spices: after outlining a sauce for duckling and rabbit he adds, "Et *nota* que en yver l'en y met plus gingembre pour estre plus forte d'espices, car en yver toutes saulces doivent estre plus fortes que en esté" (p. 236; §292).

A recipe for roasted rabbits alone was in the *Viandier* before *Y* copied it, and all four manuscripts agree about this dish. *Y* added an extension for rabbit pie; *VAT* appears to have tried to make the procedure for this latter preparation a little more explicit. Because rabbits are considered to be of a cold and dry nature,[1] a layer of pork slices about them while roasting is useful.

40. Chappons de haulte gresse

VAT **Chappons de haulte gresse en pasté. Sans larder; vuidiez la gresse en ung plat et y faictes faire[1] la dodine en la gresse mise et boullye[2] en paelle de fer, et du persil, du vin et du verjus; et puis y faictes des souppes longuetes ou plates ou autres petites, sans toster.**

Recipe 37 deals with pullets roasted and in a pasty, but Recipe 38 deals with only roast capons. *VAT*, for whom meats baked in a pie seem to have held some attraction[3] —of which predilection we have just had a hint in Recipe 39 where he amplifies the directions for rabbit pie—inserts a recipe for baked fat capons that will in part make good the omission from Recipe 38 of this variety of preparation.

Fat capons furnish the grease for a *dodine* and can be baked without the addition of fat (that is, moisture) in the form of bacon. *Dodine* remains a term in modern cuisine for a rich stew or galantine that is made for duck from onions, herbs and red wine.[4] In the *Viandier* any serving sauce may be consumed either poured over its meat or presented along side it, in bowls into which the pieces of meat may be dipped as they are eaten. According to the present recipe, this dodine constitutes a side dish to be eaten with bread sops.

Concerning the *dodine*, it is remarkable that the preparation of this serving sauce is not accorded at least a line or two of explanation on its own account somewhere in the *Viandier*. Even in the *Menagier*'s listing of sample menus a *dodine* enters explicitly into

---

[1] Magninus Mediolanensis, *Regimen sanitatis*, ch. 17. In the *Opusculum de saporibus* of Magninus, ed. Lynn Thorndike, *Speculum*, 9 (1934), p. 187, young rabbit roasted ("assaturis cuniculorum et pullorum parvorum") is served with the sauces mentioned by *VAT* for rabbit pie: cameline or verjuice. The perceived affinity between the meats of young rabbit and pullets may explain why *VAT* inserted a recipe for baked capon immediately after baked rabbit.

[1] *faire* followed by *a* stroked out.

[2] *boullye* followed by *veriust* stroked out.

[3] *VAT* adds the possibility of preparing a pastry version in a number of recipes, for instance 46 and 124. In Recipe 121 *VAT* even suggests that a fish be baked in an oven without any mention that it is to be enclosed in a pastry shell. In the *Du fait de cuisine*, likewise from the beginning of the fifteenth century, a higher proportion of the recipes are for pies of one sort or another than in the earlier versions of the *Viandier* or in the *Menagier de Paris*.

[4] The *Viandier*'s Recipe 54 specifies a *dodine* for mallard duck. The recipe for *dodine* offered there by *MAZ* is identical with the usual modern preparation.

no fewer than twelve of the fifteen meat dinners.[5] Yet the *Menagier* himself clearly did not consider that *dodine* warranted any study other than the directions offered incidently for its preparation in the *Viandier*'s Recipe 54 for mallard duck.[6] What is strange also is that the *Menagier* does not even name the sauce whose preparation he describes.

The *souppes* that form an integral part of this dish afford a means of eating the *dodine*, here as later in the dish for duck (Recipe 54, below).[7]

41. Lievres en rost

VAL *Lievrez en rost. Sans laver, halés en la broche, lardés,*
MAZ Lievres en rolz. Soient alez en broches sans lavez, puis ladez,[1]
BN *Lievres en rost. Lardés, sans laver;*
VAT **Lyevres en rost. Sans laver, lardez le;**

VAL	*rostis; a la cameline;*	*ou en rost, parboulis, lardés;*
MAZ	rotis; et maingier a la cameline;	- - - - - -
BN	*a la cameline;*	- - - - - -
VAT	**et le mengez a la cameline,**	- - - - - -

VAL *—aucuns les bacinnent de tele sauce comme ung bourbier de sangler.*
MAZ †—et aulcuns la bacinent come bourbis de saingler.
BN *—et le bassinent aucuns de telle saulce comme bourbier de sanglier.*
VAT — ‡

VAT **ou au saupiquet, c'est assavoir en la gresse qui en chiet en la lechefricte, et y mettez des ongnons menuz couppez, du vin et du verjus et ung pou de vinaigre, et le gectez sur le lievre quant il sera rosti, ou mettez par escuelles.**

MAZ †et en pasté, pourboulir et larder; —
BN *Item, lievres en pasté, parboulli et lardé;*
VAT **Et en pasté, par grans pieces soient pourboulues et puis lardeez;**

---

[5] *Menagier de Paris*, in the Fourth Article of the Second Distinction §§28–42; pp. 91–100. In fact there are only fourteen meat dinner menus because the tenth, which more or less reproduces the last fish dinner, is for a lean meal.

[6] *Menagier*, §152; p. 181.

[7] A trivial consideration of the sense of the words *soupe* and *souper* is offered by Jules-Louis Lewal, "Etymologie et transformations des noms de repas," *Bulletin de la Société archéologique de Tarn-et-Garonne* (Montaudan: Forestié, 1884), pp. 161–180.

[1] *ladez*: *sic*.

† The texts following this sign are in reverse order in the manuscript.

‡ The text following the second occurrence of this sign should be read at the point of its first occurrence.

BN	*a la cameline ou anpoudré d'espices.*
VAT	**a la cameline; - - - - - ‡—et aucuns les bacinent de**
VAT	**telle saulce comme ung bourblier de sanglier quant ilz sont en rost.**

Roast hare differs from roast rabbit in that this larger animal is not parboiled as is rabbit before roasting—although quite exceptionally *VAL* shows an alternative procedure here, not copied by other manucripts and presumably therefore original with *VAL*. According to this alternative hare *may* be parboiled before being larded and roasted. However, the alternative looks very much as if it may be merely an error for what *MAZ*, *BN* and *VAT* all copied, and that is the treatment for hare baked in a pie.

Y improved the order of the elements of these recipes by moving the note about the basting sauce ("et le bassinent aucuns") to a position ahead of the passage about baking the hare. *VAT* inserts in this place a recipe for *saupiquet*, a variety of serving sauce, but then decides at the end to copy the mention about the *bourbier de sanglier* anyway.[2] Realizing, though, that this *bourbier* is far out of place, *VAT* adds "quant ilz sont en rost" so that the *bourbier* will be understood to be a basting sauce for roast hare and not, as the *saupiquet*, a presentation sauce.

This *Bourbier de sanglier* is not quite what a modern, literal translation of its name would seem to make it. A recipe for the sauce is given in §42. *Saupiquet* is described here by *VAT* because it is a sauce that is not in exceptionally common use, although Chiquart in his *Du fait de cuisine* does offer recipes for both a *saupiquet* on rabbit and a *Saupiquet de poisson*.[3] Grease and onions and vinegar are the basic ingredients in a *saupiquet*, but it is the vinegar that lies at the origin of its name.[4]

42. Bourbier de sanglier

VAL	*Bourbier de sanglier.*	*Premierement metre en yaue*
MAZ	Bourbier de sangler.	Prener le et mecter en aigue
BN	*Bourbier de sanglier.*	*Metés en eaue*
VAT	**Bourbier de sanglier frez.**	**Premierement il le convient mettre en eaue**

VAL	*bolant et tost retraire, metre rostir, baciner de sauce*
MAZ	buillant et tantost les tirés, puis le mecter rotis et bacinez en la saulce
BN	*boullant et tirés tantost et rosticés en broche et le bacinés de saulce*
VAT	**boullant et bien tost retraire et mettre rostir et baciner de saulse**

VAL	*faite d'espices:*		*gingembre, canelle, girofle, graine*
MAZ	faicte d'espices:	assés	gigimbre, cannelle, giroffle, grainne
BN	*d'espices,*	*c'est assavoir*	*gingembre, canelle, girofle, graine*
VAT	**faicte d'espices,**	**c'est assavoir**	**gingenbre, canelle, girofle, grainne**

---

[2] *VAT*'s spelling of the name of the sauce is curious. *Cf.* Recipe 42, below.

[3] *Du fait de cuisine*, §14, f. 36r, and §36, f. 62v, respectively.

[4] "Et aguste le de vin aigre si pour mesure qu'il ne soit pas tropt poignant ne pou" (*Du fait de cuisine*, f. 36r). A recipe for this sauce is given also by the *Menagier de Paris*, §152; p. 181. As well, *Le saupiquet pour connin ou pour oiseau de riviere* appears at §284; p. 233 in the *Menagier*.

VAL	- -	- - - - - -	*et du pain halé trempé en vin*
MAZ	de paradis	- - - - -	et du pain alez tramper de vin,
BN	*de paradis,*	- - - - -	*du pain hallé trempé en vin*
VAT	**de paradiz**	**—et mieulx qui peult,**	**du pain bruslé destrempé de vin**

VAL	*et verjus et vin aigre,*	-	*et le baciner;*	*quant*
MAZ	verjus et de vin aigre;	-	- - -	puis quant
BN	*ou verjus et vin aigre;*	*coullés*	*et bacinés;*	*puis quant*
VAT	**et de verjus et de vinaigre,**	-	**et l'en baciner;**	**et puis quant**

VAL	*il sera cuit,*		*despeciés par morceaux,*	*metez boulir*
MAZ	ilz sera cuit,	se le	despiciez par pieces	et mecter boulir
BN	*il sera cuit,*		*despiecés par morssiaux,*	*puis le boulliés*
VAT	**il sera cuit,**		- - - - - - - -	- - - -

VAL		*avec vostre saulce;*	*et soit claret, noir.*
MAZ		dedans vostre saulset	soit cleret et noir.
BN		*en saulce;*	*et soit cleret et noir.*
VAT	**si[1] bacinez**	**tout ensemble;**	**et soit clairet et noir.**

At the end of Recipe 41, *VAT* refers to a sauce that he calls *bourblier de sanglier*. This is the only time in the *Viandier* when the name of this sauce (or, less likely, dish) is spelled with an *l*: *bourblier*.[2] In Recipe 42 the name is uniformly written *bourbier*, even in *VAT*. In the *Menagier de Paris*, however, where the present recipe is similar to the version in the *Viandier* copied by *VAT*, the spelling is consistently *bourbelier*.[3] And in the *Du fait de cuisine* Chiquart has either *bourbully*, *bourbulleys* or *bourbouleis*.[4]

All four manuscripts agree closely on the text. *VAT* alone omits a detail near the end, about cutting up the meat and boiling it in its basting sauce; and *VAT* repeats an instruction ("si bacinez tout ensemble"), which seems superfluous in any case.

---

[1] *si* followed by *len* stroked out.

[2] *MAZ(X)* writes *bourbis de saingler* in Recipe 41.

[3] *Menagier de Paris*, §146; p. 179. "Du bourbelier, c'est le nomblet, combien que en cest endroit l'en dit bien *nombletz* d'une part et *bourbelier* de l'autre" (*idem.*, §91, p. 158).

At the end of §146 the *Menagier* notes: "Et ceste saulse est appellee *queue de sanglier*, et la trouverez cy aprés." Both the sauce here for the *Bourbelier* and the *Menagier*'s *Queue de sangler* (§293; p. 235) resemble the *Queue de sangler a la sausse chaude* found in the *Recueil de Riom*, §13.

[4] *Du fait de cuisine*, §54, ff. 5r, 67v, 78v–80v. For Chiquart (f. 78v and 79r) the *bourbulleys* clearly has the sense of an "Esay" (Cotgrave) or breast of boar, and is not merely a variety of boiled sauce or a dish of a meat boiled in a sauce (*cf.* the *OED, s. v. burble*, and *REW*, §1386, *bullare*). The original sense has been perhaps a little muddied.

43. Toute venoison fresche

MAZ	Et nota que toute venoison fresche,	qu'il n'est point bacinee;
BN	*Toute venoison freiche.*	*Sans baciner;*
VAT	**Toute venoison fresche.**	**Sans baciner;**

MAZ	se doit maingier a la cameline.
BN	*est mengié a la cameline.*
VAT	**a la cameline.**

Z inserts this *Nota* into the *Viandier*; it is modified by *Y* and copied in turn by the *Menagier*.[1] The sentence concludes the section on roast meats and amounts to a blanket, catch-all recipe for the roasting of all non-domestic meats. It may have been conceived as a counterpart to Recipes 6 and 7 among the earlier boiled meats.

The brevity of the treatment allotted to the meat of game animals is noteworthy and implies that such meat was not commonplace, at least in roast form,[2] on the tables of the *Viandier*'s patrons.

44. Pijons rostis

VAL	*Pigons. Rostis atout les testez sans lez piez,*	*au cel.*
BN	*Pijons. Rostis a toutes les testes,*	*au sel menu;*
VAT	**Pijons. Roustiz atout les testes et sans les pietz,**	**au sel menu;**

BN	*et en pasté aussy.*
VAT	**et en pasté, au sel menu ou au vin ou a la ciboule avec la gresse du pasté.**

The pigeon or dove is one of the most common of edible birds up until the sixteenth century.[1] Pigeon pie seems to have held particular interest for either *Y* or at least *VAT*. Consideration of the possibility of presenting the bird baked in such a dish is added by *Y*; *VAT*, however, further lists several alternatives for the serving of this pie. The most significant variant in this paragraph is that *MAZ(X)* has inexplicably chosen to omit it entirely.

In the series of recipes that begins with this present one and continues up to Recipe 59, most of the birds being prepared are to be roasted, and generally speaking this is without

---

[1] *Menagier de Paris*, §147; p. 180.

[2] *Cf.* Recipes 6, 7 and 8, above, among the boiled meats.

[1] Just as every aristocratic estate had its fishpond, stocked with the more delectible or useful varieties of fish, so too the domestic dovecot was a commonplace source of fresh fowl on the mediæval high board. Concerning the consumption of fowl, both domestic and wild, in the *Viandier*, see Antoinette Saly, "Les oiseaux dans l'alimentation médiévale d'après le *Viandier* de Taillevent et le *Menagier de Paris*," *Manger et Boire au Moyen Age*, vol. 2, pp. 173–179.

previously being parboiled. Partaking as they do of the nature of air, birds are considered by physicians to be moist as well as warm, and therefore parboiling is not appropriate.[2]

45. Menus oiseaux

VAL *Menus oiseaux.*
MAZ Menus oysaulx en rolz.
BN *Menus oysiaux.*
VAT **Menuz oyseaulx comme allouetes, cailles, mauvilz et autres.**

VAL *Plumés a sec,* - - - - - - - - -
MAZ Plumey les a sec, puis ostés les gavions et les bronailles
BN *Plumés ausec, puis* - - - - - - - -
VAT **Soient plumez a sec sans eaue, puis** - - - - - - - -

VAL *brulez sans fumee, enhastez* - - - -
MAZ et le bruler a feu sans fumer et les hastés, - - - - - -
BN *brullés* - - - - *et metés en broche* - - - - - -
VAT **les boullez ung pou et les enhastez atout les testes et les pietz**

VAL *par le costé,*
MAZ - - - - - - - -
BN *par le costé,*
VAT **par de costé et non pas de long, et mettés des lesches**

VAL *du lart entre deux;*
MAZ et la ribelete de lart entredeux et des
BN *et la ribete de lart entre deux;*
VAT **ou ribeletes de lart ou des tronsons de saulcisses entre deulx;**

MAZ feulles de loriez, et emplisiez les ventres de fin froumaige fondant

VAL - - - - - - - *au sel menu.*
MAZ et miole[1] de beuf; et se mainge a sel menu, - - - -
BN - - - - - - - *au sel menu, et lessiés les piés.*
VAT - - - - **et les mengiez au sel menu;** - - - -

MAZ et se servent a couvert entre deux escuelles ou entre deux plas.
VAT **et en pasté, au fromage de gain mis ou ventre.**

---

2 "Animalia quedam sunt complesionis calide et humide ratione corporis humani tantum quemadmodum carnes castrati et gallinarum pullorum et culumborum et multe alie" (Albini, *De sanitatis custodia*, part 2, dist. 2, tract. 2, ch. 1; *ed. cit.*, p. 76). See Nada Patrone, "Trattati medici," concerning the influence that Albini's teaching enjoyed.

1 *miole* could more easily be read as *ionole*.

All manuscripts copy this recipe for "small birds,"[2] which designation *VAT* feels it useful to illustrate with the examples "larks, quail and thrush." *VAT*'s penchant for clarifying the text is again evident immediately after this, as he adds the phrase "sans eaue" to the "a sec" he undoubtedly finds in his source. In the following passage, though, he blunders, reading "boullez ung pou" for what was probably "brullés a feu [*or* en feu] sans fumee"—by which operation the down on the carcass of the small birds is to be singed away after their feathers have been plucked. Once again *VAT* tries to clarify the sense of a passage, by changing here "par le costé" to "par de costé et non pas de long"; and in the subsequent phrase *VAT* intends the more common word *lesches* to help explain the proper culinary term *ribeletes*.[3]

The arrangement of the alternating bird-and-bacon sandwich on the spit is reminiscent of a shish kebab,[4] with *VAT* even suggesting a substitute for the bacon, and *MAZ(X)* in the fifteenth century inserting savory laurel leaves as well. While only *MAZ(X)* recommends laurel leaves in this recipe, later, in the *Gelee de poisson* (Recipe 68) only *VAT* (again, a fifteenth-century manuscript) includes these leaves among the ingredients. They are present also in *VAT*'s version of the spice list, Recipe 170.[5]

A culinary tradition which stuffed these small birds with cheese[6] seems to have influenced the additions which *MAZ(X)* and *VAT* make, though at different points in the paragraph and with regard to different dishes.

The strange postscript appended by *BN* is likely to have been written in *Y* in some form—perhaps as a marginal notation?—because it is picked up by the *Menagier* where it appears in a more reasonable position: "Menuz oiseaulx. Plumez a sec et laissiez les piez, et embrochiez ... ."[7] This is in fact the order of operations reproduced in the *Viandier*'s next recipe.

46. Plouviers, videcoqs

BN	*Plouviers, videcoqs.*	*Plumés asec, brullés*	*et lessiés*	– –
VAT	**Plouviers et videcoqz.**	**Plumez a sec** –	**et laissiez les testes**	

[2] The term "small birds" is common in mediæval French cookery. Chiquart refers to *petis oyseaux*, *oysellés* and *oysellons*. Magninus provides a list of examples of such small edible fowl in ch. 17 of his *Regimen sanitatis*: "Turtures, columbe juvenes, sturnelli, alaude, pluverii, passeres, et relique aves minute que capiuntur in bladis ut turdi, meruli."

[3] This second word may not have been current because *BN* misspells it *ribete*.

[4] See the article by Claudia Roden, "The Spread of Kebabs and Coffee: Two Islamic Movements?" in *Food in Motion: The Migration of Foodstuffs and Cookery Techniques*, Oxford Symposium 1983, 2 vols. (London: Prospect Books, 1983), vol. I, p. 74.

[5] See also *baye* in *VAT*'s recipes 183 and 184.

[6] *Fromage de gain* is a rich cheese with a high butter-fat content; it would be described accurately by *MAZ*'s phrase "fin froumaige fondant."

[7] *Menagier de Paris*, §151; p. 181.

BN *les piés, enhastés par le costé; et mengiés au sel menu.*
VAT **et les pietz, enhastez de long; et soient mengiez au sel menu,**
et aultres y veullent la cameline; et en pasté, au sel mennu sans
y mettre point de fromage.

This recipe for plovers and woodcocks is clearly an addition of *Y*. *VAT* continues to demonstate his independence as he copies his source,[1] cutting off the heads of the birds as well as their feet, spitting them lengthwise rather than transversally (as had been specified in the previous recipe for small birds in general), and suggesting an alternative serving sauce. As also in the previous paragraph, *VAT* adds a treatment for these birds baked in a pie.

47. Perdris

VAL *Perdris. Plumés a sec, ostez le gavion, copez*
MAZ Cigne. Plumey les a sec et ostez les gavions et coppez
BN *Perdrix. Plumés asec,* – – – – – –
VAT **Perdriz. Plumez a sec** – – – – – –

VAL *lez piez et lez testez, refaitez en yaue boullant, tirez*[1] *tost,*
MAZ les colz et les piez et les reffaicte en aigue buillant – –
BN – – – – – *reffaites en eaue boulant,* – –
VAT – – – – – **et reffaictes en eaue boullant,** – –

VAL – – – – – *esfondrez, lavez, boutonnez de lart;*
MAZ ou sur les charbons vif, puis esfondrez,[2] lavez et lardez et rotis;
BN – – – – – – – – – – – *boutonnés de lart;*
VAT – – – – – – – – – – – **puis lardez**

VAL – – – – – *au cel menu.*
MAZ – – – – – et maingier au sel menuz.
BN – – – – – *au sel menu; et en pasté auxi,*
VAT **et ostez testes et piez; au sel menu; et aucuns en pasté,**

BN *au sel menu.*
VAT **au sel menu; et aucuns les despiecent et detranchent par menuz morceaulx et mettent entre deulx platz avec de l'eaue froide et du sel,**
et puis mettent eschauffer sur le charbon tant que l'eaue boulle,
et puis les menguent; et dient que c'est tres bonne saulce.

---

[1] The *Menagier de Paris* (§155; p. 183) reproduces *BN*'s version of this paragraph, that is to say, a version that is likely very close to *Y*.

[1] *tirez*: the scribe wrote *tuez*.

[2] *esfondrez*: the word appears to be *nussnndres*.

The recipe for partridge belongs to the oldest versions of the *Viandier*—even though *MAZ(X)* copies in error here the name of the dish that follows in his source. This bird is to be parboiled in order to render it a little more moist and plump.[3] For the same purpose of adding moisture, the meat is to be larded before being roasted. *Y* adds a brief note about baking in a pastry shell.

Variants abound in the various versions of this recipe. *Y* appears to omit the direction, found in *VAL* and *MAZ*, about removing the gizzard, the feet[4] and the head of the bird, although *VAT* does insert it, out of place. A similar direction about eviscerating the bird and cleaning it is likewise omitted by *Y*.

The alternate preparation outlined by *VAT* for the partridge (which has already been roasted, one assumes, because the liquid will be referred to as a "sauce") consists apparently of boiling the bird in brine in a covered dish.[5] It may be recalled that salt is a condiment of the same nature as any other spice in the Middle Ages. As a "sauce" it becomes important in this section on fowl.[6]

48. Turturelles

BN *Truterelles. Auxi comme perdrix sans boutoner.*

VAT **Turturelles.** - - - - - - - - - **Plumez a sec et reffaictes en eaue boullant sans larder; au sel menu; et en pasté sans teste; et qui veult, soit doré; et au tuer**[1] **soit fendue en la gorge de la teste jusquez aux espaules; et soit mengié au poivre jaunet.**

The turtle-dove was judged by *Y* to be a wildfowl whose gastronomic appeal was sufficient to warrant the inclusion of a recipe for it in the *Viandier*. *BN* offers the more abbreviated form of this recipe, while *VAT* adds an uncertain number of amplifications and refinements to *Y*'s text. The passage in *VAT*, "et qui veult, soit doré ... au poivre jaunet," has been copied erroneously from the following recipe.

The yellow pepper sauce prescribed in *VAT* for serving turtle-dove pie is not commonly used in the *Viandier*, even though a recipe for it is written as the first item in the section of boiled sauces later in the work (Recipe 164). All of the other manuscript copies specify it as a serving sauce for swan in the following recipe.

---

[3] The *Regimen sanitatis* of Magninus Mediolanensis indicates why such parboiling would be considered useful in the case of a partridge: "Perdices ... declinant ad aliquantum frigiditatem et siccitatem et sunt sicut galline deserte et habent proprietatem constringendi ventrem asse et elixe" (ch. 17).

[4] *MAZ(X)* changes *colz* to *piez*, conceivably a scribal error.

[5] A similar procedure is followed in the preparation of roast salmon in Recipe 124.

[6] The *Menagier de Paris* (§156; p. 183) similarly appends possible alternate serving sauces for roast partridge: water, rose-water and wine; or three parts rose-water with one part orange juice and wine. Chiquart's *Calunafree de perdrix* prepares the bird in the same way as in the *Viandier* but reboils the meat in camelin sauce and onions with a little mustard and verjuice (*Du fait de cuisine*, §47, f. 72v).

[1] *tuer* written first as *cuer*, the *c* then being changed into a *t* with a high cross bar.

49. Cygnes

VAL	*Cygnez.*	*Plumez a sec,*	– –
MAZ	– –	Plumey les comme une oye,	– –
BN	*Cinne.*	*Plumés aussi comme une oe,*	*eschaudés*
VAT	**Paon, cine.**	[See the following recipe.]	

VAL	– – – – – – – – – –	*fendu*
MAZ	et soit arsonné atout les piez;	et an cute soit fenduz
BN	*et arsonnés*[1] *et cuisiés a tous les piés;*	*et au cuer*[2] *soit fendu*

VAL	*de la teste*	*jusques aux espaulez;*	*doré*
MAZ	dois[3] la teste	jusques aux espaulles;	et soit dorrer, qui . l veult,
BN		*jusques aux espaules;*	*qui veult, soit doré;*

VAL	*ou verdi;*	*au poivre jaunet.*
MAZ	ou verdi; et maingier	a poivre jane.
BN	– – *et mengiés*	*au poivre jaunet.*

Swan and peacock share what was almost universally considered to be a tough and melancholic nature;[4] according to *VAT*, they share as well a similar method of preparation for the hardy diner. The passage, introduced by *Z*, which concerns the plucking of the swan, refers to Recipe 36 where, mysteriously, only one of the manuscripts, *MAZ*, says anything whatsoever about actually preparing the fowl dealt with there, a goose. Furthermore, for the swan the feet are left on; for the peacock of Recipe 50, to which *VAT* assimilates the swan, head and tail will be left on; yet in the case of the goose in the earlier recipe, wings, neck and feet were all removed.

The yellow pepper sauce is not commonly used in the *Viandier*, even though a recipe for it is the first in the section of boiled sauces later in the work (Recipe 164).

Apart from any gastronomic pleasure they may, or may not, have afforded gourmets in the late Middle Ages, certain ornamental birds assumed ceremonial functions in the course of banquets. By the fourteenth century the practice had become established in courtly

---

[1] *arsonnes* followed by *anxi comme* stroked out.

[2] The word is clearly *cuer* and not *tuer*, though this second reading would certainly make more sense; *cf.* the *VAT* text for the combined Recipes 49 and 50: "l'en tue comme ungne oue."

[3] *dois* should likely be read as *devers*.

[4] Magninus, *Regimen sanitatis*, ch. 17; *Nef de santé*; various *Tacuina sanitatis*, for example those which are published by Luisa Cogliati Arano in *The Medieval Health Handbook, Tacuinum sanitatis* (New York, 1976). "Et teus chars [of the swan], ki user les veut, si les use au poivre noir fort, car quant plus est fors tant vaut miex por se malise amender" (Aldobrandino, *ed. cit.*, p. 132). *Cf.* also p. 131 in Aldobrandino concerning peacocks: "Sor totes autres chars d'oisiaus ont il le char plus grosse et plus dure et plus tart se cuisent a la forciele, fors li chars de l'ostriche . . . ." The *Menagier de Paris* offers a recipe for swan (§157; p. 183) that is close to the *BN* version, but groups the peacock with a number of other birds that for the most part are wild.

circles of publicly declaring a commitment over a cooked and, normally, redressed,[5] swan, peacock or heron at the moment at which it was to be carved and consumed.[6]

50. Paons

VAL	*Paon.*	*Ainsy comme le cyne;*
MAZ	Pavons saulvaiges.	Pavons saulvaiges qui naist es montaignes soit
BN	*Paon.*	*Seignier auxi comme le cine, lessiés la teste*
VAT	**Paon, cine.**	**L'en tue comme ungne oue et laissiez la teste**

VAL	- - - - - - - - - - - - - - - - -
MAZ	plumez conme le signe puis soit boullir en vin et ung pol d'aigue,
BN	*et la queue,*
VAT	**et la queue;**

VAL	- - - - - - - - - - - - -	-
MAZ	puis soit tresbien larder et rotiz en la broche.	-
BN	*lardés et arsonnés*	*et dorés;*
VAT	**soit lardé ou arçonné**	**et soit rosti doré;**

VAL	*au sel.*	
MAZ	- - - - - - -	Il est meilleur a maingier froit que chault,
BN	*mengiés au sel menu.*	
VAT	**et soit mengié au sel menu.**	- - - - - - - - - - - -

MAZ	et se garde bien longuement. L'on y treuve trois viandes de chart:
VAT	**Et dure au loings bien ung moys depuis qu'il est cuit; et feust ores**

MAZ	ly une est semblable a chart de beuf, l'autre a chart de lievre,
VAT	**moisy dessus, ostez le moysy, vous le trouverez blanc, bon et sade**

MAZ	et l'aultre a chart de pardrix.
VAT	**par dessoubz.**

---

[5] See below, Recipes 213 and 214.

[6] Among French literary compositions of this period see, for example, Jacques de Longuyon, *Les vœux du paon* (*c.* 1310) ed. R. Graeme Ritchie, in *The Buik of Alexander* (Scottish Text Society, 1927); Jehan le Court (Brisebare), *Le restor du paon* (*c.* 1325), ed. R. Carey (Geneva, 1966); Jehan de la Motte, *Le parfait du paon* (1340), ed. R. Carey (Chapel Hill: University of North Carolina, 1972); *Les vœux de l'epervier* (1310), ed. G. Wolfram and F. Bonnardot (Metz, 1895); *Les veus du hairon* (*c.* 1340), ed. T. Wright, in *Political Poems and Songs Relating to English History* (Rolls Series) (London, 1859), vol. 1, pp. 1–25. Among the chronicles of the period see Pierre de Langtoft, *Chronicle*, ed. T. Wright (London, 1868); vol. 2, p. 368: *Anno Domini millesimo tricentesimo vj°*.

MAZ(X) specifies in his title that the particular peacock dealt with in this recipe is of the wild variety, and he repeats this identification with further precision in his first line. (See the comment to Recipe 52, below.)

Though there is no specific instruction about cutting the peacock's throat, as there is in §49 for the swan, *Y* says that the bird should be bled like a swan[1]—which instruction is copied by the *Menagier*.[2] Because *VAT* attempts to combine the recipes for peacock and swan, he reproduces the reference found in the previous recipe, that these birds should be killed in the same way as a swan.

Concerning *VAT*'s obscure direction, "lardé *ou* arçonné," see the following recipe. Neither *BN* nor *VAT* make any mention of parboiling the peacock, even though *MAZ(X)*'s direction would seem eminently sensible, but both rather mount it directly upon the spit for roasting.[3]

Both *MAZ(X)* and *VAT* add notes about the meat's durability.[4] It would seem that what it lacked in immediate appeal, warm off the spit, roast peacock made up for over time. It is worth noting that such self-preserving qualities in a meat were important.

51. Faisans

VAL	*Faisans. Plumez a sec, baconnez ou arçonez,*	– –
MAZ	Faisans. Plumez les a sec et soit arsoné ou bociné,[1]	et qui . l veult
BN	*Faisans. Plumés asec et boutonnés, arsonnés,*[2]	*et qui veult*

---

[1] The *Enseignements* begins its recipe for swans and peacocks by instructing the cook: "Premierement en traez le sanc par les testes touz vis, aprés si les fendez par dessus les dos jusques es espaulles e les esfondrez ... " (p. 183, l. 80; *Petit traité*, p. 218).

[2] *Menagier de Paris*, §153; p. 181. The *Menagier* has little regard for peacocks, grouping them with pheasants, storks, herons, bustards, cranes, bitterns and cormorants as fowl of secondary gastronomic value. The *Viandier* considers many of these birds separately, although they seem generally to belong to the long-beaked species deprecated by Magninus: "Et universaliter carnes avium habentium collum longum et rostrum longum degentium in aquis omnes sunt illaudabilis nutrimenti et difficilis digestionis et generant humorum melancholicum" (*Regimen sanitatis*, ch. 17).

[3] At f. 15r of the *Du fait de cuisine* Chiquart quotes a somewhat mutilated version of the following piece of "folk" wisdom:

> Si volucris verrat, qui torret eam, procul errat;
> Sed procul ab igne volucrem de flumine torre.

Hans Walther, *Proverbia sententiaeque latinitatis medii aevi* (Göttingen, 1963–1969), vol. 4, §29436. While "birds that drag along the ground" are certainly roasted in the *Viandier*, waterfowl (Recipes 52–55) are subjected to exactly the same treatment.

[4] St. Augustine himself transmits the durable myth about the incorruptability of peacock flesh in book 21, ch. 4 of the *City of God Against the Pagans*, ed. and tr. William M. Green, 7 vols. (London: Heinemann and Cambridge, Mass.: Harvard University Press, 1972), vol. 7, pp. 14–17.

[1] *bocine*: a faint *s* is written over the *e*.

[2] *arsonnes*: the manuscript has *et sonnes*.

VAT **Faisans. Plumez a sec, bouconnez ou arçonnez, et qui veult**

VAL *soit reffait en eaue chaude, rosté atout la queue et la teste;*
MAZ reffait en aigue chaude, rotis atout les piez et la teste
BN *soit refait en eaue boullant atout la teste*
VAT **soit reffait en eaue chaude et soit rosty atout la teste sans plumer,**

VAL -
MAZ et la quehue; - - - - - - - - - - - - - - -
BN *et la queue;* - - - - - - - - - - - - - - -
VAT **et atout la queue; envelopez de drappeaulx moulliez qu'ilz ne ardent;**

VAL *qui veut,* *si coppe la queue et le col,* - -
MAZ - - - - - - - - - - - - - - - - - - -
VAT **et se vous voullez, ostez la teste, la queue et les[3] ailles et rostissiez**

VAL - - - - - - - - *puis quant il sera cuit, lez ratachier*
MAZ - - - - - - - - et puis quant il sera cuit, si les
VAT **sans larder, s'il est gras et bon; et au mettre ou plat ataichiez**

VAL *au corps.*
MAZ estaichié a une cheville de bois; et ne
VAT **a buchettes la teste, la queue et les ailles en leurs places;** -

MAZ doit pas estre cuit le colz ne la quehue.
BN - - - - - - - - - - - - - *au sel menu soit mengié.*
VAT - - - - - - - - - - - - - **et mengiez au sel mennu.**

Before pheasants are put on a spit to be roasted, *Z* makes it optional to subject them to a plumping or tenderizing in hot water. A further choice of procedure then existed: either the pheasants could be roasted whole, without having the head feathers or tail plucked—as *VAT* alone specifically states—or, alternatively, the body itself, stripped of its appendages, could be roasted, the head, tail and wings set aside and then reattached to the body when this has finished cooking.

In the first case *VAT* alone indicates the mechanics of protecting the feathered appendages from the flame, by wrapping them in a damp cloth. In the second, *MAZ(X)* alone explains that the appendages are not themselves to be cooked. Though not so called here, this second treatment for roast pheasant might well be termed *faisan revestu*, resembling as it does the *Cisne revestu en ses plumes et atout sa pel* that we shall see in Recipe 72. This is an *entremets* for which the chef had to remove the whole skin of the swan before cooking it.

There seems to be some hesitation in certain manuscripts, near the beginning of the recipe, about what exactly is to be done to the pheasant after it is plucked and before it is

[3] *les* followed by *elles* stroked out.

mounted on the spit. The *baconnez* of *VAL* is clear enough, although the *ou* that follows the verb raises a question. This *ou* remains in both *MAZ* and *VAT*, but now the verb has been changed to *bociné* in the one and *bouconnez* in the other, neither of which forms is satisfying if we read them with a *c*, which is clear in both manuscripts, rather than the *t* that seems called for. Only the reading offered by *BN*, *boutonnés, arsonnés* (ms.: *et sonnes*!) makes sense, yet it should be noted that, according to the *Menagier*, the verb *boutonner* properly involves a *piquage* with cloves rather than with pork fat.[4]

52. Cigognes

VAL	*Segoingnez.*	*Plumez a sec,*	- - - - -	*getez*
MAZ	Cigogne.	Soit apparoillier	conme le signe;	-
BN	*Sogoingnes.*[1]	*Soient plumees*	*comme une oe,*	-
VAT	**Sigongnes.**	**Soient plumees**	**aussi comme une oue**	-

VAL	*en eaue boullant, copez lez ellez,*	*laisiez lez piez*	- -
MAZ	- - - - - - - -	- - - - -	- -
BN	- - - - - - - -	*lessiés les piés*	- -
VAT	- - - - - - - -	**et laissiez les pietz**	**et la queue**[2]

VAL	*et la teste,*	- - - - -	*et l'arçonnez et flamés*
MAZ	- -	- - - - - -	- - - - - - - -
BN	*et la teste,*	- - - - -	*soient arsonnee et emflambee*
VAT	**et la teste,**	**et soient mises en rost,**	**arçonnees et flambees;**

VAL	*tresbien;*	- -	*au sel menu.*
MAZ	- -	et maingier	a sel menuz.
BN	*tresbien;*	- -	*au sel menu.*

The order of the recipes at this point in the *Viandier*, for stork, heron, mallard and bustard, shows some variety among the manuscripts. Because individual manuscripts may have altered the sequence in which they copied these recipes from their respective sources,[3] the order determined here for this present edition is practically arbitrary. *MAZ(X)* seems to have decided initially to skip the recipes for peacock, pheasant and heron, going directly to the recipe for stork (§53) after he copies the recipe for swan; for this latter (§49) he had no title, though, the name *Cigne* having been used previously (§47) to identify the recipe for partridge! He must then have decided to include pheasant and heron after all, and ultimately to have come back to the peacock (§50)—which he qualifies as a wild bird.

---

[4] "Il y a difference ... entre boutonner et larder, car boutonner est de girofle et larder est de lart" (*Menagier de Paris*, p. 173, l. 12; p. 88). *Cf.* *boutonner de clou de girofle* in Recipe 200, below.

[1] *Sogoingnes*: the first letter is lost in a hole in the manuscript.

[2] *queue* followed by *soient* stroked out.

[3] See the chart in the Introduction, above.

The sequence of recipes to posit most safely as being "original" is normally the one found in *VAL*; it is the order of the recipes in *VAL* that has been followed, for good reason, in the rest of this edition. Yet in this current chapter, the recipe for *Herons* makes reference to the recipe for *Segoingnez* which appears after it in *VAL*. While such a reference "forward" may be quite understandable when the nature of the two things being compared is sufficiently different to lead the author to classify them in different groupings,[4] an order in which stork *precedes* heron seems, because of their similarity and because of this very reference, a little more likely. This is the sequence followed by *Y*.[5] In subsequent recipes both stork and heron will be referred to as independent models for the preparation of other waterfowl.

Despite an inversion found between Recipes 54 and 55 in the three later manuscripts, I have retained the order mallard/bustard as it is found in *VAL*.

MAZ(X) does not have a great deal of interest in this recipe for stork, being content to limit the directions for preparing this bird to a terse "like the swan"; the recipe for swan is what he has just copied, untitled. *Y* must have shown "plucked as a goose," but then follows *O* and *Z* for the remainder of the recipe.

As far as preparation is concerned, the stork's wings alone are removed, the remainer of the bird is mounted on a spit and then thoroughly singed.

For this and the following waterfowl, the standard serving "sauce" is fine salt, a dressing that is appropriate for what was generally conceived to be the moist nature of this type of bird.

53. Herons

VAL	*Herons. Seigniés, fendus jusques aux espaulez,*	– – –
MAZ	Haron. Soit signé et fendus jusques aux espaulles	– – –
BN	*Heron. Soit seingnié et fendu jusques aux espaules,*	– – –
VAT	**Heron. Soit seigné ou fendu jusques aux espaules**	**comme dit est**

VAL	– – – –	*apareilliez comme une cegoingne.*
MAZ	– – – – –	et apparoilliez conme la sigoigne devant dicte;
BN	– – – – – –	– – – – – – – – – –
VAT	**du[1] cine et du paon, et soit appareillié**	**comme la sigongne;**

MAZ	ou plumez asec et reffaict en aigue chaude, coppés		les halles
BN	– – – – – – – – – –	*†et lessiés*	– –
VAT	– – – – – – – – – –	– – – –	– –

---

[4] Such a reference forward is seen, for instance, in Recipe 130. The treatment of dogfish (Recipe 123), a round sea-fish, is compared with that of ray (Recipe 136), a flat sea-fish.

[5] The recipe for stork precedes the one for heron in *Z* as well, although the recipe for pheasant is made to intervene. The text copied by *MAZ(X)* even draws attention to this order by reading "la sigoigne devant dicte," as if the position was not to be expected—or perhaps as if the writer himself had just rearranged these recipes.

[1] *du* followed by *sit* stroked out.

† The texts following this sign are in reverse order in the manuscript.

MAZ et les piez et la teste, et les arsonnez et flamez tresbien; -
BN *les piés et la teste; †puis arssonné et emflambé tresbien et doré;*
VAT - - - - - - - - - - - - - - - - -

MAZ et maingier au sel menuz.
BN *et mengies au sel menu.*
VAT - - **au sel menu ou a la cameline.**

A curious variant occurs in *VAT*'s version of the first line of the recipe for heron as he writes that the bird is to be bled *or* slit to the shoulders. The carcass of the heron is to be prepared as a stork: what this means is that the wings alone are to be removed, the bird is then spitted and singed. This treatment is explicitly confirmed by *BN* who adds that the bird should be glazed as well, a procedure that has already been followed for the swan.[2] *MAZ* offers an alternative preparation: all members, including the feet and head, are to be removed—the treatment accorded the goose by *MAZ*[3]—and the bird, after being spitted, is to be singed as before.

VAT suggests cameline as an alternative sauce to plain salt.[4]

54. Malars de riviere

VAL *Malars de riviere. Plumez a sec, coppez col, piez et ellez,*
MAZ Malart de reviere. Soient plumez asec, coppez le colz et les alles,
BN *Malars de riviere. Plumés a sec* - - - - -
VAT **Malartz de riviere. Plumez a sec** - - - - -

VAL - *rostisiez;* - - - - -
MAZ lavez, rotiser, - - - - - et retener la graisse
BN - *et rosticiés,* - - - - - *et retennés la gresse*
VAT - **et mis en broche sans teste et sans pietz; et recueillez la**

VAL - - - - - - *fatez la dodine de lart, de verjus ou*
MAZ graisse pour faire la dodine, laquelle doit estre faicte de lart et
BN *gresse pour faire la dodien;*[1] *et la faites de lait ou de vin ou*
VAT **gresse pour faire la dodine, et la faictes de lait ou de vin ou**

---

2 Recipe 49.

3 Recipe 36.

4 Aldobrandino (*ed. cit.*, p. 132) likens the flesh of the heron—which, he warns, is "perilleuse a menger"—to that of the stork and the swan, and advises with heron the use of an even stronger sauce made of black pepper. A hot pepper sauce is indeed specified for heron by the *Enseignements* (p. 183, ll. 73–75; *Petit traité*, p. 217).

1 *dodien*: *sic*.

VAL	*de vin*	*et de la poudre;*	- - -	*metez sur*
MAZ	de verjus avecques oignons, vin, parressi;			puis vercel sur les
BN	de vergus. - - - - - -		- - -	- -
VAT	**de verjus** - - - - -	**avec du persil; et**		

VAL *tosteez de pain, ou boullir par quartiers dedans la dodine.*
MAZ tostees de pain, et aulcum le boillent avec la doine[2] par quartiers.
VAT **souppes longuetes, tenves, brullees;**
et soit mengié au sel menu.

While the four manuscripts agree generally on the preparation and roasting of the mallard— *VAT* implies that the wings of the bird are to be left on, though—there are variants in the section dealing with the *dodine*. This *dodine* is a type of gravy whose base is the drippings from the roasting bird itself, to which liquid, according to *VAL*, are added lard, spice and either verjuice or wine.[3] *VAL* had originally not mentioned anything about the drippings; *Z* indicates that these are indeed to be put to use, although what *Z* may have specified as other ingredients in the *dodine* is conjectural. For these ingredients *MAZ* shows verjuice *and* wine, and has onions and parsley rather than spice powder.[4] *Y* is responsible for a serious error, copied by *BN* and *VAT*, in which the word *lart* has become *lait*, and as a consequence of the change the insertion of the word *ou* makes wine and verjuice alternatives to this milk.[5] For his *Malars de riviere* the *Menagier* offers two possible sauces which contain the following ingredients: the drippings, onions fried in them, lard and parsley; or, alternatively, the drippings, onions fried in them, verjuice and half wine, half vinegar.[6] To this latter sauce the *Menagier* interestingly gives the name *saupiquet*,[7] of which name the latter element, *piquet*, is probably inspired by the vinegar in the mixture. The only occurence of this sauce in the *Viandier* is in *VAT*'s version of Recipe 41, the recipe for roast hare, where we find that *VAT* lists exactly those ingredients of the *Menagier*'s second sauce: drippings, onions, wine, verjuice and vinegar.

---

[2] *doine*: *sic*.

[3] The modern "dodine de canard" is normally made from duck, onions, herbs (the parsley found in the fifteenth-century versions of *MAZ* and *VAT*), and red wine.

[4] Both parsley and spice powder are combined in the *Dodine de tous oyseaulx* of the printed *Fleur de toute cuisine* (f. 42r). The manner of presentation of these roast birds and *dodine* in the *Fleur de toute cuisine* may help to clarify one of the *Viandier*'s serving options: the cook is to place three or four squares of toast in a plate, "puis mettez les oyseaulx dessoubz et le bouillon dessus."

[5] Curiously the printed version of the *Viandier* (ed. Pichon and Vicaire, p. 177) perpetuates this error in a recipe for a *Dodine de layt sur tous oyseaux de riviere*.

[6] *Menagier de Paris*, §152; p. 181.

[7] Chiquart devotes a whole recipe to the method of preparing *saupiquet*: *Du fait de cuisine*, §36, f. 62v. In an English recipe edited by Austin (p. 77) the *dodine/saupiquet* is called "Pikkyll pour le Mallard." See also Recipe 40, above.

A final element in this recipe involves the particular use to which the *dodine* is put. It may be soaked into sops of toast or it may, according to *VAL* and *MAZ*, alternatively serve as a cooking broth in which the quartered bird is seethed.[8]

55. Outardes, gentes, grues

VAL	*Oitardes, gentez,*[1] *gruez.*	*Comme segoingnez.*
MAZ	Ostardes, gentes et gruees.	Soient apparoilliez conme la sigoinge.
BN	*Vistardes,*[2] *grues, gantes.*	*Cuissiés comme la seigoingne.*
VAT	**Outardes.**	**Comme la sigongne;**
	au sel menu; et grues semblablement.	

The treatment of stork (Recipe 52), to which this recipe for bustards, gannets and cranes alludes, calls for plucking, de-winging, spitting and singeing.[3] *VAT* apparently chooses to omit gannets from the category of fowl dealt with here, but does explicitly repeat the condiment with which the stork was served and which is likewise to be used here, fine salt.

56. Butors

BN	*Butor. Aussi comme une*[1] *segoine.*	
VAT	**Butor. Comme la sigongne;**	**au sel menu.**

The bittern is an addition of *Y*. The model for its preparation is again the stork of Recipe 52; this seems to indicate at least that the wings of the bittern are to be removed before the bird is spitted and singed.

57. Cormorans

VAL	*Cormorans.*[1]	*Come lez herons.*
BN	*Cormorant.*	*Comme un haron.*
VAT	**Cormorant.**	**Aussi comme le heron; au sel menu.**

---

[8] The *Menagier* mentions both possibilities for using the two sauces he prescribes for his mallard.

[1] *gentez*: the manuscript shows *goutez*.

[2] *Vistardes*: the rubricator's cue for the initial is clearly a *v*, but this might have been misread for an *o* in *BN*'s source.

[3] The *Menagier de Paris* refers to the swan rather than to the stork as a model for the treatment of his *Outardes, grues, gentes* (§153; p. 181).

[1] *une* followed by *seigoi* stroked out.

[1] *Cormorans*: the scribe wrote *cormans*.

MAZ(X) omits the recipe for cormorants. The model for the preparation of the cormorant is the heron, whose recipe, according to *BN* (Recipe 53), is the same as for the stork (Recipe 52)—the wings alone of the bird being therefore removed. What is unique in this recipe is that the finished roast is to be glazed.

58. Poches ...

VAT **Poches et telles manieres d'oiseaulx de riviere. Ainsi comme le heron.**

The spoonbill, representing a type of riverbird, and the teal, which will be dealt with in the next recipe, are *VAT*'s addenda to the section of the *Viandier* that is concerned with wildfowl. The spoonbill is considered to take after the cormorant, and is therefore to be glazed, presumably with its head and legs left on like a heron.

59. Sarcelle

VAT **Sarcelle. Semblablement ainsi comme le mallart de riviere.**

The recipe for teal seems a curious afterthought. Assimilated quite naturally to the mallard (Recipe 54), it is to be divested of its head and feet. The *dodine* that is prepared as a serving sauce for a mallard must be intended to fulfil the same function for the teal.

60. Pourcelet farci

VAL	*Porcelet farcy.*	*Eschaudez, lavez;*	
MAZ	Pourcelet falcis.	Soit eschauder en l'aigue et plumez,	puis
BN	*Pourcel farci.*	*Soit eschaudé et bien lavé*	*et*
VAT	**Pourcelet ou cochon farsy.**	**Soit eschaudé et bien lavé**	**et**

VAL	– – – –	*faitez la farce des yssuez*
MAZ	mectre en broches;	et soit faicte la saulce de l'issue du pourcellet
BN	*rosti;*	*et la farce de l'essue du pourcelet*
VAT	**mis en la broche;**	**la farce faicte des yssues du cochon**

VAL	*et du porc,*	*moiaux d'eufs cuis,*	*formage de*
MAZ	et rotielles de porc cuit	et mieuf d'euf,	fromaige
BN	*et de char de porc cuite*	*et des moyeux d'oeufs cuis,*	*du fromage de*
VAT	**et de chair de porc cuite**	**et des moyeulx d'oeufz,**	**de fromage de**

VAL	*gaing,*	*chastaingnez cuite*	*et du cel,*
MAZ	fondant,	et chastaignes cuites tresbien	et sel
BN	*gain,*	*chataingnes cuites et pelees*	*et de bonne poudre d'espices,*
VAT	**gain,**	**de chastaignes cuites, pelees,**	**et de bonne pouldre d'espices,**

VAL	*broiez,*	*boutez tout ensemble,*
MAZ	et tout broyer ensamble,	puis mecter dedans le pourcellet et[1]
BN	- - - - - -	*et metés ou ventre du pourcelet,*[2]
VAT	- - - - - -	**et mettez tout ou ventre du pourcelet et**

VAL	- - - -	*metez em*[3] *broche, bacinez de vin aigre, de*
MAZ	cousez le partuis,	et en rotissant bacinez de vin aigre et de
BN	- - - - - -	*puis rostir et baciner de vin aigre et de*
VAT	**puis cousez**[4] **la fente**	**et mettez en rost, de vinaigre et de bon**

VAL	*saing boulant;*	*au poivre jaunet.*
MAZ	sain brullant et sel;	et soit maingier a poivre janet.
BN	*sain boulant;*	*mengier au poivre jaunet.*
VAT	**sain boullant;**	**et le mengiez au poivre jaunet tout chault;**
	et aucuns pareceulx le menguent a la cameline.	

In two of the manuscripts, Roast Stuffed Suckling Pig occupies an anomalous position, coming as it does at the end of a section of game birds and immediately preceding a chapter division marking the beginning of a series of *entremets*.[5] In *VAT*, the recipe is included in the chapter on roasts at a point between other four-footed animals and roast domestic fowl. A safe assumption might be that *VAT* anticipated the recipe for stuffed piglet at the earlier point in the book because he considered it more appropriately located among the roasts than among the *entremets*. But this is the other aspect of the problem: as *Y* undoubtedly copied the *Viandier*,[6] stuffed piglet was not among the *entremets* but, as seems to have been the case in *BN* and *MAZ*, was appended to the section on roast game birds! Unless one of the very early copies of the *Viandier* displaced stuffed piglet from an earlier position, and this peculiar location remained "uncorrected" until perhaps *VAT*'s copy, or unless one of the very early copies of the *Viandier* attempted, inaccurately, to insert this recipe into the collection as a new *entremets*, then we should have to make another assumption, and that is that the chapter title for the *entremets* has somehow become misplaced and that stuffed piglet is indeed to be understood to be an *entremets*.[7]

---

[1] *et* followed by *cusez* stroked out.

[2] *pourcelet*: the last letter is missing in a hole in the manuscript.

[3] The last stroke of *em* is very faint.

[4] *puis cousez*: *puisez*, with *cou* inserted above.

[5] Following this recipe *MAZ* has written "Chappitre d'entremés" and *BN* has "Ensuivent les entremez." *VAL* contains no indication of a chapter division.

[6] The Table in the Vatican manuscript shows the same order of recipes here as in the other manuscripts. We may speculate that in copying this Table at the beginning of his version, *VAT* may have decided that the recipe for *Porcellés farciet* was out of place and ought to be moved to an earlier position.

[7] In the *Enseignements*, *Char de porcelez en rost* appears at the end of a series of recipes for four-footed animals (p. 182, l. 46; *Petit traité*, p. 216). Roast Stuffed Suckling Pig occurs regularly

As for variants, *MAZ* shows the most interesting ones. Rather than *lavez* he has written *en l'aigue*; this phrase in *MAZ* may indeed conceivably be a misreading for *lavez*, but *MAZ(X)* also inserts an instruction *plumez* not found elsewhere, and the sense of this verb is problematic. The word is used in a similar context by *VAL* in Recipe 35; at that place goat kid and lamb are subjected to the treatment usually indicated by the verb after being dipped in boiling water. The *Menagier*, whose text is similar to *Y* in the essentials of this recipe, reads at this point: "Soit eschaudé en eaue boulant, puis pelé."[8]

MAZ(X) calls the stuffing a *saulce*, although in Recipe 66 for stuffed poultry *MAZ*, along with all of the other manuscripts, calls a similar stuffing a *farce*. *MAZ* describes the pork stuffing as *rotielles* or *rouelles*. As in Recipe 45, *MAZ(X)* is not happy with the designation "fromage de gain" and substitutes "fromaige fondant."[9] *MAZ(X)* adds salt to both the stuffing and the basting sauce.

The *Menagier de Paris* makes no mention of basting this meat.

The yellow pepper serving sauce (see Recipe 164, below) is still called for as a dressing for piglet in the *Recueil de Riom*.[10]

Entremés (MAZ, BN, VAT)

61. Faux grenon

VAL	*Faux grenon.*	*Cuisiez en vin et en eaue dez foyez, des guisiers*
MAZ	Faulx grenons.	Cuisez en aigue et en vin des foyes et des jousiers
BN	*Faus guernon.*	*Cuisiés en vin et en eaue des foies, des guissés*
VAT	**Faulxgrenon.**	**Cuisiez en vin et en eaue des foyes, des juisiers**

VAL		*ou char de veau,*	*hachiez bien menu,*	*frisiez*
MAZ	de poulaille	ou char de viaul,	puis trainchiez bien menuz	et frissiez
BN	*de poulaille*	*ou de char de veel,*	*et la dehachiés bien menu*	*et frisiés*
VAT	**de poulaille**	**ou de chair de veel,**	**puis la hachiez bien menu**	**et frisiez**

---

as a dish in English cookery books (Austin, pp. 40 and 82; the *Liber cure cocorum*, p. 36), but is nowhere qualified as a dish similar in function to the French *entremets*. Likewise undistinguished among the recipes in the *Sent soví* (ch. 13) is one that is quite close to the *Viandier*'s: *Con se fercez porcel ab fformatge*.

[8] *Menagier de Paris*, §142; p. 178. At §245, p. 216, the *Menagier* says that pigs' trotters should be "bien cuiz et tresbien plumez."

[9] In Recipe 45 *MAZ(X)* had specified *fin froumaige fondant*. The *fromage de gain* is normally used in the *Viandier* wherever the cook desires a cheese which will blend well with other ingredients and produce a mixture of homogenous consistency.

[10] "A couchons, poivre jaunet de gingibre, de girofle, et greyne, et du verjust, et du pain" (*Recueil de Riom*, §37).

VAL	*en saing de lart;*	*broiez gingembre,*	*canelle,*	*girofle,*	–
MAZ	en sain;	puis broyer gigimbre,	cannelle,	giroffle,	–
BN	*en sain de lart;*	*puis broiés gingembre,*	*canelle,*	*girofle,*	*graine*
VAT	**en sain de lart;**	**et puis broyez gingenbre,**	**canelle,**	**giroffle,**	**grainne**

VAL	– –	– – – –	*vin et en verjus, boullon de beuf*
MAZ	– –	– – – –	vin, verjus, boillon de beuf
BN	*de paradis,*	– – – –	*vin, verjus, bouillon de buef*
VAT	**de paradiz,**	**et destrempez de**	**vin, verjus et boullon de beuf**

VAL	*ou de celui mesmez,*	*moiaux de eufs*
MAZ	– – – – – – – – – – – – – –	et des moyeuf d'euf
BN	*ou d'icellui mesmes,*	*et moieux d'oeufs*
VAT	**et du boullon mesmes des foyes, juisiers et veel,**	**et des moyelz d'oeufz**

VAL	*grant foison,*	*collez*		*dessus vostre grain,*	
MAZ	grant foisson,	coulez	parmi l'estermine	dessus vostre grain,	puis
BN	*grant foisson,*	*coullés,*		*deffaites de vostre grain*	*et*
VAT	**grant foison,**	**et coulez**		**dessus vostre grain**	**et**

VAL	*faitez boullir emsemble*	– – – –	*un pou de pain,*	*du*
MAZ	mecter boulir ensamble;	– – – –	– – –	–
BN	*faites bien boulir ensemble, et*	– – – –	*un pou de pain*	*et de*
VAT	**faictes bien boullir ensemble;**	**et y mettent aucuns**	**ung pou de pain**	**et de**

VAL	*saffrein;*	– – – – –	*sur jaune coleur, aigret de verjus;*
MAZ	– –	et doit estre bien lyant,	sur jane couleur, aigre de verjus;
BN	*saffran;*	*et doit estre bien liant,*	*sur jaune couleur, aigret de vergus;*
VAT	**saffran;**	**et doibt estre bien lyant,**	**sur jaune couleur, aigret de verjus;**

VAL	*au drecier*	– – –	*poudrez*	*poudre de canelle.*
MAZ	et adressiez	– – –	– –	poudre de cannelle par dessus.
BN	*au dressier,*	– – –	– –	*poudre d'espicez de canelle.*
VAT	**et au dressier**	**par escuelles**	**mettez**	**dessus pouldre de canelle.**

According to *MAZ*, *BN* and *VAT*, the recipe for *Faux grenon* opens a chapter of what are termed *entremets*. Originally such a dish was prepared for presentation between courses and was considered for that reason to be less substantial, an interlude in the succession of serious meat, fowl and fish preparations. The *entremets* fulfilled the same function as farces later did between the acts of a theatre play. In time, perhaps as the main courses demanded less of the cook's attention, and certainly by the beginning of the fifteenth century,[1] his

[1] *Cf.* the *entremés eslevé* of a fully manned Castle of Love under siege in Chiquart (*Du fait de cuisine*, §10, f. 30r), and the series of *entremets* in the last section of *VAT*'s copy of the *Viandier* itself (Recipes 215–219).

artistry and skill were turned toward the *entremets* as a means of exercising his culinary skill and challenging the resources of his imagination. This dish became the chef's personal creation, an invention, or *subtletie* as the English called it, that was designed primarily to impress the diners before whom it was displayed. The *entremets* in Recipes 61–74 of the *Viandier* belong more to the earlier notion of what this course should be; they consist generally of porridges, jellied meats and stuffings.

By the time at the end of the fourteenth century that the *Menagier* was written, the *entremets* forms one of the concluding elements of a meal.[2]

The *Faux grenon* is essentially a spiced meat pâté, yellow in colour, stiff in consistency and with a distinct taste of verjuice. As an *entremets* it is considered an incidental dish.

Among the variants in this recipe are *BN*'s scribal error where *dessus* seems to have been written for *deffais* or *deffaites*. *MAZ(X)* omits bread and saffron from the ingredients—even though *Z* has added the notation that the mixture is to be both stiff and yellowish.[3] When copying the garnish to be used in presenting the dish, *BN* automatically wrote *d'espicez* after the word *poudre*.

62. Menus drois ...

VAL	*Menus drois: de piés, de foyez et de jusiers.*	*Faitez cuire en vin*
BN	*Menus doies: piés, foies, guisiers.*	*Faites cuire en vin*
VAT	**Menuz piez, foyes et juisiers.**	**Mettez cuire en vin**

VAL	*et en eaue tresbien;*	*metez vostre grain,*	*quant il sera cuit,*
BN	*et en eaue tresbien;*	*si metés vostre grain,*	*quant il sera cuit,*
VAT	**et en eaue tres bien,**	**et les mettez**	– – – –

[2] See the series of menus in the *Menagier de Paris* (ed. Brereton and Ferrier, p. 124 f.; ed. Pichon, p. 91 f.) where suggested *entremets* include a boar's head, stuffed shoulder of mutton, and the gastronomic creation known as Pilgrim capons (see Chiquart's *Du fait de cuisine*, §45). According to Olivier de la Marche, the *entremets* was served at the conclusion of a banquet in 1454: *Mémoires*, ed. H. Beaune and J. d'Arbaumont, 4 vols. (Paris: Renouard, 1883–1888), vol. 4, pp. 348 and 369.

[3] Essentially the same recipe as the *Viandier*'s is found already in the *Enseignements* (p. 182, l. 62; *Petit traité*, p. 217) near the beginning of the work between recipes for the most common domestic fowl, capons, hens and geese. It bears the title *Faus grenon* as in *BN*, though it is not designated as an *entremets*. It seems to be considered a variety of poultry dish, and the possibility of substituting minced veal for the minced chicken gizzards and livers is not mentioned. The *Menagier de Paris* (§235; p. 211) reproduces substantially the same recipe as is in the *Viandier*, but makes both toast and saffron optional ingredients by saying for both of these, "aucuns y mectent . . . ." It may be that this choice had been introduced already by *Z* and that *MAZ(X)* decided to ignore it, preferring to depend entirely upon the egg yolks for both colour and consistency. Later in the *Menagier* (§246; p. 216) there is a *Potage party* which is explicitly a variety of *Faulx grenon*. Chiquart's recipe for *Morterieulx* (also called *Ung chaut mengier* and *Faugrenon*) is similar to the *Viandier*'s *Faux grenon* except that in the *Du fait de cuisine* (§52, f. 77r) it is a *parti* version in two colours with two garnishes, as is the *Menagier*'s recipe at §246; p. 216.

VAL *en un plat, du percin, du vin aigre par dessus.*
BN *en un plat, et du percil et du vin aigre par dessus; autrement,*
VAT **en ung plat, et du persil et du vin aigre par dessus.**

BN *en lieu de percil et de vin aigre, metés lait lié de moieux d'oeufs et de pain, de la poudre d'espices et un pou de saffren; et dressiés sus les escueilles sanz percil et vin aigre.*

The proper name for this dish is given by *VAL*: *Menus drois*. The term, denoting the delicate parts of an animal,[1] was apparently not familiar enough to the scribes of *BN* and *VAT* who, respectively, read *menus doies* and *menus piez*. The word *piez* in *VAT* may be a misreading for *doiez* or may well be one of the ingredients (as indeed we see it in *VAL*), the word *drois* having been missed in the copying.[2]

The dish appears to be an alternate preparation for the preceding *Faux grenon* which uses poultry livers and giblets.[3] It differs in part from this previous recipe in the inclusion of parsley, and in the use of vinegar—whose taste is to predominate—rather than verjuice.[4]

---

[1] In his edition of the *Menagier de Paris* Pichon noted that the *menus droits* of a stag were the "morceaux recherchés, réservés au seigneur qui les mangeoit souvent après la chasse même" (p. 156, n6). Tilander (*Glanures*, p. 75) declared that the *menus droits de poulaille* are "le gosier et le foie."

[2] In any case the two words *drois* and *dois* seem to have become confused in the later history of this recipe. A Middle English derivative of this recipe was *Pettitoes* which combined minced liver, heart and lungs of a pig with an acid liquid such as lemon juice, and egg yolk for colour and thickening; pig's feet are boiled with the other meat, but are split and served only as a garnish on the finished dish. In the *Tractatus* (part II, §9) there is a recipe for parts of a goose, "collum vero cum capite, pedibus, aliis intestinis," cooked in wine with sage, parsley and hyssop, and vinegar or verjuice.

For some writers the term *dois* has to do with the size and shape of the slices into which a prepared food is cut. The *Platine en françois* has a recipe for *Potaige frumentin ou menusdetz*: "Le potaige frumentin se fait forment ainsi que nous avons dit des lozans / mais l'on les decouppe plus menuement ... " (f. 72). A recipe for *Fromentee* will follow in the *Viandier*.

[3] In the 1490 edition of the *Viandier* that was published by Pichon and Vicaire with their edition of manuscript versions, the fifteenth-century printer indicated that among the ingredients of *Faulx grenon* are "des menus droits de poulaille, comme foyes, de jusier" (p. 154).

[4] The *Menagier de Paris* has a dish called *Droiz au persil et au vinaigre* (p. 180, l. 18; p. 100) that seems to be the *Menus drois* of the *Viandier*. The dish appears in English under the name of *A disshe mete for Somere* ("Take garbage of capons ande of hennes ... ": Arundel manuscript 334, ed. Warner in *Antiquitates Culinariae*, p. 58; ed. Hieatt and Butler in *Curye on Inglysch*, part V, p. 156), where it is served cold, at night, with ginger and cinnamon added to the parsley and vinegar. Austin also published two recipes for a dish called *Garbage* (pp. 9 and 72) which uses chickens' heads, feet, livers and gizzards; the treatment of these giblets varies somewhat from what the *Viandier* shows.

MAZ(X) has not copied this recipe. *BN*, on the other hand, provides another possible preparation for this particular meat, substituting for two of the ingredients, the parsley and vinegar, a number of others which combine to constitute quite a different type of dish: egg yolks, saffron, bread, spices and milk. This alternative, a yellow *Menus drois*, would be a little less unlike the *Faux grenon* of the previous recipe. In fact it bears rather a strong resemblance to the version of the *Faus guernon* found in the *Enseignements*.[5]

63. Formentee

VAL	*Formentee. Prenez forment*	*appareliė,*	– – – – – –
MAZ	Fromentee. Prener froument,	espailliez	– – – – – –
BN	*Formentee. Prennés forment*	*bien esleu, puis le mouilliés de eaue tiede*	
VAT	**Fromentee. Prenez fourment**	**et l'appareillez**	– – – – – –

BN	*et le liés en un drapel, puis batés du petail dessus bien fort atant qu'il*

VAL	– – – –	*lavez bien*	*et metez cuire*	*en yaue;*
MAZ	– – – –	et lavez tresbien,	– – – –	
BN	*soit tout espouillié,*	*et lavés tresbien*	– – – –	*en eaue;*
VAT	– – – –	**et lavez tres bien,**	**puis le mettez cuire**	**en eaue;**

VAL	*quant il sera cuit*	*cil l'esprenez;*	*et prenez lait*
MAZ	puis le mecter cuire	et le purer;	puis bouler lait de vaiche
BN	*et quant il sera tresbien cuit*	*si le purés;*	*et prennés lait de vache*
VAT	**et quant il sera cuit**	**si le purez;**	**puis prenez lait de vache**

VAL	*boullu,*	*puis metez dedens vostre formentee,*	*faites boullir,*
MAZ	une onde	et mecter vostre froument dedans et	mecter boulir et
BN	*boulli une onde,*	*puis metés cuire dedans vostre forment,*	
VAT	**boully une onde**	**et mettez le froment dedans et**	**faictes boullir**

VAL		*remuez souvent;*	*quant il sera*[1] *ung pou reffroidy,*
MAZ		remuer souvent;	puis quant ilz sera bien reffroidiez,
BN		– – – –	*et tirés arriere du feu, et*
VAT	**une onde,**	– – – –	**et tirez arriere du feu, et**

VAL	– – – –	*fillez moiaux d'eufs ou*
MAZ	– – – –	fillez dedans moyeuf d'euf bien batus
BN	*remués souvant, et*	*fillés dedans moyeux d'uefs grant foison, et*
VAT	**remuez souvent, et**	**fillez dedans moyeulx d'oeufz grant foison; et**

BN	*qu'il ne soit pas trop chaut quant l'en les filera dedans, et remués dedans*

---

[5] *Enseignements*, p. 182, l. 61; *Petit traité*, p. 217.

[1] *sera* followed by *la* expunctuated.

VAL	*collez dedens le forment*	*du saffren bien pou;*	– – – –
MAZ	– – – – – – –	et ung poul de saffrain	– – – –
BN	*puis fines espices*	*et saffran un pou;*	
VAT	**aucuns y mettent espices**	**et saffren et de**	**l'eaue de la venoison;**

VAL	*du succre assez soit mis dedens le pot;*	*acuns y metent espices;*
MAZ	et succre assés par dessus le pout;	et aulcuns y mectent espices;

VAL	*doit estre jaunet.*
MAZ	et doit estre bien janet et lyant.
BN	*et doit estre un liant et jaunet; et aucuns y metent de l'eaue de la venoisson.*
VAT	**et doit estre jaunette et bien liante.**

Fromentee is a common dish in mediæval cookery and is a type of cream of wheat made with milk and egg yolks.[2] *BN* or its immediate source has, rather surprisingly,[3] added the most substance to the text of this recipe, indicating in detail the steps by which the wheat is to be prepared, and emphasizing that the egg yolks should not be stirred into too hot a wheat mush. Where the other manuscripts observe merely that spices are an optional ingredient, *BN* makes them obligatory.

With the word *ou*, *VAL* shows that saffron is one of those optional ingredients, whereas in *Z* saffron becomes a requirement. *Y* omits the sugar which was an ingredient in both *VAL* and *MAZ*—even though *MAZ(X)* seems to have misread just where the sugar was to go. *Y* adds a curious ingredient toward the end of his copy of the recipe, venison broth; as *BN* copies it, this is the only optional ingredient in the whole recipe; for *VAT* the venison broth is optional, as are the spices and the saffron, which *Z* seemed to make a requirement by using the word *et* rather than *VAL*'s *ou*. The *Menagier de Paris*, in which *fourmentee* is the initial item in the chapter on "Entremés, fritures et dorures," makes it clear that venison broth is intended as a possible alternative for milk on meat-days.[4] Similarly the *Menagier* explains that for him the saffron is to be an optional supplement to the egg yolks in case the yellow colour is not sufficiently pronounced.[5]

Fromentee is served particularly as a side-dish: "Le sanglier salé se mengut a la fourmentee."[6]

---

[2] The dish turns up in English cookery books under the name Furmenty (for instances, see Austin, or Hieatt and Butler). See also the *Recueil de Riom*, §11.

[3] This is a rare instance in which *BN* contains specific details not found in the other manuscripts.

[4] "A jour de poisson, l'en prend lait; a jour de char, du boullon de de la char" (*Menagier de Paris*, §234; p. 210).

[5] Recipe 207 indicates that *fromentee* has the reddish-yellow colour of saffron. *Fromentee* similarly provides a recognized standard for the thickness of a mixture in Recipes 199 and 207.

[6] *Menagier*, §91; p. 158. The *Menagier*'s menus make it very clear that *fromentee* was regularly served with venison on meat-days, or with porpoise or dolphin, the lean equivalent of venison, on fish-days. In the Anglo-Norman lexical treatise of Walter of Biblesworth which dates from the end

64. Garlins / Taillis

VAL	*Garlins.*	*Prenez figues et resins,*	*lait d'amandes*
MAZ	– –	Prenez figues, raisins	et lait d'amandres
BN	*Taillés.*	*Prennés figues et raysins,*	*lait d'almendes,*
VAT	**Tailliz.**	**Prenez figues, roisins**	**et lait d'amendes**

VAL	*boullu;*	*prenés eschaudés,*	–
MAZ	et mecter boulir ensamble;	puis prenez eschaudez,	gaitellet
BN	– – – – – – –	*et eschaudés*	*et galetes,*
VAT	**boully,**	**eschaudez,**	**galettes**

VAL	*croustez de pain blanc copez menu,*
MAZ	et croutes de pain blanc menus coppez,
BN	*croute de pain blanc coupé menu,*
VAT	**et crouste de pain blanc couppé menu par petiz morceaulx quarrez**

VAL	*metez boullir*	– – – – – – – –
MAZ	et faicte boulir tout ensamble	– – – – – – – –
BN	*et faites boullir le lait;*	*prennés saffran pour lui donner couleur,*
VAT	**et faictes boullir vostre lait,**	**et saffren pour luy donner couleur,**

VAL	– –	– – – – – – – –	*tant qu'il soit*
MAZ	– –	– – – – – – – –	tant qu'ilz soit
BN	*et sucre,*	*et puis metés boullir tout en samble*	*tant qu'il soit*[1]
VAT	**et succre,**	**et puis mettez boullir tout ensemble**	**tant qu'il soit**

VAL	*bien liant pour taillier.*
MAZ	bien lyant pour tailliez.
BN	*bien liant pour tailler.*
VAT	**bien lyant pour taillier; et mettre par escuelles.**

The name of this dish varies according to the manuscript in which it is copied. The *Y* manuscripts seem to agree that the name is derived from the verb *taillier*, "to cut," this being the final step in this recipe, and the one that is to determine the consistency to which the whole mixture is to be cooked.[2] Because the *Menagier* has *taillis* as the form

---

of the thirteenth century we find that the service of on exemplary meal opens with the presentation of a boar's head, "tot armé," followed immediately by *veneysoun ou* [with] *la fourmenté*: Richard Wright, *A Volume of Vocabularies* (2nd ed.; n.p.: privately published, 1882), p. 173.

For other uses of this porridge see Austin, pp. 14 and 91. See also Recipe 118, below.

[1] *soit*: the last three letters are missing in a hole in the manuscript.

[2] The names *taylez*, *taylys*, *taylours* are found in fifteenth-century English cookery manuscripts.

of the word for its title,[3] it may be safe to assume that *BN* wrote a less common version of the name. The dish is called *Garlins* by *VAL* alone, evidently a more archaic variant of the name; the meaning of this latter word is not known.[4] Among the recipes added at the end of the *VAT* manuscript is a *Tailliz de Karesme* (Recipe 207) that is virtually identical to the dish we have here. Both are meatless preparations, although Cotgrave describes the sixteenth-century *taillis* as "A Hachee; or made-dish of Crevisse, the flesh of Capons, or Veale, bread, wine, salt, veriuice, and spices; also, a kind of gellie."

Apart from the apparent change in name, the recipe has undergone several other modifications over time. *Z* has added *galettes* (flat cakes) to the *eschaudés* (wafers) and white bread, all of which are to be chopped small—into cubes according to *VAT*. *Y* has added saffron and sugar to the whole pot. The use of sugar remains rare in the traditional body of *Viandier* recipes. Though *Y* introduces it here in this recipe for *Garlins/Taillis*, and all four manuscripts call for it in the recipe for a yellow sauce on fish (§88), the primary function of sugar in the *Viandier* is still medicinal (Recipes 90, 93–95, below).[5]

VAT indicates that the finished, cut pudding should be served in bowls.

65. Millet

VAL	-	*Eschaudez, lavez en .ii. pairez*[1] *de eauez,*	-	*metez*
MAZ	-	Eschaudez le deux ou trois fois,		puis le mecter
BN	*Millot.*	*Mouilliés le en eaue chaude en trois peres,*		*puis le metés*
VAT	**Milet.**	**Moulliez le en trois paires d'eaue chaude,**		**puis le mettez**

VAL	*lait de vache;*	*n'i metez point la cullier*	*jusques*
MAZ	en lait de vaiche fremiant,	et n'y mecter poin de cuilliez	jusques
BN	*en lait de vache fremiant,*	*et n'y metés point de cueillier*	*jusques*
VAT	**en lait de vache fremiant,**	**et n'y mettez point la cullier**	**jusquez**

VAL	*a ce qu'il ait boullu*	- - - - -
MAZ	ad ce qu'il aye bien boulir;	puis le mecter jus du feu,
BN	*ad ce qu'il ait bien boulli;*	*puis le metés jus du feu*
VAT	**ad ce qu'il ait boully; et**	**puis le mettez jus de dessus le feu**

BN *et le batés*[2] *du dos de la cueillier,*[3] *puis le remetés sur le feu,*

---

[3] *Menagier de Paris*, §237; p. 211. Here, in what the *Menagier* calls "Tailliz a servir comme en Karesme," apples are substituted for the figs listed by the *Viandier*, undoubtedly for practical reasons of availability.

[4] "Origine incertaine; peut-être à rattacher à l'afr. *walingre* m. (m.neerl. WALLINGE, 'sorte de patisserie' GilMuisK 1,112,20, *FEW*, 17, 492b; Barbier, *ZfSL*, 55, 408)" (*Dictionnaire étymologique de l'ancien français*).

[5] See Santich, *Two Languages*, Chapter 8.

[1] *pairez*: the manuscript shows *panez*.

[2] *bates*: the manuscript shows *baces*.

[3] *cueillier* followed by *iusquez* which is stroked out.

VAL – – – – – – – – – – – – – – *tant qu'il*
MAZ et ung pol de saffrain; – – – – – – et
BN *et un pou de saffran, et metés boullir tant qu'il*
VAT **et y mettez ung peu de saffren et puis le mettez boullir tant qu'il**

VAL *soit espés.*
MAZ soit bien espés.
BN *soit bien espés.*
VAT **soit assez, et puis le dreciez par escuelles.**

In *VAL* the recipe for *Millet* continues, with neither break nor title, immediately after the last word of the recipe for *Garlins*. Such a blunder may be explicable as a result of the scribe's inattention, but suggests too that the source from which he was copying may have contained this recipe for *Millet* in such a way, perhaps added marginally in such a position, that *VAL* believed it was intended as an addition or an alternative to the *Garlins*. *MAZ* likewise does not indicate a title for this recipe; the *MAZ* copy is peculiar, however, in that from this point on recipes *with* names become rarer than those without. *BN* misspells *millot* for *millet*.[4]

While *VAL* is content to wash the grains of millet twice, *Z* suggests either two or three washings, and *Y* says flatly to wash three times, specifying that warm water should be used. *VAL* directs that milk is to be added to the washed millet, whereas *Z* alters this to read that the millet should rather be poured into simmering milk; *Z* further mentions that, after having boiled, this mixture should be removed from the fire and saffron added.

The instruction to stir with the back of the spoon, even though this does not appear in *VAT*, is probably an addition by *Y* because the phrase is picked up by the *Menagier*.

66. Poullaille farcie

VAL *Poulaille farcie. Prenez la et li copez le gavion,*
MAZ Poulaille farcie. Prener voz poullailles et les coppés les gavions,
BN *Poullaille farcie. Prennés vostre poulaille et leur coupés le gavion,*
VAT **Poullaille farcie. Prenez vos poullez et leur couppez le gavion,**

VAL *eschaudez, plumez,* – – – –
MAZ puis les eschaudez et plumez – – – – –
BN *puis les eschaudés et plumés, et gardés la pel saine,*
VAT **puis les eschaudez et plumez, et gardez que la peau soit sainne**

VAL – – *ne lez refaites pas; boutez un tuel*
MAZ – – et ne les reffaicte pas; puis mecter ung tuel
BN – – *et sans refaire; prennés un tuel*
VAT **et entiere, et ne la reffaictes point en l'eaue; puis prenez ung tuel**

[4] The spelling of the name of this dish in the *Menagier de Paris* is *milet* (§136; p. 176). The author of the *Menagier* places the dish not among the *Entremets* but earlier, among the "Potages lians sans chair."

VAL – – – – *entre la char et la pel et l'enfflés,*
MAZ – – – – – entre chart et pel et enfflez
BN – – – – – *et le boutés entre le cuir et la char et l'enflés,*
VAT **de chaume ou autre, et le boutez entre cuir et chair et l'enflez,**

VAL *puis la ffendés entre lez espaulez et n'y faitez pas grant trou,*
MAZ par entre les espaulles et n'y faicte pas tropt grant trou,
BN *puis la fendés entre les espaules et ne faites pas trop grant trou,*
VAT **puis le fendez entre les espaules et n'y faictes pas trop grant trou,**

VAL *laissiez a la pel toutez lez membres.*
MAZ et lessiez tenir a la pel les alles, le col
BN *et lessiés tenans a la pel les elles et le col*
VAT **et laissiez tenant a la peau les cuissetes, les ailles et le col**

VAL – – – – – – – *Pour faire la farce, prenez*
MAZ a tout la teste et les piez. Et pour faire la farce,
BN *atout la teste et les piés. Pour faire la farce, prennés*
VAT **atout la teste et les pietz aussi. Et pour faire la farce, prenez**

VAL *veel cuit, rouelle de porc cuit, du braon de la poulaille,*
MAZ chart de vel cuit et rouelles de porc et des broyons de poullaille cuis,
BN *char de mouton, de veel, du porc, du blanc des poullés,*
VAT **chair de mouton, de veel, de porc, du brun des poulletz,**

VAL *hachiez tout ensemble,* – – *broiez*
MAZ et achés tout ensamble, – – puis broyer en ung mortiez
BN *hachiés tout ensemble tout cru, puis les broiés en un mortier,*
VAT **et hachiez tout ensemble tout cru, puis les broyez en ung mortier,**

VAL *avec grant foison d'eufs cuis, chastaignez cuitez, formage*
MAZ avec grant foisson d'euf et de chastaines cuites et fin froumaige
BN *et oeufs tous crus* – – – – – *aveques fromage*
VAT **et des oeulfz tous cruz** – – – – – **avec de bon frommaige**

VAL *de gaing, pourdre d'espices, bien pou de saffren;*
MAZ et poudre d'espices, ung pol de saffrain,
BN *de gain et bonne poudre d'espices et un pou de saffran;*
VAT **de gain et de bonne pouldre d'espices et ung bien pou de saffren;**

VAL *salez; emplez vostre poulaille;* – –
MAZ et de sel; emplir la poulaille et recousez le trou.
BN *et sallés apoint; puis emplez vos poulés et recousés;*
VAT **et sallez a point; puis emplez voz poullez et recousez le trou;**

VAL *de vostre remaignant faitez pomez durez,*
BN *et du demourant de vostre farce faites en ponmes aussi come pastiaux*
VAT **et du remenant de vostre farce faictes en pommez comme parciaulx**

VAL *metez boullir en boullon de beuf,*
BN *de garde, et metés cuire en bouillon de buef ou en eaue boulant,*
VAT **de guede, et mettez cuire en boullion de beuf et en eaue boullant,**

VAL *du saffran grant foison, a petit boullon;*
BN *et du saffren grant foison, et qu'il ne boulent pas trop fort qui ne se*
VAT **et du saffran grant foison, et qu'ilz ne boullent mie trop fort qu'ilz ne se**

VAL *destrempés de la fleur de moiaux d'eufs,*[1] *coullez bien;*
BN *despiecent;* - - - - - - - - - - - - - *puis les*
VAT **despiecent;** - - - - - - - - - - - - - **puis**

VAL *metez en une neufve broche rostir;* - - - -
BN *enbrochiés en une broche de fer bien deliee.* - - - -
VAT **enhastez voz poulletz en une broche de fer bien liees et les pommes aussi.**

VAL *coullez dez moiaux pardessus en rostissant—aucuns le font sans couler.*

VAL *Pour la dorer,*
MAZ Et pour la dourez,
BN *Pour faire les dorees,*
VAT **Et pour les dorer ou couvrir de vert ou de jaune: pour le jaune,**

VAL *prenez moiaux d'eufs cuis, broiez du saffren avec;*
MAZ prener moyeuf d'euf, broyer, et du saffrain avecques;
BN *prennés grant foisson des moieux d'oeufs avec du saffron broié et*
VAT **prenez grant foison de moyeulx d'oefs et les batez bien et ung pou**

BN *batu tout en semble, et les en dorés;*
VAT **de saffren avec, et mettez la doreure en ung plat ou autre vaissel;**

VAL *qui veult dorure vert si broie la verdure sans saffren,*
MAZ et qui lez veult dorez vers, sans saffrain broyer de la verdure
BN *qui veult doree verde si prengne la verdure*[2] *broiee,*
VAT **et qui veult doreure verte si braye la verdure**

---

[1] Flour is to be soaked in egg yolks.

[2] *verdure* followed by *doree* stroked out.

VAL	*moiaux d'eufs grant foison*	*batus,*	*passez parmy l'estamine*
MAZ	avec moyeuf d'euf,	– –	passi par l'estermine
BN	*puis des moyeux d'oefs grant foison*	*bien batus,*	*passés par l'estamine,*
VAT	**avec les oeufz; et**	– –	– – – – –

VAL	*et dorez:*	*quant la poulaille sera cuite,*
MAZ	et dourez	la poullaille quant elle est cuite
BN	*et prennez la doreure et en dorés*	*quant vostre poulaille sera cuite;*
VAT	– – – – – – – –	**aprés ce que vostre poulaille sera cuite**

BN	*et vous pourés dressier vostre broche ou vessel ou sera vostre doreure*
VAT	**et voz pommes, drecieez vostre broche ou vaissel ou vostre doreure sera**

VAL	*getez la dorure au loing*	– – – – – – –
MAZ	et gectiez vostre dourure y dessus	– – – – – – –
BN	*et y jetés du lonc vostre doreure*	*et remetés au feu afin que*
VAT	**et gectez tout du long vostre doreure**	**et remettez au feu affin que**

VAL	– – – – – – –	*par deux ou par .iii. foys.*	
MAZ	– – – – – – –	deux ou trois fois,	et garder
BN	*vostre doreure ce prenne,*	*par ii foies ou par iii,*	*et gardés*
VAT	**vostre doreure se preigne,**	**par deux fois ou par trois,**	**et gardez**

MAZ	qu'elle n'arde.
BN	*qu'elle n'aist pas trop fort feu.*
VAT	**que vostre doreure n'ait grant feu qu'elle ne arde.**

There are three parts to this recipe for stuffed poultry: the preparation of the bird itself, the making of the stuffing and the procedure for glazing the roasting meat. Altogether it is one of the longest recipes in the *Viandier*.[3]

Poulaille farcie is a common *entremets*: Chiquart includes this preparation among the many such *entremets* which compose his grand *Chastel d'Amours*.[4]

---

[3] A similar *entremets* of stuffed and glazed chicken is copied at Recipe 195. Rodinson refers to two separate recipes in the *Wusla* (p. 157) in which a chicken skin is stuffed with a paste of the chicken's meat. Similarly the *Kitab al-tabij* (trans. Huici Miranda, p. 59) contains a recipe for stuffed boneless chicken. See also in the *Liber cure cocorum*, p. 26, the *Capons in Cassolyce*; in the *LVII Ricetti*, §16, *Capponi ripieni*; and the mention in the *Sent soví*, p. 221, of how to "Ffasir gallina que no y aga os." Recipe 21 for *Affare gallina piena* in Libro "A" of the Anonimo Meridionale resembles the *De gallina implenda* of the *Liber de coquina*, part II, §20.

[4] *Du fait de cuisine*, f. 32r: "Et es creneaux de ladicte basse court soient poullez escorchiez et revestuz et dorés, et herisons dorés, et pomes dorees feites de chars, pot d'Espaniz fait de cher tout dorés . . . ."

There are few significant variants in the first part of the recipe. Where *VAL* has "toutez lez menbres," *Z* enumerates wings, neck-with-head, and feet. To these specifics *VAT* adds, unnecessarily, the *cuissetes* or chicken legs.

For the stuffing, *Y* adds mutton to the list of meats to be minced and deletes the specification of *rouelles* of pork found in the earlier manuscripts. The word for brawn seems to have caused some difficulty, perhaps to *Y*, because *BN* and *VAT* write respectively that white or dark meat from the chicken is to be used. *Y* further modifies the list of ingredients for the stuffing by omitting chestnuts.[5]

MAZ(X) omits the whole section on the making of little balls from any left-over stuffing.[6] Because of this omission it is difficult to see whether *VAL*'s direction for making a sort of egg-yolk basting for these stuffing balls may have been in *O* or whether it was added by *VAL* himself or by an immediate source; the supplementary note in *VAL*, "aucuns le font sans couler," seems to point to the latter explanation. A rare instance of a scribal error in *VAT* appears as, copying *bien deliee*—which describes the slender iron spit—he write *bien liees*, making the past participle plural to agree with *poulletz* but retaining the feminine of *broche*.

The two colours of glazing are mentioned by *VAT* in the introductory phrase of the third part of the recipe. *Y* probably had the direction "et mettez la doreure en ung plat ou autre vaissel"—which corresponds with the form of the direction found later in *BN* and *VAT*: "dreciez vostre broche ou vaissel ou vostre doreure sera." However, *BN*, apparently not understanding the reason for this step, omits it and, impatiently, directs the cook to go ahead "et les en dorés." An omission for another reason occurs later as *VAT* felt that the direction to "glaze the chicken" when it is cooked was superfluous[7] because the recipe proceeds to tell how the operation should be done. This quasi-duplication of directions was already in *VAL* because he explains, briefly, the way in which the glazing is to be carried out. The method of glazing will be amplified by *Y*. Strangely, *BN*'s misreading of *voz pommes* by *vous pourés* does not seriously affect the sense of the passage. A most satisfactory version would imply a colon after *dorés*, as in *VAL*.

---

[5] These ingredients used to stuff chicken are identical to those used to stuff suckling pig (Recipe 60), except that chestnuts are included by all manuscripts and a little saffron is used. While not used in the mixture with which the bird is actually stuffed, saffron is specified for the balls that are to be made from the surplus stuffing.

[6] *Pommes* are made also in Recipes 95 and 195, below. Glazed meat-balls or rissoles are called *pome-dory* in Middle English: see Hieatt and Butler, part II, §§42 and 59; and part IV, §182 (*Forme of Cury*, ed. Warner, §174); and the *Liber cure cocorum*, p. 37. In the *Viaunde e claree* the name of the dish has become *Poume d'orages* and *Pomme de orages* (ed. Hieatt and Jones, §1, p. 862).

[7] The *Menagier de Paris*, following *Y*, writes, "Passez par l'estamine pour la verdure, et en dorer poulaille quant elle sera cuicte, et vos pommes, et dreciez vostre broche ou vaissel ... " (§242; p. 214).

67. [Unnamed]

MAZ Prener poulés[1] et les mecter par quartiers, puis les mecter sousfrire dedans ung poult avec ribelletes de lart en houschant souvent le poult, et le tenir couvert moult bien; puis quant ilz est bien souffrir, prener boillon de beuf et les mecter dedans pour cuire; et puis batez moyeuf d'euf, verjus et saffrain et fillez dedans, et soit bien lyant; et dressiez les quartiers par plas et sur chascun plas la ribelete de lart par les quartiers, et puis, par dessus, vostre brouet.

There seems to be no similar recipe for chicken cooked with pork in any other early cookery book. Here is a clear instance of *X*'s professional resourcefulness, whether as a practising cook he has incorporated one of his own recipes—for which no name existed, or at least was copied by *MAZ*—or whether he (or *MAZ*) has found this recipe among those of the secondary source that he followed after the end of his source-copy of the *Viandier*.

68. Gelee de poisson ...

VAL	*Gelee de poison qui porte limon ou de char.*	*Metez*	*cuire*[1]	- - -
MAZ	Prener poisson qui porte lymon ou de chart	et mecter	-	avec vostre grain
BN	*Gelee de poisson qui porte limon ou de char.*	*Metés*	*cuire*	- - - -
VAT	**Gelee de poisson a lymon et de chair.**	**Mettez le**	**cuire**	- - - -

VAL	*en vin et en verjus et vin aigre,*	- -
MAZ	en vin ou en vin aigre et verjus;	- -
BN	*en vin, verjus et vin aigre*	*et de l'eaue,*
VAT	**en vin et en verjus et en vinaigre,**	**et aucuns y mettent de l'eaue ung pou;**

VAL	*un pou de pain qui veut;*	*prenez*	*gingenbre, canelle,*
MAZ	- - - - - - - - -	puis broyer	gigimbre, cannelle,
BN	*et aucuns y metent un pou de pain;*	*puis prennés*	*gingembre, canelle,*
VAT	- - - - - - - - -	**puis prenez**	**gingenbre, canelle,**

VAL	*girofle,*	*grene de paradis,*	*poivre long,*	*noys muguetez,*	*saffren,*
MAZ	giroffle,	graine de paradis,	poivre long,	noix noiguetes,	saffrain,
BN	*girofle,*	*grain de paradis,*	*poivre lonc,*	*nois mugaites*	*et saffren,*
VAT	**girofle,**	**grainne de paradiz,**	**poivre long,**	- - -	-

VAL	*cilion folion,*	*broiez*	*et le liés en ung blanc drapel*
MAZ	cilion folion,	et broyer bien,	puis liez en ung drappel
BN	- - -	*broiés*	- - - - - -
VAT	- - -	- - -	- - - - - -

---

[1] *poulés*: The principal ingredient here may also be understood as *poules*, of course.

[1] *cuire* followed by *me* expunctuated.

VAL	- - - - - - - - -	- - - - - - -
MAZ	- - - - - - - - -	- - - - - - -
BN	*et deffaites de vostre bouillon*	- - - - - - -
VAT	**et deffaictes de vostre boullon**	**et passez parmy l'estamine,**

VAL	*et metez*	*boullir*	*avec vostre poisson ou char,*	- - - - -
MAZ	et mecter	boulir	avec vostre poisson ou chart,	- - - - -
BN	*et metés*	-	*aveques vostre grain,*	- - - - -
VAT	**puis mettez**	**boullir**	**avec vostre grain;**	**puis prenez feulles de**

VAT **lorier, espic, garingal et maciz et les liez en vostre estamine sans la**

VAT **laver, sur le marc des autres espices, et mettez boullir avec vostre grain,**

BN	*et l'escumés tant come il sera sus du feu,*[2]	- - - - - -
VAT	**et le couvrez tant comme il sera sur le feu,**	**et quant il sera jus du feu**

VAL	*et l'ezcumez*[3] *tourjours*	*jusques a ce qu'il soit drecié;*
MAZ	et l'escumez tout jours	jusquez adce que soit dressiez;
BN	*si l'escumés*	*atant qu'il soit drecié;*
VAT	**si l'escumez**	**jusqu'a tant qu'il sera drecié;**

VAL	*quant il sera cuit,*	-
MAZ	puis quant ilz sera cuit,	-
BN	*aprés que il sera drecié,*	*si purés*
VAT	**et puis quant il sera cuit,**	**si purez**

BN *vostre boullon en un vessel de boies et le lessiés ressuir;*
VAT **vostre boullon en ung net vaissel de boys tant qu'il soit rassiz;**

VAL *metez vostre grain refroidir sur une nappe;*
MAZ mecter vostre grain sur une blanche nappe reffroidiez,
BN *et metés vostre grain sur une blanche nappe,*
VAT **et mettez vostre grain sur une nappe blanche,**

VAL	*ce c'est poison,*	*le peler*	*et nestoier*	*et getez lez peleurez*
MAZ	- - - -	et soit peler	- -	et gectier les parures
BN	*et ce est poisson*	*si lez pellés*	- -	*et metés les peleures*
VAT	**et se c'est poisson**	**si le pelez**	**et nettoiez**	**et gectez voz pelleures**

---

[2] *sus du feu*: the manuscript shows *sus le feu qu*, *le* and *qu* stroked out and *du* inserted above *le*.

[3] The scribe wrote two words, *lez cumez*. Aebischer read them as *lez cuvrez*.

VAL	*ou boillon,* – – – – – – – – – – – – – –
MAZ	sur vostre boillon, – – – – – – – – – – – – –
BN	*en vostre bouillon jusquez atant qu'il soit coullé la derreniere foies,*
VAT	**en vostre boullon jusqu'a tant qu'il soit coullé la derniere foiz,**

VAL	*sans le troble;*[4] *et ne fault pas attendre*
MAZ	– – – – – – – – – – – – – – et puis coulez;
BN	*et gardés que vostre boullon soit cler et net;*
VAT	**et gardez que vostre boullon soit cler et net;**

VAL	*qu'il soit froit a le couler; metez vostre grain par escuellez;*
MAZ	– – – – – – – – – – – – – – – –
BN	– – – – – – – *puis dressiés vostre grain pessevelez;*
VAT	– – – – – – – **et puis dreciez vostre grain par escuelles;**

VAL	*remetez vostre boillon en boullant,*
MAZ	et remecter boulir
BN	*et metés vostre bouillon sur le feu en un vessel cler et net*
VAT	**et aprés remetez vostre boullon sur le feu en ung vaissel cler et net**

VAL	– – – – *escumez tourjours;* – – – – – – – –
MAZ	– – – – et escumez tousjours; puis mecter vostre poisson
BN	*et faites boulir,* – – – – – – – – – – – – – –
VAT	**et faictes boullir,** – – – – – – – – – – – – – –

VAL	– – – – – – – – – *dreciez*
MAZ	ou chart par plas et dressiez vostre boillon
BN	– – – – – *et en boullant metés*[5] *vostre bouillon*
VAT	– – – – – **et en boullant gectez**

VAL	– – – *sur vostre grain et poudrez dessus*
MAZ	– – – – – – – – – – et poudre dessus
BN	*en vos escuelles par dessus vostre grain, poudrés dessus*
VAT	**sur vostre grain et pouldrez, sur vos platz**

VAL	*vos escuellez* †
VAT	**ou escuelles ou vous avez mis vostre grain et vostre boullon,**

---

[4] *troble*: the second and third letters are indistinct. The word should perhaps be read as *troblé*.

[5] *metes*: *faites* stroked out, with *metes* written above.

† The text after the second of these signs followed at this point in the manuscript.

VAL *fleur de canelle et massis.* - - - - - -
MAZ fleurs de cannelle et mascit; puis mecter voz escuelles
BN *fleur de canelle et du matis;*[6] *et puis metés vos escuelles*
VAT **de la fleur de canelle et du macis; et mettez voz plas**

VAL *†en lieu*[7] *froit,*
MAZ en lieu froit. - - - Et qui fait gelee il n'y fault pas dormir.
BN *en lieu froit.* - - - - - - - - - - - - -
VAT **en lieu froit pour prendre. Et qui veult faire gelee, il ne fault pas qu'il dorme.**

BN *Et se vostre bouillon n'est bien net,* - *si le coulés parmi une nape*
VAT **Et se vostre boullon n'est bien net et cler, si le coulez parmy une nappe**

BN - *en ii ou en trois doubles;* *et soit sallé apoint.*
VAT **blanche en deulx ou en trois doubles;** - - - - **et sur vostre**

VAT **grain mettez colz et pietz d'escrevisses; et loche cuite se c'est poisson.**

The jelly described here is to be made only with a fish whose skin is covered with a natural oil[8]—or, alternatively, with what seems to be any type of meat.[9] *MAZ*'s apparent aversion to titles leads him to use in his first line the title found in his source, but without dropping from it the word *de* which, without the word *gelee*, no longer has any sense.

Jelly was an important culinary confection, functioning as both a practical preservative for meats and a sort of presentation sauce for cold dishes. More perhaps than in other preparations, cooks developed their own preferences in the matter of the ingredients

[6] There is a similar hesitation between *matiz* and *maciz* in the manuscripts of the *Menagier*, §64; p. 148 and §317; p. 248.

[7] *lieu* followed by *fo* expunctuated.

[8] When fish are roasted, it is this oil on the surface of the skins that lends a blue cast to their surface. According to the *Viandier*, the fish skins are to be added to the bouillon in the course of making this jelly so that their natural gelatin will help the mixture to set. In his *Tresor des pouvres* Arnaut de Villeneuve gives the following advice to the man who is careful about his health: "Tout poisson de limon comme tenche, anguille, carpe, lemproye et aultres gras poisson de limon tant de mer come d'eaue doulce ... vous sont contraires." *Cf.* also Deschamps: "Carpes, barbeaux sont lymoneux" (*Œuvres d'Eustache Deschamps*, vol. 8, p. 339; l. 116). Tilander (*Glanures*, p. 157) defined *limon* as "mucosité, glaire."

[9] "*Gelatina* est piscium sive carnium quaedam mucilago coagulata, quae nascitur de illis, quando post alixationem servantur infrigidata in aceto" (*Alphita*, p. 293). See also the *Sanitatis conservator*, ed. Hugo Faber, *Eine Diätethik aus Montpellier* (Leipzig, 1924), p. 21, in which a *gelatina* is made from certain fish and *cum aceto et speciebus aromaticis*. The *Menagier de Paris* has a *gellee de char* that is similar to that of the *Viandier*, and one of whose variants allows the use of "lus, tanches, bresmes, anguilles, escrevisses et losche" on fish-days (§251; p. 218).

composing jellies as well as of the methods by which dependable jellies could be made.[10] The foremost consideration in the composition of a good jelly—apart, of course, from the ready availability of animal gelatin among the ingredients entering into it—was the variety of spices chosen.[11]

The list of spices in this jellied fish or meat dish in the *Viandier* is subject to variation. *Y* simplifies this list by omitting *cilion folion*[12] which is common to *VAL* and *MAZ*. *VAT* further simplifies by omitting both the nutmeg and the saffron. This simplification by *VAT* is more apparent than real, however, because *VAT* adds four new herbs and spices,[13] allowing them to blend with any trace of the others that may remain on the bolting cloth. The error made by *MAZ* in writing *noix noiguetes* for *noix muguetes* seems to be a case of echoic transcription.

BN misread *l'escumés* for *le couvrés*, and later *pessevelez* (presumably not noticing a bar on the descending stroke of the *p*) for *par escuelez*.

Y in particular is responsible for several additions intended to improve this recipe. *Z* amplifies "en lieu froit" (as it appears in *VAL* after "poudrez dessus vos escuellez") into "puis mectez voz escuelles en lieu froit"; *VAT* then adds the obvious "pour prendre."

Of the two spices used to garnish the plate of jellied fish or meat, *fleur de canelle* represents powdered cassia buds which possess a flavour similar to but more delicate than normal cinnamon.[14]

One of *VAT*'s finishing touches, the use of lobster or crayfish parts, is found in the *Menagier*.[15]

---

[10] Chiquart alone (f. 116r *seq.*) has three distinct recipes for jelly—including one in Latin for a *gelicidium*—and mentions dishes using a jellied meat or fish several times in the *Fait de cuisine*. See also the *Geleye* in the *Viande e claree*, §9; the *Gelee* in Meyer's *Recettes culinaires*, §25; the *Geladia a carn ho a pex* in the *Sent soví*, Ch. 146; and the *Gelee de pesson* in the *Enseignements*, p. 185, l. 154 (*Petit traité*, p. 222). The *Libro per cuoco* contains both a *Gelatina per zaschuna carne* (§31) and a *Gellatina communa e bona de pesse* (§33), specifically for tench (*ed. cit.*, pp. 72 and 73).

[11] "Poissons en gellee. La gellee se fait d'eau, vin, et vin aigre, et pour la garder longuement y convient mettre beaucoup d'espices ... ": *Platine en françoys* (Lyon, 1505), f. 98r.

[12] In the *Menagier* recipe (§251; p. 218), the equivalent to *cilion folion* appears to be *folium de macis*: this term describes the inner skin around a nutmeg kernel, under the husk which itself is normally ground to make the spice mace. Heyd (vol. 2, pp. 599–601) defines *folium* as the leaf of the cinnamon tree.

[13] These additions make the *Viandier*'s jelly resemble somewhat more that found in the *Menagier*; this latter still incorporates two further spices, zedoary and cubeb. Three of the additional ingredients in *VAT* are found in the *Recueil de Riom*'s recipe for *Une gelee de cher de poulailhe, lappereaux et de cochons* (§9): "maxis, espic et garingal."

[14] Pegolotti has a separate entry for *Fiori di cannella*: "Fiori di cannella vogliono essere saldi e netti di fusti e di polvere, e sono di colore alcuna cosa più chiaro che colore di gherofani, e voglionsi tenere molto bene turati perchè meglio si conservi il suo olore, e sono fatti a modo di bottoni cosie fatti ... ," and there follows in his text the sketch of what resembles a clove (p. 374).

[15] The *Menagier* uses the *cuisses* and the *queue* of the crustacean; one wonders whether *VAT*'s

69. Lamproie fresche a la saulce chaude

VAL *Lamproie frache a la saulce chaude. Soit saingnie*
BN *Lemproie franche a la saulce chaude. Soit saingnee par la gueule*
VAT **Lamproye fresche a la saulce[1] chaude. Soit seignee par la gueulle**

VAL - - - - - - - - - - *d'une broche,*
BN *et lui ostés la langue, et y covient bouter une brouche pour mieux*
VAT **et luy ostez la langue, et convient boutter une broche pour mieulx**

VAL - - *gardez le sanc —c'est la graisse—ratissiez bien la*
BN *saignier, et gardés bien le sanc car c'est la gresse,* - - -
VAT **seigner, et gardez bien le sang car c'est la gresse,** - - -

VAL *broche d'un coustel,* - - - *eschaudez comme une anguille,*
BN - - - - *puis la covient eschauder come une anguille*
VAT - - - - **puis la convient eschauder comme une anguille**

VAL *rosticiez en une broche;* - - - - - - - -
BN *et rostir en broche bien deliee;* - - - - - - - -
VAT **et rostir en une broche bien deliee, et doibt estre mise et percee**

VAL - - - - - - - - *affinez gingembre, canelle,*
BN - - - - - - - - *puis affinés gingembre, canelle,*
VAT **travers en guise de une ou de deux; puis affinez gingenbre, canelle,**

VAL - *graine, nois muguetez, bien pou de pain brulé*
BN *girofle, graine de paradis, nois mugaites et bien pou de pain brullé*
VAT **girofle, grainne de paradiz, noix muguetes et ung peu de pain brulé**

VAL *trempé*[2] - - *en vin aigre,* - - *ung pou de vin;*
BN *trempé en sanc et en vin aigre et* - - *du vin un pou, et*
VAT **trempé ou sang et en vinaigre et, qui veult, ung pou de vin, et en**

VAL - - - - - *coulez, faitez boulir tout ensemble une onde;*
BN *deffaites tout ensemble* - *et faitez boulir une onde,*
VAT **deffaites tout ensemble** - **et faictes boullir une onde,**

VAL *metez vostre lamproie boullir avec toute entiere;*
BN *et lemproie toute entiere;*
VAT **et puis mettez vostre lamproye avec toute entiere;**

---

colz is correct.

[1] The scribe wrote *sauc* then wrote an *l* over the *c* and finished the word.

[2] *brule trempe*: the words are written *trempe brule* with signs to show that their order should be reversed.

VAL	*ne soit pas trop noir;*	*metez du sanc boullir avecques.*	
BN	*et ne soit pas trop noire.*	- - - - - -	
VAT	**et ne soit mie la saulce trop noire**	- - - - - - -	**—et c'est**

VAT **quant la saulce est clere; mais quant ell'est espesse, que l'en l'apelle boe, elle doibt estre noire. Et aussi n'est pas necessité que la lamproye soit boullye avec la saulce: ainsois on apporte la lamproye toute seiche devant la table et puis met on la saulce clere, ou la boe, sur la lamproye ou par escuelles; et se doibt coupper la lamproye par pieces de long, et envoyé en platz par la table; et touteffoiz aucuns frians la veullent avoir toute seiche avec la saulce de la lechefricte et de sa sueur au sel menu ou plat mesmes ou elle a esté aportee.**

MAZ(X) misses this recipe for fresh lamprey; he errs here in the same way as he did in Recipe 47 by copying the proper title, *Lamproye fresche*, but then allowing his eye to fall to the following recipe for lamprey in galantine and copying that recipe under the wrong name. The name of the dish in this first recipe distinguishes it from the following dish, which is cold lamprey.

The recipe has been modified in a number of ways at different times. In several instances either *Z* or *Y*—without a copy by *MAZ* we cannot of course guess what *Z* may have had—has been responsible for a slight rewriting of the text which may clarify it. Toward the beginning *BN* and *VAT* explain just how the lamprey is to be bled, and the use of the spit-stick, mentioned by *VAL*, in this operation. The instruction found in *VAL*, "ratissiez bien la broche d'un coustel," must have bewildered *Y*, for both *BN* and *VAT* omit the line. This instruction should probably have read "ratissiez la *bouche*" rather than "*broche*." In the *Menagier*[3] the operation of scraping out the mouth of a lamprey with a knife is compared with a similar operation in preparing *au cel*.[4]

The spice list for this recipe, already quite extensive, is augmented in *BN* and *VAT* by the inclusion of cloves.[5] Lamprey was generally held to be a particularly moist creature whose flesh required a treatment designed to dry it for safe consumption. The warm and dry spices of the cooking sauce here would exert this effect.[6] To the liquids is added—explicitly now, whereas previously this addition was only implied—the blood, a thickener,

---

[3] *Menagier de Paris*, §185; p. 192.

[4] Compare Chiquart's preparation of a lamprey: "La gorge racle fort d'un bon coutellet affin qu'il n'y demoure point de ces ossés qui y sont ... " (*Du fait de cuisine*, §27, f. 53r).

[5] This addition was probably made by *Z*, as is the case in the following recipe, §70.

[6] The *Regime tresutile* even specifies that lampreys be exposed to the warming and drying of wine from the moment they are killed: "Pour oster leur viscosité est bon de les bouter en vin toutes vives et illec les laissier mourir et puis les preparer avecques saulse et galentin [*sic*] qui est espisse fort bonne; et ainsi les preparent les cuysiniers des grans seigneurs" (*ed. cit.*, p. 77). *Lamproie a la galentine* is in fact the subject of the next recipe.

which has been set aside and which *VAL*'s version mentions as an ingredient only in a concluding afterthought.

The interesting variant in this recipe is *VAT*'s long addendum that bears both upon the sauce and upon the way in which the dish may be served. A thicker, black sauce, called "mud," is likewise a possibility. The *Menagier*'s recipe for *boe*, the primary sauce he recommends for use on lamprey, and an alternative to his thinner *saulce chaude*, is identical to what the *Viandier* has outlined, with the exception of an exchange of pepper for cloves and an addition of sufficent dark toast to give the proper opacity to the finished dressing.[7]

70. Lamproie a la galentine

VAL	*Lamproie a la galentine.*	*Saingnié comme dit est,*	*garder*[1]
MAZ	Lamproye fresche.	Soit signee[2] la lamproie	et bien garder
BN	*Lemproie en galentine.*	*Saingniez la comme dist est*	*et gardés*
VAT	**Lamproye en galantine.**	**Seignez la comme devant,**	**gardez**

VAL	*le sang, cuisiez en vin aigre,*	– –	*ung pou de aue;*
MAZ	le sang, puis mecter la cuire en vin aigre	– –	et ung pol d'aigue;
BN	*le sanc, puis la metés cuire en vin aigre*	– –	*et en eaue bien pou;*
VAT	**le sang, puis la mettez cuire en vinaigre**	**et en vin**	**et en ung pou d'eaue;**

VAL	*quant elle sera cuite*	*si la traiés hors du feu,*	*metez*
MAZ	– – – – – –	puis l'ostés hors du feu	et mecter
BN	*et quant elle sera cuite*	– – – – –	*metés la refroidier*
VAT	**et quant elle sera cuite**	– – – – –	**si la mettez refroidier**

VAL	*sus une nappe;*	*prenez pain brullé*	*deffait de*
MAZ	sur une nappe;	puis prener pain bruler	et deffaicte de vostre
BN	*sur une nape blanche;*	*prennés pain brullé*	*et deffaites de vostre*
VAT	**sur une nape;**	**puis prenez pain brulé**	**et le deffaictes de vostre**

VAL	*boillon*	– –	*parmy une estamine,*	*metez le sanc avec boullir,*
MAZ	boillon	– –	– – – – – –	et puis mecter boulir et aussi le sang,
BN	*boullon*	*et coullés par l'estamine,*		*et boullés le sanc avec,*
VAT	**boullon**	– –	**parmy une estamine,**	**et puis mettez boullir le sang avec,**

VAL	*movez souvent;*	*quant il sera bien,*[3]
MAZ	et mouver bien qui n'arde;	et puis quant il sera bien boulir,
BN	*et remués bien qui n'arde;*	*et quant il sera bien boully,*
VAT	**et mouvez bien qu'il ne arde;**	**et quant il sera bien boullu,**

---

[7] The *Menagier*'s *boe* is used also on porpoise, which fish is assimilated to pork in its treatment (§203). See Platine, "Les sauces 'légères' du Moyen Age," *L'Histoire*, 35 (June 1981), pp. 87–89.

[1] *garder* followed by *lai* expunctuated.

[2] *signee*: *sic*.

[3] A word may have been omitted here.

VAL	*metez*	*en une geste de fust,*	*mouvez tourjours*
MAZ	si le vercez en ung mortié	ou en ung aultre vaisseaul	et movez bien
BN	*si verssés en un mortier*	*ou en une jate*	*et movés souvant*
VAT	**si versez en ung mortier**	**ou en une jatte nette**	**et mouvez tousjours**

VAL	*jusques a ce qu'il soit froit;*	*affinez gingembre,*	*canelle,*
MAZ	jusques adce qu'il soit reffroidis;	puis affiner gigimbre,	cannelle,
BN	*jusquez ad ce qu'il soit refroidié;*	*affinés gingembre,*	*canelle,*
VAT	**jusquez ad ce qu'il sera refroidié;**	**puis affinez gingenbre,**	**fleur de canelle,**

VAL	-	*noix muguetez,*[4] *graine, poivre long*	*deffait*
MAZ	giroffle,	graine de paradis, poivre long, noix nuguetes	deffaicte
BN	*girofle,*	*graine de paradis, nois mugaites, poivre lonc*	*et deffaites*
VAT	**giroffle,**	**grainne de paradis, noys muguettes, poivre long**	**et deffaictes**

VAL	*du boulon,*	*metez dedens;*	*et metez vostre poisson dedens;*
MAZ	de vostre boillon;	- - - -	- - - - - - - -
BN	*de vostre boullon*	*et metés dedans;*	*puis metés vostre poisson avec,*
VAT	**de vostre boullon**	**et mettez dedans;**	**et puis vostre poisson avec,**

BN	*dedans une jate, comme devant est dit;*	- - - - - - -
VAT	**dedans une jatte comme devant,**	**et la mettez en vaissel de fust**

VAL	- -	*doit estre noir.*	
MAZ	- - -	et doit estre bien noir.	
BN	- - -	*estre noir.*	
VAT	**ou d'estain:**	- - - - -	**si avez bonne galentine.**

A previous recipe, §68, has presented a general-purpose jelly for the serving and preserving of fish; this present recipe for jellied lamprey follows the other in natural order in the *Viandier*, with a recipe for fresh lamprey intervening. The sequence of the three recipes is still maintained in *VAT*, even though he copies three other non-fish recipes before these.

For this dish the lamprey is to be boiled in a preliminary step.[5] It is *Y* who indicates explicitly that following its cooking the lamprey is to be allowed to cool; the simple instruction in *VAL* and *MAZ*, "metez sus une nappe," is sufficient to imply that this is to be a cold dish. A plate *en galentine* could be eaten immediately after its preparation, or this sauce could be depended upon—as the *gelee de poisson*—to act as a preservative when the fish was meant to be eaten later.

---

[4] *muguetez* inserted above the line.

[5] The title of this recipe in the *Menagier de Paris* is merely *Lamproye boulye* (§185; p. 193). According to the *Menagier*, whose text is virtually identical to that copied by *VAT*, this first step is to be merely a parboiling: "Quant elle sera cuicte verdelecte . . . ."

The broth which remains from the boiling of the lamprey is mixed with the lamprey's blood and, thickened with dark toast, forms the base for the cold black galantine in which the lamprey will be served.[6]

71. Ris engoulé ...

VAL	*Ris. Cuire en gresse, a jour de char. Eslisiez, lavez*
BN	*Ris engoullé au jour de mengier char. Cuisez le et le lavés*
VAT	**Rix engoullé a jour de mengier chair. Eslisiez le rix et le lavez**
VAL	*- - en yaue chaude, metez essuier contre le feu,*
BN	*tresbien en eaue chaude et metés seichier contre le feu,*
VAT	**tres bien en eaue chaude et le mettez essuyer contre le feu,**
VAL	*metez cuire en lait de vache fremiant; broiez saffren*
BN	*et metés cuire en lait de vache fremiant; puis du saffran,*
VAT	**puis le mettez cuire en lait de vache fremiant; puis broyez du saffren**
VAL	*pour rougir, deffait de vostre lait de vache; metez*
BN	- - - - - - - - - - - - -
VAT	**pour le roussir, et qu'il soit deffait de vostre lait; et puis mettez**
VAL	*dedans du gras et du boillon.*
BN	*et du gras de bouillon de buef.*
VAT	**dedans du gras boullon du pot.**

The method of preparing rice that the *Viandier* presents here consists of a series of steps that show little variation from manuscript to manuscript.[1] The title as modified by *Z* or *Y* is more descriptive of the finished dish. The recipe for this dish in the *Menagier* is very close in form to *Y*, with the notable exception that where *VAL* and *VAT* intend the use of the saffron "pour rougir" and "pour roussir," the Menagier has "pour le jaunir."[2]

---

[6] In the *Enseignements* (p. 185, l. 144; *Petit traité*, p. 221) a recipe for *Galentine a la lampree* is similar to ours. *Lampreys in galentyn* appears in a number of early English cookbooks including the *Forme of Cury* and Harleian ms. 279. Chiquart, at f. 111r of the *Du fait de cuisine*, refers to a dish called *galatine de lamproyes*; for the same dish the word is spelled *galatina* at f. 114r. In the *Opusculum de saporibus* of Magninus Mediolanensis (p. 188) a *gelatina* serves as a preservative for fish: "Si quis velit conservare per plures dies . . . ." In his *Regimen sanitatis* Magninus writes as if galantine were the standard sauce for various types of eels: "Anguilla ... et murena et lampreda requirent pro sapore galentinam ex fortibus speciebus" (part 3, ch. 20). For a history of the term galantine see the *Dictionnaire étymologique de l'ancien français*.

[1] The *Enseignements* uses the term *angoulee* to designate a type of *blanc menger* (p. 184, l. 124; *Petit traité*, p. 220).

[2] *Menagier de Paris*, §243; p. 214. The term *engoullé* derives from *goules*, "red," and by extension, "embellished, decorated." The quality of the saffron used would determine the shade of red or orange colour produced in the dish.

The serving of this dish is explicitly limited to meat-days because of the inclusion in it of animal products, milk and beef bouillon. According to Recipe 195, among the fifteenth-century additions of *VAT*, the meat-days of the week were Sunday, Tuesday and Thursday.

72. Cigne resvestu

VAL *Cisne revestu en ces plumes et atout sa pel.*
BN *Entre mes de cine revesté de sa piau atoutes les plumes.*
VAT **Entremez d'un cigne revestu en sa peau atout sa plume.**

VAL – – – *L'enflés par entre lez espaulez comme de poulaille farcie,*
BN – – – *Enflés le d'un tuel par entre les espaules,*
VAT **Prenez le cigne et l'enflez par entre les espaulles,**

VAL – – – – – – – – – *et que le col soit avec la pel,*
BN *fendés le au lonc par dessoubz le ventre, puis lui ostés la piau atout le*
VAT **et le fendez au long du ventre, puis ostez la peau atout le**

VAL *lez ellez* *et lez piez avec le corps,*
BN *col coppé aprés les espaules et les ellez, les piés tenans au corps,*
VAT **col couppé emprés les espaules, les piez tenans au corps,**

VAL *metez em broche* – – – *boutonnez comme poullaile;*
BN *puis rostir* *ou arssonner,* – – – – – –
VAT **et puis mettez en broche et arçonnez,** – – – – – –

VAL – – *quant il sera cuit* *soit revestu en sa peau,*
BN *dorer* *quant il sera cuit;* *et soit revestu en sa piau,*
VAT **et dorez; et quand il sera cuit, soit revestu en sa peau,**

VAL *et que le col soit droit;* – *au poivre jaunet.*
BN *et que le col soit bien droit*[1] *ou plat; et mengier au poivre jaunet.*
VAT **et le col soit bien droit ou plat; et soit mengié au poivre jaunet.**

The swan which is skinned, cooked and then reassembled to something resembling a life-like state, with the glorious, pristine whiteness of its feathers unharmed, is called, quite properly, an *entremets* in *BN* and *VAT*.[2] The procedure by which the skinning and re-dressing are carried out is that which has been outlined in Recipe 66 for the *Poulaille farcie*. This model is indicated by *VAL* but not by *BN* or *VAT*; quite to the contrary,

---

[1] *droit*: the first letter is missing in a hole in the manuscript.

[2] For a modern, rather whimsical evaluation of this dish, see Barbara K. Wheaton, "How to Cook a Swan," *Harvard Magazine*, 82 (1979), pp. 63–65.

these latter manuscripts point out that rather than being slit transversally from shoulder to shoulder, as was done previously in the case of poultry, the skin of the swan is to be opened along its belly.

Before the swan is roasted, *VAL* says that it should be "boutonnez comme poullaile," yet there is no indication of any such procedure in Recipe 66.[3] In Recipe 37, however, for *Poles rosties*, *MAZ* (alone) has copied that the bird is to be larded, and it may well be that this is the step which *VAL* has in mind here to be applied to the swan.

In the *Menagier*[4] the *Cingne revestu en sa pel a toute la plume* is identical to what is found in *VAT* but has been moved from the *entremets* section to the section on roast meats, which it concludes, being placed immediately after the *Viandier*'s Recipe 50 for roast swan.

73. Froide sauge

VAL	*Froide sauge.*	*Prenez vostre poulaille*
MAZ	Brouet vergay de poullaille.	Mecter cuire vostre poullaille
BN	*Une froide sauge.*	*Cuisés bien la poulaille*
VAT	**Une froide sauge.**	**Prenez vostre poulaille**

VAL	*et metez cuire*	*en eaue,*	*puis metez reffroidir;*	
MAZ		en aigue,	et puis le mecter reffroidier;	puis
BN		*en eaue,*	*puis la metés refroidier;*	
VAT	**et la mettez cuire**	**en eaue,**	**puis la mettez reffroidier;**	**et puis**

VAL	*broiez*	– –	*fleur de canelle,*	*graine, girofle,*
MAZ	broyer	gigimbre,	cannelle,	giroffle et graine de paradis,
BN	*broiés*	*gingembre,*	*canelle,*	*girofle, graine de paradis,*
VAT	**broyez**	**gingenbre,**	**fleur de canelle,**	**grainne et girofle,**

VAL	– – – – –	– –	*percil, sauge le plus, du pain,*
MAZ	– – – – –	puis broyer	parressi, saulge le plus et du pain
BN	*broiés bien sans couller;*	*prennés*	*percil et sauge, du pain*
VAT	**sans couller,**	**puis broyez**	**pain, persil et sauge,**

VAL	*ung pou de saffren,*	*et passe*[1] *la verdure pour estre vert gay,*
MAZ	et ung pol de saffrain,	et passi par la verdure pour estre vergay,
BN	*et un pou de safran*	*et de la verdure pour estre vergay,*
VAT	**et ung pou de saffren**	**en la verdeur, qui veult, pour estre vertgay,**

[3] Concerning the sense of the term *boutonner*, see Recipe 51, n4.

[4] *Menagier de Paris*, §158; p. 184.

[1] *passe*: "let it predominate."

VAL	*coullez parmy l'estamine;*	- - - -	*de moiaux d'eufs cuis,*
MAZ	et coulez par l'estermine;	et	des moyeux d'euf cuis
BN	*et coullés par l'estamine;*	*et aucuns y metent*	*moyeux d'uefs durs*
VAT	**et le coulez par l'estamine;**	**et aucuns y coullent**	**des moyeulx d'oeufz cuis durs**

VAL	*deffaitez de bon vin aigre;*	*sans boullir;*	- -
MAZ	deffait de bon vin aigre,	et sain boulit;	- -
BN	*et deffont de vin aigre;*	- - -	- -
VAT	**et deffaictes de vinaigre;**	- - -	**et despeciez**

VAT	**vostre poulaille par moittiee, par quartiers ou par membres,**

VAL	*metez dedens vostre poulaille par menbrez,*	*et aubins d'eufs*
MAZ	et mecter sur vostre poulaille mise par membres.	- - -
BN	*et metés sur vostre plat.*	- - -
VAT	**et mettez par platz et la saulce dessus;**	**et se il y a eu des**

VAL	*cuis durs dessus.*
VAT	**oeufs durs, despeciez par morceaulx au coustel et non mie a la main.**

Another cold dish, a companion piece of chicken for the cold fish of Recipes 68 and 70, the *Froide sauge* is considered to be a type of sauce with which cold chicken can be served.[2] It is at the same time a counterpart for the following dish, the *Soux de pourcel*. Powdered cinnamon is specified here by *VAL* and *VAT* as it is specified in the other cold, jellied dishes, the *Gelee de poisson* and the *Lamproie a la galentine*. In such dishes the sauce mixture is not heated, so that ordinary ground cinnamon would not dissolve sufficiently.

When the green herbs are added to the spices, *VAL* and *MAZ* indicate, quite reasonably in view of the name of the dish, that the sage is to predominate; the text in *Y* must have read "sauge le plus du pain," because *BN* is able to misunderstand this.[3] Similarly in the following phrase *BN* mistakenly changes "de safran *en* la verdure" to "de safran *et de* la verdure."

The egg yolks in vinegar are made optional by *Y*. The additional notation, to the effect that this sauce is not to be boiled, is garbled by *MAZ(X)*, and perhaps by *Z*, to such an extent that *Y* left it out altogether. The *Froide sauge* is indeed to be a cold sauce, however, and *VAL*'s notation is quite important. The name that *MAZ(X)* gives the dish, while it is descriptive, is a result perhaps of not understanding clearly the real nature of the dish.

2 The recipe for *Saugee* in the *Viaunde e claree* (§3) is very similar to the *Viandier*'s version of the dish, except for the substitution of English galingale for French grains of paradise, and the omission of parsley. This *Saugee* is to be served over pig's trotters or any *char freide*.

3 Curiously, the *Menagier de Paris*, whose text follows that of *VAT* fairly closely, has "Broyez du pain ... percil le plus, sauge, et ung pou de saffran" (§44; p. 215).

74. Soux de pourcelet

VAL	*Sourps de porcelet.*	- - - - - - - - - - - - - -
MAZ	- - - -	Prener les piez, la quehue,[1] les oroilles et le
BN	*Soulz de pourcel.*	- - - - - - - - - - - - - -
VAT	**Soux de pourcel.**	- - - - - - - - - - - - - -

MAZ groin du pourcel et cuilz bien avec sel, vin et aigue et puis soit

VAL	*fait comme froide sauge*	- - - - - - -
MAZ	faicte la saulce conme froide sauge	- - - - - - -
BN	*fait aussi comme d'une froide sauge*	*et rasisse en eaue chaude et*
VAT	**faictes ainsi comme une froide sauge**	- - - - - - -

VAL	- - -	*sans metre nulz eufs et moins de sauge.*
MAZ	- - -	sans euf, et y aie moings de sauge;
BN	*lavé tres bien*	*sans metre nulz oeufs et mout de sauge.*
VAT	- - -	**sanz mectre saffren ne nulz oeufz—et qu'il y ait moins**

MAZ		et, deppuis que vostre char sera reffroidiez,
VAT	**de sauge que de persil.**	

MAZ mecter vostre saulse par dessus.

This dish is closely related to the preceding, both of them being preparations for cold meats. This pork recipe is as well expressly a derivative of the *Froide sauge*.[2] They are related particularly in their common use of vinegar.[3] A dish that was probably called

---

[1] *quehue*: ms. *quehnee*.

[2] The English recipes edited by Austin combine our §§73 and 74, calling the dish "Pigge or chiken in Sauge" (p. 72). A similar recipe for the pork alone is §29 in the *Forme of Cury*, and on p. 32 of the *Liber cure cocorum*. According to Magninus, "Possunt ... carnes porcine frigide comedi in estate cum aceto et petrosilino in principio refectionis" (*Regimen sanitatis*, part 3, ch. 20): this was, then, a sort of cold appetizer for summer, and for the *Viandier* clearly qualified as an *entremets*.

[3] According to the *Sent soví*, piglet is served in summer in a *soux* made with vinegar and rue: "Porcell donats d'ivern en ast, e d'estiu en sols ab hurugua" (ch. 41). For the author of this work, *soux* is always a preparation that involves steeping the meat or fish in a vinegar sauce. Grewe cites S. J. Honnorat, *Dictionnaire provençal-français*, 4 vols. (Digne: Repos, 1846–48): "*solz*, viande ou poisson au vinaigre." See also the recipe in the *Tractatus*, part II, §17 that begins, "Sulta, id est *souet* in gallico, hoc modo fit: ... "; and the study by Marianne Bouchon, "Latin de cuisine," *Archivum latinitatis medii ævi (Bulletin DuCange)*, 22 (1951 & 1952), pp. 62–76; *Sulta*, p. 74.

A variant reading in the *Northern-European Cookbook*, §7, found in manuscript "Q" (§6 in the edition by Kristensen) prefaces the recipe with the phrase, "If one wants to make a *sylt* ... ." It likewise concludes, "This *sylt* may last three weeks." Rudolf Grewe explains that the word *sylt* "is the Old German *sulza* (modern German *Suelze*), Old French *soulz*, Old Catalan *sols* and may be translated as 'headcheese'" (*Northern-European Cookbook*, p. 19).

Turbot a la soussie was a lean alternative to *Soux de pourcel*.[4]

The enumeration in *MAZ* of the cuts of the piglet to be used in this dish seems to echo what is copied in the *Enseignements*: "Les iiii piez e les orilles e le groing en souz."[5] The other ingredients in this version include parsley, spices (unspecified) and vinegar.

Of the manuscripts *BN* blunders the worst by reading *moins* as *mout*, thus radically changing the nature of the recipe. *VAT*, always explicit, excludes saffron from his version of what we might call a sort of "Froide persil."[6]

VAT is unique in specifying the use of parsley with the sage in this sauce. Because of its inherent warmth and dryness, sage had long been recognized as a useful dressing for moist meats; according to the Commentary to lines 62–63 of the *Regimen sanitatis salernitanum*, sage was "universally" used with roast geese and young pigs "pour extraire et desecher en partie leurs humidités et viscosités."[7]

Potages lians [sans char] (BN)

75. Comminee de poisson

VAL	*Conminee de poisson.*	*Cuit en yaue*		*ou fruit en*
MAZ	– – – – – –	Cuisiez en aigue	vostre poisson	ou soufriés en
BN	*Comminee de poisson.*	*Cuit en aue*		*ou frit en*
VAT	**Comminee de poisson.**	**Cuit en eaue**		**ou frit en**

VAL	*huile;*	*affinez amandez*	*deffetes*	*du boullon*	*ou de*
MAZ	huille;	puis affinez amandres	– – –	de vostre boillon	ou de
BN	*huille;*	*prennés almendes*	*destrempees*	*de vostre boullon*	*ou de*
VAT	**huille;**	**affinez amendes**	– – –	**de vostre boullon,**	**de**

VAL	*puree*	*ou d'eaue boullie,*	*et en faitez lait;*	*fetez boullir;*
MAZ	puree de pois,	– – – –	et en faicte lait;	et le faicte boulir;
BN	*puree de pois*	*ou de eaue boullie,*	*et en faites du lait;*	*et metés boullir;*
VAT	**puree de poys**	**ou d'eaue boullye,**	**et faictes lait;**	– – –

[4] See Recipe 137, below.

[5] *Enseignements*, p. 181, l. 22; *Petit traité*, p. 214.

[6] In the balance between the herbs, the *Menagier de Paris* (§245; p. 215) goes even further than *VAT* and rules out the use of any sage, eggs or bread. As *MAZ* indicates (and the *Enseignements* before him), only certain parts of a suckling pig were appropriate for this dish; the *Menagier* specifies the groin, ears, tail, foreleg (*jarretz cours*, "hand of pork"), and trotters.

[7] *Le Regime tresutile et tresproufitable*, ed. Cummins, p. 58. In *VAT* parsley, sharing the same properties as sage, is displacing this latter herb and is used on fat capons (Recipe 40) and in the *dodine* for mallard duck (Recipe 54); the sauce known as "cold sage" is still indicated for roast hen (Recipe 37).

VAL	*affinez gingembre,*	*commin,*	*deffait de vin et de verjus,*
MAZ	puis affinez gigimbre	et conmyn,	deffaicte de vin et de verjus et
BN	*prennés gingembre*	*et comin,*	*defait de vin et de verjus et*
VAT	**puis affinez gingenbre**	**et du commin,**	**deffait de vin et de verjus et**

VAL	*metez boullir avec vostre lait;*	*pour maladez,*	*y fault du succre;*
MAZ	mecter boulir avec vostre lait;	et pour malade	il y faudroit du succre.
BN	*metés boullir aveques vostre lait;*	– – – –	*et y faut du sucre.*
VAT	**mettez boullir avec vostre lait;**	**et pour malades**	**il y fault du succre.**

VAL *dreciez sur vostre grain d'anguille.*

The only manuscript to show a chapter division in its text at this point is *BN*, which has "Potaiges lians" just before the recipe for *Comminee de poisson*. In *VAT* the last item in the next section, which contains dishes appropriate for the sick, is a repetition of the present *Comminee de poisson*, for which, instead of detailing the recipe, *VAT* has written merely "Querez es potages lyans sans char." That is undoubtedly what the full title should be for the chapter that begins with Recipe 75. Such is, in fact, the rubric that is found at this point in the *VAT* Table: "Potaiges lyans sans chair." Several of the dishes here are conceived as *maigre* versions of the basic dishes which have appeared already among the "potages lians de char" (Recipes 10–30).

The generic name of the present dish, *comminee*, derives from the predominant spice in it, the seed cumin. Despite the limitation that *VAL* places on the use of the preparation ("dreciez sur vostre grain d'anguille"), the name affixed to the recipe *comminee de poisson* implies that it is suitable for any fish.[1] *VAL* may have had an eye on the following recipe.

When almond milk is made, *MAZ(X)* omits boiled water as an alternative to the fish bouillon or pea puree.[2] *BN* uses sugar whether the sauce is for an invalid or not.

---

[1] In the *Menagier de Paris* the title of the dish is slightly different: *Comminee a jour de poisson* (§99; p. 162). The title in the *Viandier* could be understood to have exactly the same sense. In the *Menagier* this recipe follows the *Comminié de poullaille* (which is the *Viandier*'s Recipe 12) and refers back to it for most of the ingredients.

The name of this preparation was known in antiquity: Apicius has a *Cuminatum in ostrea et concilia* whose ingredients, other than the cumin, are, however, unlike those of the *Viandier*'s recipe for comminee: *De re coquinaria*, Book I, §15; Apicius, *L'art culinaire*, ed. & tr. Jacques André (Paris, 1974), p. 10. See also Jacques André, *L'alimentation et la cuisine à Rome* (Paris, 1981), p. 195.

[2] The *Menagier* likewise mentions only puree or bouillon. The use of puree of white peas is very common as a base in dressings for fish in the late Middle Ages. The *Du fait de cuisine* even provides the cook with a recipe for puree of peas at the very beginning of its section on fish (f. 49r). Chiquart wishes to ensure that the cook have an adequate supply of this puree on hand before he begins to elaborate any of the recipes that follow in that fish section. The *Y* version of the *Viandier* occasionally inserts boiled water as an alternative for puree in the following fish dishes (*e.g.* in Recipes 77 and 79); this substitution suggests either that the taste for pea puree may not have been universal or that the availability of white peas, even dried, was not dependable.

76. Brouet vergay d'anguilles

VAL	*Brouet vert gay d'anguilles.*	*Escorchiez, eschaudeez,*	*metre cuire*
BN	*Brouet vergay d'anguilles.*	*Escorchiés*[1] *ou eschaudés,*	*metés cuire*
VAT	**Brouet vertgay d'anguilles.**	**Escorchees ou eschaudees,**	**mettez cuire**

VAL	*en vin et en eaue; deffait de*	*percil et de saffren, pain,*	*ung pou de*
BN	– *en eaue; et*	*percil, pain, saffren*	*bien pou en*
VAT	**en vin et en eaue; et puis broyez**	**pain, persil, saffren**	**bien pou en**

VAL	*la verdure,*	– – – – –	*deffait du boillon,*
BN	*la verdure,*	– – – – –	*deffait de vostre bouillon,*[2]
VAT	**la verdeur**	**pour le faire vertgay,**	**et le destrempez de vostre boullon; et**

VAL	*gingenbre*	*deffait de verjus,*	*tout boullu emsemble;*
BN	*puis gingembre*	*deffait de verjus*	*et tout boully en semble;*
VAT	**puis broiez gingembre**	**deffait de vostre verjus**	**et tout boullez ensemble;**

VAL	*et du formage.*
BN	*et de bon formage*
VAT	**et y met on de bon frommage despecié par bons loppinetz quarrez,**

BN	*qui velt.*
VAT	**qui veult.**

Just as the previous recipe, the *Comminee de poisson*, offers a lean or meatless counterpart to the *Comminee de poulaille* described earlier in §12, so too this recipe for a *Brouet vergay d'anguilles* is an alternative on fasting days for the *Brouet vertgay* designed for any type of *grain* in Recipe 26.

The text in *VAL* is, exceptionally, not clear. The first *deffait* does not make sense as a past participle. The words "pain un pou de la verdure" seem likewise to be an error and may perhaps represent a original "pain ung pou en [*or* dens] la verdure," even though in *BN* and *VAT* the directions read "saffren bien pou" rather than bread.

BN omits wine from the pot in which the eel is to be boiled.[3]

77. Gravé de loche

VAL	*Gravé de loche.*	*Deffay pain halé*	–	*de puree de pois,*
MAZ	Graigné de louche.	Deffaicte pain halez	–	de puree de pois
BN	*Gravé de loche.*	*Prennés pain hallé,*	–	*puree de pois ou eaue boullie,*
VAT	**Gravé de loche.**	**Prenez pain hallé,**	**du vin,**	**de la puree de pois**

[1] *escorchies*: the last three letters are missing in a hole in the manuscript.

[2] *bouillon* followed by *ou de puree de pois* which is stroked out.

[3] The dish which is to follow, *Gravé de loche*, uses only puree or boiled water.

VAL – – – *passé parmy l'estamine;* – – –
MAZ – – – et passis par l'estremine et mecter boulir;
BN *ou eaue boullie, passez parmi l'estamine, puis metés boullir;*
VAT **ou eaue boullie, et passez tout parmy l'estamine et mettez boullir;**

VAL *prenez gingembre, canele, girofle, graine, saffren*
MAZ puis affiner gigimbre, cannelle, giroffle, graine, saffrain
BN *et prendre de fines espices sans poivre, et du saffren*
VAT **puis affinez gingenbre, canelle, giroffle, graine, saffran**

VAL – – – – – – – *deffait de vin aigre, prenez oignons*
MAZ – – – – – – – deffaicte de vin aigre, et y mectés des oignons
BN – – – – – – – *deffait de vin aigre, puis dez oingnons*
VAT **pour luy donner couleur, deffait de vinaigre, puis des ongnons**

VAL – – *fris, metez boullir emsemble;*
MAZ munussiez friz en huille et mecter boulir tout ensemble;
BN *minciés fris et boullir tout ensemble; puis*
VAT **missez et friz en huille et mettez boullir tout ensemble; et**

VAL *frisiez vostre loche sans farine,* – – – – – –
MAZ frisiez vostre louche sans farine, – – – – – – –
BN *frisieés vostre loche en huillesans farine, et ne la metés pas boullir*
VAT **frisiez vostre loche sans farine, et ne la mettez point boullir**

VAL – – – – – – – *dreciez le boullon dessus;*
MAZ – – – – – – – puis dressiez vostre boillon dessus;
BN – – – – – – – *mes dressiés sur vostre boullon.*
VAT **mais la mettez par escuelles et dreciez vostre graine;**

VAL *et qu'elle soit bien.*
MAZ et qu'elle soit bien eslimonee et lavee avant tout.
VAT – – – – – – – – – – – – – – – – **et doibt estre jaune.**

This dish may perhaps be considered a counterpart to Recipe 18, the *Gravé de menus oiseaux ou de tel grain comme on veult*, although there are considerable differences between the two in ingredients and in cooking.[1]

BN in particular has garbled his source. In the interest presumably of brevity he reduces the spice list of ginger, cinnamon, cloves and grains of paradise to the collective "*fines espices* without pepper"—a qualified substitution he made in Recipe 20 as well, though in that earlier place the *fines espices* are without saffron. In Recipe 16, furthermore,

[1] The *Viande e claree* offers a recipe entitled "La maniere coment l'en deit fere gravee" (§29). It is for pike and bream as well as for capons and fat hens.

fines espices include ginger, cinnamon, cloves, grains of paradise and cinnamon powder, though there is at that particular point no mention of either pepper or saffron, either to be omitted or included.[2]

In the next stage of the recipe, in which onions are added to the *gravé*, *Z* introduces the preliminary operation of frying these onions in oil. *BN*, however, somehow transfers the mention of oil to the operation that immediately follows, the frying of the fish.

The conclusion of the recipe found in *VAL* probably results from an inability to read or to understand the word *eslimonee* that is found in *MAZ*. This term was probably a part of the culinary idiom of the day; Chiquart makes use of the words *esmorcher* and *amorcher* to denote the same act of removing the slime (*limon*) from fish whose skin bears a coating of this substance.[3]

Y has added water as an alternative to puree for the liquid base of the *gravé*. *VAT*, perhaps in recollection of the previous recipe for *Brouet vertgay d'anguilles* where the cooking liquids are puree or water or wine, adds wine to the other two possibilities for the *gravé* in *Y*.[4] This puree, it might be noted, is made from white peas and is a common base for fish sauces. At the very beginning of Chiquart's chapter on fish dishes—which chapter with some affectation he calls "Tractatus de piscibus cum salsis eisdem piscibus incombentibus"—even before considering any recipes for fish, he dictates a process for making the white-pea puree: "Fault que les escuiers de cuisine soient tresbien fournix et pourveux de grant quantité de pois blancs pour faire les potageries pour ung chescun jour de la feste partinens aux poyssons."[5]

78. Chaudumet a becquet / beschet

VAL	*Chaudumet a becquet.*	*Rosticiez vostre poisson;*
MAZ	Civel de beschet.	Soit le beschet rotis;
BN	*Chaudumel au bescuit de brochiez ou de lusiaux.*	*Rosticiés vostre poisson*
VAT	**Chaudumel au bescuit.**	**Rotissiez vostre poisson;**

VAL	- -	*prenez gingenbre, pain et saffran destrempez de puree*
MAZ	- -	puis broyez pain, gigimbre et saffrain, destremper de puree
BN	*sur le gril;*	*prennés pain, puree de pois ou eaue boullie,*
VAT	- -	**puis prenez pain, puree de pois ou eaue boullie,**

---

2 Concerning culinary spices in general at this time, see Bruno Laurioux, "De l'usage des épices dans l'alimentation médiévale," *Médiévales*, 5 (1983), pp. 15–31.

3 *Du fait de cuisine*, ff. 53r, 61r, 70v. "Nim frische ele und wasche in abe den slim mit kalter aschen ... " (*Guter Spize*, ed. Hajek, §18, p. 20).

4 The *Menagier de Paris* has no corresponding recipe for a *gravé de loche* but does list among his menus (§177; p. 95) a dish called *Ung gravé d'aloes* which is perhaps the same as the *Viandier*'s §18.

5 *Du fait de cuisine*, §22, f. 49r. *Cf.* the *Menagier de Paris*, §29; p. 134.

VAL	*puree*	*ou d'eaue boullie,*	*vin et verjus avec,*
MAZ	puree de pois	ou d'aigue boulie et	mecter en icelle aigue vin et verjus,
BN	*vin, verjus, gingembre, saffran,*		
VAT	**vin, verjus, gingenbre et saffren,**		

VAL	*boullez emsemble,*	*getez sus vostre grain;*	
MAZ	puis mecter boulir tout ensamble	et gectier sur vostre grain	et y
BN	*coullés et faites boullir*	*et metés sur vostre grain*	*et la*
VAT	**coulez et faictes boullir,**	**puis gectez sur vostre grain**	**et,**

VAL	– – –	– –	*ung pou de vinaigre;*	*soit jaunet.*
MAZ	– – –	– –	mecter ung pol de vin aigre;	qui soit janet.
BN	*boullés dedans;*	– –	– – – – – –	*et soit jaunet.*
VAT	– – –	**qui veult,**	**ung bien pou de vinaigre;**	**et soit jaunet.**

The name of this dish shows an interesting mutation from copy to copy. *VAL* has simply "pike stew," using the word *becquet* for the *Esox lucius*. *MAZ(X)* is not happy with the generic name of the dish and simplifies this to *civel*; at the same time he modifies the spelling of the fish to *beschet*.[1] In *Y* we find the term *chaudumet* retained, spelled with an *l*,[2] but the qualification is changed to *au bescuit* from *a* (or *de*) *beschet* (or *besquet*). What is significant is that *BN* adds the further qualification *de brochiez ou de lusiaux*. These fish in *BN* are merely pike—by another name—and pickerel. The old name for pike, *becquet* and *beschet*, now appears as a generic designation of the dish itself. The sense of *bescuit* is apparent in the *Enseignements* which has as a name for this recipe *Luiz au bescuit*: "Premierement rosti, e puis en moust ou en sidre paré en une paele, e fet boullir; e prenez poudres de toutes manieres d'espices e du pain, destrempez du bescuit qui est en la paele, e puis metez en escueles, le pesson dedenz."[3] It is clear that for the *Enseignements* this method of preparing pike involves two stages of cooking, a roasting and a boiling; this is perhaps the original meaning of the word *bescuit*. In the *Enseignements*, however, the term now designates the liquid, a sort of sauce of fish juices, must and cider which remains in the pan after the second cooking, and it is in this sense that the author of *Y* uses the word *bescuit* in his version of Recipe 78.

---

[1] In Chiquart's *Du fait de cuisine* the fish is spelled *bechés* (f. 117v). See Paul Barbier, "Noms de poissons," *Revue des langues romanes*, 67 (1933–1936), p. 286.

[2] Chiquart's scribe, Jehan de Dudens, writes both *chaut de mes* and *chaudemés*. The *chaudumé* is a type of sauce; in the *Roman du comte d'Anjou* (*c.* 1316) the famous catalogue of delicate foods contains "les gros bequés chaudumés, si com il sont acoustumés des keus qui sevent lez sentances de l'atorner" (ll. 1139–1140, ed. Mario Roques). The *Menagier de Paris* offers a comment that the *chaudumé* is made for freshwater fish in a way similar to that followed for the *soucié* or *soutié* for sea-fish, except that saffron, nutmeg and verjuice are substituted for the herbs in the *soucié*; "et doit estre fin jaune et bouly et mis tout chault sur le poisson froit" (§277; p. 232).

[3] *Enseignements*, p. 186, l. 182; *Petit traité de cuisine*, p. 223.

The *Menagier de Paris* offers a brief outline of a *Chaudumé* for red mullet. It is composed of verjus, spice powder and saffron, and is therefore similar to what is found in the *Viandier*.[4]

Most curiously, all of the manuscripts but *BN* treat the *chaudumet* as if it were merely a serving sauce. Only *BN* reveals some echo of a boiling step for the fish—although the object of *la* in the direction "la boullés dedans" leaves some uncertainty about what really was intended.

79. Une soringne / soringue

VAL	*Une soringne. Eschaudez - - - vos anguillez, copez*
BN	*Une[1] soringne. Eschaudés ou escorchiés vos anguilles et descouppés*
VAT	**Une soringue. Eschaudez ou escorchez l'anguille, puis couppez**
VAL	*par tronsons, et - oignons par rouellez, percil esfeulié,*
BN	*par tronçons et - oingnons par rouelles et percil effueillié,[2] et*
VAT	**par tronçons et missiez ongnons par rouelles et persil effusilié, et**
VAL	*metez tout surfrire en huile en ung pot couvert sur lez charbons;*
BN	*frisiés tout en semble en huille; - - - - - - - -*
VAT	**mettez tout souffrire en huille; - - - - - - - -**
VAL	*prenez pain halé, trempé en puree de pois - - -*
BN	*prennés pain hallé et puree de pois ou eaue bouillie,*
VAT	**puis prenez pain hallé, puree de poys ou eaue boullie**
VAL	*et vin plain, - - metre boullir avec; prenez gingembre,*
BN	*du vin plain, coullés et metés en semble boullir; prennés gingembre,*
VAT	**et du vin plain, coullez et mettez avec boullir; puis prenez gingenbre,**
VAL	*canele, girofle, grene, saffren*
BN	*canelle, girofle - - - - et saffran*
VAT	**canelle, girofle, grainne de paradiz, et saffren pour luy donner**
VAL	*- - deffait de verjus, boully avec,*
BN	*- - deffait de verjus, et metés boullir aveques;*
VAT	**couleur, et deffaictes de verjus et mettés avec boullir;**
VAL	*non pas trop plain, liant, assavourez de vin aigre.*
BN	*et ne soit pas trop - liant, et ait saveur bien aigre.*
VAT	**- - - - - - et la savourez de vinaigre.**

[4] *Menagier de Paris*, §199; p. 198.

[1] The cue letter for the capital is missing because of the hole in the manuscript.

[2] *effueillie*: the *u* is missing for the same reason.

Just as *MAZ* passed over the recipe for eel broth (§76), he now omits this recipe for *Soringue* of eels.

The *soringue* is a dish of fried eel chunks that are served in a particular sauce. This latter is a thick, dark broth used exclusively with eels and is characterized in its taste by onions, wine and spices.[3] In the *Viandier*, the *soringue* serves as a recognized standard measure of viscosity for other sauces (for example, in the *Broet georgié*, Recipe 15). In *VAL* alone we find a meat-day counterpart for this *Soringue d'anguilles*, the *Soringue de haste menue de porc* (Recipe 17); the parallel between these two dishes is so deliberate that a number of phrases in *VAL*'s texts are similar.[4] The ingredients in both sauce preparations are similar as well, though beef bouillon and ample wine are used as the base rather than puree of peas and ample wine. It is *VAL* again, at the end of this §79, who cautions, with the same adjective *plain*, against allowing the taste of the verjuice, which is used to macerate the spices, to predominate over the other flavours.

There are only a few variants among the manuscripts copying Recipe 79. Where *VAL* directs that the eel is initially to be scalded—in order to remove the *limon* or slime from its skin: the skin is to be left on—*Y* offers the cook an option by saying *eschaudés ou escorchiés*, that is, either clean the eel *or* skin it.[5] Then *Y* later inserts the option of boiled water as an alternative to puree of peas.[6] *BN* omits *graine de paradis* from the spice list.[7] *VAL* seems to have had some partiality for this dish, adding notes in his own copy about cooking method and about what the final taste and consistency should be.[8]

---

[3] Though the *Menagier* calls his dish a "Soringue d'*anguilles*," it seems to be implicit for the various versions of the *Viandier* that eels are the principal ingredient. The generic name *soringue* would appear to derive from the root *sor*, "dark red" (which appears also in *hareng sor*, "red herring"). In this regard see the recipe for *Sorree* in the manuscript B.L. Royal 12.c.xii (ed. Meyer, §19, p. 53; transcribed as *Soree* in the edition of Hieatt and Jones, §19, p. 867): the dish consists of fried eels in a red sauce. Whether *-ingue* and *-engue* have anything to do with *anguilla* must probably remain moot. See Rudolf Grewe's edition of the *Sent soví*, p. 55, for a comment on the sense of the Catalan verb *sosengar* and the Provençal *saurengar*.

[4] One of *VAL*'s variants here in this eel recipe is an echo of a direction in Recipe 17: "Metez frire ... en ung pot sur lez charbons."

[5] See the verb *eslimoner* in Recipe 77, and Recipe 77, n3.

[6] The *Menagier*'s version of this recipe is copied from a source which is dependent on *Y*. The *Menagier* does not include water as an option, however, the basis for the broth being simply puree (§127; p. 173).

[7] Some slight latitude must have been allowed in the choice of spices for this dish. Chiquart's *Du fait de cuisine* (§34, f. 61r) offers a very detailed description of the preparation of a *Sorengue d'anguilles brune*. In its substance this version is identical to what we find in the *Viandier* except that among the spices pepper is included and saffron omitted. Although nameless, a recipe for this dish in the *Tractatus* (part III, §3: "Quandoque in aqua [murena vel anguilla] dequoquitur cum decoctione, ... ") calls for sage and herb bennet as well as parsley.

[8] The *Menagier* adds at the end of his recipe for *Soringue d'anguilles* that the broth should be *claret*.

80. Brouet sarrasinois

VAL	*Brouet saraginois. Escorchiez anguillez,* - - - - - - -
MAZ	Brouet serrazinés. Escourchiez anguilles et les coppés par tronssons
VAT	**Brouet sarrasinois.** - - - - - - - - - - - - -

VAL	*poudrez de cel, frisiez en huille; prenez gingembre,*
MAZ	sans poudre de sel et les frissiez en huille; puis prener gigimbre,
VAT	- - - - - - - - - - - - **Prenez** - -

VAL	*girofle, canele, graine, garingal, poivre long, saffren,*
MAZ	cannelle, giroffle, graine, garingal, poivre long et du saffrain
VAT	**canelle,** - - - - - **poivre long, et saffren**

VAL	*deffaite de vin et de verjus;*
MAZ	et deffaicte de vin et de verjus;
VAT	**pour luy donner coulleur, deffait de vin et de verjus;**

VAL	*faitez boullir emsemble et vos anguillez avec;*
MAZ	et faicte boulir tout ensamble et voz anguilles avecques;
VAT	**et faictes tout boullir ensemble et vos anguilles avec;**

VAL	*et ne soit pas trop liant: il ce lie de ly mesmez.*
MAZ	et ne soit pas troupt lyant.
VAT	**et ne soit pas trop liant car il se lye de luy mesmes.**

This recipe for eels is distinct from the previous one in several respects. Along with its different colour, the characteristic feature of the *Soringue* is its onion-vinegar taste.

The Saracen eel broth consists of chunks of eel fried and then boiled in a spicy, yellowish sauce.[1] No bread is needed as a binder in this dish because, according to *VAL* and *VAT*, the mixture with the eel will thicken on its own.[2]

The remarkable variant in this recipe is found in *VAT*'s version. Not only does he feel safe in omitting any mention of the whole cooking process, which is similar in any case to that of the previous recipe for *Soringue*, but four spices—more than half the total

---

[1] According to Rudolf Grewe, what is characteristic about Arabic cookery in the preparation of the Catalan dish known as *Carn a la sarreynesca* is that cooking is begun with all of the ingredients cold and together (*Sent soví*, §181, n1). See also C. Anne Wilson, who generalizes that Arabic cooking consists typically of frying a food before boiling it: "The Saracen Connection: Arab Cuisine and the Mediaeval West," *Petits Propos Culinaires*, 7 (1981), p. 15. The juxtaposition of the two verbs *frire* and *boullir* in the *Viandier* seems to suggest an "arabic" sequence of cooking steps. *Cf.* Recipe 188, below.

[2] The *Menagier de Paris* explains that it is the fish that will effect the necessary binding: "Boulir tout ensemble avec les anguilles, qui d'elles mesmes font lyoison" (§123; p. 172).

number—are dropped from the sauce that is to be used in the second cooking stage. The remaining saporous spices, the cinnamon and pepper, impart quite a different flavour to the sauce than is produced by the broad variety of spices listed in *VAL* and *MAZ*. The *Menagier de Paris* has a spice list and order that are identical to what was copied by *MAZ*. In general the texts of the recipe as it appears in *MAZ* and in the *Menagier* are very close; however, the *Menagier* writes "poudrez de sel" before the eels are fried,[3] so that we may assume that *MAZ(X)*'s "sans poudre de sel" reflects an idiosyncrasy on his part.

81. Lemprions

MAZ Lemprions. Prener vouz lemprions et les eschaudés et nectoyés tres-bien, puis les frissiez en huille; et prener bon vin bastart et moustarde ou aultre bon vin vernoy[1] et y mecter du succre—mais en vin bastart ne fault poin de succre pource qu'il est doubz de sa nature—et y mecter gigimbre et flour de cannelle plus que de gigimbre, et soit tout bien passis ensamble; puis gectez par dessus les lemprions sans boulir.

This dish of lamprill resembles the previous one slightly in that the eels are fried to begin with; there is, however, no mention of the lamprill being cut into pieces, and it is not to be boiled in its sauce as is the eel in the Saracen Brewet of Recipe 80. A cinnamon powder is specified here as in the *Lamproie a la galentine* (Recipe 70) because the sauce is to be made up cold and then poured over the lamprill, presumably as a dressing after it has cooked. It is the taste of the cinnamon that is to predominate in this dish.[2]

The expository style of *MAZ* is noticeably less laconic here than in the traditional recipes of the *Viandier*.

---

[3] Salt applied to a meat will tend to make it bleed as it is grilling. The *Enseignements* has a version of the Saracen eel broth that it calls *Sarraginee* and that requires the pieces of eel to be salted before being fried (p. 184, l. 131; *Petit traité*, p. 221). For other recipes for this dish see the *Browet sarasyneys blanc* (in which there is no mention of eels) in Meyer's *Recettes culinaires*, §17; Hieatt and Butler, part I, §18 and part II, §55 (this second being for beef); the Arundel ms. 334, p. 316, *Brewet sarsyn*; *Brudo saracinescho* in Libro "A" of the Anonimo Meridionale (§27, ed. Boström, p. 11); *Brodo saracenico* (for capons *or* sea-fish) in the *Libro della cocina* (ed. Faccioli, p. 33); and *Brodio sarracenio* in the *Liber de coquina* (II, §8, ed. Mulon, p. 401). Again the warning of Barbara Santich against "culinary *faux amis*" is perhaps apropos here (*Two Languages*, pp. 67–68).

[1] *vin vernoy*: probably an error for *vin vermoil*. Compare this with "moustarde et vin vermoil" in Recipe 171.

[2] In Chiquart's *Roux de lamproye* the cook is to use "cynamomy grant foyson" (*Du fait de cuisine*, §27, f. 53r).

82. Civé d'oistres

VAL	*Cyvé d'oittrez.*	*Eschaudez,*	*lavez,*
MAZ	Civé d'ostres.	Eschaudez tresbien vous orstres[1]	et les
BN	*Civé d'oistres.*	*Eschaudés les tresbien,*	– –
VAT	**Civé d'oistres.**	**Eschaudez les**	**et les lavez bien**

VAL	*parboullez,*	*puis les frisiez avec oignons menus;*
MAZ	pourbouler ung pol,	puis les frissiez avec oignons menuz menusiez;
BN	– – – –	*frisiés en huille;*
VAT	– – – –	**et frisiez en huille; et**

VAL	*prenez pain halé,*	*destrempez de puree ou d'eaue boullie,*
MAZ	puis prener pain halez,	destramper de purez de pois ou d'aigue boulie
BN	*prennés pain halé*	*trempé en puré de pois ou en eaue*
VAT	**puis prenez pain hallé,**	**puree de poys ou de l'eaue**

VAT	**des oistres ou elles auront esté eschaudees ou d'autre eaue boullue**

VAL	–	*vin et verjus avec;*	*affinez gingembre, canele,*
MAZ	–	et vin, verjus avecques;	affinez gigimbre, cannelle,
BN	–	*et vin plain, coullés;*	*puis gingembre, canelle,*
VAT	**chaude**	**et du vin plain et coullez;**	**puis prenez canelle, gingenbre,**

VAL	*graine, girofle,*	*saffren*	*deffait*
MAZ	giroffle	– – – – – – –	–
BN	*girofle, graine de paradis*	*et saffran,*	*deffaitez*
VAT	**girofle et graine de paradiz**	**et saffren pour coulourer,**	**deffait**

VAL	*de vin aigre,*	– – – – – –	*metez boulir*
MAZ	et vin aigre,	– – – – – –	mecter tout boulir
BN	*de vin aigre,*	*et oingnons fris en huille, et*	*faites bien boullir tout*
VAT	**de vinaigre,**	**et ongnons friz en huille, et**	**faictes boullir**

VAL	*avec les*[2] *oistrez.*		
MAZ	ensamble avec les orsties.		
BN	*en semble;*	*et soit bien liant*	*et jaunet et sallé apoint.*
VAT	**ensemble;**	**et soit bien lyant;**	– – – – –

VAT	**et aucuns n'y mettent pas boullir les oistres.**

---

[1] *ostres*: the scribe began by writing *orste*, which he stroked out, and then wrote *orstres*. Neither the *t* nor the second *r* of the second word are well formed, so that this word appears as *orstoies*.

[2] *les* followed by *ost* stroked out.

Y has made a few minor modifications in the recipe for oyster stew, but in the main the dish appears the same in all four manuscripts.[3] The initial parboiling of the oysters is missed by *Y*. Verjuice is further deleted from the list of possible alternate liquids for the sauce base, and onions are introduced into the recipe with the sauce rather than at the time of the frying of the oysters themselves. And it is *Y* who first notes that the sauce is to be very thick.

A rare mention of the judicious use of salt is made by *BN*.[4] *MAZ* does not mention saffron among the other spices—probably in error, because *BN* even remarks that the colour of this *civé* should be yellowish.

83. Soupe en moustarde

MAZ – – – – –
BN *Soupe en moustarde. Prennés des oeufs pochiés en huille tous*
VAT **Souppe de moustarde. Prenez de l'uille en quoy vous avez frit**

BN *entiers sans esquaille, puis prennés d'icelle huille, du vin, de l'eau,*
VAT **ou poché voz oeufz, et du vin et de l'eaue**

MAZ Prenez oignons menusiez et les frissiez en huille et les mecter
BN *des oingnons fris en huille,*
VAT – – – – – – –

MAZ en aigue, vin et verjus, le tout boulir en une peelle de fart;
BN – – – – – *boullés tout ensemble;*
VAT – – – – – **et boullez tout en une paelle de fer;**

MAZ puis prener croutes de pain rotis
BN *prennés leches de pain halé sur le gril,*
VAT **et puis prenez la crouste du pain et mettez haller sur le grail,**

MAZ et les despeciez par morceaulx quarrez et mecter boulir avec;
BN *puis en faites morssiaux quarrés et metés boullir aveques;*
VAT **puis en faictes morceaulx quarrez et mettez boullir avec;**

---

[3] A very similar recipe for "otres, id est *oistres*" is found in the *Tractatus*, part III, §1 (p. 389); the dish of oyster stew in the *Enseignements* (p. 187, l. 220; *Petit traité*, p. 226) is a poor relative of this. *Cf.* also the English *Oystres in cevey* contained in Austin (p. 100) and in the *Forme of Cury*, §123. The *Menagier*'s treatment of *Civé d'oistres* (§130; p. 174) seems to take after both *Z* (the oysters are fried with the onions) and *Y* ("du vin plain"). The *Civé d'oetres* (§32) is one of the more detailed recipes in the *Recueil de Riom*.

[4] Chiquart regularly indicates that a dish is to be salted to taste. In the *Viandier* only Recipes 66, 155, 180 and 194—all but the first being later additions in *MAZ* or *VAT*—contain any similar directions.

MAZ	– – – – – – – – – – – – – – – – – –
BN	*puis hastés*[1] *vostre boullon et ressuiés vostre soupe, puis la verssés*[2]
VAT	**aprés purez vostre boullon et ressuyez vostre souppe et la versez**
MAZ	– – – puis destramper moustarde,
BN	*en un plat; puis de la moustarde dedans*[3] *vostre boullon,*
VAT	**en ung plat; puis mettez en vostre paelle de vostre boullon**
MAZ	et faicte boulir tresbien.
BN	*et la boullir;*
VAT	**ung pou de moustarde bien espesse, et faictes tout boullir.**
BN	*puis metés vos souppes en vos escuelles et metés dessus.*

This meatless dish consists of a sauce—comprising (perhaps) oil-poached eggs, oil-fried onions and mustard—poured over sops of squared toast. It is unlikely that the eggs mentioned by *BN* and *VAT* should be included in this dish; only *BN* says that they are to be in the sauce, and *MAZ* does not even mention either the eggs or the oil in which they have been poached. The passage "Prennés des oeufs pochiés en huille ... " may have been displaced somehow from the following *Civé d'oeufs*—which *BN* has mutilated and which does in fact require whole eggs that are poached in oil.

It is regrettable that this and the following recipe are cut away in *VAL* because two explanations for the lack of agreement among the remaining manuscripts at the beginning of Recipe 83 are possible, and the confusion might well have been clarified by *VAL*. The first possibility is that the recipes for *Soupe en moustarde* (§83) and *Civé d'oeufs* (§84) may have appeared in reverse order in *O*,[4] and that the *Soupe en moustarde* was designed to use the oil in which the eggs of the other recipe had just been poached. This is the tenor of the text in *VAT*.[5] The two dishes are apparently to be prepared in tandem. The manner in which Recipe 84 ends in both *MAZ* and *VAT*—"puis faictes soupes en moustarde come devant"—indicates clearly that at least *Z* (if not *O*) realized that the logical sequence for the two recipes is the opposite of what was actually copied by *MAZ*, *BN* and *VAT*. The present order of these recipes in the *Viandier* has at least the logic of presenting the *Civé d'oeufs* as part of a series of dishes for poached eggs (Recipes 84–87).

---

[1] *hastes* in the manuscript should probably be understood as *hostes*, that is, Modern French "ôtez."

[2] *versses*: the last letter is lost in the hole in the manuscript.

[3] Following *de*, two or three letters may have been lost in the hole in the manuscript.

[4] At the end of Recipe 85, *VAL* alone refers to "la souppe comme devant"; the other three manuscripts do not have "comme devant" but rather "la souppe en la [*or* a la] moustarde."

[5] As well as in the *Menagier de Paris*, in which the order of these two recipes is indeed *Civé d'oeufs*, then *Soupe en moustarde*. The second recipe begins, as in *VAT*, "Prenez de l'uille en quoy vous avez pochez vos oeufz ... "(§132; p. 175).

An alternative explanation for the variants at the beginning of this recipe is that the version in *O* was similar to what we read in *MAZ*. The recipe begins with fried onions to which water, wine and verjuice (not mentioned by the other manuscripts) are added; for some reason *Y* preferred that oil be used in this liquid base rather than verjuice, and began his version in a manner similar to what we read in *VAT* (and similar as well to the text copied by the *Menagier*). Why *BN* should have added the actual eggs, mentioned only incidentally by *Y*, remains something of a mystery, but may perhaps be simply a matter of taste—a deliberate insertion rather than an error. The same sort of speculation is invited by the omission of the onions in *VAT*.[6]

Y adds a note about retrieving the sops of toast from the bouillon and allowing them to drain before finishing the sauce. As the recipe is copied in *MAZ*, the sops appear still to be in the pan when the mustard is added, and they will be subjected to a final boiling with the mustard.

84. Civé d'oeufs

MAZ – – – Pouchés euf en huille, puis prener oignons fris en huille
BN *Civé d'oeufs. Pochiés en huille,* – – – – – – – – –
VAT **Civé d'oeufz. Pochez en huille, aprés frisiez oingnons en huille**

MAZ par rouelles et mecter boulir vin, verjus et ung pol de vin aigre
VAT **par rouelles et mettez boullir avec du vin, du verjus et du vinaigre**

MAZ tout ensamble; et quant vous dresserez vostre boillon
VAT **et faictes boullir tout ensemble; et quant vous drecerez vostre boullon**

MAZ se le dressiez sur vostre grain; et sera noir lyant;
VAT **si le dreciez sur vostre grain; et ne soit pas lyant;**

MAZ puis faictes Soupes en moustarde, come devant.
BN *comme dessus est dit de la Souppe en moustarde.*
VAT **et puis faictes des Souppes en moustarde, comme devant.**

The first of four recipes for eggs—all of them poached—this *civé* is expressly related to the previous recipe for *Soupe en moustarde* by all three manuscripts that contain it.[1] *BN* has abbreviated the recipe severely, copying little more than a variant of the final phrase which no longer makes much sense.

---

[6] Onions are likewise not mentioned in the *Menagier*'s version of this recipe—which is similar to what is in *VAT*, but which reproduces the conclusion found in *BN*.

[1] Together with the previous recipe and part of the following recipe (for *Civé* or *Brouet d'Alemagne*), this *Soupe en moustarde* was on the fragment of the *VAL* roll which was cut off.

MAZ and *VAT* do not agree whether the sauce is to be stiff (*liant*). It is probable that the "noir lyant" written by *MAZ* was "non lyant" in other manuscripts; the *Menagier* reads "et soit non lyant."[2]

85. Brouet d'Alemagne d'oeufs

VAL[1]	...	
MAZ	– – – – – –	Pouchés euf en huille et mecter
BN	*Civé d'Almengne.*	*Des oeufs pochiés en huille, et*
VAT	**Brouet d'Almaigne d'oeufz.**	**Pochez en huille,**

VAL		...		*en huile,*
MAZ	lait d'amandres boulir	et oignons fris par rouelles		– –
BN	*lait d'almendes boulli*	*et oingnons par rouelles fris,*		– –
VAT	**layt d'amendes boully**	**et oingnons par rouelles friz**		**en huille,**

VAL	*faitez boullir emsemble;*	*affinez gingembre, canelle,*
MAZ	et faicte boulir ensamble;	puis affiner gigimbre, cannelle,
BN	*et boulli tout en semble;*	*affinés gingembre, canelle,*
VAT	**et mettez boullir ensemble;**	**puis affinez gingenbre, canelle,**

VAL	*girofle, graine,*	*ung pou de saffran*	*deffait de verjus,*
MAZ	– graine de paradis	et ung pol de saffrain,	deffaicte de verjus,
BN	*girofle, graine de paradis*	*et saffren*	*destrempé de verjus,*
VAT	**girofle, grainne de paradiz**	**et ung pou de saffren**	**deffait de verjus,**

VAL	*metez avec*	*sans trop boulir;*	*jaunet, liant,*	*non pas trop;*
MAZ	et mecter avec	sans tropt boulir;	soit lyant,	non pas tropt jane;
BN	– – –	*sans trop boulir;*	*soit bien liant et*	*non trop jaune;*
VAT	**et mettez avec**	**sans trop boullir;**	**et soit bien lyant et**	**non pas trop jaune;**

VAL	*et la souppe* – – – –	*comme devant,*	*qui veult.*
MAZ	et la souppe en moustarde,	– – –	qui veult.
BN	*et la soupe a la moustarde*	*comme devant,*	*qui veult.*
VAT	**et la souppe en la moustarde,**	– – –	**qui veult.**

---

[2] *Menagier de Paris*, §131; p. 174. The *Menagier* makes no reference to the *Soupe en moustarde*, which follows in his collection. He does specify that every bowl (presumably for two persons) is to receive three or four eggs, with the sauce poured over them, when *Civé d'oeufz* is served.

[1] The beginning of this recipe has been cut away in *VAL*.

The *Brouet d'Alemagne d'oeufs* is the meatless counterpart to the *Brouet d'Alemagne de char* (Recipe 22). These two broths utilize quite similar cooking methods and spices, although nutmeg enters into the meat version of it but not into the egg broth.

This dish is also related to the previous two dishes by its ingredients, and expressly to §83 by the last line of the text. The reference to §83 indicates that the *Soupe en moustarde* and the *Brouet d'Alemagne* could properly appear in the same menu.

What subsists of this recipe in the four manuscripts is remarkably concordant. The only significant variant here is *MAZ*'s omission of cloves.[2] The generic name *civé* written by *BN* seems quite appropriate, onions being fried with the eggs as in the previous *Civé d'oeufs*, and there seems likewise no reason that Recipe 22 could not have been called a *Civé d'Alemagne de char*.

86. Lait de prouvance / Lait lié

VAL	*Lait de prouvance.*[1]	*Boullez lait de vache une onde,*
MAZ	– – – –	Boulés laic de vaiche une unde,
BN	– – – –	*Et lait de vache soit boulli une onde*
VAT	**Lait lyé de vache.**	**Soit boully une onde**

VAL	*puis mis lors dessus le feu;*	*quant il sera ung pou froit,*
MAZ	puis soit mis hors du feu;	et quant il sera ung pol reffroidiez,
BN	*et mis hors du feu,*	– – – – – – – – – –
VAT	**et puis mis hors du feu,**	– – – – – – – – – –

VAL	*fillez dez moiaux grant foison passés parmy l'estamine;*
MAZ	passez moyeux d'euf par l'estermine;
BN	*puis fillés moieux d'oeufs grant foisson, ou par l'estamine;*
VAT	**puis y fillez des moyeulx d'oeufz grant foyson, ou par l'estamine;**

VAL	*soit liant,*	*sur jaunete couleur;*	– – –
MAZ	et soit bien lyant,	sur jane couleur	et non pas tropt;
BN	*et soit bien liant,*	*sus jaune coulleur*	*et non pas trop;*
VAT	**et soit bien lyant,**	**sur jaune coulleur**	**et non pas trop;**

VAL	*pochés dez eufs en eaue*	*et lez metez avec sans boullir.*
MAZ	puis pouchés euf en aigue	et les mecter avecques sans boulir.
BN	*puis pochiés les en eaue*	*et les moieux avequez sans boullir.*
VAT	**puis pochez des oeufz en eaue**	**et les mettez avec sans boullir.**

[2] The *Menagier's Brouet d'Alemaigne d'oeufz* contains all five of the spices in *Y* (§125; p. 172).

[1] *prouvance*: there are three vertical strokes between *pro* and *vance*.

As with the preceding two recipes, and the following one, this recipe is for a dish in which poached eggs are used, being served in a warm sauce of cow's milk thickened with egg yolks.

The major textual difficulty posed by the various manuscripts is in the name of the dish. *Lait de prouvance* (perhaps *Prouvance*), the name shown by *VAL* alone, is not unknown in other mediæval cookery books.[2] However, *VAT* (*Y*?) prefers to make use of a sort of generic name that has at least the virtue of being more descriptive. In *BN* this recipe was copied, without a break in the text and without a title, directly after the *Civé d'Almengne*, although on the face of it the two recipes seem distinct enough not to invite a deliberate association or to allow an accidental confusion.

In *VAL* and *MAZ* the egg yolks are to be sieved, but *Y* understands that the verb *filler* usually means to pour one ingredient directly into another so that "filtering" the yolks is considered to be a different operation; "filler ... par l'estamine" is made optional.[3]

The adjective *jaunete* in *VAL* is glossed by *Z* as "jaune et non pas trop."

87. Brouet vert d'oeufs et de fromage

VAL	*Brouet vert d'eufs et de formage*	– – – – – –	
MAZ	– – – – – – – – –	Prener parressi, sauge,	
BN	*Brouet d'oeufs et du fromage.*	*Prennés percil et sauge*	
VAT	**Brouet vert d'oefz et de frommage.**	**Prenez persil et ung pou de sauge**	
VAL	*et de saffren*	– –	*et pain trempé*
MAZ	saffrain,	fromaige,	et pain tramper,
BN	*et bien pou de saffren en la verdure,*		*et pain trempé*
VAT	**et bien pou de saffren en la verdeur,**	– –	**et pain trempé et**
VAL	*deffait de puree ou d'eaue;*	*prenez gingembre*	
MAZ	deffaicte de puree de pois ou d'aigue boulie;	puis affinez gigimbre,	
BN	*deffait de puree de pois,*	*et gingembre*	
VAT	**deffaictes de puree ou d'eaue boullie,**	**et puis gingenbre**	

[2] The *Northern-European Cookbook* has a recipe for *Hwit moos* ("White mush"), §16, which resembles the simple sauce of the *Viandier*'s recipe into which the poached eggs are placed.

The *Enseignements* (p. 185, l. 137; *Petit traité*, p. 221) has a preparation called *Let de Provence*, though this does not resemble the *Viandier*'s dish at all. It consists of crushed almonds, parsley, onions and eels(!), all fried together and garnished with saffron and pepper. One is tempted to think that there might have been some contamination here from a recipe for a *Soringue*! In the *Viandier*, what is somewhat mysterious is that the Table at the beginning of the Vatican manuscript lists both a *Lait lié* (§89) and a *Layt de provence* (§94). Both are located in this chapter of "Potaiges lyans sans chair": the *Layt lié* occurs at a point in the list which corresponds to our Recipe 86, whereas the *Layt de provence* has been written in—perhaps as an addition, a correction?—at the very end of the chapter. (See the chart in the Introduction, above.)

[3] The *Menagier de Paris* shows, with no option, "puiz y filez par l'estamine" (§133; p. 175). The *Menagier* also adds ginger and saffron to the sauce and, probably because of the latter spice, sees no need to describe what the finished colour should be.

VAL	*deffait de vin;*	– – – –	*metez le formage dedens*
MAZ	deffaicte de vin;	– – – –	puis mecter le fromaige dedans
BN	*deffait de vin,*	*et metés boullir;*	*puis metés du fromage dedans,*
VAT	**deffait de vin,**	**et mettez boullir;**	**puis mettez le frommage dedans**

VAL	*et lez eufs poichez en eaue;*	*soit liant,*	*vert gay;*
MAZ	et euf soient pouchiez en aigue;	et soit lyant,	vergay;
BN	*les oeufs quant ils seront pochiés en eaue;*	*et soit liant,*	*vergay;*
VAT	**et les oeufz quant ilz seront pochiez en eaue;**	**et soit lyant,**	**vertgay;**

VAL	*sans pain, qui veult en metre;*	*dez amandes, qui veult.*[1]
MAZ	et aulcuin n'y mectent poin de pain,	mais des amandres.
BN	*et aucuns y metent point de pain,*	*mais du lait d'almendes.*
VAT	**et aucuns n'y mettent point de pain,**	**mais y mettent layt d'amendes.**

Though called a "brouet vert" this dish could properly as well be termed a "brouet vert gay" or "vergay"—as indeed it is described by all four manuscripts at the end of the recipe. It bears a close relationship to the *Brouet vergay d'anguilles* (Recipe 76) and to the *Brouet vergay* for meat (Recipe 26), all three broths combining parsley, saffron, ginger and cheese with the particular main ingredient in each case.[2]

Two copies of this recipe show obvious errors. *VAL* does not mention either of the green ingredients. *MAZ* inserts cheese at tht beginning of the recipe, with the herbs and saffron, as well as later at the proper point when the poached eggs are added into the sauce. *Y* has made a couple of changes: the amount of saffron to be used is limited; the whole sauce, before the addition of the cheese and eggs, is to be boiled.

The concluding note about substituting almonds for the bread—or perhaps adding them to it—is somewhat garbled in *VAL*, but clarified, or interpreted, by *Z*.[3]

88. Une saulce jaunette de poisson

Val	*Brochet ou perche.*	Pellee,
MAZ	– – – – – – – – – – – – – –	Soit fris en huille
BN	*Une saulce jaunete sur poisson froit ou chaut.*	*Frit en huille*
VAT	**Une saulce jaunette de poisson froit.**	**Frit en huille**

---

[1] The punctuation to be used in this line in *VAL* is not obvious. It is possible also to understand a variety of alternatives: *sans pain, qui veult, en metre; dez amandes, qui veult*—or perhaps *sans pain; qui veult, en metre* ... —or even *sans pain, qui veult; en metre dez amandes, qui veult.*

[2] The *Viandier*'s dish can be compared also with an English one called a *Pench of egges*, a recipe for which was edited by Hieatt and Butler, part II, §38. This latter dish contains no green herbs, however.

[3] The *Menagier de Paris* has "Aucuns n'y mettent point de pain, maiz en lieu de pain couvient lart" (§124; p. 172)—this last word being apparently a misreading of the *Viandier*'s *layt*.

VAL	*sans farine;*	- - - - - - - - -
MAZ	sans farine;	- - - - - - - - -
BN	*sans farine.*	*Brochet ou perche: pellee, frite en farine;*
VAT	**sans farine;**	- - - - - - - - -

VAL	*affinez amandez,*	*deffait de vin et de verjus le plus,*
MAZ	affiner amandres,	deffaicte de vin et de verjus,
BN	*affinés almendes*	*et y metés du vin le plus ou du verjus, un pou d'eaue,*
VAT	**affinez amendes,**	**deffaittes de vin le plus et de verjus**

VAL	*coullez,*	*faites boillir;*	*affinez gingembre,*	*canelle,*	*giroffle,*
MAZ	et coulez;	- - - -	et affinez gigimbre,	cannelle,	giroffle,
BN	*coullez*	*et faites boullir;*	*prennés gingembre,*	*canelle,*	*girofle,*
VAT	**et les coulez**	**et faictes boullir;**	**puis affinez gingenbre,**	- -	**girofle,**

VAL	*graine,*	*un pou saffren,*	*deffait de boullon,*
MAZ	graine	et ung pol de saffrain,	deffaicte de vostre boillon
BN	*graine*	*et saffran,*	*deffaites de vostre boullon*
VAT	**grainne de paradis**	**et ung pou de saffren**	**et deffaictes de vostre boullon**

VAL	*metez boullir,*	*du succre avec.*	
MAZ	et faicte boulir,	et du succre avec;	et soit lyant.
BN	*et metés boullir,*	*du sucre avec;*	*et soit bien liant.*
VAT	**et mettez bien boullir,**	**et du succre avecques;**	**et soit bien lyant.**

Two dishes consisting of fried fish in a sauce conclude this chapter of meatless "potaiges lians."[1] In the first of these the name appears to have suffered several layers of garbling. The original form of the name may well have been similar to what appears in *VAT*: *Une saulce jaunette de poisson.* At some early stage, however, the title contained the qualification that this dish was for fried fish (as distinct from roast fish[2] or boiled fish[3]): *poisson froit.*[4] That this past participle was probably in the title from an early date can

[1] The Table in *VAT* mentions two further recipes that will end this chapter but that were not copied by *VAT*: an unidentifiable *Poivre cure de poisson* (which Pichon and Vicaire guess to be *Poivre civé* or *poivre curé*) and a *Layt de provence.* The *Saulce jaunette* is related to the *Poivre jaunet* for which a recipe will be given in §164, though the present sauce obviously lacks the other's pepper.

[2] In the *Chaudumet a becquet* (§78).

[3] As for the *Comminee de poisson* (§75).

[4] This is the form of the past participle of *frire* found in Recipes 33 *MAZ*, 98 *MAZ*, 99 *MAZ* and 106 *VAL*—and so perhaps also in what *Z* wrote of this last recipe. In Recipe 88 *Y*, however, *froid* could be either "fried" or "cold," whereas in Recipe 136 it almost certainly means "cold." In the *Du fait de cuisine* Chiquart lists in the menu for the dinner of the second day a dish called "ung broet georgé sur poysson frit" (f. 63r); the recipe for this *Broet georgé* (§37, f. 63v) is

be seen in the way *VAL* makes no reference at all to the way in which the fish is to be cooked but, remarkably, does stipulate that this cooking (by whatever means may be used) be done *without* the fish being coated with flour, this being a normal or at least common procedure before fish is fried. *BN* has clearly misunderstood the meaning of the word *froit* and has added the words *ou chaud* in order not to limit the usefulness of this recipe; this addition only entrenches the error.[5]

The specific mention of pike and perch, two of the fish most likely to be fried whole, is intended solely to direct that these fish in particular should be skinned before frying. The title *Brochet* found in *VAL* is explicable only as an unusual error by him: the recipe is not for the preparation of pike but for the preparation of a dish whose main interest, from the cook's point of view, is the thick, yellowish, sweet, spiced, hot sauce with which any fish similar to pike and perch can be served.

A further interesting change occurs in this recipe as *Y* makes wine rather than verjuice the principal liquid ingredient in the sauce.

BN writes, curiously, both that the fish should be "frit ... sans farine" and then that pike and perch should be "frit en farine."[6] Finally, *VAT* omits cinnamon from his spice list.

89. Gravé de perche

VAL	*Gavé[1] de parche.*	*Cuite, la perche fricte sans farine,*
MAZ	Grainé de louche.	Soit cuite et frite sans farine,
BN	*Gravé de perche.*	*Soit cuite, pelee et frite sans farine,*
VAT	**Gravé de perche.**	**Soit cuite, pelee et fritte sans farine,**

VAL	*ou poison froit,*	*comme loche;*
MAZ	ou aultre poisson froit[2] come louche,	il se fait a la louche;
BN	*et de poisson froit auxi frit*	*et fait comme de loche;*
VAT	**et de poisson froit ainsi frict,**	**fait comme de loche;**

VAL	*non pas si jaune,*	*bien liant.*
MAZ	et non pas se jane,	mais bien lyant et rousset.
BN	*non pas si jaune,*	*mais rous et tresbien liant.*
VAT	**non pas si jaune,**	**mais roux et bien lyant.**

---

essentially the same as for the *Viandier*'s *Saulce jaunette sur poisson froid*. See also the several dishes for "poysson frit" among Chiquart's banquet menus, ff. 109r, 110v, 111r (three different dishes), etc.

[5] The *Menagier de Paris* copies this same phrase, "sur poisson froit ou chault" (§135; p. 175).

[6] The author of the *Menagier* seems quite emphatic in ruling out the possibility of dredging his fish in flour: "Frisiez en huille sans point de farine loche, perche pelee, ou autre de ceste nature."

[1] *Gavé/*: *sic*.

[2] *froit*: the scribe wrote *seroit* using an abbreviation for *er*.

The recipe for *gravé* or *grané* of perch, though brief, has, like the previous recipe, undergone a number of minor modifications which may have confused the various manuscripts' readers. The recipe was originally designed for perch, but any fried fish (*poison froit* as *VAL* writes) could be prepared in the same way. In fact this *gravé* is meant to be merely a variation of the *Gravé de loche*, whose preparation has already been given in Recipe 77; in that recipe the loach is fried without being first dredged in flour, and the text of the present recipe refers back to the earlier procedure for guidance.

The title of the recipe in *MAZ* seems to be an error—*louche* written instead of *perche*—unless we understand that *MAZ(X)* had preferred to make loach the principal fish of this dish and then added the alternative of any fish that is "cold" (or "fried"), similar to a loach.[3] In this case it is difficult to see how this *Grainé de louche* (in *MAZ*) would be different from the previous *Graigné de louche* of Recipe 77. It must be assumed that the amount of saffron in the *Gravé de perche* would have to be reduced in order to make the colour of the dish less yellow and more russet-coloured than the *Gravé de loche*.

Pour malades *(BN, VAT)*

90. Couleis d'un poulet

VAL	*Coulis de poullez. Cuisiez en eaue tant qu'il soit*
MAZ	Colis d'ung poulet. Cuisiez le poulet tresfort en aigue,
BN	*Couleis d'un poulet. Cuisés en eaue tant qu'il soit*
VAT	**Couleiz d'un poulet. Cuisiez le en eaue tant qu'il soit ainsi comme**
VAL	*tout pourri, broiez os et tout,*
MAZ	puis le broyer tout et les os aussi, puis
BN	*bien pourri de cuire, et broiés atout les os en un mortier, puis*
VAT	**tout pourry de cuire, et le broyez atout les os en ung mortier, puis**
VAL	*deffetez de vostre boullon, coullés, metez boullir; qui*
MAZ	deffaicte de vostre boillon et couler; – – – – – et
BN	*deffaites de vostre boullon et coullés, metés boullir; et qui*
VAT	**deffaictes de vostre boullon et coulez, puis le mettez boullir; et qui**
VAL	*veult, poudre de succre par dessus.*
MAZ	y mecter du sucre; et ne soit pas tropt lyant.
BN	*veult, poudre de sucre par dessus; et non pas trop liant.*
VAT	**veult, il y met pouldre de succre par dessus; et ne soit mie trop lyant.**

[3] It is possible also to imagine that *MAZ* may have blundered in not writing "come perche" instead of "come louche" as an illustration of another fish similar to the loach. This dish is not considered by the *Menagier* who does, however, specifically name only the loach and the perch in his recipe for a *Potage jaunet ou saulse jaunecte sur poisson froit ou chault*, which recipe corresponds to the *Viandier*'s §88.

The chapter on foods for the sick begins with a most simple dish consisting of strained chicken that optionally is sweetened.[1] There is very little scope for variation in the copying of this recipe. Perhaps the only noteworthy peculiarity among the four versions is that *MAZ* seems to want to abbreviate the text.

It is also worth noting that none of the six dishes for the sick in the *Viandier* is omitted by any of the manuscripts.

Sugar, being naturally warm and moist in its qualities, is considered an appropriate foodstuff for the sick, particularly if the sickness is melancholic in nature; it enters frequently into the composition of therapeutic preparations, both here in the *Viandier* (in four of the six sick-dishes) and elsewhere.[2] Originally sugar was considered to be primarily a medication, as were many culinary herbs, and even into the fifteenth century it continued in princely households to be stored and distributed by the official apothecary.[3]

91. Eaue rose d'un chappon ou poulle

VAL *Eaue rousse de chappon ou de poulle pour malade.*
MAZ – – – – – – – – –

[1] In his "Titre des viandes pour les malades" Chiquart offers a recipe for *Ung coulleys* of chicken in which almonds are ground with the chicken (*Du fait de cuisine*, §71, f. 102r). No sugar is used by Chiquart; in fact, he excludes as well the use of any spices in this dish unless it be on the express orders of the patient's doctor, who will assess exactly what type of foods may most safely and beneficially be consumed. English recipe books call this simple preparation a *coleys* or *colys* (see Austin, p. 10, for example). For other versions of the dish see the *Brou de gualines per confortar* in the *Sent soví* (ch. 188), and the recipe for chicken broth which in the *Tresor des pouvres* of Arnaut de Villeneuve begins "Pour nourrir les hommes anciens, decrepis et foibles ... " (Lyon: Claude Nourry, 1527, f. 51r). The famous physician concludes this last recipe with the direction that the dish be given to the elderly "car ce chauldeau confortera moult."

[2] What the *Viandier* specifies as a garnish for this dish is sugar powder. This was commercially available as an item of trade at the beginning of the fourteenth century. "Polvere di zucchero sono di molte maniere, cioè di Cipri e di Rodi e di Soria e del Cranco di Monreale e d'Allessandria, e tutte si fanno in pani di zuccheri interi, ma perchè non sono tanti cotti come gli altri zuccheri che si sostengono in pani, e poi ch'è fatto i pani per lo travasare che se ne fa da una contrada a un'altra e d'un paese in altro si si disfanno i pani e ritornano in polvere di zucchero, e però si chiama polvere di zucchero" (Pegolotti, p. 363). See also Heyd, vol. II, pp. 687 and 691; and Paul Dorveaux, *Le sucre au Moyen Age*, Bibliothèque Historique de la France Médicale (Paris, 1911).

Concerning the increasing use of sugar in European cookery, see Barbara Santich, *Two Languages*, ch. 8: "A Taste for Sugar" (pp. 232–275); and the article by C. Anne Wilson, "Sugar: The Migrations of a Plant Product During 2000 Years," *Food In Motion: The Migration of Foodstuffs and Cookery Techniques*, 2 vols. (London, 1983), vol. 2, pp. 1–10. Sugar is used in most of the fifteenth-century additions of *MAZ* (Recipes 171–177), and in one-half of the edible additions at the end of *VAT*.

[3] See Graubard, p. 132; and Mara Castorina Battaglia, "Notizie sui farmaci usati alla corte di Savoia dai 1300 al 1440," *Minerva Medica*, 69 (1978), §171, p. 525.

BN	*Eaue rose d'un chappon ou poulle.*
VAT	**Eaue rose d'un chappon ou poulle.**

VAL	*Mettez*	– –	*en ung pot*	–
MAZ	Mecter vostre chappon ou une poule	– –	en ung pout	–
BN	*Metés*	– –	*en un pot*	*de terre*
VAT	**Mettez vostre poulle ou chappon**	**tout a sec**	**en ung pot**	**de terre**

VAL	*tout neuf,*	– – – –	– – –
MAZ	tout neuf	bien plomber,	– – –
BN	*tout nuef*	*pleumé par dedans,*	*et soit bien net;*
VAT	**tout neuf**	**qui soit plommé**	**et bien net;**

VAL	*n'y mettez ne yaue ne autre chose;*	*ung pou de saffren, qui veult;*
MAZ	et n'y mecter poin d'aigue	senon ung pol de saffrain;

BN	*le couvrez tres bien qui n'en puisse y estre*[1] *ne fust ne alaine nullement,*
VAT	**et couvrez bien le pot tellement qu'il n'en puisse rien yssir,**

BN	*et metés le pot bien apoint, et le chappon ou poulle dedans icellui,*

VAL	*asseés vostre pot*	*dedens une poelle plaine d'eaue*
MAZ	puis asseés vostre pout	dedans une peelle plaine d'aigue et
BN	*et le asés*	*en une*[2] *paielle plaine d'eaue*
VAT	**et mettez vostre pot**	**dedans une paellee d'eaue**

VAL	*que le pot soit moullié;*	*qu'il soit couvert que fumee n'en ysse;*
MAZ	que le pout se mecte jusques a colet et	telement couvert que fumee n'en yssce,

VAL	*faitez*[3]
MAZ	et faicte se[4]
BN	*et faites boullir icellui pot dedans icelle paielle, assis dedans,*
VAT	**et faictes boullir**

VAL	*jusques ace que le chapon soit cuit;*	– – –
MAZ	jusques adce que le chappon soit bien cuit;	– – –
BN	*tant que le chappon soit bien pourri de cuire;*	*ostés le chappon*
VAT	**tant que vostre chappon soit cuit dedans le pot;**	**puis ostez vostre chappon,**

---

1 *estre*: understand *istre*, "come out, escape."

2 *une* followed by *pail* stroked out.

3 It is not necessary to understand an infinitive after *faitez* as Aebischer supposes, *Vallesia*, 8 (1953), p. 95: in a culinary sense, *faire* means simply "to subject to a process," as in English "meat well done." *Cf.* "les faire par ii ou par iii foiz" in Recipe 195.

4 *se*: understand *ce*.

VAT	**et ostez l'eaue du pot qui sera yssue et venue du chappon tout a sec,**

VAL	– – –	*donnez l'eaue au malade.*
MAZ	– – –	et le donner a malade
BN	– – –	*et donnez au malade l'eaue qui sera issue du chappon,*
VAT	**comme dit est,[5]**	**et donnez au malade,**

MAZ	car ce reconforte moult et donne grant substance.
BN	*car elle reconfforte bien le malade et si y prant grant substance le dit malade.*
VAT	**car ell'est tres bonne pour reconforter et tout le corps y prent substance.**

The adjective *rousse*—a russet, tawny or brownish-yellow colour[6]—written in *VAL* has become *rose*, "pink," in the two manuscripts dependent upon *Y*. Although colours are always difficult to define, it seems that *Y* introduced an error into the manuscript tradition: juices from a chicken are more yellowish than pink.

Though *MAZ(X)* omits the name of this recipe—as he is coming more and more to do—his first line is clearly inspired by a title he read in his source, and he writes "mecter vostre chappon ou *une* poule ... ." There are no serious disagreements among the manuscripts, although many minor variants arise from additions and deletions at various times the work was was copied. By adding *tout a sec* at the beginning, and by repeating this at the end ("tout a sec comme dit est"), *VAT* identifies the crucial condition in the preparation of this *Eaue rousse de chappon*: the liquid being produced for the invalid is solely that which the chicken exudes. All manuscripts dwell later upon means by which the vapour must be contained within the cooking pot.[7] This latter is in fact a sort of double boiler with a close-fitting inner lid. According to *Z* this pot should be enamelled (*i.e.* glazed), while *Y* adds a specification that the pot be "earthenware."

The verb *faitez* in *VAL* does not need a following pronoun or infinitive, despite attempts by other copies to provide one or the other.[8]

92. Chaudeau flament

VAL	*Chaudeau flamen.*	*Metez boullir ung pou d'eaue,*	– –	
MAZ	Chaudel flamant.	Mecter boulir ung pol d'aigue	et de vin	et puis
BN	*Chaudiau flamenc.*	*Metés de l'eaue bouillir,*	– –	*puis*
VAT	**Chaudeau flament.**	**Mettez ung pou d'eaue boullir,**	– –	**puis**

[5] *tout a sec comme dit est* inserted above the line.

[6] According to other passages in the *Viandier*, *roux* is the colour of lightly toasted bread (Recipe 28 *VAL*), or of onions lightly fried in oil (Recipe 147 *VAT*). The use of saffron (optional in *VAL* and *MAZ*; omitted by *Y*) would merely confirm the natural colour of the chicken juices.

[7] *Cf.* the direction in Recipe 192: "Affin qu'il n'en ysse point d'alainne." In the preparation of his own *Restaurand* for a sick person, Chiquart likewise places a capon in the air-tight inner flask of a glass double boiler; he includes as well along with the fowl a bag of precious jewels that will ensure the efficacity of this sick-dish (*Du fait de cuisine*, §65, ff. 93v f.). See also the recipe in the *Viande e claree* (§6) whose rubric is "A quire char saunz fu."

[8] See the same usage in Recipe 18 *VAL*, above.

VAL *prenez moiaux d'eufs batus, destrempez de vin blanc,*
MAZ bactez mioust d'eufz - - - - - -
BN *moieux d'ouefs bien batus, destrempés de vin blanc*
VAT **prenez moyeulx d'oeufz batus sans l'aubun et destrempez de vin blanc**

VAL *fillez en vostre eaue quant elle aura bien boully*
MAZ et fillez en vostre pout quant elle aura boullir
BN *et versés a fil dedans vostre eaue,* - - - - - - *et du sel,*
VAT **et versez a fil en vostre eaue** - - - - - -

VAL *et sera un pou refroidie; faitez boullir;* - - - - -
MAZ et sera ung pol reffroidier; puis reffaicte boullir et garder qui n'arde;

BN *et maués*[1] *tresbien, et metés arriere du feu;*
VAT **et remuez tresbien qu'il ne tourne, et y mettez du sel arriere du feu;**

VAL *qui veul, du verjus.*
MAZ et aulcuns y mectent du verjus.
BN *et aucuns y metent un pou de verjus.*
VAT **et aucuns y mettent du verjus ung bien pou.**

Flemish caudle is a common invalid's dish in the fourteenth and fifteenth centuries. The *Menagier* selects it to appear at the head of his section on "Potages pour malades."[2] Among the *Viandier* manuscripts *MAZ* directs that the wine is to be added into the water at an initial stage in the preparation of the dish rather than mixed later with the beaten egg yolks. *Y* changes the procedure for adding these yolks to the boiling water: where *VAL* and *MAZ* have the water off the fire and cooled somewhat, *Y* cautions that the boiling water will set the egg mixture unless this is constantly stirred. Even *MAZ(X)* inserts a warning that the yolks might "burn."

93. Gruyau

VAL *Gruyau.* - - - - - - -
MAZ - - - - - - - Espailliez bien vostre gruyau[1]
BN *Gruiau d'orge. Espaillés le*
VAT **Ung gruyau d'orge mondé. Et s'il n'estoit mondé, appareillez le,**

---

[1] *et maues*: this may be for *et moues* (*i.e.* "mouvez") or be a poor reading of *remues*, the verb written by *VAT*.

[2] The *Menagier de Paris*, §303; p. 241. The recipe here is similar to what is found in *VAT*. The *Menagier* adds a note concerning quantities: if this caudle is for only one person, the cook should use five yolks. A *Caudel ferree*, which includes seedless raisins, is found among the recipes of the manuscript B.L. Royal 12.C.xii (§5 in the *Recettes culinaires* edited by Meyer, p. 50 and in the "Two Anglo-Norman Culinary Collections" of Hieatt and Jones, p. 866); see also Hieatt and Butler, part I, §5; part II, §31; part IV, §§17 and 43; etc.

[1] *gruyau*: the manuscript shows something like *gricyae*.

VAL *Fait comme forment,* – – –
MAZ et le lavez conme froment et le pillez bien en ung mortier,
BN *et pillés bien come dit est du forment,* – – –
VAT **pillez bien comme fourment en ung mortier**

VAL *metez cuire, purez, metez boullir avec lait d'amandez*
MAZ puis le mecter cuire – – – – – – avec laic d'amandres
BN *puis le metés cuire et le purés et metés boulir aveques lait d'almendes,*
VAT **et le mettez cuire et le purez et le mettez boullir avec lait d'amendes,**

VAL – – – – *et collez.*
MAZ – – – – et soit coulez, qui voudra;
BN *du sucre et sel; aucuns le coulent et broient;*
VAT **et y mettez du sel et du succre; et aucuns le broient et coullent;**

MAZ et ne soit pas tropt lyant.
BN *et non pas trop liant.*
VAT **et ne doibt mie estre trop lyant.**

The term *gruau* appears to be understood by *MAZ(X)* to mean barley, although both *BN* and *VAT* have "barley gruel" as the name of this dish.[2] *Z* amplifies the laconic "fait comme forment"[3] that is found in *VAL*, having to do with the standard preliminary preparation of the cereal grains to be used in dishes for the sick.[4] *MAZ(X)* omits the instruction to mash (*purer*: "wring out"?)[5] the boiled barley grains. The verb *espaillier* of the recipe, which designates a process by which the barley grains are cleaned (*mondé*), is explained by *BN* in Recipe 63.[6]

[2] The title of the corresponding dish in the *Menagier de Paris* (§304; p. 241) is "Orge mondé ou gruyau d'orge," a curious composite of the versions found in *BN* and *VAT*. A similar recipe for *Ordiat* is given in the *Sent soví* (ch. 97), where the author cautiously makes the sugar an optional garnish dependent upon the nature of the illness from which the patient suffers: "Si es hom qui no aya ffebra, mit hi sucre blanc e la dareria." The warmth of sugar would be dangerous for an individual with a choleric or sanguine disease.

[3] This comparison refers to Recipe 63. Among the "autres menues choses" appended by the *Menagier* to his collection of food recipes is a paragraph which begins, "Monder orge ou fourment pour faire froumentee" (§337; p. 271).

[4] For the use of creamed cereals and cereal soups as dishes for the sick in the Middle Ages, see A.M. Nada Patrone, *Il cibo del rico ed il cibo del povero* (Turin, 1981), p. 121.

[5] In his recipe for *Avenast*, an invalid's dish similar to the *Viandier*'s *Gruyau*, Chiquart says of the oats after they have been boiled, "Si en purés [*express*] l'eaue" (*Du fait de cuisine*, §75, f. 105r).

[6] Chiquart describes the preparation of oats for an *avenast*: "Si prenne son avenat et le moule grain a grain en tant qu'il n'y demoure que le propre grain de l'avenast et, estre ainsi delit et mondé, si le lavés en trois ou en quatre eaues tedes ... "(*ibid.*). This cleaning process, which is

94. Couleis de perche

VAL	*Coulis de perche.*	*Comme de poullet, destrempé de lait d'amandes.*
MAZ	Colis d'unne perche.	– – – – – – – – – – –
BN	*Couleis de perche.*	– – – – – – – – – – –
VAT	**Ung couleiz de perche.**	– – – – – – – – – – –

MAZ	Soit cuite en aigue et garder bien le boillon;	puis broyer amandres
BN	*Cuisés la en eaue et gardés le bouillon;*	– – – – – –
VAT	**Cuisiez la en eaue et gardez le boullon;**	**puis broiez amendes**

MAZ	et de la perche avec, et deffaicte de boillon,	couler et faicte boulir,
BN	– – – – – – – – – – –	*et metés boullir*
VAT	**et de la perche avec, et deffaictes de boullion**	**et mettez tout boullir**

MAZ	de sucre avec	et ung pol de vin;	et
BN	*et coulez, et puis du sucre;*	– – – –	*et doit tout*
VAT	**et coullez, et y mettez du succre;**	– – – –	**et doibt**

MAZ	soit claret.	
BN	*estre cler et net;*	*et bien pou de vin blanc, qui veult.*
VAT	**estre liant et claret;**	**et y met on ung pou de vin blanc, qui veult.**

This particular cullis offers a counterpart to the chicken cullis of Recipe 90 and would be useful for meatless days. *VAL* is content merely to indicate the similarity between the two, and to indicate too that, being a fish dish for lean days, this cullis is made with almond milk.

The perch is generally recognized as being a safe fish for anyone to eat, containing few superfluities,[1] and therefore appropriate for serving to an invalid.[2]

The only significant variant among the manuscripts deriving from *Z* concerns the order in which the broth is to be sieved and boiled. According to *MAZ* and the *Menagier*,[3] it is the sieved liquid which is to be boiled. *Y* makes the wine optional; it is not mentioned at all in the *Menagier*.

---

necessary with any grain, results in what becomes known in the fifteenth century as *espeaulte*, from the verb *espaillier*: "Grueu ou avenat pour lequel faire convient avoir de l'espeaulte ou aveine mondé": Bartolomeo Sacchi, *Platine en françoys* (Lyon, 1505), p. 204.

[1] The *Regimen sanitatis* of Magninus Mediolanensis ranks the perch as the very best of all freshwater fish: "Et mihi apparet que perca et lucius [the *lux* in Old French: "pike"] mediocris obtinent primum gradum supposito que sint pingues" (ch. 18).

[2] Lawrens Andrewe wrote, "Percus ... is a holsome mete for seke people": "The Noble Lyfe & Natures of Man, of Bestes serpentys, fowles and fisshes that be moste knowen," in Frederick James Furnivall, ed., *Early English Meals and Manners* (London, 1868), p. 120.

[3] *Menagier de Paris*, §307; p. 242. This version of the recipe applies to tench, sole, and crayfish or lobster, as well as to perch.

The term *liant* of *VAT* ("doibt estre liant") is suspect, or else purely relative in sense, because by its nature a cullis is of a runny consistency.

95. Blanc mengier d'un chappon

VAL	*Blanc mengier d'ung chappon pour ung malade.*	*Cuisiez*
MAZ	Blanc maigier d'ung chappon.	Cuisiez le chappon
BN	*Blanc mengier d'un chappon.*	*Cuisés le*
VAT	**Blanc mengier d'un chappon pour ung malade.**	**Cuisiez le**

VAL	*en yaue;*	*broiez amandez grant foison,*
MAZ	en aigue tant qu'ilz soit bien cuit;	puis broyer amandres grant foison
BN	*en eaue tant qu'il soit bien cuit;*	*et broiés almendes grant foison*
VAT	**en eaue tant qu'il soit bien cuit;**	**et broiez amendes grant foison**

VAL		*du broion du chappon,*	– – – –
MAZ	et	du chappon le bram	et soit bien broyer
BN	*et*	*du blanc d'un chappon*	*bien broié et*
VAT	**et, avec ce,**	**de braon du chappon,**	**et qu'il soit bien broyé**

VAL	*deffaitez de vostre boillon,*	*passez parmy l'estamine;*
MAZ	et deffait de vostre boillon,	passez par l'estermine;
BN	*deffaites de vostre bouillon,*	*passés parmi l'estamine;*
VAT	**et le deffaictes de vostre boullon et**	**passez tout parmy l'estamine;**

VAL	*faitez boullir tant qu'il soit liant pour taillier,*
MAZ	puis mecter boulir tant qu'il soit bien cuit et lyant pour tailliez,
BN	*puis metés boullir tant qu'il soit bien liant pour tailler,*
VAT	**et puis mettez boullir tant qu'il soit bien liant comme pour le taillier,**

VAL	*versez en une escuelle;*	*fillez demie douzene*
MAZ	puis vercel en une escuelle;	et mecter sur les escuelles et
BN	*puis verssés en une escueille;*	*puis metés frioler demie dousaine*
VAT	**puis versez en une escuelle;**	**et puis mettez frioler demie douzainne**

VAL	*d'amandez peleez*	*et les asseez sur la moitié du bout de vostre escuelle,*
MAZ	des amandres	– – – – – – – – – – – –
BN	*d'almendes pellees*	*et les assés sur le bout en la moitié de vostre escueille,*
VAT	**d'amendes pelees**	**et les asseez sur le bout en la moictié de vostre plat,**

VAL		*en l'autre moitié*	*des pepins de pomme de grenade et du succre.*
MAZ	et	– – – –	des pupins de ponmez de grenade et du succre.
BN	*et*	*en l'autre moitié*	*pepins de pomme de garnade, et sucrés par dessus.*
VAT	**et**	**en l'autre**	**des pepins de pomme de grenade et les succrez par dessus.**

The last of the dishes for the sick is a variation of a very common dish on the mediæval table.[1] This white dish may perhaps derive its name, as do so many other standard culinary preparations, from the net colour of its ingredients; in the *Viandier*'s *Blanc mengier* these main ingredients are almonds and the white meats of chicken. In the *Enseignements* and in English recipe collections, *blanc mengier* is presented as though intended for normal, everyday use. Even though in the *Viandier* this dish appears in the chapter on food appropriate for invalids, it is noteworthy that two of the scribes, *MAZ(X)* and *BN*, choose indeed not to copy the qualification "pour ung malade" in the title of Recipe 95.

The four versions of the recipe are remarkably concordant. Only in the final garnishing touch does *Y* introduce a modification by saying that the decorative almonds are to be sauteed slightly before being stood on end in the surface of the *Blanc mengier*. The darker colour of these almonds in *BN* and *VAT* would effectively set them off more from the white of the dish. Sugar is an appropriate additional garnish on this sick-dish, acting both as a warming and moistening therapeutic and as a well recognized digestive.[2]

96. Comminee de poisson

VAT **Comminee de poisson. Querez es potages lyans sans char.**

Because *Comminee de poisson* (Recipe 75) begins the section of "Potages lians [sans char]," it is reasonable to assume that this must have been a staple dish in the fourteenth century,

---

[1] See J.-L. Flandrin, "Internationalisme, nationalisme et régionalisme dans la cuisine des XIVe et XVe siècles," *Manger et boire au moyen âge* (Nice, 1982), vol. II, pp. 75–91. Recipes for varieties of *Blanc manger*, calling for either rice or almonds, are found in the *Enseignements* (p. 184, l. 119; *Petit traité de cuisine*, p. 220) and in the *Menagier de Paris* (§107; p. 165). Though this latter is textually very close to the *Viandier* and bears the title *Blanc mengier de chapons pour malades*, it is copied among the "Potages lians de chair." The *Du fait de cuisine* has for the sick both a *Blanc mangier de chappons* (§74, f. 104r) and a variation of this, a *Blanc mangier de perdrix* (§74a, f. 104v). Both the *Menagier* and Chiquart use white ginger in their dish, although, always cautious, Chiquart makes the inclusion of this spice dependent upon the approval of the patient's doctor. See also *Blank-mang(e)* in the *Forme of Cury* (§36 and §192; in Hieatt and Butler, part IV, §§38 and 200, the name of the dish is transcribed as *Blank maunger*), *Blamang* and *Blamanger* in Austin (pp. 21 and 85), and *Blonc manger* in the *Liber cure cocorum* (p. 9). A similar dish called *Blonc desore* in the *Liber cure cocorum* (p. 12) consists of rice, almond milk, chicken and sugar, with a fried-almond garnish as in the *Viandier*; ginger and white wine are added to these ingredients in the *Blanc desirree* of Meyer's *Recettes culinaires* (§1), and the garnish is pomegranate seeds. In the *Sent soví* (§49), the *Manjar blanch* is composed of chicken, almonds and rice as it is in the English recipes; *cf.* also the recipe *De menjar blanch de malat* in the *Libre del coch*, §144. *Biancomangiare* is a staple in the *Libro della cocina* and the *Libro per cuoco* (ed. Faccioli, pp. 38 and 64). The version of the dish found in Grewe's *Northern-European Cookbook* (§32) makes no use of rice.

[2] See Aldobrandino who says of sugar: "Est caus et moistes ou premier degré, et si est moult covignable a le nature de l'homme user" (p. 159, *s.v.* *canamiel*: "sugar cane").

as well as one considered, at least by *VAT*, to be sufficiently nutritious and digestible to be served to the sick. The recipe at the earlier point in the *Viandier* does indicate that, with the addition of sugar, it is indeed appropriate as invalids' food: "Pour malades," he had written in §75, "il y fault du succre."

Chapitre de poisson d'eaue doulce (MAZ, BN, VAT)

97. Lux

VAL	*Lux. Cuis en yaue;*	*a sauce vert*
MAZ	– Cuisiez le lux en aigue	et maigier a la saulse verde
BN	Lus. *Cuit en eaue;*	*a la saulce cameline ou vert,*
VAT	**Lux. En eaue;**	**a la saulce verte,**

VAL	*ou galentine, a cameline.*
MAZ	ou a la galentine.
BN	*ou a la galentine faite come bonne cameline.*
VAT	**ou en galentine, comme bonne cameline soit faicte.**

Freshwater fish constituted a fundamental staple in the diet of the European population during the Middle Ages. A very thriving industry of pisciculture was based upon the extensive exploitation of inland ponds, and ensured both the aristocratic gourmet and the ordinary person a good quantity of fish at affordable prices as well as a wide range of varieties.[1]

The large pike[2] shares with the perch the first prize for excellence among freshwater fish according to Magninus,[3] and so its position here at the beginning of the section of fish

[1] Eels were the principal crop farmed in these *viviers*. The estate of the Count of Flanders raised 264,000 eels in the year 1187 alone! See Raymond Delatouche, "Le poisson d'eau douce dans l'alimentation médiévale," *Comptes rendus de l'Académie d'Agriculture de France*, June 22, 1966, pp. 793–798.

[2] Which fish or fishes are identified by the names *lux* and *brochet* (Recipe 98) is somewhat of a problem. *Lux* is glossed by DuCange as a large *brochet*: "Lux semble être un gros brochet" (*s.v. luceus*). However, Émile Littré commented in his review of Douët-d'Arcq's edition of the *Petit traité de cuisine* that for the pike "*lus* est l'appellation primitive, du latin *lucius*; à côté s'est formé le sobriquet *brochet*, ainsi dit de la forme du museau. Les deux noms ont vécu quelque temps ensemble et finalement le nom populaire a éliminé l'autre": *Histoire littéraire de la France*, 27 (1877), p. 29. In the *Regime tresutile* (p. 72), *lucius* is the name of the fish in the Latin text, whereas *brochet* is used for the same fish in the French commentary on that text.

Concerning the farming of freshwater fish in the late Middle Ages, see Roger Grand, *L'Agriculture au Moyen Age* (Paris, 1935), ch. 6, pt. 3, pp. 535–546: "La pisciculture et la pêche."

[3] *Regimen sanitatis*, ch. 18. See also Hugo Faber, *Eine Diätethik aus Montpellier ("Sanitatis conservator"), dem Ende des 14. Jahrhunderts entstammend* (Leipzig, 1924), p. 20. Dishes using perch have already been included in the *Viandier* in Recipes 88 and 94; the readily digestible nature of the perch makes the latter dish appropriate for the sick.

recipes is quite understandable.

Regularly for these fish preparations—almost to the extent of seeming to fulfill a sort of formula—each recipe in the *Viandier* indicates the manner in which the fish should be cooked, and then for each cooking procedure, if more than one is feasible, the serving sauce or sauces with which the fish should be eaten.

The sauces suitable for boiled pike are shown in *VAL* to be either green sauce[4] or the cold preparation known as galantine.[5] The text in *VAL* is somewhat obscure here because the phrase *a cameline* seems to designate a third presentation sauce, yet the absence of a conjunction (*ou* seems called for here) makes an interpretation conjectural. *MAZ(X)* has no mention of this cameline sauce. It is in *Y* that we find expressed quite clearly what may well have been *VAL*'s intention: "galentine faite comme bonne cameline," one may serve boiled pike as a cold dish in a galantine made in the manner of cameline sauce.

There is no recipe in the *Viandier* for galantine alone.[6] In Recipe 70, however, lamprey is served in a galantine that is black, made of the eel's blood and nutmeg together with those ingredients that normally enter into cameline sauce. Fortunately, the *Enseignements* contains a recipe specifically for *Galentine a luis*,[7] which appears immediately prior to its *Galentine a la lampree*. The ingredients entering into this pike galantine—pepper, cinnamon, ginger and strong vinegar—are virtually identical to those of the cameline sauce, itself cold and unboiled, for which the *Viandier* (in *VAL*) specifies the ingredients at Recipe 155: pepper, cinnamon, ginger, vinegar and verjuice.[8] It is therefore likely that the recipe for pike that *VAL* copies in Recipe 97 provided for only two preparations, of which the second, the galantine dish, was to have the ingredients of cameline sauce.

---

[4] The *Viandier* provides a recipe for green sauce later at §161, among the non-boiled sauces. This was one of the most commonly prepared sauces in the late mediæval kitchen.

[5] See Recipes 68 for *Gelee de poisson*, and 70 for *Lamproie a la galentine*, above. The *Enseignements* specifies for pike both of these two sauces as well as one other: "Luz a lassausse verte. Luiz a la galentine. Luiz au bescuit" (p. 186, l. 182; *Petit traité*, p. 223).

[6] See the recipe for *Gelatina* in the *De saporibus* of Magninus (*ed. cit.*, p. 188); for *Gelatina de pescie* in Libro "A" of the Anonimo Meridionale, §57 (*ed. cit.*, p. 16); and for *Galantina piscium* in the *Liber de coquina*, part IV, §1 (*ed. cit.*, p. 413). "Lucii vel tenche in aqua dequoquuntur et cum salsa viridi vel camelina comeduntur. Et qui voluerit in galatina diu servari poterunt: dequoquitur in aqua" (*Tractatus*, part III, §8; *ed. cit.*, p. 390). See also the two versions of *Pike in galentine* in Austin (p. 101); the *Geladia* in the *Sent soví* (§146); the *Menagier*'s brief reference to *galentine de poisson froit* (§129; p. 174; and, in the *Edificio di Ricetti* (not paginated) the recipe "a conzelare ogni zelatina cosi de stade come de inverno" that is specifically for pike. Rather than for pike, the bourgeois author of the *Menagier* provides a recipe for *Galentine pour carpe* among his "Saulses boulyes" (§283; p. 233); *cf.* Recipe 102, below.

[7] *Enseignements*, p. 184, l. 141; *Petit traité*, p. 221.

[8] Later copies of the *Viandier* expand this spice list, notably by the addition of grains of paradise—melegueta pepper—but the essence of cameline sauce remains the cinnamon and vinegar.

98. Brochet

VAL	*Brochet.*	*Rosti, au chaudiumé;*	*le froit,*
MAZ	– –	Soit rotis, au chauduné;	ou fris,
BN	*Brochet.*	*Rosti, ou chaudumel;*	*le frit en potaige—comme dist est,*
VAT	**Brochet.**	**Rosty, au chaudumé;**	**et le frit, en potage ou**

VAL	– – – *rosti, au cel, vin et poudre.*
MAZ	a la jauce.
BN	*"en la jance."*
VAT	**a la jance.**

What is peculiar about this recipe for pickerel and the previous recipe for pike is that the cooking methods specified in them do not bear the slightest resemblance to one another. It is as if the recipe for *Brochet* should be subsumed under *Lux* and be merely a continuation of it: pike—boiled, roasted or fried. This is indeed the procedure for the very next fish: barbel boiled, roasted or fried (Recipe 99). If Littré is correct and *brochet* is merely a more recent name for *lux*,[1] we might imagine that at some early stage in the copying of the *Viandier* a scribe, possibly the original author himself, tried to insert the name *brochet*, by which the fish was perhaps more popularly known, into the recipe for pike but that this annotation was soon misunderstood to introduce a distinct recipe for another sort of fish. The difference between *lux* and *brochet* seems, however, to be that which exists between "pike" and "pickerel."[2]

The four manuscripts do not agree on the text that describes the saucing of the fried pickerel. *VAL* seems to allow a second treatment there for roasted pickerel, and *Z* calls the sauce *jance*[3]—apparently a term that *MAZ(X)* does not recognize, writing instead clearly *jauce*. The *ou* of *VAT* ("en potage *ou* a la jance") seems to allow an alternative presentation for fried pickerel, but this is probably an error. The text of *BN* indicates that

---

[1] See Recipe 97, n2, above. Bartolomeo Sacchi (1421–1481), known as Platina, has in his *De honesta voluptate* a paragraph on the *Lucius fluvialis*. The French version of this work regularly amplifies on the original; as well as expanding from five lines to thirty-seven lines Platina's description of the pike, the French version uses two names to refer to this fish: "Du lus ou bechet. Le lus ou bechet est ung poysson de fleuve qui a large gorge et les dens agues et devoure les petis poyssons ... ": *Platine en françoys* (Lyon, 1505), f. 95v.

According to J.-P. Sosson, "La part du gibier dans l'alimentation médiévale" (p. 351), at the end of the fourteenth century in Flanders pickerel were a seasonal food, being consumed in quantity especially between September and February.

[2] In an article on the pike ("Noms de poissons," *Revue des langues romanes*, 63 (1925), p. 10), Paul Barbier concludes "que *luz* est le brochet arrivé à son plein développement et que *brochet* doit être le nom du même poisson quand il est moins gros." He cites Eustache Deschamps (*c.* 1350) for whom "*lus*, *brochet* et *carreau* ... doivent indiquer diverses étapes dans la croissance de l'*Esox lucius* L."

[3] The *Viandier*'s recipe for *Jance* is at §168 among the boiled sauces. *Jance* is the principal ginger-based dressing in mediæval cuisine.

only one type of preparation is intended, and this must be some sort of ginger stew. In the following recipe (§99) *VAT* probably copies more accurately: "au potaige a la jance."

99. Barbillons

VAL	*Barbillons. En eaue, au poivre aigret;*
MAZ	Barbillons. Soient cuit en aigue, maingier a la rappee;
BN	*Barbillons. Cuis en eaue, au poivre egret;*
VAT	**Barbillons. En eaue, au poivre aigret;**

VAL	*lez rostis, au verjus;*	*lez frois, au potaige ou a la jance.*
MAZ	et les rotis, au verjus;	et les fris, a poutaige.
BN	*les rostis, au verjus;*	*le frit, en potaige comme dessus est dit ensuivant,*[1]
VAT	**et les rostiz, au verjus;**	**et les friz, au potaige a la jance.**

BN *ou a la jance sup.*[2]

The order of the recipes *Barbillons* and *Bar* is probably that which is found in *VAL* and *BN*, despite what might be considered the logic of the reverse sequence. The logical manuscripts, *MAZ(X)* and *VAT*, do rearrange the order of the two recipes, but the *barbillons* is likely still to be the more common or favoured of the two fish, lending itself as it does to a broader variety of ways of cooking and of serving.

The sauce known as *rappee*, which *MAZ(X)* substitutes for sharp pepper sauce as a dressing on boiled barbel, does not appear in any other recipe in any extant manuscript of the *Viandier*. The name of this sauce can, however, be read twice in the Table of the Vatican manuscript.[3] In Recipe 27, copied in all four manuscripts, a broth called *Rappé* is made of ginger, verjuice and wine and is used as a dressing on a fried meat together with a mash of tart fruit (currants or verjuice grapes). Once again the *Menagier de Paris* proves valuable in furnishing a recipe for a *Saulse rappee* that is likely to be close to what *MAZ(X)* intends: it is a simple combination of crushed unripe grapes and ground ginger.[4]

---

[1] After the word *dit* the scribe wrote *euß*. Pichon and Vicaire interpreted this as an abbreviation for *ensuivant*.

[2] After the word *jance* the scribe wrote *sup le bar*, making no break in the text between this and the following recipe. The meaning of *sup* is not clear. Pichon and Vicaire suggest "*supra*." The word may belong with the following recipe for bass, §100.

[3] See the chart in the Introduction, above. Note particularly in the *VAT* Table, §29, *Jambon de porc a la rappee* and, among the unboiled sauces, §164, *Rappee*.

[4] *Menagier de Paris*, §294; p. 237. The *Recueil de Riom* (§47) echoes *MAZ* in recommending *saulse rappee* for *barbeaux*, and provides a recipe for this: "Pouldre de gingibre blanc, et du poivre, et du verjust de grain reffait ou boullon destrampé de verjust." A similar recipe is read at §40: "A la sausse rappee, il fault mectre tremper du pain en verjust et puis coler. Et prandre le verjust en grain, et l'esgrenez, et le reffere ou boillon de poisson, et puis mectre dedans la saulce." Another variety of the sauce, a sort of syrup in this case, is found in the *Tractatus*, part I, §19: "Rapa

The sauce for which *MAZ(X)* substitutes this *rappee*, *poivre aigret*, is likewise unmentioned elsewhere in the *Viandier*. Again, though, the *Menagier* does refer to it, as an alternative name for the sauce *poivre jaunet* which is served on the barbel in winter.[5] In the *Viandier*'s Recipe 164 this latter sauce is shown in *VAL* and *MAZ* to be a combination of ginger, pepper, saffron and verjuice,[6] and so does in fact bear at least some resemblance to the *rappee* of *MAZ(X)*. The ginger mixed with the tart taste of the verjuice produces a "sweet-and-sour" or bitter-sweet effect appropriate for a fish of few superfluities such as the barbel.[7]

100. Bar

VAL	*Bar.*	– – – – – –		*A saulce vert.*
MAZ	Le bar.	Bar soit cuit en aigue et	maingier	a la saulce verde.
BN	*Le bar.*[1]	*Cuit en eaue et sel,*	*mengiés*	*a la saulce verte.*
VAT	**Bar.**	**Cuit en eaue;**		**a la saulce vert.**

The *Menagier de Paris* reproduces this recipe for bass, but without making any mention of the addition of salt to the water in which it is to be cooked.[2] For the standard Green

vel mulsa hoc modo fit: tempore vindemearum, accipitur mustum optimum, dulce dequoquitur et despumatur usque ad mellis spissitudinem, et servetur. Dat sinapy condimentum, et valet in aliis causis plurimis" (ed. Mulon, p. 383).

[5] "Barbillons rostiz au vertjus. ... *Item* en hiver au poivre egret ou jaunet, car c'est tout ung" (*Menagier*, §169; p. 187). See also in the *Menagier*, §281; p. 232, where a recipe is provided for the standard boiled sauce *Poivre jaunet ou aigret*. In the *Viande e claree* (§19), a recipe for a sauce called *Pevre gresse* calls for ginger, pepper, bread and ground fresh grapes; the pepper in particular distinguishes this from the alternative sauce specified in the *Viandier* for Barbillons. The most recent editors of the *Viande e claree*, Hieatt and Jones, guess that the grape juice for the sauce *Pevre gresse* would be "probably sour" (ed. cit., p. 870). Concerning the qualification *gresse*, they speculate upon a connection with *aigre* and *aigret*; Cotgrave shows an archaic word *Aigras* which he glosses "Veriuyce."

[6] The later manuscript versions, *BN* and *MAZ2*, add vinegar as well to the verjuice and wine.

[7] See Durante da Gualdo, *Tesoro*, according to whom the *Triglia balbona* (*Mullus barbutus*) is warm in the first degree and dry at the beginning of the second degree. Such qualities are exceptional in a fish.

[1] The recipe for *Bar* continues without break in the same paragraph as the previous recipe for *Barbillons*.

[2] *Menagier*, §168; p. 187. In general most of the recipes for fish in the *Menagier* show considerable indebtedness to the *Viandier*. Salt was in common use, both in the boiling of fish and as a garnish for cooked fish; it was considered useful with fish because "li sels amende lor malice et le wiscosité qu'il ont. ... Cil qui sont cuit en ewe pure et au sel valent miex des autres, mais qu'il soient mangié a saveur de gyngembre, de poivre, de canele et d'autres espesses" (Aldobrandino, p. 177). *Cf.* Recipes 105, 109 and *passim*, below.

Regarding the names of the *bar* and *barbel*, see Paul Barbier, "Noms de poissons," *Revue des langues romanes*, 63 (1925), p. 10.

Sauce see Recipe 161, below.

101. Alose [d'eaue doulce]

MAZ – Soit baconee, salee, cuite, et maingier
BN *Alouse. Soit baquee et sallee, cuite en eaue;*
VAT **Aloze. Soit baconee, salee et cuite en eaue;**

MAZ a la moustarde ou a la siboule; – – – – – –
BN *a la moustarde ou a la ciboulle* – – *ou a la saulce vert;*
VAT **a la moustarde ou a la ciboule et au vin et a la saulce vert;**

MAZ et le rotis, a la cameline.
BN *la rostie, a la cameline; et au fort, en vin blanc*
VAT **et la rostie, a la cameline; et la cuite[1] au four, a ung pou de vin blanc**

BN *et verjus et poudre d'espices par dessus.*
VAT **et de pouldre d'espices mis cuire avecques la lecchefrite au four;**

et aucuns y mettent de la cameline et non autre chose.

The shad appears not to have been among the *Viandier*'s earliest listing of freshwater fishes, but to have been inserted by *Z*. The three manuscripts copying this recipe agree generally on the two possible treatments, for boiled and roast shad, which are copied by *MAZ*; but interestingly *Y* introduces a new method of cooking a fish, baking it in an oven. For this last novelty, *VAT* can even suggest particular procedures that he has practised or heard about.

The Table at the beginning of *VAT* specifies correctly that the fish dealt with in this recipe are *Alozes d'eaue doulce*. All manuscripts will copy a recipe two chapters later (Recipe 143) for an *Alose* that is classified as a flat sea-fish.

102. Carpe

VAL *Carpe. Cuite en yaue, a la saulce vert*
MAZ Carpe. Soit cuite en aigue et maingier a la saulse verde
BN *Carpes. Cuites en[1] eaue, a la saulce vert*
VAT **Carpes. Cuites en eaue, a la saulce vert**

VAL *ou galentine.*
MAZ ou a la galentine.
BN *ou a la galentine comme la lemproie.*
VAT – – – – **autelle comme lamproye.**

---

[1] In *VAT* the second half of this recipe for *aloze* is in a separate paragraph, as if for a new fish.

[1] *en* followed by *a* stroked out.

There is close agreement among the manuscripts on the ways of preparing this common fish.[2] *VAT*, however, has blundered in omitting the possibility of serving carp as a cold dish in galantine; the comparison with the lamprey is consequently misleading.

103. Perche

VAL	*Perche. Cuite en yaue, pelee,*	*a vin aigre,*
MAZ	Perche. Perche soit cuite en aigue, pellee, et maingier	a parressi
BN	*Perche. Pellee, cuite en eaue,*[1]	*au percil*
VAT	**Perche. En eaue, et pelee,**	**au vinaigre**

VAL	*a persin,*	*ou en coulis;*	*la frite,*	*en potaige gravé.*
MAZ	et a vin aigre.			
BN	*et vin aigre,*	*en*[2] *coulis;*	*la frite,*	*ou en potage gravé.*
VAT	**et au**[3] **percil,**	**ou au couleiz;**	**et la fritte,**	**au gravé.**

The perch cullis, a sick-dish, has been outlined in Recipe 94.

The term *gravé* is used here by *VAL* and *BN* as an adjective qualifying a sort of *potaige* made from fried perch: after being fried, the fish would be put into a pot with a sauce similar to that described in the *Gravé de loche* (Recipe 77), a standard preparation; we have in fact already seen the *Gravé de perch* in Recipe 89.

104. Tanche

VAL	*Tanchez.*	*Eschaudeez,*
MAZ	Tanche.	Soit eschaudee en aigue, puis cuit, et maingier
VAT	**Tanche.**	**Eschaudee en eaue,**

VAL	*a la saulce vert;*	*lez fruitez, en potaige;*	*eschaudez*	*et limonez,*
MAZ	a la saulse verde;	et la frite, en poutaige;	ou l'eschauder	– –
VAT	**a la saulce verte;**	**et la fritte, au potaige;**	– – –	– –

---

2 J.-P. Sosson has found that in Flanders at this time on the table of Guillaume d'Ostrevant carp were the preferred fish. Especially and clearly was this so in Lent: "Pour 39 semaines [the period Sosson studied]: 10,757 carpes, 542 brochets, 33 anguilles et 21 brèmes .... Les carpes s'y taillent la part du lion" ("La part du gibier dans l'alimentation médiévale," p. 351).

The *Menagier* contains a recipe for *Galentine pour carpe* (§283; p. 233). That carp lends itself to a jellied treatment is recognized even by Eustache Deschamps: "Carpes, barbeaux sont lymoneux" (*Œuvres*, vol. 8, p. 339; l. 116). See Recipe 68, above.

1 *eaue* followed by *mengie a la sauce vert* stroked out.

2 Before *en* part of a letter is apparent beside a hole in the manuscript but it is impossible to tell what the letter might have been.

3 *au* followed by *perche* stroked out.

VAL *fendés sur lez dos,* - *a fine poudre,*
MAZ et la fender sur le dolz, - puis mecter du sel et de la fine poudre
VAT **et la renversee, rostie et pouldree de pouldre de canelle,**

VAL *liez de fil, rostir sur le greil,*
MAZ y dedans et le rajouster ensamble et lyés, puis le rotissiez sur le gril
VAT - - - - - - - - -

VAL *moller en vin aigre, coller en rostissant de huille de nois;*[1]
MAZ et la moillie en vin aigre et la oignés en rotissant de huille d'olive;
VAT **et soit plungee en vinaigre et ung pou d'uille.**

VAL *a la cameline.*
MAZ et la maingier a la cameline.

A member of the carp family, the tench was a popular eating fish in the fourteenth and fifteenth centuries[2]—even though *BN* for some reason chooses to omit it from his copy. Three cooking methods for the tench are mentioned: boiling, frying[3] and roasting.[4] The

---

[1] *nois* written *mois* with the first stroke of the *m* expunctuated.

[2] This favour was enjoyed by the tench despite the reserve expressed by Lawrens Andrewe in his treatise on fish (published by Furnivall in his *Early English Meals and Manners*, p. 122): "It is a sweete fisshe but it is evyll to disiest." Durante da Gualdo indicates in fact that the tench is by nature cold in the second degree as well as moist, likewise in the second degree, qualities rendering it potentially quite harmful for human consumption unless the method of cooking and the serving sauce countered them adequately. Andrewe's comparison of the tench to an eel explains perhaps in part the use in the *Viandier* of the *renversé* procedure, normally reserved for the eel: "*Tenca* is tench of the fresshe water, and is fedde in the mudde lyke the ele and is moche lyke of colours."

[3] The Italian recipe collection in the Musée Masséna at Nice contains a version of the dish which the *Viandier* calls *Tanche frite, en potaige*: "*Thenche ad brodecto* per xii ricchi giucti. Tolli tre tenche grosse, et tolli ii libri di mandorle, et tolli tre onze di spetie, et tolli pertosinoli bona quantita & menta & salvia pocha; et tolli le tenche tenute in sale un poco, bene lavate, et mictele ad frigere; et quan sonno fricte polverizale di bone spetie; et tolli le mandorle et lavale col gusio et mannale & stemperale con acqua chiara & colale si che sia spesso, et mecti il lacte ad bollire in un vasello per se; & mictivi quantita di specie & d'agrazzo o d'aceto & lu sugo dell'erbe che tu ay tucte; queste cose micti ad imocta(?) ad foro, et fa bollire et mestalo spesso; et quan e bollito mictive il pesce, & trai indireto per ministrare. Questo brodecto vole essere giallo & verde, & agro d'agrazzo o d'aceto" (ff. 7v–8r).

The *Forme of Cury* contains a *Tenches in cyvee* which begins likewise, as does the *Viandier*'s option, with fried tench (§120; Hieatt and Butler, part IV, §123); see also Hieatt and Butler, part III, §9, for a dish of the same name which begins with boiled tench.

[4] In his *Opusculum de saporibus* (*ed. cit.*, p. 188) Magninus Mediolanensis specifies sauces for tench that are similar to those found in the *Viandier*. For the boiled tench, green sauce is to be provided; for roast tench, "impleatur cum petrosillo et pulvere specierum et agresta intus et

method known as *renversé* was commonly practised for the eel, but the term and procedure seem to be introduced into this recipe for tench with either *Y* or perhaps *VAT* himself.[5] The procedure consisted of slitting a fish along the back, folding it on itself along its belly, applying the appropriate sauce on the inner and outer surfaces of flesh and skin, and then lacing the two edges together.[6] While *VAL* and *MAZ* say that fine powder is put on the fish while it is roasting, *VAT* specifies the use of cinnamon, but later fails to make any mention of a serving sauce. In the other manuscripts this serving sauce is cameline, a dressing in which cinnamon predominates.

A detailed recipe for the confection of *Pouldre fine* is offered by the *Menagier*. It comprises white ginger, cinnamon, cloves, grain of paradise and sugar.[7]

105. Bresme

VAL	*Bresme.*	*Cuite en yaue*	*ou rostie,*		*a la sauce vert;*
MAZ	Roussaille.	Soit cuit en aigue	ou roustie	et maigier[1]	a la saulce verde;
BN	*Bresme.*	*Soit cuite en eaue,*	– –	*mengié*	*a la saulce vert;*
VAT	**Bresme.**	**Cuitte en eaue,**	– –		**a la saulce verte;**

VAL	– –	– –	*et en pasté, a poudre d'espicez et*
MAZ	– –	– –	et en pasté et poudre d'espices.
BN	*en rost,*	*au verjus;*	*ou en potaige poudree de fine poudre d'espices,*
VAT	**et la rostie,**	**au verjus;**	**et en pasté, pouldree d'espices,**

VAL	*au sel.*
MAZ	– – Soit cuite en aigue et en vin pour maingier au vin aigre.
BN	*au sel menu.*
VAT	**au sel menu.**

extra. Et addatur aliquantulum de oleo olivarum in agresta que apponatur ab extra." *Cf.* the very similar recipe for *Tinche rinvesciate* in the *LVII Ricette* (§45). The parsley mentioned here is the main ingredient of the green sauce used on tench when it is merely boiled. This internal and external saucing for the roast tench in Magninus implies the *renversé* treatment indicated by the *Viandier*. Parsley, possessing a nature that is extremely warm and dry, both in the third degree according to Constantinus, Platearius, Aldobrandino and others, is generally relied upon in mediæval cookery to counteract and neutralize any superfluous coldness or humidity in other foodstuffs.

[5] The term is used again in the *Viandier* only by *VAT* in Recipe 107. In the *Roman du comte d'Anjou* (*c.* 1316), Jehan Maillart wrote, "J'avoie tances / que en appele renversees": ed. Mario Roques (Paris, 1931), ll. 1142–1143.

[6] The *Menagier de Paris* suggests inserting a thin lath, presumably well oiled, between the two skin surfaces before the "reversed" fish is sewn together (§172; p. 187).

[7] *Menagier de Paris*, §314; p. 247. Exceptionally, quantities are specified in this recipe, although both Brereton and Ferrier (p. 329) and Pichon (p. 247, in the recipe and in n3) show great hesitation interpreting the abbreviations.

[1] *maigier*: *sic.*

For this recipe *MAZ* copies the name of the following dish, an instance of an error to which for some reason—the position of the titles or rubrics in his source manuscript?—he seems peculiarly prone.[2] It is true though that the two recipes, 105 and 106, are rather similar textually, the two fish here, bream and roach, being similar in nature and in fact readily hybridizing together.[3]

Three dishes are possible for the bream according to the *Viandier*: the fish can be boiled, roasted or served in a pasty. For the first two methods *VAL* and *MAZ* mention a common serving sauce, green sauce, but *Y* makes a distinction: for boiled bream the green sauce is indeed appropriate—as it is in the previous recipe for boiled tench and in the following recipe for boiled roach[4]—but on roast bream plain verjuice should rather be used.[5]

BN strangely misreads *potaige* for *paste*.

MAZ(X) appends a peculiar passage at the end of this recipe, apparently as an alternative to boiling bream in just plain water. However, this passage is identical to what *VAL* has in Recipe 117 for crayfish, a recipe which will be omitted by *MAZ(X)*. This seems to be yet another instance of a misplaced text in the *MAZ* manuscript.

106. Poulaille / Baissaille / Rossaille

VAL	*Poulaille.*	*Cuite en eaue, a la saulce vert;*
MAZ	– –	Soit cuite en aigue et maingier aux aillés vers;
BN	*Baissaille.*	*Cuite en eaue, a la saulce verte;*
VAT	**Rossaille.**	**En eaue, a la saulce vert;**

VAL	– – – – – –	*en rost, au verjus;*
MAZ	et la salee, a la moustarde;	la rotie, a verjus;
BN	– – – – – –	*en rost au verjus;*
VAT	– – – – – –	**en rost, au verjus.**

VAL	*la froide,*	*a la jance ou au potaige.*
MAZ	et la frite,	a la jasse ou en poutaige.
BN	*la frite,*	*a la jance ou en potage comme devant.*

[2] In this respect see specifically the treatment that *MAZ* accords Recipes 47, 70 and 119.

[3] Pichon and Vicaire quote Pierre Belon, *La nature et diversité des poissons* (Paris, 1555), to the effect that "la rosse est un poisson qui tient de la brême et du gardon" (p. 27, n1).

[4] The *Enseignements* goes so far as to make a generalization: "Tout pesson d'eve douce qui est cuit en eve est bon a la verte sausse" (p. 186, l. 188; *Petit traité*, p. 223). Freshwater fish are considered to be more cold and humid in nature than those of the sea because of the warming and drying effects of salt (*Régime de santé*, f. 63v).

[5] One might conjecture that the roasting process is expected to dry and particularly to warm this freshwater fish to the point where a parsley sauce is no longer required or safe. Verjuice, on the other hand, is considered to be moderately cold and dry by nature.

A variety of names is used to identify the fish in this recipe, all of them designating species of comparatively small fish but all of them apparently related to the roach.[1] Randle Cotgrave glosses *rosse* as "The Roche-fish; also, a small red-tayled lake-fish, not much unlike a Mennow; also, as *Poule de mer*." The word *poulaille* in *VAL* is undoubtedly a collective form for this *poule de mer*.[2] *Baissaille* in *BN* may be a generic designation for any lowly, insignificant, fish—even one perhaps that is not esteemed particularly highly.

As with the bream in the previous recipe, this fish affords a good range of possibilities for cooking and saucing.

One significant variant turns up here, in *MAZ*, although it appears at first examination to be two variants: a different sauce for the boiled fish, and a mention of the saltwater roach and its serving sauce. These details are quite likely the product of a single case of haplography. In the same way as *MAZ(X)* picks up titles from following recipes, he seems also here to have transposed a whole line of the text that is in Recipe 107 for eels—copying even the name of the sauce, *aillez vers*: the phrases appear in *VAL*'s version of Recipe 107.

107. Anguilles

VAL	*Anguillez.*	*Cuitez en eaue,*[1]	*aux aillez vers;*
MAZ	– – –	Cuisez en aigue et maingier	aux hauls vers;
BN	*Chevriaux.*[2]	*Cuis en eaue,*	*aux aulx vers;*
VAT	**Anguilles.**	**En eaue,**	**aux ailletz vertz;**

VAL	*les salleez,*	*a la moustarde;*	*en rost, aux aillez blans;*
MAZ	la sallee,	a la moustarde;	en roz, aux aillés blans;
BN	*lez sallees,*	*a la moustarde;*	*en rost aux aillez blans et,*
VAT	**la salee,**	**a la moustarde; et**	**en rost, aux aulx blans;**

VAL	*qui veult,*	– – – –	– – – –	*comme une lamproie;*
MAZ	– –	– – – –	– – – –	– – – –
BN	*qui veult,*	*au verjus; en rost*	*a la sauce chaude*	*comme la lemproie;*
VAT	– –	**la renversee,**	**a la saulce chaude**	**comme une lamproye;**

---

[1] The *Menagier de Paris* affirms that "Gardons et rosses—c'est la friture" (§188; p. 194). The fish *gardon* appears in the *VAT* Table (§122) but is not copied by any manuscript of the *Viandier*. For *gardon*, the small white fish normally translated nowadays as "roach," Cotgrave reads, "A certain freshwater fish that resembles the chevin; onely his head is lesse, and bodie broader; Some hold it to be the freshwater Mullet; others (more probably, though Gesner say otherwise) the Roche, or a kind thereof." The recipe for *Cheveneaux* will be the second after this.

[2] See *pole*, fish No 323 in Paul Barbier, "Noms de poissons," *Revue des langues romanes*, 57 (1914), p. 329; and *rosse*, fish No 325, *ibid.*, p. 331.

[1] Following the word *eaue* a phrase was inserted above the line by means of a caret but was subsequently scraped off; nothing of this insertion is legible, even under ultraviolet rays.

[2] The *BN* scribe has written *chenriaux*.

VAL *en pasté, a la poudre.*
MAZ et en pasté, a poudre d'espices.
BN *en pasté, soient poudrés d'espices;*
VAT **et en pasté, pouldré d'espices, aux aulx blans; et auccuneffois**

BN *ou en potages.*
VAT **au potaige, comme dessus es "Potaiges."**

Eels constituted an important part of the lean diet in the Middle Ages and, according to the *Menagier*'s menus, were normally served in various forms among the meat dishes of non-fish dinners and suppers. Even Alexander Neckham in the twelfth century writes of catching eels ("in vivario sive in stanno deprensi") by an assortment of means then currently practised, including a spear (*fuscina*) specifically designed for taking eels.[3]

Eels can be prepared in a number of ways. They can be boiled, whether they are fresh or salted—although the sauce will naturally be different in each case—they can be roasted,[3] or they can be baked in a pasty.[4]

The four manuscripts agree in most respects in their copies of this recipe, but there are two later additions for which *Y* is probably responsible. A variety of the roasting procedure calls for a hot sauce, for which a reference is made to Recipe 69, the *Lamproie fresche a la sauce chaude*. For this procedure *Y* may have recommended that the eel be turned inside out along its belly, as was done with the tench (Recipe 104); *BN*, however, perhaps not understanding what was meant by the term *renversee*, needlessly repeats the phrase "en rost."[5] *Y* further suggests that eel can be eaten in a stew. To clarify, *VAT* refers back to the section on "Potaiges lyans sans chair," where the cook might adapt such a recipe as §76 for *Brouet vertgay d'anguilles*, §79 for *Une soringue* (of eels), or §80 for *Brouet sarrasinois* (of eels).

108. Chevesnes

VAL *Cheneveaux. Cuit en eaue, a sauce vert;*
MAZ Chenernes. Cuisiez en aigue et maingier a la saulce verde;

---

[3] *De utensilibus*, in Richard Wright, *A Volume of Vocabularies* (2nd ed., n.p.: privately printed, 1882), p. 92. See also Recipe 97, n1, above, concerning the very large place accorded eels in mediæval pisciculture.

[3] The author of the *Sent soví* (§198) agrees with the *Viandier* in recommending that roast eel be eaten with a garlic white sauce. At the conclusion of its recipe for *Alleata*, the *Liber de coquina* notes, "Potes comedere cum piscibus dure digestionis, sicut morua et cetera" (part II, §67). An *Alliata bullita* is attested by DuCange, vol. I, p. 185c.

[4] The *Enseignements* has "Anguilles en pastez. *Item*, anguilles salees, cuites en eve, a la moustarde" (p. 186, l. 187; *Petit traité*, p. 223). See also the *Anguille in pastillo* of the *Tractatus*, part III, §3.

[5] *BN* did not copy the recipe for tench (§104) in which the *renversé* technique of preparation was used. The *Recueil de Riom* has a recipe for *Les anguilles reversees, et les brochereux, et carpes a la garentine* (§28): the spices used on the reversed eel here (grains of paradise, cloves, nutmeg and mace) would seem to be the same as for a cold galantine.

VAL	*en rost, au verjus.*
MAZ	et les rotis, a verjus.

The chub, related to both the carp and the minnow, is known by four different versions of a name in the *Viandier*. *MAZ* has *chenernes* (for *chevernes*), whereas *VAL* (who writes a form with a metathesis of the *n* and *v*), *BN*[1] and the *VAT* Table show a diminutive *cheveneaux* and *chevesneaulx*.[2] Cotgrave shows "The Chevin, or Pollard-fish" for *Chevesne.*

This is a boney fish, not very firm or tasty, whose flavour deteriorates rapidly. Both *BN* and *VAT* omit this recipe from their copies—*BN* perhaps accidentally—and the *Menagier de Paris* does not mention it either.

109. Truite

VAL	*Truitez. Cuitez en eaue,*	*a la cameline;*
MAZ	Tructes. Cuictes en aigue et maingier	a la cameline;
BN	*Truites. Cuites en eaue, mengier*	*a la cameline;*
VAT	**Truite. En eaue,**	**a la cameline;**

VAL	*ou en pasté, au sel menu, a pouldre d'espicez, qui veult.*
MAZ	ou en pasté, ou sel menu ou a poudre d'espices.
BN	*en pasté, au sel menu.*
VAT	**et en pasté, au sel menu.**

The second possible way of preparing trout, in a pie, seems to have been quite widely practised.[1]

Y eliminates the option of eating trout pie with spice powder. The *Menagier* mentions neither salt nor spice powder as possible garnishes for his pie, but only that it may be covered with broad strips of bacon on meat-days.[2]

---

[1] In *BN* the title *Chevriaux* was copied above the preceding recipe for eels (§107). Pichon and Vicaire note (p. 27, n2) that this name in *BN* stands for the fish "chevennes."

[2] In the *Enseignements* the name of the chub seems to be *chavesoz*: "Loches e chavesoz a lassausse verte; cuites e frites, a la moustarde" (p. 186, l. 193; *Petit traité*, p. 224). It seems clear that this text should read "Loches e chaves[n]ez a lassausse verte, cuites; e frites, a la moustarde."

[1] See the *Liber de coquina*, part IV, §8: *De troitis in pastillo: pastillum de troitis*; Libro "A" of the Anonimo Meridionale, §81: *Pastello de trocte*; and the *Libro della cocina*, p. 46: *Del pastello dele trote.* All offer exceptionally long and detailed articles on this dish.

[2] *Menagier*, §179; p. 190. The bourgeois author of the *Menagier* devotes a paragraph to distinguishing between several varieties of trout available at different seasons throughout the year. The recipe for *De troitis in pastillo* in the *Liber de coquina, loc. cit.* concludes in much the same fashion as in the *Menagier*: "Et tempore carnis, potes ponere lardum loco olei." *Cf.* also the commentary concerning trout in the *Regime tresutile*: "On le prent et mect en pastés avecques espisses" (p. 73).

110. Pinperneaulx

VAL	*Pinperneaulx.*	– –	*Rostis,*	*au verjus vert ou blanc.*
MAZ	Pipenalx.[1]	– –	Soient rotis et maingier	a verjus verd ou blanc.
BN	*Pimperniaux.*	*Eschaudés,*	*rosticés, mengiez*	*au*[2] *verjus.*
VAT	**Pinperneaulx.**	**Eschaudez,**	**rostiz,**	**au verjus vert.**

Unlike most other freshwater fish in this chapter, the grig—a small, lithe eel[3] —is considered suitable for only one sort of preparation.

111. Loche

VAL	*Loche.*	*Cuite en eaue;*	*premierement, cuire du formage,*
MAZ	Louche.	Soit cuite en aigue;	et premierement, cuisiez du fromaige
VAT	**Loche.**	**En eaue,**	**a la moustarde, et y met on du frommage;**

VAL	*persil*	*—qu'il ne soit pas trop;*
MAZ	et du parressi avec ung pol de vin,	et qu'il ne soit pas du tout cuit; et

VAL	*lavez, eschaudez bien la loche, metez boullir avec le formage;*
MAZ	eschauder tresbien la louche et puis la mecter avec vostre fromaige boulir;

VAL	*et au dressier,*	*du verjus esgrené et des groisellez.*
MAZ	et y mecter adressiez	du verjus de grain ou des grousselles cuites en aigue.

VAT	**et la fricte en potaige, et y**[1] **du frommaige au cuire, qui veult.**

A small fish, thriving in mountain streams, the loach is omitted in *BN*'s copy of the *Viandier*, despite the high regard in which it was held by Magninus.[2] The older versions of the *Viandier* offer only one manner of doing loach, making use of a sort of cheese fondu

---

[1] *Pipenalx*: *sic.*

[2] *au* followed by *vin* stroked out.

[3] "Pimperneaulx ont luisant et delyé pel et ne sont point lymonneux comme sont anguilles" (*Menagier de Paris*, §181; p. 191). The lack of *limon* on this variety of eel would make it inappropriate for a jellied or galantine preparation.

[1] The scribe may have omitted a word after *y*.

[2] The *lopia* is ranked fourth in Magninus's order of desirability, after *perca*, *lucius* and *vendosie*, in the *Regimen sanitatis*, part 3, ch. 18. *Vendoises* are mentioned in the *VAT* Table as part of the subject matter to be dealt with in the *Viandier* that followed but, seemingly having suffered the same fate as *gardons*, are not treated in any extant manuscript. It may be speculated that *BN*'s omission of this recipe for loach was perhaps prompted by the absence of this particular species in the regular merchant traffic and the private fish ponds upon which his patron normally depended for supplies of fish.

into which *MAZ(X)* adds a touch of wine; they serve the fish with a mash of tart grapes or currants.

For this type of dish, clearly explained and unique in the *Viandier*, *Y* substitutes a recipe for a plain—one is tempted to say, pedestrian—boiled loach that is eaten with mustard,[3] and then concludes this part of the recipe with a vague direction about the use of cheese. A new paragraph at the top of f. 67r in the Vatican manuscript contains the line beginning "et la fricte en potaige . . . ." This new treatment here for loach is similar to that which may be accorded to a pike (Recipe 98), a barbel (Recipe 99) or a perch (Recipe 103); however, the inclusion of "du frommaige au cuire" in preparing fried loach is surely inspired by the earlier recipe for the boiled fish in *VAL* and *MAZ*.[4]

112. Gaymeaux

VAL	*Gaymeaux.*[1]	*En eaue et oignons;*
BN	*Guemual.*[2]	*Cuit en eaue et oingnons minciés bien menu; mengier*
VAT	**Gymiau.**	**En eaue et de l'ongnon missié;**

VAL	*a la moustarde.*
BN	*a la moustarde; et du fromage, qui veult.*
VAT	**a la moustarde.**

The name of this fish should read *Gaymiau* in the *VAT* copy.[3] The variant in *BN*, "et du fromage qui veult," may have been copied accidentally from the end of the previous recipe for loach.

113. Meinuise

VAT **Meinuise. En eaue et de l'ongnon missé; a la saulce vert ou aux bons aulx.**

It is possible that this recipe for small fry is original with *VAT*. It does not appear in even the Table to the contents of *VAT*, which Table was copied or compiled before the

---

[3] In the *Enseignements* loach is to be eaten with mustard if it is fried (p. 186, l. 193; *Petit traité*, p. 224).

[4] The *Menagier de Paris* writes a version of this recipe that is probably close to what was in *Y*: "Loche cuite en eaue, au percil et au bon frommage, mengee a la moustarde. La fricte en potage et a l'aillet vert. La cuicte en eaue ou a la moustarde soit mengee; et au frire soit effleuree ["floured"] celle qui sera fricte" (§182; p. 191). *BN* may well have have been dismayed by the disorder in *Y*!

[1] The initial letter was written as an *E*.

[2] The name of the fish as *BN* writes it could be *Guennial*.

[3] The manuscripts of the *Menagier de Paris* (§183; p. 192) have *Gaymeau*, *Gaymiau* and *Waymel*. The identity of this fish remains somewhat of a mystery. *Cf. FEW*, vol. 21, p. 257b; *DEAF*, "G": col. 419; and Tobler-Lommatzsch, vol. 4, col. 45: *gaimel*.

body of the *Viandier* was written out. In the *Enseignements*, "menuise de luiz ou d'autre pesson"[1] are fingerlings. *VAT* may be reminded of this variety of fish dish by the similar way in which this and the previous recipe for *Gaymeaux* make use of chopped onion in the cooking water. The next recipe will deal with another small fish, the young of the lamprey.

114. Lamproions

VAL	*Lamproions.*	- - - -		*A la saulce chaude*
MAZ	Lamprions.	Soit cuit en aigue	et maingier	a la saulce chaude,
BN	*Lamprions.*	*Cuis apoint ou fris,*		*a la saulce chaude*
VAT	**Lamproyons.**	- - - -		**A la saulce chaude**

VAL	*comme la lamproie, non pas d'espices, au cel menu.*
MAZ	- - - - - et ne soit pas tropt espesse;
BN	*comme la lamproie;* - - - - - - - - -
VAT	**comme lamproye;** - - - - - - - - -

MAZ	- - - - - - - et en pasté, a la saulce d'espices;
BN	*le boully en eaue, a la moustarde; et en pasté, poudré d'espices.*
VAT	**en eaue, a la moustarde; et en pasté, pouldré d'espices,**

MAZ	- - - - - - - - - - - et la frite a la saulce cameline.
VAT	**a la cameline gectee dedans les pastez.**

The *Viandier*'s recipe for lamprill evinces a continual accretion, reflecting what must have been strong culinary interest in this fish.

The original, briefest form of the recipe is in *VAL*: the reference in the word "comme" is to the recipe for *Lamproie franche a la saulce chaude* (§69), but in the case of this lamprill fine salt is to be stirred into the hot sauce rather than the mixture of spices. For "pas d'espices," *MAZ(X)* writes "pas trop espesse"; he may perhaps have thought that the text meant that the sauce should be less dense, less opaque than in the earlier recipe, clearer because it contains fewer spices and less toast.[1] No mention of the method of cooking the lamprill is felt necessary by *VAL* because the recipe for lampreys is implicitly to hold in this regard too.

Z makes some modifications to this recipe. Because the young lamprey is so small that roasting on a spit is difficult, and in reality impractical,[2] boiling is suggested as the

---

[1] *Enseignements*, p. 185, l. 170; *Petit traité*, p. 223. Fingerlings are not dealt with by the *Menagier*, even though *menuise vive* were regularly sold in the streets of Paris: see Guillaume de la Villeneuve, *Les crieries de Paris*, ed. Étienne Barbazan, *Fabliaux et contes*, 2 vols. (Paris, 1808); vol. I, p. 277.

[1] In Recipe 69 *VAT* distinguishes between, on the one hand, a variety of sauce for lamprey that is "clere" and not dark, and, on the other, one that is "espesse" and dark, this latter sauce being the one called *boe*.

[2] Even for the fully-grown lamprey the cook is warned that the spit must be very slender (Recipe 69).

method by which the fish should be cooked—even though *BN*, apparently doubting that boiling is an entirely satisfactory way of cooking lamprill, suggests that it should be fried as well. In any case, a second stage in the preparation of this dish would remain a boiling of the small fish in the lamprey hot sauce, as this has been modified. *Z* adds one further type of dish: lamprill baked in a pastry shell.

On his own, *MAZ(X)* suggests a third possibility, fried lamprill in cameline sauce. *Y*, too, feeling the need for another variation of a dish that is not quite so complex as the first involving the hot lamprey sauce, suggests a rather plain boiled lamprill to be eaten with a mustard sauce.[3]

115. Santoilles

VAT **Santoilles. Au brouet comme en potaige; a la cameline gectee es pastez.**

In the *VAT* Table the spelling of the name of this small type of freshwater lamprey, or lampern, is *setailles*.[1] The fish does not appear in the *Menagier de Paris*. For *VAT* these lampern are closely related to the young of the lamprey: not only is there a close similarity in one of the dishes which may be prepared from them, but *VAT* has altered the order of the recipes as this appears in his Table. This Table shows *Lamproyons/Setailless/Ables/Escrevisses*; *VAT* copies *Meinuise/Ables/Lamproyons/Santoilles/Escrevisses*—perhaps a slightly more logical sequence, but one in which lampreys and lamprill still remain together.

116. Ables

VAL	*Ablez.*	*En eaue,*	– – – – –	*a la moustarde.*
MAZ	Abletes.	Abletes cuites	avec parressi et maingier	a la moustarde.
BN	*Ables.*	*Cuis en eaue,*	– – – *mengié*	*a la moustarde,*
VAT	**Ables.**	**En eaue,**	– – –	**a la moustarde.**

BN *non*[1] *autrement.*

---

[3] The *Menagier de Paris* has in essence the three dishes contained in *Y* but has characteristically subjected them to his own modifications: the lamprill are to be roasted, or rather semi-roasted ("rostiz verdeletz") before being boiled in the hot sauce; or, alternatively, boiled and eaten with mustard (as in *Y*); or, alternatively, baked in a pasty, after which, the *Menagier* advises, "gectez la saulse chaude [the standard lamprey hot sauce] dessus les pastez et faictes boulir" (§184; p. 192).

[1] Besides this form of the word, and the *santoilles* that *VAT* writes ahead of his copy of the recipe, Godefroy shows as variants *setoille*, *satouillie* and *sautoille*—this last form being attested in Godefroy by Pichon and Vicaire's reading of *VAT*.

[1] *non*: the first *n* of the word is a pair of abbreviations for "and," as if the scribe had begun to copy the "and" that follows the word "moustarde" in both the preceding (§112 in *BN*) and the following (§114) recipes.

The use of parsley in the water when cooking bleak is indicated by *MAZ* but it must also have been in both *Z* and *Y* because the *Menagier* picks it up for his treatment of *Ables*.[2]

117. Escrevices

VAL	*Eccrevissez.*	*En eaue et en vin, mangier au vin aigre.*
BN	*Escrevices.*	*Cuites en eaue et en vin aigre, mengiez au vin aigre.*
VAT	**Escrevisses.**	**Cuites en eaue et en vin, au vinaigre.**

Crayfish reasonably occupy the concluding position of the chapter of freshwater fish in the *Viandier*. Similarly, at the end of the second chapter of sea-fish *Y* will place another type of *escrevices*, this time, though, qualified as *de mer* (Recipe 151)—that is to say, lobster. At that point in the book, the recipe copied by *BN* and *VAT* for *Escrevices de mer* is almost identical to the one above.

MAZ has already reproduced this recipe for crayfish at the end of the recipe for bream—which dish he calls *Roussaille*, using the title of the following recipe!

Chapitre de poisson de mer ront (MAZ, BN, VAT)

118. Porc de mer

VAL	*Porc de mer.*	*Fendu au long par le dos,*
MAZ	Poisson de mer ront soit	fenduz a long par le dolz
BN	*Porc de mer.*	*Fendu au lonc par le dos,*
VAT	**Porc de mer.**	**Fendu au long par le dos,**

VAL	- - - - - - -	*fendu par leschez comme venoison;*
MAZ	et	mecter par lesches conme venoison;
BN	*puis cuit en eaue et*	*coupés par lechies come venoison; puis*
VAT	**puis soit cuit en eaue et puis**	**taillié par lesches comme venoison; puis**

VAL	*prenez vin et eaue de vostre poisson,*		*affinez*
MAZ	prener vin et aigue de vostre poisson,	puis	affinez
BN	*prennés du vin, de l'eaue de vostre poisson,*		*affinés*
VAT	**prenez du vin et de l'eaue de vostre poisson,**	**et aprés**	**affinez**

VAL	*gingembre,*	*canelle,*	*giroffle,*	*grene,*	*poivre long,*
MAZ	gigimbre,	cannelle,	giroffle,	graine de paradis,	poivre long,
BN	*gingembre,*	*canelle,*	-	*graine,*	*poivre lonc*
VAT	**gingenbre,**	**canelle,**	**giroffle,**	**grainne de paradiz,**	**poivre long**

[2] *Menagier de Paris*, §187; p. 194.

VAL	*ung pou de saffren*	*et de pain*	*et du boullon;*
MAZ	saffrain	et du pain;	et faict vostre boillon clairet;
BN	*et un pou de saffren;*	– –	*et faites bon boullon cleret,*
VAT	**et ung peu de saffren;**	– –	**et faictes bon boullon claret,**

VAL	*ne soit pas jaune,*	*comme*
MAZ	et ne soit mie tropt jane,	ainsi conme
BN	*et ne soit pas trop jaune;*	*et sert l'en come*
VAT	**et ne soit mie trop jaune;**	**et en sert l'en[1] ainsi come**

VAL	– – – – – – – –	*ung Blanc mengier.*
MAZ	– – – – – – – –	ung Blanc maigier.
BN	*par maniere d'un entremés sus*	*un Blanc mengier.*
VAT	**par maniere d'un entremez avec**	**ung Blanc mengier.**

All of the manuscripts except *VAL* show a division of chapters at this point in the *Viandier*, and even the *VAT* Table has "Poisson de mer ront."[2] *MAZ(X)*, who more and more frequently will not copy even the title of a recipe, has written the rubric "Chappitre de poisson de mer" over this recipe for porpoise, and then nonsensically repeated *Poisson de mer ront* at its beginning as if this were the name of the dish as well.

The porpoise (in English the name translates literally as "hog fish") enjoyed a reputation as a distinct genre or type of sea-fish in the fourteenth century. Magninus classifies all fish according to their degree of resemblance to the porpoise. The *De saporibus* stipulates sauces that are warmer and more "acute" according as the meat of a fish is "grosser" and approximates the "bestial" or "pork-like" nature of that of the porpoise.[3]

The four versions of this recipe are remarkably concordant. Only *Y* has made substantive changes in the tradition, inserting a direction about cooking in water, omitting bread as an ingredient in the sauce, and suggesting toward the end of his version that this dish might serve as an *entremets* over (*BN*), or with (*VAT*), a white dish. The phrase that *VAL* and *MAZ* have at this last point, "[ainsi] comme ung blanc mengier," may have

[1] *len* inserted above the line.

[2] The *Menagier de Paris* aphoristically makes an interesting seasonal distinction between the two general categories of round and flat sea-fish: "Ront en yver, et plat en esté" (§190; p. 194).

[3] "De piscibus ... sciendum est quod quanto sunt grossioris carnis et difficilioris digestionis et maioris superfluitatis et humoris nature tanto indigent saporibus calidioribus et acutioribus. ... Unde sequitur quod pisces bestiales et specialiter porcus marinus assatus vel elixatus indiget salsa calidiori et acutiori. Et similiter intelligatur in aliis piscibus secundum quod magis vel minus appropinquant porco marino" (Magninus Mediolanensis, *Opusculum de saporibus*, *ed. cit.*, p. 188). The sense of the word *bestiales* used by Magninus is clarified in the *Regime tresutile et tresproufitable* (*ed. cit.*, p. 74): "Les poissons grans comme bestes—comme est le porc marin et le chien de mer [the dogfish or shark of the *Viandier*'s Recipe 123] et aussi le poisson nommé daulphin ... sont difficiles a digerer et engendrent gros nourrissement et de grande suparfluité." The *Regimen sanitatis salernitanum*, with commentaries, of which this French *Regime* is a translation, is very largely—in places, textually—indebted to the *Regimen sanitatis* of Magninus himself.

the sense that *VAL* and *MAZ* allow to be understood, that this dish is comparable in appearance to a *blanc mengier*. However, it has neither the colour, the texture nor the taste of the standard white dish, to say nothing of the ingredients.[4] The clue to the sense of the phrase "comme ung blanc mengier" lies in the direction that has already been given that the fish ("bestial" meat that it is) is to be sliced like venison. What the author of the *Viandier* has in mind is a fairly common mediæval dish in which venison is served with rice or with furmenty: this is the *entremets* of Recipe 63, and is itself made with the broth of the venison it accompanies. For the *Menagier* a standard *entremets* is venison and furmenty; on lean days he assumes that the substitute will be porpoise and furmenty.[5]

The very position of the porpoise at the head of the *Viandier*'s chapter of round sea-fish is not readily explicable. Gastronomically it was not held in any particular esteem. It may be that cooks looked upon the porpoise as exemplary of round sea-fish in general in the same way as physicians such as Magninus did.

Several apparent errors are noticeable in the various copies. *BN* omits cloves from among the spices; and *VAL* writes "et du boullon" rather than (perhaps) "et faites boullon."

119. Maquerel frais

VAL	*Maquereaulx frais.*	*Affaitez par l'orelle*	*et rostir*
MAZ	Gornaulx,[1] rougés.	Affaictier les par l'oroille	et les rotissiez
BN	*Maquerel frais.*	*Affaitié par l'oreille*	*et rostir*
VAT	**Maquerel frez.**	**Affaictié par l'oreille**	**et rosty**

VAL	*sur le greil;*		*a la cameline;*	– – –
MAZ	sur le gril;	et maingiez	a la cameline	ou a vin aigre et
BN	*sur le gril;*	*mengier*	*a la cameline;*	– – –
VAT	**sur le grail;**		**a la cameline;**	– – –

BN *poudre fine; et liés d'un filet tout entour qui ne se despiecent;*

[4] A remote possibility exists that the phrase "comme ung blanc mengier" is spurious. Speculating upon the nature of an *entremets* in general, Pichon, in his edition of the *Menagier de Paris* (vol. I, p. xlii, n3) cites the *Viandier*'s recipe for porpoise, but only as this was copied in the no-longer-extant version of Saint-Lô. "Dans le Ms. de Saint-Lô, il est dit que le *porc de mer* doit être coupé par lesches et *détourné* [*atourné*: "dressé"?] *par manière d'entremets sur un blanc doublier* ["nappe"]." No similar phrase, referring either to an *entremets* or to a *blanc mengier*, was written in the *Menagier*'s recipe for *Porc de mer, Marsouin, Pourpoiz* (§203; p. 198). The *Menagier* has only "dreciez comme venoison," implying that this was a very common type of preparation.

[5] *Menagier de Paris*, the first, fourth and fifth menus for lean dinners (ed. Brereton and Ferrir, §§46, 49, 50, pp. 181–182; ed. Pichon, §§XX, XXIII, XXIV, pp. 101–103). In the *Menagier* the fish is called variously *marsouin* and *pourpois*. For other instances of this combined dish, see the *Furmenty with purpaysse* in Austin, pp. 17 and 105; and *le riz avecques la venoyson dou daulphin*, *i.e.* dolphin, a dish contained in the banquet menus of the *Du fait de cuisine*, ff. 110r and 113r.

[1] The capital letter is a *D*.

VAL	*en pasté, a la poudre.*
MAZ	et en pasté, et poudre d'espices et a la cameline ou a sel menuz;
BN	*et en pasté, a poudre d'espices, - - - au sel menu;*
VAT	**et en pasté, pouldre d'espices, a la cameline; - - -**

MAZ	et les salés, - - - au vin ou a la siboule.
BN	*le sallé, - - - au vin et a la siboulle*
VAT	**et s'il est sallé, cuit en eaue et mengié au vin et a la ciboule**

BN	*- - - - ou a la moustarde.*
VAT	**ou a la calongne ou a la moustarde.**

Mackerel in a relatively fresh state is alone considered by *VAL*, but *Z* added a recipe for the salted variety. Two dishes—for which the fish is cooked by roasting or is baked in a pasty—are possible for fresh mackerel; and one—which naturally involves boiling[2]—is mentioned for salted mackerel. In every case a number of alternate sauces is provided. Most peculiar among the variants is the serving sauce for the pasty: where *Z* gives a choice between cameline and fine salt, *BN* copies only fine salt and *VAT* copies only cameline. Both of these possibilities must surely have been transmitted by *Y* from *Z*, yet each of the two versions dependent upon *Y* chooses a different sauce to copy.[3] For the salted mackerel the *Menagier* specifies wine and scallions.[4]

The position of the recipe for mackerel in the *Viandier* appears to have been deferred by *Y*. Where in *VAL* and *MAZ* mackerel is accorded an early place in the order of round sea-fish, *Y* passed it by when copying his series of fish recipes, but then did pick it up later just after the dogfish (§123), giving it a new position which is still reflected in the order shown in the *VAT* Table. For some reason, though, *VAT* insults mackerel once again by copying even salmon—a fish of decidedly secondary ranking—ahead of it.

120. Gournault, rouget, grimondin

VAL	*Gournalx, rougez.*	*Affaitez par le ventre,*
MAZ	Rouget.	Affaictiez les par le ventre
BN	*Gornault, rouget, grimodin.*	*Soient affectés parmi le ventre et*
VAT	**Gournault, rouget, grimondin.**	**Affaittiez par le ventre et**

[2] Freshwater fish could be caught or cultivated locally, but sea-fish were apt not to be caught within a day or two's journey of market and were, for purposes of preservation, frequently salted. These salted sea-fish are in mediæval cookery almost invariably subjected to a routine boiling as a preliminary step in preparing them for safe and palatable consumption at the table. The procedure was considered more or less automatic and, as here, might not even be mentioned in a recipe.

[3] With seeming perversity the *Menagier* writes, "En met on en pasté, et pouldre dessus" (§195; p. 196).

[4] *Ibid.* A set of recipes for fresh and salted mackerel similar to those in the *Viandier* is contained in the *Enseignements* (p. 186, l. 201; *Petit traité*, p. 224).

VAL	*lavez,* - - - - - - - - - -
MAZ	- - - - - - - - - - - - -
BN	*lavés bien, puis soient mis en la paielle et du sel dessus,*
VAT	**lavez tres bien et puis mis en la paelle et du sel dessus,**
VAL	- - - - *metez boullir, et du cel;*
MAZ	- - - - et les cuisiez en aigue et sel
BN	*puis de l'eaue aprés et metés cuire,* -
VAT	**et de l'eaue aprés et mettez cuire,** -
VAL	*a la cameline;* - - - - - -
MAZ	et maingier a la cameline; - - - - et les rotis,
BN	*et mengier a la cameline;* - - - - - -
VAT	**et mengiez a la cameline; et se vous le voulez mengier en rost,**
VAL	*ou fendus au long du dos,* - - - *rostis;*
MAZ	- - - - - - - - - - - - - - - - - -
BN	*les espaules soient fendus au lonc du dos et puis laver et metre rostir;*
VAT	**soient les espaules fendues au long du dos et puis lavez et mettez rostir;**
VAL	- - *plungier en verjus souvent;* - -
MAZ	- - - - - - - - - - - a fine poudre,
BN	*qui veult, plongier en verjus souvent et poudrés*
VAT	**et puis les plungez en verjus bien souvent et pouldrez**
VAL	*mangier au verjus.*
MAZ	du verjus et vin aigre.
BN	*d'espices.*
VAT	**de pouldre d'espices par dessus; et soient mengez au verjus;** - -
VAT	**et qui les veult en pasté, a la cameline.**

The composition of the group of fish for which this recipe is appropriate varies a little from manuscript to manuscript,[1] but there is no doubt that for the fourteenth-century French gastronome they represented the best of all possible sea-fish. Magninus begins his ranking of sea-fish with the *rogetus*[2] and *gornatus*, the red mullet and the gurnard; he then lists, in

[1] In the Introduction, above, see the general chart of the contents of all the manuscripts. Perhaps the most remarkable sequence for these fish appears in the *VAT* Table where *Gourneaulx* is the second fish of the "Poisson de mer ront" but where *Grimondins* and *Rouget* are not written until the end of the chapter. Equally strange is the appearance of *Lamproyes* at this latter point in the *VAT* Table, yet no recipe for lamprey (either sea-lamprey or the freshwater variety) has been copied by the *Viandier*.

[2] The red mullet is held by Magninus to provide the supreme standard by which the excellence of all other sea-fish should be measured (*Regimen sanitatis*, Ch. 18, "De piscibus"). *MAZ*, having mistakenly used the title of this recipe, *Gornaulx, rougés*, at the head of the previous recipe, is content now simply to write *Rouget* for this Recipe 120.

descending order of preference, *plagicia* (plaice, Recipe 133, at the head of the *Viandier*'s section of flat sea-fish), *solea* (sole, Recipe 135) and *merlengus* (whiting, Recipe 122).[3] To the premier grouping of *gourneault* and *rouget*, *Y* adds a third, related fish, *grimondin*, the red gurnet.[4]

Boiling[5] and roasting are the original methods of cooking these fish, but *VAT* adds a brief mention of an optional baked dish for them. For the first two methods, variants occur where *Z* puts spice powder into the vinegar in which the fish is to be dipped from time to time as it roasts. This note is in fact all that *MAZ(X)* has copied of the instructions for roasting, but he does for some reason add vinegar to the single serving sauce of verjuice. *Y* adds a number of refinements: of primary interest is the note that salt should be put on the fish *before* the water, rather than *with* the water as is stated in *VAL* and *MAZ*. This technique of dredging the red mullet in salt becomes a model procedure for the cook, and will be referred back to later in the recipes for the conger (Recipe 121) and for the dogfish (Recipe 123).

121. Congre

VAL	*Congre. Eschaudez,*	*metez cuire en eaue, sallez;*	
MAZ	Congre. Eschauder conme anguilles,	cuisiez en aigue;	–
BN	*Congre. Eschaudés comme l'anguille et*	*cuit en eaue,*	*le sallé come*
VAT	**Congre. Eschaudé comme une anguille,**	**cuit en l'eaue**	**et sallé comme**

VAL	– –	*aucuns*	– – – –	*rostissent sus le greil;*
MAZ	– –	et aucuns	– – – –	rotissent sur le gril;
BN	*le rouget;*	*et aucuns,*	*quant il est cuit,*	*le rosticent sur le gril;*
VAT	**ung rouget;**	**et aucuns,**	**quant il est cuit,**	**le rotissent sur le grail;**

VAL		*a la saulce vert.*	– –	
MAZ	et le maingent	a la saulce verde	ou a la jane.	
BN	*mengiés*	*a la saulce verte.*	– –	
VAT	**et se mengue**	**a la saulce;**	– –	**ou mis ou four, qui veult.**

The conger can be boiled or roasted on a grill as with the previous set of fishes. As also in the previous recipe, *VAT* appends the possibility of baking this fish in an oven, apparently

---

[3] These fish conform most closely to the desired characteristics in sea-fish: the best sea-fish are scaley, with layered white flesh that is of subtle taste, faint smell and some durability; their habitat should be deep, agitated (*i.e.*, highly oxygenated) northern waters. These criteria are echoed by most health handbooks of the period: see, for instance, Giacomo Albini, *De sanitatis custodia* (*c.* 1341), part 2, dist. 2, tract. 2, ch. 8, ed. G. Carbonelli (Pinerolo: Tip. Sociale, 1906), pp. 81–82; and the anonymous *Sanitatis conservator* (ed. Faber, *Ein Diätethik aus Montpellier*, p. 20).

[4] This fish is of the same family, *Trigla*, as the gurnard and is a cousin of the red mullet.

[5] The *Enseignements* contains a recipe for "gornars cuiz en eve a la sausse cameline destrempee de vin aigre" (p. 187, l. 214; *Petit traité* p. 225). Vinegar is the usual liquid in cameline sauce.

a novel cooking technique which is not suggested by the *Menagier*. Where *VAL* and *MAZ* mention roasting as an independent option, *Y* indicates that it is really a second cooking stage to be used at the chef's discretion only after the fish has already been boiled.

The term *eschauder* means literally "to scald"[1] but, as it is used here, a subsequent procedure, for which this is a prepararation, may as well be implied by it: that would be the skinning of the fish. The *Menagier* writes quite explicitly about the conger, "eschaudez le, et estauvez ['remove the skin'] comme une anguille."[2] Where an eel is so treated previously in the *Viandier*, at Recipes 76 and 79, the texts read "escorchees *ou* eschaudees" and "eschaudez *ou* escorchez."[3] The verb *escorcher*, literally "to skin," may implicitly indicate the exposure of a fish to a dry heat, perhaps over an open flame, as a preliminary step to skinning it, whereas *eschauder* would indicate the use of a wet heat, an immersion or dousing in boiling water.

The technique by which the fish is coated with salt or dredged in salt has already been outlined by *Y* in the previous recipe, for *Rouget*.

In the category of blunders we may point out that *VAT* did not copy which type of sauce was to be prepared and served with boiled conger. And similarly, in the same passage as copied by *MAZ*, an unknown sauce may be *poivre jaunet* (of Recipe 164) or merely, and more likely, *jance*.

122. Merluz

VAL	*Mellus.*	*Metez tramper en charree trois jours,*	*lavez,*
MAZ	– –	Mecter le tramper en charree trois jours,	puis la lavez
VAT	**Merluz.**	**Mectez tremper trois jours en eaue**	**et puis le lavez**

VAL		*frisiez en huille sans farine;*		*aux aulx.*
MAZ	tresbien et	frissiez en huille sans farine;	et le maingiez	aux haulx bouliz.
VAT	**tres bien et**	**frisiez en huille sans farine;**	**et le mengiez**	**aux aulx de**

[1] "*Eschauder*. To scald, or cast hot liquor upon" (Cotgrave). In §76 of his *De observatio ciborum* (sixth century), Anthimus says of the vessel into which milk is drawn from a cow, "Vas ille fictile sit et bene scaldaetur": ed. Shirley Howard Weber (Leiden, 1924), p. 48. "The process of formation of the English word *scald* is here seen: from *calda*, hot water, the verb *excaldare* was formed with the sense of, 'to rinse out with hot water'" (*ibid.*).

[2] *Menagier de Paris*, §198; p. 197.

[3] In his recipe for *Brouet vergay d'anguilles* (§122; p. 171), the *Menagier* glosses the verb *escorchiez*: "*id est*, estauvez." Brereton and Ferrier gloss *estauver* as "to remove skin (from fish)." Commenting upon the *Menagier*'s use of the word *estauvez* in this recipe, Pichon wrote, "D'après les nombreux passages du *Viandier* où ce mot est employé, et surout d'après celui-ci, je crois qu'il signifie: dépouiller l'anguille de sa peau (peut-être en l'exposant à la vapeur de l'eau, en *l'étuvant*)" (p. 171, n5). The French word seems to have been influenced by the sense that survives today in the English word *scorch* (see the *Oxford English Dictionary*) because Littré cites (*s. v. écorcher*) among others an example where this sense seems quite likely: "Estuiz de cuir escorchiez aux armes de France. *Invent. des livres de Charles V*, art. 262."

la roye; et aucuns le menguent a son eaue mesmes come l'en fait venoison, a la moustarde.

The two manuscripts that identify the fish for which this is the recipe show a word for stockfish that is derived from the Latin *merluccius*, in French *merluche*: "hake."[1] The Table in the Vatican manuscript shows "white fish," *Mellanz* (that is, *Gadus merlangus*), which is related to the cod (*Gadus morhua*), but unless it too was available in a dried state it has nothing to do with this recipe in the *Viandier*.

The first step in the preparation of this dish is to reconstitute the dried fish. For this *O* has specified the use of a solution of water and *charree*, this latter substance being what Cotgrave translates as "buck ashes," the wood ash left after lye has been leached from it.[2] *VAT* writes that the fish should be soaked rather in water alone.[3]

There is no disagreement about the cooking method to be employed for this fish, once it has been reconstituted. Where variants do appear is in the making of the sauce in which the fried fish is to be dressed. *VAT* writes a phrase, "aux aulx de la roye." The recipe for ray fish (§136) does indeed call for a new type of garlic cinnamon sauce known as *aulx camelins*, but the way in which *VAT* refers to it, if what is to be used is in fact this particular sauce, seems strange. Besides, the *Menagier* suggests another variety of sauce that likewise incorporates garlic, a *jance d'aulx*.[4] These two sauces are not at all similar, the first being a cinnamon-based sauce and the second a ginger sauce. In fact the only thing the two have in common is the garlic which is in their names. Another recipe may shed some light upon what *VAT* meant when he wrote "aux aulx de la roye": in the version of the recipe for cameline garlic sauce (Recipe 156) written by *VAL* and *MAZ*, one of the ingredients indicated by both, and by them alone, is ground ray-fish liver—an exceptional sort of ingredient among the standard sauces. It may well be that because of this ingredient the cameline garlic sauce became known also as *Aulx de la raie*—even

---

[1] At the end of his recipe for *Merlus*, the *Menagier de Paris* notes, somewhat doubtfully, "Merlus est fait, ce semble, de morue" (§204; p. 199). "*Merlucius, Merlus*: 'Merlan, morue, merluche'" (L. Stouff, *Ravitaillement et alimentation en Provence aux XIVe et XVe siècles*, p. 472). Recipe 126 in the *Viandier* will deal with fresh cod. The *Platine en françoys* has a description of the fish hake: "Le merlus est ung poysson de mer [et] n'a guieres d'escaille et est forment semblable au luz ou bechet. En la mer par toute la province de Narbonne s'en trouve beaucop. C'est ung poysson doulx a menger ... " (f. 95r). The table at the beginning of this work shows the spelling *Merluz*.

See also the recipes for *Einem stoc vische* in the *Guter Spize* (§20, p. 21) and for *Einen gutten stockfisch* in Eberhard (§23, p. 90), both of which are for a more complex dish than is provided for in the *Viandier*.

[2] See also the use of *cendre gravelee* later in Recipes 178 and 179.

[3] The *Menagier* indicates likewise that water alone is to be used to soak the fish; as for the duration of this soaking, he contradicts the *Viandier* quite firmly: "Tremper une nuit seulement." Aebischer reads this line in *VAL* as, "Metez tramper en charrée, tousjours lavez" (*ed. cit.*, p. 97).

[4] The *jance d'aulx* is an alternative for mustard as the serving sauce for stockfish in the *Menagier*. The possibility of using either garlic or mustard may have been introduced by *Y*.

by *VAT* who, in Recipe 156, will no longer even specify the inclusion of ray liver in its composition.

The mention of venison by *VAT* refers the reader back to the treatment of salted stag and boar meat in Recipe 7: this venison, after being minced and boiled in water, is eaten with mustard. To serve this particular dish the cook is told, "Dressiez vostre venoisson, et de son aigue avecques" (*MAZ*).[5]

123. Chien de mer

VAL	*Chien de mer. Cuit comme rouget*	*et*
MAZ	Chien de mer. Cuisiez le conme le rouget,	puis
BN	*Chien de mer. Affaitiés comme la congre,*	*et quant il*
VAT	**Chien de mer. Affaictié come le rouget et cuit en eaue,**	**et quant il**

VAL	- - - *peler;*	*a cameline.*
MAZ	- - - le peler;	et le maingier aux haulx camelins.
BN	*sera cuit soit appareillié come raie;*	*aus aulx blans ou a la cameline.*
VAT	**sera cuit soit pellé come roye;**	**et mengié aux aulx camelins.**

Dogfish is a name given to a number of fish but which are mainly of two families, *Squalus* and *Scyllium*. Physically, dogfish is a small, slender shark and, boneless like a shark, to be prepared for eating needs only be eviscerated, cooked and skinned.[1]

There is disagreement among the *Viandier* manuscripts over the preparation of this fish. All manuscripts recognize two phases in handling dogfish in the kitchen, and generally agree that comparisons with procedures followed in the preparation of certain other fish will provide useful help. For *VAL* and *MAZ* the first phase is the cooking, for which the fish must be eviscerated and dredged in salt after the manner of the red mullet (Recipe 120). For *Y* the verb *affaitter*, "to clean," can be used in the more general sense of "prepare for cooking," which sense includes both eviscerating and salting. For these procedures the red mullet still provides a useful model, but *BN* refers rather to the conger (Recipe 121), perhaps because the shape of the two fish is a little more similar, or perhaps because he wishes to include an initial scalding step for the dogfish preparatory to skinning it.[2]

The second phase in the preparation of this fish follows the actual boiling, and that is the skinning of it. *Y* compares this procedure to that to be followed for the ray, but in Recipe 136 for *Raie* we read nothing about skinning in either *BN* or *VAT*; only *MAZ* even mentions skinning—and that with no comments at all about anything particular to be noted in this procedure. The reference here to the ray would remain a mystery if it were not again for the *Menagier de Paris* whose text, as so frequently and so fortunately

---

[5] In the *Menagier*'s recipe for porpoise (*Porc de mer*, *Marsouin*, *Pourpoiz*: §203; p. 198) we read that the boiled fish should similarly be "mis en ung plat dedens son eaue comme venoison."

[1] This fish is the *canis marinis* of Magninus's category of *pisces bestiales* (see Recipe 118, n2, below.)

[2] A scribal misreading of *rouget* for *congre* is likewise not at all beyond the realm of possibilty.

happens, casts dependable light on the *Viandier*'s obscurities. In his recipe for dogfish[3] the *Menagier* refers the cook to the procedures presented for the brett, a fish for which the bourgeois author seems to have a predilection.[4] In this earlier recipe of the *Menagier* we read: "Brecte affaictié comme ung rouget, cuicte comme une raye et ainsi pelee, mengee aux aulx camelins." This text is clearly inspired by the *Viandier*'s Recipe 123; the usefulness of the comparison between the dogfish and the ray bears therefore upon both the cooking and the skinning, and as well upon a direction that we read in Recipe 136 for ray: "Mettre cuire par pieces" (*VAL*). All of this means, then, that the variant that is found in *BN*, "*appareillié* comme raie" (rather than "*pellé* come roye"), is, surprisingly, not a serious *lapsus* or inexactitude. *Y* may very well have written that the dogfish "soit cuit et pellé come raie." One very important feature of this dish, though, and one which is never explicitly stated, is that the dogfish is to be cut into pieces like the ray.

124. Saumon frais

VAL	*Saulmont frais.*	*Soit boutonnez, gardez l'escune pour le frire;*
MAZ	Salmon fres.	Soit baconné et garder l'eschinee pour frire
BN	*Saumont frais.*	*Soit bagué et gardés l'echine pour rostir;*
VAT	**Saumon frez.**	**Baconné, et gardez l'eschine pour rostir;**

VAL	- -	- - - - - - - - - - -
MAZ	en la paelle;	- - - - - - - - - - -
BN	- - -	*puis despeciés par dalles, cuissés en eaue,*
VAT	- - -	**puis le depeciez par dalles et soit cuit en eaue,**

VAL		*du vin et du cel au cuire;*		*au poivre jaunet ou*
MAZ	et y mecter	du vin et du sel au cuire;	et la maingier	a poivre janet ou
BN	*et*	*du vin et du sel a cuire;*	*mengiés*	*au poivre jaunet ou*
VAT	**et**	**du vin et du sel au cuire;**	**et soit mengié**	**au poivre jaunet ou**

VAL	*a la cameline;*	- - - - - - - - - - - - - -
MAZ	a la cameline;	- - - - - - - - - - - - - -
BN	*a la cameline.*	- - - - - - - - - - - - - -
VAT	**a la cameline;**	**et le mectent aucuns ressuyer sur le grail au mengier;**

VAT	**et en pasté, qui veult, pouldré d'espices, et soit mengié a la cameline;**

VAL	*le sallé,*	*cuit en yaue,*	- - - -
MAZ	et le salez,	- - - - - - -	maingier a vin et
VAT	**et s'il est sallé,**	**soit cuit en eaue sans sel et**	**mengiés au vin et**

---

[3] *Menagier de Paris*, §192; p. 195.

[4] "Est la brecte aussi comme chien de mer, maiz brecte est plus petite, et plus doulce et meilleur ... " (*Menagier*, §191; p. 194).

VAL	*a la cibole;*	– – *en pasté, a la pouldre.*
MAZ	a la siboule;	et la fresche en pasté aveques espices et sel.
VAT	**a la ciboule miciee.**	

A very common edible fish in the Middle Ages—not very highly esteemed by connoisseurs or physicians, but readily procured throughout most of Europe, and relatively cheap—the salmon could be dealt with in the kitchen in as broad a variety of ways, according to the *Viandier*, as most other fish. Both fresh and salted salmon were normally available[1] and for each the *Viandier* offers two possible treatments.

Fresh salmon undergoes a two-stage cooking process. Originally the first stage consisted of a frying, but *Y* changes this to roasting. In the second stage the fish was boiled, exposing it to the warming and drying effects of wine and salt. The instruction "gardez l'eschine," which is found copied more or less accurately in all of the manuscripts, merely advises the cook not to filet or de-bone the salmon until after it has been cooked in the first stage, whether this is by frying or by roasting, and the flesh has been rendered somewhat more firm or cohesive. *VAL* and *MAZ* imply that the bones may be removed for the boiling, the second stage of cooking; *Y* is more precise, suggesting that the fish be picked apart in layers of flesh, which layers, when boiled, will better absorb the wine and salt of the pot.

Concerning the variants *boutonnez*, *baconné* and *bagué*, see Recipe 51, n4, above.

The salted salmon can be either boiled or, according to *VAL*, baked in a pie. *Z* writes that only fresh salmon is suitable for a pastry dish, but he does not move the mention of this dish from its position after the consideration of boiled salted salmon. What he does do, though, is to include salt in his recipe for salmon pie made from fresh salmon, thus achieving the same effect. *Y* transposes this whole passage to its logical place at the end of the section dealing with fresh salmon.[2]

125. Mulet

VAL	*Mullet.*	*Comme maqueraux.*
MAZ	–	Soit cuit conme le malquerez.
BN	*Mulet.*	*Aussi comme maquerel.*
VAT	**Mulet.**	**Ainsi come le[1] maquerel.**

[1] *BN* copies only the recipe for fresh salmon.

[2] The text of the recipe for fresh and salted salmon in the *Menagier* (§200; p. 198) is very close to what is read in *VAT*. A recipe for salmon of both sorts is found in the *Enseignements* (p. 186, l. 181; *Petit traité*, p. 223) but is very brief, one of the shortest for fish in the whole of that collection of recipes. In common with the *Viandier*, the *Enseignements* suggests that fresh salmon be eaten with a hot pepper sauce. This use of pepper, favoured by the *Enseignements* but generally shunned by the *Viandier*—which tends instead to prefer grains of paradise, melegueta pepper—suggests by itself that this dish was a traditional, long-established one. Chiquart, on the other hand, directs that salmon should be served with only cameline sauce (*Du fait de cuisine*, ff. 56v and 69v).

[1] *le* followed by *mq* stroked out.

While mackerel is dealt with by *VAL* and *MAZ* (and therefore presumably by *O* and *Z*) at a location six recipes previous to this point in the *Viandier*, at §119, it was left aside by *Y* in favour of the red mullet, conger, stockfish and dogfish. *VAT* reinserts it in his copy of the *Viandier* immediately prior to this recipe for grey mullet.

126. Morue fraiche

VAL	*Morue fraiche.*	*Aparellié comme rouget,*
MAZ	La fresce.	Apparilliez ainsi conme le malquerel
BN	*Morue franche.*	*Appareillier et cuire comme le rouget,*
VAT	**Morue fresche.**	**Appareillee et cuite come ung rouget,**

VAL		*vin au cuire;*			*a la jance;*
MAZ	et y mecter	du vin a cuire,	et	maingier	de la jasse;
BN	*et*	*du vin a la cuire;*	*qui veult,*		*a la jance;*
VAT	**et**	**du vin au cuire;**		**mengee**	**a la jance;**

VAT	**et y met l'en, qui veult, des aulx, et aucuns non;**

VAL	*le sallé,*	*a la moustarde ou au beure frais.*
MAZ	et la salee,	a la moustarde ou a beurre fresc fondu par dessus.
BN	*et la sallee,*	*a la moustarde ou au beurre frais fondu dessus.*
VAT	**la salee,**	**a la moustarde ou beurre fraiz fondu.**

Cod, like salmon, is available both fresh and salted, but the ways the *Viander* offers for preparing it as a dish are fewer and simpler.

MAZ very inattentively copies this recipe without break or title immediately after the *Mullet* (Recipe 125), for which he does not copy the title either. In the first line of this recipe for cod he echoes the line, "ainsi conme le malquerel," which he has just written for the grey mullet.

An optional serving sauce in *VAT* is similar to a possible dressing mentioned in the *Enseignements*; this latter collection has recipes for both the fresh and the salted cod.[1] The *VAT* option is likely the unboiled sauce listed in the Table to that manuscript (§169) as *Une bonne sausse de jance pour morue aux aulx*, even though *jance* or *janse* is normally a boiled sauce.[2]

According to J.-L. Flandrin, the relatively frequent use of butter in the *Viandier*, as here in the optional sauce for salt cod, marks this cuisine as belonging to the northern parts of France.[3]

---

[1] "E se veut mengier a la blance aillie d'aus e d'alemendes, destrempee de vin aigre ... " (*Enseignements*, p. 186, l. 206; *Petit traité de cuisine*, p. 225).

[2] See the *Viandier*'s Recipes 166–168. All three *jances* in Chiquart are boiled mixtures of white ginger, grains of paradise and verjuice, with various other ingredients (*Du fait de cuisine*: §43, f. 69r; §46, f. 72r; and §58, f. 83r).

[3] Butter is also an ingredient in Recipes 150, 153, 188, 190 and 206, below. In other recipe

127. Grapois

VAL	*Grapois. Leschié tout cru,*		*cuit en eaue;*
MAZ	Crappois. Eschaudez le tout cruz,	puis soit	cuit en aigue pour
VAT	**Grappois. Leschié tout cru et**		**cuit en eaue pour**

VAL	*servir avec les pois.*
MAZ	servir avec les pois.
VAT	**servir avec les poys come de lart. Et aucuns l'essuyent ung pou sur le feu; et qui met l'eaue es poys, ilz en vallent mieulx.**

Whale meat was generally available in a salted state[1] and had therefore to undergo a preliminary operation of boiling. *MAZ(X)* requires this salt meat to be immersed in hot water before being cooked.

The dishes for which whale meat could be prepared were limited. Its most common appearance on a table was with a pea puree in the equivalent to the modern pork and beans when this was prepared for a meatless day.[2]

The last recipe for a round sea-fish that *BN* copies is for fresh cod (§126). He omits this recipe for whale as well as those for all of the remaining fish in this chapter, passing on to the first items in the division of flat sea-fishes.

128. Egreffin

VAL	*Egreffin.*		*Comme rouget; le froit,*
MAZ	– – – – – –	Soit cuit	conme le rouget; et le fris
VAT	**Moruaulx[1] et aigreffins.**		**Come la morue et aigreffins**

---

collections, such as the *Du fait de cuisine*, almond butter rather than cow's-milk butter is called for; almond butter is used nowhere in the *Viandier*. See Jean-Louis Flandrin, "Le goût et la nécessité: sur l'usage des graisses dans les cuisines d'Europe occidentale (XIVe–XVIIIe siècles)," *Annales: Économies, Sociétés, Civilisations*, 38 (1983), pp. 369–401.

[1] "Craspoiz, c'est baleine salee ... " (*Menagier*, §207; p. 200). In one of his menus for a "disner de poisson," the *Menagier* lists, among other dishes, "harens, graspoix, anguilles salees," apparently a series of salt fish (ed. Brereton and Ferrier, p. 181, §47 in the Fourth Article of the Second Distinction; ed. Pichon, p. 102).

[2] "E se a ce [that is, on a fish-day] ou en Karesme il y a craspoiz, l'en doit faire les craspoiz comme de lart a jour de char" (*ibid.*, §29; p. 136); this dish of what Pichon calls *Lard sur les pois* has just been described by the *Menagier* in the same paragraph. A similar dish using porpoise, the lean counterpart of venison, is *Porpeis avec la puree*: see *Maniere de langage*, ed. Paul Meyer, *Revue critique d'histoire et de littérature*, num. comp. 1870 (Paris, 1873), p. 393; repr. in Lozinski, *Bataille de Caresme*, p. 191.

[1] *moruaulx* followed by *com* stroked out; either the scribe was about to forget *aigreffins* or else this fish was not clearly part of the title to this recipe in his source. It may be, too, that the *VAT* scribe is himself responsible for combining these two recipes while he is copying them.

VAL *a la jansse.*
MAZ soit maingier a la jasse.
VAT **soient appareilliez.**

Immediately after copying the recipe for fresh cod (§126), *VAT* inserts a recipe for codling which is to be prepared in the same way as cod. Since haddock is closely related to cod and is generally of the size of a smaller cod, *VAT* adds *Aigreffins* to this "new" recipe, anticipating a little thereby the recipe for haddock that will appear two fishes later in his source. Even the text of this new double recipe reveals something of the hesitant way it was put together.

Frying is not found as an option in the recipes for either red mullet or cod.[2]

129. Orfin

VAT **Orfin. Affaittié par l'oreille, en rost; a la cameline.**

This recipe for garfish was added by *Y*. The *Menagier* has a version of it that begins as *VAT* does, but in which the fish is to be boiled.[1]

130. Brete

VAL *Brete.*[1] *Cuire comme raye, affaitié; aux aulx camelins.*
MAZ Brete. Soit cuit conme le rouget et maingier aux haulx camelins.
VAT **Braytte. Cuite come une raye.**

There is disagreement among the manuscript copies of this recipe about just which fish it is whose handling is to provide the model for the treatment of the brett.[2] There is, though, perhaps what amounts to at least partial agreement about what this treatment should be, since the red mullet is to be eviscerated by its belly and the ray by its "navel."[3]

---

[2] The *Menagier*'s recipe is for haddock alone and probably reproduces *Y*: "Aigrefin appareillié comme le rouget ... " (§201; p. 198). For the second part of this recipe the *Menagier* blunders quite exceptionally as a result of reading *froid* ("cold") for *froit* ("fried"): "Et le couvient ung pou laissier froidir en son eaue."

[1] *Menagier de Paris*, §202; p. 198.

[1] *Brete*: written *rete* in *VAL* where this recipe continues immediately after the word *jansse* of the recipe for *Egreffin*. The source used by *VAL* would seem not to have had capitals that were a part of the word.

[2] "Et est la brecte aussi comme chien de mer, maiz brecte est plus petite, et plus doulce et meilleur; et dist l'en que c'est la fumelle du chien, et est brune sur le dos et le chien est roux" (*Menagier de Paris*, §191; p. 194).

[3] There is a virtual accord among the manuscripts provided that we punctuate *VAL*, "cuire, comme raye affaitié," and provided we understand *cuire* in the other two versions to include the eviscerating procedure as well as the actual cooking.

For cooking, the red mullet is to be salted and then boiled, while the ray is to be cut up, boiled and skinned—in that order. The *Menagier*, whether reading a source close to *VAT* or following his own practice or that of some third party, refers to the treatment accorded both fish as models, indicating that the brett is to be cleaned through its belly (like the red mullet) and skinned after being cooked (like the ray).[4]

VAT has so little interest in this fish that he does not copy the serving sauce appropriate for it. As it happens, this sauce is the same as for the ray.

131. Colin

VAT **Colin. Come morue.**

A variety of cod, and resembling it, the coalfish (*Pollachius virens*: "green pollack") is to be prepared like a cod (Recipe 126). No recipe for *Colin* is found in the *Menagier*; this may well be an insertion made by *VAT* into his version of the *Viandier*.

132. Truite saulmonoise

VAL *Truite saulmonoise. - - - Cuite en yaue et vin; a cameline.*
VAT **Truitte saumonneresse. Tronçonnee, cuite en eaue et en vin; a la cameline.**

The last item of this particular chapter, the salmon trout, has the distinction of being copied both here, as a variety of round sea-fish, and later by *VAT* (in Recipe 142) as a flat sea-fish. The *Menagier* does not include a recipe for salmon trout but does, in his chapter on freshwater fish,[1] write out a recipe for plain trout that is the same as the *Viandier*'s recipe here for saltwater salmon trout. In both cases the fish is to be cut into slices or steaks two fingers thick, boiled in water and red wine, and served with cameline sauce. The *Viandier*'s recipe for freshwater trout (§109) mentions neither cutting nor wine.

Chapitre de poisson de mer plat (BN, VAT)

133. Pleis

BN *Pleis. Affetiés par devers le dos au dessoz de l'oreille,*
VAT **Pleys. Affaictiez par devers le doz dessoubz l'oreille,**

BN *soit bien cuite; pour saulce metés du vin*
VAT **bien lavee, cuitte come ung rouget, a saulse de vin**

---

[4] "Brecte affaictié comme ung rouget, cuicte comme une raye et ainsi pelee, mengee aux aulx camelins" (*ibid.*). It might be noted that the *Menagier*'s recipe for brett is the first in his section on sea-fish; it therefore precedes those for both *Rouget* and *Raye*.

[1] *Menagier de Paris*, §179; p. 190.

BN *et du sel par dessus; et qui en veult en potaige, soit frite sans farine.*
VAT **et de sel; et qui veult en potaige, soit cuite sans farine.**

In those two manuscripts derived from *Y*, the *Viandier*'s chapter on flat sea-fish opens with recipes for plaice, flounder and sole. The first fish at that same point in *VAL* and *MAZ* is the ray, the fourth to be treated by *BN* and *VAT*.

It may be that *BN* miscopied his original very slightly. In the sauce for boiled plaice he writes "du vin et du *sel par dessus*," yet this use of salt upon the fish is, as we have seen, the peculiar feature in the method of *cooking* the red mullet (Recipe 120), and not in the serving of it. The text of the *Menagier* instructs the cook to eviscerate the fish by slicing it beneath the gill, backwards, to clean it, and then to set it in a pan—"et du sel dessus"—and to boil it as one would a red mullet.[1] This method of preparing and cooking plaice will provide an important model for the treatment of a number of flatfish (flounder, sole, turbot) which are to be examined later in this chapter of the *Viandier*. The casual nature of the reference here in *BN* to the cooking method for *Pleis* ("soit bien cuite") is all the more surprising.[2]

134. Flais

BN *Flais. Auxi come la pleis.*
VAT **Flaiz. Appareilliee comme pleiz, a la saulce vert, cavelee come la pleiz.**

Flounder is considered to be related to plaice and will receive the same treatment when being cooked.[1] The term *cavelee* appearing in *VAT* seems to be either a misreading for the name of another fish, *carrelez*,[2] which is a smaller sort of plaice, or else a poor copy of the word *tavelee*, "spotted, speckled."[3] The *Menagier* scorns the flounder simply because the *carrelet* is available in the same season and is preferable to it.[4] His recipe for plaice includes the *quarrelet* as well: "Plays et quarrelet sont aucques d'une nature. La plus grant est nommee *plaiz* et la petite *quarrelet*, et est *tavellee* [my emphasis] de rouge sur le dos; et sont bons du flo [high tide] de mars et meilleurs du flo d'avril."[5]

---

[1] *Menagier de Paris*, §211; p. 202. The *Menagier* does not reproduce the recipe for a stew of plaice fish, the dish that is found in *BN* and *VAT*.

[2] In Recipe 135, *BN* will direct the cook who is working on a sole: "Cuisés comme pleis"!

[1] The *Enseignements* considers plaice and flounder together, offering two recipes for them. The first of these is for the boiled fish, eaten with a wine sauce; the second makes use of an herb-and-spice galantine (p. 187, l. 209; *Petit traité*, p. 225).

[2] These *carreletz* will be mentioned again by *VAT* in the meatless version of the dish called *Tuillé* (Recipe 206).

[3] The *Menagier* uses this term to describe the red gurnard: "Le grimondin est ... tanné, tavellé et de diverses couleurs" (§199; p. 197).

[4] *Menagier de Paris*, §220; p. 204. Earlier in the *Menagier* the name of the fish is *carreletz* (§120; p. 171).

[5] *Menagier*, §211; p. 202.

It seems likely that the source that *VAT* was following intended a separate paragraph for the fish *Carelet* or *Carrelez* to be inserted between Recipes 134 and 135. The sole text for this entry would be "Come la pleiz."

135. Solles

MAZ	– Soit eschaulder	et apparoilliez	– –	
BN	*Solles. Eschaudés*	*et affeitiés*	*et cuisés*	
VAT	**Solles. On les doit[1] eschauder**	– – –	**et puis cuire et affiner**	

MAZ	conme plays,	et maingier a la saulce verde,	au chaudumé;
BN	*comme pleis;*	– – – – – – – – – –	–
VAT	**come la pleiz en eaue,**	**et mengier a la saulce vert;**	– – –

MAZ	et la rotiez	sur le gril	– – –	et au verjus d'usille.
BN	*et qui veult rostie,*	– –	*sans escharder,*	– –
VAT	**et en rost, qui veult,**	– –	**sans eschauder,**	**au verjus;**

BN	*et aucuns l'escorchent devers le dos,*	*et au verjus;*	*et la frire*
VAT	**et escorchent aucuns le dos;**	– – –	**et la fricte,**

BN	*sans ferine*	*et sans eschauder,*	*mengier au verjus.*
VAT	– – –	**sans eschauder,**	**en huille.**

The fish sole allows a variety of culinary preparations. Three cooking methods are mentioned here: boiling, roasting and frying; the last is added by *Y*.

In the first section, on boiled sole, *VAT* uses the verb *affiner* in the sense of "finish off," referring to the method that is followed in the preparation of plaice. The same reference to plaice is remarkable in *MAZ* because he and *VAL* have not even copied the *Viandier*'s recipe for this fish; *BN*'s reference back to Recipe 133 is likewise useless because for plaice *BN* has written merely "soit bien cuite"! *VAT* at least indicates that for plaice the cooking method is to be the same as for the red mullet (Recipe 120): salted, then boiled. The *Menagier* has what seems to be an echo of *VAT*'s verb *affiner*: "Mectre en la paelle, et du sel dessus, et de l'eaue; puis faire cuire, et *a la parfin* mectre du sel avec."[2]

In the section on roast sole *VAT* changes the verb *escharder* ("to scale, remove the scales from") of *BN* into *eschauder* ("to scald"). The *Menagier*, presumably in the *Y* tradition with *BN*, has *escharder* at this point in the recipe.[3] For the same dish both *BN*

---

[1] *doit* inserted above the line.

[2] *Menagier de Paris*, §213; p. 203.

[3] "L'en les rostit sur le grail et du feurre [*straw*] moullié entredeux; et celles ne doivent point estre eschardees ... " (*ibid.*) It should be noted, though, that all three manuscripts of the *Viandier* that contain this recipe show *eschauder* at the beginning for boiled sole, whereas the *Menagier* has *escharder et affaictier*.

and *VAT* copy only normal verjuice as the serving sauce, but the *Menagier* "keeps" the sorrel verjuice which is seen in the *MAZ* version of the *Viandier*.[4] If indeed the *Menagier* derives more or less directly from *Y*, it seems, at least in the case of this recipe and on the basis of this choice of sauce, that we should postulate the existence of a Y_1, copied from *Y*, affording a common source for *BN* and *VAT* but with no direct influence upon the *Menagier*. The *MAZ(X)* scribe did not at first copy this recipe for sole but began the chapter on flat sea-fish with the next recipe, the one for ray. In *MAZ* this paragraph, which is headed *Raye*, is prolonged by a succession of recipes for six other fish, all but one of which are found in *VAL* and in the same order as is followed by *VAL*, but all of which are copied without any name and without any separation between them. The eighth and last recipe in this apparent miscellany is the same as the present Recipe 135. It remains somewhat of a mystery, though, why *MAZ(X)* should first have passed by this recipe for sole but then have returned to it later after copying the recipe for sturgeon (§146), neither naming the fish the recipe was designed for nor distinguishing it from any other recipe linked together in that paragraph. At the very least we must hypothesize that *MAZ* or *MAX(X)* was copying from *two* versions of this particular section of the *Viandier*.

136. Raie

VAL	*Raye. Appareilliez par le nombryl,* – – –
MAZ	Raye. Apparilliez la par le nombril, – – –
BN	*Raie. Soit appareillié par endroit nombril et gardés le foie, et la*
VAT	**Roye. Appareilliee par endroit le nombril et gardez le foye, et la**

VAL	*metre cuire par piecez;* – – – – – –
MAZ	despiciez par pieces et cuilz, – – – et puis le pelez;
BN	*metés par pieces, cuisés fort comme pleis, puis pellés;*
VAT	**despeciez par pieces et la cuissiez come une pleiz, et puis la pelez;**

VAL	*mengier froide aux aulx camelins; soit le foie tirié hors qu'il*
MAZ	et maingier froide aux haulx; et ne cuisiez le foye astant
BN	*mengiés* – *aux aulx camelins.*
VAT	**et la mengiez tyede aux aulx camelins; et du foye aucuns font des**

---

[4] This mention of *verjus d'usille*, sorrel verjuice, in *MAZ* is the only instance of its use in the *Viandier*. The herb sorrel, whose leaves contain the oxalate of potash that gives them a characteristic acid taste, was fairly common in fifteenth-century salads (*cf.* the *Nef de santé*, *s. v. ozeille*). Even among Chiquart's recipes sorrel verjuice was frequently called for, particularly as a dressing for roasted fish—as is the case here in the *Viandier*. Specifically, fried sole is to be served with "verjust de oyselle et de orenges" (*Du fait de cuisine*, f. 56v). Magninus Mediolanensis suggests serving boiled capons and pheasants in summer "cum succo acedule viridis" (*De saporibus*, *ed. cit.*, p. 187).

VAL	*ne cuise trop.*
MAZ	conme la raye.
VAT	**tostees et mettent du frommage de gain bien tenve pardessus; et est bonne viande et bien friande.**[1]

This recipe for ray is the first for flat sea-fish to be copied by *VAL*[2] and offers, in the matter of skinning, a type of procedure for another fish of the same general nature, the dab (Recipe 138), as well as for the dogfish (Recipe 123) and brett (Recipe 130) that were classified as round sea-fish in the previous chapter.[3]

With regard to cooking, the comparison with plaice made here by *Y* seems at first sight to be quite useless because neither *BN* nor *VAT* say anything in particular about cooking plaice, except that it should be well boiled (*BN*) and that it should be boiled in the same fashion as a red mullet (*VAT*). On further examination, though, we find that the procedure for cooking red mullet requires the fish to be coated in salt before being boiled, and it appears to be this dredging procedure that is intended for the ray.

A sauce called cameline garlic is specified as a dressing for the boiled ray.[4] This is not too common a sauce. Its strength[5] makes it appropriate for tougher fish such as the dogfish (Recipe 123) and the brett (Recipe 130), and in one use it is even designated aptly as "aulx de la roye" (Recipe 122). What is notable about this sauce is that one of the ingredients in it is liver from the ray fish itself.[6] Because of the shorter cooking time required by the liver, relative to the fish itself, *VAL* and *MAZ* provide useful practical warnings that this liver should not be overdone.

137. Turbot

VAL	*Turbot.*	*Appareilliez comme plais,*	*pelé vers*
MAZ	– –	Apparoilliez conme la plis et cuisiez	et puis la pelez par
BN	*Turbot.*	*Appareillié et cuit comme une pleis*	*et puis peler par devers*
VAT	**Turbot.**	**Appareillié et cuit come une pleiz**	**et puis pelé par devers**

[1] *et bien friande* added in a lighter hand.

[2] And the first in *MAZ* as well, although the recipe for sole that precedes in the two *Y* manuscripts must have existed in his original because he copies this after the recipe for sturgeon (§146). The ray is the first flat sea-fish to be dealt with by the *Menagier de Paris* as well (§210; p. 201), where the text devoted to it is quite extensive and only partially related to that of the *Viandier*.

[3] Concerning the manner of evisceration prescribed here, Gunnar Tilander glosses the word *nombril* as "l'anus d'une raie, pris par mégarde pour le nombril" (*Glanures lexicographiques*, p. 183).

[4] Chiquart also designates "aulx camellins" as the proper dressing for a ray fish: "La roye [se doibt donner] aux aulx camellins qui soient fais es amendres et de son feie" (*Du fait de cuisine*, f. 56v).

[5] In Recipe 156 below we see that the principal ingredients of *Aulx camelins* are cinnamon, garlic and ray liver. Both cinnamon and garlic are particularly warm and dry, garlic to the fourth degree, the most extreme, in each quality (Platearius, Crescentius, Aldobrandino, etc.).

[6] Hence the designation found in Recipe 122. The *Menagier* suggests the use of a galantine for cold ray.

VAL	*le dos;*	- - - - - -		*a la saulce vert.*
MAZ	le dolz;	- - - - -	et maingier	a la saulce verde.
BN	*le dos;*	- - - - - -	*mengiés*	*a la saulce verte ou au verjus.*
VAT	**le doz,**	**et doit estre par pieces;**	**et mengié**	**a la saulce vert ou en souz.**

The variant found in *BN* and *VAT* concerning the serving sauce for turbot is not easily explained. The *Menagier de Paris* notes that turbot and brill (*Barbue*, the subject of the next recipe) are much the same fish, differing only in size, and further indicates that they are to be cooked and served in the same way.[1]

The *Menagier* suggests that turbot be eaten either with green sauce or in a preparation called *soucie* or *soucié*.[2] *BN* has changed the phrase *en souz* (as in *VAT*), or something similar to this, to *au verjus*, perhaps because of an inability to understand the meaning of what he read.[3] The Table to the *VAT* version of the *Viandier* does indeed list an unboiled sauce called *Une soussie*, which is very likely to be that sauce whose recipe appears in *VAL*, *MAZ* (twice) and *BN* under the functional name of *Saulce a garder poisson* (§162). The *Menagier* in fact combines both of these names in the recipe that corresponds to the *Viandier*'s §162: "Ung soutyé [var. *un soucié*] vergay a garder poisson de mer."[4] This sauce makes a cold dish that is a meatless alternative to the *Soux de pourcel* we saw earlier (Recipe 74).

138. Barbue

BN	*Barbues. Cuites et appareilliés comme turbot*	*et puis*
VAT	**Barbue. Appareilliee come turbot**	**et puis, qui veult,**

BN	*pellés comme raie;*	*mengier*	*a la saulce vert ou au souciee.*
VAT	**pelee come roye;**	**et se mengue**	**a la saulce vert ou en souz.**

The brill is similar to the turbot, according to the *Menagier*, and is prepared and sauced in the same way.[1] For the sauce known as *soucie* or *souz*, see Recipe 162, *Saulce a garder poisson*.

---

[1] *Menagier*, §214; p. 203.

[2] According to the manuscript of the *Menagier* that is in the Bibliothèque royale, Brussels: "ou mis au soucié" (ed. Pichon, p. 203). The Paris, *BN* 12477 manuscript (preferred by Brereton and Ferrier, §214) has "ou mis au succre," an unlikely variant. In the section of this work that contains the meal menus, the Fourth Article of the Second Distinction, Brereton and Ferrier read a dish as *Turbos a la soucye* (p. 180, l. 10; this is *Turbos à la soucie* in Pichon, Menu 15, p. 100), and *Turbos au succre* (p. 182, l. 6; *Turbot à la soucie* in Pichon, Menu 21, p. 102).

[3] One may imagine also that the word *souz* could very well look like *ueriuz* if it were written with an abbreviation for the *er*. See also *BN*'s copy *au souciee* in the next recipe where the *au* must clearly have been an *en* in his original.

[4] *Menagier*, §277; p. 231. The gender of the word seems to be masculine in this passage. "*Nota* que le mot *soutyé* est dit de *soux*, pource qu'il est fait comme soux de pourcel ... " (*ibid.*).

[1] *Menagier de Pairs*, §215; p. 203. For this author the turbot is preferable to the brill.

139. Bresme

VAL	*Bresme.*	- - - -	*En yaue,*	*a cameline;*
MAZ	- -	- - - - -	- - - - - - - - -	- - -
BN	*Bresme.*[1]	- - - - -	- - - - - - - - -	- - -
VAT	**Bresme.**	**Eschaudee et cuite**	**en eaue come turbot, et mengee**	**a la cameline;**

VAL	- - - - - - - - - - -	*ou en pasté,*
MAZ	- - - - - - - - - - -	Soit eschaudee et mise en pasté
BN	- - - - - - - - - - -	*Eschaudés, en pasté,*
VAT	**et en rost sans eschauder, au verjus;**	**et en pasté, eschaudee,**

VAL	*a la poudre.*			
MAZ	et poudré d'espices;	- - - -	et maingier	a la cameline.
BN	*poudree d'espices;*	*ou cuite en eaue;*		*a la cameline.*
VAT	**pouldree d'espices;**	- - - -	**et se mengue**	**a la cameline.**

Bream can be prepared either by boiling or in a pastry shell or—an addition made by *VAT*—roasted.[2] *MAZ(X)* is interested in only the pasty of bream; *BN* copies this first and then adds the boiling procedure afterwards.

140. Lymande

VAL	*Limonde.*	*Doit estre cuite comme plais,*	*a la saulce*
MAZ	- -	oit cuite conme la plis,	a la saulse
VAT	**Lymande.**	**Appareilliee et cuite come une pleiz, et mengee**	**a saulce**

VAL	*du vin;*	- -	*ou au gravé.*
MAZ	de vin;	- -	ou au grain, qui . l veult.
VAT	**de vin et de sel;**		**ou faictes en gravé.**

There are actually two procedures here for the preparation of the dab: it can be either boiled or fried. In the latter case it is served in the stew known as a *gravé*.[1]

The only variant in this recipe for *Lymande* (apart from *VAL*'s spelling of the fish, *Limonde*) is found in the *MAZ* reading of *grain* for *gravé*.

---

[1] *Bresme*: the cue for the initial letter is missing in a hole in the manuscript.

[2] The *Menagier de Paris* has a recipe only for boiling bream or for baking it in a pie (§216; p. 203).

[1] The *Menagier de Paris* likewise offers two possible preparations, both of them involving frying. The second corresponds to the second treatment outlined in the *Viandier*: "Ou friz par moitié [*i. e.* half-fried] et mengiez au civé ou au gravé" (§212; p. 202).

141. Doree

VAL *Doree. Soit appareillee*
VAT **Doree. Appareilliee et cuite en eaue[1] come barbue, a la saulce de**

VAL *par la teste, puis rostie, au verjus.*
VAT **cameline; et en rost, fendue par la teste au long, au verjus; et en pasté, poudre d'espices, a la cameline.**

The John Dory, or Saint Peter fish, is amply treated by *VAT* yet all but ignored by the other manuscripts. The *Menagier* says that it may be boiled or roasted—the first two treatments outline by *VAT*—but speaks only of verjuice as a sauce.[2] The possibility of baking this fish in a pasty may be an addition by *VAT*.

142. Truitte saumonneresse

VAT **Truitte saumonneresse. Doibt estre pellee, et teste et tout, et cuitte en eaue ou en rost; et menger au verjus.**

Salmon trout has already been treated by two of the manuscripts, *VAL* and *VAT*, at the end of the chapter on round sea-fish (Recipe 132). There seems to be no similarity between the present recipe and the other.

This particular fish is not mentioned in the *Menagier*,[1] nor is this second occurence of it in *VAT* anticipated in the *VAT* Table. Following *Lymande* and *Doree*, paragraphs that *VAT* has already copied, though not in that order, the *VAT* Table concludes its enumeration of flat sea-fish with *Carreletz.*[2]

143. Alose de mer

VAL	*Alose.*	- - - *Rostir sus le greil*
MAZ	- - - - -	Soit pourboulie et rotier sur le gril,
BN	*Alouse cratoniere.*	*Parboullir et rostir sur le gril,*
VAT	**Aloses.**	**Come dit est dessus avec le poisson ront,**

[1] *et cuite en eaue* inserted above the line by means of a caret. The scribe began to insert the phrase after *Doree* but wrote only *et*; this *et* is repeated after with the remainder of the phrase.

[2] *Menagier de Paris*, §218; p. 204.

[1] Unless this is the *vermeille* variety of trout mentioned by the *Menagier* among his freshwater fish—at §179; p. 190, and at p. 174, l. 27 (Brereton and Ferrier); p. 90 (Pichon).

[2] In the Introduction, above, see the outline of the contents of all of the manuscripts. The person who compiled the *VAT* Table exercised what must have seemed to be a certain ichthyological reasoning in moving the series of shad, seal (?: *Fuccus*), bleak, sturgeon, cuttlefish, cockles and mussels back among the round sea-fish of the earlier chapter. Concerning the *carreletz*, see Recipe 134, above. For the seal, see Lawrens Andrewe (ed. Furnivall, p. 118): "Focas is a see bulle . . . ."

VAL	*ou en broche;*		*a cameline.*	
MAZ	ou en broche sans boulir;	et maingier	a la cameline.	
BN	*ou en broche sans parboulir;*	*mangier*	*a la cameline;*	*fruites comme ables.*
VAT	– – – – – – – – –	– –	– – –	**et frit comme alozes.**

The shad was treated previously, and in more detail, as a freshwater fish (Recipe 101). The marine shad migrates into fresh waters in order to spawn, and some varieties are found as far inland as some lakes in Switzerland and Italy.

The present recipe allows for this saltwater fish only to be roasted, one of several possibilities that have been prescribed for the freshwater shad. *Z* adds a parboiling stage depending upon whether a grill or a spit is to be used in the roasting process.[1] *VAT* tries to abbreviate the entry, but without success: rather than "avec le poisson ront" he should have written "avec le poisson d'eaue doulce."[2] Clearly, given the greater variety of dishes possible in the earlier recipe, this was not the *Viandier*'s intention.

Y seems to add a variant for fried shad, according to *BN* and *VAT*. An unusual procedure for frying *ales* is mentioned by the *Menagier*.[3] However, the comparison made at the end by *VAT* ("frit comme alozes") either refers to the *freshwater* shad (Recipe 101) or else is nonsense. A further possibility is that the phrase belongs to the treatment of another fish altogether that *Y* has fitted between *Aloses* and *Ables*. The corresponding passage in the *Menagier* reads, as a separate recipe for a different fish, "Fuites [var. *fenes*], comme alozes."[4] The fish inserted by *Y* and echoed in the *Menagier* may well have been *fruités*, for *fritel* or *froitel*: small fry.

The parboiling stage, mentioned for the roasted shad, remains a prerequisite for this fried shad as well.

144. Ables / Alles de mer

BN	*Ables.*	*Rostir en filopant;*	*mengier a la moustarde.*
VAT	**Alles de mer.**	**Rosties en filopant;**	**a la moustarde ou a la sausse de vin.**

---

[1] The sense of the generic name *Alose cratoniere* found in *BN* is not clear but may refer to the manner of cooking this shad which makes use of a *cratis*: "grill." "Sanis autem convenit preparatio [of fish] per frissuram et post ipsam assatorum super cratem" (G. Albini, *De sanitatis custodia*, *ed. cit.*, p. 82). Because parboiling is required only if the fish is to be roasted on the grill, this method of cooking would seem to expose it to a drier, more direct heat than if it were mounted on a spit.

[2] In the *VAT* Table the *Alozes d'eaue doulce* (§120) are far out of place, following the *Escrevisses* (Recipe 117), the last item of the *Viandier*'s actual recipes, and this may have led the scribe who was writing the body of *VAT* to consider them to belong to the category of round sea-fish.

[3] "Ales ... pelees, puis cuictes en l'eaue ung trespetit, puis enfarinees, frictes a l'uille ... " (§219; p. 204). These directions are similar to what is found in *VAT* for smelt (Recipe 145).

[4] *Menagier de Paris*, §177; p. 188. Brereton and Ferrier gloss *fene* only as a "kind of freshwater fish." In the *Menagier* the recipe is copied between *Aloze* and *Carpe*.

The identity of the fish which *Y* introduced into the *Viandier* at this point is problematic. According to both *BN* and the *VAT* Table, the name of these fish is *Ables*, which would be bleak, a freshwater fish resembling carp.[1] However, *VAT* writes *Alles* (or perhaps *Allés*), a form of name that is reproduced in the *Menagier*,[2] and these fish would be the *ale* that Godefroy defines as a sardine or anchovy, both being a variety of small, herring-like fish.[3] It seems likely that *Y* wrote the name as we find it in *VAT*. [4] While Chiquart has neither *ables* nor *alles*, he does mention *anchues* and *anchoyes* among his sea-fish dishes.[5] As Pichon and Vicaire point out, the modern treatment for anchovies, cutting them into strips, would tend to confirm this identification of *Alles de mer*.[6]

145. Esperlans

VAL	*Aspellens.*	*En pasté,*	*hostez hors,*
MAZ	– –	Mectez les en pasté,	puis les hostés hors de pasté, puis
VAT	**Esperlans.**	**En pasté**	**et puis ostez hors du pasté, et**

VAL	*friolés en farine et huille;*	*a la jance ou*
MAZ	les friolés avec farine et huille;	a la jauce ou
VAT	**enfarinez et les frisiez en huille; et les mengez**	**a la jance ou**

VAL	*aux aulx vers.*
MAZ	aux haulx vers.
VAT	**aux aulx vertz; ou tous friz, a la moustarde.**

---

1 "Able: f. a blay, or bleake, fish" (Cotgrave). See Recipe 116, above.

2 *Menagier de Paris*, §219; p. 204. The recipe here is in its first part the same as is copied by *BN*. The most recent editors of the *Menagier*, Brereton and Ferrier, gloss *ale* only as a "small flat fish." *Cf.* the English "alewife," a fish of the herring family.

3 Magninus mentions the herring, *allec*, in Chapter 17 of his *Regimen sanitatis*. See *alix* in Nada Patrone, *Il cibo del rico*, p. 335, and the *REW*, §4001. See also Jacques André, *L'Alimentation et la cuisine à Rome* (Paris, 1981), p. 112; and the comment by Pérez in his edition of Ruperto de Nola's *Libro de Guisados*: concerning the fish called *variales*, "Se trata del humilde y popular boquerón del Mediterráneo." According to Pérez, this fish is also called *alcha*, *alache* and *haleche*.

4 The *Enseignements* also has *Alles*: "Tout pesson d'eve douce qui est cuit en eve, est bon a la verte sauce. Alles a la moustarde" (p. 186, l. 189; in this line of the text the editor inexplicably changes the name of the fish to *Ables*. In the *Petit traité de cuisine*, p. 224 and n1, the editors there, Pichon and Vicaire, do not understand that *alles* marks the beginning of a new recipe but rather change the name of the fish to *allés* and gloss "*hallés*, c'est-à-dire grillés"). Just before this point in the text of the *Enseignements*, there is a recipe for *Espellens*, as in the *Viandier*, and a passage that seems to read, "Cules a la moustarde" (p. 186, l. 196; *Petit traité*, p. 224): see the more recent editor's discussion of these two passages (*Bataille de Caresme*, p. 171).

5 *Du fait de cuisine*, f. 16v. Sardines are fried and eaten with mustard, as in this recipe for *Alles*; anchovies are eaten with parsley (f. 56v).

6 "Le mot *en filopant* qui vient après et qui signifie *couper en filets* corroborreroit cette opinion, les anchois s'apprêtant ordinairement ainsi" (*Le Viandier de Guillaume Tirel, dit Taillevent*, p. 30, n8).

Though the initial treatment of smelt may appear strange, the three manuscripts copying this recipe agree: these fish are to be baked in a pasty and then removed from it in order to be fried. It is tempting to suppose an error to have been committed early in the tradition, by which "li os ostés" ("remove the bones") became *VAL*'s "hostez hors." This instruction would have been enlarged upon in later versions. If such a misreading did indeed occur, we may understand two possible preparations for smelt, baking (of deboned smelt) and fried.

146. Esturjon

VAL	*Esturgon.*	*Eschaudez, fendez par le ventre,*	*la teste*
MAZ	– –	Eschauder et fendez par le ventre	et la teste
BN	*Esturjon.*	*Eschaudés par le ventre*	*et soit la teste*
VAT	**Esturjon.**	**Eschaudez le et le fendez par le ventre,**	**et la teste**

VAL	*coppee en .ii. tronssons,*	*lez autrez*
MAZ	coppés en deux tronsons	et les aultres tronsons
BN	*fendue en ii et coupé du corps,*	*et tous les autres tronçons*
VAT	**couppee et fendue en deulx**	**et tous les autres tronçons**

VAL	*fendus,*	*cuire en vin ou en yaue,*
MAZ	qu'il se peuvent fendre fender aussi,	et cuisiez en aigue
BN	*soient fendus ceux qui se pevent fendre;*	*soient cuis en vin, en eaue,*
VAT	**fendus**[1] **qui se pourront fendre,**	**et soit cuit en vin et en eaue,**

VAL	*que le vin passe,*	*metre froidir;*
MAZ	et que le vin passe,	et lessiez reffroidier;
BN	*et que le vin passe,*	*puis traire et refroidier;*
VAT	**et que le vin passe,**	**et puis le traiez et laissiez reffroidir;**

VAL	*et mengier a persil et au vin aigre.*	
MAZ	et maingier a parressi ou au vin aigre.	
BN	*puis mengiés au vinaigre et du percil*	*et seel.*
VAT	**et aprés le mettez en vinaigre et en persil.**	

While the *Viandier* classifies sturgeon as a flat sea-fish, in the *Menagier* this recipe is placed between stockfish and whale among the round sea-fish. There, the bourgeois author suggests a variation in the form of a warm dish of sturgeon making use of spices in the bouillon.[2]

The *Recueil de Riom* specifies a serving sauce for sturgeon consisting of parsley, vinegar and onions.[3]

---

[1] *fendus* inserted above the line by means of a caret.

[2] *Menagier de Paris*, §205; p. 199: "comme ce feust venoison." In recommending a sauce for sturgeon Chiquart agrees with the *Viandier* but adds onions: "Les esturjons au persy, oygnions et vin aigre" (*Du fait de cuisine*, f. 56v).

[3] *Recueil de Riom*, §43.

147. Seiche

VAL	*Perche. Pellee, mise par morceaux,* – – –
MAZ	– Soit paree et mise par morceal et puis le mecter
BN	*Seiche.* – – *Soit par morssiaux despecié, puis la metés*
VAT	**Seiche. Soit pellee et par morceaux despeciee, puis la mettez**
VAL	– – – – – – – – – – – – – – – – – *metez frire,*
MAZ	en une peele sans aigue et la saichiez tresbien avec sel, – –
BN	*en une paielle de fer et du sel aveques, et metés sus*
VAT	**en une paelle de fer et du sel avec, mettez sur**
BN	*le feu et remuez souvent tant qu'elle soit bien nestoié,*
VAT	**le feu, remuez et la retournez souvent tant qu'elle soit bien nettoiee,**
VAL	*versez en une nappe et l'estandez bien;*
MAZ	puis vercel sur une nappe et l'estordez tresbien;
BN	*et puis la metés en eaue en une nape et l'espingiés bien;*
VAT	**et puis la mettez en une nappe et l'espreignez tant qu'elle soit**
VAL	*coullez de fleur, frisiez en huille et oignons avec,*
MAZ	et colez en farine et la frisiez en huille avec des oignons,
BN	*puis l'emfarinés, puis soit frite en huille* – – –
VAT	**assez seiche,** – – – – **et puis la frisiez en huille aux ongnons**
VAT	**qui ne soient pas si tost mis en la paelle comme les morceaulx de la seiche**
VAL	– – – – – – – – *metez sus de la poudre;*
MAZ	– – – – – – – – puis poudré de fine poudre d'espices;
BN	– – – – – – – – *et poudrés d'espices;*
VAT	**car ilz seroient trop roux; et au dressier y mettez la pouldre d'espices sus;**
VAL	– *aux aulx,*
MAZ	et maingier aux haulx
BN	*mengier aux aillés verdelés*
VAT	**et soit mengee aux aulx blans deffaiz de vinaigre; et si la peult on mengier**
VAL	*gravé, ou verjus.*
MAZ	ou au grainné ou au verjus.
BN	– – – – – – – – – *ou a vergus.*
VAT	**au gravé ou potaige qui veult;** – – **et l'enfarinent aucuns.**

Despite the name of the fish that is given by *VAL*,[1] this recipe is clearly for the cuttlefish, a logical first item in the series of molluscs with which this chapter of the *Viandier* concludes.

[1] In *VAL* the cue for the capital letter at the beginning of the name of the fish is an *s*, clearly

In the *Menagier de Paris*, this recipe is the last in the chapter of flat sea-fish, following three of the molluscs found in the *Viandier*.[2] The *Menagier* distinguishes between *seiche conree* (that is, "cured cuttlefish") and *seche fresche*: for the first, he copies the *Viandier*'s recipe very closely, and adds twice as much material again in the form of further advice for the preparing, cooking and serving of this fish.

BN makes a mistake in instructing the cook, when the fish has been fried in salt, "puis la metés en eaue en une nappe." There should be no mention of water at all; the word *eaue* may have been suggested in some copy by the words *en une*.

In *VAT* we find knowing advice about the length of time the onions should be fried.[3] Whether accidentally or deliberately *VAT* omits mentioning that the pieces of fish are coated in flour, taking up this procedure merely as a possibility at the end of his version.

The phrase *tant qu'elle soit bien nestoié* points to the need to purge the cuttlefish of the inky fluid it secretes. The *Menagier* indicates that a frying in salt is effective in causing the fish to exude this ink.[4]

148. Oestres

VAT **Oestres. Cuites en eaue et puis frictes en huille avec ongnons; et mengié au civé ou a la poudre ou aux aulx.**

This recipe for oysters originates in *VAT*. Oysters are not mentioned in the *Menagier de Paris*. The dish bears some resemblance to what is read in the *Enseignements*.[1]

149. Hanons

VAL	*Hanons.*	- - - - - - - -	*Eschaudez,*	-
MAZ	– –	Elisiez bien deux ou trois fois	et les eschaudez	et lavez
BN	*Hanons.*	*Esliere*	*et eschauder*	*et laver*
VAT	**Hannons.**	**Soient bien esleuz,**	**eschaudez**	**et lavez**

visible beside the *P* drawn by the illuminator. Paul Aebischer reads this name in *VAL* as *Parche* (despite the fact that the first vowel is clearly an *e*), but notes that this name is an "erreur qui se trouve aussi dans *N* [the Bibliothèque Nationale manuscript]": *Vallesia*, 8 (1953), p. 98. Pichon and Vicaire read *BN* as *Perche*, which, again clearly, the word in BN is not. Aebischer changes the *Parche* he reads in *VAL* to *Seiche* presumbably on the authority of *VAT* alone.

[2] *Menagier de Paris*, §224; p. 205.

[3] This preparation may be related to what the *Enseignements* calls *Seiches en chivé d'oignons, assez frites en uile* (p. 187, l. 218; *Petit traité*, p. 225).

[4] "Aucuns, aprés ce qu'elle est pellee et mise par morceaulx, la tiennent et remuent longuement en la paelle pour gecter son humeur et sa liqueur, laquelle l'en doit souvent gecter et purer. Et quant elle ne gecte plus riens, l'en l'essuye comme dessus" (*Menagier*, *loc. cit.*).

[1] "Oistres en civé, cuites en eve avant e oignons, au poivre e au safren e a l'aillie d'alemandes" (p. 187, l. 220; *Petit traité*, p. 226).

VAL	– – *frisiez en huille*	*et oignons avec,*	*et de la*
MAZ	tresbien, puis frissiez en huille	et en oignons	et de la
BN	*tresbien, puis frioler en huille*	*aveques oingnons*	*et y*[1]
VAT	– – **et aprés friolez en huille**	**et en ongnons miciez, avec**	

VAL	*poudre.*	– –
MAZ	poudre fine;	et des haulx.
BN	*poudrés de la poudre d'espices;*	*aux aillés vers.*
VAT	**pouldre d'espices;**	**et mengiez aux bons aulx blans.**

Cockles and mussels were apparently commonly available foodstuffs in the fourteenth century, at least in some parts of France: all four manuscript copies of the *Viandier* have included recipes for them, and the *Menagier de Paris* enlarges upon these recipes when in turn he comes to copy them. In both *VAL* and *MAZ* they occupy the last two positions in the chapters on fish; *Y* later appends a recipe for lobster after them.

Z has amplified the recipe for cockles somewhat by adding, in particular, directions designed to ensure that the meat of this mollusc is in good condition and clean before it is fried.[2] There appears to be some confusion about a verb that *Z* introduces, here and in the next recipe: *eslisiez.* In both instances *BN* writes a supposed infinitive, *esliere*, and *VAT* uses the past participle of the verb *eslire.* At its previous occurences in the *Viandier, esleu* is used with regard to wheat (Recipe 63 *BN*) and garden cress (Recipe 153 *BN*), and *eslisiez* is an imperative used about rice (Recipe 71 *VAL* and *VAT*). The meaning of the word is perhaps not always understood by the scribes. *Eslisiez* is likely a derivative of *lise*, meaning "sand."[3] What the *Viandier* intends is that the cook take care that no grain of sand (or dirt) remain among the wheat, rice or garden cress, or on the flesh of the shellfish he is about to cook. Later copyists, including the *Menagier*, understand the verb to be *eslire*, "to cull."

The serving sauce for cockles varies from manuscript to manuscript. The *Menagier* agrees with *BN*,[4] but *VAT* leaves the herbs out of his garlic sauce.[5]

150. Moules

VAL	*Moullez.*	– – – – – – – –	*Cuitez en vin*
MAZ	– –	Elissiez tresbien et lavez iii ou iiii fois	et cuisiez en aigue,
BN	*Moules.*	*Esliere bien* – – – – –	*et cuire en eaue*
VAT	**Moules.**	– – – – – – – –	**Cuites en eaue**

[1] *et y* followed by *frioles* which is stroked out.

[2] The *Menagier de Paris* prefaces his copy of *Y*'s version of *Hanons* with detailed advice on how to distinguish between fresh cockles and those that "sont de vielle prise" (§221; p. 204).

[3] Tobler-Lommatzsch: "Slamm"; Godefroy: "Sable en général, terre molle, glaise."

[4] "Mengiez aux ailletz vers clarectz"; the *Menagier* then adds directions on how to obtain the green colour in this sauce (*loc. cit.*).

[5] See the two sauce recipes at §157 and §158.

VAL		*et aue,*		*persil avec;*
MAZ		vin	et sel	et beurre fres;
BN	*un pou*	*et du vin*	*et du sel;*	- - - - - -
VAT		**et du vinaigre avec,**		**et de la mente, qui veult; et puis,**

VAT **au drecier, de la pouldre d'espices, et aucuns y veullent du beurre;**

VAL	- - - - - - -	- - - - - -	*aux aulx.*
MAZ	et maingier au vin aigre.	- - - - - -	- - -
BN	*mengier au vin aigre.*	- - - - - -	- - -
VAT	**mengier au vinaigre**	**ou au verjus vert**	**ou aux aulx vertz:**

et si en fait on du civé, qui veult.

As in the previous recipe for cockles, *Z* adds a direction here for cleaning mussels of sand or dirt.

VAT makes a surprising number of changes in this recipe, referring to practices that are only in part reflected by other manuscripts of the *Viandier*. While the *Menagier* repeats the version of this recipe that is copied by *BN*,[1] he too appends an alternative that involves boiling with old verjuice and parsley. This preparation is then served with fresh butter: "C'est tresbon potage," he comments.[2]

The *civé* mentioned by *VAT* would be prepared by frying the mussels with onions in oil, as was done with both the oysters and the cockles.

151. Escrevices de mer

BN *Escrevices de mer. Cuire en vin et en eaue ou au four;*
VAT **Escrevices de mer. Cuites en vin et en eaue ou mises ou four;**

BN *mengiés au vin aigre.*
VAT **et mengiez en vinaigre.**

An addition by *Y* to the end of the chapters on sea-fish, this recipe for lobsters, or sea crayfish, apparently did not suggest any variants in either *BN* or *VAT*. Where the *Menagier de Paris* deletes the salt from the *Viandier*'s recipe for mussels (§150), he adds it here when cooking lobster.[1]

---

[1] The notable difference in the *Menagier*'s echo of *Y* is that he contradicts *Y* and *Z* by writing "sans sel" when mussels are cooking (§222; p. 204). *VAT*, it should be noted, omits salt at this point.

[2] This butter is indicated by *MAZ* as an ingredient in the cooking pot, though *VAT* shows it as an optional garnish.

[1] The *Menagier* also provides a gloss for the name of this crustacean: "Escrevisses de mer doivent estre cuictes en four, et dit l'en *langoustes* ... " (§223; p. 205). Chiquart indicates that *langoustes* are to be served with vinegar, as in the *Viandier* (*Du fait de cuisine*, f. 56v).

Escrevices de mer are not mentioned in the *VAT* Table, but in any case the compiler of the Table has transferred both *Hannons* and *Moules*, along with *Aloze* (Recipe 143), *Fuccus* (seal, not mentioned in any existing manuscript of the *Viandier*), *Ables* (Recipe 144), *Esturjon* (Recipe 146) and *Seiche* (Recipe 147), back to the chapter on round sea-fish.

Viande de Quaresme *(BN)*

152. Flans, tartes en Karesme

VAL	*Flans, tartez en karesme*	*qui ont saveur de formage.*
MAZ	Pour faire flaons et tartres en karesme	qui auront savour de fromaige.
BN	*Pour faire flaons et tartes en quaresme.*	
VAT	**Pour faire flans ou tartres en karesme.**	

VAL	*Prenez rufvez,*[1] *laitancez de lux, de carpes,*
MAZ	Prener tanches, lue[2] et carpes et parexpaler les ruves et les laictances,
BN	*Prennés tenches, lus, carpes*
VAT	**Prenez tenches, lux, carpes**

VAL	*du saffren*	– – – – – –	*destrempé de lait d'amandez*
MAZ	et du saffrain,	broyer tout ensamble	et destremper de laic d'amandres
BN	*et almendes,*	*broiés tout ensemble,*	*et du saffron pour un pou de couleur*
VAT	**et amendes**	**et broyez tout ensemble,**	**et du saffren pour ung pou coulourer,**

VAL		*et de vin blanc;*	*metez du succre et le poisons*
MAZ		et de vin blanc;	puis en faictes flaons et tartres;
BN	*donner,*	*puis deffaitez de vin blanc*	*et en faites vos flans*[3] *et tartres;*
VAT		**puis deffaictes de vin blanc**	**et puis emplez voz flans et tartes;**

VAL	*avec lez letancez sans lez airestez; faitez vos flaons et vos tartez.*
MAZ	et que y soit fourt que les arestes et les testes.
BN	*puis sucrés par dessus quant ilz seront cuitez.*
VAT	**et quant ilz seront cuitz mettez du succre dessus.**

BN *Item, en autre maniere: prengnés anguilles et en ostés les testes et les getés et les queuez ossi, et broiés bien le remanant avec saffren deffait d'un pou de vin blanc; puis emplés vos flans et sucrés du sucre quand ils seront cuis.*

---

[1] *rufvez*: the manuscript appears to read *eufuez*. Aebischer imagined "Prenez *et filez* laitancez" (*ed. cit.*, p. 99).

[2] *lue*: *sic*.

[3] *flans* followed by *et sucres du sucre* which is stroked out, and then the phrase *et en faites vos flaons* is repeated.

The order of the recipes at this point in the *Viandier* varies from manuscript to manuscript.[4] In *VAL* and in the *VAT* Table (but not in the text of *VAT* itself), the recipes for fish and for crustaceans are followed immediately by the chapters on sauces, and these latter are followed in turn by the supplementary recipes 152 and 153.[5] In *BN* this supplementary material, which is headed by a chapter title, "Viande de quaresme"—a title unique among all the manuscripts and only partially accurate—is inserted between the fish and the crustacean recipes; then the sauce recipes follow the crustaceans. In *MAZ* and in *VAT* the series fish/crustaceans is followed by the supplementary material, augmented in *VAT* by Recipe 154, after which the sauces are copied.

What may have happened to account for this diversity in the order of the recipes in the various manuscripts is that *O* composed a *Viandier* that concluded with a sequence of fish/crustaceans/sauces; to this, *VAL*, or some copy before *VAL*, seems to have appended Recipes 152 and 153. *Z* then tried to improve the overall sequence of recipes by rearranging the order of these additional pieces, inserting them just ahead of the chapter on sauces. They are, after all, designed for, or at least appropriate for, use on meatless days, and therefore seem to belong in principle with the fish recipes. The first dishes in this Recipe 152 are in fact fish preparations. This rearranged sequence is maintained by *Y*, *BN* temporarily passing over cockles, mussels and lobster in favour of the two supplementary recipes, §152 and §153.

For some reason that is not clear—he may perhaps have had access to more than one manuscript of the *Viandier*—the compiler of the Table that appears in *VAT* seems to have "restored" the supplementary material (Recipes 152 and 153), augmented by two further recipes for various pies, to the position we may conjecture they "originally" occupied, as this is seen in *VAL*, at the very end of the book. For no very good reason this present edition adheres to the sequence of recipes found in *MAZ*, a sequence that was thus presumably established by the efforts of *Z*.

The Lenten custard pies of Recipe 152 are represented in the *Enseignements* by a recipe that is quite similar to what we find in *VAL* and *MAZ*.[6] Even more interestingly, the long addition made by *BN* at the end of the *Viandier* recipe is textually close to a second recipe for *Flaons en Caresme*, which precedes the other, in the *Enseignements*.[7] A variation of this eel flan turns up later as *Flaons cochus* (Recipe 194) among the additions copied by *VAT*.

Apart from this "extra" recipe offered by *BN*, though, it is clear that *VAL* and *MAZ* on the one hand, and *BN* and *VAT* on the other, are not describing the same dish. For *VAL* and *MAZ* this is a "roe pie," the fish milt and roe lending a cheese-like flavour to the

---

[4] See the chart in the Introduction, above.

[5] The *VAT* Table promises two further recipes, "Pour faire aultres flans et tartes" and "Pour faire pastés en pot" (§§178 and 179).

[6] "Se vos volez fere pastez qui aient savor de fromage, ou flaons en Caresme" (*Enseignements*, p. 186, l. 174; *Petit traité*, p. 223).

[7] "Se vos volez fere flaons en Caresme, prenez anguilles si en ostez les arestes . . . " (*Enseignements*, p. 185, l. 166; *Petit traité*, p. 222).

custard filling—hence the qualification found in the title for the dish in *VAL* and in *MAZ*.[8] For *BN* and *VAT* there is no mention of roe being a distinct ingredient: as apparently conceived by *Y* this is merely a multiple-fish pie, similar to fish pies that abound in Chiquart and in English cookery manuals of the period.[9] That these are two distinct dishes is confirmed by the *Menagier* who makes of the *Viandier*'s recipes three paragraphs under the general heading of "Flaons en Karesme": the first of these is *BN*'s saffron eel tart; the second is the recipe using fish roe—"flaons ont saveur de frommage quant l'en les fait de laitances de lus, de carpes ... "; and the last employs "char de tanches, lus, carpes."[10]

Among the variants in the recipe—most of which arise from the different concepts that *O* and *Y* had of the nature of the dish—we might observe that tench is added by *Z* to the pike and carp mentioned by *VAL* as a source for the roe. According to *VAL*, sugar is included in the pie, whereas *Y* uses the sugar as serving garnish.

153. Poree de cresson

VAL	*Pour faire poree de cresson.*	– – –
MAZ	– – – – – –	– – –
BN	*Poree de cresson.*	*Metés parboullir,*
VAT	**Poree de cresson.**	**Prenez vostre cresson et le faictes boullir**

VAL	*Hachiez menu,*	– – –	– – – – – –
MAZ	Hachés croisson assés et	grant foison	et une poignis de brectes
BN	– – – – –	– – –	*une poingnié de betes*
VAT	– – – – –	– – –	**et une pongnee de bettes**

VAL			*frisiez en huille,*
MAZ	avec,		frissiez en huille
BN	*avequez,*	*puis la tornez et hachiés et*	*friolés en huille,*
VAT	**et mettés avec,**	**puis la miciez et**	**friolés[1] en huille**

---

[8] The French word *ruves* turns up in the name of the English dish *Rygh in sawce* (*Forme of Cury*, §105). Properly this term refers to only the hard roe or eggs of the female fish; *laitancez* denotes the soft roe or milt of the male.

[9] Chiquart, *Du fait de cuisine*, §29, f. 55v, *Tartres de poyssons*; Austin, p. 47, *Tartes of fysshe*; *Liber cure cocorum*, p. 41, *Chewetes on fysshe day*.

[10] *Menagier de Paris*, §247; p. 216. It is tempting to imagine that the disappearance of the word *laitances* and the appearance of the fish *tanches* may have been occasioned by the same scribal error. It may be noted in passing that the fish specified for this pie in *Y* are those that, possessing a skin coating of *limon*, lend themselves particularly to making good jelly or galantine: see Recipe 68, above.

[1] The manuscript reads *frioles et hachiez en huille* with the word *hachiez* stroked out.

VAL *boullez tresbien;* - - - -
MAZ et puis le mecter boulir en lait d'amandres; - - - - -
BN *puis la metez boullir en lait d'almendes;* - - - - -
VAT **et puis la mettez boullir en lait - - - si vous la voulez telle;**

VAL - - - - - - - - *metez du formage avec, qui veult.*
MAZ - - - - - - - - - - - -
BN *ou charnage, a la char ou au beurre ou au fromage;*
VAT **ou en charnage, en l'eaue de la chair ou au frommage,**

MAZ et saler appoint.
BN *soit sallee apoint, et le cresson soit bien esleu.*
VAT **ou toute crue sans riens y mettre, se vous la voulez ainsi. Et est bonne**

VAT **contre la gravelle.**

Poree is a term which originally referred to a dish made of *poireaux*, leeks, but by the time the *Viandier* uses the term it had come to designate any sort of stew made of leafy vegetables in general.

In Recipe 154, *VAT* lists four types of *poree*, those made from chard, cabbage, turnip greens and, lastly, leeks—the *poreaulx* for which the dish had become known. Chiquart speaks of a *porree verde*, as if this might be a standard dish made from any leafy vegetables—what we might today call vegetable greens or just "greens." In the *Du fait de cuisine* this *porree verde* is to be served at a dinner in the same menu as large joints of beef and mutton.

The possibility of including a handful of chard, the green part of whose leaf can be stewed like spinach, is introduced into this recipe by *Z*. The recipe as modified by *Z* is reproduced in its essentials by the *Menagier*.[2] As *VAT* observes in a concluding remark, the medicinal properties of garden cress, particularly for the urinary tract, were well established in the doctrine of contemporary physicians. Aldobrandino distinguishes between river cress and garden cress: the garden variety is warm and dry at the beginning of the third degree, that is, in the extreme, and "destoupe les voies du fie et des rains, et fait bien oriner."[3]

154. D'autres menuz potaiges ...

VAT **D'autres menuz potaiges come poree de bettes, chouz, navetz, poreaulx, veel au jaunet, et potaiges de ciboulles sans autre chose, poys, feves frasees, pillez ou coullez ou atout le haubert, chaudun de porc, brouet**

[2] *Menagier de Paris*, §50; p. 140.

[3] *Le Regime du corps*, p. 172. Among the cries of street vendors in Paris at this time were "Cresson de fontaine!" and "Bon cresson orlenois!" (Guillaume de la Villeneuve, *Crieries de Paris* in Étienne Barbazan, *Fabliaux et contes*, vol. 1, pp. 276–286).

aux yssues de porc—femmes en sont maistresses et chascun le sçait faire; et des trippes, que je n'ay pas mises en mon Viandier, sçait on bien comment elles se doibvent mengier.

VAT still uses the word *poree* in the sense of a sort of vegetable stew, as it was used by other manuscripts in the previous recipe for *Poree de cresson.*[1]

The *veel au jaunet* is undoubtedly similar to one of the *au jaunet* recipes for mutton, tripe or leg of beef that are provided by the *Menagier.*[2]

A recipe for a *Chaudun de porc* has been copied by all four manuscripts as the first item (Recipe 10) in the chapter on "Potages lyans." The next item in the present listing, *Brouet aux yssues de porc*, suggests that the *chaudun* of Recipe 10 may also be considered to be a *brouet*; indeed, it is so called in the *Liber de coquina*, II, §59.

Saulces non boullues (VAL, MAZ2, BN, VAT)

155. Cameline

VAL	*Cameline.*	*Broiez gingembre,*	*grant foison de canele,*	-
MAZ	- - - - - -	Broyés gigimbre,	cannelle grant foison,	-
MAZ2	Saulse cameline.	Broyés gigimbre	et cannelle grant foison,	giroffle,
BN	*Cameline.*	*Broiés gingembre,*	*canelle grant foizon,*	*girofle,*
VAT	**Pour faire cameline.**	**Prenez gingenbre,**	**canelle et grant foison,**	**girofle,**

---

[1] This is the nature of the dish that is generically called *Poretam viridem* in the *Tractatus* (part V, §3). The recipe for *Omnis poreta communiter* that follows in the *Tractatus* (part V, §4) provides even more universally applicable directions.

For the *Menagier*, *poree* has also become a generic term for the leafy vegetables themselves. These include "bectes, feuilles de violectes, espinars et laictues, orvale" (§225; p. 207). Boiled cabbage must have been very common in the diet of the time: the *Menagier* assumes that his cook will have a ready supply of cabbage water to draw upon as an ingredient (§§281 and 282; pp. 232 and 233).

[2] *Menagier*, §§68–70; p. 149. The yellow colour in each case is supplied by saffron. The boiled sauce known as *poivre jaunet* is, in the *Y* manuscripts, one of the most commonly used serving sauces for cold-complexioned meats. It is indicated for use with goose (Recipe 36), for turtle-dove (Recipe 48), and for suckling pig (Recipe 60).

An example of a recipe for preparing mutton, veal or beef tripe can be read in the *Sent soví*, §183. The same Catalan cookbook contains recipes for *Porada o cebada* (§§95 and 96; and Appendix I, §69); these dishes correspond perhaps to the *Viandier*'s *poree de poreaulx* and *potaige de ciboulles*. The *Sent soví* has as well a recipe for *Janet a tota carn* (§154) in which the meat is chopped into pieces and cooked in a sauce comprising ground liver, parsley, saffron, spices, wine, vinegar and egg yolks. See also the *Potatge de janet de moltó*, *Janet de gallines* and *Janet de cabrit* in the *Libre del coch*, §§39, 40 and 41.

VAL	- - - -	-	*poivre long;*	
MAZ	graine de paradis,	mastic,	poivre long;	colez
MAZ2	graine de paradis,	mastic,	poivre long qui . l veult;	et puis coulez
BN	*graine,*	*macis,*	*poivre lonc qui veult;*	*puis coullés*
VAT	**grainne de paradiz,**	**mastic,**	**poivre long qui veult;**	**puis coullez**

VAL	*halé*	*trempé en vin aigre*	*et verjus,*	*tout coullé ensemble.*
MAZ	pain halez	tramper en vin aigre,	- -	coulez tout ensemble.
MAZ2	pain halés,	tramper en vin aigre,	- -	et atramper tout apoint
BN	*pain*	*trempé en vin aigre,*	- -	*et atrempés tout*
VAT	**pain**	**trempé en vin aigre,**	- -	**et passez**

MAZ2	et salez.
BN	*et sallés apoint.*
VAT	**et sallez bien a point.**

The chapter on unboiled sauces is opened in all four manuscripts of the *Viandier* by the recipe for cameline sauce, one of the most widely used on the late mediæval table. When *MAZ(X)* recopies the series of sauce recipes from some second manuscript, he begins again with cameline. To distinguish between the first and the second series of recipes at this point in the Mazarine's *Viandier* I have assigned the siglum *MAZ2* to the latter. Of the unknown source manuscript used by *MAZ(X)* we can say, at the very least, that it appears to derive from a parent other than *Z*, and that it did show titles for each of these sauces.

Cameline is basically a cinnamon sauce—hence the recommendation to the cook that the cinnamon be measured generously. Where *jance* (Recipes 166–168) is essentially a ginger sauce and is boiled, *cameline* has cinnamon as its predominant ingredient and is unboiled.[1]

Although the spice list for cameline in *VAL* is relatively brief, subsequent copies testify to a progressive accretion until it becomes, next to the fish preservative of Recipe 162,[2] the richest of all of the sauces in this chapter. Into this list of ingredients *Z* adds grains of paradise and a substance that is copied in *MAZ*, *MAZ2* and *VAT* as mastic;[3] *Y*, in turn, adds cloves and at the same time makes the pepper optional. *BN* alone writes "mace"

[1] "*Camelinus*—fercula et salsamenta ... alia cinereum fere colorem usurpant et vocantur celebrato nomine camelina, quia colorem pilorem cameli pretendunt. J. Godard *Ep*. 223" (Latham, *Dictionary of Medieval Latin)*. "*Camelinus*—of a camel; with reference to a camel-coloured sauce" (*ibid.*). The translator of Bartolomeo Sacchi's *De honesta voluptate* (the *Platine en françoys*) writes *sausse canelline* as if there were a relationship between the name of the sauce and its main ingredient, *canelle*. See the comment of Hieatt and Butler in *Curye on Inglysch*, p. 213, *s.v. Sawse camelyne*.

[2] Preserving sauces tended always to depend upon the combination of a wide variety of potently warm and dry ingredients, rather than upon any single warming and drying spice.

[3] In *MAZ*'s copy of Recipe 112, the word could be *mascic*. Mastic, a lentisk resin tasting strongly of pine tar, was used medicinally in the Middle Ages; the illustrations that Tobler-Lommatzsch (vol. 5, col. 1238) has gathered are exclusively medical. Castorina Battaglia has a

rather than "mastic." This spice should almost certainly have been written as "mace" in all cases; we can understand how a spelling such as *mascit* in *Z* could have led to a copyist's error. The word is variously spelled *macy*, *macis*, *marcis*, *maciz*[4] and *macit* at this period. Later cookery books include plain nutmeg[5] as well in their recipes for cameline sauce.[6]

If properly used by *MAZ2* and *BN*, the verb *atremper* indicates a tempering of the warmth of the spices by the cool vinegar. Perhaps not understanding the technical sense of this verb, or not seeing any need for the word, *VAT* writes simply *passer*: "sieve."

The use of verjuice with the vinegar is not mentioned by any manuscript other than *VAL*.[7]

---

description of fourteenth-century commercial mastic in her "Farmaci," §102, p. 519: "Masties (Olio masties): Mastice. 'L'olio di mastice di Mesue della seconda descrizione era a base di mastice in olio rosato omfagino (de olive immature) e vino spiritoso; si cuoceva a bagno maria sino a consumazione del vino'" (C. Rubiola, C. Masino, "Inventario, debiti e crediti di un manoscritto de spezieria toscana del sec. XIV," *La Farmacia Nuova* (Turin), vols. 4-5-6 (1966), pp. 36–37. See Pegolotti, p. 370; W. Heyd, *Histoire du commerce du Levant au moyen-âge*, 2 vols. (Leipzig, 1885–86), vol. 2, pp. 633–5; and R. Landry, *The Gentle Art of Flavoring*, tr. B.H. Axler (London and New York, 1970), pp. 156–157.

Mastic is extremely rare in mediæval European cooking. It is not used in the *Enseignements*, in the *Menagier* or in the *Du fait de cuisine*. To my knowledge it is not in any mediæval Italian recipe collection, in English cookery of the period, nor in the *Sent soví* or the Portuguese Cookbook. See Wilson, *Petits Propos Culinaires*, 7 (1981), p. 14 and n. 3. Its presence in the *Viandier* remains doubtful.

[4] In the *Menagier de Paris*'s recipe for *Hericot de mouton* (§64; p. 148) one of the manuscripts shows *maciz*, whereas the two others have *matiz*. In the *Viandier*'s *Hericot* (Recipe 4 *VAT*) the spice is *macis*. And it should be noted that in Recipe 7 *MAZ* writes *mascit* for mace.

[5] "Le *mascie* est li fuelle de le nois muscate qui demeure entor lui ausi com les fueilles qui demeurent antor les noisetes" (Aldobrandino, p. 190). See Colin Clair, *Of Herbs and Spices* (London and New York, 1961), pp. 65–66; and W. Heyd, *op. cit.*, pp. 644–648.

[6] *Menagier*, §271; p. 230. Chiquart's cameline sauce (*Du fait de cuisine*, §44, f. 69v) combines toast, wine, vinegar, cinnamon, ginger, grains of paradise, cloves, pepper, mace, nutmeg, sugar and salt. The simplest form of cameline may well be that unnamed blend of cinnamon, sugar and vinegar (or verjuice when it is in season) described in the *Sanitatis conservator* (*ed. cit.*, p. 18). See also the plain, unnamed cameline sauce in the *Northern-European Cookbook*, §6; the *Salsa camallina* in the *Sent soví*, §51, which is likewise comparatively simple; the *Salsa camelina* in the *Tractatus*, part V, §11 (*ed. cit.*, p. 394); and the *Salsa camellina* in the *Libre del coch*, §109 and n1. The same name was used to identify what is clearly a wide variety of mixtures.

[7] In the *De saporibus* of Magninus (*ed. cit.*, p. 187), the cameline sauce specified for roast rabbit makes use of verjuice in summer and wine and vinegar in winter. The choice of liquid creates a relatively cooler or warmer sauce, appropriate to the season.

156. Aulx camelins

VAL	*Aulx camelins.*	*Broiez canele et pain;*	*deffetez de vin*
MAZ	– – – –	Broyés cannelle, pain et haulx;	deffaicte de vin
MAZ2	Haulx camelins.	Broyer cannelle, haulx et pain;	deffait de vin
BN	*Aulx camelins.*	*Broiés canelle et pain et aulx*	*et deffaites de vin*
VAT	**Aulx camelins.**	**Broyez aulx, canelle et pain**	**et deffaictes de vin**

VAL	*aigre*	*et de verjus; broiez avec du foye de raye.*
MAZ	aigre	et de verjus; et y broyés du foye de la roye avec.
MAZ2	aigre.	
BN	*aigre.*	
VAT	**aigre.**	

Cameline garlic sauce is not merely a variant of the previous cameline sauce. More simple than the regular cameline, this mixture comprises just two main ingredients, the cinnamon that gives it its character, and garlic. *VAL*'s omission of this garlic is purely an oversight. The use of this sauce is not as widespread as that of regular cameline: in the *Viandier* it is in fact recommended as a dressing only for fish.[1]

The use of ray fish liver, a thickener, in *VAL* and *MAZ* only, and apparently suppressed by *Y*, is mentioned in the *Menagier de Paris* as a desirable option.[2]

157. Aulx blans

BN	*Aulx blans. Prennés aulx et pain, deffaites de verjus.*
VAT	**Aulx blans. Broyez aulx et pain et deffaittes de verjus.**

A series of garlic sauces follows the previous recipe for cameline garlic. This first variety in Recipe 157 is the most plain, but seems to have been inserted in the *Viander* by *Y*.

158. Aulx vers

VAL	*Aulx vers.*	*Broiez pain,*	*pecil;*	– –	*defaitez de verjus.*
MAZ	– –	Broyés pain, haulx,	parressi,	gigimbre;	destramper de verjus.
BN	*Aulx vers.*	*Broiés aux et pain*	*et verdeure,*	– –	*deffaites de verjus.*
VAT	**Aulx vers.**	**Broiez aulx, pain**	**et verdeur**	– –	**et deffaictes ensemble.**

For green garlic sauce there is only limited agreement about what should be used to produce the green colour. The *Menagier* suggests that the green could be provided by

[1] For stockfish (Recipe 122), dogfish (Recipe 123), brett (Recipe 130) and ray (Recipe 136). Both the *Menagier de Paris* (§273; p. 230) and the *Du fait de cuisine* (f. 56v) state that this sauce is called "Aulx camelins pour raye."

[2] *Menagier*, §273; p. 230.

parsley, sorrel[1] or rosemary, or by any combination of those.[2] The *Menagier* further states that the white and green garlic sauces are appropriate for dressing goslings and beef; the *Viandier*'s Recipe 36 for roast goose and gosling, and Recipe 3 for boiled beef, do indeed call for the use of these sauces.

In the *VAT* Table, between *Aux vertz* (Recipe 158) and *Aux aux harens fraiz* (Recipe 159), the scribe has written in the names of two further sauces, *Rappee* (§164) and *Aux atout la cotelle* (§165), the recipes for which, if indeed they appeared in his source, are passed over later in the body of the *Viandier* that was copied by *VAT*, along with all of the following sauce recipes but Recipe 159. *MAZ* alone mentions the use of the first sauce, *rappee*, recommending it for boiled barbel in Recipe 99 as an alternative to boiled yellow pepper sauce.

According to the *Menagier de Paris*, *Rappee* is made of ground verjuice grapes and ginger, with some whole verjuice grapes used as a topping garnish.[3] The nature of the second sauce, *Aux atout la cotelle*, can only be guessed, but in the next recipe we see unpeeled garlic used in a sauce.

159. Aulx a harens frais

VAL	*Aulx a harens frais.*	*Sans peller et sans couler.*
MAZ	– – – –	Broyés haulx sans parez, deffaicte de vin, et
BN	*Aulx a herans frais.*	*De moust, d'aulx sans peller, et broiez et dreciez*
VAT	**Aulx a harens frez.**	**Deffaictes de moult ou de verjus.**

MAZ les testes d'arens avec.
BN *atout les peleurez.*

This sauce, appearing in the *Menagier de Paris* in a slightly different form from what we read here,[1] is referred to nowhere else in the copies of the *Viandier* that have survived. The characteristic of *Aulx a harens frais* is that it has a coarse texture, including as it does among its ingredients the exterior skins of the garlic buds, unfiltered from the final sauce. This feature suggests that the sauce is likely related to the *Aux atout la cotelle* whose name appears in the *VAT* Table (§165); it is also likely to be a close relative of the following, a smoother-textured sauce described, but unnamed, in *MAZ* alone (Recipe 160).

---

[1] Chiquart uses sorrel to colour his green garlic sauce for eel (*Du fait de cuisine*, f. 72v; see the *Viandier*'s Recipe 107, above). The commentary to l. 62 of the *Regimen sanitatis salernitanum* indicates that sage can be used to produce a green garlic sauce in which the taste of the garlic will be somewhat allayed; this sauce is used on goose—although, the commentator avers, only by the common people.

[2] *Menagier de Paris*, §274; p. 231.

[3] *Ibid.*, §294; p. 237. In the *Viandier*'s broth called *Rappé* (Recipe 27) the major ingredients are the same as in the *Menagier*'s *Rappee* sauce. Concerning the most appropriate use of this sauce, the bourgeois author notes that "en juillet, quant le vertjus engrossist, est au jambon ou pié de porc."

[1] *Menagier*, §275; p. 231.

The present recipe underwent a variety of alterations from copy to copy, but the sauce remains apparently a simple and familiar preparation. It is the last sauce recipe that *VAT* copies from the traditional corpus of the *Viander*.

A question may be raised whether this sort of garlic sauce is to be used *on* fresh herring,[2] or whether it could possibly represent a late avatar of the classical *garum*. In this latter preparation, though, it must be admitted that the herring was decidedly not fresh.

160. [Unnamed]

MAZ Broyés haulx parés et amandres parees, destramper de verjus.

MAZ(X) has inserted a last garlic recipe into this chapter on unboiled sauces; as usual, *MAZ* has failed to name it. The *De saporibus* of Magninus Mediolanensis states that roast hens and pheasants should be eaten with a sauce that Magninus calls *Alleata cum amigdalis*. That sauce is likely to be what is described here.[1]

161. Saulce vert

VAL	*Saulce vert.*	*Grant foison de percil esfeulié sans lez tigez, gingenbre*
MAZ	– – –	Broyés gigimbre et parressi ensamble
MAZ2	Saulse verde.	Broyer parressi, pain, gigimbre, sauge;
BN	*Saulce verte.*	*Prennés pain, percil, gingembre,*

VAL	*pelé, du pain blanc sans haler,*	*broiez;*	*destrempez*
MAZ	et pain blanc sans halés,	et broyés tout ensamble;	destramper
MAZ2		– – – – – –	destramper
BN		*broiés bien,*	*et defaites*

VAL	*de verjus et de vinaigre*	*et collez.*
MAZ	de verjus et de vin aigre le plus.	
MAZ2	de vin aigre ou de verjus.	
BN	*de verjus et de vin aigre.*	

---

[2] Being an oily fish the herring is highly perishable and so is often met as a foodstuff in its smoked, pickled or salted form. Mongers did, however, regularly cry "Herans frais!" in the streets of Paris (see Guillaume de Villeneuve, *Les Crieries de Paris*, ed. Étienne Barbazan in *Fabliaux et contes*, vol. 1, p. 277). The *Bataille de Caresme et de Charnage* sees "Harens fres a la blanche aillie" recruited into the army of Lent (ed. Lozinski, l. 190). In the *Enseignements*, fresh herrings are eaten with garlic, among other possible garnishes (p. 187, l. 216; *Petit traité*, p. 225). In the *Tractatus* (part V, §19), fresh herring is roasted and the sauce for it is made as in *MAZ*, with its head.

[1] *Ed. cit.*, p. 187.

Green sauce is the first of the ginger sauces in the *Viandier* because most sauces based on ginger are boiled and will appear in the next chapter, "Saulcez boulluez," Recipes 164 ff. Used primarily on boiled fresh fish, this is a relatively simple mixture of ginger and parsley—to which greenery *VAT* adds sage—with verjuice and vinegar.[1] It is on the whole a mild sauce, used as a dressing wherever the meats or fishes are themselves relatively temperate in nature.

162. Saulce a garder poisson / Une soussie

VAL	*Saulce a garder poison.*		*Pain, percil, sauge,*
MAZ	– – – – – – – – – –	Broyés	pain, parcil, sauge,
MAZ2	Saulses pour garnir[1] poissons de mer.	Prener	pain, parressi, saulge,
BN	*Une saulce a garder poisson de mer.*[2]	*Prennés*	*pain, percil et sauge,*

VAL	*salmonde,*	– –	*gingenbre,*	*canelle,*	*girofle, noys muguetez,*
MAZ	sanemonde,	– –	gigimbre,	cannelle,	giroffle, noix muguetes,
MAZ2	salemonde,	– –	gigimbre,	cannelle,	
BN	*salmonde,*	*vin aigre,*	*gingembre,*	*fleur de canelle,*	

VAL	*poivre long,*			– – – –	*saffren*	
MAZ	poivre long,			– – – –	saffrain	
MAZ2	poivre long,	giroffle,	graine de paradis,	ung pol de	saffrain,	noix nuguetes;
BN	*poivre lonc,*	*girofle,*	*graine de paradis,*	*poudre de*	*saffren*	*et noix mugaites;*

VAL	– – – –	*deffait de vin et de verjus;*
MAZ	et ung pol de pain;	destramper de vin et de verjus et soit coulez
MAZ2	– – – –	destramper de vin aigre
BN	– – – –	– – – – – – – – –

[1] The *Enseignements* (p. 181, l. 19; *Petit traité*, p. 214) lists the ingredients for what it calls "la savor verte sans aux": pepper, ginger, parsley and sage, with verjuice or vinegar or wine. Magninus provides a little more detail for his *Salsa viridis*, which he honours by according it first mention in his sauce book: "Recipe petrosilli m [manus] i, rorismarini quartum m, unius panis assi ad quantitatem unius ovi, zingiberi albi 3 [dram] i, gariolfili xiii. Fiat salsa cum aceto sed in estate apponatur minus de speciebus et in hyeme plus. Iterum in hyeme in predicta salsa ponatur aliquantulum vini vel quod acetum sit minus forte" (*ed. cit.*, p. 187). Ingredients for a green sauce in the *Sanitatis conservator* (*ed. cit.*, p. 19) are parsley, mint, a little salt, all of this in vinegar; a little garlic is optional. See also the *Salsa viridis* in the *Tractatus*, part V, §10; p. 394; the *Salsa vert* in the *Sent soví*, §167; the *Salsa verda* in the *Libre del coch*, §139; and the *Saulse verd* of the *Recueil de Riom*, §39.

[1] *garnir*: the word is not distinct.

[2] The phrase *poisson de mer* is repeated.

VAL - - - - - *metez sur vostre poisson,* *coullez.*
MAZ par l'estermine, vergay, et mecter sur vostre poisson ;
MAZ2 - - - - - et mecter sur vostre poisson quant tout sera passez,
BN - - - - - - - - - - - - *quant tout sera passé,*

MAZ et aulcuns y mectent la sanemonde a toute la racine.
MAZ2 et soit vergay; et aulcun y mectent la sanemonde a tout la racine.
BN *soit vergay;* *et aucuns y metent la salmonde a tout la rassine.*

In keeping with the principle that a preservative should employ as varied a combination of herbs and spices as possible in order to warm and dry the meat or fish to which it is applied, this *Saulce a garder poison* contains three herbs and either six or seven spices. Given the large number of ingredients, it is surprising that there is among the four copies such relative agreement on the text of this recipe. *Y* (*BN* at any rate) adds grains of paradise to the spices found in *VAL* and *MAZ*.

The form of the word for herb bennet is a little hesitant from copy to copy; the *MAZ(X)* scribe even writes *sanemonde* (in accord with its Latin etymon, which held that the herb was both *sana* and *munda*) on both of its occurrences in his first copy of the recipe; however, when he comes to repeat the recipe (as *MAZ2*), he copies *salemonde* (the form written by *VAL*, *BN* and the *Menagier*[3]) in its first occurence, but returns to *sanemonde* for the second.

These variations in spelling or in form within *MAZ* allow a guess about the composition of the version of the *Viandier* that is found in the Bibliothèque Mazarine. The person who decided to write *sanemonde* in the last line of *MAZ2* ("et aulcun y mectent la sanemonde a tout la racine"), when what he had in his source for these repeated recipes was probably *salemonde*, was—again, in all likelihood—not the *MAZ* scribe himself. It was *X*, or *X*'s source, who recopied these sauce recipes from a *Y* source. He was sufficiently learned a person—an observation that can in no wise be made of the *MAZ* scribe himself—to recognize in his *Y* source a form of the name of the herb that was not etymologically proper, and to change it on its second occurence. The adjunction of the recipes numbered 118 to 133 in *MAZ* (what in this edition we call *MAZ2*) must surely date from some copy before the extant *MAZ* was produced.

While *VAT* does not copy this sauce for preserving fish, in his Table he has written, after the name *Sausse vert* for Recipe 161, the name of another sauce that he copies as *Une soussie* (§168 in the Table). When we turn to the *Menagier*, we find that the *Viandier*'s Recipe 161 for *Une saulce a garder poisson de mer* (as it is called in *BN*) turns up with the name *Ung soutyé vergay a garder poisson de mer*.[4] The generic name *Soussie* (with some

---

[3] *Menagier de Paris*, §277; p. 231.

[4] *Ibid.* "*Nota*," explains the author, "que le mot *soutyé* est dit de *soux*, pource qu'il est fait comme soux de pourcel. Pour poisson de eaue doulce ainsi se fait *chaudumé*, fors tant que l'en y met nulles herbes; et en lieu de herbes l'en y met saffran et noix muguectes et vertjus; et doit estre fin jaune et bouly et mis tout chault sur le poisson froit" (§277). In the Pichon edition of the *Menagier* (p. 231) the name of the sauce is read as *un soucié*. The *Libre del coch* contains a *Solsit*

uncertainty on our part about form and gender) seems therefore to have been introduced into the *Y* tradition in some copy before *VAT*.

This sauce has already been used by *Y* for the serving of brill (Recipe 138, above). At that point it is called both *souciee* and *souz*.

A second sauce listed at this point in the *VAT* Table is apparently a rather specialized garlic *jance* for cod. It is titled quite descriptively *Une bonne sausse de jance pour morue aux aulx*. This would seem to be the variety of *jance* mentioned by *VAT* alone in Recipe 126 for boiled fresh cod.

Saulces boullues (VAL, BN) ❧

163. La barbe Robert

VAT **La barbe Robert, autrement appelee la Taillemaslee.**

This sauce is not listed in the Table at the beginning of the *VAT* manuscript. A recipe for a *Saulce barbe Robert* is contained in the *Fleur de toute cuisine*: "Prenez oignons menus fris en saing de lart ou beurre selon le jour, verjus, vinaigre et moustarde, menue espice et sel et faictes bouillir tout ensemble. Ceste saulce sert a connins rostis et poisson frit tant de mer que d'autres oeufz fris [*sic*]."[1]

164. Poivre jaunet

VAL	*Poivre jaunet.*	*Broiez gingembre,*	*saffren*
MAZ	– – –	Broyés gigimbre, poivre long,	saffrain – –
MAZ2	– – –	Broyer poivre, gigimbre,	saffrain, pain alez,
BN	*Poivre jaunet.*	*Broiés gingembre,*	*saffren, pain hallé, et*

VAL	– – – – – –	*et girofle qui veult,*
MAZ	– – – – – –	et aulcuns y mectent graine de giroffle,
MAZ2	deffaicte de vin aigre	
BN	*deffaites de vin aigre*[1]	

---

de gallines o de moltó (§123); its editor, Veronika Leimgruber, glosses the generic term *solsit* as simply a "brou de carn amb espècies" (p. 138). According to Rudolf Grewe in his presentation of the *Northern-European Cookbook*, the *Sylt* of §7 is the Old German *sulza* (modern *Suelze* and Old Catalan *sols*); the term can be translated as "headcheese." See also the *Libre de sent soví*, §148, p. 166, n2.

[1] Ed. Pierre Pidoux (Paris, 1548), f. 45v. Pichon and Vicaire demonstrate that the family of printed sixteenth-century cookbooks of which the *Fleur de toute cuisine* is a member derives quite directly from the *Viandier*, and constitues what might be termed a later stage in its tradition. A sauce called simply "Robert" is listed among other sauces in the *Condamnacion de Bancquet* of Nicole de la Chesnaye (ed. P.L. Jacob in his *Recueil de farces, soties et moralités du quinzième siècle* (Paris, 1859), p. 310). The fifteenth-century printed edition of the *Viandier* has a dish that uses a "Saulce Robert" on "Pastés de poules" (ed. Pichon and Vicaire, p. 170).

[1] *vin aigre* followed by *et de verius* stroked out.

VAL *ung pou de verjus;* *boullir quant vollez*
MAZ deffaicte de verjus et de vin aigre; puis boulez quant vous voudrois
MAZ2 et la mecter boulir;
BN *et faites boullir;*

VAL *drecier.*
MAZ dressiez vostre viande.
MAZ2 – – – – – – et ung pol de giroffle et du verjus.
BN – – – – – – *et aucuns y metent graine et girofle au verjus.*

Two of the manuscripts, *VAL* and *BN*, as well as the *VAT* Table, recognize a new chapter that begins with this recipe for yellow pepper sauce.[2] The sauces that are grouped here require the ingredients to be boiled together and are brought warm to the table. There they function either as a presentation dressing over a meat or fish, or they are served in bowls, set to the side of the main dish, into which the person dining will dip a piece of meat or fish before eating it. In all of these boiled sauces the primary ingredient is either ginger and pepper or, in the case of the *jances* and the *poitevine*, ginger alone.

The yellow pepper sauce of this recipe 164 derives its characteristic colour from the saffron in it. It differs from the following black pepper sauce primarily in the absence of this saffron in the latter.[3]

Among the manuscript versions *Y* differs by introducing toast as a thickener; though the bread is toasted only lightly (*hallé* rather than *brullé*: see the next recipe), this addition changed the nature of the original yellow pepper sauce. *MAZ* writes "graine de giroffle," meaning perhaps "clou de giroffle."[4] Instead of this, *BN* writes "graine *et* giroffle," specifying two distinct spices; and *MAZ2* modifies the phrase to read "ung pol de giroffle."

165. Poivre noir

VAL *Poivre noir. Broiez gingembre et poivre ront, pain brulé,*
MAZ – – – Broyés gigimbre, poivre ront et pain bruler,
MAZ2 Poivre noir. Broyer gigimbre, poivre ront, pain bruler,
BN *Poivre noir. Broiés gingembre et pain brullé et poivre,*

[2] *VAT* has none of these recipes, even though he copied the names of all of them into his Table.

[3] The *Sanitatis conservator* has a recipe for a *piperatum* which is made "cum ... modico ... croco, quod tamen maxime in hyeme competit" (p. 19). The recipe for *Piperata* in the *Liber de coquina* (part II, §68) distiguishes between this yellow pepper sauce and the following black pepper sauce by the presence or absence in the mixture of saffron, and by the choice of bread or of toast. This recipe states that pepper sauce is used *pro vaccinis, cervinis vel caprinis*: for beef, stag-meat or goat-meat.

[4] As indeed *MAZ* will write in Recipe 173, and *VAT* in Recipes 192, 200 and 201. We may of course also insert some punctuation in the phrase and understand that *MAZ* intended, as *BN* did, two spices: "graine [de paradis], de giroffle." The word *granne* alone is used occasionally by Chiquart to designate *graine de paradis* (*e. g.*, ff. 37r, 69v).

VAL	*deffait de verjus et de vin aigre;*	*fetez boullir.*
MAZ	deffaicte de vin aigre et d'ung pol de verjus	et faicte boulir.
MAZ2	deffaicte de vin aigre	et faicte boulir.
BN	*deffaites de vin aigre et de verjus*	*et faites boullir.*

Where long pepper,[1] saffron and light toast are used in the yellow pepper sauce of the previous recipe, the black pepper sauce described here calls for round pepper[2] and dark toast.

166. Saulce / Jance au lait de vache

VAL	*Saulce de lait de vache.*	*Broiez gingenbre,*	*moiax d'eufs,*
MAZ2	Jasse de lait de vaiche.	Prenez	myeux d'euf
BN	*Jance au lait de vache.*	*Broiés gingembre,*	*moieux d'oeufs,*

VAL	*destrempés de lait;*	*faitez boullir.*
MAZ2	deffait de lait de vaiche,	et faictes boulir.
BN	*deffaites de lait de vache,*	*et faites boullir.*

The term *jance* is not known to *VAL*, these two ginger preparations in Recipes 166 and 167 being termed by him simply "sauces." Neither these *jances* nor the *Jance de gingembre* of Recipe 168, added by *Y*, is copied by *MAZ* in his first version of the sauces.

The warm and moist qualities of ginger make it particularly valuable as a condiment where only a very temperate sauce is required. It can be used to moderate the strength of other ingredients with which it is mixed (the extremely dry pepper or garlic of Recipes 164–5 and 167), or its own temperate virtues can be reinforced by such ingredients as we find in the present recipe.

This milk variety of *jance* is a simple boiled combination of ginger, egg yolks and cow's milk. It is not used with a dish in any existing copy of the *Viandier*.

167. Sauce / Jance aux aulx

VAL	*Sauce de aulx.*	*Broiez gingembre, aulx, amandez,*	*desfaitez*
MAZ2	Jansse aux haulx.	Broyer gigimbre, aux, amandres,	deffaicte
BN	*Jance aux aulx.*	*Broiés gingembre, aux, almendes,*	*desfaites*

VAL	*de verjus,*	*faitez boullir;*	*du vin blanc, qui veult.*
MAZ2	de verjus;	– – –	et y mecter du vin blanc.
BN	*de bon verjus.*	– – –	– – – – – –

[1] According to Platearius, *piper longum*, otherwise known as *macropiper*, is warm and moist in its qualities. It is appropriate for use on meats that are by nature cold and relatively dry, such as fresh boar (Recipe 7), geese (Recipe 36) and swan (Recipe 72). See also Aldobrandino, p. 184. On the various peppers see Colin Clair, *Of Herbs and Spices*, pp. 67–72; and Pegolotti, *ed. cit.*, p. 427.

[2] This variety of pepper is known as *piper nigrum* or *piper rotundum*, or *melanopiper*; it is the modern "black pepper." It is considered to be very warm and dry.

Garlic *jance* uses almonds as a binder rather than the egg yolks and milk of the previous recipe.[1] We met this sauce previously in the *Viandier* under the name of *Aillez blans* when it was used on roast eels (Recipe 107). In the *Du fait de cuisine* Chiquart's *Jance*[2] is used on roast poultry, and combines ginger, grains of paradise, almond paste, garlic, white wine and verjuice.

168. Jance de gingembre

BN	*Jance de gingembre. Prennés gingembre et almendes sans aux et deffaites de verjus, puis boullez; et aucuns y metent du vin blanc.*

The name of this sauce, *Jance de gingembre*, is tautological. The recipe for it, appended—perhaps by *Y*[1]—after the other varieties of *jance* have been described, makes what we might term your basic boiled ginger sauce. In fact the *Menagier* titles this recipe merely *Jance*.[2]

169. Une poitevine

VAL	*Une poitevinee.*	*Broiez gingenbre*	-	*et graine,*
MAZ	- - - -	Broyés gigimbre,	-	- -
MAZ2	Sause portemie.	Broye gigimbre,	giroffle,	graine de paradis,
BN	*Saulce poetevine.*	*Broiés gingembre,*	*girofle,*	*graine de paradis*

VAL	*pain brulé et vos foyez,*	*deffaitez de*
MAZ	pain bruler et le foye de vostre poulaille rotis,	deffaictes de
MAZ2	foyes, pain brulez,	- -
BN	*et de*[1] *vos foies, pain brullé,*	- -

VAL	*verjus;*	*faitez boullir avec du rost;*
MAZ	verjus et de vin;	et y mecter la graisse du rolz boulir aveques.
MAZ2	vin, verjus;	et faicte boulir, et la graisse de vostre rost;
BN	*vin et verjus;*	*et faites boullir, et de gresse de rost dedans;*

---

[1] See also the *Alleatum* in the *Sanitatis conservator*, p. 19; the *Alleata alba* and the *Sapor albus* on sturgeon, both in the *De saporibus* of Magninus, pp. 187 and 188; and the *Alleata* of the *Liber de coquina*, part II, §67; p. 410.

[2] The spelling that Chiquart's scribe, Jehan de Dudens, gives the word varies among *jance*, *jense*, *jensse* and *jansa* (ff. 26r, 67r, 69r, 72r, 83r).

[1] The source followed by *MAZ2* may have contained the *Jance de gingembre* but our scribe has been selective in the sauces he copies from this source.

[2] *Menagier de Paris*, §288; p. 234. The bourgeois author still insists upon adding "ung pou d'aulx" to the ginger and almonds of his "plain" *jance*. The same sauce (without garlic) is called *Salsa alba* in the *Sanitatis conservator*, p. 19. In the *Recueil de Riom* (§36) we read: "A grosse poulaille, de la jansse d'amendes de gingibre blanc et de verjust."

[1] *et de vos*: the manuscript reads *et des vos*.

VAL *verdissiez sur vostre rost, dreciez par escuellez.*
MAZ2 puis vercel sur vostre rolz adressiez par escuelles.
BN *puis verssés dedanz vostre rost ou vous dressiés par escueilles.*

That the name of this ginger sauce was not very generally known is apparent in the copy *MAZ2* makes of it. His *Portemie*[2] is a misreading of the form correctly copied by the *VAT* Table: *Une poitevine*. This is the name generally agreed upon when the sauce is recommended earlier in the *Viandier*, in the recipe for roast capons, hens and cockerels (Recipe 38).[3]

170. Espices qui appartienent / Espices qu'il fault ...

BN *Espices qui appartienent en cest present Viandier, premierement:*
VAT **Espices qu'il fault a ce present Viandier:**

BN *gingembre, canelle, girofle, graine de paradis, poivre lonc, macis,*
VAT **gingenbre, canelle, giroffle, graine de paradis, poivre long, espic,**

BN – – – *espices en poudre: fleur de canelle, saffran, garingal,*
VAT **poivre ront,** – – – – **fleur de canelle, saffren,** –

BN *noys mugaites.*
VAT **noiz muguectes, feulles de lorier, garingel, mastic, lores, conmin, succre, amandes, aulx, ongnons, ciboules, escalongnes.**
S'ensuit pour verdir: persil, salmonde, hoseille, fueille de vigne ou boujons, groseillier, ble vert en yver. Pour destremper: vin blanc, verjus, vinaigre, heaue, boullon gras, layt de vache, layt d'amendes.

Several of the foodstuffs listed by *VAT* in his paragraph as sources for green food-colouring do not, in fact, appear to be called for at all in the *Viandier*, at least such as we have it. There has been no mention of vine leaf or of unripened wheat, for instance. Considering, though, that the list is in part a series of suggested alternatives, the absence of a specific mention of these two items among the recipes should not be considered an oversight.

The identity of the "espice" *lores* in *VAT* is uncertain.

---

[2] When this sauce was mentioned in Recipe 38, *MAZ* wrote *portemine*.

[3] The *Menagier de Paris* copies this recipe (at §289; p. 234), adding toast to the ingredients and stating, as *Y* does, that the grease from the roast poultry should likewise be added to the sauce. (*Cf.* the procedure to be followed in making *dodine* for roast duck in Recipe 54.)

[Additional Recipes *(MAZ)*]

171. [Cameline Mustard Sauce]

MAZ Prener moustarde et vin vermoil et poudre de cannelle, et de succre assés, et tout deffaicte ensamble; et soit espés conme cannelle; ce est bons a tous rolz.

The *MAZ* scribe concludes his first copy of the *Viandier*'s sauces—from which two or three *jances* have been omitted—by the foot of his p. 142, according to the modern pagination of the Mazarine manuscript. At the top of p. 143 he begins a series of seven recipes, several of which are much more extensive and complex than what is generally found in the common material of the *Viandier* before this point. All of these recipes are untitled, as is the case with all of the sauce recipes *MAZ* has just copied, and appear to be for dishes that are unique among early French cookery manuals. The first two are for further sauces; the remainder are for a variety of other preparations.

Despite the indication here in Recipe 171 that this sort of mustard sauce (a mustard cameline?) is suitable for roast meats, the *Viandier* has suggested previously that mustard sauce should be used on boiled meats, specifically on boiled salt pork and mutton (Recipe 3) and on boiled salt boar (Recipe 7).[1]

Sugar has become a standard ingredient in these latter additions by *MAZ*, no fewer than five of the seven recipes indicating that it is a requirement.

The phrase "espés conme cannelle" should probably be "espés conme cameline."

172. [Marjoram Sauce]

MAZ Prener jus de marjoliaine doubce, aigue et atant de vin blanc et y mecter du gigimbre et vin, ung pol de giroffle, de cannelle et de succre.

There is no other use of marjoram in the *Viandier*.

173. [Stewed Poultry]

MAZ Cuisiez tresbien toumeaulx[1] de beuf—et garder la moille d'une part —et puis tirés vostre chart et ostez tout le gras du pout, et puis mecter dedans le demourant de vostre brouet maigre cuire chappons, poullés, pingons, perdris et quelcunque viande que vous voudrez; et

[1] Mustard, *sinapis*, is held by all authorities to be dangerously warm and dry, in the fourth degree for both qualities (Platearius, Crescentius, Aldobrandino, etc.). The earlier use by the *Viandier* of a mustard sauce on boiled meats, such as pork, which are themselves cold and moist seems the more reasonable application. One can only wonder whether, alas, the cook responsible for commenting "Ce est bons a tous rolz" was guided more by his palate than by his reason!

[1] *toumeaulx*: understand *trumeaulx*, "knuckle (of beef)."

poullés, pingons, perdris et quelcunque viande que vous voudrez; et y mecter cuire avec poivre ront, tout[2] entiers, et raisins de karesme entiers et la moille de beuf, puis passez pain blanc sans halez avec le boillon; affinez gigimbre, cannelle et noix miguetes, cloux, avec vin blanc grant foisson et verjus, et y mecter du saffrain et du succre; et dourez vostre poulaille entiere et le brouet dessus.

Thomas Austin published an English recipe for a dish that seems quite similar to this and is called *Pertrich stewyde.*[3]

174. [Stewed Mutton]

MAZ Prener mouton par pieces et cuilz en ung poult a pol d'aigue et y mecter du vin, adjouster oignons menus menusiez et parressi menu menusiez; et y mecter dedans de la poudre fine, du saffrain et du verjus et ung pol de vin aigre.

A similar recipe for mutton stew is published by Austin.[1] In the English recipe ginger, ground pepper and salt are used in addition to saffron and may be understood to be included here in the general term "poudre fine."

175. [Tortes of Herbs, Cheese and Eggs]

MAZ Prener parressi, mente, bedtes, espinoches, letuees, marjolienne, basilique et pilieux, et tout soit broyer ensamble en ung mortiez et destramper d'aigue clere et espreignez le jus; et rompés oeuf grant foison avec le jus et y mecter poudre de gigimbre, de cannelle et poivre long et fin fromaige gratusiez et du sel, tout batez ensamble; et puis faicte vostre paste bien teine[1] pour mectre en vostre bacin et la grandeur du bacin, et puis chassez bien vostre bacin et puis y mecter du sain de port dedans et puis vostre paste aprés dedans le dit

---

[2] *tout*: though the scribe has written what appears to be *but*, it is likely that the word should be *tout*. Whole pepper is specified in the English version of this recipe edited by Austin: "Take the pertryche, an stuff hym wyth hole pepir ... " (*Two Fifteenth-Century Cookery-Books*, p. 9). As well, the *Menagier* writes *tout*—"ysope, ozeille toute, marjolaine ... "—to describe unbroken sorrel (§277; see Brereton and Ferrier's Note to this passage).

[3] *Loc. cit.*.

[1] *Ibid.*, p. 72: *Stwed mutton.*

[1] *teine*: the sense of the word, which is indistinctly written, is plainly the *tenve* that was copied in Recipes 54, 136 *VAT*, and 201.

bacin et mecter vostre bacin sur les charbons et remecter dedans la paste du sain de porc; et quant il sera fonduz mectez[2] vostre grain dedans vostre paste et le couvrez de l'autre bacin et mecter du feu dessus conme dessoubz et lessez vostre tourtel[3] ung pol sechiez, puis descouvrés le bacin dessus et mecter sur vostre torte par bone maniere v myeux d'euf et de la fine poudre, puis remecter vostre bacin dressez conme devant et le lessez po a pol cuire et a petit feu de charbon et regarder souvent qu'elle ne cuise tropt; puis mecter du succre dessus a dressiez.

The *Menagier* has a recipe that begins, "Pour faire une tourte," and that is clearly related to this, though not entirely dependent upon it.[4] The dish is a sort of herb quiche.

Spinach, of Arabic origin as a foodstuff, is of relatively late introduction into European cookery.[5]

176. [An Egg Dish]

MAZ Prener des gastiaulx blans ou aultre pain blanc bien sec, puis le gratusiez; et prener du brouet de la chart de beuf ou de la poulaille et la mecter en ung bel pout et mecter boulir sur les charbons a petit feu, et mecter saffrain et fin fromaige gratusiez dedans; et premierement mecter vostre pain dedans vostre brouet quant il boudra; puis, adressiez, fillez euf, et les faicte espés conme ris; et, a dressiez sur les euf, mectez du fromaige gratussiez.

Eggs are poached hard in this yellow cheese sauce, and then served dressed in it as well, with grated cheese as a garnish.

177. [Clary Fritters]

MAZ Prener harbe qui se appelle orvale et la broyer et deffaicte de aigue clere, et y mecter et bater avec farine bien buretelee; et y mecter du miel avec et ung pol de vin blanc et le batez ensamble tant qu'il soit cleret; puis frissiez en huille per petites cuillerez conme l'on fait

---

2 The scribe wrote *mectez dedans* and then stroked out the second word.

3 *tourtes* appears to have been changed to *tourtel*.

4 *Menagier de Paris*, §250; p. 218.

5 See Wilson in *Petits Propos Culinaires*, 8 (1981), pp. 23–24. See also the use made of spinach in the dishes 96 and 190 of the *Libre de sent soví*; this collection dates from 1324.

buignés; et mecter bien de romany sur chacun fritel; et espreignés vous fritelles entre deux tranchens pour esgoutez l'uille, puis les mecter en ung bel pout neuf pres du feu; et mecter du succre a dressiez sur vous plat.

In the *Liber de coquina* another version of this recipe for fritters offers a broad choice in the matter of flavouring by specifying elderflowers or any other flower.[1]

Clary sage (*Salvia sclarea* L.) has tall flowering spikes and a taste reminiscent of grapefruit.[2]

S'ensuivent aucuns remedes et experimentz touchans le fait des vins et autres choses (VAT)

178. Pour amender moust ou vin nouvel ...

VAT **Pour amender et faire vermeulx moust ou vin nouvel pour vendre tantost. Mettez en ung muy de vin a la mesure de Paris iii deniers pesant de saffren moullu et destrempé du moust mesmes et, en chascun muy, plain pot de miel qui tiengne ii deniers de vin a xvi deniers boully en une paelle, et le faictes tresbien mouvoir et puis le laissiez refroidier; et, ce fait, prenez une plainne escuelle de farine de fromment et destrempez ces trois choses emsemble; si sera bel et bon pour boire et vendre tantost.**

The section on wines forms a natural supplement to the *Viandier*. Whatever may have been the source that *VAT* drew upon for these "recipes," such practical advice for the care of wines was not unusual in late mediæval household manuals,[1] and appears also in

---

[1] "Flores sambuci vel alios flores quoscumque volueris" (*Liber de coquina*, part III, §7: *De fristellis*). The name of the *Viandier*'s recipe may perhaps have been *Fritels*.

[2] Theodora FitzGibbon, *The Food of the Western World* (New York, 1976), p. 405. See also Colin Clair, *Of Herbs and Spices*, p. 142; and Robert Landry, *The Gentle Art of Flavoring*, p. 68.

[1] The *Menagier de Paris* itself is the best example of this type of manual, of course. In the Brereton and Ferrier edition a section on curing the various ills to which wine is subject is found at pp. 133–135 (in the Pichon ed., vol. 2, pp. 67–70). There is no apparent influence, one way or the other, between the *Menagier* and the Vatican copy of the *Viandier* with respect to this chapter. Among early printed books the *Edificio di ricette* (Venice, 1541; tr. as *Bastiment de receptes*, Lyon, 1541) contains recipes for improving wine and vinegar, but again these seem not to bear any close similarity to what we read in the *Viandier*. In their edition of the *Viandier* Pichon and Vicaire suggest that Taillevent may have compiled this section separately and then appended it onto his collection of culinary recipes (p. 63).

fourteenth-century cookery books.[2]

This first prescription aims at improving the taste of must or new wine, and at giving it a rich red colour.

179. Pour garder vin d'engresser ...

VAT **Pour garder vin d'engresser et d'estre trouble. Mettez en ung muy de vin plaine escuelle de pepins de vin rouge seichiez et puis boulliz; et prenez lye de vin blanc et la faictes seichier et puis l'ardez tant qu'elle deviengne cendre; et en prenez plainne escuelle et mettez ou vaissel sans riens mouvoir.**

180. Pour tous vins degresser

VAT **Pour tous vins degresser. Prenez une escullee de pepins de vin rouge seullement seichiez et molluz, et de la gresse de la maniere ou couleur du vin plaine escuelle et ung levain de paste de ung denier, et demie livre d'alun et deux cloches de gingenbre et ung pou de cendre gravelee, toutes ces vi choses bien moulues et bien batues mettez ou vaissel et puis mouvez bien d'un court baston, fendu devant le bout en quatre, tant que l'escume en saille—et ne soit le baston que ung pié dedans le vaissel; et puis le vertochiez.**

These two recipes, 179 and 180, deal with the prevention and cure, respectively, of the development of an abnormally high degree of viscosity in wine, which condition may or may not be accompanied by a cloudy appearance. In all likelihood this is the "disease" qualified by Pasteur as slimy wine spoilage, *vin gras*, and is prevalent in wines with a relatively high alcoholic content. The bacteria responsible for this type of spoilage are generally controlled in modern winemaking by the addition of sulphur dioxide. It is probable that the tannic acid of the pulverized grape seeds, the sulphate of the alum,[1] and the tartar of the burnt

[2] In this category one may cite for instance the *Tractatus de modo preparandi et condiendi omni cibaria et potus* (Paris, Bibliothèque Nationale, manuscript lat. 7131, f. 94r), where there is a series of restorative recipes for wines. Of these the last, beginning "At vinum sit vendibile . . . ," requires the admixture of saffron, honey and wheat flour just as in the *Viandier*'s Recipe 178. The edition of the *Tractatus* published by Marianne Mulon is preceded (pp. 373–374) by an examination of similarities between this series of wine recipes on f. 94r and v and the chapter on wines in the *Viandier*.

[1] Balducci Pegolotti (p. 411) lists thirteen varieties of alum current in the commerce of the first half of the fourteenth century; these differ according to source and to nature. See L. Liagre, "Le commerce de l'alun en Flandre au moyen-âge," *Le Moyen Age*, 61 (1955), 176–206.

lees of the wine[2]—all of this rendered a little less unpalatable by the admixture of ginger in Recipe 179—would act as an efficient bactericide in much the same way as sulphur dioxide.

The verb *vertochier* or *vertocher* appears in Recipe 180 and at the end of four of the following recipes. Where it is not used, in Recipes 182 and 184, the verb found is *estoupper*. The two verbs would seem to have a synonymous sense but DuCange glosses the first as "mettre un tonneau en état de servir."[3]

181. Pour garir vin boucté

VAT **Pour garir vin boucté. Pour ung muy de Paris mettez plain pot de forment boullir tant qu'il soit baien, puis le purez et mettez reffroidier; et prenez des aubuns d'oeufz bien bastus et escumez, et mettez tout ou vaissel et mouvez a ung court baston fendu en iiii au bout qui n'aviengne pas a la lye qu'elle ne trouble; et mettez avecques une livre de surmontain moulue, et soit pendue a ung fillet en ung sachet de toille au bondon du vaissel.**

182. Pour garir vin bouté ...

VAT **Pour garir vin bouté ou qui sente le fust, le mugue ou le pourry. Prenez deux denrees de gingenbre et deulx denrees de citail et soient bien batuz emsemble, puis mettez celle poudre boullir en ii quartes de vin et l'escumez bien; puis le mectez chault ou vaissel et le mouvez bien jusques au fons; puis l'estouppez bien et le laissiez reposer tant qu'il soit rassiz.**

According to DuCange, "*Vin bouté* dixerunt, pro *Vin poussé*, vinum vitiatum." The spoilage known as *poussé* is one of the types of lactic spoilage in wines studied by Pasteur.[1] In appearance, such wine may show a fine haze or precipitate, or a silky streaming cloud; its taste is often describable as "mousy," or as of sauerkraut. The lactic acid bacteria form glutinous threads in the wine, which accounts for the English term "ropy" applied to it. Particular bacillae are responsible for this ropiness or gelation, by the formation of dextrans from the sucrose in grape wines. These bacillae are found in wines of relatively low alcoholic content.[2]

---

[2] Concerning this *cendre gravelee* see the *Tresor de la langue française*, vol. 9, p. 453a; Boileau, *Livre des métiers*, ed. G.B. Depping (Paris, 1837); part 2, §XXIV, p. 331: *cendres clavelées*; and Pegolotti, p. 416, *s. v. cenere gravella*.

[3] DuCange, vol. 9, p. 391a. See the Glossary, below.

[1] M.A. Amerine, H.W. Berg and W.V. Cruess, *The Technology of Wine Making* (Westport, Conn., 1972), p. 581.

[2] *Ibid*. p. 583.

Contrary to the treatment prescribed for the next type of wine disease, the amount of oxygen introduced by stirring the various ingredients into a cask of ropy wine will not unduly feed lactic acid bacteria.

183. Pour garir vin qui trait a aigreur

VAT **Pour garir vin qui trait a aigreur. Prenez, pour ung muy de vin, une pinte du vin qui sera du vaissel mesmes et mettez boulir, et mettez demye once de baye moulue et la destrempez de vin tout chault; et mettez ou vaissel sans le mouvoir ne tant ne quant; et le vertochez.**

Acetic spoilage is caused by acetic or vinegar bacteria. In modern times moderate amounts of sulphur dioxide control acetification. The *Viandier* makes use of the prussic acid in bay leaves to accomplish the same end. It may be because acetic acid bacteria require oxygen for growth and for acetification that *VAT* advises as little movement of the treated wine as possible.

184. Pour garir vin enfusté

VAT **Pour garir vin enfusté. Prenez, pour ung muy, demie livre de succre et deux onces de succre, demie once de baye moulue, et destrempez tout ensemble et mettez ou vaissel sans le mouvoir. Ou, aultrement: prenez charbons tous vifz et les mettez ou tonnel, puis l'estouppez tresbien et le laissiez trois jours en ce point.**

The scribe seems to have repeated the word "sugar" for some other ingredient in this recipe.

The term *enfusté* is an alternative for the expression *qui sente le fust* that was copied in Recipe 181. It refers to the woody taste acquired by a wine from the tannin of improperly prepared wooden casks.

185. Pour vin qui a la seive brisiee

VAT **Pour vin qui a la seive brisiee. Prenez plaine escuelle de tan et plain poing de pois et les meslez ensemble et mettez ou vaissel; et le vertochez sans mouvoir.**

Tannins are amorphous astringent substances that precipitate gelatin from a solution. It would seem that their function here, and that of the peas, is to treat a wine malady whose nature is similar to that of the *vin bouté* above.

186. Pour esclarcir vin roux en yver

VAT **Pour esclarcir vin roux en yver. Mettez en ung muy demie livre d'amandes nouvelles et les destrempez du vin mesmes et les mettez ou vaissel sans mouvoir; et a vin roux desroussir en esté, prenez deux pongnees de feulles de franc meurier pour ung muy et les mettez ou vaissel sans le mouvoir, et puis le vertochez.**

The prescription for lightening the colour of *vin roux* is in two parts, according to the season of the year. We may speculate that the "winter" recipe is the more commonly used, but that new almonds would be available only after harvest-time in the autumn. Curiously, the Latin treatise in the Bibliothèque Nationale, ms. lat. 7131, indicates only the first of these procedures, that which is appropriate in winter: "Ad vinum derosyr [*sic*] in tempore hyemali accipe libram unam de amigdalia concussis vino distemperatis et in tunella mitte bene movendo cum vino" (f. 94v).[1] The mulberry leaves specified by the *Viandier* for use in summer are mildly acidic in nature.

For the same effect, the *Menagier* suggests using holly leaves which are to be put into the cask of wine through the bung-hole.[2] The *Menagier* makes no reference to different treatments for different seasons of the year.

187. Pour vin vermeil esclarcir

VAT **Pour vin vermeil esclarcir. Mectez dedans le tonnel xl aulbuns d'oeufz batuz et bien escumez et, avec ce, plain poing de sel et deux onces de poivre moulu, et destrempez tout emsemble du vin mesmes et mettez ou vaissel et mouvez tout ensemble, lye et tout; et puis vertochez et laissiez reposer.**

This recipe bears a certain resemblance to one found in the *Tractatus*: "Ad clarificandum vinum turbidum, accipe duas uncias spice nardi, et uncias duas de pomis pulverizatis, et .XI. albumins ovorum, et manum plenam salis communis; insimul incorpora, et in tunellam pone bene movendo cum virgulis."[1] Scribal lapses of one sort or another seem to have operated in the fate of this recipe.

[Additional Recipes *(VAT)*] ❧

[1] *Tractatus de modo preparandi et condiendi omnia cibaria*, part I, §10; ed. cit., p. 382.

[2] *Menagier de Paris*, p. 134, l. 14; p. 68.

[1] *Tractatus*, part I, §3; ed. cit., p. 381.

188. Potaige appellé Menjoire

VAT **C'est ce qui appartient qui veult faire potaige appellé menjoire. Premierement, le grain qui y fault: paonneaulx, faisans ou perdriz et, qui n'en peult finer, plouviers, grues, allouettes ou autres menuz oiseaulx, et fault rostir ledit grain en la broche; et quant il sera pres cuit, especiallement comme grans oyseaulx, paonneaulx, faisans ou perdriz, fault les mettre par membres et les frire en saing de lart en une paelle de fer et puis les mettre ou pot ouquel on vouldra faire son potaige; et pour faire ledit boullon fault le boullon d'un trumeau de beuf et du pain blanc hallé sur le grail, et mettre tremper pain et semez du dit boullon et coullez par l'estamine; puis fault fleur de canelle, cynamome, gingenbre de Mesche, ung pou de girofle, de poivre long et graine de paradiz, et de l'ypocras selong la quantité que on veult faire du potaige; et deffaictes lesdictes espices et ypocras emsemble et gectez dedans le pot avec le grain et le boullon et tout fere boullir ensemble, et y mettre ung bien pou de vinaigre, et qu'il ne boulle guaires; et y mettre du succre compettemment; et selon les faisans convient mettre sur ledit potaige hosties dorees quant il est drecié, ou annis blanc ou vermeil, ou pouldré de grenade. Et qui le vouldroit faire a jour de poisson, convient prendre amendes entiers sans peler et les laver tres bien et puis broyer et affiner en ung mortier, et couler parmy l'estamine; et, s'il n'y a assez liqueur, prendre ung pou de pain blanc ou de la chappleure de deux ou de trois pains blans pour avoir ung pou de puree clere dont les poys ne soient pas trop boyans; et ung pou de vin blanc ou vermeil et ung pou de verjus et deffaire lesdictes amendes et pain, tout couler par l'estamine; et fault autelles espices comme a celuy devant dit, et le grain, c'est assavoir perches, brochetons, colz d'escrevisses et loche la plus belle qu'on peult finer: et fault frire tout ledit grain en beurre fraiz—ou sallé, et le dessaller. Puis dreciez vostre grain es platz et mettez le boullon dessus, et y mettez annis blanc ou vermeil ou la grenade, ou des amendes pelees —et les roussir ung pou en ung petit de beurre frez sur le feu.**

The thirty-three recipes that conclude *VAT*'s extended version of the *Viandier* are *unica*.[1] While a number of them resemble recipes found in other cookery manuals of the period,

[1] The material copied here may be covered by the rubric which precedes Recipe 178 in the manuscript: "S'ensuivent aucuns remedes et experimentz touchans le fait des vins *et autres choses*." We should perhaps understand a comma after the word *vins*.

they are not as a group attributable to any single known source. The types of dishes described in these final recipes are quite broadly varied and include stews, glazings and elaborate "architectural" *entremets*. Rather than constituting a further development of a particular chapter of the traditional *Viandier*, these additional recipes probably represent the annexation of some individual's collection of commonly used "favourites." They are preparations that, with only one or two exceptions, have not already been described in the *Viandier*, and that in many cases probably did not exist as recognized dishes at the time when *VAL* or even *BN* was copied. If these last preparations in *VAT* have a predominant character it is that they tend to be somewhat more complex than those that precede. They are perhaps more likely to reflect aspects of gastronomic taste and culinary art in France at the beginning of the fifteenth century.

There are two distinct recipes for the preparation called *Menjoire*. In them the ingredients vary according to whether the dish is to be prepared for meat-days or for lean days. In the first, the game birds are roasted and then cooked in a spiced bouillon. In the second, fish is fried in butter[2] and then served under a broth of almond milk (which may or may not be extended with puree of peas, wine and verjuice) and spices. The serving garnish is, for the first, saffron-coloured wafers[3] in a quantity appropriate to the number of birds, and, for the second, sauteed almonds. For both, aniseed or pomegranate seed offers an optional alternative. The only common feature between these two dishes is the use of the same spices and the same optional garnishes.

A number of features of this *Menjoire* suggest that it may be of Arabic inspiration. According to Wilson a two-fold cooking method, in which the sequence is a frying followed by a boiling, is characteristic of Saracen cuisine.[4] The combination of vinegar and sugar produces a bitter-sweet taste which again is typical of Arabic cookery.[5] And the use of the exotic anise or pomegranate seeds as a garnish seems to confirm a Saracen influence upon this dish.[6]

Several ingredients in this recipe are novel for the *Viandier*. The author now distinguishes a type of ginger that he calls *gingenbre de mesche*. In the middle of the fourteenth century Italian merchants classified ginger into three types: *baladi*, the Arabic name for

[2] The *Menagier de Paris* offers a recipe for the desalting of butter: §354; p. 266.

[3] The usual sense of the verb *dorer* in the *Viandier* is "to glaze (a food with a mixture containing egg)," but *hosties dorees* are more apt to be wafers which have received a sprinkling of saffron, as in the procedure outlined for Platina's *Soupes dorees*: *Platine en françoys* (Lyon, 1505), f. 81r.

[4] C. Anne Wilson in *Petits Propos Culinaires*, 7 (1981), p. 15. *Cf.* this same sequence of cooking steps followed in the *Brouet sarrasinois*, Recipe 80, above.

[5] *Idem*. See also Platine (pseud.), "Les sauces 'légères' du Moyen Age," *L'Histoire*, 35 (June 1981), pp. 87–89. The phenomenon of the bitter-sweet taste is well recognized in mediæval cookery, however: "Si volueris acrum dulce facere, ponas ibi succum citrangulorum cum zucara" (*Liber coquina*, part IV, §16; and part II, §25). In his recipe for a peacock sauce (§11), Chiquart suggests the same mixture of vinegar and sugar as is in the *Viandier*, "affin que il soit ung aigre doulx." *Cf.* also the *Libre del coch*, §38. Sugar will be an ingredient in fourteen of the twenty-eight edible recipes appended by the compiler of the *VAT* manuscript.

[6] Wilson, *Petits Propos Culinaires*, 8 (1981), p. 21 and n7.

common ginger; *colombino*, referring to the port in Travancore, called Columbum or Kolam, through which the ginger was shipped; and *micchino*, indicating that the spice had passed by way of Mecca.[7] The *Menagier* describes the differences between the last two varieties: "*Nota* que troiz differances sont entre gingembre de Mesche et gingembre coulombin: car le gingembre de Mesche a l'escorche plus brune, et si est le plus mol a trenchier au coustel, et plus blanc dedens que l'autre. *Item* meilleur est et tousjours plus cher."[8]

Alongside *canelle* we now find a new variety of cinnamon called *cynamome*. This second, having a Latinate name common in pharmaceutical treatises, represents a finer sort of the spice.[9] The *Menagier* does not use the term at all, whereas Chiquart writes only of *cynamomi* and never of *canelle*.

Hippocras, a spice-flavoured wine, is normally a cordial and rarely an ingredient in a dish, as here. The *Menagier* provides a recipe for "pouldre d'ypocras," which mixture of spices may have been kept on hand in the kitchen for use as a culinary ingredient.[10]

In early recipes in the *Viandier* sugar is used only exceptionally, and then normally only to provide additional warmth and moisture to an invalid's food by being grated on top of it as a garnish. In the fifteenth century the admixing of sugar *into* "everyday" dishes seems to have become quite general. No fewer than fourteen of these last preparations in the *Viandier* call for the admixture of sugar.[11]

Pomegranate seed is seen in the *Viandier* only in this recipe. Aniseed is found only here and in the next recipe.[12]

---

[7] Colin Clair, *Of Herbs and Spices*, p. 61. On *gingembre mesche, gingembre de Mesche*, see Tilander, *Glanures lexicographiques*, pp. 168–169.

[8] *Menagier de Paris*, §272; p. 230. The *Menagier* indicates that both *pouldre de gingembre coulombin* and *gingembre mesche* could be purchased *a l'espicier* (Brereton and Ferrier, p. 186, l. 8; Pichon, p. 111).

[9] *Cinnamomo* is called *cannella fina* in the druggist's handbook *Ricettario fiorentino di nuovo illustrato* by Neri Neri, Giovanni Batista Benadu, Francesco Rosselli and Giovanni Galletti (Florence: Marescotti, 1597). According to the merchant Pegolotti, though, there is no difference between the two: "Cannella, cioé cennamo" (*ed. cit.*, p. 361). *Canelle* and *cynamome* are used together in Recipe 206 also.

[10] *Menagier de Paris*, §317; p. 248. This *ypocras* could be bought (presumably in powdered form) from the local spicer (Brereton and Ferrier, p. 190, l. 5; Pichon, p. 122). See also Tilander, *Glanures lexicographiques*, pp. 206–207.

[11] The *Menagier* (Paris, *c.* 1393) makes sparing use of sugar; Chiquart (at the court of Savoy, 1420) uses it almost as commonly as any other spice. Concerning the utilization of sugar in French and Italian cookery of the fourteenth and fifteenth centuries, see Flandrin and Redon, pp. 402–403.

[12] *Grains de mil grane*, pomegranate seeds, are rare in both the *Menagier* and the *Du fait de cuisine* and are used there as a garnish, as they are here: in the first, on a jellied dish (§253; p. 221), and in the second, on a fish pie called *Broet de Savoye* (§26, f. 52v). The pomegranate as an edible fruit was introduced into Europe through the influence of Saracen cookery: see Wilson in *Petits Propos Culinaires*, 7 (1981), pp. 14–15. As for *anis vermeil*, this condiment appears in the *Menagier* as an *espice de chambre* (p. 186, l. 20; p. 112).

Knuckle of beef is suggested as an ingredient here because, as is mentioned in Recipe 191, this is considered a good cut of meat which does not possess any objectionable taste. On the contrary, the marrow in the bones of this joint adds its delicate flavour to the stock.

189. Lassis de blanc de chappon

VAT **Lassis de blanc de chappon. Mettez cuire vostre chappon avec trumeaulx de beuf, puis prendre tout le blanc du chappon et le charpir ainsi qu'on charpiroit lainne, et prendre des autres membres du chappon et mettre par pieces et les frire en sain de lart tant qu'ilz soient ung petit roux, et les dreciez en platz et mettez par dessus ladicte charpie; puis pelez amendes, broiez et deffaictes de vostre boullon et y mettez du vin blanc et du verjus; et prenez gingenbre de Mesche paré et le mettez en pouldre, et grainne de paradiz les deux partz et du succre competemment et qu'il soit doulx de succre; puis fault des amendes blanches pelees et les frire en sain de lart ou en sain de porc doulz,[1] et que les amendes soient piquees dedans le potaige quant il sera drecié; et soit assez liant tant que les amendes se puissent tenir droictes; et semez par dessus de l'annis vermeil.**

The *Enseignements* gives the name *Laceiz* to a type of *blanc mengier* in which the chicken meat is cut or raked into long strips and is then cooked with a little sugar.[2] The term *laceiz*[3] seems to denote a dish in which the meat or fish has been shredded into its fibres, this form of the meat or fish then being called *charpie*. This latter term was applied by *VAT* (alone) to the *Frase de veel* (Recipe 33), in which dish the meat is sliced very finely.[4] In the present recipe only the white meat of the chicken is to be so shredded, the dark meat, fried, forming the base of the dish.

---

[1] *ou en sain de porc doulz* inserted above the line by a different hand.

[2] *Enseignements*, p. 184, l. 122; *Petit traité*, p. 220. An alternative preparation, called *angoulee*, requires the rice to be cooked in the chicken broth or in almond milk.

[3] The *Buch von guter spise* has a chicken preparation which it calls *lazis* (§40).

[4] DuCange glosses the mediæval Latin *carpeia* as "Portio cibaria Monachica sic dicta, ut videtur a *Carpia*, nostris *Charpie*." Niermeyer (*Mediae Latinitatis Lexicon minus*, p. 146b) confirms that this *carpeia* was current in the thirteenth century in the sense of "hash." See A. Thomas in *Mélanges Louis Havet* (Paris, 1909), pp. 506–507; and *TLF*, vol. 5, p. 572a. *Charpie* was a useful method of disposing of leftovers: "Quant du luc fraiz est demouré de disner au souper, l'en en fait charpie," notes the frugal *Menagier* (§174; p. 188). See also the dish called *Arpa*, for shredded chicken, in the *Tractatus*, IV, §4.

190. Gravé d'escrvisses

VAT **Gravé d'escrevisses. Prenez amendez, lavez sans eschauder ne plumer, et broyez; puis fault avoir de la puree de poys clere et escrevisses grosses et belles et les cuire, les deulx pars eaue et le tiers vin, et ung pou de vinaigre qui veult; puis purez et laissiez reffroidir et mettez les pietz et les colz d'un costé, et les mettre hors de leur cotte;[1] puis vuidiez les charcois dedans, batez et broiez tres bien comme les amendes et deffaictes tout emsemble de puree de poys, de vin et de verjus, et tout couller ensemble par l'estamine; puis prenez gingenbre, ung pou de cynamome, ung pou de grainne de paradiz, et de girofle ung pou moins que de graine, et ung pou de poivre long; et prenez les pietz et les colz des escrevisses et frisiés en ung pou de beurre, qu'ilz soient secz comme loche fricte; et mettez boullir en une paelle ou en ung beau pot net et deffaictes les espices d'un pou de vin et de verjus et y mettre succre assés largement et boullir tout ensemble, et saler doulx; et qui y veult mettre fricture, faire le peult; et qu'il soit assez lyant tant qu'il puisse couvrir son grain.**

This *gravé* is a dish comprising both a sauce, itself composed of lobster (or crayfish) meat that is reduced to a pâté and spiced, and the whole meat itself of the claws and neck of the lobster.

The text of the recipe may be confusing because the author sees the two preparations, sauce and meat, proceeding simultaneously: in the midst of the succession of steps that must be followed to make the sauce, he mentions that the unground, whole meat of the lobster is to be fried; then he returns to the sauce, the next step for which requires boiling. A *gravé* consists normally of bits of fried meat served with a thick sauce poured over it, as distinct from a *potage* in which the meat is cooked, as the last step in its preparation, in the sauce with which it is to be served.

The reference to fried loach is specifically to Recipe 77, *Gravé de loche*.

The instruction found toward the end of this recipe, "saler doulx," indicates that salt is to be added sparingly.[2]

191. Ung rozé a chair

VAT **Ung Rozé a chair. Prenez amendes sans peler et broiez tres bien, puis prenez boullon de beuf, vin et verjus et deffaictes voz amendes et coulez par l'estamine; puis prenez vostre grain—c'est assavoir poictrine**

---

[1] *et les mettre hors de leur cotte* inserted above the line by a different hand.

[2] "*Doux de sel*. Fresh, unsavorie, not throughly seasoned" (Cotgrave).

de veau et poulaille entiere ou par quartiers, qui soient cuitz ensemble avec ung trumeau de beuf ou autre bon endroit—puis frire son grain en sain de lart tant qu'il soit rousset; puis prenez cynamome fine, non guaires, gingembre de Mesche blanc, et de menues espices comme grainne de paradiz, girofle et poivre long; et pour donner couleur convient avoir tornesoc et orcanet—et est l'orcanet aussi duisable comme le tornesoc, qui en peult finer, pour cause qu'il n'a pas si vive couleur que le tournesoc—et le convient mettre tremper en ung peu d'eaue chaude plus que tyedde iii ou iiii heures, et aprés le convient gecter en son pot et le remuer tres bien aprés ce que sondit potaige aura boullu; et mouvoir tres bien tant qu'il ait couleur semblable a couleur de rosee.

Similar to the *Dyapré* (Recipe 205) and to the *Tuillé* (Recipe 206), this *Rozé* for meat-days differs from them particularly in being of a somewhat more distinct colour. The colouring agents, the important ingredients in this otherwise quite ordinary dish, are on the one hand a variety of orchil lichen which, used in powdered form, produces a violet-reddish colour,[1] and on the other alkanet, a common source for red dyes in the Middle Ages—even though the author of *VAT* suggests ("*qui en peut finer*") that it was not too readily obtainable.[2] It is not clear whether these colorants are to be used in combination ("convient avoir tornesoc *et* orcanet") or, as the comment about the suitability of alkanet suggests, as alternatives according to the depth of hue desired in the *Rozé*.[3]

In Recipe 205 the dish of this present recipe is called "le grain d'amendes et de rozé."

[1] See A.L. Smith, *Lichens* (Cambridge, 1921), p. 412. *Tornesaut* is used on two occasions in the *Du fait de cuisine* (ff. 30r and 60r) to produce a distinct *blue* colour in a dish: "Pour faire la potagerie de l'azur, prennés tornesaut grant foyson et mectés tramper dedans le lait ... " (f. 30r). As with modern litmus, of which it is at the origin, the orchil lichen will turn red in the presence of an acid and blue in the presence of an alkali. For cooks, then, this colouring agent is particularly valuable.

[2] Chiquart has a *Broet rossee* that is identical to the *Viandier*'s *Rozé a chair* except that alkanet alone provides the distinctive colouring. The Savoyard author dictates as well a note on the preparation of this dye: "Et quant vostre boullon bouldra, si prennés bonne et grande casse a frire belle et tresbien necte, et mectés tresbon oyle bel et cler dedans et le eschauffés tresbien; et, lui estant bien chaut et boullans, lancés de bon orcannete dedans qui soit bien nectoyés, et le coysés et osthés bien et appoint; et puis le coulés bien et nectment a ung cousté d'estamine sur beaulx platz, et puis en mectés dedans vostre boullon en si bon point, et ainz que la coulleur dudit boullon soit plus sur la couleur rosee que de goules" (*Du fait de cuisine*, §8, f. 28r; exactly the same procedure of boiling alkanet in clarified oil is prescribed again at ff. 58v and 60r of this work). It is perhaps worth noting that the *Viandier* specifies water as the leaching agent here in Recipe 191, but pork fat later in Recipe 199. On the culinary use of alkanet, see Colin Clair, *Of Herbs and Spices*, p. 110.

[3] In English recipe books (*Forme of Cury*, §52; Austin, p. 24; *Liber cure cocorum*, f. 13) the

192. Une Trimolette de perdrix

VAT **Une Trimolette de perdriz. Premierement fault les appareillier et les rostir en broche tant qu'ilz soient presque rostiz, puis les oster de la broche et mettre par quartiers ou les laissier entiers et mettre en ung beau pot net; et missier ongnons les plus menuz que on pourra et les frire en ung pou de saing de lart et de boullon de beuf et gectez dessus lesdictes perdris, et le hocher souvent; puis avoir des foyes de poulailles avec ung petit de pain et les haller bien sur le grail et puis mettre tremper et couller par l'estamine et gecter en son pot sur son grain de perdris; et aprés prenez cynamome fine, ung pou de gingenbre, du clou de girofle et ung pou plus largement de grainne de paradiz, de poivre long et deffectes les espices de bon ypocras; et, ce fait, tout mettre en son pot et couvrir son pot tres bien affin qu'il n'en ysse point d'alainne; et gecter du succre dessus, et quant on le voudra oster du feu et y mettre ung bien pou de vinaigre dedans; et qu'il ne boulle point.**

The *Trimolette* is a piquant sauce that is served particularly over partridge.[1] Made with poultry livers,[2] this mixture is rather thick in consistency and, following the final addition of vinegar, slightly sharp in flavour.[3]

---

name *rosee* is generally given to a preparation containing roses or rosewater. See the *Curye on Inglysch*, p. 211, *s.v. rose(e)n*. The *Menagier de Paris* uses sandalwood as the source of a pink culinary dye (§84; p. 154), as does the *Du fait de cuisine* (*poudre sandre*, f. 37r, in the *Broet tyolli*, §13).

[1] *Trimolette* does not appear to be the name of the finished dish which combines partridge and a sauce, but only of the sauce itself. In his *Condamnacion de Banquet* (*c.* 1500) Nicole de LaChesnaye prescribes

> Pour viande bien douillecte,
> Le perdrix et la trimollecte.

(Ed. P.L. Jacob in *Recueil de farces, soties*, p. 332.) Similar to the *Viandier*'s dish is the *Tigellada de perdiz* that appears twice in the Portuguese cookbook edited by Newman, at ff. 4v (p. 2) and 15r (p. 13). *Cf.* also the *Recueil de Riom*, §14.

[2] Both the *Tresmollete de perdrix* (§12, f. 34r) and the *Calunafree de perdrix* (§47, f. 72v) in the *Du fait de cuisine* make use of chicken liver to produce a thick, dark sauce.

[3] Chiquart's *Tresmollete* is likewise to be tangy: "Mectés dedans du succre et non pas tant qu'il oste le gust du verjust, car il ne doibt pas estre sur le doulx" (f. 34v).

193. Brouet de daintiers de cerf ...

VAT **Brouet de daintiers de cerf et cervoisons. Premierement, fault tres bien eschauder et laver en eaue boullant les deintiers de cerf, et bien cuitz puis reffroidiz, et aprés tailliez par morceaulx quarrez—ne trop gros ne trop menuz—et les frire en sain de lart et mettre en la paelle mesmes du boullon de beuf; et y mettre du persil effueillié et de la poudre fine competemment qu'il ne soit pas trop fort d'espices; et pour leur donner liqueur fault avoir ung petit de cameline—ou prendre ung foye ou deux de poulaille et ung petit de pain blanc et les couller et mettre en son pot en lieu de cameline—et y gecter ung pou de vinaigre et deffaire ses espices de vin et de vertjus, les deux partz verjus et le tiers vin—ou en lieu de verjus, groiselles; et le saller competemment.**

The term *cervoison* as it is used here seems to designate not merely the modern French *cervaison*, "stag meat" or "the stag-hunting season,"[1] but rather "the young of the stag," whose antlers are not yet fully formed.[2] The *Regimen sanitatis salernitanum* includes testicles among pork meat, brain and marrow as particularly nourishing foods, though the commentary to the *Regimen* specifies that they must be from young animals.[3] It may be superfluous to note that stag's testicles were considered a delicacy.[4]

The substitution of *groiselles* for verjuice implies that what is meant by *groiselles* is unfermented currant juice.

194. Flaons cochus

VAT **Flaons cochus. Prenez craisme et moyeulx d'oeufz bien batus, puis les mettez dedans la craisme; et avoir darioles plus grandes que ceulx que on fait; et y deffaire dedans de la pouldre fine ou blanche; puis avoir grosses anguilles de plain poing et les eschauder et rostir tres bien, et mettre par tronçons et les mettre debout esdiz flaons, en chascun trois ou quatre; et les succrer grandement quant ilz sont cuitz, et les laissiez reffroidier.**

---

[1] *Menagier de Paris*, §90; p. 156.

[2] According to Godefroy the normal term in Old French for the young of the stag is *cervot*, *cervoz*. For the writer of Recipe 193, *cervoison* would seem to be a collective form of that noun.

[3] The French translation of the relevant passage in the commentary reads: "Et est yci a noter diligemment que les coullons des bestes agees esquelles la semence est mixtionee ne sont pas de bonne nourriture, mais les coullons des bestes jeunes impotentes de herser et esquelz n'est pas encore la semence fermentee, sont souffisanment de bon nourrissement s'il sont bien digerez" (*Regime tresutile et tresproufitable*, ed. Cummins, p. 32).

[4] See Gunnar Tilander, *Nouveau mélange d'étymologie cynégétique* (Lund, 1961), p. 52, *s.v.* *deintiez*.

The generic name for these open custard tarts is a derivative of the low Latin *flatones*, "placentae species" (DuCange); the qualification *cochus* may represent the Latin past participle *coctutum* for *coctum*, "cooked,"[1] or the word may be a Picard form cognate with the Francian *cossu*.[2]

The *Enseignements* has a recipe for *Flaons en Caresme* in which the ingredients include cooked eel meat which is mashed, ginger, saffron and wine.[3] The *Viandier*'s *Flaons cochus* are the result of a richer mixture that combines cream—this is the only occasion on which cream is used in the book—and egg yolks to produce a true custard into which the slices of cooked eel are set. The generous use of sugar here is reminiscent of *Y*'s addition of sugar to the *Flaons en caresme*, of which one variety is for eels, in Recipe 152.

There is no recipe for *darioles* in the *Viandier*, in the *Enseignements*, in the *Menagier de Paris* or in the *Du fait de cuisine*.[4] English recipe books, however, mention *darioles*, *darials* and *daryols* frequently, and it is apparent that, though the basis for these is a custard similar to that of the flan, the *dariole*, at least as it was made in England, makes use of a wider range of ingredients. These include such foodstuffs as marrow and fruit.[5] *VAT* writes as if *darioles* were the pastry tart-shell; to hold three or four sections of a large eel, these shells would indeed have to be quite large.

The composition of *pouldre fine ou blanche* was apt to vary from kitchen to kitchen but the *Menagier* provides his notion of what the ingredients of *pouldre fine* should be:

---

[1] For the reformed Vulgar Latin past participle *-utus* of verbs in *-uere*, see M.K. Pope, *From Latin to Modern French* (Manchester: Manchester University Press, 1934), §§1050 and 1056; Édouard Bourciez, *Eléments de linguistique romane* (4th ed.; Paris: Klincksieck, 1956), §93; Charles H. Grandgent, *An Introduction to Vulgar Latin* (Boston: D.C. Heath, 1934; repr. New York: Hafner, 1962), §438. The palatal sound in this word *cochus* seems to point to an origin in the south of France, in the Iberian peninsula or in the north of Italy (Bourciez, *Éléments*, §180 b). These flans are apparently to be cooked in a water bath, much as the procedure is in cooking a modern custard.

[2] The *TLF* (vol. 6, p. 256b) dates at 1378 the same instance of the word *cossu* as is cited in Godefroy (vol. 9, p. 210c); this latter glosses the word as "riche, à son aise."

[3] *Enseignements*, p. 185, l. 166; *Petit traité*, p. 222. The *Recueil de Riom* has a brief recipe for open-faced pies called *Tartes pellerines* which use cheese, "et y aura dedans de l'anguille par groz petiz transons, en chascune tarte .v. ou .vi. transons, et qu'ilz ne soient pas tropt grans" (§31). Barbara Santich points out a certain similarity between these *Flaons cochus* and the *Menagier*'s *Tarte jacobine* (§248; p. 217): "In one recipe for Tarte jacobine (also known as Flaons cochus), chunks of eel were stood upright in the pastry case and the custard mixture was poured over" (*Two Languages*, p. 270).

[4] *Darioles* are included in several of the menus compiled by the *Menagier*, but he provides no recipe for making them. According to Ernest Gamillscheg, *dariole* is a Picard word and is probably a derivative of the verb *dorer*: see the *Zeitscrift für romanische Philologie*, 40 (1920), p. 519. It is true that saffron is a common ingredient in the English *darioles*.

[5] Austin, pp. 47, 53, 55, 56, 75; *Liber cure cocorum*, p. 38, "darials"; *Forme of Cury*, §183 (Hieatt and Butler, part IV, §191), "daryols."

ginger, cinnamon, cloves, grains of paradise and sugar.[6]

195. Doreures

VAT **Doreures. Entremetz pour ung jour de feste ou pour ung convy de prince aux trois jours maslés de la sepmaine, comme dimenche, mardi et le jeudi. Pour farsiz et pommeaulx: convient, pour les pommeaulx, de la chair de porc crue—il ne peult challoir quelle—dont les poulles soient farcies. Et convient, aprés que la poulaille est tué, rompre ung pou de peau de la teste, et avoir ung tuyau de plume et souffler dedans tant qu'elle soit bien plaine de vent, et puis les eschauder et aprés les fendre par dessoubz le ventre et les escorchier; et mettre les charcois d'un costé. Et convient, pour faire la farce pour farcir la poullaille, du blanc, du lart hachié avec la chair, et fault des oeufz, de bonne poudre fine, du pignolet et du roisin de Corinde, et en farsir la peau de la poulaille, et ne l'emplir pas trop qu'elle ne crieve, puis la recoudre; et convient la boullir en une paelle sur le feu et ne le fault guaire laisser cuire, et puis les brochez en broches gresles; et quant les pommeaulx seront bien faictz les convient mettre cuire avec ladicte poulaille et les tirer quant ilz seront durciz; et avoir les broches des pommeaulx plus gresles de la moittié ou plus que celles de la poullaille. Et aprés fault avoir de la paste batue en oeufz tellement qu'elle se puisse tenir sur la paelle, et quant la poullaille et les pommeaulx seront presque cuitz les oster et mettre sur sa paste:[1] et prendre de la paste a une cuillier nette, en remuant tousjours, et mettre par dessus sa poulaille et ses pommeaulx tant qu'ilz en soient dorez, et les faire par ii ou par iii foiz tant qu'ilz en soient bien couvertz; et fault prendre du feul d'or ou d'argent et les enveloper —et fault avoir ung petit d'aubun d'oeuf et les arrouser affin que le fueil tiengne mieulx.**

---

[6] *Menagier de Paris*, §314; p. 247. *Pouldre blanche* normally contains ginger, cinnamon and nutmeg. Earlier in the same work the bourgeois author advises that both of these compounds can be purchased ready-made at *l'espicier* of *les Halles* or the Porte de Paris (Brereton and Ferrier ed., p. 190, ll. 5–6; Pichon ed., p. 122). See Tilander, *Glanures lexicographiques*, p. 206.

[1] *mettre sur sa paste*: understand *sa paste* as object of *mettre*, not of *sur*.

The title found over this recipe appears to be somewhat inappropriate unless, of course, *Doreure* was indeed the name conventionally applied to such a dish of stuffed, glazed chicken skin as is described here. The dish may be compared with what is found in Recipe 66 for *Poulaille farcie*. In the last stage of the present recipe, very thin leaves of beaten gold or silver are to be stuck onto the "chicken";[2] the use of this gold-leaf may explain the name *Doreure*. The cost of such ornamentation would naturally, as the subtitle indicates, limit the dish's use to the exceptional occasions of a princely banquet.[3] The following recipe, for *Coqz heaumez*, states that gold and silver are suitable materials to decorate what is set before aristocratic banqueters; for others mere tin is adequate.

After the second sentence—which amounts to a partial listing of the ingredients for the stuffing—there are four distinct steps in the preparation of this dish: removing the skin from the chicken, making the stuffing to be inserted carefully into the chicken skin or formed into balls,[4] cooking by boiling and roasting, and finally glazing. The carcass of the chicken is not itself to be stuffed, cooked and glazed, but merely provides the white meat (*du blanc*) which is to be ground with the pork and other ingredients for the stuffing. All references to "poulles" and all but the first reference to "poulaille" are to the pseudo-chicken, the stuffed skin.

The stuffing uses fruit not seen in the earlier recipe for *Poulaille farcie*. These pine nuts and seedless currants will be combined in three other dishes in this last section of the *Viandier*, in Recipes 197, 208 and 212.

The glazing compound used on the stuffed chicken in Recipe 66 is a simple mixture of beaten egg yolks and either saffron or "greenery" (*i.e.* parsley); here the author writes of

---

[2] Chiquart refers to this type of glazing procedure on several occasions, a procedure that makes use of what he terms *orpati*, which must be gold-leaf (*Du fait de cuisine*, ff. 14r, 47v, 77r). He writes also of "folliés de pasté pour faire les doreures" (f. 76v) and of a "folliet d'or" (f. 77r), both of which are provided by his pastry chef.

[3] Concerning the meat-eating days of the week in the middle of the fourteenth century, we have the following from a conversation manual:

> —Apolone, faites nous savoir / quants Quatuor tempres / a il en cascun an?
> / Que sont che, Quatuor tempres? /
> —Ce sont junes que Nostre Sire / ha ordenees a jeuner / es quatre tamps de l'an. /
> —Et en quels jours eskieent elles? /
> —Elles eskient toutdis les merkedis, les venredis / et les samedis.

Livre des mestiers (*c.* 1340), ed. Jean Gessler, 4 vols., with 2 introductory vols. (Brugges: Gruuthuse, Sainte-Catherine, Desclée-DeBrouwer, 1931), vol. 1, p. 25. On the whole question of regular weekly fast days in mediæval France, see Fernand Cabrol and Henri Leclercq, *Dictionnaire d'archéologie chrétienne et de liturgie*, 15 vols. (Paris: Letouzey & Ané, 1920–1953), vol. 7 (1927), part 2, col. 2481–2501: *Jeûne*; and Michel Mollet, *La vie et la pratique religieuses au XIVe siècle et dans la première partie du XVe, principalement en France* (Paris: Centre de Documentation Universitaire, n.d.)

[4] Chiquart makes use of "pomes dorees feictes de chars" as part of an *entremets* (f. 32r). See also the *Poume d'oranges* in the *Viande e claree* (§1).

"paste batue aux oeuf" (Recipe 196) and "paste batue d'oeufz" (Recipe 213). This glazing *paste* is likely a mixture of eggs and flour.[5] When roasted in two or three layers on the chicken skin and on the balls of stuffing, it will provide them with a firm coating that is as functional—given the pliability of the stuffed chicken skin and the soft balls of stuffing—as it is decorative.

196. Coqz heaumez

VAT **Coqz heaumez. Mettez cochons rostir, et poulaille comme coqz et vielles poulles, et quant le cochon sera rosty d'une part et la poulaille d'autre convient farsir la poullaille—sans escorcher, qui veult; et la convient farsir[1] de paste batue aux oeuf; et quant ell'est doree la convient mettre a chevauchons sur le cochon, et fault ung heaume de papier collé et une lance fichié a la poittrine de la dicte poullaille, et les fault couvrir de fueil d'or ou d'argent pour les seigneurs, ou de feul d'estain blanc, vermeil ou vert.**

As is the case with the preceding dish, this "armed cock" falls clearly into the category of *entremets*; one might even say it presents an early sort of *coq-à-l'âne*.

As in the previous and following recipes, decorations of gold-leaf, silver-leaf and tin-leaf allow the host publicly to acknowledge the social distinctions to be made between the guests at his table.

197. Tourtes parmeriennes

VAT **Tourtes parmeriennes.[1] Prenez chair de mouton ou de veau ou de porc et la hachiez competemment; puis fault avoir de la poulaille et faire boullir et despecier par quartiers, et fault cuire ledit grain avant qu'il soit hachié, puis avoir poudre fine et l'en espicier tres bien raisonnablement et frire son grain en sain de lart; et, aprés, avoir de grans pastez descouvers—et qu'ilz soient plus hault dreciez de paste que autres pastez et de la grandeur de petitz platz—et faictz en maniere de creneaulx, et qu'ilz soient fortz de paste affin qu'ilz puissent**

---

[5] In later recipes the author writes explicitly "aubuns d'oeufs et de fleur batue tout ensemble ... et mettre de la paste en ladicte escuelle ... " (Recipe 202); and "les dorer de paste et de fleur" (Recipe 211).

[1] *farsir* appears to be an echo of the same verb written earlier and should probably instead have been *dorer*—particularly as the following phrase reads "et quant ell'est doree .... ."

[1] The word *Tourtes* is centred on the page and the epithet *parmeriennes* is squeezed a little after it as if this qualification were an afterthought.

porter le grain; et, qui veult, on y met du pignolet et du roisin de Corinde meslez parmy le grain et du succre esmié par dessus, et mettre en chascun pasté iii ou iiii quartiers de poullaille pour fichier les bannieres de France et des seigneurs qui seront en la presence, et les dorer de saffren deffait pour estre plus beaulx—et qui ne veult pas tant despendre de poullaille, ne fault que faire des pieces plates de porc ou de mouston rosty ou boully. Et quant ilz sont rempliz de leur grain, les fault dorer par dessus le grain d'un petit d'oeufz bastuz ensemble, moyeulx et aubuns, affin que le grain se tiengne plus ferme pour mettre les bannieres dedans; et convient avoir fu fueil d'or ou d'argent ou du fueil d'estain pour les dorer avant les banieres.

Parma pie is relatively well known as a dish in the fifteenth century. It is called *Torte parmigiane* on Italian tables of the day;[2] and Chiquart offers recipes for two types of *Tortre parmeysine*, one for fish and one for pork and fowl—this latter type resembling quite closely what we find in the *Viandier*.[3]

The *Viandier* allows either mutton, veal or pork to be used with poultry in the pie, whereas the *Du fait de cuisine* specifies pork alone but allows cockerels to be substituted for chicks, depending upon the season of the year and the consequent availability of chicks. Chiquart's recipe affords an understanding of the proportions of the various ingredients, that is, the relative quantities of them considered proper in this mixture: for three to four large pigs, he directs the cook to dress 300 pigeons, 200 chicks (or, alternatively, 100 cockerels) and 600 "little birds."

The combination of pine nuts and seedless current grapes was seen in the previous recipe. To these two fruits Chiquart adds figs, dates and plums in *Tortes parmeysines*, as well as an assortment of herbs (sage, parsley, hyssop and marjoram), all meticulously prepared. A creamy cheese and 600 eggs function as binders in the same way as the *Viandier*'s lard.

The gold-, silver- or tin-leaf decoration is a standard finish for this dish, as are the little banners implanted in the surface of the dish as it is presented before the host and his honoured guests.[4]

---

[2] C.G. Carbonelli, *Come vissero i primi conti di Savoia da Umberto Blancamano ad Amedeo VIII: Raccolti di usi, costumanze, tradizioni e consuetudine mediche, igieniche, casalinghe tratti dai documenti degli archivi sabaudi* (Milan: Miglietta, 1931), p. 178, n2.

[3] *Du fait de cuisine*, §40, f. 65v, and §21, f. 43v.

[4] "Prennés vostre or party et le mectés pardessus vostres tortes parmeysines en maniere d'un eschaquier [checkerboard], et de la poudre du succre par dessus. Et quant l'on en servira, que sur chescune torte soit mise une banderete des armes d'un chescun seigneur qui de cestes tortes parmeysines sera servi" (*ibid*., f. 47v).

198. Tostees dorees

VAT **Pour faire Tostees dorees, prenez du pain blanc dur et le trenchiez par tostees quarrees et les rostir ung pou sur le grail; et avoir moyeulx d'oeufz batuz et les envelopez tres bien dedans iceulx moyeulx; et avoir de bon sain chault et les dorer dedans sur le feu tant qu'elles soient belles et bien dorees et puis les oster de dedans la paelle et mettez es platz, et du succre dessus.**

The *Tostees dorees* are to some extent a counterpart to the *Souppes dorees* that turn up in English cookery books, [1] but whereas the sop is a piece of plain bread in a broth, the *tostee* is a dish that is prepared with grilled bread[2] and whose characteristic colour derives from a soaking in egg yolks and a frying in lard.

The dish is similar to modern "French toast."

The word *dedans* ("les envelopez tres bien dedans") should be understood as having *les* (the *tostees*) as object; the object of the verb *envelopez* is the egg yolks: the beaten yolks are to be enclosed in the toast.[3]

199. Blanc menger party

VAT **Blanc menger party. Prenez amendes eschaudees et pelees et les broyez tres bien et les deffaictes d'eaue boulue, puis pour faire la lieure pour les lyer fault avoir du ris batu ou de l'amydon; et quant son layt ara esté boulu le fault partir en plusieurs parties—en deux potz, qui ne veult faire que de deux couleurs et, qui le veult faire, en iii ou en iiii parties; et convient qu'il soit fort lyé autant que seroit Froumentee, tant qu'il ne se puisse reprendre quant il sera drecié ou ou plat ou en l'escuelle. Puis prenez orcanet ou tornesoc, ou asur fin, ou persil ou salmonde, ou ung petit de saffren coullé avec la verdure affin qu'il tienge mieulx sa couleur quant il sera boullu; et convient avoir du saing de porc et mettre tremper dedans l'orcanet ou tournesoc, et l'azur pareillement. Et gectez du succre dedans le lait quant il bouldra pour tirer arriere, et le sallez et remuez fort tant qu'il soit renforcy et ayt prins sa couleur telle que luy vouldrez donner.**

---

[1] *Sowpes dorry* in the *Forme of Cury*, §82 and in *Curye on Inglysch*, IV, §84; *Sowpys dorry* in the *Diversa servicia*, *Curye on Inglysch*, II, §65; *Sowpus dorre* in the *Liber cure cocorum*, p. 14; and *Soppes dorre* in Austin, pp. 11, 90 and 114. All of these recipes involve almonds and wine, and, normally, saffron, ginger and sugar.

[2] Cotgrave glosses "*Tostée*: f. A toast of bread: Pic [*i. e.* Picard]." See a similar recipe in Eberhard, *Gut kuchenn vonn eyerrn* (§14), in which bread is used.

[3] The same "post-positional" use of *dedans* is seen in the following recipe.

This *Blanc menger party* is a variation of the standard, but multi-versioned, white dish. The *Viandier* already contains another variation of this generic preparation in Recipe 95, the *Blanc mengier d'ung chappon pour ung malade*. The present recipe has no chicken in it but depends for its character upon a parti-coloured appearance.

The coloured sections into which the dish is divided can be in strips or in equal portions, either halves, thirds (in segments of a circle, presumably) or quarters. The *Du fait de cuisine* contains a similar "*Blanc mangier parti* de quatre couleurs tout en [ung] plat, c'est assavoir d'or, d'azur, de goules et d'argent."[1] In the *Viandier* the colours that would be produced by the ingredients listed are red (from the alkanet), red or blue (from the *tornesoc*, an orchil lichen),[2] blue (from the *asur fin*, probably finely powdered lapis lazuli[3]) and green (from parsley or herb bennet, with a little saffron thrown in for a *vergay* effect). The alkanet, orchil and *azur* are to be steeped in boiling lard, and then probably filtered, as a preparatory step to their use.[4]

The phrase "quant il bouldra pour tirer arriere" should be understood to imply a word such as *assez* before *pour*. The word *renforcy*, "thickened," appears as *forced*, *enforced* and *aforcyd* in English recipes, though usually with the sense of "seasoned" or "made substantial."[5] Here, however, the author is merely insisting upon the necessity that the almond milk mixture be heavy or viscous enough that the various colours of the *blanc mengier*, set side by side in the same dish, not be able to run together (*se reprendre*).[6] The thickening of the mixture is effected by the rice flour or starch, new products in the *Viandier* and mentioned at the beginning of the recipe.[7]

---

[1] *Du fait de cuisine*, §9, f. 28v. Chiquart specifies the following sources for his four colours: gold—saffron; blue—*tournesaut*, soaked in almond milk; scarlet—the oil in which *orcanite*, alkanet, has been boiled; and silver—starch (alone).

[2] See the use of both *orcanet* and *tornesoc* in Recipe 191, above. *Tournesot* is likewise used by the *Menagier de Paris* "pour faire gellee bleue" §252; p. 220). The *Menagier*'s recipe for *Lait lardé*, which is normally yellow from saffron and eggs, offers an interesting optional variant: "Qui le veult faire vert, si prengne du tournesot" (§259; p. 225). As with litmus, the colour produced by the dye from orchil lichen varies according to the acidity or alkalinity of the mixture to which it is added.

[3] See Pegolotti, p. 372.

[4] See above, Recipe 191, n2.

[5] Austin, pp. 3, 6, 17, 29, 41, 46, 55; *Forme of Cury*, §§3, 40, 44.

[6] Compare this past participle with the adjective *fort* used to describe the consistency of the batter from which crêpes are to be made in Recipe 202.

[7] For the making of starch at this time see *Viaunde e claree*, §21: *Amydon*; *Curye on Inglisch*, part V, §3; and Austin, p. 112. The process was already described by Pliny the Elder in his *Natural History*, book 18, ch. 17, ed. and tr. H. Rackham, 10 vols. (London: Heinemann, and Cambridge, Mass.: Harvard University Press, 1938, repr. 1950), vol. 5, pp. 238–239. The *Viande e claree* also contains a particoloured dish (*De amydoun*) of wheat starch, sugar and almond milk which is boiled and then fried (§13).

200. Layt lardé

VAT **Layt lardé. Prenez du lait et le mettez boullir sur le feu, et avoir moyeulx d'oeufz batuz, puis descendez le lait de dessus le feu et le mettez sur ung pou de charbon et fillez les oeufz dedans; et qui veult qu'il soit a chair, prenez lardons et les couppez en deux ou trois morceaulx et gectez avec le lait boullir; et qui veult qu'il soit a poisson, il n'y fault point mettre de lardons; mais gecter du vin et du verjus avant qu'on le descende pour faire brosser, puis l'oster de dessus le feu et le mectez en une nappe blanche et le laissier esgouter, et l'enveloper en ii ou en iii doubles de la nappe et le pressourer tant qu'il soit dur comme foye de beuf; puis le mettre sur une table et le taillier par leesches comme de plainne paulme ou trois doys, et les boutonner de clou de girofle; puis les frire tant qu'ilz soient roussés; et les dressiez, et jectez du succre dessus.**

A recipe for a similar dish called *Lait lyé* was copied by *VAT* at §86. The name for the present dish, *Layt lardé*, may be explained in one of three ways: by the presence in it of *lardons*, pieces of bacon; by the way the compressed, curdled milk is cut—as the *Menagier de Paris* says, "comme lesche de lart"[1]; or by the way in which the solid milk is interlarded with whole cloves, an operation for which the *Viandier* uses the term *boutonner* but for which the *Menagier* says "lardé de giroffle et de pignolet."[2] The dish may be served in conjunction with *Tourtes de layt*: see the end of Recipe 201.

The text of the *Menagier* helps explain the term *brosser* as well. While not distinguishing explicitly between preparations for meat-days and for meatless days, the bourgeois author advises the cook, after the milk and eggs of his *Lait lardé* have boiled, "Hostez hors du feu et laissiez tourner; ou sans oeufz les fait l'en tourner de vertjus." It is the acidity of the verjuice in particular that is responsible for making the milk curdle, *brosser*.

Despite its presence here among the fifteenth-century additions to the *Viandier*, this dish was by no means a late innovation in mediæval cuisine. The earliest known European recipe collection, the German compilation from the beginning of the thirteenth century

---

[1] *Menagier de Paris*, §259; p. 224. See also Austin, pp. 17 and 85: *Let lory*; the *Forme of Cury*, §§68 and 81 (Hieatt and Butler, part IV, §§69 and 83): *Lete lardes* and *Leteloryе*; and the *Liber cure cocorum*, p. 13: *Lede lardes*. The *Lette lardes* published by Austin (pp. 35 and 92) and in the *Forme of Cury* (§68) is similar to what is copied for this recipe in the *Viandier*, but is particoloured. See the green-and-yellow curdled-milk dish in the next recipe. *Cf.* the preparations called *Mylk rost* in the *Diversa servicia*, §25 (Hieatt and Butler, part II, p. 66); *Ein gebraten milch* in the *Buch von Guter Spize*, §25, p. 23; and *Spaecket mialk* in the *Northern-European Cookbook* (§18).

[2] *Menagier*, *loc. cit.*

which has been studied by Rudolf Grewe, contains a recipe for *Spaecket mialk* which is virtually identical to this *Layt lardé*.[3]

201. Tourtes de layt

VAT **Tourtes de layt. Prenez du lait et le mettez boullir sur petit feu de charbon, et convient avoir des oeufz entrejectez ou atout l'aubun, qui veult; et quant il boust le departir en deulx vaisseaulx, puis avoir la verdure de persil et couller avec la moittiee de ses oeufz; et prendre du vin et du verjus et le gecter dedans tant qu'il soit bien brossé, puis le mettre reffroidir que on y puisse tenir la main; et avoir une estamine de deux pietz de long, puis prenez une culleree ou deux dudit lait et l'envelopez deux ou trois tours dedans l'estamine, puis le frocter au mains bien et fort; et quant il sera prins et dur l'oster de l'estamine, mettez refroidir et y piquer deux ou trois renges de cloux de girofle, et aprés les frire en sain de lart tant qu'ilz soint roussettes. Et les convient servir avec le layt lardé en ung plat, moictiee ung et moittiee aultre.**

Although this dish is called *Tourtes de layt*, there is no mention of a pastry shell—the basis for what both the *Du fait de cuisine* and the *Menagier* call *tartres*—used to hold the custard. The reader may wonder whether the name of the dish is authentic. Deep-fried after being formed, these *tourtes* can be handled safely with the fingers and do not need a shell.

The procedure to be followed after the milk is boiling remains rather obscure. A reasonable guess might be that half of the milk is to be coloured green (with ground parsley) and half coloured yellow (with beaten eggs). Then each mixture is curdled in its respective container and cooled.[1]

The dish appears to be similar to the previous one except that the *Layt lardé* of Recipe 200 is cut into bacon-like slices before being fried. In one of the *Menagier*'s sample dinner menus, *tourtes de lait* are served together with *lait lardé*.[2]

201A. Buignetz et roysolles de mouelle

VAT **Buignetz et roysolles de mouelle.**

---

[3] *Northern-European Cookbook*, §18.

[1] See the notes to the previous recipe.

[2] *Menagier de Paris*, ed. Brereton and Ferrier, p. 179, l. 22; ed. Pichon, p. 98. The two dishes that precede these during the second serving of a *disner de char* are *crespes* and *pastez noirroiz*, both of which are among these later additions to the *Viandier* in the Vatican manuscript (Recipes 202 and 208).

Of the recipe for marrow fritters and rissoles, only this title has been copied. The scribe seems to have decided not to copy the recipe, but passed on to the next title and its recipe.

The *Menagier* mentions that *Bingnetz de mouelle* are to be made by preparing the marrow as would be done for *Pastez norroiz* (the *Viandier*'s Recipe 208, below) and then placing it in pastry, or covering it with batter, made of flour and egg yolks, and finally deep frying the resultant turnover in lard.[1] For *Roysolles de mouelle* the *Menagier* merely appends what appears to be a variant for a more common pork rissole:[2] "A la cour des seigneurs comme monseigneur de Berry, quant l'en y tue ung beuf, de la mouelle on fait rissolles."[3]

Austin has published an English recipe for *Ryschewys of marow* that combines flour, egg yolks, sugar, salt, ginger and saffron to make a "cake" onto which is placed a paste of marrow, sugar and ginger; "& fold hem to-gederys, & kytte [cut] hem in the maner of Rysschewes, & frye hem in freyssche grece."[4]

202. Crespes grandes et petites

VAT **Crespes grandes et petites. Les grandes a ung pot a cirop ou en ung paellon d'arain, et les petites a une paelle de fer; faire les convient en aubuns d'oeufz et de fleur batue tout ensemble, et avoir une escuelle de bois creuse et du sain chault et mettre de la paste en ladicte escuelle, —et qu'elle ne soit pas trop forte—et hochier la main dedans la paelle[1] dessus sain chault; et les garder de trop roussir. Et pour petites crespes convient batre moyeulx et aubuns d'oeufz et de la fleur parmy, et qu'elle soit ung petit plus troussant que celle des grandes crespes; et qu'on ait**

---

[1] *Menagier de Paris*, §258; p. 224. The recipes the *Menagier* places after these are for *Lait lardé* (the *Viandier*'s Recipe 200) and for *Roissoles*, for *Crespes* (Recipe 202) and for *Pipefarces* (Recipe 203).

[2] This is the variety of rissole that Chiquart presents in his collection of recipes, although he adds fruits to the *Menagier*'s ingredients of hashed pork, eggs and spices (*Du fait de cuisine*, §51, f. 76r).

Alice Vollenweider has suggested a connection between the Italian *raviolo* and the French *rissole* that would pass by the forms *raniolo, raynolle, raysole, roussole* and *ruissole*: "Der Einfluss der italienischen auf die französische Kochkunst im Spiegel der Sprache (Historischer Ueberblick)," *Vox Romanica*, 22 (1963), pp. 418–432. The *Rafioli friti* in the *Libro per cuoco* (§62) do indeed bear a remote resemblance to the *Menagier*'s pork rissole.

[3] *Menagier de Paris*, §261; p. 226. See Pichon and Vicaire's note 1 on p. 124 of their edition of the *Viandier*.

[4] Austin, p. 44. The *Northern-European Cookbook* offers a recipe entitled "How one prepares a pie of deer marrow" (ed. cit., §20).

[1] The word *paelle* in the direction "hochier la main dedans la paelle" should, for the cook's sake, undoubtedly read *escuelle*.

petit feu tant que le feu[2] soit chault, et avoir son escuelle de boys percee ou fons et y mettre de la paste et puis, quant tout est prest, couler et faire en maniere d'unne petite boucle ou plus grande, et au travers de la boucle une maniere de ranguillon de paste mesmes; et laissier cuire ou sain tant qu'ilz soient rondelettes.

The batter employed for large and for small crêpes differs by the presence or absence of egg whites and by the thickness of the mix. The relative consistency is relevant because of the technique outlined for dropping the batter into the shallow pan of hot grease: large crêpes are formed by causing the batter to overflow its bowl, held above the pan, by plunging a hand into this batter; small crêpes are made with thicker batter which is allowed to drain through a hole in the bottom of the bowl.[3]

In the section of the recipe dealing with the smaller crêpes, the passage "qu'on ait petit feu tant que le feu soit chault" does not seem reasonable. It may be that the scribe should have written "tant que le *sain* soit chault."

The normal garnish for *crespes* was a sprinkling of sugar.[4] *Crespes* may be served with *Pipesfarces*: see Recipe 203, below.

203. Pipesfarces

VAT **Et qui veult faire des Pipesfarces, convient avoir de bon frommage de gain par grosses lesches comme le doy, et les enveloper en la paste des petites crespes et puis les boutter en son sain chault; et les gardez d'ardoir; et quant ilz sont seiches et jaunettes les drecier, et les crespes avec.**

There is no break in the text between this recipe and the preceding one for crêpes. As the end of the paragraph here indicates, *Pipesfarces* may be served together with the *Crespes.*[1]

---

[2] *le feu* should probably read *la paelle*.

[3] The *Menagier* specifies the use of "une escuelle percee d'un pertuis gros comme vostre petit doy" (§262; p. 226). A very similar technique is advised for the forming of *Blaunche escrepes* in the *Viaunde e claree*: "Metez vos quatre deis dedens la bature pour haster ... et metez vostre dei denz le partuz del esquele ... " (§2). For another example of this common dish see §161 in the *Sent soví*: "Qui parla con se deuen ffer crespes de pasta e d'ous."

[4] See the *Crispa* and *Crispella* in the *Liber de coquina*, part III, §§5 and 6, where either honey is suggested as an alternative for sugar.

[1] In three of the *Menagier*'s sample menus (Brereton and Ferrier, p. 177, l. 14; p. 179, l. 16; p. 180, l. 21; Pichon, pp. 95, 98, 100) the third service ends with "crespes et pipefarces." Under a name that is perhaps even more descriptive, the *Sent soví* (§159) has the same dish as the *Pipesfarces*, called *Lesques de ffromatge gras*; for a garnish these pasties are rolled in sugar. See also the *Resoles de paste e d'ous e de fformatge* in §150 of the same work. In the *Libre del coch* the *Viandier*'s dish is termed *Lesques de formatge freschs* (§129). It is probably also the dish called

Their name is descriptive of the appearance of these pasties, although the *Menagier*'s directions for making them show that the fingers of soft cheese are merely dipped into (*touiller* is the verb used by the *Menagier*[2]) the batter, or coated with it (in the *Viandier*, *enveloper*). The batter that is specified (and that is called for in the following recipe for *Alouyaulx* as well) is that which is used to make the smaller size of crêpes; this is a thicker, heavier mixture than is used to make the larger variety and will therefore coat the cheese more thickly.

204. Alouyaulx

VAT **Alouyaulx. Prenez mouelle de beuf ou de la gresse qui est ou rongnon de beuf et trenchier par morceaulx longs et gros comme le doy d'un homme, et reffaire la mouelle de beuf en eaue chaude—et ne faire que boutter et tirer, et la gresse plus largement; et avoir ung trumeau de veau et oster la chair des os le plus emsemble qu'on pourra, et la mettre par lesches tenves comme une espesse oublee et les estandre sur ung dressouer net; et enveloper les morceaulx de mouelle en ses lesches de veau et ung petit de sel blanc et de pouldre fine ou blanche; puis avoir une broche de fer bien gresle et les embrocher; puis avoir de la paste tele qu'il convient aux petites crespes et les en dorer quant ilz sont bien cuitz au regart de ceulx de mouelle.**

There are two types of *Alouyaulx* mentioned here, that of beef marrow wrapped in slices of veal, and that of suet—the layer of delicate, tasty fat that surrounds veal and beef kidney—likewise wrapped in thin slices of veal.[1] A gauge of the proper thickness of these

---

Les oblyes farcies de frommage in the *Recueil de Riom* (§33): there the preparation is likewise deep-fried, and is then served with a sprinkling of sugar.

Cheese is regarded as a type of digestive, appropriate for the conclusion of a meal: "Fromages ... conforte l'estomac et fait bien le viande avaler s'il est mangiés apriés ce qu'on a pris grant quantité de viandes, especialement quant eles sont crasses et abominables [nauseating]" (Aldobrandino, *ed. cit.*, p. 180). See also the commentary to lines 106–110 of the *Regimen sanitatis salernitanum* (p. 85 in the Cummins edition of the French translation).

[2] *Menagier de Paris*, §264; p. 227. "Dip" is the Brereton and Ferrier gloss of *toulliez*; Pichon suggests "rouler, sausser."

[1] Austin has edited recipes for *Allowes de mutton* and *Alows de beef or de motoun* (pp. 83 and 40) in which marrow or suet are wrapped in slices of mutton or beef; the marrow or suet is mixed with other substances that would tend to absorb its grease and allow a more cohesive ball to be formed. The *Menagier de Paris* has a recipe for *Allouyaux de beuf* that wraps slices of leg of beef around marrow or, more simply, around "gresse de beuf" (§139; p. 177). There is no mention in any of these recipes of coating the outer meat with a flour-and-egg batter as the *Viandier* does. The *Recueil de Riom*, however, mentions a dish called *Pastez de veau et d'alouestes* (§34), whose recipe includes a fine cheese and beef marrow.

veal envelopes is provided by the *oublee*, a very common wafer available commercially.[2]

For both the marrow and the suet there is a preliminary plumping stage in which each is dipped in hot water, briefly for the marrow and at greater length for the suet.[3] Marrow is a visceral substance and as such is recognized as having a cold and moist nature.[4] For that reason it should be immersed in the water only briefly. With the plumped marrow warmed somewhat without its natural moisture having been too much increased, the last phrase in the recipe indicates that it must be exposed to the warming and, in particular, drying effects of the open flame for a time which is relatively longer than that required for the suet.

The verb *dorer* is used for the application of crêpe batter around the meat roll. This term may refer to the mere action of coating something with a prepared liquid, which may harden when cooked, and is therefore a glazing; or it may refer to the actual colour of the batter—which is made with eggs and will gild the meat. The yellow colour of the coated meat roll and its relatively small size may explain the origin of the name of this dish: "small larks." The outer layer of veal may also have been rolled in such a way as to form the projecting "head" and "wings" of a lark.

205. Dyapré

VAT **Dyapré. Tout pareil comme le grain d'Amendes et de Rozé cy devant, mais ne luy convient pas baillier si forte couleur et ne le fault pas tant remuer dedans le pot comme le Rozé; et y fault du succre assés competemment, autant a l'un potaige comme a l'autre; et convient foison grain qui soit frit en sain de lart ainsi comme[1] l'autre.**

The recipe for *Dyapré* is based upon two other recipes, the *Rozé a chair* described in §191 and the *Tuillé* whose recipe will be copied next in the manuscript.[2] Both of these other

---

[2] These wafers were sold in the streets of Paris by the *oubloier*: see Guillaume de Villeneuve, *Crieries de Paris* (ed. cit.), vol. 2, p. 285, l. 170.

[3] The *Menagier de Paris* provides in another recipe a description of how to plump marrow: "Mouelle de beuf qui est reffaicte: c'est a dire que l'en met icelle mouelle dedens une cuillier percee, et met l'en icelle cuillier percee avec la mouelle dedens le boullon du pot a la char et l'y laisse l'en autant comme l'en laisseroit ung poucin plumé en l'eaue chaude pour reffaire; et puis le met l'en en eaue froide. Puis couppe l'en la mouelle ... " (§258; p. 223).

[4] "La moule de l'eschine a complexion [de le moule] des autres os du cors; si est froide et moiste et tient le nature de le cerviele" (Aldobrandino, ed. cit., p. 134.

[1] *comme* followed by *de* which is stroked out.

[2] The name of the dish seems to have undergone a slight modification to *Diacre* in Meyer's *Recettes culinaires*, §22 (also ed., Hieatt and Jones, manuscript "B," §22; p. 867, and in the *Diversa cibaria* in *Curye on Inglysch*, part I, §22. The vague designation in the *Viandier*'s recipe "grain d'amendes" likely is intended to refer the reader to the parti-coloured white dish of Recipe 199, this being, like the *Rozé a chair*, a colourful, spiced almond-and-meat preparation. Cotgrave

dishes use ground almonds to provide substance for the sauce in which veal or chicken (the unspecified *grain*) is served. In the *Rozé* the hue produced by alkanet and orchil is a distinct red; in the *Dyapré* not as much of the colouring agent is to be stirred in, so that the reddish tint will be less pronounced.

Sugar is a necessity in this dish, as in the *Tuillé*—in default of the verjuice used in the *Rozé*—as an insurance that the orchil will in fact produce a red colour rather than blue. While not specifically mentioned, the *Dyapré* should, according to Recipe 206, contain the spices listed for the *Rozé*, *viz.* a little fine cinnamon, ginger, grains of paradise, cloves and long pepper, as well as the "succre assés competemment."

206. Tuillé

VAT **Tuillé. Prenez amende sans peler, lavez et broyez tres bien, puis prenez boullon de beuf, du vin et du verjus et deffaictes voz amendes et broyez tres bien; puis mettez telles espices comme au Rosé et au Diapré, fors qu'il y fault plus de canelle et de cynamome; et y fault autel grain de poullaille et de veau, et le frire en sain de lart; et y fault du succre assez compettemment—et qu'il soit doulx de succre.** ***A jours de poisson:*** **et qui veult changer lesdiz potaiges a jour de poisson et qui ne pourroit finer de vertjus**[1]**, poys avoir de l'eaue boullue et deffaire les amendes sans peller; puis pour le grain fault perches et brochetz et les boullir tant que on les puisse plumer, puis les frire en beurre fraiz; et avoir espices pareilles au Dyapré et au Rozé: gingenbre, cynamome et moins espices; et qui n'aroit poisson d'eaue doulce, prenez solles, carreletz, lymandes; et y convient du succre largement ou plus que es potaiges dessus diz es jours de chairs; et soient compettemment sallez.**

This dish, *Tuillé*, the preceding *Dyapré* and the *Rozé a chair* (Recipe 191) share several features and are recognized as being similar in nature by the author. For this reason, perhaps, the recipe here is not quite as explicit as recipes elsewhere in this final series of the Vatican collection.

In the meatless version of this dish, perch, pike, sole, plaice and dab are all of delicate taste, are appropriate alternatives to the chicken and veal of the meat version, and are

---

defines *diapré* as "Diaperd, or diapred; diversified with flourishes, or sundrie figures." It has been suggested that the fabric design produced at Ypres in Flanders gave rise to the pattern known as "d'Ypres" or diapered. In his *Miroir de mariage* (l. 1236), Deschamps uses the qualification *d'Yppre* in a sense which his editor glosses as "de diverses couleurs": *Œuvres complètes de Eustache Deschamps*, 11 vols., vols. 1–6 ed. Auguste Henri Édouard, marquis de Queux de Saint-Hilaire, vol. 7–11 ed. Gaston Raynaud (Paris: Firman Didot, 1878–1903), vol. 9, p. 43.

[1] *vertjus* stroked out. The scribe's intention is unclear.

appropriately fried in butter—this in itself an unusual procedure.[2] Their delicate flavour makes them appropriate, too, for the almond-based sauce used in all three dishes.

The sense of the name *Tuille* or *Tuillé* is not clear.[3] In the *Menagier*'s recipe for *Tuille de char*, lobster meat is ground together with the almonds. At the point of serving, after the sauce has been poured over the fried meat in individual bowls, the *Menagier* indicates a step not found in *VAT*: "Sur le potage de chescune escuelle .iiii. ou .v. queues d'escrevices, et du succre pardessus pouldré."[4] The appearance of the overlapping lobster tails is of a tiled roof and this may also account for the name of the dish.[5]

---

[2] Normally fish in the *Viandier* are fried in oil (*e. g.* in Recipe 135 *VAT*).

[3] The *Menagier de Paris* shows *tieule de char* in several dinner menus (Brereton and Ferrier, p. 176, l. 21; p. 177, l. 32; p. 182, l. 22; Pichon, pp. 94, 96, 103); however, in the recipe section of the *Menagier*'s Second Distinction, the names of the dish are *Tuille d'escrevisses* (§77; p. 152) and *Tuille de char* (§118; p. 170). The British editors gloss the word *tieule* only as a "dish made with prawns."

The present edition has settled on the form *tuillé* in the belief that a past participle more likely described the dish, both for its shape and for its colour. The increase of the amount of cinnamon to be mixed with the colorants of the *Rozé* would indeed produce a dark orange tile-colour. See Zanger, pp. 19, 37 and 48. The colour of a dish at this time normally played a greater role in determining its name than did its shape: *cf.* *dyapré* and *rozé*. The name of the *Broet tyolli* in Chiquart (§15, f. 36v) makes use of the same past participle; for this tile-colour, Chiquart's recipe requires sandalwood powder: "Or prennés de la poudre sandre selon la quantité du boullon pour luy donner couleur, et de celle y mectés tant qu'il hait la couleur qu'il doibt avoir" (f. 37r).

A curious error has appeared in the *VAT* Table as the scribe wrote *Tuilleis* for *Taillis* back at Recipe 64: he may have been thinking of this dish, or may merely have malformed the letter *a*.

[4] *Menagier de Paris*, §118; p. 170.

[5] This is indeed the image of the dish the *Menagier* seems to want to present when he refers to his *Tuille d'escrevisses* (§77; p. 152). The interesting passage reads: "Qui veult faire tuille d'escrevisse, ainsi [as in the previous recipe for *Gravé d'escrevisses*, the *Viandier*'s Recipe 190] se peut il faire, maiz forment les escailles des escrevisses." I believe Pichon is correct when he speculates that "cette phrase signifie que la tuille d'escrevisses se fait comme le gravé, sauf qu'on met dessus les écailles, ou sauf qu'elle est dressée de manière à représenter des écailles d'écrevisse" (p. 152, n1). Brereton and Ferrier do not understand the sense of this passage, or of the verb *forment* which they read as an adverb, and insert another verb: "maiz [broyez] forment les escailles . . . "—as if the lobster shell is to be eaten.

The image of a tile roof is quite clear in Chiquart's *Escrevisses farcies* (§68). After removing the lobster meat, the cook is to set the shells aside and make a paste of the meat. "Puis," Chiquart directs the cook, "prennés les croysses des escrevisses de dessus reservees et mectés de la dicte farce dedans une croyse et une autre abouchés sus, et si les mectés l'une au contraire de l'autre" (f. 99r).

There exists a remote possibility of a connection between the *Tuillé* and the Portuguese *Tigellada de perdiz* (f. 4v; ed. Newman, p. 2). This dish is cooked in a *tigella*, a crock or "clay baking dish" (Newman, p. xviii).

207. Tailliz de Karesme

VAT **Tailliz de Karesme. Prenez amendez pellees et broyez tres bien en ung mortier, puis ayez eaue boullue et reffroidiee comme tiedde et deffaictes les amendes et coulez parmy l'estamine, et faictes boullir vostre lait sur ung petit de charbon; puis prenez des eschaudez cuitz de ung jour ou de deux et les tailliez en menuz morceaulx come gros dez; puis prenez figues, dates, et raysins de Daigne et trenchez lesdictes figues et dates comme les eschaudez et puis y gettez tout et le laissiez especir comme Frommentee; et mettre du succre boullir avec; et fault mettre boullir une onde ou deux ledit lait d'amendes; et pour luy donner coulleur convient avoir du saffren pour le coulourer comme Fromentee; et qu'il soit doulx salé.**

Tailliz is a common dish in French and English cookbooks of the fourteenth and fifteenth centuries. The *VAT* copy of the *Viandier* has already provided a recipe for *Tailliz* at §64, a dish which *VAL* calls *Garlins* and *BN* calls *Taillés*: this is a sweet, yellow pudding of figs, raisins and almond milk, thickened and cut into slices for serving. It has no meat in it. The present *Tailliz de Karesme* seems identical to the earlier dish except for the inclusion here of dates, and the qualification that the raisins should be from Digne.[1] The Lenten *Tailliz* is also to be salted, although only very mildly.[2]

The *Menagier*'s *Tailliz a servir comme en Karesme* is a yellow apple-and-raisin pudding made of almond milk thickened with biscuits (*eschaudez*), thin cakes (*gallectes*) and white breadcrusts. The *Menagier* adds that "l'en en sert en Karesme en lieu de riz."[3]

208. Pastez nourroys

VAT **Pastez nourroys. Prenez chair cuite bien menue hachiee, pignolet, raisin de Corinde et frommage de gain esmié bien menu, et ung pou de succre et ung petit de sel.**

The name of this dish—a rich mixture of meat, fruit and cheese—may be related to the Latin *nutritus*, meaning "food, nourishment," perhaps as an adjective, "nutritious"; more likely, though, the qualification *nourroys* is cognate with the English "Norse."[1] The recipe

---

[1] "Roisins de Digne (c'estassavoir qu'ilz sont petiz et n'ont aucuns noyaulx dedens ne pepins quelzconques) ... " (*Menagier de Paris*, §212; p. 246).

[2] Compare this *doulx salé* with the *saler doulx* of Recipe 190.

[3] *Menagier de Paris*, §237; p. 211. There is no recipe in the *Menagier* for a *tailliz* that, like the *Viandier*'s Recipe 64, is not qualified as being for Lent.

[1] Norse pasties must therefore have been seen somehow as a national dish, in much the same way as the German broth, English broth, Saracen broth, Poitevin sauce, Parma tortes, and the Spanish specialty of Recipe 211. The *Menagier* contains Pisa tortes and Lombardy custard; Chiquart has also a Savoy broth and a Spanish *gratunee*.

for these pasties is somewhat reminiscent of the *Tortes parmeriennes* of Recipe 197, at least in its use of chopped meat and in its choice of the fruit to be mixed with that meat.

There seems to be little relationship between the *Viandier*'s dish on the one hand, and the *Pastez norreis* of the *Enseignements*,[2] the *Pastez norroiz* of the *Menagier*[3] and the *Pasté nurry* and *Pastez nurriz* of Chiquart[4] on the other. All three of these latter dishes contain spices, but none of them has either fruit or cheese.

No direction is given by the *Viandier* about how the pie is to be cooked. The remarkable feature of the Norse pasties in the other three books is that they are not to be baked but are to be deep-fried in lard; the same procedure is specified in the *Viandier*'s next recipe, for *Petis pastez lorez*. It is tempting to assume that the *Pastez nourroys* of Recipe 208 should likewise be deep-fried.

209. Petis pastez lorez

VAT **Pour faire petis pastez lorez. Comme pastez d'un blanc ou au dessoubz, et les frire et qu'ilz ne soient pas si hault de paste; et qui veult faire des Laictues et des Oreillettes fault faire couvercles de pastez, les ungs plus grans que les autres, et les frire en sain de lart porc doulx tant qu'ilz soient durs comme cuitz en ung four. Et qui veult, on les dore de fueil d'or ou d'argent ou de saffren.**

There is no rubric for this recipe, even though there is a break between the paragraph containing it and the paragraph for *Pastez nourroys*, Recipe 208. Both recipes are apparently for deep-fried pasties.

The verb *faire* is understood, repeated, before "Comme pastez d'un blanc . . . ." Either the cook is to make his pasties the size of the coin known as a *blanc*,[1] or else he is to make them to the same size as those which could be *bought* for a *blanc*. Because of the additional specification concerning the height of the *petis pastez lorez*, there must have been certain generally recognized standard sizes of pastry shells according to their cost on the market.[2]

---

[2] *Enseignements*, p. 185, l. 170; *Petit traité*, p. 223.

[3] *Menagier de Paris*, §258; p. 223. This dish, apparently a popular one with the *Menagier*, is prescribed for ten of his twenty-three menus (pp. 175–182 and 92–103 respectively in the two editions).

[4] *Du fait de cuisine*, §50, f. 75r.

[1] The *Menagier de Paris* describes the size of a pad for a bung hole as being "du large d'un blanc" (Brereton and Ferrier, p. 134, l. 30; Pichon, p. 69). According to Pichon, "Les blancs frappés sous le règne de Charles VI, avoient 11 à 12 lignes de diamètre" (p. 69, n. 1). In the recipe for *Pastés de lorais* that Pichon and Vicaire reproduce from the fifteenth-century printed edition of the *Viandier*, the pastry shells are described as being three fingers in diameter: "petis pastés bien fais à bouter les trois doys" (*Le Viandier de Guillaume Tirel dit Taillevent*, p. 171).

[2] As the *Menagier* also indicates, pastry shells were available commercially from *pâtissiers*, the price of these shells being related to their size. The cod liver for the *Menagier*'s *Pastez norroiz* is

Laictues and *oreillettes* appear listed as dishes, among *crespes*, *losenges* and *pastelz noirroix*, in the *Menagier*'s sample menus.[3] Their names may describe the appearance of these pasties, whose oversize upper crusts may be shaped into lettuce leaves or "ears." The word *lorez*, stressed on the first syllable, may be, like the modern French *loure*, a derivative of the Latin *lura*, "satchel, purse," so that the pasties are seen as resembling small bags as in a bagpipe.[4]

Since no mention is made of the contents of these pasties, it is likely that they are still to be filled with what went into the *Pastez nourroys*—chopped meat, fruit and cheese—of which preparation the *laictues* and *oreillettes* may merely be other fanciful variants. The close relationship between Recipes 208 and 209 is all the more likely for the want of a rubric before the second.

210. Herissons

VAT **Herissons et Petz[1] d'Espaigne. Prenez chair crue, hachiez la plus menue que faire se peult; puis fault roisin de Daingne, frommage de gain esmié et tout meslez emsemble avec pouldre fine; puis ayez des caillettes de moutton, eschaudez et lavez tres bien—et non pas en eaue trop chaude qu'ilz ne se retraient—et les emplez de ladicte chair hachiee, et puis les coudre d'unne petite brochette de boys.**

Hedgehogs and Spanish "pots" are presented under the same title apparently because they share the same filling of finely chopped meat, small seedless grapes, creamy cheese and spices—what is commonly called the *farce*. While the *Viandier* specifies raw meat, there is no explicit direction about how these ingredients in the *farce*, and the sheep's stomach containing them, are to be cooked.

---

to be "haschiez et mis en petis pastez de .iii. deniers piece" (§258; p. 223). Pichon and Vicaire interpret the *Viandier*'s "pastez d'un blanc" in this way: "C'est le prix qui donnoit la mesure du pâté. Autrefois, le pain étoit souvent désigné par son prix qui restoit le même en tout temps, mais dont la taille diminuoit en temps de disette. A cette époque (de 1384 à 1405) le blanc à 6 et 5 deniers de titre (moitié argent, moitié cuivre) valoit 10 deniers et quelquefois 12 (Le Blanc, *Traité des monnoyes de France*, Paris, 1696, p. 411)" (p. 128, n1).

[3] *Menagier*, ed. Brereton and Ferrier, p. 178, l. 18; p. 182, l. 27; ed. Pichon, pp. 96, 103. See also in the *Sent soví*, p. 220, the mention of a dish called *Orelletes de pasta levada*. The *Recueil de Riom* offers the following recipe which, while perhaps related to the *Viandier*'s dish, does little to help us understand clearly the nature of this dish: "Lez lectues et lez ozillectes. Faictes de paste. Et avoir des amendez batues sans coler et mectre par dessus les ozillectes et les lectues, et frire en l'uile. Et du sucre" (§27).

[4] *FEW*, vol. 5, p. 465a, *lura*: "Schlauch." The dish may be related remotely to the English *Bursews* (*Forme of Cury*, §179).

[1] *petz*: the word is written *potz* here, but *petz* at the beginning of Recipe 211.

The *Menagier de Paris* mentions *Heriçons*, but only in order to dismiss the dish as not worth the effort required to make it.[2] In an English cookery book edited by Austin the *Viandier*'s dish appears as *Yrchouns*, an anglicization of the French *herissons*. In that English recipe, which begins, "Take pigges mawys (stomachs), & skalde hem wel ... ," the meat to be chopped is pork, the prepared stuffing is sewn into the pig's stomach, and the whole is mounted on a spit for roasting. The name of the dish may have been suggested by the bloated appearance of the stuffed stomach. In the English recipe, however, there is a more deliberate effort to make the dish resemble a hedgehog: slivers of almonds spike the outer surface of the skin, then the whole "animal" is roasted and glazed.[3]

211. Petz d'Espaigne

VAT **Et qui veult faire des Petz d'Espagne, fault prendre de petiz liberons[1] de terre en maniere de petites esguieres de terre et les moullier d'aubun d'oeuf par dedans affin que la farce se tiengne mieulx, puis les emplir et mettre boullir sur le feu en paelle ou chaudiere; et puis quant ilz sont bien cuitz les tirer et laissier esgoutter; et, quant ilz sont froitz, cassez lesdiz potz et ne despeciez rien; puis avoir broches greslettes—et non pas si menues aux herissons—et fault faire petites pommettes et mettre en brochettes en deux ou en iii renges; et puis les dorer de paste et de fleur.**

The name of this dish is clearly *Petz d'Espaigne* as the scribe writes it at this point, even though in the double title at the beginning of the previous recipe he wrote *Pots d'Espaigne*. The *Du fait de cuisine* mentions a *Pot d'Espaniz fait de cher tout dorés* as part of an *entremeés eslevé*;[2] the *Menagier* lists *Pes d'Espaigne* and *Petz de Espaigne* among his sample menus.[3]

The dish is clearly an *entremets* of the same sort as in Recipe 210. The paste of meat, fruit and cheese is moulded into the shape of a flower-pot; small balls of the same paste, impaled on sticks inserted into the "pot," will represent the flowers sprouting from it.[4]

---

[2] "Les heriçons sont faiz de caillecte de mouton et est grant fraiz et labor et pou d'onneur et de prouffit. Et pour ce *nichil hic*" (*Menagier de Paris*, §366; p. 269). *Herisons dorés* are mentioned by Chiquart as part of an *entremets* (*Du fait de cuisine*, f. 32r), but there is no recipe for them.

[3] "Take blaunchid Almaundys, & kerf hem long, smal, & scharpe, & frye hem in grece & sugre; take a litel prycke, & prykke the yrchons, An putte in the holes the Almaundys, every hole half, & eche fro other; ley hem then to the fyre; when they ben rostid, dore hem sum wyth Whete Flowre, & mylke of Almaudys, sum grene, sum blake with Blode, & lat hem nowt browne to moche, & serue forth" (Austin, p. 38).

[1] This word is probably an error for *biberons*.

[2] *Du fait de cuisine*, f. 32r.

[3] *Menagier de Paris*, p. 178, l. 21 and p. 182, l. 30; pp. 97 and 103.

[4] This ingenious creation is found also in the *Forme of Cury* under the name *Potews*, §177. Into the hole left by the roasting-spit the cook is to insert *steles*, "stalks."

The "stuffing" mentioned in this recipe is probably the same as is used in the previous dish, with which this recipe is linked in the manuscript. The semi-cooked balls of this mixture are to be roasted and glazed, just as in the dish called "hedgehogs."

212. Espaules de mouton farcies. Motes et mangonneaulx

VAT **Espaules de mouton farcies. Motes et Mangonneaulx. Les convient mettre cuire en une paelle sur le feu et des cuissotz de mouton et de porc—et qu'ilz ne soient pas trop cuitz—puis les mettre reffroidier; et fault oster la chair de autour des otz et la hachier bien menu et la chair des Mangonneaulx et des Mottes pareillement; puis avoir du pignolat et du raisin de Corinde, et avoir une grande allumelle d'oeufz fritz au blanc lart, puis les trenchez par menuz morceaulx comme dez gros, et gardez qu'ilz ne soient pas ars; puis prendre toutes lesdictes mistions et du frommage de gain esmié et mettre tout en une paelle ou jatte nette et tres bien mesler; puis convient avoir des ratiz de mouton et les estandre et mettre de la pouldre fine avec les os dedans sans farce, puis enveloper les os et les farcir, et puis les enveloper du ratis de mouton et les coudre de brochettes de boys pour tenir la chair qu'elle ne chee d'entour l'espaule, ainsi que compaignons sçaivent bien la maniere. Et pour les Motes qui se font en maniere de petites tourtelettes, et les Mangonneaux ainsi longs que petites andoulles, et les enveloper de son dit ratis et les dorer d'oeufz bien et suffisamment; et au surplus, faire ce que au cas appartient.**

This recipe, at the beginning of a series of more ostentatious *entremets*, contains two related procedures. The first of these, for stuffed shoulder of mutton, demands a certain professional expertise; as the author says, the procedure is to be carried out in a masterly fashion, "ainsi que compaignons sçaivent bien la maniere." The *Menagier* rejects this dish from his treatise on cookery, "*quia nichil est nisi pena et labor*."[1] For Chiquart the professional cook, however, the stuffed shoulder of mutton may demand great effort and care but it is certainly worthwhile as a display dish. It seems also to have become one of the obligatory set-pieces for a formal banquet, much in the manner of the *Hures de sengliers dorees*, the boar's head.[2] Chiquart's detailed recipe for stuffed shoulder of

[1] *Menagier de Paris*, §365; p. 269. The *Menagier* will also reject the *Heriçons*, his next entry, for the same reason.

[2] For other versions of the Recipe 212 see the *Liber de coquina*, part II, §42 (ed. Mulon, p. 407): *De spatula implenda*; and the *Libro per cuoco* (ed. Faccioli, p. 87): *Spalle de castron implite*. The most detailed recipe in the *Recueil de Riom* is for these *Espaulez de mouton farcies, et moctes, et mangomaux rotis es plas* (§12).

mutton is designed expressly to "donner entendement a celluy qui haura la charge de faire lesdictes espalles."[3]

The two recipes, in the *Viandier* and in the *Du fait de cuisine*, are similar. Chiquart indicates that meat from the same number of legs of mutton (hind legs) is to be used as there are shoulders to be stuffed. The delicate part of the operation is that the shoulder joints must not be disturbed: "Si laissés les os desdictes espalles que de une chascune espalle ilz se tieingnient tous ensemble, et si les gardés tresbien de despiecer et de dessevrer d'ensemble." The mixture of chopped meat, fruit, eggs and cheese, for the towers and mangonels as well as for the stuffed shoulder, can be placed in one of two ways within the sheet of what the *Viandier* calls *ratiz* and Chiquart calls *toyles* (cauls or peritoneal membrane; in modern French, *toilette* or *crépine*). According to the *Viandier*, the membrane is first wrapped around the bones and then stuffed; Chiquart, on the other hand, tells his cook to spread a layer of stuffing upon the membrane, and then on this bed, he says, "Couchés et estandés les os d'une chascune espalle qui [so that they] se tiengnent ensemble, et si n'estent point le jangot mais ilz soient tresbien entiers et tiengnent les .iii. os d'une chescune espalle sans estre desevrés l'un de l'autre." Finally the membrane is closed with wooden pins and given a moderately realistic shape, with the joint in a bent position. The whole shoulder is placed carefully upon the grill, roasted and glazed, being turned—as always, with great care—when necessary.

Any excess stuffing, according to the *Viandier*'s recipe, is to be formed into small, squat towers and into mangonels, each sheathed in a piece of membrane, roasted and glazed.

213. Cignes revestuz

VAT **Cignes revestuz de leur peau. Les convient souffler et escorcher, et eschauder avant l'escorcher, et les fendre par dessoubz le ventre et oster les charcois, puis rostir les charcois en une broche et les dorer, en tournant, de paste batue d'oeufz, aubun et moyeu ensemble; puis les tirer de la broche et laissiez reffroidier, puis les vestez de leur pel, qui veult; et convient avoir petites brochettes de boys et mectre au col pour le soustenir droit comme s'il estoit vifz. Et est a feste le second mectz.**

This dish and the following one of *Paons revestuz* are a pair of the more common *entremets* of the period. The *Cigne revestu* has already been described in Recipe 72, a recipe offering much more procedural detail than is provided in the later version here. That the author is trying to abbreviate his directions is apparent in the awkward way he inserts the instruction *eschauder*. Scalding must, of course, be the first step before the skin can easily be separated in one piece from the carcass of the bird. This latter step is accomplished, as we saw in

---

[3] *Du fait de cuisine*, §64, f. 90r.

Recipe 72, by means of blowing through a straw inserted through a small hole in the bird's skin.[1]

214. Paons [revestuz]

VAT **Paons. Les convient souffler et enfler comme les cignes et les rostir et dorer pareillement; et se doivent servir au dernier metz; et quant ilz sont revestuz convient avoir broches de boys gresles et tenves pour passer parmy les plumes de la queue, ou ung pou de fil d'archal pour drecier les plumes comme se le paon faisoit la roe.**

A companion piece to the preceding dish, the *Paon revestu* seems to be a relatively more recent addition to the stock of colourful *entremets* reproduced in the *Viandier*.[1] Chiquart, dictating his *Du fait de cuisine* in 1420, makes the *Paon escorchiés et revestus* merely part of a very complex *Entremés eslevé*.[2] For the tough, unappetizing carcass of the peacock, however, the canny *maistre queux* of the Duke of Savoy substitutes a more succulent roast goose; this courtly *supercherie* was one of the gastronomic advantages of the *escorchié-et-revestu* procedure!

As in the *Du fait de cuisine* much attention is paid in the *Viandier* to the use of slender sticks to prop the neck and the tail of the "re-dressed" peacock into an impressive, life-like pose.

---

[1] The same procedure is followed in Recipe 66 for *Poulaille farcie*, and is quite common in Chiquart's work for the court of Savoy.

[1] See also the stuffed peacock in the *Libro della cocina*, ed. Faccioli, p. 40.

[2] This particular *entremets* in the *Du fait de cuisine* (§10, ff. 30v–33r) illustrates the extent to which cooks in princely households by the beginning of the fifteenth century had become designers of spectacular three-dimensional tableaux whose function was in large part to present a selection of the cooks' most prodigious culinary creations. Chiquart's *Entremés eslevé* is a *Chastel d'Amours* consisting of four battlemented towers, each lit from within, manned by miniature defenders bloodily repelling a vigorous siege launched from ships on a stormy painted sea. At the base of each tower are major display dishes: a fire-breathing boar's head, a large pike cooked in three ways, a fire-breathing skinned-and-redressed swan (the *Viandier*'s Recipe 213, with modifications) and a fire-breathing roast suckling pig. In the centre of the courtyard, the Fountain of Love emits rosewater and spiced wine; over the fountain is a dovecot containing all manner of flying birds, all presumably cooked and ready to be eaten. Around the perimeter of the courtyard, by the parapets of the curtain walls, are some dozen other stuffed birds or edible moulded figures (including *veneürs avecques leurs cornes*). This gastronomic monster is borne from beneath by four persons; also hidden from view behind the walls of moulded meat are three or four musicians, both instrumentalists and singers. The whole confection, at least as a structural and sculptural tour-de-force, is of the same nature as the *Viandier*'s Recipes 215–218.

The *Paon revestu* of Chiquart occupies something of a position of honour by itself in the castle courtyard beside the central Fountain of Love (f. 31v).

215. Le Chevalier au Cigne

VAT **Entremetz de paintrerie. Qui veult faire le Chevallier au Cigne a son droit, convient avoir xii pieces de boys legierettes dont les iiii qui seront droictes soient plus fortes que les autres, et tout assembler et clouer bien fort; puis avoir du plonb comme la large d'une table de iii piez de long et autant de le, et y fauldroit bien de ii a iii tables de plonb, et le faire en maniere d'un petit coffre qui ait comme ung piet de parfont qu'il puisse tenir deux ou iii seaulx d'eaue; et faire une petite nasselle de parchemin collé ou sera mis l'ymage du dit Chevallier au Cigne. *Item*, fault la semblance d'un petit cigne qui soit fait de parchemin collé et couvert de minu vair ou de duvet blanc; et fault une petite chaynete semblable d'or pendue au col dudit cigne ataichié a ladicte nacelle parmy ladicte carre de plonb; ouquel carre convient iiii rouelles bouttees et iiii chevrons pour bouter ça et la; et y fault de la toille taintte a ondes en maniere d'eaue, et qu'elle soit clouee au hault du carre affin que on ne voye point les hommes qui seront dessoubz.**

The term *paintrerie*, here and in Recipe 218, is a derivative not of *pain* but of the past participle of *peindre*. This *entremets* and the next three following it depend largely for their effect upon the skill of carpenters, metal workers and particularly artists and painters, rather than upon any culinary talent of a chef. They contain, in reality, nothing edible and amount essentially to elaborate, thematic conversation pieces introduced and carried, or wheeled about, in order to entertain guests at a banquet.[1]

The legend of the Knight of the Swan must have been one of the most common in late mediæval aristocratic circles.[2]

---

[1] Olivier de la Marche describes a more developed instance of the same category of entertainment, which he terms *entremectz mouvans*. During a banquet intricate scenes, mounted on wheeled platforms, are towed or pushed throughout the hall to the delight and wonderment of the guests. See *Mémoires d'Olivier de la Marche, maître d'hôtel*, ed. H. Beaune and J. d'Arbaumont, 4 vols. (Paris, 1883–1888), vol. 3, p. 134. The same author also mentions that less voluminous *entremets* were placed upon certain of the banquet tables (*ibid.*, p. 184).

[2] See the *Roman du Chevalier du Cygne et de Godefroid de Bouillon*, ed. M. de Reiffenberg and A. Bornet, 3 vols. (Brussels, 1846–1859). See also the comment by Pichon and Vicaire, p. 132, n2. This particular theme for an *entremets* remained just as dependable a means to raise banqueters' interest one or two generations after the Vatican copy of the *Viandier* was produced. Olivier de la Marche records that, in the course of a banquet arranged at Lille by Philippe de Bourgogne in 1454, a tableau similar to the *Viandier*'s *Chevalier au Cigne* was mounted upon the main dining table and occupied most of its surface (*op. cit.*, vol. 2, p. 342).

216. Une tour

VAT **Une tour. Qui veult faire une tour couverte de toille tainte comme se c'estoit maçonnerie, convient iiii fenestres aux iiii quarrés de la la tour, et qu'il y ait semblable comme[1] Sarrasins et Mores faisans semblant de tirer a l'Omme sauvage qui les vouldroit assaillir. Et, pour faire l'Omme sauvaige, convient ung bel homme hault et droit vestu d'une robe de toille et chausses et soullers tout tenant ensemble, et que ladicte robbe soit toute couverte de chanvre paint. Et en la tour il fault comme la figure d'ung jeune valleton qui deguisé soit comme Enfant sauvaige; et qu'il ait des pelotes de cuir plainnes de bourre ou des estaint tains en maniere de pierres pour gecter contre ledit Homme sauvage.**

This tower is clearly of the same genre as the preceding *entremets* and the two following ones, an *ouvrage de paintrerie*.

The subject represented in this piece is problematic. It is likely to be inspired by a scene from a narrative in vogue at the beginning of the fifteenth century.[2]

217. Saint George et sa pucelle

VAT **Pour faire l'ymage saint George et sa pucelle. Convient faire une grande terrasse de paste ou de legier boys comme celuy de quoy on fait les pavoiz, et faire la semblance d'un cheval sellé et bridé, et l'ymage de saint George sur ledit cheval et ung dragon soubz les pietz dudit cheval, et la pucelle qui mainne le dit dragon lyé de sa sainture parmy le col.**

The story of St. George saving the princess and slaying the dragon is related in Jacobus da Voragine's *Legenda sanctorum*.[1] The tale seems to have enjoyed a flush of popularity at the beginning of the fifteenth century: in 1429, at Thonon, the Duke of Savoy even organized a two-day dramatic spectacle during which the sacred life of St. George was represented.[2]

---

[1] *semblable comme*: the same phrase is found in Recipe 219.

[2] See Madeleine Jarry's study of the theme in fifteenth-century tapestries, "L'homme sauvage," *L'Oeil*, 183 (March 1970), pp. 14–21; and, concerning the relationship between food and the *homme sauvage*, Marie-Christine Pouchelle, "Les appétits mélancoliques," *Médiévales*, 5 (1983), "Nourritures," pp. 81–88.

[1] A modern English translation of the *Golden Legend* is available, by Granger Lyan and Helmut Ripperger (New York, 1969; orig. ed. 1941); the story of St. George is at p. 323. The French version of the relevant passage (from the Lyons edition of Mathieu Husz, 1488, f. K6r) is reproduced *in extenso* by Pichon and Vicaire in their edition of the *Viandier*, p. 134, n2.

[2] "Vi era ... San Giorgio che lottava contra un dragone costruito e lavorato con gran cura": F. Cognasso, *Amedeo VIII*, 2 vols. (Turin, 1930); vol. 1, p. 124.

218. Saincte Marthe

VAT **Pour faire l'ymage saincte Marthe. Convient faire l'ymage saincte Marthe, le dragon de son long en costé elle et une chainne d'or lyee au col du dragon don celle saincte le tendra, comme elle le conquist. Et se peult faire ledit personnage par deux personnes, qui veult, ou d'ouvrage de paintrerie de telle haulteur et grander[1] que on veult.**

The story of St. Martha is also contained in Voragine's *Golden Legend.*[2] It narrates the taming and killing of the dragon Tarascon by the sister of Lazarus and Mary Magdalene, who arrived by boat on the shores of the south of France.

219. Entremetz plus legiers

VAT **Entremetz plus legiers. Convendroit faire terrasses de pain bis et faire comme une damoisselle assise sur la terrasse, laquelle terrasse soit couverte de fueil d'estain vert et herboyé en semblance d'erbe vert; et y fault ung lyon qui ara ses ii pates de devant et la teste ou giron de la damoiselle; et luy peult on faire une gueule d'arain et la langue d'arain tenve et les dens de papier collé a ladicte gueulle; et y mettre du canfre et ung petit de coton, et quant on vouldra servir devant les seigneurs y bouter le feu. Et qui veult faire la semblance d'un loup, d'un ours, d'un asne royé, de serpent ou quelque autre beste, tant privee que sauvage, se pevent faire semblables comme le lyon, chascun endroit soy.**

It is difficult to see that the first of these "easier" *entremets* would require much less ingenuity and effort to create than, say, the previous *Ymage saincte Marthe.* Whatever the animal to be built by following this "recipe," the remarkable feature of the completed *entremets* is that the animal will be able to exhale flames at the proper moment. For safety's sake, sheets of brass are used to form the animal's tongue and mouth, within which camphor is burned on a cotton wick.[1] The fire-breathing boar's head in Chiquart consumes alcohol as well as camphor: "Pour donner entendement ou maistre queux qui haura la charge desdictes hures pour faire qu'elles donnent et lancent feu par la gorge, si prennés ung doublet de cire et si l'enveloppés tout d'environ de coton qui soit moilliez en

---

[1] *grander*: *sic*

[2] See Lyan and Ripperger, *op. cit.*, p. 391 f. The relevant passage from the French translation of Lyons, 1488, f. R4r, is reproduced by Pichon and Vicaire, p. 135, n1.

[1] As was mentioned concerning Recipe 214, Chiquart ignites simultaneously three fire-breathing animals incorporated into a single grand *entremets* (*Du fait de cuisine*, f. 30v).

eaue ardent fine et puré d'un pou de canfre."[2] Since camphor does not burn by itself, the *Viandier*'s mention of camphor must imply that it is in an alcohol solution.[3]

220. La poulse pour ung chappon gras

VAT **La Poulse pour ung chappon gras. Amassez la gresse du chappon et le foye aussi et passez par l'estamine avec boullon de beuf, et destrempez ung pou de gingenbre avec verjus et mettez boullir en une paelle tout ensemble et lyez de moyeulx d'oeufz batuz, et du succre largement; et levez les ailles et cuisses de vostre chappon et versez vostre sausse dessus.**

With regard to the name of this preparation, Pichon and Vicaire speculate interrogatively that "C'est très probablement une faute pour saulse?"[1] An error in the copying of such a common word as *saulse*, properly read and written as it is at the end of this recipe, seems unlikely. Furthermore, it is difficult to imagine the use of a definite article ("*La* saulse pour ... ") rather than an indefinite article in such a case.[2]

What is described here seems in effect to be a variety of basting or presentation sauce. The *Menagier* contains a recipe for a *Saulse d'un chappon rosty*. Its ingredients are not really similar to what is in the *Viandier*, but the text concludes, "et poucer fort comme ung poucin."[3] The same verb is used at another place in the *Menagier* where a chick

---

[2] *Ibid.*, f. 25r.

[3] This camphor is "the Arabic *kafur*, valued as a disinfectant against the pest. There are two forms of the substance, the rare and valuable camphor found in lumps in the stems of *Dryobalanops aromatica*, a tree of Sumatra, and the now common distillate from the camphor laurel, *Cinnamomum camphora*, of China and Japan. ... Both forms were known at the time of Pegolotti" (Pegolotti, *ed. cit.*, p. 415). It would doubtless be in an alcoholic distillate of camphor that the *Viandier*'s author would soak his wick.

[1] *Le Viandier de Guillaume Tirel dit Taillevent*, p. 136, n1.

[2] A distant possibility is that the word *poulse* may be a derivative in the singular of the late Latin *puls* and its plural *pultes*, which DuCange glosses as "obsonia quae coctione praeparantur" (DuCange, vol. 6, p. 566c). As used here the term appears to designate a substantial yellow syrup with which a meat is served. By combining both ground liver and egg yolks with the other ingredients, the *poulse* is certainly thick. In Occitanian the plural which derives from this Latin word is *polses* and is glossed as a "bouillie de farine, de maïs ou de blé" (Alibert, *Dictionnaire Occitan-Français*). In Classical times the *puls* was any sort of porridge: see Jacques André, *L'alimentation et la cuisine à Rome* (Paris, 1981), p. 144 and *passim*. See also *pous* in Godefroy, vol. 6, p. 358a, and Tobler, vol. 7, col. 1669.

The *Sent soví* has a recipe (§62) for an egg-yolk sauce for geese and capons that is similar to the *Viandier*'s preparation. The roasting fowl is first stuffed with boiled garlic. It is suggested that the basting sauce be used later as a dip for sops. The *Viandier*'s preparation bears no close relationship to the *Saulse pour ung chappon ou poule* in the *Menagier* (§295; p. 237).

[3] *Menagier*, §278; p. 232.

(*poucin*) is dressed to counterfeit a young partridge; in this recipe the cook is instructed to "pousser les cuisses [of the chick] pour faire la char plus courte."[4] The *Poulse* of the *Viandier*'s recipe appears to be a treatment for capons designed to render their meat more tender.

[4] *Ibid.*, §241; p. 212. Brereton and Ferrier interpret the words *pousser* and *courte* literally: a young partridge has shorter legs than a chick! It is, however the *char* that the recipe aims to render *plus courte*. At p. 232, for the word *poucer* Pichon refers to the passage at p. 212 saying, "Nous avons déjà vu ... qu'on poussoit les cuisses du poucin pour faire la char plus courte."

ENGLISH TRANSLATION OF THE *VIANDIER*

English Translation

This English translation of the *Viandier* is based upon the version contained in the Vatican manuscript. Italics identify material which is not in the *VAT* copy but which is read in one or more other manuscript versions; the labelling of such words and passages as a variant (*var.*) indicates that this material offers alternative ingredients or procedures to those shown in *VAT*.

The recipe numbers appearing in this translation correspond to the numbers used above in the edition of the four manuscripts. The French name which is shown below for each recipe is that which identifies the recipe in the edition, and may not have exactly the form of the name which is written in *VAT*.

Here begins the Viandier of Taillevent,
chief cook of the King of France,
in which are contained the following things:

Firstly:*

To Remove Excess Salt from any Sort of Pottage [**1**]
To Remove the Burnt Taste from any Sort of Pottage that Is Said To Be Burnt [**2**]
Gross Meats, Boiled [**3**]
Hericoc of Mutton [**4**]
Larded and Boiled Meats [**5**]
Stag and Roe-Deer Venison [**6 & 8**]
Boar Venison [**7**]
Capons with Herbs [**9**]

Thick Pottages

Chaudun of Pork [**10**]
Cretonnee of New Peas and New Beans [**11**]
Cuminade of Poultry [**12**]
Cuminade of Almonds [**13**]
Cinnamon Brewet [**14**]
Georgié Brewet [**15**]
Russet Brewet [**16**]
A Vinegar Dish [**17**]
Gravy of Small Birds [**18**]
White Brewet of Capons [**19**]
Boussac of Hare [**20**]
Houdons of Capons [**21**]
German Brewet [**22**]
Hotch-Potch of Poultry [**23**]
Subtle English Brewet [**24**]
Verjuice Brewet [**25**]
Bright-Green Brewet [**26**]
Rappé [**27**]

* The table that is copied at the head of the Vatican manuscript announces the contents of the *Viandier* only up to Recipe 169. It lists a number of recipes that are not, in fact, actually copied, and does not show several that are. It is reproduced above, in the Introduction, along with the contents of all of the manuscripts.

Veal Stew [**28**]
Hare Stew [**29**]
Rabbit Stew [**30**]
Mutton and Beef in Stewed Green Vegetables
Leg of Pork in Rappée
Capon in Verjuice
Capon and Knuckle of Beef in Yellow Sauce
Salt Ham with Chine of Pork and Chitterlings with Peas or Leeks
Roast Fresh Ham with Leeks, Eaten with Hot Pepper Sauce

Roasts

Kid [**35**]
Lamb
Geese, Pork [**36 & 31**]
Veal [**32**]
Calf's Tripe [**33**]
Mutton [**34**]
Pullets [**37**]
Capons, Hens, Cockerels [**38**]
Rabbits [**39**]
Fat Capons in a Pasty [**40**]
Hares [**41**]
Bourbier [of Boar] [**42**]
Any Venison [**43**]
Pigeons [**44**]
Small Birds [**45**]
Plovers, Woodcocks [**46**]
Partridges [**47**]
Jellied Meat
Jellied Fish
Turtle-Doves [**48**]
Swans [**49**]
Peacocks [**50**]
Pheasants [**51**]
Storks [**52**]
Herons [**53**]
Bustards [**55**]
Mallards [**54**]
Bitterns [**56**]
Small Bitterns
Cormorants [**57**]
Spoonbills [**58**]
Teal [**59**]
Stuffed Suckling Pig [**60**]

Entremets

Faulx Grenon [**61**]
Pettitoes (*Menus droits*) [**62**]
Frumenty [**63**]
Cold Sage [**73**]
Soux [**74**]
Tuilleis [**64**]
Millet [**65**]
Stuffed Poultry [**66**]
[*Unnamed*] [**67**]
Fish and Meat Jelly [**68**]
Fresh Lamprey [**69**]
Lamprey in Galantine [**70**]
Fancy Rice (*Ris engoulé*) [**71**]
Entremets of a Redressed Swan [**72**]

Thick Meatless Pottages

Cuminade of Fish [**75**]
Bright-Green Brewet of Eels [**76**]
Gravy of Loach [**77**]
Chaudumel of Pike [**78**]
A Soringue [**79**]
Saracen Brewet [**80**]
Oyster Stew [**82**]
Mustard Sops [**83**]
Egg Stew [**84**]
German Brewet [**85**]
Thickened Milk [**86**]
Green Egg Brewet [**87**]
Yellowish Sauce [**88**]
Gravy of Perch [**89**]
Pepper Fish Civet
Provençal Milk [**86**?]

For the Sick

Chicken Cullis [**90**]
Pink Water [**91**]
Flemish Caudle [**92**]
A Barley Gruel [**93**]
A Perch Cullis [**94**]

Hereafter Follows how to Make the Aforementioned Things

Firstly

1. Pour dessaller ...: To remove excess salt from any sort of pottage without adding or removing anything. Take a clean white cloth and spread it over your pot, turning it frequently; the pot should be off the fire.

2. Pour oster l'arsure ...: To remove the burnt taste of a pottage. *First empty your pottage into a new pot, then* take a little leaven and tie it up in a small clean cloth and throw it into the pot; do not leave it there long.

2A. *Pour ce mesme: For the Same. Take walnuts and grind them thoroughly, wash them and boil them with your meat.*

[Boiled Meats]

3. Bouliture de grosse chair: Gross Meats, such as Beef, Pork and Mutton, Boiled. Cooked in salted water and eaten as follows: beef, in summer, with green Garlic Sauce, in winter, with white Garlic Sauce; pork and mutton also, if fresh, with a good Green Sauce *of parsley, sage and hyssop* made without wine; and if salted, with mustard.

4. Hericoc de mouton: Hericoc of Mutton. Sautee your raw mutton in bacon grease and cut it up into pieces together with finely minced onions *in a covered pot, stirring often*; moisten with beef broth and wine, and add verjuice, mace, *parsley,* hyssop and sage *and optionally saffron*; boil all together. *The neck, shoulder and breast of mutton is good for this dish.*

5. Bouli lardé: Larded and Boiled Meats. Take your meat, whether of domestic animals or game, lard it and set it to cook in water and wine, with mace alone and optionally saffron.

6. Venoison de cerf fresche: Fresh Stag and Roe-Deer Venison. Parboiled, and larded its full length *on the inner side of the meat, then boiled in a change of water*, with mace and a generous quantity of wine; cook it well; eat it with Cameline Sauce. In a pasty: the meat parboiled and larded *with fine spice powder put in*; eaten with Cameline Sauce.

7. Sanglier: Fresh Wild Boar Venison. Cooked in wine and water *and boiled again*; eaten with Cameline Sauce or sharp Pepper Sauce. Salted wild boar and stag. *Soak your meat, then wash it and discard the first bouillon, wash the meat in fresh water and let it cool on a cloth; then slice it and boil it briefly in a mixture of equal parts of water and wine. Peel the skin off roasted chestnuts, put on a plate and set out your meat together with its broth.* Eaten with Mustard Sauce.

8. *Chevreau sauvage:* *Roe-Deer. Prepared and eaten in the same way as Stag, above. In a pasty: parboiled and larded; eaten as above.*

9. Chappons, veel, aux herbes: Capons with Herbs, or Veal with Herbs. Set them to cook in water, bacon fat, parsley, sage, hyssop, dittany, wine and verjuice; saffron and ginger are optional.

Thick Pottages

10. Chaudun de porc: Chaudun of Pork. Cook the pork tripe in water, then cut it up and fry it in bacon grease; then take ginger, long pepper and saffron, and toast moistened in beef broth *because the broth of the tripe smells of dung*, or, alternatively, in cow's milk, and strain this; then, just before serving, add in boiled verjuice grapes and egg yolks, and boil.

11. Cretonnee de pois nouveaulx: Cretonnee of Fresh Peas. Cook them until they can be pureed, then puree them and fry them in bacon grease; then bring cow's milk to a boil, and soak your bread in it; grind ginger and saffron, infuse them in your milk, and boil; then take chickens cooked in water, break them into quarters, fry them and set them to boil with the other mixture; remove from the fire and pour in a great quantity of egg yolks *and serve*.

11A. Cretonnee de feves nouvelles: Cretonnee of Fresh Beans. Same as for the Peas, above.

12. Comminee de poullaille: Cuminade of Poultry. Cook the poultry in wine and water, then quarter it and fry it in bacon grease; then moisten a little bread in your broth, strain it and set it to boil with your meat; add in a very little ginger and cumin; beat a large quantity of egg yolks and pour them into your pottage when it is off the fire, and be careful that it does not set.

13. Comminee d'almandes: Cuminade of Almonds. Thoroughly cook your poultry in water, quarter it and sautee it in bacon grease; then grind almonds, moisten them in your broth and set them to boil with your meat; add ginger and cumin infused in wine and verjuice. It always binds by itself.

14. Brouet de canelle: Cinnamon Brewet. Cook your poultry in wine or in water, or cook any other meat, quarter it and sautee it; then grind unpeeled, dry almonds and a great deal of cinnamon, moisten them with beef broth and strain them, and boil them well with your meat, along with verjuice; and add ground *ginger*, cloves and grains of paradise. It should be thick and strong.

15. Brouet georgié: Georgié Brewet. Take any fowl and cut it up; fry parsley leaves and finely minced onions lightly in bacon grease; then add chicken livers and toast, steeped in wine and beef broth, and boil everything together; then add ground ginger, *cloves* and saffron, infused in verjuice. Your bouillon should be whitish brown and thick like a Soringue.

16. Brouet rousset: Russet Brewet. Take any meat, sliced onions and parsley leaves and fry these lightly in bacon grease; strain bread and liver into beef broth and wine, and set this to boil with your meat; then add ground ginger, cinnamon, cloves, grains of paradise, cassia buds, infused in verjuice. It should be russet-coloured.

17. Haste menue de porc / Une vinaigrete: A Vinegar Dish. Roast chunks of pork viscera *on a spit*, but do not overcook them; cut them up, slice onions and fry them together lightly in pork grease, or in any other grease, in a pot over a low fire, stirring frequently; when they have fried enough, add beef broth and *predominantly* wine over your meat and boil; then grind *ginger*, grains of paradise and a little saffron, infuse these in vinegar, and boil everything together. It should bind itself and be reddish brown.

18. Gravé de menus oiseaux: Gravy of Small Birds or of any other meat. Fry them thoroughly in bacon grease; moisten toast in beef broth, strain it and put it with your meat; then add in ground ginger and cinnamon, and a little verjuice, and boil together. It should be thin and not too thick.

19. Blanc brouet de chappons: White Brewet of Capons. They are cooked in wine and water, broken apart by members and fried in bacon grease; then grind up almonds, the dark meat from your capons and *chicken* livers, steep this in your broth and boil it with your meat; then grind ginger, *cinnamon,* cloves, galingale, long pepper and grains of paradise, and boil everything thoroughly together; and add in well beaten *and strained* egg yolks. It should be quite thick.

20. Boussac de lievres, connins: Boussac of Hares or Rabbits. Sear them on a spit or on the grill, then cut them up by members and fry them in bacon grease; infuse burnt toast in beef broth with wine in it, strain it and boil everything together; then add ground ginger, cinnamon, cloves and grains of paradise, infused in verjuice. It should be dark brown and not too thick.

21. Hondous de chappons: Hondons of Capons. Cook them in wine and water, break them apart by members and sautee them in bacon grease; moisten a little toast in your broth and boil your meat in it; then grind ginger, cinnamon, cloves and grains of paradise, and infuse them in verjuice. It should not be too thick.

22. Brouet d'Alemagne de char: German Brewet of Rabbits or Poultry, for meat-days. Cut up your meat and fry it with chopped onion in bacon grease; grind a large quantity of almonds and steep them in wine and beef broth, and set this to boil with your meat; then add ground ginger, cinnamon, cloves, grains of paradise, nutmeg and a very little saffron, infused in verjuice. It should be yellowish and thick.

23. Hochepot de poullaille: Hotch-Potch of Poultry. Break your poultry apart by members and fry it in bacon grease; steep a little burnt toast and chicken livers in wine and beef broth, and set your meat in this to boil; then add ground ginger, cinnamon and grains of paradise, infused in verjuice. It should be clear and dark, but not overly so.

24. Soutil brouet d'Angleterre: Subtle English Brewet. Grind together chestnuts that have been cooked and peeled, egg yolks cooked in wine, and a litte pork liver, moisten this with a little warm water, and strain it; grind ginger, *cinnamon,* cloves, *long pepper, grains of paradise, galingale, spikenard,* and saffron for colour, and boil everything together.

25. Brouet de verjus: Verjuice Brewet of Poultry or of any Other Meat. Cook your meat, with bacon fat for taste, in such a mixture of wine, water and verjuice that the taste of the verjuice predominates; then grind ginger, *and a little bread moistened in the bouillon,* and strain this with a great quantity of raw egg yolks, and boil it; then, when your meat has sauteed, dress it with this.

26. Brouet vergay: Yellow-Green Brewet. Cook any meat in wine, water and beef broth, with bacon fat for taste; then your meat should be sauteed; grind ginger, saffron, parsley and, optionally, a little sage, raw egg yolks and bread, and strain all of this, moistened with your bouillon and a little verjuice; and, if you wish, some good cheese.

27. Rappé: Rappé. *Sear your meat on the spit, then* fry your meat in bacon grease; steep bread in beef broth, strain and throw it over your meat; grind ginger, infuse it in verjuice and wine, and put it over your meat; then get currants or verjuice grapes *boiled in water* and set the meat in this (*var.*: *use these as a garnish when the meat is served in bowls*).

28. Civé de veel: Veal Stew. Roasted on a spit or on the grill, without overcooking, cut up into pieces and fried in grease with chopped onions; steep burnt toast in wine and beef broth or in pea puree, and boil your meat with this; then add ground ginger, cinnamon, cloves, grains of paradise, and saffron for colour, infused in verjuice and vinegar. It should be thick, there should be enough onions, the bread should be dark and sharp with vinegar, and it should be yellowish.

29. Civé de lievres: Hare Stew. It should be black and the bread well burnt in order to give it colour; it is made of the same ingredients as Veal Stew, and the hare should not be washed.

30. Civé de connins: Rabbit Stew. It should be strong and not quite so dark as the Hare Stew, nor so yellow as the Veal Stew, but between the two; and it should be made of the same ingredients as the Veal Stew.

Here Follow Roast Meats

31. Porc rosti: Roast Pork. Eaten with verjuice. And some people put garlic, onions, wine and verjuice in the pan with the drippings from the roast and make a sauce with it. Also, in a pasty *with saffron and spice powder*, eaten with verjuice.

32. Veel rosti: Roast Veal. Strongly parboiled, larded *and roasted*; it is eaten with Cameline Sauce. In a pastry, with spice powder, bacon fat and saffron; it is eaten with verjuice.

33. Fraise de veel: Calf's Tripe, called **Charpie**. Take your cooked meat, cut it up small and fry it in bacon grease; then grind ginger and saffron, mix with beaten raw eggs and pour this on your meat in the frying pan; serve garnished with spice powder or green verjuice.

34. Mouton rosti: Roast Mutton. Eaten with fine salt, with Cameline Sauce, or with verjuice.

35. Chevreaux, aigneaux: Roast Kids, Lambs. Plump them briefly in boiling water and sear them a little on the spit and then lard them; eat them with Cameline Sauce.

36. Oyes: Roast Geese and Goslings. *Pluck them dry, then plump them in hot water and cut off the wings, neck and feet; roast them without larding;* they are eaten with white or green Garlic Sauce, with black Pepper Sauce or with Jance *or with boiled Garlic Sauce*; and some people eat them with Saint Merry Sauce, that is with garlic steeped in the broth of the goose offal or in any other greasy water; and some gourmets take the goose or gosling, when it is roasted, to the goose butchers of Saint Merry or Saint Severin or the Baudés Gate to be cut up into pieces and slices in such a way that in each piece there is skin, flesh and bone; and they do it very neatly. (*Var.*: *And the offal should be washed* *once or twice in salted water, and set it about the goose—that is the liver, head, wings, feet and the other offal; this should be put to cook in a pot with salt meat, and then let cool; it is eaten with vinegar and parsley before the goose is roasted because it is the first thing to be eaten of the goose, and is called "goose giblets".*)

37. Poulés rostis: Roast Pullets (var.: *Hens*) and Chicks. *They should be plucked in water, larded and roasted;* they are eaten with Cold Sage Sauce *or with Cameline Sauce or with verjuice.* In a pasty *with spice powder and pieces of bacon fat*, they are eaten with green verjuice in the summer or without sauce in the winter.

38. Chappons, gelines, hetoudeaux: Roast Capons, Hens and Cockerels. Eaten with Must Sauce in summer, or with Poitevin Sauce or Jance in the winter: this latter sauce is made in the winter like Must Sauce, that is with wine and sugar boiled together.

39. Connins rostis: Roast Rabbits. They should be parboiled, larded and set to roast; they are eaten with Cameline Sauce. In a pasty they should be parboiled and larded and set either whole or in large pieces in the pastry with spice powder; they are eaten with Cameline Sauce or with verjuice.

40. Chappons de haulte gresse: Fat Capons in a Pasty. Without larding; empty the grease into a dish and make the Dodine Sauce out of this grease boiled in a metal pan, with parsley, wine and verjuice; and then make sops, long or flat or small, untoasted.

41. Lievres en rost: Roast Hare. Without washing, *seared on the spit,* larded *and roasted*; eat with Cameline Sauce or with Saupiquet Sauce that is made out of the grease that falls into the dripping pan, chopped onions, wine, verjuice and a little vinegar; this is poured over the hare when it has roasted, or set out in bowls. *And as it is roasting some people baste it with a sauce as for a Bourbier of Boar.* In a pasty, large pieces of hare are parboiled and larded; eaten with Cameline Sauce *or sprinkled with spice powder.*

42. Bourbier de sanglier: Bourbier of Fresh Wild Boar. The breast should first be put into boiling water and quickly withdrawn and set to roast *on a spit*, and baste it with a sauce made of spices—that is, ginger, cinnamon, cloves, and grains of paradise of the best variety—and toast that has been moistened in wine, verjuice and vinegar *and strained*; then, when it has cooked, baste it all together (*var.: when it has cooked, cut it into pieces and set it to boil in your sauce*). It should be clear and dark.

43. Toute venoison fresche: *Note that* fresh venison generally is not basted; *it is eaten* with Cameline Sauce.

44. Pijons rostis: Pigeons. Roasted with their heads and without their feet; eaten with fine salt. In a pasty, eaten with fine salt or wine or shallots, with the grease of the pasty.

45. Menus oiseaux: Roasted Small Birds, such as larks, quail, thrush, and others. Plucked dry without water *then remove the gizzards and the viscera*, then boil them a little (*var.: sear them in a clear flame*), and mount them on a spit with their heads and feet, sideways and not lengthwise, and put between every two of them slices or rashers of bacon or slices of sausage *and bay leaves*; *and fill the bellies of the birds with a mixture of good rich cheese and beef marrow;* they are eaten with fine salt *and they are served at table between two bowls or between two plates.* In a pasty, with cream cheese in their bellies.

46. Plouviers, videcoqs: Roast Plovers and Woodcocks. Pluck them dry, *sear them,* and leave their heads and feet on, mount them lengthwise on the spit; they are eaten with fine salt, and some people prefer Cameline Sauce. In a pasty, with fine salt without putting in any cheese.

47. Perdris: Roast Partridge. Pluck them dry, *remove their gizzards,* cut off their heads and feet, plump them in boiling water, *eviscerate and wash them,* then lard them (*var.*: *interlard them*); eaten with fine salt. For some people, in a pasty, with fine salt. And some people cut them up and slice them into small pieces and put them between two dishes with water and salt and set them to heat over a low fire until the water boils; then they eat them, and they say that that is a very good sauce.

48. Turturelles: Roast Turtle-Doves. Pluck them dry and plump them in boiling water without larding; eat them with fine salt. In a pasty with the head removed.

49. ***Cygnes***: *Roast Swan. It is plucked dry like a goose, mounted on a spit and roasted with its feet still on; when being killed, its throat should be slit from its head to its shoulders; optionally it may be glazed; it is eaten with yellow Pepper Sauce.*

50. Paons: Roast Peacock. It is killed as a goose (*var.*: *swan*), the head and the tail are left on; it is larded and mounted on a spit and glazed as it roasts; it should be eaten with fine salt. *It is better eaten cold than warm, and can be kept for a long time.* It lasts well for a month after being cooked, and if it should be mouldy on the surface, just remove the mouldiness and you will find it white, good and sound underneath. *Peacock offers three types of meat: one similar to beef, another similar to hare, and a third much like partridge.*

51. Faisans: Roast Pheasant. Pluck dry, interlard, mount on a spit, and optionally plump it in hot water; the bird should be roasted without plucking its head or tail, which are wrapped in damp cloths to prevent their burning. Alternatively, remove the head, tail and wings and roast the bird without larding, if it is good and fat; when serving it, attach the head, tail and wings in their places with sticks *the neck and tail should not be roasted.* Eat it with fine salt.

52. Cigognes: Roast Storks. They should be plucked like a goose, *plumped in boiling water, the wings cut off,* and the feet, tail and head left on, and they should be set to roast on a spit, and singed *thoroughly*; eaten with fine salt.

53. Herons: Roast Heron. It should be bled or (*var.*: *and*) its throat slit down to the shoulders, as is done for a swan and a peacock, and it should be prepared as a stork; *or pluck dry and plump it in hot water, cut off its wings, feet and head* (*var.*: *leave on its feet and head*) *mount it on a spit and singe it*; eaten with fine salt or Cameline Sauce.

54. Malars de riviere: Roast River Mallards. Pluck them dry, and mount them on a spit without head or feet *or wings*, and catch the grease in order to make the Dodine Sauce. This is made from milk or wine or verjuice *from bacon fat, verjuice, onions, wine* and parsley *and spice powder*; and make long, thin, toasted sops *over which the Dodine is poured, or else boil the quartered birds in the Dodine*; it should be eaten with fine salt.

55. Outardes, gentes, grues: Roast Bustards, *Wild Geese, Cranes.* As with a stork; eaten with fine salt.

56. Butors: Roast Bittern. As with a stork; eaten with fine salt.

57. Cormorans: Roast Cormorant. As with a heron; eaten with fine salt.

58. Poches ...: Roast Spoonbills and similar river birds. As with a heron.

59. Sarcelle: Roast Teal. Just the same as with a river mallard.

60. Pourcelet farci: Roast Stuffed Suckling Pig or Piglet. It should be scalded, washed well and put on the spit. The stuffing is made from the viscera of the piglet, from cooked pork, *cooked* egg yolks, a rich cheese, cooked, peeled chestnuts, and good spice powder (*var.*: *and salt*); all of this is *ground together and* put into the belly of the piglet, and the cut is sewn up; then put it to roast *basting it* with vinegar and good boiling grease *and salt*; eat it with hot yellow Pepper Sauce—some lazy persons eat it with Cameline Sauce.

Here Follow the *Entremets*

61. Faux grenon: Faulxgrenon. Cook poultry livers and gizzards, or veal, then chop them up very fine and fry them in bacon grease; grind ginger, cinnamon, cloves and grains of paradise and infuse these in wine, verjuice and beef broth, and (*var.*: *or*) in that broth of the livers, gizzards and veal; add a great quantity of egg yolks, pour this over your meat and boil everything thoroughly together. Some people add a little bread and some saffron. It should be quite thick, yellowish, and sharp with verjuice. When serving in bowls, sprinkle cinnamon powder over top.

62. Menus drois: Pettitoes: feet, livers and gizzards. Set them to cook thoroughly in wine and water, and put them on a plate with parsley and vinegar over them *or, instead of parsley and vinegar, put on milk thickened with egg yolks and bread, spice powder and a little saffron; and serve it in bowls without parsley and vinegar.*

63. Formentee: Frumenty. Clean grains of wheat *in warm water, wrap it in a cloth and beat heavily on this with a pestle until all the chaff has separated*, and wash it well and cook it in water; when it has cooked, mash it; bring cow's milk to a boil, put the wheat into it and bring it to a boil again *stirring frequently*; remove this from the fire and stir frequently and add a great quantity of *well beaten* egg yolks, *and it should not be too hot when they are added*; and some people add spices and *a little* saffron and venison water (*var.*: *and a good quantity of sugar added into the pot*). It should be yellowish and quite thick.

64. Garlins / Taillis: Taillis. Take figs, grapes, boiled almond milk, cracknels, *galettes* and white bread crusts cut into small cubes and boil these last items in your milk, with saffron to give it colour, and sugar, and then set all of this to boil until it is thick enough to slice. Set it out in bowls.

65. Millet: Millet. Soak it in three changes of hot water, then put it into simmering cow's milk—and do not put a spoon into this until it has boiled; then remove it from the fire *and beat it with the back of the spoon*, put in a little saffron and then set it to boil until it has boiled enough *is very thick*. Then set it out in bowls.

66. Poullaille farcie: Stuffed Poultry. Take your hens, cut their neck, scald and pluck them, and be careful that the skin remains undamaged and whole, and do not plump the birds; then take some sort of straw and push it between the skin and the flesh, and blow; then cut the skin between the shoulders, not making too large a hole, and leave the legs *with the feet*, wings, and neck *with the head* still attached to the skin.

To make the stuffing, take mutton, veal, pork and the *cooked* dark meat of chickens, and chop up all of this raw, and grind it in a mortar, together with *a great quantity of* raw eggs, *cooked chestnuts,* a good rich cheese, good spice powder and a little saffron, and salt to taste. Then stuff your chickens and sew up the hole again. With any leftover stuffing make *hard* balls, using a great deal of saffron, the size of packets of woad, and cook them in beef broth and boiling water gently, so they they do not fall apart. Then mount your chickens and the balls on very slender iron spits.

To glaze them or cover them with green or yellow: for the yellow, take a great quantity of egg yolks, beat them well with a little saffron, and set this glazing in a dish of some sort; and should you want a green glazing, grind the greenery with the eggs *without saffron, and put this through the strainer and apply it*: after your poultry and your balls of stuffing are cooked, place your spit in the dish with the glazing mixture two or three times and cast your glazing the full length of the spit, then put it back on the fire so that your glazing will take; and watch that your glazing does not have so hot a fire that it burns.

67. [Unnamed] *Quarter chickens and sautee them in a pot with rashers of bacon, stirring frequently and keeping the lid tight; then, after frying, take beef broth and cook them in it; then add beaten egg yolks, verjuice and saffron. It should be quite thick. Serve the quarters on plates, and on each plate place a rasher of bacon and then pour your broth over top.*

68. Gelee de poisson ...: Fish and Meat Jelly. *Take any fish whose skin is covered with a natural oil, or any meat, and* cook it in wine, verjuice and vinegar—and some people add a little water (*var.*: *a little bread*); then grind ginger, cinnamon, cloves, grains of paradise, long pepper, *nutmegs, saffron and chervil [?]* and infuse this in your bouillon, strain it (*var.*: *tie it in a clean cloth*), and put it to boil with your meat; then take bay leaves, spikenard, galingale and mace, and tie them in your bolting cloth, without washing it, along with the residue of the other spices, and put this to boil with your meat; keep the pot covered while it is on the fire, and when it is off the fire keep skimming it until the preparation is served up; and when it is cooked, strain your bouillon into a clean wooden vessel and let it sit. Set your meat on a clean cloth; if it is fish, skin it and clean it and throw your skins into your bouillon until it has been strained for the last time. Make certain that your bouillon is clear and clean *and do not wait for it to cool before straining it.* Set out your meat in bowls, and afterwards put your bouillon back on the fire in a bright clean vessel and boil it *constantly skimming*, and pour it boiling over your meat; and on your plates or bowls in which you have put your meat and broth sprinkle ground cassia buds and mace, and put your plates in a cool place to set. Anyone making jelly cannot let himself fall asleep. If your bouillon is not quite clear and clean, filter it through two or three layers of a white cloth. *And salt to taste.* On top of your meat put crayfish necks and legs; and cooked loach, if it is a fish dish.

69. Lamproie fresche a la saulce chaude: Fresh Lamprey in a Hot Sauce. The lamprey should be bled by its mouth, and its tongue removed; you should shove a skewer into it to help bleed it, and keep the blood because that is the grease *and scrape the inside of the mouth with a knife*, then scald it as you would an eel and roast it on a very slender spit inserted through it sideways once or twice. Then grind ginger, cinnamon, cloves, grains of paradise, nutmegs and a little burnt toast moistened in the blood together with vinegar and, if you wish, a little wine; infuse all of this together and bring it to a boil, and then put your lamprey whole into it. The sauce should not be too dark—that is, when the sauce is thin, but when the sauce is thick, and is called "mud", it should be dark. Also, it is not necessary for the lamprey to be boiled with the sauce; rather the lamprey is brought dry to the table and the thin sauce, or the "mud", is poured over the lamprey or is served in bowls; and the lamprey should be cut into pieces lengthwise and sent to the table on plates; nevertheless, some gourmets insist on having it dry with the sauce, made of the drippings and fine salt, served in the same plate in which it is brought.

70. Lamproie a la galentine: Lamprey in Galantine. Bleed a lamprey as previously, keeping the blood, then set it to cook in vinegar and wine and a little water; and when it is cooked, set it to cool on a cloth; steep burnt toast in your bouillon, strain it, and boil it with the blood, stirring to keep it from burning; when it is well boiled, pour it into a mortar or a clean *wooden* bowl and keep stirring until it has cooled; then grind ginger, cassia buds, cloves, grains of paradise, nutmegs and long pepper and infuse this in your bouillon and put it, and your fish with it, in a bowl as was said; and put it in either a wooden or pewter vessel, and you will have good gelatine.

71. Ris engoulé: Fancy Rice for Meat-Days. Cull the rice and wash it thoroughly in hot water and set it to dry by the fire, then cook it in simmering cow's milk; then add ground saffron infused in your milk, to lend it a russet colour, and greasy *beef* broth from the pot.

72. Cigne resvestu: An *Entremets* of a Swan Redressed in its Skin with all its Plumage. Take the swan and inflate it between its shoulders *as with Stuffed Poultry* and slit it along its belly, then remove the skin together with the neck cut off at the shoulders, and with the legs remaining attached to the body; then fix it on a spit *interlarded as poultry*, and glaze it; and when it is cooked, it should be redressed in its skin, with the neck either straight or flat; it should be eaten with yellow Pepper Sauce.

73. Froide sauge: A Cold Sage. Cook your poultry in water, then set it to cool; grind ginger, cassia buds (*var.*: *cinnamon*), grains of paradise and cloves, and do not strain them; then grind bread, parsley and sage, with, if you wish, a little saffron in this greenery to make it a bright green, and sieve this; and some people add strained, hard-cooked egg yolks steeped in vinegar *; do not boil.* Break your poultry apart into halves, quarters or members, set it out on plates with the sauce over *and hard-cooked egg whites on top.* If you used hard eggs, cut them up with a knife rather than breaking them by hand.

74. Soux de pourcelet: Soux of Piglet. *Take the feet, tail, ears and snout of the piglet and cook them thoroughly with salt, wine and water, and then* proceed as for a Cold Sage, but without using any saffron or eggs, and with less sage than parsley *; and as soon as your meat has cooled, put your sauce over it.*

Thick Meatless Pottages

75. Comminee de poisson: Cuminade of Fish. The fish are cooked in water or fried in oil; grind almonds *infused* in your broth, in pea puree or in boiled water, and make almond milk *and set it to boil*; grind ginger and cumin, infused in wine and verjuice, and put it to boil with your milk. If this is to be a sick-dish, there must be sugar in it.

76. Brouet vergay d'anguilles: Bright-Green Brewet of Eels. Skin them or scald them, cook them in wine and water; grind bread and parsley, with a very little saffron in the green to make it yellowish green, and steep this in your broth; then grind ginger that is infused in verjuice, and boil everything together. If you wish, little cubes of a good cheese can be used.

77. Gravé de loche: Gravy of Loach. Take toast, wine and either pea puree or boiled water, put all of this through the strainer and set it to boil; then add ground ginger, cinnamon, cloves, grains of paradise, and saffron for colour, infused in vinegar, and chopped onions fried in oil, and boil everything together; and fry your loach *in oil* without flouring it, and do not boil it but set it out in bowls with your broth over top *; and it should be thoroughly washed of the natural oil on its skin before all else.* It should be of a yellow colour.

78. Chaudumet a becquet / beschet: Chaudumel of Pike *or Pickerel.* Roast your fish *on the grill*; then grind bread, ginger and saffron, and steep this in pea pure or boiled water, wine and verjuice, strain, and boil; then pour this on your fish and, if you wish, a very little vinegar. It should be yellowish.

79. Une soringne / soringue: A Soringue. Scald or skin the eel, then slice it across and set it to sautee in oil *in a covered pot over a low fire* with sliced onions and parsley leaves; take toast, pea puree or boiled water, and wine—with the wine predominating—strain it and put it with the other to boil; then add ground ginger, cinnamon, cloves, grains of paradise, and saffron for colour, infused in verjuice; boil all of this. Season it with vinegar.

80. Brouet sarrasinois: Saracen Brewet. *Skin eels, cut them across and fry the slices in oil without having (*var.*: after having) dredged them in salt;* grind *ginger,* cinnamon, *cloves, grains of paradise, galingale,* long pepper, and saffron for colour, infuse these in wine and verjuice and then boil it all together with your eels. It should not be too thick because it thickens by itself.

81. Lemprions: *Lamprill. Take your lamprill and scald and clean them thoroughly, then fry them in oil; take good bastard wine and mustard, or any other good red wine with sugar—though with bastard wine sugar is unnecessary because it is sweet by nature—and add to it ginger and, in greater quantity, cassia buds, sieved together; and pour this over the lamprill without boiling.*

82. Civé d'oistres: Oyster Stew. Scald oysters and wash them well, *parboil them a little* and fry them in oil *together with chopped onions*; take toast, pea puree or the water in which the oysters were scalded, or any other hot, boiled water, and a generous proportion of wine *and verjuice*, and strain this; then add in ground cinnamon, ginger, cloves, grains of paradise, and saffron for colour, infused in vinegar, and onions fried in oil, and boil all of this together. It should be stiff *and yellowish, and salted to taste.* Some people do not boil the oysters in this.

83. Soupe en moustarde: Mustard Sops. Take the oil in which you fried or poached your eggs *without shells*, with wine and water *and chopped onions fried in oil*, and boil everything in an iron pan; then take crusts of bread, toast them on the grill, cut them into square pieces and add them to boil with the other; then strain your bouillon, and drain your sops and drop them on a plate (*var.*: *bowl*); then put a little very thick mustard into your bouillon pan and boil everything *and pour it on top of the sops.*

84. Civé d'oeufs: Egg Stew. Poach eggs in oil, fry sliced onions in oil and set them both to boil with wine, verjuice and vinegar; and when you serve your bouillon, set it out poured over your meat. It should not be thick. Then make Mustard Sops as above.

85. Brouet d'Alemagne d'oeufs: German Egg Brewet. Boil together eggs poached in oil, boiled almond milk and sliced onions fried in oil; then grind ginger, cinnamon, cloves, grains of paradise and a little saffron infused in verjuice, and add these to the other ingredients without boiling too much. It should be quite thick and not too yellow. With Mustard Sops *as above*, if you wish.

86. Lait de prouvance / Lait lié: Thickened Cow's Milk *Provençal Milk*. Cow's milk should be brought to a boil and then removed from the fire, then *when it has cooled a little* add in a large quantity of egg yolks either directly or after having put them through the strainer. It should be quite thick and somewhat yellowish, though not too much. Then poach eggs in water and put them with this without boiling.

87. Brouet vert d'oeufs et de fromage: Green Brewet of Eggs and Cheese. Take parsley and a little sage, with a very little saffron in this green, and bread steeped in *pea* puree or boiled water; then add in *ground* ginger, infused in wine, and set it to boil; then add in cheese, and eggs after they have been poached in water. It should be thick and bright green. Some people do not put in any bread, but they do add almond milk.

88. Une saulce jaunette de poisson: A Yellowish Sauce for Fried *Cold or Warm* Fish. *Pickerel or perch are skinned and* fried in oil without being dredged in flour; grind almonds, steep them in a mixture of wine and a little verjuice, strain them and boil; then add ground ginger, *cinnamon,* cloves, grains of paradise and a little saffron, infused in your broth, and boil all of this well together with sugar. It should be quite thick.

89. Gravé de perche: Gravy of Perch. Perch, or any other fish *such as loach*, should be cooked, skinned and fried without flour; the dish is prepared as Gravy of Loach. It is not so yellow but rather russet-coloured, and quite thick.

Dishes for the Sick. Brewets and Other Things

90. Couleis d'un poulet: Chicken Cullis. Cook it in water until it is falling apart and grind it, along with its bones, in a mortar, then steep it in your broth and strain it; if you wish, ground sugar can be sprinkled over the top. It should not be at all too thick.

91. Eaue rose d'un chappon ou poulle: Pink Water of a Capon or Hen. Put your hen or capon dry into a new earthen pot that is glazed and very clean *without any water and with only a little saffron*, and cover the pot so tightly that nothing (*var.: no vapour*) can escape; set your pot to boil in a pan of water *that comes up to the neck of the pot and covers the pot so that vapour cannot escape* until your capon is cooked in the pot; then remove your capon and pour from the pot the water which has exuded from the capon—which, as was said, was dry; give this *the water which has come from the capon* to the invalid, because it provides good sustenance and the whole body is nourished by it.

92. Chaudeau flament: Flemish Caudle. Set a little water to boil; then beat egg yolks, without the whites, mix them with white wine and pour gradually into your water *when it has boiled and cooled a little; then boil it again, watching that it does not burn* stirring it well to keep it from setting; add salt when it is off the fire. Some people add in a very little verjuice.

93. Gruyau: A Gruel of Husked Barley. If it is not husked, prepare it: pound it in a mortar like wheat, cook it and mash it; then set it to boil with almond milk, with salt and sugar. Some people grind it and strain it. It should not be at all too thick.

94. Couleis de perche: A Perch Cullis. Cook a perch in water and keep the broth; then grind almonds and the perch together, steep them in broth, put everything to boil;

then strain it and add in a little sugar. It should be rather thin. A little white wine can be added.

95. Blanc mengier d'un chappon: An Invalid's White Dish of Capon. Cook a capon in water until it is well done; grind a great quantity of almonds together thoroughly with the dark meat of the capon, steep this in your broth, put everything through the strainer and set it to boil until it is thick enough to slice; then dump it into a bowl. Then sautee a half-dozen skinned almonds and sit them on end on one half of your dish, and on the other half put pomegranate seeds with a sprinkling of sugar on top.

96. Comminee de poisson: Cuminade of Fish. See in the section of thick meatless pottages.

Here Follows about Freshwater Fish

97. Lux: Pike. *Cooked in water,* eaten with Green Sauce, or in a galantine made like good Cameline Sauce.

98. Brochet: Pickerel. Roasted, eaten as a *Chaudumé*. Fried, in a pottage or *as is said* in Jance. *Roasted, eaten with salt, wine and spice powder.*

99. Barbillons: Barbel. *Cooked* in water, eaten with sharp Pepper Sauce. Roasted, eaten with verjuice. Fried, in Jance pottage *as above.*

100. Bar: Bass. Cooked in water, eaten with Green Sauce.

101. Alose [d'eaue doulce]: Shad. It should be larded, salted and cooked in water; eaten with Mustard Sauce, or with shallots and wine, or with Green Sauce. Roasted, eaten with Cameline Sauce. Baked in an oven, using a dripping pan in the oven; with a sauce made of a little white wine, *verjuice* and spice powder; and some people put nothing other than Cameline Sauce on it.

102. Carpe: Carp. Cooked in water, eaten with Green Sauce or in galantine like lamprey.

103. Perche: Perch. *Cooked* in water and skinned, eaten with vinegar and parsley; or in a cullis. Fried, in a gravy *pottage.*

104. Tanche: Tench. Scalded in water, *then cooked,* and eaten with green sauce. Fried, in a pottage. Inside-out, roasted, sprinkled with cinnamon powder (*var.: salt and fine spice powder; sew the two edges together with thread and roast the fish on the grill*), dipping it into vinegar and *basting it with* a little *walnut* (*var.: olive*) oil *while it is roasting*; eat it with Cameline Sauce.

105. Bresme: Bream. Cooked in water *or roasted,* eaten with Green Sauce. Roasted, eaten with verjuice. In a pasty, sprinkled with spice powder, eaten with fine salt. *It should be cooked in water and wine to be eaten with vinegar.*

106. Poulaille / Baissaille / Rossaille: Roach. *Cooked* in water, eaten with Green Sauce (*var.: green Garlic Sauce*). Roasted, eaten with verjuice. *Fried, eaten with Jance or in a pottage as above.*

107. Anguilles: Eels. *Cooked* in water, eaten with green Garlic Sauce. Salted eels, eaten with Mustard Sauce. Roasted, eaten with white Garlic Sauce *or, alternatively, with verjuice.* Inside-out, with Hot Sauce as for a lamprey. In a pasty, sprinkled with spice powder, eaten with white Garlic Sauce. And occasionally in a pottage as in the section on pottages, above.

108. *Chevesne*: *Chub. Cooked in water and eaten with Green Sauce. Roasted, eaten with verjuice.*

109. Truite: Trout. *Cooked* in water, eaten with Cameline Sauce. In a pasty, with fine salt *or spice powder.*

110. Pinperneaulx: Pimpernels. Scalded, roasted, and eaten with green *or white* verjuice.

111. Loche: Loach. *Cooked* in water; *first, partially cook cheese, parsley and a little wine; wash and scald the loach well, then set it to boil with your cheese*; it is eaten with Mustard Sauce *it is served with verjuice grapes or currants cooked in water.* Some people put in cheese. Fried, in a pottage, with cheese as it is cooking.

112. Gaymeaux: Waymel. *Cooked* in water with chopped onion, eaten with Mustard Sauce.

113. Meinuise: Small Fry. In water with chopped onion, eaten with Green Sauce or with a good Garlic Sauce.

114. Lamproions: Lamprill. *Cooked in water, or fried,* eaten with Hot Sauce like a lamprey *without spices* (*var.*: *not too thick*) *with fine salt.* In water, eaten with Mustard Sauce. In a pasty, sprinkled with spice powder, with Cameline Sauce in the pasty. *Fried, eaten with Cameline Sauce.*

115. Santoilles: Lampern. In a brewet as for a pottage. With Cameline Sauce in pasties.

116. Ables: Bleak. *Cooked* in water *with parsley*, eaten with Mustard Sauce.

117. Escrevices: Crayfish. Cooked in water and wine, eaten with vinegar.

Round Sea-Fish

118. Porc de mer: Porpoise. Slit along its back, cooked in water and sliced into slabs like venison; then take wine and the bouillon of your fish, and grind ginger, cinnamon, cloves, grains of paradise, long pepper and a little saffron *and bread* and make a good, light broth. It should not be at all too yellow. It is served by way of an *entremets* with (*var.*: *on top of*) a White Dish.

119. Maquerel frais: Fresh Mackerel. Cleaned out by its gill and roasted on the grill; eaten with Cameline Sauce *or with vinegar and fine spice powder*; *bind it around with a net so it will not break apart.* In a pasty, sprinkled with spice powder, eaten with Cameline Sauce *or with fine salt.* If the mackerel is salted, it is cooked in water and eaten with wine and shallots or scallions, or with Mustard Sauce.

120. Gournault, rouget, grimondin: Gurnard, Red Mullet, Red Gurnard. Clean it out through the belly and wash it thoroughly, put it in the pan with salt over it and water afterwards, and cook it; eat it with Cameline Sauce. And if you want to eat it roasted, the shoulders should be slit along the back, then it should be washed and set to roast; dip it frequently in verjuice and sprinkle it over with spice powder; it should be eaten with verjuice *and vinegar.* Alternatively, in a pasty, with Cameline Sauce.

121. Congre: Conger Eel. Scalded like an eel, cooked in water and salted like a red mullet; and some people, when it is cooked, roast it on the grill; eaten with *Green* Sauce. Alternatively, it can be put in the oven.

122. Merluz: Hake. Soak it in water for three days, then wash it thoroughly and fry it, without flour, in oil; eat it with Rayfish Garlic Sauce. Some people eat it in its own broth as you do venison, with Mustard Sauce.

123. Chien de mer: Dogfish. Cleaned like a red mullet and cooked in water; and when it is cooked, it should be skinned (*var.*: *prepared*) like a ray; eaten with cameline Garlic Sauce (*var.*: *white Garlic Sauce, Cameline Sauce*).

124. Saumon frais: Fresh Salmon. *It should be* larded, and keep the spine in it for roasting (*var.*: *frying in a pan*); then pick it apart by layers, and cook it in water and wine, with salt; it should be eaten with yellow Pepper Sauce or with Cameline Sauce. Some people set it to dry on the grill for eating. Alternatively, in a pasty, sprinkled with spice powder, and eaten with Cameline Sauce. If it is salted, it should be cooked in water without salt and eaten with wine and chopped shallots.

125. Mulet: Grey Mullet. As with the mackerel.

126. Morue fraiche: Fresh Cod. Prepared and cooked like a red mullet, with wine when cooking; eaten with Jance. Some people put garlic with it, and others do not. Salt cod is eaten with Mustard Sauce or with melted fresh butter *over it*.

127. Grapois: Whale Meat. Sliced raw and cooked in water, to be served, like pork, with peas. Some people dry it a little over the fire. The peas are better if you put them in the bouillon.

128. Egreffin: Codlings and Haddock. Both should be prepared like cod. (*var.*: *Haddock cooked like red mullet; when fried, eaten with Jance.*)

129. Orfin: Garfish. Cleaned through its gill, roasted; eaten with Cameline Sauce.

130. Brete: Brett. Cooked like a ray *like a red mullet; eaten with cameline Garlic Sauce.*

131. Colin: Coalfish. Like a cod.

132. Truite saulmonoise: Salmon Trout. Sliced across, cooked in water and wine; eaten with Cameline Sauce.

Flat Sea-Fish

133. Pleis: Plaice. Cleaned out towards its back beneath the gill, thoroughly washed, and cooked like a red mullet; eaten with a sauce of wine and salt *over it*. And, if you wish, in a pottage, the fish being cooked (*var.*: *fried*) without flour.

134. Flais: Flounder. Prepared like plaice, eaten with Green Sauce.

135. Solles: Sole. They should be scalded *and cleaned*, then cook and finish them in water like a plaice; eat them with Green Sauce *in a Chaudumé*. Alternatively, roasted *on the grill*, without scalding *though some people skin the back of the fish*; eaten with *sorrel* verjuice. Fried in oil, *without flour and* without scalding; eaten with verjuice.

136. Raie: Ray. Clean it out through the area of its navel, and set the liver aside; cut the fish into pieces and cook it like a plaice, and then skin it; eat it warm with cameline Garlic Sauce. Some people toast slices of the ray liver and put a creamy cheese very thinly on top; this is a good dish and very dainty.

137. Turbot: Turbot. Prepared and cooked like a plaice, and then skinned over its back, and it should be in pieces; eaten with Green Sauce or in *soux*.

138. Barbue: Brill. Prepared like a turbot and then, if you wish, skinned like a ray; it is eaten with Green Sauce or in a *soux*.

139. Bresme: Bream. Scalded and cooked in water like a turbot; eaten with Cameline Sauce. Roasted without scalding; eaten with verjuice. In a pasty, scalded, sprinkled with spice powder; eaten with Cameline Sauce.

140. Lymande: Dab. Prepared and cooked like a plaice, and eaten with a sauce of wine and salt. Or make a gravy with it.

141. Doree: John Dory. Prepared and cooked in water like a brill, eaten with Cameline Sauce. Roasted, slit lengthwise from the head, eaten with verjuice. And in a pasty, with spice powder, eaten with Cameline Sauce.

142. Truitte saumonneresse: Salmon Trout. It should be skinned, its head and everything, and cooked in water or roasted; eaten with verjuice.

143. Alose de mer: Shad. As is said above among the round fish. *They should be parboiled and roasted on the grill, or else roasted on a spit without parboiling; they are eaten with Cameline Sauce.* They are fried like shad (*var.*: *bleak*).

144. Ables / Alles de mer: Anchovies. Cut into strips, roasted; eaten with Mustard Sauce or in wine sauce.

145. Esperlans: Smelt. *Put them* in a pasty and then take them out of the pasty, dredge them in flour and fry them in oil; eat them with Jance or with green Garlic Sauce. Or simply fried, eaten with Mustard Sauce.

146. Esturjon: Sturgeon. Scald the sturgeon and slit it along its belly, its head should be cut off and split in half, and all the other slices split that can be split; it should be cooked in wine and water, with the wine predominating; then remove it and let it cool, and afterwards set it out in vinegar and parsley.

147. Seiche: Cuttlefish. It should be skinned and broken into pieces, then put into an iron pan *without water*, with salt; put it on the fire *to fry*, stir it and turn it over frequently until it is quite clean, then put it on a cloth and pat it until it is quite dry; then flour it and fry it in oil, along with onions, which are not put into the pan as soon as the pieces of cuttlefish because they would get too browned. When serving, sprinkle it with spice powder; it should be eaten with white Garlic Sauce made with vinegar. It can also be eaten in a gravy or a pottage *or with verjuice*. Some people dredge it in flour.

148. Oestres: Oysters. Cooked in water and then fried in oil with onions; eaten as a stew or with spice powder or with Garlic Sauce.

149. Hanons: Cockles. They should be cleaned of all dirt, scalded and washed, then sauteed in oil with chopped onions and spice powder; eaten with a good white Garlic Sauce.

150. Moules: Mussels. *Clean them of all dirt and wash them three or four times*, cook them in water with vinegar (*var.*: *wine and water, with salt*), with mint (*var.*: *with parsley*) if you wish. Serve them with spice powder, and some people use *fresh* butter; eat them with vinegar or with green verjuice or with green Garlic Sauce. Or, if you wish, a stew can be made of them.

151. Escrevices de mer: Lobsters. Cooked in wine and water, or put in the oven; eaten in vinegar.

152. Flans, tartes en Karesme: To Make Flans or Tarts in Lent *which will taste* *of cheese.* Take *the roe and milt of* pike and carp, and almonds, and grind everything together, along with saffron to add a bit of colour, then steep this in white wine; then fill your flans and tarts *with sugar, the deboned fish and the roe*; when they have cooked sprinkle sugar on top. *In a different way: take eels and remove their heads, throwing them away along with the tails, and grind up the remainder with saffron infused in a little white wine; then fill your flans, and powder them with sugar when they have cooked.*

153. Poree de cresson: To Make Stewed Cress. Take your garden cress and boil it (*var.*: *parboil it*), along with a handful of chard, then chop it up fine, sautee it in oil and then put it to boil if you so wish. On non-fasting days [it may be cooked] either in meat broth, *or in butter,* or with cheese *added,* or just plain without putting anything in it, should you like it that way. *It should be salted to taste, and the garden cress should be well culled.* It is good against gallstones.

154. D'autres menuz potaiges ...: Other Lesser Pottages, such as stewed chard, cabbage, turnip greens, leeks, veal in Yellow Sauce, and plain shallot pottage, peas, frenched beans, mashed beans, sieved beans or beans in their shell, pork offal, brewet of pork tripe—women are experts with these and anyone knows how to do them; as for tripe, which I have not put in my recipe book, it is common knowledge how it is to be eaten.

Unboiled Sauces and How to Make Them

155. Cameline: To Make Cameline Sauce. *Grind* ginger, a great deal of cinnamon, cloves, grains of paradise, mace and, if you wish, long pepper; strain bread that has been moistened in vinegar, strain *everything together* and salt as necessary.

156. Aulx camelins: Cameline Garlic Sauce. Grind garlic, cinnamon and bread, and steep this in vinegar *and verjuice; grind ray liver with this.*

157. Aulx blans: White Garlic Sauce. Grind garlic and bread, and steep this in verjuice.

158. Aulx vers: Green Garlic Sauce. Grind garlic, bread and greenery, and steep this together *in verjuice.*

159. Aulx a harens frais: Fresh Herring Garlic Sauce. *Grind unpeeled garlic*, steep it in must (*var.*: *in wine*) or in verjuice *along with the herring heads; and serve it with the garlic peelings in it.*

160. [*Unnamed: Almond Garlic Sauce?*] *Grind peeled garlic and peeled almonds, and steep them in verjuice.*

161. Saulce vert: *Green Sauce. Grind untoasted white bread, a great quantity of parsley leaves with peeled ginger and sage; steep this in a mixture of vinegar and a little verjuice, and strain it.*

162. Saulce a garder poisson / Une soussie: *A Sauce to Preserve Sea-Fish. Grind bread, parsley, sage, herb bennet, vinegar, ginger, cassia buds* (var.: *cinnamon*), *long pepper, cloves, grains of paradise, saffron powder and nutmegs; infuse this in wine and verjuice* (var.: *vinegar*), *strain it and put it on your fish. It should be yellowish green. Some people put in the herb bennet with its whole root.*

Boiled Sauces

163. La barbe Robert: Robert's Beard Sauce, otherwise called *Taillemaslee.*

164. Poivre jaunet: *Yellow Pepper Sauce. Grind ginger, long pepper, saffron—and some people add in cloves with* (var.: *a little*) *verjuice—and toast; infuse this in vinegar* (var.: *verjuice*), *and boil it when you are about to serve your meat.*

165. Poivre noir: *Black Pepper Sauce. Grind ginger, round pepper and burnt toast, infuse this in vinegar* (var.: *and a little verjuice*) *and boil it.*

166. Saulce / Jance de lait de vache: *Cow's Milk Jance. Grind ginger and egg yolks, infuse them in cow's milk, and boil.*

167. Sauce / Jance aux aulx: *Garlic Jance. Grind ginger, garlic and almonds, infuse them in good verjuice, and boil. Put white wine in it* (var.: *if you wish*).

168. Jance de gingembre: *Ginger Jance. Grind ginger and almonds, but no garlic, infuse this in verjuice, then boil it. Some people put white wine into it.*

169. Une poitevine: *Poitevin Sauce. Grind ginger, cloves, grains of paradise, burnt toast and roasted chicken liver; infuse this in* (var.: *wine and*) *verjuice and boil it with the grease from the roast; baste the roast with it and serve it in bowls.*

170. Espices qu'il fault a ce present viandier: Spices Necessary for This Present Recipe Book: ginger, cinnamon, cloves, grain of paradise, long pepper, aspic, round pepper, cassia buds, saffron, nutmegs, bay leaves, galingale, mace, laurel leaves [? *ms*: *lores*], cumin, sugar, almonds, garlic, onions, shallots and scallions. The following for a green colour [*or*, to give a tart taste]: parsley, herb bennet, sorrel, vine leaves or vine shoots, currants and green wheat in winter. For steeping: white wine, verjuice, vinegar, water, greasy broth, cow's milk and almond milk.

[**Additional Recipes** *(MAZ)*]

171. [*Cameline Mustard Sauce*]: *Take mustard, red wine, cinnamon powder and enough sugar, and let everything steep together. It should be thick like cinnamon. It is good for any roast.*

172. [*Marjoram Sauce*]: *Take sweet marjoram juice and equal quantities of water and white wine, and add to these ginger and wine, a little cloves, cinnamon and sugar.*

173. [*Stewed Poultry*]: *Thoroughly cook knuckle of beef, setting the marrow to one side; remove the meat and skim all the grease from the pot; then, in the lean bouillon that remains, cook capons, pullets, pigeons, partridge and any other meat you may wish; with this cook whole round pepper, whole raisins and the beef marrow, then strain untoasted white bread with the bouillon; grind ginger, cinnamon, nutmegs and cloves, with a great quantity of white wine, and verjuice; add in saffron and sugar. Glaze your whole poultry, and [serve with] the broth over top.*

174. [*Stewed Mutton*]: *Take pieces of mutton and cook them in a pot with little water; add wine, finely chopped onions and finely chopped parsley, fine spice powder, saffron, verjuice and a little vinegar.*

175. [*Pies of Herbs, Cheese and Eggs*]: *Take parsley, mint, chard, spinach, lettuce, marjoram, basil and wild thyme, and grind everything together in a mortar, moisten with pure water and squeeze out the juice; break a large number of eggs into the juice and add powdered ginger, cinnamon and long pepper, a good quality cheese, grated, and salt; beat everything together. Then make very thin pastry to put in your dish, of the size of your dish, and then line your dish with it; coat the inside of the dish with pork fat, then put in* *your pastry, put your dish on the coals and again coat the inside of the pastry with pork fat; when it has melted, put your filling in your pastry and cover it with the other dish and put fire on top as well as underneath and let your pie dry out a little; uncover the top of the dish and put five egg yolks and fine spice powder carefully over your pie; then replace the dish as it was before and let it gradually cook in a low coal fire; check often to see that it is not overcooking. Put sugar over the top when serving it.*

176. [*An Egg Dish*]: *Take white cakes or any very dry white bread and grate it; put beef or poultry bouillon in a fine pot and set it to boil over a low fire of coals; add in saffron and a good quality cheese, grated, first putting your bread into your bouillon when it boils. On serving, strain eggs and make them as thick as rice and garnish with grated cheese on the eggs.*

177. [*Clary Fritters*]: *Take the herb called clary and grind it, steep it in pure water and beat well sieved flour into this; add in some honey and a little white wine and beat these together until smooth; then fry small spoonfuls of this mixture in oil, as is done for fritters, and put rosemary generously on each fritter; squeeze your fritters between two blades to drain off the oil, then put them in a fine new pot beside the fire. Dress them on a plate with sugar.*

Here Follow Some Remedies and Experiments Concerning Wines and Other Things *(VAT)*

178. Pour amender moust ou vin nouvel ...: To Improve Must or New Wine, or to Make it Red for an Early Sale. For a hogshead of wine, Paris measure, take three pennyweight of ground saffron that has been infused in the must itself; for each hogshead, boil a full two-pennyweight pot of honey together in a pan with sixteen pennyweight of wine, stir this well and cool it; then take a bowlful of wheat flour and steep these three things together. It will be fine and good to drink and sell at an early date.

179. Pour garder vin d'engresser ...: To Keep Wine from Becoming Slimy and from Being Cloudy. Put into a hogshead of wine a bowlful of red-wine grape-seeds that have been dried and then boiled; then take lees of white wine, dry them, roast them until they becomes ash, and put a bowlful of them into the vessel without stirring.

180. Pour tous vins degresser: To Remove the Sliminess from any Wine. Take a bowlful of grape-seeds, dried and ground, from red wine only, a bowlful of grease of the same colour as the wine, a pennyweight of dough leaven, a half-pound of alum, two buds of ginger, and a little burnt lees; put all six of these things, thoroughly ground and beaten, into the vessel and, with a short stick that is split into four at the end, stir them well so that the mixture froths up. The stick should extend only a foot into the vessel. Then the wine can be drawn.

181. Pour garir vin boucté: To Cure Ropy Wine. For a Paris hogshead set a potful of wheat to boil until it is bursting, then puree it and let it cool; take well-beaten and skimmed egg whites and put both of these things into the vessel and stir it with a short stick, split into four at the end, that does not reach the dregs and disturb them; hang a pound of ground laser-wort in a cloth bag on a string through the bung-hole of the vessel.

182. Pour garir vin bouté ...: To Cure Ropy Wine, or Wine that has Taken on the Smell of the Cask, or a Musky or Musty Taste. Beat two pennyworth of ginger together with two pennyworth of zedoary and set this powder to boil in two quarts of wine, skimming well; then pour it while it is hot into the vessel and stir it right to the bottom, then stop the vessel up tightly and let the mixture sit until it has settled.

183. Pour garir vin qui trait a aigreur: To Cure Wine that is Turning Bitter. For a hogshead of wine, boil a pint of that same wine and in it steep a half-ounce of ground bay leaves; put this in the vessel without stirring in the slightest. The wine can then be drawn.

184. Pour garir vin enfusté: To Cure Wine with a Woody Taste. For one hogshead take a half-pound of sugar, two ounces of sugar [?] and a half-ounce of ground bay leaves, steep all this together and put it into the vessel without stirring. Alternatively, put live coals into the cask, stop it up tightly and let it sit like that for three days.

185. Pour vin qui a la seive brisiee: For Wine with Broken Bouquet [?]. Mix together a bowlful of tannin and a handful of peas, and put them into the vessel. Draw the wine without stirring.

186. Pour esclarcir vin roux en yver: To Clarify Deep-Red Wine in Winter. Into one hogshead, without stirring, put a half-pound of new almonds steeped in that same wine. To lighten the colour of deep-red wine in summer, into one hogshead, without stirring, put two handfuls of mulberry leaves. The wine can then be drawn.

187. Pour vin vermeil esclarcir: To Clarify Claret Wine. Take forty egg whites, beaten and skimmed well, a handful of salt and two ounces of ground pepper, and steep everything together in some of the wine itself; put this into the cask and stir everything together, lees and all. Let it sit, and then the wine can be drawn.

[**Additional Recipes** *(VAT)*]

188. Potaige appellé menjoire: How to Go about Making the Pottage Called *Menjoire*. First, the meat that should be used: young peacocks, pheasants or partridge, or if these cannot be found, plovers, cranes, larks or other small birds; this meat should be roasted on the spit and, when it is almost done, the large birds in particular—the small peacocks, pheasants or partridge—should be broken by their members and then fried in bacon grease in an iron pan; then put them into the pot in which the pottage is to be made. To make this bouillon you need the broth of a knuckle of beef, and white bread toasted on the grill, and set the bread to soak in this broth and strain it; then you need ground cassia buds, cinnamon, Mecca ginger, a few cloves, long pepper and grains of paradise, and a quantity of hippocras suitable for the amount of pottage you want to make; infuse these spices together in the hippocras, add them to the pot with the meat and the broth, and boil everything together, with a very little vinegar, and let it only just come to the boil; and put in an adequate amount of sugar. Depending upon the person making it, this pottage can be dressed with glazed wafers on top, or with red or white anise, or it can be sprinkled with pomegranate seeds.

And should you wish to make it on a fish-day, you should take whole, unskinned almonds, wash them carefully, bray and grind them in a mortar and put them through a strainer; if there is not enough liquid, take a little white bread, or slices from two or three white loaves to have a little thin puree in which the peas are not too mushy, a little white or claret wine and a little verjuice, steep the almonds and bread in this and put everything through the strainer; and you need such spices as were mentioned above; for meat you need perch, pickerel, crayfish necks, and the finest loach you can find, and all of this meat should be fried in fresh butter—or in salted butter that is desalted. Then set out your meat on plates and pour the bouillon over it, with white or red anise on top, or pomegranate seeds, or skinned almonds that have been toasted a little on the fire in a little fresh butter.

189. Lassis de blanc de chappon: Shredded White Capon Meat. Cook your capon with knuckle of beef, then take all the white meat of the capon and shred it as you would card wool; break the remainder of the capon into pieces and fry them in bacon grease until they are slightly russet-coloured, set them out on plates and put the shredded white meat on top; then skin almonds, grind them and steep them in your broth, putting in some white wine and verjuice; powder peeled Mecca ginger and grains of paradise, in a proportion of one to two, and enough sugar to make it sweet. Then you need skinned white almonds; fry them in bacon grease or in rendered pork grease and stand them in the pottage when it is set out; it should be thick enough for the almonds to stand upright; and sprinkle red anise over the top.

190. Gravé d'escrevisses: Gravy of Crayfish. Get almonds, wash them without scalding or skinning them, and grind them; then you need thin pea puree; and cook fine big crayfish in a mixture of two parts water and one part wine, with a little vinegar if you wish; then drain them and let them cool, and set the claws and necks to one side and remove the shells from them; remove the meat from the body, grind and bray this as you would almonds, steep it in pea puree, wine and verjuice, and put all of it together through the strainer. Then get ginger, a little fine cinnamon, some grains of paradise, fewer cloves, and a little long pepper; fry the crayfish claws and necks in a little butter—they should be dry like fried loach—and put them to boil in a pan or in a good clean pot; infuse the spices in a little wine and verjuice, add in a generous amount of sugar and boil everything together; salt to taste. And you can put fried meat in this if you wish. It should be thick enough to cover its meat.

191. Ung rozé a chair: A Pink Dish for Meat-Days. Grind unskinned almonds well, then take beef broth, wine and verjuice and steep your almonds in it and strain them; then take your meat—that is, breast of veal, or whole or quartered chicken cooked with knuckle of beef or with some other good cut of beef—fry this meat in bacon grease until it is a russet colour; then take a very small amount of fine cinnamon, white Mecca ginger, and lesser spices such as grains of paradise, cloves and long pepper. For colour you should have orchil and alkanet—alkanet is as suitable as orchil, if you can get it, because its colour is not so pronounced as is that of orchil; it should be soaked in a little water, which is hot and not just warm, for three or four hours; then put it into the pottage after it has boiled, and stir it thoroughly until it has the colour proper for a Pink Dish.

192. Une trimolette de perdrix: A *Trimolette* of Partridge. The partridge must first be prepared and roasted on a spit until almost done, then taken off the spit and either quartered or left whole, and put into a good new pot; mince onions as fine as possible, fry them in a little bacon grease with beef broth, and put them over the partridge, stirring often; then get chicken livers with a little bread and toast them thoroughly on the grill, steep and strain them, and add them over the partridge in the pot; then take fine cinnamon, a little ginger, somewhat more cloves, grains of paradise and long pepper, and infuse these spices in good hippocras; then add all of this to the pot and cover it tightly so that no vapour can escape; and put sugar on it. And when it is about to be taken off the fire, add a very little vinegar into it; it should not boil.

193. Brouet de daintiers de cerf et vervoisons: Brewet of Stag Testicles. They must first be thoroughly scalded and washed in boiling water, and well cooked, then cooled, cut into moderate-sized cubes and fried in bacon grease. Into the same pan put beef broth, parsley leaves and just enough spices that it not be too strongly spiced; to provide a liquid, a little Cameline should be used or else take one or two chicken livers and a little white bread, strain them in the pot in place of Cameline; put in a little vinegar, and infuse the spices in wine and verjuice in a proportion of one to two, or, instead of verjuice, currant juice; and salt to taste.

194. Flaons cochus: Rich [?] Flans. Add well-beaten egg yolks to cream; get pastry shells of a size that is larger than normal; steep fine or white spice powder in the egg-and-cream mixture; then get large eels the size of a fist, scald them, roast them well, slice them and stand the round sections in the flans, three or four in each; put a lot of sugar on top of them when they are cooked, and let them cool.

195. Doreures: Glazings [Glazed Stuffed Chicken]. An *entremets* for a feast day or for a princely banquet on the three meat-days of the week, namely, Sunday, Tuesday and Thursday. For stuffings and meatballs: you need, for the balls, raw pork—the cut of pork does not matter—with which the hens are to be stuffed. After the poultry is killed, you should make a break in the skin by the head and blow through a hollow feather until the skin is inflated, then scald the poultry and cut them under the belly and skin them; put the carcasses to one side.

To make the stuffing for the poultry you should have white meat, bacon chopped up with the meat, eggs, good fine spice powder, pine-nut paste and currants, and stuff the skin of the poultry with it, without overfilling and bursting it, then sew it up again; this should be boiled in a pan on the fire and should be allowed barely to cook, then mount them on slender spits. And when the meatballs are well made they should be set to cook with the poultry, and take them out when they have hardened; for the balls, get spits that are half as thick or less as those for the poultry.

After that, you should have an egg batter such that it will stay blended in the pan. When the poultry and the meatballs are almost cooked, remove them and put them in the batter; take the batter in a clean spoon, constantly stirring, and put it over the poultry and the meatballs until they are glazed with it; and do it twice or three times so that they are well coated with it. Then you need to take gold-leaf or silver-leaf and wrap them in it; you need to dampen them with a little egg white for the leaf to stick better.

196. Coqz heaumez: Helmeted Cocks. Roast piglets and such poultry as cocks and old hens; when both the piglet and the poultry are roasted, the poultry should be stuffed—without skinning it, if you wish; it should be [glazed] with an egg batter. And when it is glazed it should be seated astride the piglet; and it needs a helmet of glued paper and a lance couched at the breast of the bird, and these should be covered with gold- or silver-leaf for lords, or with white, red or green tin-leaf.

197. Tourtes parmeriennes: Parmesan Pies. Take mutton, veal or pork and chop it up sufficiently small; then boil poultry and quarter it—and the other meat must be cooked before being chopped up; then get fine powder and sprinkle it on the meat very sensibly, and fry your meat in bacon grease. Then get large open pastry shells—which should have higher sides than usual and should be of the size of small plates—and shape them with crenelations; they should be of a strong dough in order to hold the meat. If you wish, you can mix pine-nut paste and currants among the meat, with granulated sugar on top; into each pasty put three or four chicken quarters in which to plant the banners of France and of the lords who will be present, and glaze them with moistened saffron to give them a better appearance. For anyone who does not want to go to such expense for poultry, all he has to do is make flat pieces of pork or of mutton, either roasted or boiled. When the pies are filled with their meat, the meat on top should be glazed with a little beaten egg, both yolks and whites, so that this meat will hold together solidly enough to set the banners in it. And you should have gold-leaf or silver-leaf or tin-leaf to glaze the pies before setting the banners in them.

198. Tostees dorees: To make Glazed Toast, slice hard white bread into squares for toast, and roast them lightly on the grill, and coat them completely with beaten egg yolks; get good hot grease and glaze them in it on the fire until they are properly glazed; then take them out of the pan and put them on plates, with sugar over top.

199. Blanc mengier party: A Particoloured White Dish. Take scalded and skinned almonds and grind them well and steep them in boiled water; then, to make the binding to bind them, you need beaten rice or starch. When the milk has boiled, it should be split into several parts—into two if you want to make only two colours and, if you wish, into three or four parts; and it should be bound very thick, as much as frumenty, so that it cannot run when it is set out on the plate or in the bowl. Then take alkanet or orchil, or fine azure, or parsley or herb bennet, or a little saffron strained with the greenery so that it will keep its colour better when it is boiled. You should have bacon grease, and set the alkanet or orchil to soak in it, and the azure likewise. And add sugar into the milk when it boils enough to be taken off the fire, and salt it, and stir it strongly until it has thickened and taken on that colour you wish to give it.

200. Layt lardé: Larded Milk. Set milk to boil on the fire; get beaten egg yolks, then take the milk down off the fire, place it on some coals and pour the eggs into it. Should you wish it for a meat-day, take rashers of bacon, cut them into two or three pieces and put them with the milk to boil; and should you wish it for a fish-day, you should not put any bacon in it; but add in wine or verjuice before it is taken down in order to make it curdle. Then take it off the fire and put it in a clean cloth and let it drain, and wrap it in two or three layers of the cloth and squeeze it until it is as hard as beef liver. Then put it on a table and cut it into slices the size of the palm of your hand or of three fingers; interlard them with cloves, then fry them until they are russet-coloured. Set them out garnished with sugar.

201. Tourtes de layt: Fried Milk. Set milk to boil on a low coal fire; you should have eggs scrambled together, or with the whites if you wish, and when the milk boils split it into two vessels; then strain parsley greenery with half of your eggs, and add in enough wine and verjuice to curdle it well, then set it to cool to the point where you can hold your hand in it. Get a bolting cloth two feet in length, take a spoonful or two of the milk and wrap it in two or three turns of the cloth, then rub it good and strongly with your hands and, when it has set and is hard, take it from the cloth; set it to cool and stick two or three rows of cloves in it, then fry them in bacon grease until they are russet-coloured. They should be served with Larded Milk in a plate, half of one and half of the other.

201A. Buignetz et roysolles de mouelle: Fritters and Marrow Rissoles.

202. Crespes grandes et petites: Large and Small Crêpes. The large ones are made with a syrup pot or a large brass pan, the small ones with an iron pan. They should be made of egg yolks and flour beaten together. Get a deep wooden bowl and hot grease, put the batter in the bowl—it should not be too thick—turn your hand in the bowl over the hot grease; and keep them from browning too much. For Small Crêpes you should beat yolks and whites together with flour, and it should be a little thicker than the batter for the Large Crêpes. Keep a low fire going until [the grease is] hot; get a wooden bowl with a hole in the bottom, put the batter in it and then when everything is ready let it run out and make a sort of little loop, or a larger one, and across the loop make a sort of tongue of a buckle with the same batter; and let the Crêpes cook in the grease until they have swollen up.

203. Pipesfarces: If you wish to make Stuffed Tubes (*Pipesfarces*), you should have good rich cheese in slices as thick as a finger, and coat them in the batter of the Small Crêpes, then drop them into hot grease, and keep them from burning. When they are dry and yellowish, set them out and the Crêpes with them.

204. Alouyaulx: Little Larks. Take beef marrow or the fat that is on beef kidney [suet] and slice it into pieces as long and as thick as a man's finger; plump the beef marrow in hot water, merely dipping it in and out, immersing the fat at greater length. Get a knuckle of veal and remove the meat from the bones in continuous pieces as much as is possible, and cut it into very thin slices the thickness of a wafer; lay them out on a clean dressing board and wrap the pieces of marrow in the slices of veal, with a little white salt and with fine or white spice powder; then mount them on a very slender iron spit; then get batter such as is used for the Small Crêpes and glaze them with it when they are well cooked—that is, as far as the marrow ones are concerned.

205. Dyapré: A Diapered Dish. Just the same as the Almond Dish and the Pink Dish, above, but it should not be given so pronounced a colour and it should not be stirred so much in the pot as the Pink Dish; you need quite a good amount of sugar, as much in the one pottage as in the other; and you need a lot of meat, fried in bacon grease just as for the other dish.

206. Tuillé: A Tiled (or Tile-Coloured) Dish. Wash unskinned almonds and grind them well, then steep your almonds in beef broth, wine and verjuice; then add in such spices as for the Pink Dish and the Diapered Dish, except that it needs more cinnamon, both ordinary and fine; and similarly it needs poultry meat and veal fried in bacon grease, and quite a good amount of sugar so that it is sweet. On fish-days: if you wish to change these pottages for fish-days, and if you cannot get verjuice, get boiled water and steep the almonds in it without skinning them; then for meat you need perch and pike, and boil them until they can be skinned, then fry them in fresh butter; and use spices as in the Diapered Dish and the Pink Dish: ginger, cinnamon and the lesser spices. If you cannot get freshwater fish, use sole, plaice and dab. And you should be generous with the sugar, more than in the above pottages for meat-days. It should be adequately salted.

207. Tailliz de Karesme: Lenten Slices. Grind skinned almonds very well in a mortar, then take lukewarm boiled water, steep the almonds, strain them and boil this milk on a few coals; take one- or two-day-old cracknels and cut them into small pieces the size of large dice; then take figs, dates and seedless grapes, cut up the figs and dates like the cracknels, and drop everything into the milk and let it become as thick as Frumenty, and add in sugar to boil with it; the almond milk should boil briefly. To give it colour you should use saffron to colour it the same as Frumenty. Salt it lightly.

208. Pastez nourroys: Norse Pies. Take finely chopped, well-cooked meat, pine-nut paste, currants, finely crumbled rich cheese, a little sugar and very little salt.

209. Petis pastez lorez: To make little *Pastez lorez*. Pasties the size of one-penny pasties or smaller, fried, with their sides not so high. If you wish to make Lettuce Leaves or Little Ears you must make pastry covers, the ones larger than the others. Fry them in refined pork grease until they are as hard as if baked in an oven. And if you wish, they can be glazed with gold- or silver-leaf, or with saffron.

210. Herissons et petz d'Espaigne: Hedgehogs and Spanish Farts (Pots). Chop raw meat as small as possible; mix seedless grapes and crumbled rich cheese together with fine spice powder; get sheep rennets, scald them and wash them thoroughly—though not in water hot enough to shrink them—and fill them with the chopped meat, and then sew them up with a little wooden skewer.

211. Petz d'Espaigne: If you wish to make Spanish Farts (Pots), you must get little jugs such as earthenware water pitchers, and moisten them on the inside with egg white so that the filling will stick better; then fill them and set them to boil on the fire in a pan or cauldron; when they are well cooked, take them out and let them drain; when they are cool, break the pots and do not disturb anything. Then get slender spits—not so small as for the Hedgehogs; and you should make little meatballs and put them on skewers in rows of two or three; then glaze them with a flour batter.

212. Espaules de mouton farcies. Motes et mangonneaulx: Stuffed Shoulder of Mutton. Towers and Mangonels. Shoulders of mutton should be cooked in a pan on the fire, as well as legs of mutton or pork—do not overcook them—then let them cool; the meat is taken off from around the bones and is chopped up very fine, and the meat for the Mangonels and Towers similarly; then get pine-nut paste, currants and a large egg omelette fried in white bacon fat, and cut them into small pieces the size of large dice, and keep them from burning; take all of these ingredients, along with crumbled creamy cheese, and put everything into a clean pan or bowl and mix them thoroughly together. Then you need sheep cauls: spread them out, sprinkle them with fine spice powder and set out the bones on them without the stuffing; then wrap up and pack around the bones, wrapping them with the sheep's caul, and sew them together with little skewers of wood to keep the meat from falling away from around the shoulder—as cook's help know how to do. The Towers are made like little pies, and the Mangonels are as long as little chitterlings; wrap them in the caul and glaze them properly with eggs. For the rest, do what is required in each case.

213. Cignes revestuz: Swans Redressed in their Skin. They should be inflated and skinned, scalding before skinning; cut into them under the belly and remove the carcass; roast the carcasses on a spit and glaze them as they are turning with an egg batter, yolks and whites together. Remove them from the spit, let them cool, then dress them in their skin if you wish. You should have little wooden skewers to put in their neck to hold it upright as if the birds were alive. This is the second serving at a feast.

214. Paons [revestuz]: Peacocks [Redressed in their Skin]. They should be blown into and inflated like the swans, and roasted and glazed in the same way. They should be in the last serving. When they are redressed you should get slender, thin sticks of wood to pass through the tail feathers, or a little brass wire to hold the feathers up as if the peacock was spreading its tail.

215. Entremetz de paintrerie: le Chevalier au cigne: Painted *Entremets*. If you wish to make the Swan Knight realistically you should get twelve light pieces of wood, four of which will be the uprights and should be stronger than the others, and assemble and nail everything strongly; then get lead in the size of a sheet three feet long and just as wide, and you would need from two to three sheets of lead, and make a sort of little coffer which is about a foot deep so as to contain two or three buckets of water. Make a little boat of glued parchment covered with minever or with white down; and you need a little golden chain hanging from the neck of the swan attached to the boat across the lead box. On this box four wheels should be affixed, and four shafts so that it can be pushed here and there; and it should have cloth painted with waves to look like water, nailed to the top of the box so that the men beneath it will not be seen.

216. Une tour: A Tower. If you wish to make a tower covered with cloth painted as if it were masonry, it should have four windows at the four corners of the tower, and there should be in them the likeness of Saracens and Moors shooting at the wild man who is trying to attack them. To make the wild man you need a tall, erect, handsome man dressed in a linen robe with leggings and shoes of matching material; and the robe should be covered completely with painted hemp. In the tower you need the representation of a young lad who is disguised as the wild boy, and he should have leather balls, stuffed with flocks of wool or yarn, painted to look like stones, to throw at the wild man.

217. Saint George et sa pucelle: To Represent Saint George and his Maiden. You need to make a broad platform of dough or of light wood such as shields are made of, and make the likeness of a horse, saddled and bridled, and the image of Saint George on that horse, and a dragon under the hooves of the horse, and the Maiden who is leading the dragon, which is bound by its neck to her belt.

218. Saincte Marthe: To Represent Saint Martha. You should make the image of Saint Martha with the dragon at full length by her side and, around the neck of the dragon, a gold chain by which the saint will hold it, as if she had tamed it. This figure can be done by two people, if you wish, or by painted work of whatever height and size you may wish.

219. Entremetz plus legiers: Easier *Entremets*. You could make platforms of coarse bread, and represent a damsel sitting on the platform, which platform should be covered with tin-leaf painted to look green and grassy; and you need a lion that will have its two front paws and its head in the lap of the damsel. And you can make it with a brass-lined mouth and a thin brass tongue, and with paper teeth glued in the mouth; and put camphor and a little cotton in the mouth and, when it is about to be served before the lords, set fire to this. If you wish to represent a wolf, a bear, a zebra, a serpent or any other animal, whether domestic or wild, they can be done in the same way as the lion, each in its own fashion.

220. La poulse pour ung chappon gras: The *Poulse* for a Fat Capon. Collect the grease from the capon, and the liver as well, and put it through the strainer with beef broth; infuse a little ginger in verjuice and set everything to boil together in a pan, and bind it with beaten egg yolks; add in a generous amount of sugar. Remove the wings and legs of your capon and pour your sauce over top.

MODERNIZING THE *VIANDIER*

Modernizing the *Viandier*

The Nature of Early French Cookery

In her survey of the genre of the mediæval cookbook Marianne Mulon comments that early recipes demonstrate "avant tout l'abus des épices."[1] And, among a surprising number of other historians who should know better, Carson Ritchie echoes this assessment by asserting quite comprehensively that "the whole of medieval cookery revolved around the use of spices."[2]

It is, of course, a simple matter to leaf through the recipes contained in the *Viandier*, or in virtually any culinary collection of the late Middle Ages, and observe that spices occupy a dominant place among the ingredients for just about any dish.[3] From this observation to a conclusion that mediæval cuisine is over-spiced and consequently indigestible is a small step, and one that, unfortunately, many observers have rashly made. Speaking specifically of the *Viandier* we may agree that the observation about the prevalence of seasonings is on the whole accurate. It is clearly true that these recipes frequently do call for "many" spices. However, unless the casual reader glancing through the *Viandier* becomes a practical cook, willing to accept a recipe as a set of instructions and to create a dish as close as is feasible to what was intended by the authors, then he or she cannot pass any serious judgement upon its gastronomic qualities or merits.

What the willing, open-minded cook will find, working with a recipe from the *Viandier*, is that the dish will very largely have the qualities that he or she chooses to give to it. This is exactly the case as it was in Taillevent's day. The reasons for the indeterminateness of the results are twofold. In the first place these written recipes do not attempt to indicate quantities, either in the net output or "yield" of any given recipe or in the amount of each ingredient that should be "measured" into the mix. These quantities, input and output, are obviously interdependent. If the recipe is to be of general usefulness, suitable to prepare either an intimate serving for six persons or for a banquet of 600, then clearly quantities

---

[1] "Les premières recettes médiévales," p. 937.

[2] Carson I. A. Ritchie, *Food in Civilization: How History Has Been Affected by Human Tastes* (New York: Beaufort and Sydney: Methuen, 1981), p. 62.

[3] Concerning the use of spices in mediæval European cookery in general, see Toby Peterson, "The Arab Influence on Western European Cooking," *Journal of Medieval History*, 6 (1980), pp. 317–340. Peterson's argument is that Europeans emulated the Arabs in their food preparation and in according spices a prestigious role in a search for the sensuous pleasures of the good life. See also Eliyahu Ashton, "The Volume of Mediæval Spice Trade," *Journal of European Economic History*, 9 (1980), pp. 753–763; Bruno Laurioux, "De l'usage des épices dans l'alimentation médiévale," *Médiévales*, 5 (1983), pp. 15–31; and, by the same author, "Spices in the Medieval Diet: a New Approach," *Food and Foodways*, 1 (1985), pp. 43–76.

cannot be specified. The cook's professional discretion will determine whatever quantity of each ingredient is reasonable for the quantity of the dish being prepared. Time and again in the *Du fait de cuisine* Chiquart advises his reader to use an amount of an ingredient that is "appoint" or is "par bonne mesure."[4] The authors of the *Viandier* do not enjoin their cooks as explicitly to use good judgement in determining quantities, but the implicit caution is nonetheless there. One of a cook's most important professional functions is to judge what quantities are appropriate for whatever dish he is preparing.

The modern cook using these recipes has exactly the same freedom as his or her mediæval counterpart. It is up to him or her to allow experience and taste to guide in determining just how much of any particular ingredient to use. It is true that in some recipes the *Viandier* text will indicate that a greater amount of one herb or spice is to be used, that the tang of the vinegar should predominate, or that the dish should have a sweet flavour or a yellow colour. But these directions imply only relative amounts of an ingredient and never the exact quantity in any absolute sense. As a fourteenth-century cook would tell you, this food is only as bitter or as thick or as spicy as you, or your master or mistress, care to make it.

Two further factors that modern detractors of mediæval foods do not seem to take into consideration are that spices at the time of the *Viandier* were exorbitantly expensive, and that they were in all likelihood much less potent than those at the disposal of most modern cooks. It has indeed been demonstrated that in the houses of the great and wealthy the consumption of costly foodstuffs, including spices, was intended to be conspicuous.[5] If hospitality and the occasional ostentatious demonstration of affluence were part of the accepted social code, few households could afford the wasteful expense of a lavish use of such spices on a regular basis. Normal everyday menus were undoubtedly more bland; not every meal was a banquet. As to the potency of the condiments for which aristocracy and bourgeoisie spent so much of their wealth, we may again wonder whether the recipe books tell the whole story. In the days before vacuum-sealed containers, when oriental spices required at the very least a full year to complete their voyage to a European port, and then another month or two to be transported to the local merchant-distributor in northern France, a great deal of their aroma, their pungency, their zest must surely have faded.[6]

---

[4] "Du fait de cuisine par Maistre Chiquart 1420," *Vallesia*, 40 (1985), p. 118.

[5] The illustration that Brunetto Latini in his *Livres dou Tresor* offers of one of the prime aristocratic virtues, Magnificence, is well known. "Est-elle," he declares, "en faire grans noces [feasts], et doner as gens grans herbegerie et grans viandes et grans presens et a cestui [the host] ne covient penser de ses despenses solement, més des autrui": ed. Francis J. Carmody (Berkeley & Los Angeles: University of California Press, 1948; repr. Geneva: Slatkine, 1975), book 2, ch. 22, p. 193.

[6] Concerning the highly developed trade routes from the East at the end of the Middle Ages, and the commercial interests, based in Venice and Genoa, which operated on them, see Robert-Henri Bautier, *The Economic Development of Medieval Europe*, tr. Heather Karolyi (London: Thames & Hudson and New York:Harcourt Brace Johanovich, 1971), especially pp. 135–144; and the *Cambridge Economic History of Europe*, 7 vols. (Cambridge: Cambridge University Press, 1952), vol. 2, ch. 5, pp. 257–354, Robert S. Lopez, "The Trade of Medieval Europe: The South,"

Indeed a clear distinction was established between imported and domestic aromatics along the line of their relative potency. According to Platina in the second half of the fifteenth century the exotic spices are more delicate than those of domestic source, the latter, because of their very strength, being appropriate for only a lower class of consumer.[7] Delicate condiments enjoyed the esteem of the aristocratic diner and the respect of his cook; excessive familiarity would breed contempt.[8]

Another assumption that some modern scholars have made after examining the recipes contained in late-mediæval culinary collections is that the aristocratic diet of this time can be characterized by a predominence of meat, in a broad assortment of forms and treatments, and a relative absence of vegetables. The recipe collections do not constitute a sound base for such a conclusion. What these written treatises are concerned with transmitting is for the most part the formulæ for creating the more complex of the made dishes, the ones in which more than an ingredient or two are to be combined or handled in some peculiar way. It would be useless to devote a recipe to the boiling of cabbage or spinach. The *Viandier* itself clearly indicates in Recipe 154 that there are still a good number of secondary preparations—several of which are for vegetables—for which no separate recipe has been written and included in this compilation, for the simple reason that anyone can do them: "Femmes en sont maistresses et chascun le sçait faire." We do know, however, that garden vegetables were universally cultivated throughout the Middle Ages for domestic consumption. In the first half of the thirteenth century John de Garland enumerates at length the vegetables that are found in his Parisian garden: cabbage, chard, leeks, garlic, onions, scallions, and so forth.[9] Market gardens of the day regularly included among

---

esp. pp. 332 ff.

[7] "Aromata, quibus in pulmentariis utimur, multifariam habentur, & omnia quidem prius ab externis in nostram provinciam importata ... Piper: ... "; "De acrimoniis, et primum de allio ... ": Bartolomeo Sacchi, *Platine de honesta voluptate et valitudine* [c. 1460] (Rome: Uldericus Gallus, 1475), book 3. "Des espices que nous usons en noz viandes y a plusieurs & diverses manieres lesquelles sont aportees par les estrangiers du pays d'orient en noz provinces. E premierement le poyvre: ... "; "S'ensuyvent les espices fortes & des petites gens. Et premierement des ailx ... ": *Platine en françoys tresutile & necessaire pour le corps humain qui traicte de honneste volupté et de toutes viandes et choses que l'omme menge ...* (Lyon: Françoys Fradin, 1505). The vulgar, strong "spices" listed by Platina include garlic, leek, fennel, cumin, anis, poppyseed, coriander, mint, celery and thyme.

[8] This appears to have been what happened to the long-standing seasoner pepper which, in the course of the fourteenth century, was displaced by the more subtle and delectable flavour of grains of paradise.

[9] Thomas Wright, *A Volume of Vocabularies* (n.pl., 1882), p. 136. Teresa McLean's list of typical vegetables is more extensive: beans, peas, leeks, onion, cabbage, cauliflower, turnip, parsnips, spinach, orach, sorrel, lettuce, endive, cress, radishes and some carrots: *Medieval English Gardens* (London, 1981), pp. 197–223. John de Garlande lists as well the herbs in his exemplary herb garden: sage, parsley, dittany, hyssop, great celandine, fennel, feverfew, columbine, rose, lily and violette (*loc. cit.*). See also: Frank Crisp, *Medieval Gardens* (London, 1924); Noël Coulet, "Pour une histoire du jardin," *Le Moyen Age*, 73 (1967), pp. 239–270; and Roger Grand, *L'Agriculture*

their commercial crops such vegetables as peas, beans, lentils, cabbage, turnips, parsnips, carrots, Swiss chard, leeks, onions, garlic, shallots, spinach, salad greens including romaine lettuce and cress, as well as mushrooms and, increasingly in the fifteenth century, tomatoes, asparagus, melons and pumpkins.[10] In the same way and for the same reasons fruits appear in early recipes only when they are to undergo some sort of culinary process, as for instance is the case with several of Chiquart's sick-dishes for quince, pears and apples.[11] Mediæval European gardens are usually well planted with a range of fruit trees that include apple, pear, peach, apricot, cherry, quince, medlar, sorb-apple, chestnut, hazel-nut and, in the more southern regions, fig, orange and almond.[12] To these fruits can be added the berries: mulberry, strawberry, gooseberry and, uncultivated and seemingly of lesser significance, raspberry.

All of these fruits and vegetables were available either from the domestic garden or in the major market towns of France in the fourteenth and fifteenth centuries. Furthermore almost all of them were "cried" by itinerent vendors who passed regularly through the streets selling an appetizing variety of produce to bourgeois housewives and cooks.[13] The professional cook of the late Middle Ages enjoyed the potential to create meals that offered a variety of the principal types of foodstuff: meat, fish, cereals, vegetables, fruits, wines, milk products, and condiments.[14] In sum, the most that can be said in the matter of normal

---

au Moyen Age (Paris, 1935), pp. 336–341.

[10] Grand, *op. cit.,* pp. 342–354. In the Second Article of his Second Distinction, dealing with *Courtillage* or gardening, the *Menagier* provides very detailed directions concerning the planting, cultivation and harvesting of comestible plants (ed. Brereton and Ferrier, pp. 118–124; ed. Pichon, vol. 2, pp. 43–53).

[11] Recipes 70, *Cuyns en pasté*: three or four quince are cored, stuffed with sugar, packed round in a pie shell with beef marrow, ginger and cinnamon, and baked; Recipe 72, *Poyres cuytes sans brase ne eaue*: pears are baked in a hermetically-sealed pot; Recipe 73, *Ung emplumeus de pomes*: applesauce is made from boiled apples, almond milk and sugar.

[12] In his early-thirteenth-century Parisian orchard John de Garlande declares that trees for the following fruit must grow: cherry, pear, apple, plum, quince, medlar, peach, chestnut, walnut, hazel-nut, fig as well as grape: "Sine quibus," he says, "mensa divitis mendicavit" (*loc. cit.*). In *Medieval English Gardens*, Teresa McLean echoes the same list, addding to it a wide range of berries (*ed. cit.*, ch. 8, pp. 224–248). See also the treatise on grafting edited by Carole Lambert, *Le recueil de Riom et la Manière de henter soutillement: Deux receptaires inédits du XVe siècle*, which offers directions for producing a variety of hybrid fruit trees; and Grand, *op. cit.,* pp. 374–393.

[13] See the multitude of cries incorporated into the poem by Guillaume de la Villeneuve on the *Crieries de Paris*, ed. Étienne Barbazan, *Fabliaux et contes de poètes françois*, 4 vols. (Paris, 1808); vol. 1, pp. 276–286.

[14] The conclusion at which Benassar and Goy arrived a decade ago after their survey of contemporary scholarly research in this area is significant: "A la fin du XIVe siècle, au XVe siècle, et dans la première partie du XVIe siècle, l'ensemble de la population en période normale, aurait disposé d'une nourriture saine, assez abondante, voire riche en viande; c'est le temps de l'Europe carnivore, d'une Europe carnivore qui arroserait le plus souvent possible ses repas de grands coups de vin." Bartolomé Benassar and Joseph Goy, "Contribution à l'histoire de la consommation alimentaire

late-mediæval diet is that the surviving recipe collections cannot be taken as evidence that all of these food elements did not enter significantly into the everyday regimen of the people for whom the recipes were written.

In its "unusual" combination of ingredients, its unfamiliar use of widely different textures or flavours in a single dish, mediæval cookery offers both a challenge to the modern cook trapped in routine and a delightful surprise to the staid or blasé gastronome. Together with these delectable, vital flavours come the distinctive colours of the various dishes, intended as much to tantalize the eye as the flavours were to stir and delight a sophisticated sense of taste. The stimulation of appetite, always a purpose of any professional cook, is at the heart of mediæval gastronomy; the means to this end, using shape, colour, texture and taste, are intimately bound to mediæval æsthetic sense. The last twenty years or so has seen an increase in careful research into mediæval alimentation and foods; a by-product of this work has in a general way been an enhanced accessibility to original recipe texts. At the same time, a cheering parallel phenomenon, consequent upon these scholarly studies, has been a conversion of the earnest academic efforts into a growing broad interest in the early European foods among modern amateur cooks. A number of works now offer relatively popular surveys of early cookery, allowing the ordinary reader to understand how largely what we eat today has been determined by what was eaten in the past.[15] The evolution of culinary techniques and of gastronomic tastes in European culture has been gradual over the years. Those who have the curiosity to step back only a little way now have the means to rediscover forgotten pleasures.

---

du XIVe au XIXe siècle," *Annales. Économies, Sociétés, Civilisations*, 30 (1975), p. 427.

[15] The ability to combine interesting writing with solid historical fact varies extensively among modern "popular" presentations of historic cuisine. Among the more successful combinations are found Alfred Gottschalk, *Histoire de l'alimentation et de la gastronomie*, 2 vols. (Paris: Editions Hippocrate, 1948)—old but still worth reading; Philippa Pullar, *Consuming Passions: A History of English Food and Appetite* (London: Hamilton, 1970 and London: Sphere, 1972); Molly Harrison, *The Kitchen in History* (Reading: Osprey, 1972); and Barbara Ketcham Wheaton, *Savoring the Past: The French Kitchen and Table from 1300 to 1789* (Philadelphia: University of Pennsylvania Press, 1983). Recent works which try, with varying degrees of competence and authenticity, to render early recipes accessible to the average modern cook are: Lorna J. Sass, *To the King's Taste: Richard II's Book of Feasts and Recipes Adapted for Modern Cooking* (New York: Metropolitan Museum of Art, 1975); Madeleine Pelner Cosman, *Fabulous Feasts: Medieval Cookery and Ceremony* (New York: Braziller, 1976); Constance B. Hieatt and Sharon Butler, *Pleyn Delit: Medieval Cookery for Modern Cooks* (Toronto and Buffalo: University of Toronto Press, 1976); Moira Buxton, *Medieval Cooking Today* (Waddesdon, Bucks: Kylin, 1983); Jeanne Bourin, *Les recettes de Mathilde Brunel: Cuisine médiévale pour table d'aujourd'hui* (Paris: Flammarion, 1983); and Josep Lladonosa i Giró, *La cocina medieval* (Barcelona: Laia, 1984). Two books of the same genre but dealing with even earlier fare are Pierre Drachline and Claude Petit-Castelli, *À Table avec César: 120 recettes romaines mises au goût du jour* (Paris: Sand, 1984); and John Edwards, *Roman Cookery: Elegant and Easy Recipes from History's First Gourmet* (rev. ed., Vancouver and Point Roberts, Wash.: Hartley & Marks, 1986).

Types of Dish

The prepared dishes of early French cuisine can in a general way be divided into two types. It is easy and appropriate to distinquish between, on the one hand, dishes that are essentially liquid and, on the other, those that are solid or that consist primarily of solids. As a consequence, in terms of eating utensils, we may distinguish between dishes that are eaten with a spoon or those that are eaten in the fingers.[16] Apart from a spoon, which was frequently provided by the host to his guest as part of the table setting, knives were the only utensils used at a table. These varied in size from the large blades wielded by the *esquier tranchant* as he carved and sliced the joints of meat, to the smaller daggers, occasionally folding pocketknives, which were normally the personal property of the diner.

With the spoon one ate vegetable purees (for instance, *pois coullés*, §154) and porridges of oats (gruel), wheat (*Fromentee*, §63) or rice (*Blanc mengier*, §95). Chunks of meat could be picked up in the fingers (carefully wiped before and after on the table runner that was set for this purpose) or speared with a one's knife. If a bowl of sauce was served, the meat could be dipped in it before being eaten. Sops (*Soupe en moustarde*, §83) and *tostees* (*tostees dorees*, §198), served cut to the size of one or two fingers, were handled in the same way. One of the advantages of pastry shells was, of course, that they allowed chopped meat and other messy foodstuffs to be consumed relatively cleanly.

Meals

The order in which the recipes have been set out in the *Viandier* indicates in only a very general way the normal sequence of their serving to a contemporary table. The *Du fait de cuisine*, which was dictated by its author at roughly the same time as the Vatican version of the *Viandier* was copied, 1420, lays out menus for dinners and suppers for both meat and lean days.[17] The overall format for these meals seems to be quite firmly established by the beginning of the fifteenth century. For the high board of the court of Savoy Chiquart is able to specify dinners consisting of two courses or servings that are composed explicitly of the following dishes:

---

[16] Notwithstanding the popular cinematographic image of the mediæval banquet as the gastronomic equivalent of an unbridled sexual orgy, a boisterous avatar of some distant barbarous sub-culture, meals were in fact bound by procedural etiquette probably more than any other regular social activity at this time. Manuals on table manners abound and offer guidelines on every conceivable aspect of proper behaviour, from sneezing at the dinner table (heaven help the barbarian who belched!) to the number of nuts (two at a time) a person might gracefully take from the nut-bowl when it was passed. Though naturally fingers were the primary utensils at the table, an insistence upon cleanliness provided a strip of towelling the length of the table-edge. The function of the meat-carver was a very important one at the noble table, and his instructions carefully defined the bite-sized "gobbets" (as the *Forme of Cury* terms them) to which he was to reduce meat. The automatic association of eating with one's fingers and vulgarity is an unfortunate modern one.

[17] *Ed. cit.*, pp. 116–118; in the translation, *Chiquart's 'On Cookery.' A Fifteenth-Century Savoyard Culinary Treatise*, pp. xxix–xxxi.

1) boiled joints of meat (beaf, mutton), with sauce; salt meats (cuts of pork, sausage), with sauce; green puree; a variety of *brouets*; and an *entremets* (*e.g.*, a glazed bore's head);

2) roast meat (goat kid, piglet, loin of veal or pork, shoulder of mutton), with sauces; roast fowl (gosling, capon, pheasant, partridge, rabbit, pigeon, heron), with sauces; *fromentee* and venison; pasties (pies, *talmoses*, flans); a variety of *brouets* and *civés*; *blanc mengier*; and an *entremets* (*e.g.*, a raised *entremets* of the Castle of Love).

Because the Count of Savoy modelled his court upon those of Burgundy and France, though on a much more modest scale, we may suppose that the users of the *Viandier* aimed to prepare meals whose content and order bore a close resemblance to those that Chiquart has prescribed.[18] The twenty-three sample menus outlined by the *Menagier de Paris* show that, at least in affluent bourgeois circles, the sequence of dishes approximates what was usual on aristocratic tables.[19] During a normal dinner we find a regular sequence of dishes: appetizers of pasties and deep-fried doughnuts; boiled meats; *potages* of *soupes, brouets, gravés, civés* or *soringues*; vegetable *poree*; then, at the heart of the meal, roasts of meat, fowl (roasted, boiled or baked in a pie), and more pasties; then, among the final servings, one or more *entremets* (of a humble, unambitious nature for this Parisian bourgeois): *fromentee*-and-venison, a cold dish or jelly of meat or fish) and an *yssue* or *desserte* of pancakes or biscuits, fruit, *dragees* and hippocras.

A Modern *Viandier* Menu

The following four recipes have been adapted from items in the *Viandier* as illustrations of the practical culinary resources that this old collection still offers.

Tailliz de Karesme: Lenten Slices *(Viandier, §207)*

This dish can be served as a warm pudding, as cold slices, as squares or as ball-shaped cookies. Serves 8-10.

Imperial	*Ingredients*	*Metric*	*Directions*
1 cup	ground almonds	250 mL	**Combine almonds and water. Steep for 5 minutes, stirring occasionally. Sieve the mixture to remove coarse grains *or* (preferably) blend mixture in electric blender until grains are absorbed. Yield—2 cups (500 mL) almond milk.**
2 cups	boiling water	500 mL	

[18] An interesting overview of all of the activities involved in conducting a formal meal, from cooking, to table-setting and serving, is afforded by Patricia Labahn in her unpublished doctoral thesis, *Feasting in the Fourteenth and Fifteenth Centuries: A Comparison of Manuscript Illuminations to Contemporary Written Sources* (St. Louis: St. Louis University, 1975).

[19] *Menagier*, pp. 175–182, §§28–50; pp. 91–103.

1/2 cup	granulated sugar	125 mL	**In pot, over low heat, combine almond milk, sugar and salt. When dissolved,**
pinch	salt	pinch	
2–3 cups	diced bread (crusts removed) *or* biscuit pieces *or* stale cake pieces	500–750 mL	**add bread, or biscuits or stale cake. Stir well.**
pinch	saffron	pinch	**Add saffron for colour if desired.**
3/4 cup	raisins	175 mL	**Add raisins, dates and figs. Cook while stirring over low heat—about 15 min.—until a thick, porridge-like consistency is obtained.**
3/4 cup	dates, cut into 3/4" (2 cm) pieces	175 mL	
6–8	large figs, cut into 3/4" (2 cm) pieces	6–8	
			Taste; add additional sugar if desired.

For garnish:

2 tsp	granulated sugar	10 mL	See below.

To serve:

Pudding: Divide mixture into desired number of portions. Sprinkle with sugar. Serve.

Slices: Lightly grease a loaf pan, line with paper, grease again. Pack the mixture firmly into pan. Sprinkle with sugar. Refrigerate. When cool, remove from pan, slice and serve.

Squares: Grease a cake pan. Layer broken biscuit (*e.g.* vanilla wafers) on bottom of pan. Turn mixture into pan. Sprinkle with sugar. Cool. Cut into squares and serve.

Cookies: Use 1 tbsp (15 mL) of mixture. Roll into a ball. Roll balls in sugar, coating thoroughly, tapping off excess sugar. Place in small paper cups. Cool. Store in tightly sealed container.

Cooking Variations: If desired, after adding the sugar and the bread, biscuits or cake to the almond-milk mixture, add the remaining ingredients, pour into prepared baking dish. Set the dish in a pan of hot water and bake in a 350° oven for 30–40 min. Serve.

Variations: The *Menagier de Paris*, written at about the end of Taillevent's life, adds chopped apples to the mixture and omits the dates and figs. It is a tasty variation of this dish. More bread/biscuits/cake pieces should be added to absorb the moisture from the apples.

Doreures: Glazings *(Viandier, §§195 & 66)*

This dish is described as an entremets for a princely banquet on the three meat-days of the week, Sunday, Tuesday and Thursday. Pork meatballs are added to the poultry dish. After cooking, both the meatballs and the bird are glazed with a crêpe batter and wrapped in gold- or silver-leaf.

The recipe given below is less ambitious. It omits the meatballs and the glazing, and adds Brie cheese to the stuffing. Other recipes of this type include a good, rich cheese (see Recipe 66), and this improves both the flavour and consistency in the dish. The recipe works equally well with a whole stuffed chicken or *stuffed chicken breasts. Serves 6.*

one 5–6-lb (2.5 kg-) roasting chicken, boned if desired

or

three whole- or six half-breasts of chicken

Stuffing:

Imperial	*Ingredients*	*Metric*	*Directions*
3/4 lb	boned, skinned, uncooked breast of chicken	350 g	**Grind or process the chicken meat, pine nuts and Brie cheese in a mortar, grinder or food processer.**
3/4 cup	pine nuts	175 mL	
1/4 lb	Brie cheese, rind removed	125 g	
1	whole raw egg, lightly beaten	1	**Add egg**
3/4 tsp	ginger	3 mL	**and spices.**
3/4 tsp	cinnamon	3 mL	
1/2 tsp	cloves	2 mL	
1/4 tsp	salt	1 mL	**Mix well until all ingredients are evenly distributed.**
6	strips of bacon	6	**Lightly sauté bacon. Drain off grease. Cut the bacon into small pieces.**
1 cup	currants	250 mL	**Add bacon bits and currants to the mixture.**

For cooking:

4-6	strips of bacon	4-6	See below.
1-1/2 cups	dry white wine	375–500 mL	

For sauce:

1/3 cup	bread crumbs	75 mL	See below.
	or		
1/4 cup	ground almonds	60 mL	

For garnish: Sprigs of parsley and toasted almond slices, if desired.

To cook and serve:

Stuffed whole bird: Preheat oven to 450°. Fill the cavity with prepared stuffing. Close opening with skewers or sew together. Place bird breast-side-up in baking pan. Pour 1 cup dry white wine and place strips of bacon over bird. Cover lightly with foil. Reduce temperature to 350° and roast till done—approximately 20 minutes per pound (*or* 450 kg)—basting frequently. Remove foil cover for last half-hour of cooking period. Remove to serving dish and keep warm.

Stuffed breasts of chicken: Preheat oven to 350°. Between pieces of wax-paper, pound the breasts of chicken until flat and thin. Distribute the stuffing evenly and press firmly onto the six pieces. Roll the breasts, secure with tooth picks and place them seam-side-down in baking dish. Add wine. Place one strip of bacon on each. Cover and cook 30–40 min. until tender, basting several times during cooking period. Remove cover for last 10–15 min. of cooking period. Transfer breasts to a platter and keep warm. Serve with sauce (below), if desired.

Sauce: Remove fat from pan juices. In saucepan heat 1/4 cup (75 mL) of the fat. Stir in pan juices. Thicken with bread crumbs *or* ground almonds. Cook, while stirring until desired consistency is reached. Strain and serve over chicken.

Garnish with parsley and toasted almonds. Serve.

Ris engoulé: Fancy Rice *(Viandier, §71)*

Because this rice dish was prepared with meat broth and milk, it could be served on days when the consumption of meat was permitted. On meatless days the rice would be cooked in almond milk or just plain water. Serves 6.

Imp.	*Ingredients*	*Metric*	*Directions*
1 cup	uncooked rice	250 mL	**Wash the rice.**
2 tbsp	butter	30 mL	**Melt butter in a saucepan. Add rice and stir till rice is coated.**
1 cup	hot milk	250 mL	**Add a pinch of saffron to hot milk and bouillon. Add liquid to rice.**
1 cup	hot beef or chicken bouillon	250 mL	
pinch	saffron	pinch	
			Cover and simmer till liquid is absorbed.

Poree de cresson*: Stewed Cress *(Viandier, §153)

The Viandier *suggests that cress is a good remedy for gallstones! Although the recipe calls specifically for garden cress, it works equally well with the watercress variety. Serves 6.*

Imp.	*Ingredients*	*Metric*	*Directions*
1 lb	cress	450 gr	**Choose greens that are young and tender. Cull and rinse the greens thoroughly. Trim stem ends of cress and remove white ribs from chard. (Discard, or reserve for another dish.)**
1/2 lb	Swiss chard	250 g	
3 cups	boiling, salted water	750 mL	**Blanch rapidly in (or steam over) boiling water. Drain and chop fine.**
3 tbsp	butter or oil	45 mL	**In heavy skillet, sauté the greens in butter or oil.**
1/2 cup	grated cheese	125 mL	**Add cheese. Simmer about 5 minutes. Stir and serve.**
	Salt to taste.		

Variation: Cook the cleaned greens in chicken or beef bouillon.

BIBLIOGRAPHY AND INDEX

Select Bibliography

Entries in this Bibliography are arranged according to subject. Within each subject category, entries are further arranged either alphabetically or according to rough chronological order.

Glossaries and Dictionaries

Alphita: *Alphita o Synonima herbarum* (a medico-botanical glossary, MSS of the 13th century) in "Sopra un vocabolario di voci tecniche del medio evo," in vol. 3, 271–322 of Salvatore de RENZI *et al.*, eds. *Collectio Salernitana, ossia Documenti inediti, e trattati di medicina appartenenti alla Scuola medica salernitana.* Naples: Filiatre-Sebezio, 1852–1859; repr. Bologna: Forni, 1967. 5 vols. Also in J. L. G. MOWAT, ed. *Sinonima Bartholomæi.* Oxford: Clarendon, 1882, 7–199; and in Piero GIACOSA, ed. *Magistri Salernitani nondum editi.* Turin: Bocca, 1901, 401 ff.

AND: STONE, Louise W. and William ROTHWELL. *Anglo-Norman Dictionary.* London: Modern Humanities Research Association, 1977– .

Cotgrave: COTGRAVE, Randle. *A Dictionarie of the French and English Tongues Compiled by Randle Cotgrave.* London: Adam Islip, 1611; 1st ed. repr. Columbia, South Carolina: University of South Carolina, 1950.

DEAF: BALDINGER, Kurt, Jean-Denis GENDRON and Georges STRAKA. *Dictionnaire étymologique de l'ancien français.* Quebec City: Laval University, 1974– . (Part of letter G only.)

DEI: BATTISTI, Carlo and Giovanni ALESSIO. *Dizionario etimologico italiano.* Florence: Barbèra, 1950–1957. 5 vols.

DuCange: DUCANGE, Charles Du Fresne, Sieur. *Glossarium mediæ et infimæ latinitatis ... cum supplementis integris D. P. Carpenterii.* Ed. Léopold FAVRE. Niort, 1883–1887; repr. Paris: Librairie des Sciences et des Arts, 1937–1938.

FEW: VON WARTBURG, Walter. *Französisches etymologisches Wörterbuch: eine Darstellung des galloromanischen Sprachschatzes.* Bonn: F. Klopp, 1928– .

Godefroy: GODEFROY, Frédéric. *Dictionnaire de l'ancienne langue française et de tous ses dialectes du IXe au XVe siècles.* Paris: F. Vieweg, 1881–1902; repr. Vaduz: Kraus, 1965. 10 vols.

GPSR: GAUCHAT, Louis, Jules JEANJAQUET and Ernst TAPPOLET. *Glossaire des patois de la Suisse romande.* Neuchâtel and Paris: V. Attinger, 1924– .

Huguet: HUGUET, Edmond. *Dictionnaire de la langue française du seizième siècle.* Paris: Didier, 1925–1967. 7 vols.

Latham: LATHAM, Ronald Edward. *A Dictionary of Medieval Latin from British Sources.* London: Oxford University, 1975– .

Latham, *Word-List*: LATHAM, Ronald Edward. *Revised Medieval Latin Word-List from British and Irish Sources*. London: Oxford University, 1965.

NG: BLATT, Franz, ed. *Novum glossarium mediæ latinitatis ab anno DCCC usque ad annum MCC*. Copenhagen: Ejnar Munksgaard, 1957– . (Letters L–O.)

Niermeyer: NIERMEYER, Jan Frederik. *Mediæ Latinitatis lexicon minus: A medieval Latin-French/English dictionary. Perficiendum curavit C. van de Kieft*. Leyden: Brill, 1976.

REW: MEYER-LÜBKE, Wilhelm. *Romanisches etymologisches Wörterbuch*. Heidelberg: C. Winter, 1911–[1920].

Richelet: RICHELET, Pierre. *Dictionnaire françois tiré de l'usage des meilleurs auteurs de la langue*. Geneva: Herman Widerhold, 1679; repr. Geneva: Slatkine, 1970.

Sainte-Palaye: SAINTE-PALAYE, Jean Baptiste de La Curne de. *Dictionnaire historique de l'ancien langage françois*. Niort and Paris: L. Favre, 1875–1882.

Schüle: SCHÜLE, Ernest, Lucien QUAGLIA and Jean-Marie THEURILLAT. "Les comptes de l'Hospice du Grand Saint-Bernard (1397–1477) ... Glossaire établi par Ernest Schüle," *Vallesia*, 30 (1975), 341–384.

SOUTER, Alexander. *A Glossary of Later Latin to 600 AD*. Oxford: Clarendon, 1949.

TILANDER, Gunnar. *Glanures lexicographiques*. Lund: Gleerup, 1932.

TLF: *Trésor de la langue française*. Paris: CNRS, 1971– .

Tobler: TOBLER, Adolph and Erhard LOMMATZSCH. *Altfranzösisches Wörterbuch*. Berlin: Weidmann, 1925– ; repr. and currently Wiesbaden: Steiner, 1955– .

Trévoux: *Dictionnaire universel françois et latin*. Trévoux: Estienne Ganneau, 1704. 3 vols.; Paris, 1721. 5 vols.; Paris: Veuve Delaune & Veuve Ganeau, 1752. 7 vols.; Paris, 1771. 8 vols.; etc. (Originally a reissue of Antoine FURETIÈRE's *Dictionnaire universel, françois et latin*. 1701).

Early Works on Foodstuffs and Cookery

Bibliographies

BITTING, Katherine Golden. *Gastronomic Bibliography*. San Francisco: n. pub., 1939; repr. Ann Arbor: Gryphon, 1971 and London: Holland Press, 1981. (Contains only relatively modern works.)

GIRARD, Alain. "Du manuscrit à l'imprimé: le livre de cuisine en Europe aux 15e et 16e siècles," in Margolin and Sauzet, *Pratiques et discours alimentaires à la Renaissance* (see below), 107–118.

SCHUMACHER-VOELKER, Uta. "German Cookery Books, 1485–1800," *Petits Propos Culinaires*, 6 (1980), 34-46.

———"Reprints of Old German Cookery Books," *Petits Propos Culinaires*, 7 (1981), 47–55.

SIMON, André Louis. *Biblioteca gastronomica*. London: Wine & Food Society, 1953. (Lists works only from the 16th century to the present.)

SIMON PALMER, María del Carmen. *Bibliografía de la gastronomía española*. Madrid: Velázquez, [1977].

VICAIRE, Georges. *Bibliographie gastronomique*. Paris: P. Rouquette, 1890; 2nd ed. London: D. Verschoyle, 1954; repr. Geneva: Slatkine, 1978.

WESTBURY, Richard M.T.B., Lord. *Handlist of Italian Cookery Books*. Biblioteca di Bibliografia Italiana, 42. Florence: Olschki, 1963.

Latin

APICIUS, M. Gavius. *De re coquinaria*: Mary Ella MILHAM, ed. *Decem libri cui dicuntur De re coquinaria et excerpta a Vinidario conscripta*. Leipzig: Teubner, 1969. Jacques ANDRÉ, ed. and trans. *De re coquinaria (De la cuisine)*. Paris: Belles Lettres, 1965; repr. 1974. Barbara FLOWER and Elisabeth ROSENBAUM, trans. *The Roman Cookery Book: A critical translation of the Art of Cooking by Apicius for use in the study and the kitchen*. London: Harrap, 1958 and London: Peter Nevill, 1958. Also John EDWARDS, trans. *The Roman Cookery of Apicius. A translation of the oldest cookbook in the world*. Vancouver: Hartley & Marks, 1984.

ANTHIMUS. *De observatione ciborum ad Theodoricum regem Francorum epistula*. Ed. Shirley Howard WEBER. Leyden: Brill, 1924. Ed. Eduard LIECHTENHAN. Leipzig: Teubner, 1877; repr. Leipzig and Berlin: Teubner, 1928; new edn. Corpus Medicorum Latinorum, 8, fasc. 1. Berlin: Academia Scientiarum, 1963. Also, Valentin ROSE, ed. in vol. 2, 43–102, of *Anecdota græca et græcolatina*. Berlin: Duerwinler, 1864–1870. 2 vols.

CONSTANTINUS AFRICANUS. *Liber de gradibus*. MS Paris, BN lat. 6891, fol. 88va–89ra. (This is virtually the same work as Isaac's *De gradibus simplicium*.)

PLATEARIUS, Matthæus. *Liber de simplici medicina, dictus Circa instans* (*c*. 1100). Fifteenth-century French trans. as *Le livre de simples medecines*. Ed. Paul Dorveaux. Paris: Société française d'histoire de la médecine, 1913.

Flos Medicinæ Scholæ Salerni (Regimen Sanitatis Salernitanum), in Salvatore de RENZI, *et al.*, eds. *Collectio Salernitana*. Naples: Filiatre-Sebezio, 1852–1859; repr. Bologna: Forni, 1967. 5 vols. (Renzi published several versions of the *Regimen Sanitatis Salernitanum*; vol. 5 contains the longest. See also *Le régime tresutile et tresproufitable* ..., below.)

ARNALDUS DE VILLANOVA. *Liber de vinis* (*c*. 1310). Ed. and trans. Henry E. SIGERIST. *The Earliest Printed Book on Wine (1478)*. New York: Schuman, 1943.

Tacuinum sanitatis in medicina. Ed. Luisa COGLIATI ARANO. Milan: Electra, n.d. Oscar RATTI and Adele WESTBROOK, trans. *The Medieval Health Handbook* Tacuinum Sanitatis. London: Barrie & Jenkins and New York: Braziller, 1976. Also Elena BERTI TOESCA, ed. *Il 'Tacuinum sanitatis' della Biblioteca nazionale di Parigi; manoscritto miniato, integralmente riprodotto in 207 fototipie con introduzione e transcrizione*. Bergamo: Istituto italiano d'arti grafiche, [1937].

MUSANDINUS, Petrus. *Summula Musandini*, in vol. 5, 254–268, of Salvatore de RENZI, *et al.*, eds. *Collectio Salernitana*. Naples: Filiatre-Sebezio, 1852–1859; repr. Bologna: Forni, 1967. 5 vols. (Incipit: *Incipit summula de preparatione ciborum et potuum infirmorum, secundum Musandinum.*)

CRESCENTIUS, Petrus (Pietro de' Crescenzi). *Commodorum ruralium* (*c.* 1285–1309). Augsburg: Johannes Schussler, 1471. French tr. as by "Pierre de Crescens." *Le Livre des Prouffitz Champestres et Ruraulx*. Paris: Jean Bon Homme, 1486. See also the extract *De diversis speciebus vitium* (between 1304 and 1309) in Emilio FACCIOLI, ed. *Arte della cucina* (see below), 3–17.

MATTHÆUS SILVATICUS (of Mantua). *Pandectæ medicinæ* (*c.* 1336). Bologna and Naples: n. pub., 1474; Venice: n. pub., 1478; etc.

Liber de coquina. Ed. Marianne MULON, in "Deux traités inédits d'art culinaire," in vol. 1 ("Les problèmes de l'alimentation"), 396–420, of the Actes du 93e Congrès national des Sociétés savantes tenu à Tours (1968), *Bulletin Philologique et Historique*. Paris: Bibliothèque nationale, 1971. 2 vols.

Tractatus de modo preparandi et condiendi omnia cibaria. Ed. Marianne MULON (see previous entry), 380–395.

MAGNINUS MEDIOLANENSIS (Maino de' Maineri). *Opusculum de saporibus*, in Lynn THORNDIKE, ed., "A Medieval Sauce-Book," *Speculum*, 9 (1934), 183–190.

———— *Regimen sanitatis*. Louvain: Johannes de Westfalia, 1482. Also pub. under the name of ARNALDUS DE VILLANOVA, as in Thomas MURCHIUS, ed. *Hec sunt opera Arnaldi de Villanova*. Lyons: Françoys Fradin, 1504.

Sanitatis conservator: *Eine Diätethik aus Montpellier dem Ende des 14. Jahrhunderts und "Tractatus medicus de Comestione et Digestione vel Regimen Sanitatis" benannt*. Ed. Hugo FABER. Leipzig University Medical Dissertations, vol. 13, July, 1921. Zeulenroda i. Thür: Oberreuter, [1924].

PLATINA DI CREMONA, Baptista (Bartolomeo Sacchi). *De honesta voluptate et valitudine ad amplissimum ac doctissimum D.B. Rouerellam S. Clementis Presbiterum Cardinalem*. N.p., n.d. [*c.* 1474]; Rome: Uldericus Gallus, 1475; Venice: Petro Mocenico, 1475; etc. An early French trans.: *Platine en françoys tresutile & necessaire pour le corps humain qui traicte de honneste volupté et de toutes viandes et choses que l'omme menge*. Lyons: Françoys Fradin, 1505. A modern English trans.: Elizabeth B. ANDREWS. *On Honest Indulgence and Good Health*. St. Louis: Mallinckrodt Chemical Works, 1967.

Hortus sanitatis. Strasbourg: Russ, [*c.* 1507]. French trans.: *Jardin de santé*. Mainz: Jean Meydenbach, 1491. 2 vols.; and Paris: A. Verard, [*c.* 1499]. 2 vols.. Vol. 1 of the French trans. has "Ortus sanitatis translaté de latin en françois"; vol. 2 has "Le traictie des bestes, oyseaux, poissons, pierres precieuses et orines, du *Jardin de santé*." Also pub. in Latin under the title *Herbarius*. Mainz: n. pub., 1484; Padua: n. pub., 1485, 1486; etc.

French

Viaunde e claree. Named from the *incipit* of a late-13th-century Anglo-Norman collection of 29 recipes "Coment l'en deit fere viaunde e claree." In Constance B. HIEATT and

Robin F. JONES. "Two Anglo-Norman Culinary Collections Edited from British Library Manuscripts Additional 32085 and Royal 12.C.xii," *Speculum*, 61 (1986), 859–882.

Enseignements. In Appendix I, 181–190, of Grégoire LOZINSKI, ed. *La Bataille de Caresme et de Charnage*. Paris: Champion, 1933. Previous ed.: Louis-Claude DOUËT-D'ARCQ, ed. "Un petit traité de cuisine écrit en français au commencement du XIVe siècle," *Bibliothèque de l'École des Chartes*, 21st year, 5th series, vol. 1 (Paris: Dumoulin, 1860), 216–224. And also Jérôme PICHON and Georges VICAIRE, eds. "Traité de cuisine écrit vers 1300," in *Le Viandier de Taillevent* (see next entry), 211–226.

Le Viandier de Guillaume Tirel dit Taillevent. Ed. Jérôme PICHON and Georges VICAIRE. Paris: Leclerc & Cormuau, 1892; new ed. Sylvie MARTINET. Paris: Techener, 1892; repr. Geneva: Slatkine, 1967 and Luzarches: Daniel Morcrette, n.d. For the Valais MS of the *Viandier*, Paul AEBISCHER, ed. "Un manuscrit valaisan du '*Viandier*' attribué à Taillevent," *Vallesia*, 8 (1953), 73–100. For an enumeration of fifteen early printed versions of the *Viandier* see Pichon and Vicaire, lii–lxviii.

Royal 12.C.xii (Thirty-two recipes from the first half of the fourteenth century): Constance B. HIEATT and Robin F. JONES, eds. "Two Anglo-Norman Culinary Collections Edited from British Library Manuscripts Additional 32085 and Royal 12.C.xii," *Speculum*, 61 (1986), 859–882. Also Paul MEYER, ed. "Notice sur le MS Old Roy. 12.C.XII du Musée britannique (Pièces diverses, recettes culinaires)," *Bulletin de la Société des Anciens Textes Français*, 19 (Paris: Firmin-Didot, 1893), 38–56.

Le Ménagier de Paris, traité de morale et d'économie domestique composé vers 1393 par un bourgeois parisien. Ed. Jérôme PICHON. Paris: Crapelet, 1846; Paris: Crapelet & Lahure, for the Société des Bibliophiles français, 1847. 2 vols; repr. Geneva: Slatkine, 1970. Also Georgine E. BRERETON and Janet M. FERRIER, eds. *Le Menagier de Paris*. Oxford: Clarendon, 1981.

CHIQUART AMICZO, Maistre. *Du fait de cuisine*. Terence SCULLY, ed. "Du fait de cuisine par Maistre Chiquart 1420 (Ms. S 103 de la bibliothèque Supersaxo, à la Bibliothèque cantonale du Valais, à Sion)," *Vallesia*, 40 (1985), 101–231. English trans.: T. SCULLY. *Chiquart's "On Cookery": A fifteenth-century Savoyard culinary treatise*. New York and Bern: Peter Lang, 1986.

Recueil de Riom: LAMBERT, Carole, ed. *Le recueil de Riom et la Manière de henter soutillement: Deux receptaires inédits du XVe siècle*. Montreal: CERES, 1988.

Provenzalische Diätetik. Auf grund neuen Materials. Ed. Hermann SUCHIER. Halle: Max Niemeyer, 1894. See also Édouard BONDURAND. "Une diététique provençale," *Revue du Midi*, 18 (1895), 191–207.

Le grant herbier en françois, contenant les qualitez, vertuz et proprietez des Herbes, Arbres, Gommes et Semences. Extraict de plusieurs traictez de medecine. Paris: Pierre le Caron, [*c.* 1498].

Jardin de santé. See *Hortus sanitatis*, above.

Le régime tresutile et tresproufitable pour conserver et garder la santé du corps humain. (A 15th-century French translation of the *Flos Medicinæ Scholæ Salerni*—see above—with commentaries attributed to Arnaldus de Villanova—see above and next entry.) Ed. Patricia W. CUMMINS. Chapel Hill: University of North Carolina, 1976.

ARNAUT DE VILLENEUVE. *Regimen sanitatis en françois*. Lyons: Claude Nourry, 1501. (See Magninus Mediolanensis. *Regimen sanitatis*, above.)

ALDOBRANDINO DA SIENA. *Le régime du corps de maître Aldebrandin de Sienne. Texte français du XIIIe siècle*. Ed. Louis LANDOUZY and Roger PÉPIN. Paris: Champion, 1911.

Livre fort excellent de Cuysine tres-utille & proffitable contenant en soy la maniere dhabiller toutes viandes ... . Lyons: Olivier Arnoullet, 1542. Also published as *Le Grand Cuisinier de toute cuisine*. Paris: Jehan Bonfons, n.d.; as *La Fleur de toute cuysine*. Paris: Alain Lotrian, 1543; as *Livre de cuysine tres utille & prouffitable*. Paris, [*c.* 1540]; and as *Le Livre de honneste volupté*. Lyons: Benoist Rigaud, 1588. (This last title should not be confused with that of Platina, above.)

Le grant kalendrier et compost des Bergiers avecq leur Astrologie, etc., Troyes: Nicolas le Rouge, [1510]; repr. Paris: Siloe, 1981. Also *Le compost et kalendrier des bergiers*. Paris: Guido Marchant, 1493; repr. Paris: Éditions des Quatre Chemins, [1926].

English

The Forme of Cury. Ed. Samuel PEGGE. London: J. Nichols, 1780. Also Richard WARNER, ed. *Antiquitates Culinariæ: Curious Tracts on Culinary Affairs of the Old English*. London: R. Blamire, 1791; repr. London: Prospect Books, n.d. (See also the following work.)

HIEATT, Constance B. and Sharon BUTLER, eds. *Curye on Inglysch. English Culinary Manuscripts of the Fourteenth Century*. Early English Text Society, S.S. 8. Oxford: Oxford University, 1985. (Includes eds. of 5 works: I, *Diversa cibaria*; II, *Diversa servicia*; III, *Utilis coquinario*; IV, *Forme of Cury*; V, *Goud Kokery*.)

Liber cure cocorum. Ed. Richard MORRIS. Berlin and London: Asher, for the Philological Society, 1862.

AUSTIN, Thomas. *Two Fifteenth-Century Cookery-Books: Harleian MS. 279 (ab. 1430) & Harleian MS 4016 (ab. 1450), with Extracts from Ashmole MS. 1439, Laud MS. 553 & Douce MS. 55*. Early English Text Society, O.S. 91. London: Oxford University, 1888; repr. 1964.

Noble Boke of Cookry ffor a Prynce Houssolde or eny other Estately Houssolde. Ed. Robina (Mrs. Alexander) NAPIER. London: Elliot Stock, 1882.

FURNIVALL, Frederick James. *Early English Meals and Manners*. Early English Text Society, O.S. 32. London: Oxford University, 1868; repr. 1931. (Recipes from Harleian MSS 276 and 5401.)

Italian

Libro della cocina por un anonimo toscano, in vol. 1, 19–57, of Emilio FACCIOLI, ed. *Arte della cucina. Libri di ricetti, testi sopra lo scalco, il trinciante e i vini dal XIV al XIX secolo*. Milan: Il Polifilo, 1966. 2 vols. Previous ed.: Francesco ZAMBRINI, ed. *Il Libro della cucina del Secolo XIV*. Bologna: Gaetano Romagnoli, 1863. (In the Tuscan dialect.)

Libro per cuoco, in vol. 1, 59–105 of Emilio FACCIOLI, ed. *Arte della cucina* (see previous entry). Also Alberto CONSIGLIO, ed. *Libro di cucina del secolo XIV*. Rome: Canesi, 1969. And Ludovico FRATI. Leghorn: Raffaello Giusti, 1899; repr. Bologna: Forni, 1970. (In the Venetian dialect.)

GUERRINI, Olindo, ed. *Frammento di un libro di cucina del secolo XIV edito nel dì delle nozze Carducci-Gnaccarini*. Bologna: Nicola Zanichelli, 1887.

ANONIMO MERIDIONALE. *Due Libri di cucina*. Ed. Ingemar BOSTRÖM. Stockholm: Almqvist & Wiksell, 1985. (Two anonymous collections in a MS dating from the beginning of the 15th century.)

MARTINO, Maestro. *Libro de arte coquinaria*, in vol. 1, 115–204, of Emilio FACCIOLI, ed. *Arte della cucina* (see above). (A Lombard author writing in the middle of the fifteenth century.)

MORPURGO, Salomone, Domenico ZANICHELLI and Giacomo ZANICHELLI, eds. *LVII Ricette d'un libro di cucina del buon secolo della lingua*. Bologna: Nicola Zanichelli, 1890.

Nice. Musée Masséna, Bibliothèque de Cessol, MS 226. (Two fifteenth-century Italian recipe collections bound together, 56 recipes in all. *Incipit*: *Tolli el panico brillato. Explicit*: *Explicit Liber Coquina. Deo gratias.*)

Cuoco Napolitano. Pierpont Morgan Library, MS B.19.

Opera nuova intitolata [E]Dificio di Ricetti .... Venice: n. pub., 1541. French trans: *Bastiment de receptes, nouvellement traduict de italien en langue françoyse*. Lyon: A l'Escu de Coloigne, 1541; Poitiers: Bouchet, 1544; etc.)

Catalan, Portuguese, Castilian, Arabic

Sent soví: GREWE, Rudolf, ed. *Libre de sent soví (Receptari de cuina)*. Els nostres clàssics, A, 115. Barcelona: Barcino, 1979. Partially ed. by José OSSET MERLE. "Un libro de cocina del siglo XIV," *Boletín de la Sociedad Castellonense de Cultura*, 16 (1935), 156–177. And by Lluís FARAUDO DE SAINT-GERMAIN. "El *Libre de Sent Soví*, Recetario de cocina catalana medieval," *Boletín de la Real Academia de Buenas Letras de Barcelona*, 24 (1951–1952), 5–71.

ROBERT [DE NOLA], Mestre. *Libre del coch*. First pub. as *Libre de doctrina per a ben servir de tallar y del Art del Coch*. Barcelona: Carles Amorós, 1520. Veronika LEIMGRUBER, ed. *Libre del coch. Tractat de cuina medieval*. Barcelona: Curial Edicions Catalanes, 1977; 2nd ed. 1982. An early Castilian trans. as by RUPERTO DE NOLA. *Libro de guisados manjares y potages intitulado Libro de Cozina*. Logroño: Miguel de Guía, 1529; repr. Bilbao: Papelera Española, 1971. Also Dionisio PÉREZ, ed. *Libro de Guisados*. Los clásicos olvidados, 9. Madrid: Companía Ibero-americana de Publicaciones, 1929. And Carmen IRANZO, ed. *Libro de cozina*. Madrid: Taurus, [1969]. (A fifteenth-work.)

Portuguese Cook Book: GOMES FILHO, Antônio ed. *Um tratado de cozinha portuguesa do sécolo XV*. Rio de Janeiro: Instituto Nacional do Livro, 1963. Also Elizabeth T. NEWMAN, ed. *A Critical Edition of an Early Portuguese Cook Book*. Ph.D. Thesis,

University of North Carolina, Chapel Hill, 1964; facs. Ann Arbor, Mich.: University Microfilms, 1983.

Confits: FARAUDO DE SAINT-GERMAIN, Lluís, ed. "*Libre de totes maneres de confits*. Un tratado manual cuatrocentista de arte de dulcería," *Boletín de la Real Academia de Buenas Letras de Barcelona*, 19 (1946), 97–134.

HUICI MIRANDA, Ambrosio. *Traducción española de un manuscrito anónimo del siglo XIII sobre la cocina hispano-magribi*. Madrid; Ayuntamiento de Valencia, 1966. (The source is an Andalusian *Kitāb al-tabīj* from the first third of the thirteenth century.)

Germanic

Northern-European Cookbook: GREWE, Rudolf, tr. "An Early XIII Century Northern-European Cookbook," *Current Research in Culinary History: Sources, Topics and Methods*. Boston: Culinary Historians of Boston, 1986, 27–45. (Proceedings of a conference at Radcliffe College, June 14–16, 1985.) The work subsists in four versions, edited as follows: two of these are contained in HARPESTRAENG. *Gamle Danske Urtebøger, Stenbøger og Kogebøger*. Ed. Marius KRISTENSEN. Copenhagen: Universitets-Jubilaeets Danske Samfund, 1908–1920; one version is found in each of Henning LARSEN, ed. *An Old Icelandic Medical Miscellany (Ms. Royal Irish Academy 23 D 43)*. Oslo: Det Norske Videnskaps-Akademi i Oslo, 1931; and Hans WISWE, ed. "Ein mittelniederdeutsches Kochbuch des 15. Jahrhunderts" (see the entry below: a version of the *Northern-European Cookbook* is imbedded in a larger recipe collection).

Das bouch von gouter spize. Aus der Würzburg-Münchener Handschrift. Ed. Hans HAJEK. Texte des späten Mittelalters, 8. Berlin: Erich Schmidt, 1958.

EBERHARD: FEYL, Anita, ed. *Das Kochbuch Meister Eberhards*. Ph.D. Dissertation, Albert-Ludwig University, Freiburg im Breisgau, 1963. Also pub. as A. FEYL. "Das Kochbuch des Eberhard von Landshut (erste Hälfe des 15.Jhs.)," *Ostbairische Grenzmarken*, 5 (1961), 352–366. (The numbering of the recipes is the same in both editions.)

Mittelniederdeutsches Kochbuch: WISWE, Hans, ed. "Ein mittelniederdeutsches Kochbuch des 15. Jahrhunderts," *Braunschweigisches Jahrbuch*, 37 (1956), 19–55.

Kochbüchlein: BIRLINGER, Anton, ed. "Kalender und Kochbüchlein aus Tegernsee," *Germania. Vierteljahresschrift für deutsche Alterthumskunde*, 9 (1864), 132–207.

Modern Studies of Foodstuffs and Early Cookery

General Studies

ANDRÉ, Jacques. *L'alimentation et la cuisine à Rome*. Études et Commentaires, 38. Paris: Klincksieck, 1961; repr. Paris: Belles Lettres, 1981.

ASHTOR, Eliyahu. "Essai sur l'alimentation des diverses classes sociales dans l'Orient médiéval," *Annales. Économies, sociétés, civilisations*, 23 (1968), 1017-1053.

AUSTIN, Gertrude Ellen. "English Food in the Thirteenth Century," *Medieval Forum*, 3 (1935–1936), 117–133.

BARBER, Richard W. *Cooking and Recipes from Rome to the Renaissance*. London: Allen Lane, 1973.

BENASSAR, Bartolomé and Joseph GOY. "Contribution à l'histoire de la consommation alimentaire du XIVe au XIXe siècle," *Annales. Économies, sociétés, civilisations*, 30 (1975), 402–430.

BLOND, Georges and Germaine BLOND. *Festins de tous les temps. Histoire pittoresque de notre alimentation*. Paris: Fayard, 1960; repr. 1976.

BOLENS, Lucie. "L'art culinaire médiéval andalou est baroque: les ruses de la science au service du goût (XIe–XIIIe siècle)," *Manger et boire au moyen âge*, II, 141–148.

BOUCHON, Marianne. "Latin de cuisine," *Archivum latinitatis medii ævi. Bulletin Du Cange*, 22 (1952), 63–76.

BOURIN, Jeanne. *Les recettes de Mathilde Brunel. Cuisine médiévale pour table d'aujourd'hui*. Paris: Flammarion, 1983.

BUXTON, Moira. *Medieval Cooking Today*. Waddesdon, Bucks.: Kylin, 1983.

CASTELOT, André. *L'Histoire à table. "Si la cuisine m'était contée ....*" Paris: Plon, 1972; repr. Paris: Perrin, 1978.

CHARBONNIER, Pierre. "L'Alimentation d'un seigneur auvergnat au début du XVe siécle," *Bulletin Philologique et Historique* (1968). Paris: Bibliothèque Nationale, 1971, 77–101.

CHELMINSKI, Rudolph. *The French at Table*. New York: William Morrow, 1985.

———"The Gluttonous Evolution of *la cuisine française*," *Smithsonian*, 16 (1985), 134–146.

CLAIR, Colin. *Kitchen and Table*. London, New York and Toronto: Abelard-Schuman, 1964.

COLLIN, Hubert. "Les ressources alimentaires en Lorraine pendant la première partie du XIVe siècle," *Bulletin Philologique et Historique* (1968). Paris: Bibliothèque Nationale, 1971, 37–75.

COSMAN, Madeleine Pelner. *Fabulous Feasts. Medieval Cookery and Ceremony*. New York: Braziller, 1976.

COURTINE, Robert J. and Céline VANCE. *Les grands maîtres de la cuisine française du Moyen Âge à Alexandre Dumas*. Paris: Bordas, 1972. Trans. by Philip Hyman and Mary Hyman as *The Grand Masters of French Cuisine: Five Centuries of Great Cooking*. New York: Putnam, 1978.

DARENNE, E. *Histoire des métiers de l'alimentation*. Meulan: Réty, 1904.

DAVIDSON, Alan, ed. *Oxford Symposium Documents 1983: Food in Motion. The Migration of Foodstuffs and Cookery Techniques*. Stanningley, Leeds: Prospect Books, 1983. 2 vols.

DELLE CINQUETERRE, Berengario (Barringer A. Fifield). *The Renaissance Cookbook. Historical perspectives through cookery*. Crown Point, Indiana: Dunes, 1975.

DRACHLINE, Pierre and Claude PETIT-CASTELLI. *À Table avec César*. Paris: Sand, 1984.

DRUMMOND, J.C. and Anne WILBRAHAM. *The Englishman's Food: A History of Five Centuries of English Diet*. London: Cape, 1939; 2nd ed. 1958; rev. ed. 1964.

DYER, C. "English Diet in the Later Middle Ages," *Social Relations and Ideas: Essays in Honour of R.H. Hilton.* Ed. T.H. ASTON, *et al.* Cambridge: Cambridge University, 1983.

EIXEMINIS, Francesc. *Com Usar Be de Beure e Menjar. Normes morales contingudes en el 'Terc de Crestia.'* Ed. Jorge E.J. GRACIA. Barcelona: Curial, 1977.

FACCIOLI, Emilio. "La cucina," in *Storia d'Italia*, 5/1: "I documenti." Turin: n. pub., 1973.

FENTON, Alexander and Eszter KISBAN. *Food in Change: Eating Habits from the Middle Ages to the Present Day.* Edinburgh: John Donald, 1986.

FIRPO, Luigi. *Gastronomia del Rinascimento.* Turin: Union Tipografico-Editrice Torinese, 1974.

FITZGIBBON, Theodora. *The Food of the Western World. An encyclopedia of food from North America and Europe.* New York: Quadrangle/The New York Times Book Co., 1976.

FLANDRIN, Jean-Louis. "Brouets, potages et bouillons," *Médiévales*, 5 (1983): "Nourritures," 5–14.

————"Différences et différenciation des goûts: réflexion sur quelques exemples européens entre le 14ème et le 18ème siècle," *Oxford Symposium Documents 1981*. London: Prospect Books, 1981, 191–207.

————"Les métamorphoses de la cuisine," *L'Histoire*, 85 (1986), 12–19.

FLANDRIN, Jean-Louis and Odile REDON. "Les livres de cuisine italiens des XIVe et XVe siècles," *Archeologia Medievale*, 8 (1981): "Problemi di storia dell'alimentazione nell'Italia medievale," 393–408.

FRANKLIN, Alfred. *La Vie privée d'autrefois*. Paris: Plon, 1888–1891; repr. Geneva: Slatkine, 1980. (Of specific interest are vol. 3: "La cuisine," vol. 6: "Les repas," and vol. 8: "Variétés gastronomiques.")

GILLI, P. "Les traités de cuisine dans la péninsule ibérique (13e–16e siècles)." Unpublished Master's Mémoire, University of Paris I, 1984.

GOTTSCHALK, Alfred. *Histoire de l'alimentation et de la gastronomie depuis la préhistoire jusqu'à nos jours*. Paris: Hippocrate, 1948. 2 vols.

GRANJA SANTAMARIA, Fernando de la. *La Cocina arábigoandaluza según un manuscrito inédito*. Ph.D. Thesis 6, University of Madrid, Faculty of Philosophy and Letters, 1960.

GRAUBARD, Mark Aaron. *Man's Food. Its Rhyme or Reason*. New York: MacMillan, 1943.

GREWE, Rudolf. "Catalan Cuisine, in an Historical Perspective," *Oxford Symposium Documents 1981*. London: Prospect Books, 1981, 170–178.

HAZLITT, William Carew. *Old Cookery Books and Ancient Cuisine*. London: E. Stock, 1886; repr. Detroit: Gale, 1968.

HÉMARDINQUER, Jean-Jacques. *Pour une histoire de l'alimentation*. Paris: Colin, 1970.

HENISCH, Bridget Ann. *Fast and Feast: Food in Medieval Society*. University Park and London: Penn State University, 1976.

HIEATT, Constance. "The Roast, or Boiled, Beef of Old England: *ore le fraunceis pur une feste araer*," *Book Forum*, 5 (1980), 294–299.

HIEATT, Constance and Sharon BUTLER. *Pleyn Delit. Medieval Cookery for Modern Cooks*. Toronto: University of Toronto, 1976. French trans. by Brenda Thaon as *Pain, vin et venaison: Un livre de cuisine médiévale*. Montreal: Aurore, 1977.

INCONTRI LOTTERINGHI DELLA STUFA, Maria Luisa. *Desinari e cene dai tempi remoti alla cucina toscana del XV secolo*. Florence: Olimpia, 1965.

JANSSEN, Walter. "Essen und Trinken im frühen und hohen Mittelalter. Aus archäologischer Sicht," in *Feestbundel voor prof. dr. J.G.N. Renaud*. Zutphen: De Walburg Pers, 1981, 324–331.

KNIBIEHLER, Yvonne. "Essai sur l'histoire de la cuisine provençale," *Oxford Symposium Documents 1981*. London: Prospect Books, 1981, 184–190.

LACROIX, Paul. *Mœurs, usages et costumes au moyen âge et à l'époque de la Renaissance*. 2nd ed. Paris: Firmin Didot, 1872.

LAURIOUX, Bruno. "Le mangeur de l'an Mil," *L'Histoire*, 73 (Dec. 1984), 90–91.

———"Les premiers livres de cuisine," *L'Histoire*, 85 (Jan. 1986), 51–55.

——— and Odile REDON. "Émergence d'une cuisine médiévale: le témoignage des livres," *Matériaux pour l'histoire des cadres de vie dans l'Europe occidentale (1050–1250): Cours d'agrégation*. Ed. H. Bresc. Nice: Université de Nice, 1984, 91–101.

LEBAULT, Armand. *La Table et le repas à travers les siècles*. Paris: Laveur, 1910.

LEVALET, Monique. "Quelques observations sur les cuisines en France et en Angleterre au Moyen Âge," *Archéologie Médiévale*, 8 (1978), 225–244.

Manger et boire au moyen âge: see MENJOT, Denis, ed. (below).

MARGOLIN, Jean-Claude and Robert SAUZET, eds. *Pratiques et discours alimentaires à la Renaissance*. Actes du Colloque de Tours, 1979. Paris: Maisonneuve-Larose, 1982.

MARTÍNEZ-LLOPIS, Manuel. *Historia de la gastronomía española*. Madrid: Editoria Nacional, 1981.

MEAD, William E. *The English Medieval Feast*. New York: Barnes and Noble, 1967.

MENJOT, Denis, ed. *Manger et boire au moyen âge*. Publications de la Faculté des Lettres et Sciences humaines de Nice, 27. Paris: Belles Lettres, 1984. 2 vols.

MENNELL, Stephen. *All Manners of Food: Eating and Taste in England and France from the Middle Ages to the Present*. London: Blackwell, 1985.

———*The Sociology of Taste: Eating and Taste in England and France from the Middle Ages to the Present*. Oxford: Blackwell, 1985.

MONTANARI, Massimo. *L'alimentazione contadina nell'alto Medioevo*. Nuovo Medioevo, 2. Naples: Liguori, 1979.

———"Valeurs, symboles, messages alimentaires durant le Haut Moyen Âge," *Médiévales*, 5 (1983): "Nourritures," 57–66.

MULON, Marianne. "Les premières recettes médiévales" in Hémardinquer, 236–240. Published also as "Recettes médiévales," in *Annales. Économies, sociétés, civilisations*, 19 (1964), 933–937.

NADA PATRONE, Anna Maria. *Il cibo del rico ed il cibo del povero. Contributo alla storia qualitativa dell'alimentazione. L'area pedemontana negli ultimi secoli del Medio Evo.* Turin: Centro Studi Piemontesi, 1981.

———"Trattati medici, diete e regimi alimentari in ambito pedemontano alla fine del medio evo," *Archeologia Medievale*, 8 (1981), 369–392.

Oxford Symposium Documents 1983: see DAVIDSON, Alan, ed. (above).

PARIENTE, Henriette and Geneviève DE TERNANT. *La fabuleuse histoire de la cuisine française*. Paris: Éditions ODIL, 1981.

PERRY, Charles. "Three Medieval Arabic Cook Books," *Oxford Symposium Documents 1981: National and Regional Styles of Cookery*. London: Prospect Books, 1981.

PETERSON, Toby. "The Arab Influence on Western European Cooking," *Journal of Medieval History*, 6 (1980), 317–341.

PIPONNIER, Françoise. "Équipement et techniques culinaires en Bourgogne au XIVe siècle," *Bulletin Philologique et Historique* (1971). Paris: Bibliothèque Nationale, 1977, 57–80.

———"Recherches sur la consommation alimentaire en Bourgogne au XIVe siècle," *Annales de Bourgogne*, 46 (1974), 65–111.

PLATINE (Jean-Louis Flandrin). "À quelle sauce les manger," *L'Histoire*, 33 (April 1981), 81-82.

———"Les sauces 'légères' du moyen âge," *L'Histoire*, 35 (June, 1981), 87–89.

PLOUVIER, Liliane. "Cuisine: et le potage fut ... ," *L'Histoire*, 64 (Feb., 1984), 79–81.

———"La gastronomie dans le *Viandier de Taillevent* et le *Ménagier de Paris*," *Manger et boire au moyen âge*, II, 149–159.

———"Taillevent, la première star de la gastronomie," *L'Histoire*, 61 (Nov., 1983), 93–94.

POUCHELLE, Marie-Christine. "Les appétits mélancoliques," *Médiévales*, 5 (1983): "Nourritures," 81–88.

PUIGGARÍ, Josep. "Notes istòriques de culinària catalana," *L'Avenç Literari*, 5 (1893).

PULLAR, Philippa. *Consuming Passions: A History of English Food and Appetite*. London: Hamilton, 1970; repr. London: Sphere, 1972. (Particularly ch. 5, "Mediæval Summer," pp. 78–117.)

RÉGNIER-BOHLER, Danielle. "Exil et retour: la nourriture des origines," *Médiévales*, 5 (1983): "Nourritures," 67–80.

REVEL, Jean-François. *Un festin en paroles. Histoire littéraire de la sensibilité gastronomique de l'Antiquité à nos jours*. Paris: Pauvert, 1979. Tr. Helen R. Lane as *Culture and Cuisine. A journey through the history of food*. New York: Doubleday, 1982; repr. New York: DaCapo, 1984.

ROBIN, Françoise. "Le luxe de la table dans les cours princières (1360–1480)," *Gazette des Beaux Arts*, 86 (1975), 1-16.

RODEN, Claudia. *A Book of Middle Eastern Food*. New York: Knopf, 1972.

RODINSON, Maxime. "Les influences de la civilisation musulmane sur la civilisation européenne médiévale dans les domaines de la consommation et de la distraction: l'alimentation," *Atti del Convegno Internazionale della Accademia Nazionale dei Lincei*, April, 1969. Rome: Accademia Nazionale dei Lincei, 1971, 479–499.

———"Recherches sur les documents arabes relatifs à la cuisine," *Revue des études islamiques*, 17 and 18 (1949), 95–165.

SABBAN, Françoise. "Le savoir-cuire ou l'art des potages dans le *Ménagier de Paris* et le *Viandier* de Taillevent," *Manger et boire au moyen âge*, II, 161–172.

SALY, Antoinette. "Les oiseaux dans l'alimentation médiévale d'après le *Viandier* de Taillevent et le *Ménagier de Paris*," *Manger et boire au moyen âge*, II, 173–179.

SANTICH, Barbara. "The Italian Influence on Mediaeval Catalan Cuisine," in vol. 1, 67–73 of *Oxford Symposium Documents 1983*. Staningley, Leeds: Prospect Books, 1983. 2 vols.

———"Mediæval Thickeners," *The Cooking Medium. Proceedings, Oxford Symposium 1986*. London : Prospect Books, 1987, 118–128.

———*Two Languages, Two Cultures, Two Cuisines: A comparative study of the culinary cultures of northern and southern France, Italy and Catalonia in the fourteenth and fifteenth centuries*. Unpublished Ph.D. Thesis, Flinders University of South Australia, 1987.

SASS, Lorna J. "The Preference for Sweets, Spices and Almond Milk in Late Mediæval English Cuisine," *Food in Perspective. Proceedings of the Third International Conference on Ethnological Food Research, Cardiff, 1977*. Ed. Alexander FENTON and Trevor M. OWEN. Edinburgh: John Donald, 1981.

———*To the King's Taste. Richard II's book of feasts and recipes adapted for modern cooking*. New York: Metropolitan Museum of Art, 1975.

SCULLY, Terence. "'Aucune science de l'art de cuysinerie et de cuysine': Chiquart's *Du fait de cuisine*," *Food and Foodways*, 2 (1987), 199–214.

———"The *Opusculum de saporibus* of Magninus Mediolanensis," *Medium Ævum*, 54 (1985), 178–207.

SERJEANTSON, M.S. "The Vocabulary of Cookery in the Fifteenth Century," *Essays and Studies by Members of the English Association*, vol. 23. Oxford: Clarendon, 1938, 25–37.

SOMMÉ, Monique. "L'Alimentation quotidienne à la cour de Bourgogne au milieu du XVe siècle," *Bulletin Philologique et Historique* (1968). Paris: Bibliothèque Nationale, 1971.

SOYER, Alexis. *The Pantropheon, or History of Food and its Preparation in Ancient Times*. London: Simpkin, 1853; repr. New York and London: Paddington, 1977.

STECCHETTI, Lorenzo (Olindo Guerrini). *La tavola e la cucina nei secoli XIV e XV*. Florence: G. Barbèra, 1884.

STOUFF, Louis. *Ravitaillement et alimentation en Provence aux XIVe et XVe siècles*. Paris and The Hague: Mouton, 1970.

TANNAHILL, Reay. *Food in History*. London and New York: Stein & Day, 1973.

VEHLING, Joseph. *Cookery and Dining in Imperial Rome*. New York: Dover, 1977. (Based on Apicius's *De re coquinaria*.)

VOLLENWEIDER, Alice. "Der Einfluss der italienischen auf die französische Kochkunst im Spiegel der Sprache (Historischer Ueberblick)," *Vox Romanica: Annales Helvetica explorandis linguis romanicis destinati*, 22 (1963), 59–88 and 397–443.

WEISS-AMER, Melitta. *Zur Entstehung, Tradierung und Lexik deutscher Kochbücher und Rezepte des Spätmittelalters*. Unpublished Master's Thesis, University of Waterloo, 1983.

WHEATON, Barbara Ketcham. *Savoring the Past. The French Kitchen and Table from 1300 to 1789*. Philadelphia: University of Pennsylvania, 1983. French trans. as *L'Office et la bouche. Histoire des mœurs de la table en France, 1300–1789*. Paris: Calmann-Lévy, 1984.

WILSON, C. Anne. *Food and Drink in Britain from the Stone Age to Recent Times*. London: Constable, 1973.

————'The Saracen Connection: Arab Cuisine and the Mediæval West," part 1, *Petits Propos Culinaires*, 7 (March 1981), 13–22; part 2, *ibid.*, 8 (June 1981), 19–27.

WISWE, H. *Kulturgeschichte der Kochkunst*. Munich: Moss, 1970.

ZUTTER-PRENTKI, Alix. *Goût et gastronomie dans le sud de l'Allemagne, 14e–16e siècles*. Doctoral Dissertation in progress. Paris, École des Hautes Études en Sciences Sociales.

On Spices, Herbs and Edible Plants

ANDRÉ, Jacques. *Lexique des termes de botanique en latin*. Paris: Klincksieck, 1956.

ARBER, Agnes R. *Herbals, their Origin and Evolution. A Chapter in the History of Botany*. 2nd ed. Cambridge: Cambridge University, 1938; repr. 1953.

BARDENHEWER, Luise. *Der Safranhandel in Mittelalter*. Bonn: Hauptmann, 1914. Philosophy Dissertation, vol. 26, Bonn, June 1914.

BERTI TOESCA, E. *Il "Tacuinum sanitatis" della Biblioteca Nazionale di Parigi*. Bergamo, 1937.

CLAIR, Colin. *Of Herbs and Spices*. London and New York: Abelard-Schuman, 1961.

CLARKSON, Rosetta E. *The Golden Age of Herbs and Herbalists*. New York: Dover, 1972. (Particularly Chapters 10: "Flowers in Food," and 12: "A Prelude to Salads.")

COULET, N. "Pour une histoire du jardin. Vergers et potagers à Aix-en-Provence, 1350–1450," *Le Moyen Âge*, 73 (1967), 239–270.

DENCE, Colin S. "Herbs and Spices through the Ages," *Herbal Review*, 4 (1978), 11–23.

FLÜCKIGER, Friedrich A. and Daniel HANBURY. *Pharmacographia: a history of the principal drugs of vegetable origin met with in Great Britain and British India*. 2nd ed.

London and Glasgow: Macmillan, 1879. French trans. as *Histoire des drogues d'origine végétale*. Paris: Doin, 1878. 2 vols.

FREEMAN, Margaret B. *Herbs for the Mediæval Household for Cooking, Healing and Divers Uses*. New York: Metropolitan Museum of Art, 1943.

GARGILIUS MARTIALIS, Q. *De oleribus* (*Liber de virtutibus herbarum*). (Third century.) First printed Rome, 1509. Ed. Valentin ROSE in vol. 2, 103–160 of *Anecdota græca et græcolatina*. Berlin: Duerwinler, 1864–1870. 2 vols.

GIBAULT, Georges. *Histoire des légumes*. Paris: Librairie Horticole, 1912.

GRAND, Roger and Raymond DELATOUCHE. *L'Agriculture au Moyen Âge de la fin de l'Empire romain au XVIe siècle*. Paris: De Boccard, 1935. (This is vol. 3 of *L'Agriculture à travers les âges. Histoire des faits, des institutions, de la pensée et des doctrines économiques et sociales.*)

GREENBURG, Sheldon. "Spices and the Shaping of our World: A Few Examples,"in vol. 2, 44–51 of *Oxford Symposium Documents 1983*. Staningley, Leeds: Prospect Books, 1983. 2 vols.

GUÉRILLOT-VINET, André and Lucien GUYOT. *Les Épices*. Paris: Presses Universitaires de France, 1963.

GUYOT, Lucien. *Histoire des plantes cultivées*. Paris: A. Colin, 1963.

HARRISON, Sydney G., G.B. MASEFIELD and Michael WALLIS. *The Oxford Book of Food Plants*. London: Oxford University, 1969.

HENSLOW, George. *Medical Works of the Fourteenth Century, together with a List of Plants Recorded in Contemporary Writing, with their Identifications*. London: Chapman & Hall, 1899; repr. New York: B. Franklin, 1972.

HUSSON, Camille. *Étude sur les épices, aromates, condiments, sauces et assaisonnements: leur histoire, leur utilité, leur danger*. Paris: Dunod, 1883.

HYMAN, Philip and Mary HYMEN. "Long Pepper: A Short History," *Petits Propos Culinaires*, 6 (1980), 44–54. Also, "Connaissez-vous le poivre long?" *L'Histoire*, 24 (July 1980), 94–95.

LANDRY, Robert. *Les soleils de la cuisine*. Paris: Laffont, 1967. Tr. Bruce H. Axler as *The Gentle Art of Flavoring*. London and New York: Abelard-Schuman, 1970.

LAURIOUX, Bruno. "De l'usage des épices dans l'alimentation médiévale," *Médiévales*, 5 (1983): "Nourritures," 15–31.

————"Et le poivre conquit la France," *L'Histoire*, 67 (May 1984), 79–81.

————"Spices in the Medieval Diet: A New Approach," *Food and Foodways*, 1 (1985), 43–76.

LECLERC, Henri. *Les épices, plantes condimentaires de la France et des colonies. Leur histoire, leurs usages alimentaires, leurs vertus thérapeutiques*. Paris: Mason, 1929.

MAURIZIO, A. *Histoire de l'alimentation végétale depuis la préhistoire jusqu'à nos jours*. Paris: Payot, 1932; repr. 1939.

MILLER, J. Innes. *The Spice Trade of the Roman Empire*. Oxford: Clarendon, 1969.

PARRY, John William. *The Spice Handbook: Spices, Aromatic Seeds and Herbs*. Brooklyn, N.Y.: Chemical Publishing Co., 1945.

————*The Story of Spices*. New York: Chemical Publishing Co., 1953.

PETINO, Antonio. *Lo zafferano nell'economia del medioevo*. Studi de Economia e Statistica, 1. Catania: Facoità de Economia e Commercio, 1951.

SAINT-LAGER, J.B. *Histoire des herbiers*. Paris: Baillière, 1885. And a supplement to this: *Recherches sur les anciens herbaria*. Paris: Baillière, 1886.

SERJEANT, Robert. "Agriculture and Horticulture: some cultural interchanges of the medieval Arabs and Europe," *Atti del Convegno Internazionale della Accademia Nazionale dei Lincei*, April 1969. Rome: Accademia Nazionale dei Lincei, 1971, 535–548.

WAKE, C.H.H. "The Changing Pattern of Europe's Pepper and Spice Imports, *ca.* 1400–1700," *Journal of European Economic History*, 8 (1979), 361–399.

On Fish

BARBIER, Paul. "Noms de poissons," *Revue des langues romanes*, 51 (1908), 385–406; 52 (1909), 97–129; 53 (1910), 26–57; 54 (1911), 149–190; 56 (1913), 172–247; 57 (1914), 295–342; 58 (1915), 270–329; 63 (1925), 1–68; 65 (1927), 1–52; 67 (1933–1936), 275–372.

BELON DU MANS, Pierre. *La Nature et diversité des poissons*. Paris: Ch. Estienne, 1555.

DELATOUCHE, R. "Les Poissons d'eau douce dans l'alimentation médiévale," *Comptes rendus de l'Académie d'Agriculture de France* (June 22 1966), 793–798.

GESNER, Conrad. *Historia animalium liber quartus qui est de piscium et aquatilium animalium nature*. Zurich: Froschoveus, 1558.

————*Nomenclator aquatilium animalium. Icones animalium aquatilium*. Zurich: Froschoveus, 1560.

GISLAIN, G. de. "Le rôle des étangs dans l'alimentation médiévale," *Manger et boire au moyen âge*, I, 89–101.

MIRA, Giuseppe. *La pesca nel medioevo nelle acque mediterranee*. Milan: Giuffre, 1937.

————*La pesca nel medioevo nelle acque interne italiane*. Milan: Giuffre, 1937.

RONDELET, Guillaume. *Libri de piscibus marinis, in quibus veræ piscium effigies expressæ sunt, quæ in tota piscium historia contineantur*. Lyons: Mattiam Bonhomme, 1554. French tr. as *L'Histoire entiere des poissons*. Lyons: Macé Bonhomme, 1558.

SAINT-DENIS, E. de. *Le vocabulaire des animaux marins en latin classique*. Paris: Klincksieck, 1947.

WICKERSHEIMER, Ernest. "Zur spätmittelalterlichen Fischdiätetik," *Sudhoffs Archiv für Geschichte der Medizin und der Naturwissenschaften*, 47 (1963), 411–416.

On Beverages

ALLEN, H. Warner. *A History of Wine*. London: Faber & Faber, 1961.

AMERINE, M.A., H.W. BERG and W.V. CRUESS. *The Technology of Wine Making*. Westport, Conn.: Avi, 1972.

BRUNELLO, Franco. *Storia dell'acquavite*. Vicenza: N. Pozzo, 1969.

DION, Roger. "Grands traits d'une géographie vinicole de la France: la viticulture médiévale," *Publications de la Société Géographique de Lille* (1948–1949), 6–45.

———*Histoire de la vigne et du vin en France des origines au 19e siècle*. Paris: Flammarion, 1959.

———"Viticulture ecclésiastique et viticulture princière au moyen âge," *Revue Historique*, 212 (1954), 1–22.

EYER, Frédéric. "La cervoise et la bière au Moyen Âge et à la Renaissance," *Bulletin Philologique et Historique* (1968). Paris: Bibliothèque Nationale, 1971, 346–363.

FORBES, Robert James. *A Short History of the Art of Distillation*. Leiden: Brill, 1948.

JAMES, Margery K. *Studies in the Medieval Wine Trade*. Ed. Elspeth M. VEALE. Oxford: Clarendon, 1971.

RENOUARD, Y. "Le grand commerce de vins au moyen âge," vol. 1, 235–248, in *Études d'histoire médiévale*. Bibliothèque générale de l'École pratique des hautes études. Paris: S.E.V.P.E.N., 1968. 2 vols.

Le Vin au Moyen Âge: Production et producteurs. Actes du IIe Congrès des Médiévistes, Grenoble, June 4–6 1971. N.p.: Société des historiens médiévistes de l'enseignement supérieur public, 1978.

Other Related Studies

BARBAZAN, Étienne, ed. *Fabliaux et contes des poètes françois des XIe, XIIe, XIIIe, XIVe et XVe siècles tirés des meilleurs auteurs*. New ed. by Dominique Martin MÉON. Paris: B. Warée; Imprimerie de Crapelet, 1808. 4 vols.

BRIDBURY, A.R. *England and the Salt Trade in the Later Middle Ages*. Oxford: Clarendon, 1955.

CASTELVETRO, Giacopo. *Breve racconto di tutte le radici, di tutte l'erbe e di tutti i frutti che crudi o cotti in Italia si mangiano*. London: Castelvetro, 1614. Ed. Luigi FIRPO in *Gastonomia del Rinascimento*. Turin: Unione Tipografico, [1973], 131–176.

COLLIN, Hubert. "Les ressources alimentaires en Lorraine pendant la première partie du XIVe siècle," *Bulletin philologique et historique* (1968). Paris: Bibliothèque Nationale, 1971, 37–75.

CRANE, Eva, ed. *Honey, a Comprehensive Survey*. London and New York: Heinemann & Crane, Russak, 1975.

CRISP, Frank. *Medieval Gardens: With some Account of Tudor, Elizabethan and Stuart Gardens*. London: John Lane, 1924. 2 vols.

DAVID, H. "L'hôtel ducal sous Philippe le Bon. Mœurs et coutumes. Les offices," *Annales de Bourgogne*, 37 (1965), 241–255.

DEERR, Noel. *The History of Sugar*. London: Chapman & Hall, 1949–1950. 2 vols.

DELORT, Robert. "L'aliment-roi: le pain," *L'Histoire*, 85 (Jan. 1986), 96–102.

———*Le commerce des fourrures en Occident à la fin du moyen âge*. Rome and Paris: École Française de Rome, 1978. 2 vols.

DOBROWOLSKI, Paweł T. "Food Purchases of a Traveling Nobleman: the accounts of the Earl of Derby, 1390–1393," *Food and Foodways*, 2 (1988), 289–308.

DORVEAUX, Paul. *Le sucre au Moyen Âge*. Bibliothèque Historique de la France Médicale, 26. Paris: Champion, 1911.

DURBEC, J.-A. "La grande boucherie de Paris. Notes historiques d'après des archives privées (XIIe–XVIIe siècles)," *Bulletin philologique et historique* (1955–1956), 65–125.

FAUREAU, Robert. "La boucherie en Poitou à la fin du Moyen Âge," *Bulletin Philologique et Historique* (1968). Paris: Bibliothèque Nationale. 1971, 295–318.

FLANDRIN, Jean-Louis. "Le goût et la nécessité: sur l'usage des graisses dans les cuisines d'Europe occidentale (XIVe–XVIIIe siècle)," *Annales. Économies, sociétés, civilisations*, 38 (1983), 369–401.

GUAL CAMARENA, Miguel. *Vocabulario del comercio medioeval*. Taragona: Diputación Provincial, 1968; 2nd ed. Barcelona: Albir, 1976.

———"Un manual catalan de mercadería (1455)," *Anuario de Estudios Medioevales* (Barcelona), 1 (1964), 431–450. (An edition of the *Libre de conexenses de spicies, e de drogues.*)

GUILHIERMOZ, P. "Note sur les poids du moyen âge," *Bibliothèque de l'École des Chartes*, 67 (1906), 161–233 and 402–450.

HEYD, Wilhelm. *Histoire du commerce du Levant au moyen-âge*. Rev. ed. publ. by Furcy RAYNAUD. Leipzig, 1885–1886; repr. Amsterdam: Hakkert, 1967. 2 vols.

JACOB, Heinrich E. *Six Thousand Years of Bread*. New York: Doubleday, Doran, 1944.

JARRY, Madeleine. "L'homme sauvage," *L'Œil*, 183 (March, 1970), 14–21.

LAFORTUNE-MARTEL, Agathe. *Fête noble en Bourgogne au XVe siècle. Le banquet du Faisan (1454): Aspects politiques, sociaux et culturels*. Université de Montréal, Institut d'études médiévales, Cahiers d'études médiévales, 8. Montreal: Bellarmin, 1984, and Paris: Vrin, 1984.

LECOQ, Raymond. *Les objets de la vie domestique. Ustensiles en fer de la cuisine et du foyer des origines au XIXe siècle*. Paris: Berger-Levrault, 1979.

LIPPMANN, Edmund O. von. *Geschichte des Zuckers seit den ältesten Zeiten bis zum Beginn der Rübenzucker-Fabrikation*. Berlin: Springer, 1929.

LOPEZ, Roberto S. and Irving W. RAYMOND. *Medieval Trade in the Mediterranean World*. New York and London: Columbia University, 1955.

MCLEAN, Teresa. *Medieval English Gardens*. London: Collins, 1981.

MINTZ, Sidney W. *Sweetness and Power: The Place of Sugar in Modern History*. New York: Elizabeth Sifton/Viking, 1985.

NENQUIN, Jacques. *Salt, a Study in Economic Prehistory*. Bruges: De Tempel, 1961.

PEGOLOTTI, Francesco Balducci. *La Pratica della Mercatura*. Ed. Allan Evans. Cambridge, Mass.: Mediæval Academy of America, 1936; repr. New York: Kraus, 1970.

POUCHELLE, Marie-Christine. "Les appétits mélancoliques," *Médiévales*, 5 (1983): "Nourritures," 81–88.

RODINSON, Maxime. "Romanía et autres mots arabes en italien," *Romania*, 71 (1950), 433–449.

SOSSON, J.-P. "La part du gibier dans l'alimentation médiévale: l'exemple des Pourvances de Guillaume d'Ostrevant au Quesnoy (23 septembre 1397–23 juin 1398)," *La Chasse au Moyen Âge (Actes du Colloque de Nice, 22-24 juin 1979)*. Paris: Belles Lettres, 1980, 347–359.

TOLKOWSKI, Samuel. *Hesperides: a History of the Culture and Use of Citrus Fruits*. London: Bale, 1938.

VERDON, Jean. "Fêtes et divertissements en Occident durant le haut Moyen Âge," *Journal of Medieval History*, 5 (1979), 303–314.

VILLENEUVE, Guillaume de la. *Les Crieries de Paris*. Ed. Étienne BARBAZAN in *Fabliaux et contes des poètes françois*, IV, 276–281. (See above.)

WILSON, C. Anne. "Sugar: the Migration of a Plant Product during 2000 Years," vol. 1, 1–10, *Oxford Symposium Documents 1983: "Food in Motion. The Migration of Foodstuffs and Cookery Techniques."* Staningley, Leeds: Prospect Books, 1983. 2 vols.

WITTEVEEN, Joop. "Rose Sugar and Other Medieval Sweets," *Petits Propos Culinaires*, 20 (July 1985), 22–28.

WOODROOF, Jasper Guy. *Tree Nuts: Production, Processing, Products*. Westport, Conn.: AVI, 1967. 2 vols.

WRIGHT, Richard. *A Volume of Vocabularies: Illustrating the Condition and Manners of our Forefathers, as well as the History of the Forms of Elementary Education and of the Languages Spoken in this Island from the Tenth Century to the Fifteenth*. N.pl.: privately printed, 1857; 2nd ed. 1882.

Glossary and Index

The numbers in the following Glossary and Index refer to Recipe numbers; if a word in a particular recipe appears in only one of the manuscripts, the siglum of that manuscript follows the Recipe number: *e. g.* **ables** 144 *BN*.

Verbs are inserted into the Glossary in their infinitive; if no infinitive is attested in the *Viandier*, a supposed infinitive is supplied for the Glossary entry, but enclosed in brackets.

The letter *y* is assimilated to the letter *i*.

Words which are common in modern French are glossed only when the presence in the *Viandier* of the things or procedures they represent might be of interest.

Abbreviations like "vol." and "p." are omitted to clarify reading of the entry itself, save in the case the *Menagier*.

ables 115, 144 *BN*; abletes 115 *MAZ*, a fresh-water fish, *Alburnus alburnus*, bleak; s.a. **alles**

affaittier, affetier, affeitier, affaictier, affecter 119, 120, 123, 129, 133, 135 *BN*, to prepare, clean, clean out, eviscerate—Tobler, 1, 171

affiner 15, 16, 17, *passim*, to make fine, grind; 135 *VAT*, to finish off

agu 28, piquant

aigneaux 35, lambs

aigreffins, egreffin, angrefin 128, a round sea-fish, *Melanogrammus aeglefinus*, haddock

aigret 61, sharp, nippy (in flavour); *cf.* **agu**

aigreur 183, bitterness, sourness (like vinegar)

aillés, aillez, ailletz: a. blans 107; **a. vertz** 107, 149 *BN*; **a. verdelés** 147 *BN*, varieties of garlic sauce; s.a. **aulx**—DuCange, I, 185c, *alliata bullita*

alaine, alainne 91 *BN*, 192, vapour; s.a. **fumee, fust**

alles de mer 144 *VAT*, a flat sea-fish, *Engraulis encrasicholus*, anchovy; s.a. **ables**

allouetes 45, 188, larks

allumelle 212, omelette—Godefroy, 1, 243b

alouyaulx 204, a preparation of marrow, veal and batter in the shape of a small lark

aloze, alose, alouse 101, 143, *Leuciscus alburnus*, a fresh-water and flat sea-fish, *Alosa alosa*, shad; **a. cratonniere** 143 *BN*—Cotgrave; Barbier, *Revue des langues romanes*, 54 (1911), 151

alun 180, alum—see Pegolotti, 367–370; Heyd, 2, 565.

amblos: see **umblos**

amendes, almendes, almandes, amandres 13, *passim*, almonds; **lait d'a.** 64, *passim*, almond milk; **grain d'a.** 204, nutmeat of almonds

amender 178, to improve

amydon 199, wheat starch

andoulles, andoylles 212, *VAT* Table §32, chitterlings

anguille 69, 75 *VAL*, 107, 121, 194, eel; **brouet vertgay d'a.** 76; **soringue d'a.** 79; **brouet saraginois (d'a.)** 80

annis blanc ou vermeil 188, 189, *Pimpinella anisum*, anise—Clair, p. 111

aours adj. 2 *VAT*, burnt—Cotgrave; Godefroy, 1, 311 *s'aourser*, "s'attacher au fond du pot, brûler"

apoint: see **point**

appareiller, apparoillier 93, 123 *BN*, 126, 135 *MAZ*, to prepare, clean (out), eviscerate (a fish)—Cotgrave; Tobler, 1, 424

arain 219, brass

archal 214, brass—Tobler, 1, 501

arçonner, arsonner 50, 51, 52, 53, 72, to fix on a spit—Godefroy, 1, 384a

arrouser 195, to moisten

arsure, arsseure 2, a burnt taste—Tobler, 1, 551

asur, azur 199, a bright blue pigment or dye, azurite or perhaps powdered lapis lazuli—see Pegolotti, p. 372

atramper 155, to temper, mix in proper proportions—Tobler, 1, 627

aubuns, aubins 73 *VAL*, 181, *passim*, egg whites

aulx, haulx 31 *VAT*, *passim*, garlic; **a. vertz** 3, 36, 107, 145, 147, 149, 150, 158; **a. blans** 3, 36, 147 VAT, 149 VAT, 157; **a. de la roye** 122 *VAT*; **a. camelins** 123, 130, 136, 156; **a. a harens frez** 159; **jance aux a.** 167; **a. atout la cotelle** *VAT* Table §165, various types of garlic sauce; s.a. **aillés**—Clair, p. 171

bacin 175 baking dish (in which a torte can be made)

baciner, bassiner 41, 42, 43, 60, to baste—Tobler, 1, 791

[**baconner, baconer**] 51, 101, 124, to wrap in slices of bacon, lard—Tobler, 1, 792

baye 183, 184, *Laurus nobilis*, bay laurel (leaf); see also **lorier**—Clair, p. 118

baien, boyans adj. 181, 188, burst, split (peas, from cooking)—Tobler, 1, 796 **baissaille** 106 *BN*, a type of fresh-water fish

balaine *VAT* Table §148, classified as a flat sea-fish, whale

bar 100, *Galeichthys marinus*, a fresh-water fish resembling a bass

barbe Robert, la 163, a sauce

barbillons 99, a fresh-water fish, *Barbus barbus*, barbel

barbue 138, a flat sea-fish, *Scophthalmus rhombus*, brill; "a kind of lesse Turbot, or Turbot-like fish, called by some, a Dab, or Sandling" (Cotgrave)

basilique 175, *Ocymum basilicum*, basil—Clair, p. 115, Freeman, p. 3

bastart: vin b. 81, a mixed wine, related to muscatel: *il est doubz de sa nature*—DuCange, 9, 393b and 8, 343b; s.a. *Romania*, 71 (1948), 529 and 86 (1966), 97

Baudés: porte B. 36 *VAT*, location of goose roasters and vendors in Paris

beschet, becquet 78, *Esox lucius*, pike—Tobler 1, 894

bescuit 78, an error for **beschet**, or else a scarlet-coloured sauce made of fish juices (?)—Tobler, 1, 940 *bescuit*, "ein Fischgericht"

betes, bettes, bedtes, brectes 153, 154, 175, *Beta vulgaris*, chard

beuf 3, 206, beef

beurre butter: **b. fraiz** 126, 150, 206; **b. fraiz ou sallé** 153, 188, 190

[**biberons**] (?) 211, a water jug, ewer; see **liberons**—Cotgrave; cf. Tobler 1, 961; *FEW*, 1, 350a; Ste-Palaye 1, 153b

blanc s.m. 209, a coin

blanc s.m. 95 *BN*, 195, white meat of a chicken

blanc mengier 118, white dish; **b. m. d'un chappon pour ung malade** 95; **b. m. party** 199

blé vert 170 *VAT*, unripened wheat (?)—*cf. Menagier*, §270: "feuille de blé"

bociné 51 *MAZ*, error for **botiné**, meaning **boutonné**?
boe 69, a thick sauce
boyans: see **baien**
bondon 180, bung-hole—Cotgrave
bouconnez 51 *VAT*, error for **boutonnez**?
boujons 170 *VAT*, vine shoots—*Menagier*, §270
boullon, boullion, boillon 7, *passim*, bouillon, broth, stock; at 88, a sauce base (of crushed almonds, wine and verjuice) which has been boiled
boulture, bouliture 3, a boiling, boiled meat; *cf. rostz* and *friture*
bouly, boully lardé 5, broth which includes bacon
bourblier, bourbier, bourbis de sanglier 41, 42, "the breast, or Esay of a wild Swine" (Cotgrave); "du bourbelier, c'est le nomblet" (*Menagier*, §91)
bourre 216, flocks of wool or hair used for stuffing—Cotgrave; Tobler, 1, 1075
boussac, boussat, bonsax, 20, a variety of prepared dish comprising a meat and a sauce—Tobler, 1, 1085
bouté, boucté 181, 182, ropy (of wine)—DuCange, 9, 393b and 1, 723c
boutonner, 51, 72 *VAL*, 124 *VAL*, to interlard (with cloves or pieces of lard, bacon) **b. de clou de girofle** 200—Tobler, 1, 1096; *cf. Menagier*, ed. Brereton & Ferrier, p. 173, l. 12; ed. Pichon, 2, p. 88.
boutter 203, 215, to cast—Tobler, 1, 1092
brayer 11, 14, 19, 33, to grind; s.a. **broyer**
braytte: see **brete**
braon, broion, broyons, bram 19, 66, 95, brawn, muscle, dark meat of poultry; *cf. du brun des poulletz*, 66 *VAT*—Tobler, 1, 1126; *A-ND*, 1, 75a; Niermeyer, 103b, *bradonis*: "jambon, ham"
brese 7, coals of fire
bresme 105, 139, classified as both a fresh-water fish (family *Cyprinidæ*) and a flat sea-fish (family *Sparidæ*), bream
brete, braytte 130, a type of round sea-fish, *Pleuronectes rhombus*, brett—*REW*, 1316
[**brisier**] 185, to bruise, break (?)—see *TLF*, 4, 982b (Etymol.)
broche 20, *passim*, spit, skewer; **b. de fer** 66; **brochette de boys** 210, 212, 213, 214
[**brochier**] 195, to put on a spit, to skewer—Godefroy, 1, 738a
brochet 88 *VAL*, 98, 206, a fresh-water fish, *Esox lucius*, pike; **brochetons** 188, pickerel
broyer 24, *passim*, to crush, blend together; s.a. **brayer**
bronailles 45 *MAZ*, bowels (?)—*FEW*, 1, 566a, b *brunna* : *bournel* "conduit, tuyau"
brosser 200, 201, to curdle: "broussé ou brossé (lait): lait tourné, grumelé, aigri" (M. Rolland, *Dictionnaire des expressions vicieuses*)—s.a. *FEW*, 1, 561a
brouet 15, *passim*, broth; **b. georgié** 15; **b. rousset** 16; **blanc b. de chappons** 19; **b. d'Alemaigne** 22, 85; **soutil b. d'Angleterre** 24; **b. de verjus** 25; **b. vergay** 26, 73 *MAZ*, 76, 115; **b. saraginois** 80, 87; **b. vert de eufs et de formage** 87; **b. aux yssues de porc** 154; **b. de daintiers de cerf** 193
buchettes 51, wooden pins—Tobler, 1, 1209
buhoreaulx *VAT* Table §65, a type of game bird, a small bittern (?); s.a. **butor**—Godefroy, 1, 758 *buordel*
buignetz 201A, 177, fritters—Tobler, 1, 1195
[**bureteler**] 177, to sieve (flour)—Tobler, 1, 1205
butor 56, bittern; s.a. **buhoreaulx**

cailles 45 quails
caillette 210, rennet, the inner lining of the fourth stomach of calves and other young ruminants
calongne 119 *VAT*, scallion, shallot; s.a. **escalongnes**
camelins: aulx c. 156, cinnamon garlic sauce

cameline s.f. 6, 155, *passim*, cameline, a cinnamon sauce

canelle, cannelle 16, *passim*, common cinnamon from cassia bark or buds; **pouldre de c.** 61, 104 *VAT*, 171, a finer cinnamon, also called *cynamome*; **fleur de c.** 16, 68, 73, (ground) cassia bark or buds; **brouet de c.** 14; **canelle et cynamome** 206—see Pegolotti, p. 361 and p. 374 *fiori di cannella*; Heyd, 2, p. 595; Clair, p. 48

canfre 219, camphor—see Pegolotti, p. 375

carpes 102, 152, carp

carre s.f. and m. 215, box, four-sided container—*cf.* Tobler, 8, 92

carreletz 134 *VAT* (?), 206, *VAT* Table §159, a sea-fish, small plaice

[caveler] (?) 134 *VAT*, to eviscerate (?); see also **taveler**

cendre 179; **c. gravelee** 180, a crude potash; "ashes made of the burnt lees, or dregs of wine" (Cotgrave); *cf.* **charree**—see Pegolotti, p. 380; Gual Camarena, 265, *cendra clavellada* ; *FEW*, 2, 758a and 759, n3.

cerf 6, 7, 193, stag

cervoisons 193, young stag (?)

chair, char 14, *passim*, flesh, meat (usually of domestic animals as distinct from **veneison**); **grosse c.** 3; **a c., es jours de c., a jour de c., a jour de mengier c.** 71, 200, 206, on non-fasting days; s.a. **charnage, poisson, maslés**

chanvre 216, hemp

chappleure 188, thin slice—Tobler, 2, 241

chappon, chapon 19, 21, 38, 173, capon; **c. de haute gresse, c. gras** 40, 220; **eaue rose d'un c.** 91; **blanc mengier d'ung c.** 95; **lassis de blanc de c.** 189; **c. aux herbes** 9; **c. au vertjus** *VAT* Table §30

charbon 17, 47, 79, 175, 176, 200, 201, 207, coals of fire

charcois 190, 195, 213, carcass—Godefroy, 2, 67c; Tobler, 2, 260; s.a. *Menagier*, ed. Brereton & Ferrier, p. 327, note to p. 247, l. 29: "entrails"

charnage 153, non-fasting days

charpir 189, to cut or draw into long filaments; to card (as wool)—Tobler, 2, 281

charpie 33, 189, a type of dish comprising strands of meat; these strands of meat themselves—DuCange, 2, 181c; Niermeyer, 146b

charree 122, "buck-ashes, the ashes whereof Lye hath bin made" (Cotgrave); *cf.* **cendre gravelee**—Tobler, 2, 282

[chasser] 175, to line (a baking dish) with pastry—der. of L. *capsa*, Fr. *châsse*? See DuCange, 2, 144c "*capsa*: arca, theca, cista, ubi aliquid reponitur"

chastaignes 7, 24, 60, chestnuts

chaudeau, chaudiau, chaudel: c. flament 92, Flemish caudle—Cotgrave; Tobler, 2, 326

chaudiere 211, cauldron

chaudumel, chaudumé, chauduńé, chaudumet 98, 135 *MAZ*, a type of sauce; **c. a becquet, au bescuit** 78—Tobler, 2, 328–9

chaudun, chauduin, chaudin 10, 154, tripe; "le chaudun, ce sont les boyaulx ... les boyaulx menuz ... et aussi en est la pance" (*Menagier*, §12)—Tobler, 2, 329

cheneveaux, chenernes 108, a freshwater fish, *Leuciscus cephalus*, chub; s.a. **chevriaux**—Cotgrave, *s. v. chenevel*

[cheoir] v.intr.: pres.3 **chee** 212, to fall

chevrel, chevreu, chevriaux, chevrieulx 35, kid, young goat; **c. sauvage** 8, roe deer

chevriaux 107 *BN*, chub (?); s.a. **cheneveaux**

chevrons 215, spars

chien de mer 123, a round sea-fish, family *Scyliorhindæ*, dogfish

chouz 154, cabbage, cole

ciboule, siboulle 44, 101, 119, 124, 154, 170 *VAT*, shallot—Cotgrave

cilion folion 68, ?, perhaps *Anthriscus cerefolium*, chervil—Clair, p. 140; s.a. *folion* in Tobler, 3, 2015; Godefroy, 4, 52 a; and *FEW*, 3, 685a

cynamome 188, 190, 191, 192, 206, a fine type of cinnamon from cinnamon bark (*cf.* the *Tractatus* (II, §11), which distinguishes between *cynamomum* and *canellam*: "Ad homines simplices et mediocres sufficiat . . . canella"); **canelle et c.** 206; s.a. **canelle**—see Pegolotti, pp. 361 and 374; Heyd, 2, p. 595; *Ricettario*

cine, cigne 49, swan; **c. revestu** 72, 213, 214

cirop: pot a c. 202 broad, shallow pan for evaporating a liquid

citail 182, zedoary—Tobler, 2, 451 *citoval*

civé, civet, civel a type of prepared dish: **c. de menus oisiaux** 18 *BN*; **c. de veel** 28; **c. de lievres** 29; **c. de connins** 30; **c. d'oistres** 82, 148; **c. d'oeufz** 84; **c. de moules** 150—*FEW*, 2, 591b

claret: see **cleret**

cler 68 *VAT*, 69 *VAT*, 94 *BN*, 188, 190, thin; *cf.* **fort**—*cf. Menagier* §255, p. 253; §263, p. 256; *passim*

cleret, clairet, claret 42, 94, 177, thin, smooth, of an even consistency (said of a mixture)

cloche de gingenbre 180, bud, root of ginger

clou de girofle 173, 192, 200, 201, clove; s.a. **girofle**

cochon 60 *VAT*, 196, piglet; s.a. **pourcelet**

cochus: see **flaons**

colet 91 *MAZ*, neck of a pot

colin 131 *VAT*, a round sea-fish, *Pollachius virens*, coalfish, coley

commin, conmin, comin 12, 13, 75, 170 *VAT*, *Cuminum cyminum*, cumin—Clair, p. 149

comminee, cominé a dish made with cumin: **c. de poullaille** 12; **c. d'amendes** 13; **c. de poisson** 75, 96

compaignons 212, cook's assistants, help; journeyman cooks—Cotgrave

compettemment 188, 206, appropriately, adequately—Tobler, 2, 627

congre 121, conger eel

connins, conis 39, conies, rabbits; **boussac de c.** 20; **brouet d'Alemagne de c.** 22; **civé de c.** 30; s.a. **lappereaulx**

convy 195, banquet—Tobler, 2, 820

coq 9, *Origanum dictamnus*, dittany (of the mint family), or possibly *Tanacetum balsamita*, costmary (of the tansy family)—Cotgrave; Clair, p. 246; Freeman, p. 7

coqz heaumez 196, an entremets

Corinde: see **roisin**

cormorant 57, cormorant

cotelle: see **aulx**

coton 219, cotton

cotte 190, the "tunic" or shell of a lobster

couleiz, coulis, colis a cullis: **c. d'un poulet** 90; **c. de perche** 94, 103—Cotgrave; Tobler, 2, 560

couler 14, *passim*, to strain, filter, sieve; **c. parmi, par, l'estamine** 61 *MAZ*, *passim*—Tobler, 2, 561

couvercle 209, pastry shell

couvert: a c. 45 *MAZ*, under cover

craisme 194, cream

crappois: see **grappois**

cratoniere: see **alouse**

crespes 202, 203, 204, a sort of pastry—Tobler, 2, 1033

cresson, croisson 153, garden cress

cretonnee 11, 11A, a sort of dish prepared with greaves—Cotgrave, *cretons*; Tobler, 2, 1043; *FEW*, 16, 314

cuillerez, culleree 177, 201, spoonful

cuissotz 212, leg (of mutton or pork)

Daigne, Daingne Digne: **raysins, roisin de D.** 207, 210 a type of small seedless grape

daintiers, deintiers 193, delicacies, testicles; "les deitez sont les couillons" (*Menagier*,

p. 172, l. 8)—Cotgrave; Godefroy, 2. 411c and 412a

dalles 124, thin slices, layers, flakes (of fish flesh)—Cotgrave; *TLF*, 6, 679a

dariole 194, a sort of pastry shell for making a pastry of the same name—Tobler, 2, 1195; *TLF*, 6, 708b

dates 207, dates—see Pegolotti, p. 378

deffaire: see **desfaire**

degresser 180, to treat wine for slimy wine spoilage; *cf.* **engresser**—*TLF*, 6, 987b

[**dehachier**] 61 *BN*, to chop, mince—Tobler, 2, 1312

delié 66 *BN*, 69, slender, slim; *cf.* **gresle**—Tobler, 2, 1382

denree 182, quantity of a product to be had for a *denier*, a small quantity—Godefroy, 2, 507 c; *A-ND*, 2, 157a; Cotgrave

[**desclairir**] 8 *MAZ*, to explain—Tobler, 2, 1253; *A-ND*, 2, 165b

desfaire, deffaire 4, 11, *passim*, to infuse, macerate (a solid in a liquid); s.a. **destremper**—Tobler, 2, 1579

[**despecier**] 73, 124, 136, 147, 211, to pick apart, break apart; cf. **estre par pieces** 137—Cotgrave

desroussir 186, to remove russet colour from (a wine)—Godefroy, 2, 646c

dessaller 1, 188, to remove salt from

destremper, destramper 11 *MAZ*, 22, 24, 36, 42 *VAT* (subst. for **tremper**), 61, 76, 92, 160, 170, 178, 220, to infuse, macerate (a solid in a liquid)—Tobler, 2, 1795

detrancher 47, to cut apart

diapré 205, 206, a prepared dish with a coloured, ornamental design on its surface (?)—*cf.* Tobler, 2, 1912

diviser past part. 8 *MAZ*, set forth, set out—Tobler, 2, 1880–1881

dodine 40, 54, a serving sauce made of the the grease of roast fowl

doies: see **menus**

dorer, dourer 48, 50, 66, 173, 195, 196, 198, 204, 209, 211, 212, to glaze (a food); 209, to gild (with a metal leaf or a glazing)

doree 141, a flat sea-fish, *Zeus faber*, John Dory

doreure 195, glazing; **d. jaune 66**; **d. verte** 72

double 1 *MAZ*, 68, 200, layer (of a cloth) —Godefroy, 9, 400c

doulx 190, 206, 207, 209, mild, sweet

drappel, drappeaulx, drappelet 2, 51, 68, cloth; *cf.* **touaille**

drecier, dressier 61, *passim*, to set out (food on table)

dressouer 204, a serving board—Cotgrave

droiz: see **menus**

droit: a son d. 215, properly, faithfully—Tobler, 2, 2079

duisable 191, suitable—Godefroy, 2, 781b

duvet 215, down

eaue: e. grasse 36, a bouillon of a fat meat; **e. rousse, rose d'un chappon ou de poulle pour malade** 91, a sick dish

effusilié 79 *VAT*: in other mss. **esfeuilié, effueillié**, *q. v.*; error for *effuillié* or *esfuilié*?

egreffin: see **aigreffins**

[**emflamber**] 52 *BN*, 53 *BN*, to singe (down from fowl); s.a. **flamber**

emplir 152, 211, to fill

endroit: bon e. 191, a good cut of meat; **chascun e. soy** 219, each in its own way, appropriately—Tobler, 3, 293

[**enfariner, emfariner**] 145, 147, to dredge, coat with flour

[**enfler**] 72, to inflate; *cf.* **souffler** 213, 214

enfusté 184, woody (taste of wine); *cf.* **qui sente le fust** 182

engoullé: ris e. 71, fancy rice, made russet with saffron—cf. Tobler, 3, 394

engresser 179, to spoil by becoming slimy (wine); *cf.* **degresser**

enhaster 45, 46, 66, to mount on a spit

ensuivant adj. 99, immediately preceeding (?)

[entrejecter] 201, to scramble together—Godefroy, 3, 287a

entremez, entremetz, entremés 72, 118, 195, 215, 219, MS rubric before 61, "certaine choice dishes served in between the courses at a feast, or banquet" (Cotgrave)

escalongnes 170 *VAT*, *Allium ascalonicum*, shallots, scallions; s.a. **calongne**—Tobler, 3, 834; Landry, p. 237

escharder 135 *BN*: error for **eschauder**?

eschauder, eschaulder 49 *BN*, 60, 66, 135, *passim*, to scald, as a preparation for skinning or husking; *cf.* *skalde* in the *Forme of Cury*, §83—Tobler, 3, 870

eschaudés, eschaudez s.m.pl. 64, 207, cracknels, pastry cooked in boiling water—Tobler, 3, 872; *TLF*, 7, 634a; Lebault, 299

eschine, echine 124, spine; **eschinee** 124 *MAZ*, *VAT* Table §32, loin (of pork)—Tobler, 3, 898

esclarcir 186, to clarify (wine)

escorchier 76, 79, 80, 135, 195, 196, 213, to remove the skin from - *FEW*, 3, 281b

escrevisses, escrevices, eccrevissez 68, 117, 188, crayfish; **e. de mer** 151, lobster; **gravé d'e.** 190

escuelle, escueille 41, 95, *passim*, bowl; **e. de bois creuse, e. percee** 202

escullee 180, bowlful

escumer 68, 181, 182, to scum, skim

esfeuilié, effueillié 79, with leaves plucked from stem; s.a. **effusilié**—Tobler, 3, 1040

[esfondrer] 47 *VAL* and possibly *MAZ*, to eviscerate—Godefroy, 3, 455 "vider"

esgouter, esgoutter 200, 211, to drain away, drip through (a filter)—Tobler, 3, 1082

esgrené: verjus e. 10, 27, 111 *VAL*, a mash of verjuice grapes; s.a. **verjus**

esguieres 211, water jugs

[eslimoner] 77 *MAZ*, to remove the slime from the skin of a fish; s.a. **limon**; in the *Du fait de cuisine* the term is *esmorcher*, *amorcher*

[eslire], esliere, (elire) 63 *BN*, 71, 149, 150, 153 *BN*, to cull, clean the sand, dirt from; "mectez boulir vos escrevisses, et quant elles seront cuictes soient eslites comme qui les vouldroit mengier, et ostez le mauvaiz de dedens ..." *Menagier*, §76; *cf.* the English expression *pyke clene*, *Forme of Cury*, §124 and §167—Tobler, 3, 1096

[esmier] 197, 208, 210, 212, to crumble, break into small pieces—Cotgrave

Espaigne: pets d'E. 210, 211, a prepared dish

[espaillier] 63 *MAZ*, 93, to remove chaff from a grain; *cf.* **espouillié** 63 *BN*—Tobler, 3, 1139

espaules de mouton farcies 212, a prepared dish

especir 207, to thicken

esperlans, aspellens 145, flat sea-fish, *Osmerus esperlanus*, smelt

espic 68 *VAT*, 170 *VAT*; **espit** 24 *MAZ*, *Lavandula spica*, aspic, spikenard

espices 33, *passim*, spices; **fines e.** 16 *BN*, 20 *BN*, 23 *BN*, 77 *BN*; **menues e., moins e.** 191, 206; **pouldre d'e.** 4, 31, 60—see Pegolotti, *spezierie grosse* and *minute*, p. 431

espicier 29, 197, to add spices to

espinoches 175, spinach

espit: see **espic**

espouillié: see **espaillier**

[espreindre] 63 *VAL*, 147 *VAT*, 175, 177, to wring, press (liquid from); *cf.* **espingiés** 147 *BN*—Tobler, 3, 1255

esquaille 83 *BN*, (egg-)shell

essuier 71, 127, to drain, dry; *cf.* **ressuir, ressuyer**

estain 70 *VAT*, 196, 219, tin, pewter

estaint 216, carded wool, woollen yarn—Cotgrave, *estain*; Tobler, 3, 1339 *estaim*

estamine, estermine 25, *passim*, bolting cloth, a strainer; **une e. de deux pietz de long** 201

estandre 147 *VAL*, 204, to (set to) drain

estoffes 29, 30, ingredients

[**estordre**] 147 *MAZ*, to wring out—Tobler, 3, 1417

[**estoupper**] 182, 184, to stop up (a cask)—Tobler, 3, 1410

esturjon 146, classified as a flat sea-fish, sturgeon

faisans 51, 188, pheasants

farce 60, 66, 195, 211, 212, stuffing, filling

farcir, farsir 196, to stuff

farine, ferine 77, 88, 89, 122, 133, 135 *BN*, flour; **f. bien buretelee** 177; **f. de fromment** 178

farsiz s.m.pl. 195, dishes of stuffed animals or fowl

fart 83 *MAZ*, iron (m.Fr. *fer*)

faux grenon, faulx grenons, faus guernon, faulxgrenon 61, an entremets, a prepared dish of ground meat—see *faus* in Tobler, 3, 1653

[**fendre**] 49, 53, 104, to split (a fish)

feul, fueil s.m. leaf (of metal): **f. d'or ou d'argent** 195; **f. d'estain** 196, 197, 209; s.a. **lorier, vigne**

feves, feuves 11, 154, *Vicia faba*, broad beans, field beans

fiens 10, dung—Cotgrave

figues 64, 207, figs

filer, filler 10, 19, 33, 63, 86, 92 *VAL* and *MAZ*, 95 *VAL*, 200, to pour; *cf.* **versez a fil** 92 *BN* and *VAT*—Tobler, 3, 1849

[**filoper**] 144, to shred, reduce to long filaments (?)—*FEW*, 3, 395a: *filope*, "frange, effilochure"

finer 188, 191, 206, to obtain—Tobler, 3, 1876

flaiz 134, a type of flat sea-fish, *Platichthys flesus*, flounder—Cotgrave

[**flamber, flamer**] 52, 53, to singe (down from fowl); s.a. **emflamber**

flaons, flans: f. en Karesme 152, Lenten flans; **f. cochus** 194—Cotgrave

fleur 202, 211, (wheat) flour; s.a. **canelle**

foie, foyes 15, 16, 17 *MAZ*, 19, 61, 62, **faye** 24 *VAT*, liver; **f. de poullaille** 23, 169, 192, 193; **f. de chappon** 220; **f. de porc** 24; goose liver 36; **f. de beuf** 200; rayfish liver 136

folion: see **cilion**

formage: see **fromage**

formentee: see **fromentee**

fort 14, 202, thick, viscous, *cf.* **cler**; **fort** 14 *VAT* and **f. d'espices** 28, 29, strongly spiced

four 151, oven

fourt 152 *MAZ*, except for (mod. Fr. *fors*)

fourment, fromment, forment 63, 93, 181, wheat; **farine de f.** 178, wheat flour

franc meurier: see **meurier**

frase, fraise, fraisse 33, tripe, "a calves chaldern" (Cotgrave)

frasees: feves f. 154, frenched beans, "pilled, or shaled beans" (Cotrave, *s. v. frezé*)

[**fremir**] 65, 71, to simmer, scald (milk)

frians 36 *VAT*, 69 *VAT*, gourmets

friand 136, tasty

fricture, friture 33 *BN*, 190, fried meat

frioler 13, 14, 21, 25, 26, 95, 149, 153, to sautee—Tobler, 3, 2266

fritel, fritelles 177, fritter

frocter 201, squeeze (curdled milk in a bolting cloth) —Godefroy, 4, 164b

froit 33, 88, 89, 98 *VAL*, 99 *VAL*, 128 *VAL*, probably the past participle of **frire**; *cf.* **froide** 106 *VAL*, where other mss. have **frite**; and cf. the past part. **fruites** in 143 *BN*

fromentee, froumentee, formentee 63, 199, 207, frumenty, a wheat porridge

fromage, fromaige, froumage, froumaige, formage 26, 46, 76, 111, 152, 153, cheese; **fin f.** 175, 176; **f. de gain** 45, 60, 66, 136, 203, 208, 210, 212, a creamy cheese, see **gain**; **f. fondant** 45 *MAZ*, 60 *MAZ*; **brouet d'oeufz et de f.** 87

fromment: see **fourment**

fruites 143 *BN*, perhaps **fruités**, s.m.pl. (?), a type of fish, small fry (?)—Godefroy, 4, 153 a; Tobler, 3, 2270; Cotgrave, *fritou*

fuccus *VAT* Table §138, a flat sea-fish, seal (?)

fumee 91, vapour

fust 70, wood; 182, (stale smell of a) cask—Tobler, 3, 2368

fust 91 *BN*, vapour, or odour, smell (as above) (?); *cf.* **alaine** and **fumee**

gay "light, or bright, of colour" (Cotgrave): see **vertgay**

gaymeaux, gaymel, gymiau, guemmual 112, a fresh-water fish, waymel—*DEAF*, "G3", 419; *cf.* Tobler, 4, 45

gain "herbe du pâturage, regain; moisson; époque de la récolte" (*DEAF*, "G1," 41–2): **fromage de g.** creamy cheese from milk of pastured cows, goats, see **fromage**

gaitellet 64, a small cake—*DEAF*, "G3," 365

galantine, galentine 70, 97, a jelly, gelatine, galantine; *cf.* **gelee de poisson**—*DEAF*, "G1," 64–5

galetes 64, a sort of thin flat cake—*DEAF*, "G1," 61

garde: see **guede**

gardons *VAT* Table §122, a fresh-water fish—*DEAF*, "G2," 178

garingal, garingel 19, 24, 68 *VAT*, 80, 170 *VAT*, **caringal** 19 *BN*, rhizome of *Cyperus longus* or of *Alpinia officinarum*, galingale—*DEAF*, "G1," 77; see Pegolotti, pp. 374–375; Heyd, 2, 612; Gual Camarena, 329; *Menagier* ed. Pichon, 2, 212, n1

garlins 64 *VAL*, name of a dish made of figs, raisins, almond milk—*DEAF*, "G2," 281

gastiaulx 176, a sort of cake—*DEAF*, "G3," 362–363

gavion 45 *MAZ*, 47, 66, neck, gizzard; *cf.* **guisiers**—*DEAF*, "G3," 416

gelee de poisson 68, fish jelly; *cf.* **galantine**

gelines 38, hens

gentes, gantes 55 wild geese—Tobler, 4, 1575

georgié: brouet g. 15, a garnished broth

geste: see **jatte**

gingembre, gigimbre 9, *passim*, ginger; **cloche de g.** 180; **g. de Mesche** 188, 189, 191, ginger from Mecca—see Pegolotti, p. 360; Clair, p. 60

girofle 14, *passim*, cloves; **clou de g.** 192, 200, 201; **cloux** 173; **graine de g.** 164—see Pegolotti, p. 373; Clair, p. 50

gournault 120, a round sea-fish of the family *Triglidæ*, gurnard

graigne or perhaps **graigné**, 77 *MAZ*, variant for **gravé**, *q. v.*

grail, greil, gril 20, 28, 29 *BN*, 78 *BN*, 83, 104, 119, 121, 124, 135 *MAZ*, 143, 188, 192, 198, grill—Tobler, 4, 514

grain 5, *passim*, the substantial part of a prepared dish, the principal solid ingredient—Tobler, 4, 519; *FEW*, 4, 235

grain: see **verjus**

graine, grainne, grene, de paradis, paradiz 14, *passim*, *Amomum melegueta*, melegueta pepper, Guinea pepper—Clair, p. 67; Landry, p. 196; see Pegolotti, p. 422, *meleghette*

grainne or **grainné**: see **gravé**

grappes 10 *VAT*, (verjuice) grapes

grappois, crappois 127, classified as a round sea-fish, whale (meat, blubber?)

[**gratusier**] 176, to grate

gravé, grainné, graigné 103, 140, 147, gravy; **g. de menuz oyseaulx** 18; **g. de loche** 77; **g. de perche** 89, 103; **g. d'escrevisses** 190

gravelee: see **cendre**

gravelle 153, gravel, urinary calculi

greil: see **grail**

grenade 188, pomegranate; s.a. **pomme de grenade**—Cotgrave

grenon, guernon: see **faux**

gresles, greslettes 195, 211, 214, slender; *cf.* **delié**

gresse, graisse 40, 44, 54, 69, 180, 204, 220, liquified fat, grease; *cf.* **sain**; s.a. **haulte gresse**

gril: see **grail**

grimondin, grimodin 120, a round sea-fish, *Aspitrigla cuculus*, red gurnard, red gurnet

groiselles, grosselles, grosseillier 27, 170 *VAT*, 193, currants, the berry and the juice—Tobler, 4, 689

grues 55, 188, cranes

gruyau 93, gruel

guede, garde 66, woad, bluing—Cotgrave; Tobler, 4, 721; s.a. E.M. Carus-Wilson, "La guède française en Angleterre: un grand commerce du moyen-âge," *Revue du Nord*, 35 (1953), 89–105.

guehnee s.f. 74 *MAZ*, ?

guernon: see **faux**

guisiers, guissés, juisiers, jousiers 61, 62, gizzards—Tobler, 4, 339; Godefroy, 9, 697b

hachier 61, 66, 197, 208, 210, to chop, chop up

haler, haller 10, 20, 27, 35, 41, 83, 188, to sear (meat), to toast; **halé** s.? 155, a piece of toast—Tobler, 4, 956

hannons 149, cockles—Cotgrave

harens, arens, herans: aulx a h. frais 159, a garlic sauce for fresh herring

haricocus: see **hericoc**

haste: h. menue, menue h. 17, lit. (what is roasted on) a small spit: "la haste menue c'est la rate, et a icelle tient bien la moictié du foye et les rongnons" (*Menagier*, §12; *cf. hastelet*, §266)

hastés imper. 83 *BN*, should probably be read as **hostés**

haubert 154, shell of peas or beans

haulte gresse: de h. g. 40, "full, plumpe, goodlie, fat, well-fed, in good liking" (Cotgrave)

herboyé adj. 219, grassy—Godefroy, 4, 458a

hericoc, hericoq, haricocus de mouton 4, a mutton stew—Tobler, 4, 919; see Cotgrave and *FEW*, 16, 164 a–b; *TLF*, 9, 685 a: "Déverbal de l'anc. verbe *harigoter*, 'déchiqueter, mettre en lambeaux'" (Chrétien, *Yvain*, 831)

herissons 210, 211, hedgehogs, a prepared dish

herons, haron 53, herons

hettoudeaulx, hetoudiaux 38, cockerels—Tobler, 4, 1089; *FEW*, 16, 116a

hochepot 23, a stew, hotch-potch; *cf.* **hochier**—Cotgrave

hochier, houchier, houschier, hocher 4, 17, 67, 192, 202, to stir, agitate—Tobler, 4, 1120

hondous, hondel, houdous, houdons 21, a kind of (chicken) stew—Godefroy, 4, 421b *hardouil, hourdouil*

hoseille, usille 135 *MAZ*, 170 *VAT*, *Rumex acetosa*, sorrel, used for verjuice and for a green food-colouring—Tobler, 6, 1335; Landry, p. 241

hosties 188, wafers; *cf.* **oublee**—Godefroy, 9, 769c; Tobler, 6, 1059

huille, uille 75, *passim*, oil; **h. de nois** 104 *VAL*, walnut oil; **h. d'olive** 104 *MAZ*

ypocras 188, 192, a spiced wine, hippocras

ysope, ysouppe 3, 4, 9, *Hyssopus officinalis*, hyssop—Clair, p. 184

yssues 36 *MAZ*, 60, viscera, tripe, offal: "*les issues d'une beste*, the head, and intralls of a beast" (Cotgrave)—Tobler, 4, 1489; *TLF*, 10, 603a

jambon *VAT* Table §29, §32, §33, ham of a pig or boar—*Menagier*,]91

jance, jansse, 36, 98, 106, 126, 145, a boiled sauce of ginger and almonds; **j. de lait de vaiche** 166; **j. aux haulx** 167; **j. de gingembre** 168—Tobler, 4, 1564

jane: la j. 121 *MAZ*, a sauce; s.a. **jaunette** and **saulce**

jatte, jate, geste 70, 212, bowl—Tobler, 4, 1596

jaunette: saulce j. 88, a thick, spiced, saffron sauce; s.a. **saulce**; *cf. veel au jaunet*, 54; *le chappon et le trumel de beuf au jaunet*, *VAT* Table 31

juisiers, jousiers: see **guisiers**

Karesme 152, Lent

laictances, laitancez 152, milt, soft roe; s.a. **ruves**—Tobler, 5, 101

laictues, letuees 175, a leafy vegetable, lettuce; 209 a prepared dish or pasty resembling this (?)

lait, laic 54, 153 *VAT*, 199, milk; **l. de vache, vaiche** 10, 11, 63, 65, 71, 86, 166, 170; **l. d'amendes** 64, 152 *VAL*, 153, 207; **tourtes de l.** 201; **l. de Prouvance** 86 *VAL*; **l. lardé** 200; **l. lyé de vache** 86 *VAT*; **jance de l. de vache** 166

lamproye, lemproie 69, 102, lamprey; **l. en galentine** 70

lamproyons, lamprions 81 *MAZ*, 114, a fresh-water fish, lamprill

lappereaulx 39 *VAT*, young rabbit

larder 5 *MAZ*, 6, 8, 32, 35, 36, 37 *MAZ*, 39, 40 41, 47, 48, 50, 51, to bard or lard or to season with pieces of pork; **bouly lardé** 5; **lardé rosti** 31 *VAL*; **layt lardé** 200, 201

lardons 200, piece of pork

large s.f. 215, breadth, width

lart 8, *passim*, bacon, back-fat, flare, fleed (esp. of a pig); **sain de l.** 27; **blanc l.** 212

lardons 200, pieces of pork for larding—Cotgrave

lassis de blanc de chappon 189, a dish of strips of capon—Godefroy, 4, 689c

lechefricte 31, 41, 69, 101, dripping-pan—Tobler, 5, 286

leches, lesches, lachez 7, 45 *VAT*, 118, 200, 203, 204, slices—Tobler, 5, 333

[**leschier**] 127, to slice; s.a. **lez**

letuees: see **laictues**

levain de paste 2, 180, (bread-)dough leaven [**lever**] 220, remove, cut off (proper meat-carving term)—Godefroy, 4, 768b; Tobler, 5, 368

lez: mettre par l. 36 *VAT*, to slice; s.a. **leschier**—*FEW*, 5, 372b

liant 14, *passim*, thick (of a liquid)

liberons 211, beakers, jugs (?); error for *biberons*, *q. v.*

lye 179, 181, 187, dregs

lier 13, 17, 80, 199, 220, to thicken, bind (a liquid); 68, to bind up; s.a. **lait**

lieure 199, a binding agent, thickener

lievres 41, hares; **boussac de l.** 20; **civé de l.** 29, 30

lymande, limonde 140, 206, a flat sea-fish, *Limanda limanda*, limanda, dab

limon 68, a natural oil, rich in protein, covering the skin of certain fish—*FEW*, 5, 348b; *cf.* Tobler, 5, 480

[**limoner**] 104 *VAL*, to clean the slime (**limon**) off (a fish); s.a. **eslimonee**—*FEW*, 5, 349a

liqueur 188, 193, liquid base for a mixture, moisture, a sauce

loche, louche 68, 111, 188, a fresh-water fish, family *Cobitidæ*, loach; **gravé de l.** 77, 89, 190

loppinetz 76, small chunks—*FEW*, 5, 421b; *cf.* Tobler, 5, 648

lores 170 *VAT*, ?, perhaps **lorés**, *lorel*, laurel; see **lorier**—Gode, 4, 738b, *laure*

lorez: pastez l. 209, small pasties

lorier, loriez: feulles de l. 45 *MAZ*, 68 *VAT*, 170 *VAT*, *Lauris nobilis*, bay laurel; see also **baye**—Clair, p. 118

lusiaux 78 *BN*, pickerel; *cf.* **lux**; s.a. **brochetons**

lux 97, 152, a fresh-water fish, *Esox lucius*, pike; s.a. **brochet**

macis, mascit, matis, maciz 4, 5, 6, 68 *VAT*, 155 *BN*, mace; s.a. **mastic**, below—Tobler, 5, 759; see Pegolotti, p. 375

malartz 54, mallard, wild duck

mangonneaulx 212, mangonel

maquerel 119, 125, a round sea-fish, family *Scombridæ*, mackerel

marc 68 *VAT*, residue—Cotgrave; Tobler, 5, 1120

marjoliaine, marjolienne 175, *Origanum vulgare*, wild marjoram (?); **m. doubce** 172, *Origanum majorana*, sweet marjoram—Clair, p. 198; Freeman, p. 10; Landry, p. 153

maslés adj. 195, having to do with butchery —*cf.* *FEW*, 6.1, 4a *macellarius*; s.a. DuCange 5, 160b, *macellus*

mastic 155 *VAT*, 170 *VAT*, mastic (or an error for **macis**, *q. v.*)—Tobler, 5, 1238

matis: see **macis**

mauvilz 45 *VAT*, thrush

meicier: see **micier**

meinuise 113, fry, fingerlings—Cotgrave; Tobler, 5, 1467

mellanz 122 *VAT* Table, a round sea-fish, *Gadus merlangus*, whiting—Tobler, 5, 1531

mellus: see **merluz**

menjoire 188, a prepared dish—*cf.* Huguet, 5, 125a, *mangeure*

mente 150, 175, *Menta viridis*, garden mint—Clair, p. 201

menus doies, drois 62, pettitoes, delicate parts of venison—*cf.* Godefroy, 4, 772c

[**menusier**] 15 *MAZ*, 22 *MAZ*, 82 *MAZ*, 83 *MAZ*, 174, mince; s.a. **micier** and **munussier**—Tobler, 5, 1468

merluz, mellus 122, a round sea-fish, *Merluccius merluccius*, hake; stockfish, dried cod—Tobler, 5, 1532

Merry: la saulse saint M. 36 *VAT*, a sauce for a goose, from (the location of) a confrerie of goose roasters, vendors in Paris

Mesche: see **gingembre**

metz, mectz 213, 214, service (of food)

meurier: feulles de franc m. 186, mulberry leaves—Tobler, 6, 273

micier, missier, meicier, misser 4, 15, 16, 22, 113, 149, 153 *VAT*, 192, to mince; s.a. **menusier**—Tobler, 6, 10

miel 177, 178, honey—see Pegolotti, p. 378

mieux: see **moyeulx**

miguetes: see **muguetes**

milet, millot 65, *Panicum miliaceum*, millet grain

miole: see **mouelle**

mistions 212, mixtures, mixes of ingredients —Cotgrave; Tobler, 6, 99

moyeulx, moyeuf, mieux, mioust 10, *passim*, (egg) yolks—Godefroy, 5, 360b

moille: see **mouelle**

moins espices: see **espices**

moisy adj. and s.m. 50 *VAT*, mouldy, mouldiness

moller: see **moullier**

[**monder**] 93, to husk, separate straw from grain; *cf.* **espaillier** - Godefroy, 10, 169a; Cotgrave, *s. v.* *mondé*

mortier, mortié 70, 93, 175, mortar

morue 126, *VAT* Table §169, a round seafish, *Gadus morhua*, cod; **moruaulx** 128 *VAT*, codling

motes, mottes 212, castles, squat towers—Tobler, 6, 352

mouelle, moille, miole 45 *MAZ*, 173, 201A, 204, marrow—*FEW*, 6.1, 633a

moules, moullez 150, mussels

moullier, moller, moillir 65, 104, to moisten, soak

moulst, moust, moult, mol 38, 159, 178, must, the freshly pressed, unfermented juice of new grapes

moustarde, moutarde 3, *passim*, mustard; **souppe de m.** 83—Clair, p. 208

mouton, moutton, mouston 3, 34, 66, 174, 197, 210, 212, sheep, mutton; **hericoc de m.** 4

mouvoir 70, 180, *passim*, to stir

mugue 182, musk—Tobler, 6, 417

muguetes, muguettes, mugaites, miguetes: nois m. 22, 68, 69, 70, 162, 173, nutmeg; **noix noiguetes** 68 *MAZ* is probably an error, and **noix minguetes** 22 *MAZ* should be read as *noix miuguettes*—see Pegolotti, p. 374; Clair, p. 64

muy 178, 179, 181, 183, "a mesure of capacity for dry and liquid products used principally in Paris which originally signified the weight of the cubic capacity of an average-sized wagon-load: 2.682 hl for wine" (Zupko, p. 116); a hogshead (of wine)—Pegolotti, p. 409

mulet, mullet 125, a round sea-fish, family *Mugilidæ*, grey mullet

[**munussier**] 77 *MAZ*, to chop up, mince (onions) (?); s.a. **menusier**

nappe, nape 1, 7, 68, 70, 147, 200, a cloth

navetz 154, turnip greens

noiguetes: see **muguetes**

nois, noix 2A, walnuts; **huille de n.** 104 *VAL*; s.a. **muguetes**

nombril 136, navel, belly (of fish)

nourroys: see **pastez**—Tobler, 6, 803

oeufz, oeux, euf 33, *passim*, eggs; **moyeulx d'o.** 10, *passim*, yolks; **aubuns d'o.** 181, 197, whites; **civé d'o.** 84; **brouet d'o. et de frommage** 87; **paste batue en o.** 195, 196, a glazing compound; **allumelle d'o.** 212, omelette

[**oigner**] 104 *MAZ*, to baste—Tobler, 6, 1020

oyseaulx: menuz o. 18, 45, small game birds

oysons 36 *VAT*, goslings; s.a. **oues**

oistres, oestres, ostres, oittrez, orstres 148, *Ostreidæ*, oysters; **civet d'o.** 82

onde, unde: bouillir une o. 7, 11, 63, 69, 86, to bring to a boil

ongnons, oignons, oingnons 15, *passim*, onions

orcanet 191, 199, *Alkanna tinctoria* or *Anchusa officinalis*, plants whose roots yield a red dye, alkanet, dyers' bugloss—Clair, p. 110

oreillettes 209, an ear-shaped pasty (?)

orelle, oreille, oroille 119, gill (of a fish)

orfin 129, a round sea-fish, *Belone belone*, garfish, sea-pike

orge 93, barley

orvale 177, *Salvia sclarea*, clary—Clair, p. 142

oublee 204, wafer; *cf.* **hosties**

oue, oe, oye 36, 49, 50 *VAT*, 52, goose; **la petite oue** 36, parts or "issues" of a goose; s.a. **oysons**

outardes, oitardes, vistardes, ostardes 55, bustard—Tobler, 6, 1360

paelle, paielle, poelle, peelle 40, *passim*, pan; **paellon** 202, small pan—Tobler, 7, 9 and 11

pain 10, *passim*, bread; **p. blanc 64**; **p. bis** 219; **p. brullé** 18, *passim*; **p. roussi** 28; **p. hallé** 83

paintrerie 215, 218, an inert, painted representation—Tobler, 7, 565

paires, peres 65, changes (of water)

paon, pavon 50, 214, peacocks; **paonneaulx** 188, young peacocks

parboullir: see **pourboullir**

parciaulx 66 *VAT*, parcel; *cf.* "tourteaulx de guede" (*Menagier*, §324), small cakes of woad; s.a. **pastiaux**

pareceulx s.m.pl. 60, lazy persons

parexpaler 152 *MAZ*, to express, squeeze out—*cf.* Godefroy, 3, 549c *espelir*; *FEW*, 3, 307a

parmerien: tourtes parmeriennes 197, Parma pies

parures 68 *MAZ*, skin parings (of a fish); s.a. **peleures**—Tobler, 7, 248

passer 155, *passim*, to sieve, pass through a sieve; pp. **passis** 81

paste 211, paste, dough; **p. batue en oeufz, aux oeuf, d'oeufz** 195, 196, 202, 213; *cf.* **un petit d'oeufz bastuz ensemble** 197

pasté 6, *passim*, a pastry shell, pie; **pastez nourroys** 208; **pastez lorez** 209

pastiaux 66 *BN*: "*pastel*—Dyers Woad (of a finer sort then that which is called *Guesde*)" (Cotrave); s.a. **parciaulx**

pavois 217, (a large shield that could be used as) a platform, display deck—Godefroy, 10, 301a

pavon: see **paon**

pel 213, skin

peler 68, *passim*, to skin (an animal or fish)

peleures, pelleures 68, skin peelings (of a fish); s.a. **parures**

pepins, pupins 95, 179, 180, pippins, seeds

perche 103, 147 *VAL*, a fresh-water fish of the family *Percidæ*, perch; **gravé de p.** 89, 188, 206; **ung couleiz de p.** 94

perdriz 47, 173, 188, partridge; **trimolette de p.** 192

peres: see **paires**

persil, percil, percin, parressy, pierressy 3 *MAZ*, 4, *passim*, *Petroselinum sativum*, parsley—*FEW*, 8, 325a; Clair, p. 211; Freeman, p. 11

[**pertussier**] 2A, to break open (a nut)—Tobler, 7, 808

petail 63 *BN*, pestle

petz d'Espaigne 211, a prepared dish—Tobler, 7, 849; Robert

pierressy: see **persil**

piez 19 *MAZ*, breast (?)

pignolet, pignolat 195, 197, 208, 212, a paste of pine nuts—Tobler, 7, 930

pijons, pigons, pingons 44, 173, doves

pilieux 175, *Thymus serpyllum* or *Menta pulegium*, wild thyme, pellamountain—Cotgrave, *s. v. polieul*; Tobler, 7, 1380 *polieul*; Freeman, p. 15

piller 7, 14, 93, 154, to grind—Tobler, 7, 936

pinperneaulx, pimperniaux, pipenalx 110, a fresh-water fish, a type of small eel, water pimpernel or pimpernol; "a grig, scaffing, spitchcocke, fawson Eele" (Cotgrave)—Littré *pimperneau*

pipesfarces 203, stuffed tubes of pastry

plain adj. **vin p.** 17, 79, 82, wine in such quantity that it predominates in a mixture

plays, pleis, plays 133, 134, 135, 136, a flat sea-fish, *Pleuronectes platesa*, plaice

plast, plaut 7 *VAL* and *MAZ*, plate; *cf.* **plat**

plat 62, 66, 68, plate, a concave vessel; 69, 72, 73, 95, a serving dish; *cf.* **plast**

plomber, plommer, pleumer 91, to enamel, glaze—Tobler, 7, 1175

plouviers 46, 188, *Charadriidæ*, plovers

plumer 35 *VAL*, 36, 60, 190, 206, to pluck feathers from, remove hair from, peel, skin, husk—Tobler, 7, 2012-2013

poches 58, *Threskiornithidæ*, spoonbills

[**pochier, pocher, poucher, poicher**] 83, 84, 85, 86, 87, to poach (eggs)

point: a p., apoint 66, 82 *BN*, as necessary, to the extent required

poys, pois 127, 154, 188, white peas; **cretonnee de p.** 11; **puree de p.** 28, 29, 75, 77, 78, 79, 82 *VAT*, 87, 190

poisson, poison 68, fish; **gelee de p. qui porte limon, p. a limon** 68; **comminee de p.** 75, 96; **a p., a jour de p.** 188, 200, on a meatless day

poitevine: saulce poitevine, poetevine 38, 169, a boiled ginger sauce; **portemie** 169 *MAZ2* is probably a error; **une poitevinee** 169 *VAL*, the same sauce

poivre: p. long 10, 19, 24, 68, 70, 80, 118, 155, 162, 164 *MAZ*, 170, 175, 188, 190, 191, 192, *Piper longum*, long pepper; **p. ront** 165, 170 *VAT*, 173, *Piper nigrum*, black or common pepper; **p. aigret** 7, 99, a sauce; **p. jaune, jaunet** 36, 48, 60, 72, 124, 164, a sauce; **p. noir** 36, 165, a sauce; **p. chault** *VAT* Table §33, a sauce—see Pegolotti, pp. 360 and 427; Clair, p. 67; Landry, p. 194

pomme de grenade 95, pomegranate; **pepins (pupins) de p.**

pommez, pommettes, pommeaulx 66, 95, 195, balls (of chopped meat)

porc 3, 31, *passim*, porc; **chaudun de p.** 9; **la haste menue de p.** 17

porc de mer 118, classified as a round sea-fish, porpoise

poreaulx 154, *VAT* Table §32 and §33, leeks

poree 153, 154, *VAT* Table §28, a stew of vegetables, a salad

pot, pout 2, 91, 177, 181, 211, pot, contents of a pot; **potz d'Espaigne** 211, see **petz**; **p. a cirop** 202, an open flat pan for reducing a liquid by boiling

potaige, poutaige 1, *passim*, food prepared in a pot, stew

poucins 37, chicks, spring chickens

poulaille 106 *VAL*, a type of fresh-water fish; s.a. **rossaille**

pouldre, poudre 6 *MAZ*, 54 *VAL*, 124 *VAL*, 148, spice powder; **p. d'espices** 4, 31, 32, 33, 39, 60, 66, 105 *VAT*, 109 *VAL*, 119 *VAT*, 120 *VAT*, 139 *VAT*, 147 *VAT*, 149 *VAT*, 150 *VAT*; **p. fine** 104, 210, 212; **fine p. d'espices** 4; **p. fine ou blanche** 194, 204: "*pouldre blanche*—a powder compounded of Ginger, Cinnamon, and Nutmeg; much in use among Cookes" (Cotgrave); and **poudre fine de gigimbre et de cannelle** 32 *MAZ*

pouldrer 68, 120, *passim*, to sprinkle with spice powder

poullaille, poulaille 13, *passim*, poultry; **comminee de p.** 12; **brouet de p.** 22; **brouet de verjus de p.** 25; **hochepot de p.** 23; **p. farcie** 66, 195

poulle, poules 91, 195, 196, hen

poullés, poulet 11, 19 *MAZ*, 37, 66, 67, 173, pullet; **couleiz d'un p.** 90

poulse 220, a gruel-like sauce—Godefroy, 6, 358a; Tobler, 7, 1669

pourboullir, parboulir, parbouller, parbouler 6, 32, 39, 41, 82 *VAL*, to parboil, to boil intensely but briefly—Godefroy, 6, 353c

pourcel, pourcelet piglet, suckling pig: **p. farsy, falcis, efarcy** 60; **soux, sourps de p.** 74

pourri 90 *VAL*, and **p. de cuire** 90, 91, disintegrating as a result of boiling (said of meat)

prendre: se p. 66, 68 *VAT*, to set, become fixed (said of a glazing); *cf.* **se reprendre**

privé adj. 219, domestic (animal)—Tobler, 7, 1909

pupins 95 *MAZ*: see **pepins**

puree de poys: see **poys**

purer 11, *passim*, to puree, mash; to strain, drain (of liquid)—Godefroy, 6, 469a–b; Tilander, *Glanures*, 211–212: "égoutter"

quehue 74 *MAZ*, tail—see various spellings in Godefroy, 10, 458c–459c

raie, roye 123, 130, 136, 138, a flat sea-fish, family *Rajidæ*, ray fish, skate; **aulx de la r.** 122, a type of sauce; **foye de la r.** 136, 156

raysins, roisins 64, grapes; **r. de Karesme** 173, dried grapes, raisins; **r. de Corinde** 195, 197, 208, 212, small seedless grapes from Corinth; **r. de Daigne** 207, 210, grapes drom Digne

ranguillon 202, tongue of a buckle—Godefroy, 6, 593b

rappé 27, a type of wine or broth made from a mash of fresh grapes—*cf.* Tobler, 8, 311: "Lauer, geringer Wein, Nachwein"; Cotgrave; *cf.* also *raspe*, a seeded grape

rappee 99 *MAZ*, *VAT* Table §29 & 164, a type of sauce made from a mash of fresh grapes

rassuir 68 *BN*; **[rasseoir]** 68 *VAT*, 74 *BN*, 182, to settle (sediment from a liquid)—Cotgrave

[ratissier] 69 *VAL*, to scrape clean—Cotgrave; Tobler, 8, 336

ratiz 212, peritoneal membrane (of animals), caul—Tobler, 8, 336

reffaire 35, 47, 48, 51, 66, 204, to plump (a foodstuff), make plump by parboiling—Cotgrave; *cf.* Tobler, 8, 549 [**renforcir**] 199, to thicken, bind; *cf.* **fort**

regart: au r. de prep.phr. 204, as regards, with respect to

renges 201, ranges, rows—Tobler, 8, 808

renversee104 *VAT*, 107 *VAT*, a method of cooking (fish) by turning inside-out—Cotgrave; Tobler, 8, 848

reprendre: se r. 199, to run (together, colours); *cf.* **se prendre**—Cotgrave; Tobler, 8, 938

ressuir, ressuyer 83, 124, to drain, let drain, dry out; s.a. **essuier**—Tobler, 8, 1078

revestu: see **cine, paon**

ribeletes, ribelletes 45, 67, bards of pork or lard: "*riblette*, a collop, or slice of bacon" (Cotgrave)

rix, ris 176, rice; **r. engoullé** 71, a prepared dish; **r. batu** 199, rice powder (a thickener)

roye: see **raie**

royé: asne r. 219, zebra—*cf. raie*, "stripe"

roisins: see **raysins**

roysolles 201A, rissoles, deep-fried meat turnovers—Cotgrave; Tobler, 8, 1422

rolz 45 *MAZ*, rôti—*cf. FEW*, 16, 683b

romany 177, *Rosmarinus officinalis*, rosemary —*FEW*, 10, 488a; Clair, p. 218; Landry, p. 219

rongnon 204, kidney; **la gresse qui est ou r. de beuf** 204, suet

rosé, rozé 205, 206, pink; **ung r. a chair** 191, a prepared dish

rotielles, rouelles 60 *MAZ*, 66, rolled pieces of meat; **rouelles** 215, wheels

rouget 120, 121, a round sea-fish, *Mullus surmuletus*, red mullet

rougir: see **roussir**

roussaille, rossaille 106, a fresh-water fish, *Leuciscus rutilus*, roach; s.a. **poulaille**—Tobler, 8, 1357 *rochaille*; s.a. Paul Barbier, *Revue des langues romanes*, 57 (1914), 331

roussir, rougir 71, 188, 191, 200, to make russet

roux, rous, rose, rousse, rousset 16, 89, 91, 147 *VAT*, 188, 189, russet, yellowish red, brown

ruves, rufvez 152, fish roe, hard roe; s.a. **laictances**—*FEW*, 16, 247b: *rogue*

sade 50 *VAT*, tasty, palatable—Tobler, 9, 37

saffren, saffrain, saffran 4, *passim*, *Crocus sativus*, saffron—see Pegolotti, p. 376; Gual Camarena, p. 412; Clair, p. 224; Freeman, p. 13

[**saichier**] 147 *MAZ*, to sautee (a fish in a pan)—Godefroy, 7, 274c

sain, saing 28, *passim*, drippings from a roast, grease (esp. of pork); **s. de lart** 10, *passim*; **s. de porc** 199; **s. de porc doulx** 189, rendered lard; **s. de lart porc doulx** 209; s.a. **gresse**

salmonde, salemonde, sanemonde 162, 199, herb bennet, common avens - *FEW*, 11, 145b

sancte *VAT* Table §155, a flat sea-fish

sangle adv. 37, by itself, without any addition—Tobler, 9, 146

sanglier 7, boar; **bourbier de s. frez** 42, a sauce

santoilles, setailles 115, lampern—Tobler, 9, 587, *setueille*; Godefroy, 7, 323b, *satouille*; s.a. A. Thomas, *Romania*, 35 (1906), 472

sarrasinois, saraginois adj. Saracen; **brouet s.** 80, an eel broth

sarcelle 59, teal

sauge, saulge 3, 4, 9, 26, 87, 161 *MAZ2*, *Salvia officinalis*, sage; **froide s.** 37, 73, 74, a sauce made with sage—Clair, p. 229; Freeman, p. 13

saulce, sausse 31, 47 *VAT*, 220, sauce; **s. vert, verte** 3, 161, *passim*; **s. saint Merry** 36; **s. de most, moust, moulst, mol** 38; **s. jaunette** 88, **la jane** 121 *MAZ*; **s. de vin** 140, 144; **s. a garder poisson** 162; **s. de lait de vache** 166 *VAL*; **s. de aulx** 167 *VAL*

saulcisses 45, sausages

saumon, salmon, saulmont, saumont 124, a round sea-fish, salmon

saupiquet 41 *VAT*: "sauce for a roasted Conie, of Onions, ginger, verjuyce, and white wine; generally, any kind of tart sauce" (Cotgrave)

seiche 147, classified as a flat sea-fish, *Sepia officinalis*, cuttlefish

seive 185, bouquet (of wine)—*FEW*, 11, 191a

sel, cel 120, *passim*, salt; **s. menu** 34, *passim*, fine salt; **poudre de s.** 80 *MAZ*; **s. blanc** 204

[**semer**] 188, to cover over with, to disintegrate ? (*cf. saimer*, "to melt (bacon fat)"—Godefroy, 7, 288b; Tobler, 9, 65)

setailles: see **santoilles**

Sevrin: carrefour saint S. 36 *VAT*, location of goose orasters and vendors in Paris

sigongnes 52, storks

solles 135, 206, a flat sea-fish, *Solea solea*, sole

soringue, soringne, seringne 15, 17 *VAL*; **s. d'anguilles** 79, a (eel) sauce of brownish colour with onions, vinegar—Cotgrave; *FEW*, 17, 18b

soubzfrire, souffrire 4, *passim*, to fry lightly, partially, to brown or sear; s.a. **surfrire**

souciee: see **soux**

souppes 40, 54, sops; **s. de moustarde, en moustarde** 83, 84, 85

soustil adj. 24, easily digested—*cf.* Tobler, 9, 984

soux, souz, soulz, sourps; soussie, souciee 74, 137, 138, *VAT* Table 168, a type of sauce, jelly or pickling brine for meat—Tobler, 9, 1023 and 995; *REW*, 8445; DuCange, *s.v. solta*

sucre, succre 38 *VAT*, 63, 64, 75, 81, 88, 90, 93–93, 152, 171–173, 175, 177, 184, 188–190, 192, 194, 197–200, 205–208, 220, sugar; **pouldre de s.** 90; **s. esmié** 197, sugar which has been broken or granulated from its loaves—see Pegolotti, pp. 362–65

succrer 95, 194, to sprinkle with sugar

sueur 69 *VAT*, drippings (from roasting lamprey)

surfrire 16, 17, 18, to simmer; "*nota* que l'en dit *surfrire* pour ce que c'est en un pot; et se c'estoit en une paelle de per, l'en diroit *frire*" (*Menagier*, §75; p. 151); s.a. **soubzfrire**

surmontain 181, *Laserpithium siler*, laserwort, hart-wort—Tobler, 9, 532

table 215, sheet (of lead); "Terme de Plombier. Espece d'ais de plomb qui a été jetté en moule et qui sert à faire des tuiaux, des cheneaux, des cuvettes, des gouttieres ou autres ouvrages" (Richelet, 2, 417b)—Cotgrave

taillemaslee 163, another name for a sauce called "la barbe Robert"

tailliz, taillés s. 64, hash; **t. de Karesme** 207—Tobler, 10, 42

[**taindre**] 215, 216, to dye; *cf.* **chanvre paint** 216—Tobler, 10, 150

tan 185, tannin

tanche, tenche 104, 152, a fresh-water fish, *Tinca tinca*, tench

tartres, tartes 152, tarts, pies

[**taveler**]: see **caveler**

teine: see **tenve**

tendre 18, supple, loose, of low viscosity—Cotgrave

tenve 54, 136 *VAT*, 204, 214, 219; **teine** 175, thin, slim, slender, slight—Cotgrave; Tobler, 10, 239; *FEW*, 13.1, 229b

terrasse 217, 219, platform, hillock

tonnel 184, cask—see Zupko, pp. 176–177; Pegolotti, p. 410

tornesoc, tournesoc 191, 199, an orchil lichen from which a colouring dye is extracted—Tobler, 10, 436; Smith, *Lichens*, p. 412-415

tostees 54, 136 *VAT*, 198, pieces of bread or another foodstuff, toasted; **t. dorees** 198, a preparation of toast dipped in egg yolk and deep fried

toster 40, to toast (bread)

touaille 1 *MAZ*, cloth, towel; *cf.* **drappel** —Tobler, 10, 339

toumeaulx: see **trumeau**

[**tourner**] 12 *VAT*, 92, to coagulate, curdle — Tobler, 10, 434

tourtel 175, **tourtelettes** 212, small cake

tourtes, torte 175, cake; **t. parmeriennes** 197; **t. de lait** 201

tourtourelles: see **turturelles**

[**traire**] 146, 183, to draw, extract

[**trainchier**] 61 *MAZ*, to slice

tranchens 177, blades—Tobler, 10, 580

trimolette 192, a sauce (for partridge)—Godefroy, 8, 52c

trippes 154, a variety of *potaige*

tronçons, tronsons 45, 79, 146, 194, round slices—*cf.* Tobler, 10, 680

[**tronçonner**] 132, to slice across a round section—*cf.* Tobler, 10, 681

trouble adj. 179, cloudy (of wine)

troussant adj. 202, binding, thick (of batter)

truite, truitte 109, a fresh-water fish, trout; **t. saulmonoise, saumonneresse** 132, 142, a fresh-water and flat sea-fish, *Salmo trutta*, salmon trout

trumeau, trumel, toumeaulx *VAT* Table §31, 173, 188, 189, 191, 204, knuckle, hock, shank (of beef, veal)—Tobler, 10, 713

tuel, tuyau 66, 195, a straw, blow-pipe—Tobler, 10, 717

tuillé 206, a prepared dish—*cf.* Tobler, 10, 338, *tiule* and *tiulee*, *tuilee*

tune *VAT* Table §156, classified as a flat sea-fish, tuna—see Pegolotti, p. 380

turbot 137, a flat sea-fish, *Scophthalmus maximus*, turbot

turturelles, truterelles, tourtourelles 48, turtle-doves

tuyau: see **tuel**

usille: see **hoseille**

vair: minu v. 215: "minever; the furre of Ermines mixed, or spotted, with the furre of the Weesell called *Gris*" (Cotgrave); "fourrure de l'écureuil du Nord, fourrure de diverses couleurs" (Godefroy, 8, 135b); see Delort, 1, 39–45; 432–436

veel, veau 9, 32, 61, 66, 191, 197, 204, 206, veal; **civé de v.** 28; **fraise de v.** 33; **v. au jaunet** 154

venoison, veneison 5, 6, 43, 63, 118, 122, meat of wild game animals; **v. de cerf, de chevrel sauvaige** 6; **v. de sanglier** 7

vendoise *VAT* Table §121, a fresh-water fish, *Leuciscus leuciscus*, dace

verdeur, verdeure, verdure 66, 158, 201, greenery, herbs which provide green colouring; for the *Menagier* (§113; p. 168), *verdeur* can mean "bitterness, sourness"; see the following

verdir 170, to give a sharp, tart or sour taste (to a dish)—*cf.* the *Menagier*, §113; p.168

verjus, vertjus 3, *passim*: "verjuyce; especially that which is made of sowre, and unripe grapes; also, the grapes whereof it is made" (Cotgrave); **brouet de v.** 25; **v. esgrenez, v. en grain, v. de grain** 10, 27, 31 *MAZ*, 37 *MAZ* and *BN*, 111 *VAL* and *MAZ*, a mash of verjuice grapes; **v. vert, v. reverdi** 3 *MAZ*, 33, 34 *MAZ*, 37, 110, 150, a type of sauce

vermeulx, mermoil 171, 178, 188, red, claret (the wine colour); in 81 **vernoy** should probably read **vermoyl**—*FEW*, 14, 289b

vernoy: see **vermeulx**

vertgay, vergay, vert gay 26, 73, 76, 87, 162, a yellowish-green colour obtained by combining green and yellow ingredients; *ung pou de saffren en la verdeur, qui veult, pour estre vertgay*; "on appelle le ver gay, la couleur du ver naissant" (Furetière); **brouet v. de poullaille** 73 *MAZ*—Cotgrave: "*gay*, light, or bright, of colour"; Tobler, 4, 39: "*gai*, bunt (Farbe)"

[**vertochier, vertocher**] 180, 183, 185, 186, 187, to broach, tap a keg(?): "*vertoquer*, mettre un tonneau en état de servir" (DuCange, 9, 391a); *n. b.*, however, that the *Tractatus* has repeatedly *in tunellam mitte* or *in tunellam pone* at the point where the *Viandier* reads *vertochez* (*ed. cit.*, pp. 361–362)

videcoqz 46, woodcocks—Godefroy, 8, 228b

vigne: fueille de v. 170 *VAT*, vine leaves (for a green food-colouring)

vin 4, *passim*, wine; **v. bastart** 81, a type of mixed red wine; **v. vermoil, vermeil, vernoy** 81, 171, 187; **v. blanc** 92, *passim*; **v. blanc ou vermeil** 188; **v. roux** 186; **v. nouvel** 178

vinaigre, vin aigre 17, *passim*, vinegar

vinaigrette, vin aigrete: une v. 17, a prepared dish in which the taste of vinegar predominates

vollaille, voulaille 15, 19 *MAZ*, fowl